INSIDE
CANADIAN
POLITICS

Alex Marland

Jared J. Wesley

OXFORD
UNIVERSITY PRESS

OXFORD
UNIVERSITY PRESS

Oxford University Press is a department of the University of Oxford.
It furthers the University's objective of excellence in research, scholarship,
and education by publishing worldwide. Oxford is a registered trade mark of
Oxford University Press in the UK and in certain other countries.

Published in Canada by
Oxford University Press
8 Sampson Mews, Suite 204,
Don Mills, Ontario M3C 0H5 Canada

www.oupcanada.com

Copyright © Oxford University Press Canada 2016

Library and Archives Canada Cataloguing in Publication

Marland, Alexander J., 1973–, author
Inside Canadian politics / Alex Marland and Jared J. Wesley.

Includes bibliographical references and index.
ISBN 978–0–19–900139–2 (paperback)

1. Canada—Politics and government—Textbooks.
I. Wesley, Jared J., 1980–, author II. Title.

JL75.M42 2016   320.971   C2015-906388-4

CONTENTS AT A GLANCE

CONTENTS

3   Federalism in Canada   81

PART II Politics and Politicking   337

10 Democracy and Elections   386

13 Diversity and Representation   494

14 Canada's Place in the World   541

FIGURES AND TABLES

Figures

Tables

INTRODUCING *INSIDE CANADIAN POLITICS*

Oxford University Press is delighted to introduce *Inside Canadian Politics*, a fresh perspective on the institutions and issues at the heart of Canada's political system. Written by scholars with experience working in public administration, the text delivers an "insider's" take on the discipline, giving chapter-length coverage to key topics in Canadian politics—from federalism, regionalism, and diversity to the party system, activism, and elections. Along the way, students are encouraged to debate and discuss the effectiveness of government mechanisms in the daily lives of Canadians. Contemporary and accessible, *Inside Canadian Politics* offers a balanced view of the theory and practice of politics in Canada.

Outstanding Features

A Critical Focus

Inside Canadian Politics delivers a variety of features designed to get students thinking about—and talking about—the issues at the heart of Canadian politics.

UP FOR DEBATE

Should Canada give more money for foreign aid?

THE CLAIM: YES, IT SHOULD!

Canada should increase its foreign aid to help combat poverty in developing nations.

Yes: Argument Summary

The scope of global need for foreign aid is incomprehensible, with malnourishment, disease, sexual violence, inadequate environmental standards, and a lack of basic education being some of the many chronic problems that are most acute in developing countries. The United Nations target for foreign aid is 0.7 per cent of an industrialized nation's gross domestic product; Canada commits roughly half of this objective. Western nations can minimize human suffering if they choose to prioritize humanitarian aid over domestic politics. There is moral and altruistic need for the federal government to build on its peacekeeping image by taking a leadership role in the international community in allocating more funds to combat global poverty. For as Bono of U2 once said, "the world needs more Canada."

Yes: Top 5 Considerations

1. Reducing global poverty has been, and should be, the primary purpose of Canadian foreign aid. There is a moral imperative for the Government of Canada, whose citizens enjoy some of the best living standards in the free world, to help those in greater need living in impoverished societies. Relying on corporations and citizens to donate to their preferred causes is not enough.
2. Canada's position as a middle power means that it can leverage the political value of funds that would have otherwise been committed to its military. Through foreign aid, Canada can reward foreign governments that prioritize improving the quality of life of its citizens, form alliances

with like-minded leaders, and redirect support from regimes with poor human rights records. This can inspire other developing nations to follow suit and reduces the conditions that lead to stateless combatants targeting Canada.
3. It is imperative that countries like Canada commit their resources in order to advance the objectives of multinational organizations like the United Nations (UN) and the Organisation for Economic Co-operation and Development (OECD). Improving human rights, promoting democracy, advancing the equality of girls and women, encouraging sustainable economic development, and distributing medicine to those in need are noble values. Without concrete, government-sponsored action, those in need are left only with unfulfilled promises.
4. So-called "economic diplomacy," whereby industrialized nations prioritize trade and economic investment in emerging economies, is a capitalist approach to solving a problem that requires a communitarian mindset. Trade liberalization may serve the interests of businesses in large economies while exploiting smaller ones, thereby worsening the plight of the poor rather than allegedly helping them.
5. Countless organizations in Canada, including the Canadian offices of global advocacy groups such as Amnesty International and Doctors Without Borders, seek to fill the foreign aid policy vacuum. Political parties should listen to these perspectives and show leadership by advancing an international development agenda.

Yes: Other Considerations

- By engaging Canadian businesses in public aid programs as opposed to using public funds, the government legitimizes attempts by profit-motivated commercial interests to present

End-of-chapter debate supplements give students the tools to debate a key topic related to the chapter—Do first ministers have too much power? Is negative advertising bad for democracy? Are affirmative action programs needed in the public service?

Zunera Ishaq, a Sunni Muslim, took the oath of Canadian citizenship in October 2015 after winning a series of court battles affirming her right to do so while wearing her niqab. The government had fought to uphold the ban on the face-covering niqab, with Conservative prime minister Stephen Harper arguing: "I believe, and I think most Canadians believe, that it is offensive that someone would hide their identity at the very moment where they are committing to join the Canadian family." The divisive issue came to the forefront during the 2015 federal election campaign, with some branding the niqab a symbol of Muslim oppression of women and others holding it up as an important religious right. How would you set the limits of reasonable accommodation in a case such as this?

These sorts of controversies and tensions are not unique to Quebec. Similar, smaller-scale debates have occurred across Canada over the course of the past century. Moreover, while ethnic and religious rights tend to dominate these discussions, reasonable accommodation also involves addressing the needs of other minority groups (including Aboriginal people, LGBTT people, allophones, people with disabilities, and others). And the requirements of reasonable accommodation apply more broadly than just to governments. Employers are also required to provide such protections for employees (see *O'Malley and Ontario Human Rights Commission v. Simpsons-Sears*). In many ways, then, conversations about reasonable accommodation tend to overlap with those concerning the need for employment equity and affirmative action in Canada.

Diversity and the Courts

Advocates of inclusion have advanced their cause by many means, including entering politics to reform the electoral process and legislatures from within, and educating the public on the depth of Canada's democratic deficit so that citizens will put pressure on

Carefully chosen photos and captions serve as case studies to spark discussion of political theory in the context of relevant events.

A Visual Focus

A dynamic design and numerous original illustrations—figures and charts, tables and maps, infographics and more—make complex information accessible to student readers.

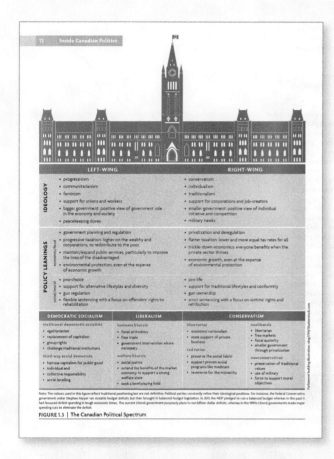

FIGURE 1.3 | The Canadian Political Spectrum

FIGURE 14.4 | Immigrants as a Percentage of Total Population in G8 Countries

Source: United Nations, "Trends in International Migrant Stock: The 2013 Revision."

Rarely does a single image so poignantly capture human suffering as the photo of Syrian toddler Alan Kurdi's lifeless body. The 3-year-old washed up on a beach in September 2015 after the inflatable boat holding his father and other refugees capsized in the Mediterranean Sea. The refugee crisis suddenly dominated the Canadian election campaign, and the Liberals pledged to bring in at least 25,000 Syrian refugees. Why do you suppose it took a heart-wrenching photograph for Canadian media, politicians and voters to pay attention to a crisis that had been going on for months?

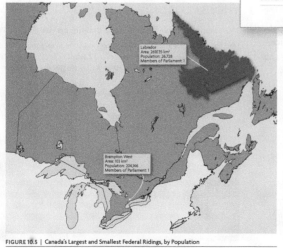

FIGURE 10.5 | Canada's Largest and Smallest Federal Ridings, by Population

Innovative Boxed Features

Four recurring boxed features offer unique perspectives on Canadian politics.

INSIDE CANADIAN POLITICS

How Were Free Votes Used to Deal with the Hot-Button Issue of Same-Sex Marriage?

Free votes are rare in Canadian legislatures, although a pair occurred on the divisive issue of same-sex marriage. In 2005, several leaders released their members from the requirement to toe the party line on Bill C-38, which became known as the Civil Marriage Act. While his ministers remained bound to support the bill by virtue of cabinet solidarity, and facing a minority government situation, Prime Minister Paul Martin allowed Liberal backbenchers a free vote on the issue. So, too, did Conservative Party leader Stephen Harper and Bloc Québécois leader Gilles Duceppe. Jack Layton chose to whip his caucus, however, obliging New Democrats to vote in favour of legalizing same-sex marriage.

The Liberal cabinet voted nearly unanimously in support of same-sex marriage; none opposed, and one member abstained. Yet the Liberals' backbench was the most divided on the same-sex marriage vote. While 59 backbench members voted in favour of the bill, 32 opposed, with 3 abstaining. Despite the free vote, members of the other parties ended up voting predictably along party lines. Even in the absence of party discipline, the Bloc was remarkably unified in its support of the bill with 43 of 54 voting in support. By the same token, the Conservative caucus was almost entirely unified in opposing the bill with 93 of 98 members voting nay, 3 yea, and 2 abstaining. Conversely, despite the requirements of party discipline, one member of the NDP—Manitoba MP Bev Desjarlais—voted against the motion, citing personal religious convictions. Desjarlais was stripped of her position in Layton's shadow cabinet as a result,

and lost a subsequent nomination race in her home constituency before resigning from the NDP caucus to sit as an independent. She ran, but finished third, in the subsequent federal election.

Bill 38 passed by a final tally of 158 to 133, with 15 not voting, and by 47–21–3 in the Senate, becoming the Civil Marriage Act with Royal Assent on 20 July 2005.

The law re-emerged as a focal point in the 2006 federal election, when Stephen Harper announced his party's intention to hold another free vote, this time on whether or not to revisit the issue. The electorate granted Harper's Conservatives a minority government, and as one of the prime minister's first acts, he introduced a motion to "restore the traditional definition of marriage without affecting civil unions and while respecting existing same-sex marriages." The motion was defeated 175 to 123, with notable divisions occurring in the Conservative and Liberal caucuses. Citing a precedent set by PC prime minister Brian Mulroney during the free vote over capital punishment, Harper released all of his members—including cabinet ministers—to vote their conscience on the motion. As a result, 6 of the 25 ministers chose to vote against the motion, joining 7 of their backbench Conservative colleagues, 85 Liberals, and all 47 Bloc and 29 NDP members. By contrast, the remaining 110 Conservative MPs voted in favour of restoring the traditional definition of marriage; only 13 opposition members, all Liberal, supported the motion. Following the vote, Prime Minister Harper pledged not to re-open the same-sex marriage issue.

THE LESSON

Leaders may publicly release their members from the constraints of party discipline, yet the results of free votes almost always break down along traditional party lines.

VOX POP

Why do you suppose that members of the legislature tend to support their party leader's position during free votes?

"Inside Canadian Politics" boxes expand the coverage of key topics with an "insider's" take on everything from the press gallery's relationship with the prime minister to the women who cracked the glass ceiling in Canadian politics.

"They Said It" boxes present the opinions of a host of political insiders, from John A. Macdonald to Rick Mercer, giving insight into what prominent Canadians had to say, write, or tweet at key moments in the country's political history.

THEY SAID IT

John Sankey, Lord Chancellor of Britain, on the "Living Tree"

John Sankey, 1st Viscount Sankey, had only recently been appointed Lord Chancellor of Britain when he famously characterized Canada's constitution as "a living tree" in a landmark ruling in the case of *Edwards v. Canada* (1929), more commonly known as the *Persons* case.

> The British North America Act planted in Canada a living tree capable of growth and expansion within its natural limits. The object of the Act was to grant a Constitution to Canada. Like all written constitutions it has been subject to development through usage and convention.

—*Edwards v. Canada (Attorney General)* (1929)

VOX POP

Many feel that constitutions must evolve to meet the changing needs of society, but not all agree on the best way to guide that evolution. Do you think that judges—who are not elected or otherwise accountable to the electorate—are best positioned to guide the development of Canada's constitution? Should changes be negotiated by politicians? What role should average citizens play?

"Vox Pop" discussion questions are peppered throughout each chapter, challenging students to evaluate and apply the material they have just read.

Opportunities Available

Knowledge of Canadian Politics and Government Preferred!

Executive Assistant

Fredericton, NB

Description

The Law Office of Kelly Lamrock, Q.C., seeks an Executive Assistant to help build our growing practice in administrative & immigration law and public policy consulting.

The Executive Assistant shall:

- Assist in the drafting and organizing of documents in complex files
- Ensure documentation of hours, invoicing of clients, and financial records
- Provide for the scheduling of meetings and travel
- Undertake research into public policy issues and co-ordinate Right to Information requests
- Develop a marketing strategy for the practice, with a special focus on multicultural communities and new Canadians
- Manage client communications and intake, and provide support to the lawyer when dealing with culturally diverse files

The position offers participation in health and insurance plans, as well as allowances for professional development and generous vacation time.

Qualifications

The successful applicant shall:

- Have a Bachelor's Degree, preferably in Political Science, Communications, or related fields
- Have experience working in communications and media relations, preferably in a public policy field
- Have excellent written communication skills
- Have experience working in public policy or government, preferably in the New Brunswick context
- Have experience working with a culturally diverse clientele in a multicultural environment, preferably with connections to communities in Fredericton
- Have experience in file management and financial reporting
- Have a demonstrated understanding of issues of social justice, equality and diversity
- Be fluent in English and French

Source: Courtesy Kelly Lamrock

"Opportunities Available" boxes present real job ads in the public service, allowing students to see where the study of Canadian politics may lead them.

BRIEFING NOTES

Reference Cases

Governments may refer cases only to the highest court in their respective jurisdictions. This means that while the federal government may refer questions, bills, or laws to the Supreme Court of Canada, provincial and territorial governments cannot. Rather, they may refer cases to their respective courts of appeal. Governments are not limited to referring their own laws for judicial review; they may choose to refer other governments', as well. Consider the pair of references concerning the federal government's proposed reforms to the Senate, as discussed in Chapter 6. The Quebec government referred federal Bill C-7 to the Quebec Court of Appeal, while the federal government referred a set of broader questions to the Supreme Court of Canada.

"Briefing Notes" boxes bring clarity to often misunderstood aspects of Canada's political system, such as the nature of equalization programs or the difference between a referendum and a plebiscite.

Additional Resources for Students and Instructors

Inside Canadian Politics is supported by a range of ancillary products designed to enhance the learning experience inside and outside the classroom.

For Instructors

- **Instructor's Manual.** A detailed guide for instructors provides extensive pedagogical tools and teaching tips for every chapter, including overviews and summaries, key concepts, essay and research assignments, and links to relevant online resources.
- **Presentation Slides.** Enhanced with graphics and tables drawn straight from the text, classroom-ready PowerPoint slides supplement lectures with summaries and key points for each chapter.
- **Test Generator.** The user-friendly software enables instructors to sort, edit, import, and distribute hundreds of questions in true–false, multiple-choice, and short-answer formats.

- **Video Guide.** Carefully chosen video clips, matched to each chapter and streamed from our companion website, provide case studies, documentary footage, and conversations that complement the themes and issues discussed in the textbook. An accompanying viewing guide provides a précis of each clip as well as discussion questions and assignment topics to inspire and guide further research.

For Students

- **Study Guide.** An online handbook for students includes chapter summaries, study questions, and lists of additional resources to help you review material from the textbook and lectures.

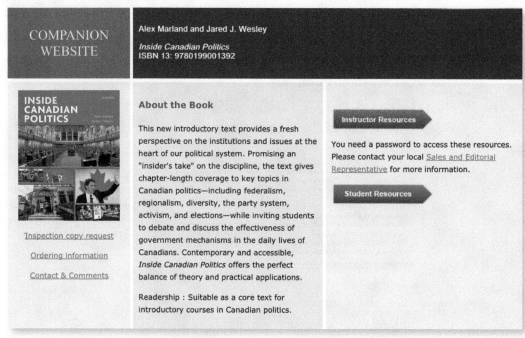

 www.oupcanada.com/Marland

Acknowledgements

Oxford University Press would like to thank the following reviewers and anonymous reviewers whose thoughtful comments and suggestions helped to guide the development of this textbook:

Mark Blythe, University of Alberta/MacEwan University
Mona Brash, Camosun College
Jay Haaland, Kwantlen Polytechnic University
Stewart Hyson, University of New Brunswick
Antonia Maioni, McGill University
Nanita Mohan, University of Guelph
Dennis Pilon, York University
Ivan Savic, Memorial University of Newfoundland
Erin Tolley, University of Toronto
Nadia Verrelli, Laurentian University

PREFACE

A Note to Instructors: Why Canadian Politics Needs "Pracademics"

In setting out to write a new introduction to Canadian politics, we wanted to produce a text that would reflect our experiences as scholars who have worked in public administration and who conduct research interviews with political insiders. We have seen the value that academic theories and models can have for the so-called "real world" of Canadian politics, when they are properly applied. We have also seen how practical experience can either dismiss or breathe life into academic concepts that, to date, have existed largely on paper. In this sense, our approach was *pracademic*, blending perspectives drawn from the worlds of practising public servants and full-time academics, to produce an insider's perspective on how Canadian politics actually works.

Pracademia has a richer history in the United States than in Canada. There, pracademically minded civil servants and researchers have long moved more easily from one career track to another, recognizing and demonstrating the mutual value of practice and scholarship. The twenty-first–century American political science community is home to a growing pracademic movement, which prides itself on applied research in contemporary politics, improved teaching, increased student engagement, enhanced societal relevance. According to two leading American pracademics:

> When we detach ourselves completely from the practical world of government and politics and become specialized and isolated from our colleagues in different subfields, we lose relevance and our scholarship loses meaning. By interacting with the political actors whom we study, we invigorate our scholarship and teaching, expand our audience, and validate ourselves and our scholarship. The fact that it is not unusual for a scholar of the legislative process not to have spoken with or personally observed a legislature does not demonstrate our objectivity; rather, this detachment should raise a red flag about our discipline's values and priorities. . . . While not every political scientist is interested in or suited to this sort of activity, the more pracademics that we have in a department, a field, and the discipline, the better off we all will be.[1]

In this sense, pracademia is a culture—a network of people who appreciate the benefits of solving real-world challenges by combining practitioner and academic perspectives. Pracademia allows policy analysts, issues managers, strategic directors, deputy ministers, political staffers, and others to take a step back from the frantic pace of day-to-day work, and assess how to better understand or improve the way they get

---

1. Michael P. McDonald and Christopher Z. Mooney, "'Pracademics': Mixing an Academic Career with Practical Politics," *PS: Political Science & Politics* 44, no. 2 (2011): pp. 252–3.

things done. At the same time, pracademia allows professors, researchers, and students to understand how things really work on the ground. Leaving the ivory tower can be daunting—even intellectually improper—to some. For those who do venture out to test their models by working alongside practitioners, it only serves to improve the foundations of their work. Thus, both communities benefit from a more holistic, pracademic perspective.

As mentioned, pracademia has been slower to develop in Canada than in the United States.[2] This has as much to do with the smaller job market (on both the academic and pratitioners' side) as it does with the persistence of three prevailing attitudes about pracademia north of the border:

1. *The gulf between academics and practitioners is decreasing.* Critics argue that academics (and their research findings) are too esoteric and divorced from actual practice, while practitioners' work is bereft of any connection to theory, evidence, or rigorous research. In reality, both sides have a long way to go to make their work relevant to the other. Academics must acknowledge the benefits of grounding their research in real-world evidence, and practitioners must be more receptive to allowing academics direct access to their day-to-day environment. By the same token, practitioners must recognize the value of taking an academic approach to evidence-based decision-making, while academics must make their research more accessible to people outside their discipline or subfield.

2. *Both sides have something meaningful to offer the other.* Critics hold that pracademia waters down "pure" academic work, and slows down fast-paced work in the public service. In fact, pracademia makes academic work more relevant, anchoring applied research in real-world problems and grounding theory in real-world experiences and evidence. Pracademia also provides academics with new avenues for research, new venues for knowledge dissemination, and new paths for career development. For practitioners, pracademia supports the push for evidence-based practices and innovation, and the desire for career growth and learning.

3. *Building pracademic networks is getting easier.* Technology allows pracademics to connect through blogs, Twitter (#pracademic), and Flipboard. Organizations like the Institute of Public Administration of Canada host events to facilitate face-to-face connections. An increasing number of secondments, internships and co-op placements, funding programs, scholarships in residence, professional graduate degrees, university courses, post-graduate certificate programs, associations, symposiums and workshops, journals and presses, and other institutions also exist that connect the academic and practitioners' worlds.

The following chapters are written from this pracademic perspective, illustrating the advantages of blending scholarly theories with practical experience, drawing evidence from both sides of the traditional divide, and exposing some of the myths and misconceptions that exist in both communities.

---

2. J.I. Gow and V. Seymour Wilson, "Speaking What Truth to Whom? The Uneasy Relationship between Practitioner and Academic Knowledge in Public Administration," *Canadian Public Administration* 57, no. 1 (2014): pp. 118–37.

A Note to Students: Why This Is More Than a Textbook

The authors of this book are "pracademics": scholars who have experience working in government. As academics, we have written research grant proposals to fund scholarly research, we have published in peer-reviewed journals, and we have taught an array of Canadian politics courses. As practising public servants, we have hurriedly prepared briefing notes in response to an emerging situation, contributed to cabinet papers that have informed government policy decisions, and supervised budding bureaucrats. With feet in both camps, we have seen, first-hand, the gaps that can exist between the worlds of political science and practical politics. Our objective in this book is to bridge these chasms, bringing together the best insights from the scholarly community and public sector. The Opportunities Available boxes you will find in each chapter reflect our pracademic approach, providing you with a look at real jobs related to the study of Canadian politics.

You have easy access to more knowledge than any previous generation in human history. You have the ability to browse entire floors of university libraries at a glance, to search for unfamiliar terms on (more or less) reliable websites, to consult thousands of scholarly papers at the click of a mouse, and even to access massive open-source databases to conduct your own primary research. These are luxuries that students of some other countries and generations have never enjoyed.

At the same time, this type of common wisdom and keystroke convenience can be just enough to make you a misinformed, cynical, and disengaged citizen. Common perceptions and online materials are fraught not only with stereotypes, deceptions, and even overt lies; they also consist of many half-truths and outdated understandings, which make it challenging for students to learn, teachers to instruct, and politicos to practise in a reliable way.

Indeed, the Canadian political consciousness hosts a great many false beliefs that contain just enough truth to carry sway among many casual observers. Public opinion, socialization, media commentary, and even some political science literature all help to perpetuate these misconceptions. In part, this is due to the gap between theory and practice discussed above.

To this end, each chapter of *Inside Canadian Politics* begins with a set of three maxims meant to dispel prominent misconceptions about our government. You should know, for example, that the average citizen has many opportunities to make a difference in Canadian politics (Chapter 1), that there is much more to the justice system than courtrooms and judges (Chapter 7), that political communication is much more than "spin" (Chapter 11), and that Canada has more clout than you might think (Chapter 14). Some political science professors and ardent students of Canadian politics might see these maxims as so self-evident that they hardly need to be stated. Yet Canadians' knowledge of their political system is so limited that these "truths" are not universally known. Competing myths and misconceptions need to be busted, not just for the benefit of students in a classroom and policy analysts at their workstations, and not simply to improve society's knowledge about itself and its politics. They need to be exposed and corrected if Canadians hope to improve their political system, develop better public policies, and achieve real progress toward addressing society's greatest challenges.

We are under no illusion that this guide will achieve these ends in and of itself. We are not expecting every student to read the entirety of what follows in these pages

↻ See About the Authors, on the inside back cover, for more information about the authors' backgrounds in the worlds of political science and public administration.

(even those who are required to do so). We do, however, hope to empower readers to challenge some of the common misconceptions that surround Canadian politics and take the discussion beyond their seminars or working groups to the issues properly at the coffee shop or bar, kitchen table or boardroom table. It is in that spirit that each chapter concludes with a debate section.

Structure of *Inside Canadian Politics*

Our challenge is to provide you with an insider's guide that will allow students to competently produce and critically consume knowledge about Canadian politics. We will give you the foundation necessary to make sense of the day-to-day goings-on in Ottawa and capital cities across Canada, without burdening you with excessive facts, figures, or trivia that would be out of date by the time this book went to press. (We are writing in the immediate aftermath of the 2015 federal election, for instance, which makes it challenging to provide up-to-date material.) And we will provide you with a set of dependable supplementary resources to further your understanding, as we cannot possibly fit everything you need to know into a single printed volume.

A quick glance through the pages of this book will show you that we have strived to provide more than simply nuts-and-bolts descriptions of the way Canadian political institutions function. We have supplemented explanations with *Inside Canadian Politics* stories that demonstrate these concepts in action. Key terms are identified in bold and are accompanied by definitions in the margins. Each chapter ends with a topical public policy debate, to show how differing approaches can lead to differences of opinion on the country's most divisive issues. We've illustrated the text with photos and cartoons, illustrative charts and figures, and innovative infographics, all meant to reinforce and build on themes developed in the main narrative. And, just so you don't have to take our word for it, we also shared thoughts from political insiders, drawn from speeches, written documents, and tweets that are presented here in segments titled They Said It. In our opinion, to get a flavour of how Canadian politics works in the real world, it is essential to consider the voices of those who operate in that world.

To help us deliver content that engages an array of perspectives, we have benefited from research assistance provided by a number of political science students, including Lori-Ann Campbell, Michael Penney, and Matthew Yong.

As you review the varied content of this book, here's what we ask: take these lessons and ideas seriously. Challenge them through your own experiences, and—should you find them wanting—tell someone about it. Debate with your classmates and your friends; discuss with your professors and family. Then take it to the next level by sending a letter to a newspaper, phoning a call-in radio program, posting a blog, tweeting about it, and/or joining a political organization. And write to us, or find us on Google: we need to know if you spotted any errors or omissions, so that we can fix them, and we would welcome ideas for how we can improve this pracademic guide.

Don't just sit there. Get *Inside Canadian Politics*.

Alex Marland, www.mun.ca/posc/people/Marland.php
Jared J. Wesley, https://ualberta.academia.edu/JaredWesley
October 2015

1 CANADIAN POLITICS

Inside this Chapter

- What is politics? What is democracy?
- What are the main cleavages in Canadian politics?
- What have been the major issues in Canadian political history?
- What do chapters in the rest of this book deal with?

Inside Canadian Politics

There are several reasons people take an introductory course in Canadian politics. Some aspire to become involved in one of the many areas in which familiarity with Canadian politics is indispensable, from social activism to public service

What the 2015 Election Means for Canadian Politics

Visit the *Inside Canadian Politics* flipboard to learn about the latest developments relating to Canadian politics.

 Go to
http://flip.it/gblag.

to constitutional law. Some feel that a better understanding of how our government works is part of being a more responsible citizen. Some take the course simply because it is a prerequisite in their political science department. Regardless of why you're here, we think you'll find this book enlightening and even entertaining. As authors we will be honest and straightforward, and we intend to challenge you to make informed judgements and arguments about the topics we will present. In return we ask that you engage with others about what you read, both within the classroom and away from it.

Students often come to the study of Canadian politics with certain ideas that are not entirely accurate. Here are three maxims you should be aware of from the outset.

 Canada's political system has changed considerably since 1867. Canada's system of parliamentary democracy was established a century-and-a-half ago, and while the constitutional order has changed remarkably little since that time—in spite of notable attempts at constitutional reform in the late twentieth century—Canada's political system has undergone significant shifts since Confederation.

 There are many different ideas and ideologies at play in Canadian politics. Some people consider it a hallmark of Canada's politics that ideological divisions are less entrenched than they are in other democratic states, especially south of the border and in Europe. Nevertheless, ideology exerts a powerful force on the political order and is, as we shall see in this chapter, one of three principal cleavages shaping the dynamics of Canadian politics.

 The average citizen has many opportunities to make a difference in Canadian politics. Canadian citizens may be feeling detached from the country's political institutions like never before—indeed, this civic alienation is reflected in declining rates of political participation and voter turnout, especially among young people—but there are abundant opportunities to become involved in politics in a variety of paid and volunteer positions. Throughout this book we'll present examples of the kinds of opportunities open to anyone with an interest in, and understanding of, Canadian politics.

Overview

This introductory chapter is a primer for the rest of the book. It summarizes some of the core concepts in politics generally and in Canadian politics specifically. This includes a brief overview of the historical dynamics that have shaped the political landscape in this country, particularly along the cleavages of geography, ethnicity, and ideology, and of the hybrid nature of the country's political institutions, which are based on British and American models. In doing so, this chapter provides the basis for understanding how major political disputes arise and are resolved within Canadian democracy. At the same time, the chapter looks at how these cleavages and institutions have presented particular challenges for Aboriginal peoples, whose role, if not influence, in Canadian politics has expanded considerably in recent decades.

Each chapter of this textbook ends with a supplement designed to help you debate a topic that is central to the study of Canadian politics. We preview the debate topic at the start of the chapter so you can keep the question in mind as you read through.

UP FOR DEBATE

Do Aboriginal and non-Aboriginal politics belong in the same political system?

Keep this question in mind as you read through the chapter. Consult the end-of-chapter debate supplement for more material to help you engage in an informed discussion of the topic.

Getting Inside Canadian Politics

Canadian politics is more interesting and complex than most people realize. As is true with most topics, understanding the basics is essential to making sense of the intricacies of current events and developments.

As you begin your journey of learning about Canadian politics, try this simple way to bring the theories and concepts in this book to life. Go online to news sources like *The Globe and Mail*, CBC News, or perhaps *The Hill Times*, or peruse an online news magazine like *Ottawa and Beyond* (bit.ly/BeyondOttawa). You could also see what's trending at the #cdnpoli Twitter hashtag. Have a look at what some of the major Canadian news stories are, how the government is involved, and who the main politicians are. Talk with your peers to see if they have the same reactions you do. Chances are, you will be exposed to different opinions. You're on your way to getting inside Canadian politics.

To the majority of citizens who do not follow developments that closely, and at times even to those who do, the landscape of Canadian politics can seem confusing. Consider the nature of representation in Canada, for instance. At any given time, a Canadian is represented by a member of the provincial or territorial legislature, by a member of Parliament, and by a senator—all three of whom may be from different political parties. (This is not to mention the individual's mayor, reeve, councillor, school board trustee, and many other official representatives at the local level.) Deciding exactly whom to approach for help with a particular government service or program, or whom to hold to account at the ballot box, can be challenging given these different layers of political representation.

Canadians are also represented by heads of government. Each province and territory is led by a premier, and the country is headed by a prime minister. As powerful as they are, and as democratic as the Canadian system is, neither of these highest-ranking leaders is directly elected by the citizens they represent. Rather, the premier and prime minister are chosen by representatives of the Queen who are appointed to their positions, rather than elected. Is this democratic?

Consider the process of making decisions about government policy. Canadians pride themselves on their universal healthcare system; despite its shortcomings, citizens consistently list it as among the most important elements of the country's political culture and identity. Yet in reality, there is no single Canadian healthcare system. There are at least 14: one for each province and territory and one at the federal level. This high degree of decentralization distinguishes Canada from other countries, in health policy and beyond. Canada is the only country in the Western world without a national department of education, for instance, leaving the determination of

decentralization The transfer of authority from central to local government, typically from the federal government to provincial/territorial governments.

curriculum, teaching standards, and so on to each provincial and territorial government. The same is true for the stock market: Canada is alone in not having a common securities regulator, but rather has several regional sets of rules and enforcement mechanisms. Likewise, taxation and regulation systems differ from jurisdiction to jurisdiction, resulting in odd anomalies. Transporting some goods, like liquor, is often easier between Canada and the United States than it is between provinces. How does a country with so much internal diversity manage to govern itself as a single political system?

To be certain, there are advantages and disadvantages to the structure of Canada's political system. With complexity can come both responsiveness and problems with accountability, for instance. Yet, to assess whether Canadian democracy functions properly and achieves the best results for Canadians requires more than a surface-level understanding of how things work. It requires you to step deep *inside Canadian politics*, as this book's title suggests.

To start you on this journey, this introductory chapter begins with an overview of the key concepts underpinning Canadian politics, providing a basic lexicon to engage in later discussions. We then identify three maxims of Canadian politics—three truths that serve as pillars supporting the information found in the remainder of the

Andrew Francis Wallace/Getty Images

Critics were divided in 2015 when the Ontario government proposed progressive new guidelines for sex education in the province's schools. Canada is the only advanced industrial country without a national education department, and curriculum and standards vary considerably among provinces and territories. In the context of sexual health and education, consider that the topic of sexual orientation is introduced to students in grade 3 in Saskatchewan but in grade 8 in New Brunswick. How would having curriculum determined by a single, central education department change the nature of education in Canada? How would it affect the ability of Canadian students and parents to influence the education system?

book. The chapter concludes with a road map to the rest of the volume, including summaries of each chapter.

Core Concepts in Canadian Politics

Before delving more deeply inside Canadian politics, it is important to take a higher-level view of some of the overarching concepts that guide politics in Canada, and elsewhere. We will not spend much space in the following chapters discussing other countries' political systems, but it is important to situate Canada within this broader global and historical perspective.

To begin, what do we mean by "politics"? The practice of politics has been around since the dawn of human civilization, as people have struggled to determine their common priorities and endeavours. These struggles tend to centre on "who gets what, and when" in terms of a community's shared resources. This, in turn, involves a competition among individuals and groups for control over the decision-making process. This pursuit of power is a cornerstone of politics in Canada today.

In modern times, the most contested communal decision-making has been exercised at the state level. Many states exist as countries, like Sweden, Turkey, Vietnam, Peru, and Mozambique. As we will see in Chapter 3, on federalism, ultimate political authority within these *unitary* states is concentrated in a single, country-wide body. Other states exist within specific countries, as in the case of regional governments in *federations* like the United States, Argentina, Germany, Ethiopia, India, Australia, and Canada. In this sense, federal countries consist of multiple states, each enjoying ultimate authority (or sovereignty) over different areas of jurisdiction.

In this sense, the Canadian federation consists of eleven sovereign states: one at the country-wide level, and ten at the provincial level. The central ("federal") government enjoys jurisdiction over the armed forces and defence, citizenship, and other pan-Canadian areas of jurisdiction, while the provinces maintain jurisdiction over healthcare, education, the administration of justice, and other local jurisdictional matters. In practical terms, Canada's three territories enjoy many of the same powers as provinces, although their autonomy remains limited by the fact that the federal government holds full sovereignty over their jurisdiction.

State decisions are made by governments. In democratic states like Canada, members of government are elected to their positions on a regular basis; in autocratic states like many in the Middle East, governments consist of religious or hereditary rulers and their appointed advisers. Thus, citizens play a more active role in democratic states than do subjects in autocracies. In liberal democracies like Canada, citizenship involves a combination of rights and responsibilities that are not enjoyed by people living in other parts of the world.

To summarize, politics in Canada involves the pursuit of political power through democratic means, with individuals and groups competing to control the levers of decision-making found in governments located in each of the country's eleven states. This competition takes place on many levels (locally, regionally, country-wide, globally), in many dimensions (cultural, territorial, intergovernmental, ideological, partisan), in many venues (boardrooms, campaign trails, courtrooms), on many issues (healthcare, education, national defence), involving many players (politicians, judges, citizens). The chapters that follow dig deeper inside Canadian politics to explain how this process unfolds.

politics Activities involving the pursuit and exercise of collective decision-making.

power The ability to control or influence other members of a political community.

state A structured political community with a single source of ultimate authority over its territory.

jurisdiction The ultimate authority to make legal decisions, or the seat of power for such decision-making.

↻ See pages 84–5 of Chapter 3 for the differences between federal and unitary systems of government.

government The body of individuals assigned to conduct the affairs of the state on behalf of the citizenry.

democracy A system of government featuring decision-makers chosen by citizens through free and fair elections.

autocracy A system of government featuring an unelected decision-maker with absolute authority.

citizen A legally recognized inhabitant of a democratic state.

liberal democracy A system in which equality, rights, and freedoms are preserved through public debate and free and fair elections.

↻ The characteristics of liberal democracy are discussed on pages 40–1 of Chapter 2, on the constitution.

Three Maxims of Canadian Politics

At this point, we offer three things that we feel every student or observer of Canadian politics should bear in mind. This is not a set of concepts that every textbook includes. However, we think it is important to present these three statements as embodiments of the key pillars of Canadian politics; they will serve as common threads for the discussions found later in this book:

1. Canadian politics is defined by the CLEAVAGES of geography, ethnicity, and ideology.
2. The INSTITUTIONS of Canadian democracy are Anglo-American hybrids.
3. Understanding Canadian politics requires some awareness of Canadian HISTORY.

1. Core Cleavages

cleavage A division that separates opposing political communities.

institution A structure that defines and constrains behaviour within a political system.

Not everyone thinks alike, which is why politics is so often divisive. In Canada, the cleavages that are mostly responsible for shaping the dynamics of Canadian politics over the past four centuries are *geography*, *ethnicity*, and *ideology*. These are not the only dividing lines in Canadian society, nor are they the only focal points for political debate and conflict. They do, however, represent the core pillars of Canadian politics, and they are the most deeply engrained in the country's political psyche. This is no coincidence. All of Canada's major political institutions—its constitution, legislature, courts, laws, political parties, and more—have been crafted with geography, ethnicity, and ideology in mind. This means that, in the "game" of Canadian politics, both the rules and players are hardwired to ensure that the competition for power occurs along fault lines defined by territory, race, language, and core beliefs about the role of the state in society and the economy. Discussed below, these various factors are mutually reinforcing: certain ethnic communities tend to be concentrated in select parts of Canada, while different regions and cultural communities tend to adhere to unique sets of ideological beliefs (Figure 1.1).

These three cleavages leave little room for additional forms of political expression and debate. The structure of Canada's political institutions means that other lines of division, such as gender and class, often fail to achieve long-term salience. As a result, issues like gender equality or income inequality, and proposed solutions like affirmative action or the redistribution of wealth, tend to be overshadowed. Instead, discussions about linguistic accommodation or the proper distribution of federal transfer funds to the provinces tend to dominate. In this sense, Canadian politics is as much about what interests are organized *into* the system as what is organized *out* of it.

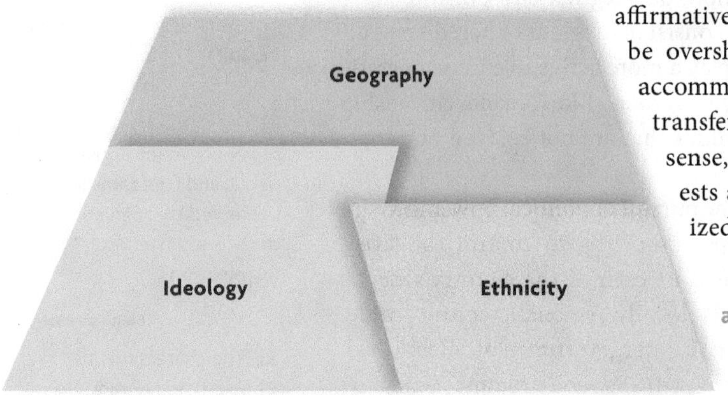

FIGURE 1.1 | Mutually Reinforcing Cleavages in Canadian Politics

a) Geography

First and foremost, Canadian democracy has always been conducted along geographic lines. The notion of who controls which territory

How do you think geography, ethnicity, and ideology align in Canada?

was fundamental to Canadian politics even prior to the country's founding in 1867. Land claim disputes among various orders of government and Aboriginal communities continue to this day, affecting everything from healthcare and education to hunting and natural resources.

It should come as little surprise that Canada's geography has come to define its politics. Canada is next only to Russia as the world's largest country in terms of land mass. The distances that divide Canadians on the west coast of British Columbia from those on the east coast of Newfoundland, or that separate people from the northern reaches of Nunavut from those at the southern tip of Ontario, can be measured as much by kilometres as by their distinct political perspectives. People in different parts of Canada have different interests, priorities, and viewpoints based on the unique shared experiences within their communities. Growing up in a harsh, remote environment shapes one's political perspective differently than growing up in a well-to-do suburb, or living in a big city. Being endowed with a wealth of natural resources like oil and gas shapes a community's economy and outlook, often putting it at odds with neighbours with fewer natural advantages. Even within closer proximity, political geography tends to divide Canadians in rural areas from those in urban ones, and those who live in economically developed areas from those who do not. All told, attitudes toward authority, community, distribution of wealth, mutual obligations, and other political beliefs vary depending on where a person lives. If you know someone from a different part of Canada, or even a different part of your province, chances are that person's political attitudes will vary from your own.

Political scientists often refer to these geographically defined communities as having unique **political cultures** that help to distinguish them from their neighbours.

political culture A society's innate political characteristics, embodied in the structure of its institutions and the beliefs of its members.

The Canadian Press/Sean Kilpatrick

You can buy 4L of milk in Toronto for as little as $3.97. It can cost you twice as much in St John's, and—as shown here—more than double that price in Iqaluit. As the card indicates, the Iqaluit price reflects a $10.52 government subsidy, meant to offset the high costs of shipping nutritious food to the far north. To what extent should the government subsidize the cost of milk and other products in remote areas? How much might your answer depend on the part of the country in which you live?

Observers often divide Canada into several regional political cultures, although the boundaries between them tend to be blurry. Some see clear divisions between Westerners, Easterners, Northerners, and central Canadians, for instance, while others see unique political cultures within these larger groups (of the Prairies, for instance, or of the Maritimes). Given the nature of power sharing in Canada, leaders of these various provincial communities have had the opportunity to build their own "small worlds" within the confines of the Canadian state.[1] This contributes to a sense of political identity whereby some citizens identify more with their province and its premier than with Canada and the idea of being "Canadian."

As one of the world's first federations, Canada sees its power divided among 13 geographically defined communities, now numbering 10 provinces and 3 territories. Across a wide range of subject areas of localized interest, from natural resources to health and education, each provincial government is entitled to govern itself according to its own laws without interference from other provinces or the central government. Known as the federal government (based in Ottawa), the latter presides over matters of national interest, including the military, foreign affairs, currency and banking, and criminal justice. Yet when it comes to the day-to-day lives of Canadians, and the day-to-day functioning of politics in the country, a growing proportion of government responsibility now falls under provincial jurisdiction.

federation A political system that distributes power between a central government and regional governments.

With the steady growth of the welfare state and Canada's emergence as a two-pronged economy based on natural resources (like oil, gas, agriculture, timber, and fish) and the knowledge sector (rooted in provincially run universities and colleges), provinces are playing a greater role than ever before. And while federal and provincial governments do collaborate on several areas of common interest, the provinces remain autonomous when it comes to defining their own policy priorities and direction. As a result, no two provinces have the same set of political priorities and processes. This has helped to ensure that Canadian politics remains defined by geography, with each province consisting of its own unique political "world."

welfare state Government programming designed to promote the economic and social well-being of citizens.

policy Overarching principles used to guide government decisions and actions.

FIGURE 1.2 | A Cultural Map of Canada

Drawing heavily on stereotypes, this illustration that appeared in *Maclean's* magazine nevertheless captures some of the cultural features unique to different parts of the country. How do you think these cultural characteristics inform the political culture of each region? How would your political outlook be influenced by, for instance, "yoga pants," "empty factories," or "floods" and "funny accents" in your home province?

Maclean's, http://www.macleans.ca/news/canada/putting-canada-on-the-map/

Even on a country-wide scale, Canadian politics has always been conducted along territorial lines. Representation in executive, legislative, and judicial branches of government is heavily influenced by geography. Federal elections are waged in each of over 300 separate districts across Canada, where constituents elect their own member of Parliament to represent the community. Similarly, each province is allotted a certain number of senators and, by convention, is entitled to representation in the federal cabinet and on the Supreme Court of Canada. These rules help to ensure that regional representation is embedded within the central institutions of the Canadian state, perpetuating the power of geography in influencing Canadian politics.

b) Ethnicity

mosaic A metaphor used to depict Canada's multicultural character, which features many distinct yet interdependent ethnocultural communities.

Ethnicity is a second dominant cleavage in Canadian politics. Corresponding with its self-image as a multicultural mosaic, Canada remains divided into many racial and linguistic communities, each with its own outlook on Canadian politics. Centuries before the first contact with European settlers, Indigenous societies were similarly divided along tribal lines. While they, too, failed to prevent the sort of internecine warfare that had defined cultures throughout the rest of the world, Aboriginal political institutions—like the brand of federalism developed by the Haudenosaunee (Iroquois)—served as models for cultural accommodation and collaboration among disparate groups.

Crown The legal concept dictating the supremacy of the monarch over the executive, legislative, and judicial branches of government.

First Nations Aboriginal groups descended from a variety of historical Indigenous nations; collectively, the earliest inhabitants of North America and their descendants, other than Métis and Inuit.

colonialism Belief in the supremacy of European settler institutions over those of Aboriginal groups, and policies and practices that support this belief.

Tragically, when they began arriving in greater numbers in the seventeenth, eighteenth, and nineteenth centuries, the European colonists failed to extend the necessary level of respect in incorporating Aboriginal people into the original institutions of the Canadian state. While the Crown signed treaties with many First Nations, establishing nation-to-nation relationships between the British and (future) Canadian governments, on one hand, and Aboriginal peoples, on the other, these arrangements were often cast aside in the name of political expediency or, worse yet, outright discrimination. As a result, for centuries, Aboriginal peoples have been defined not as the self-governing communities embodied in treaties, but primarily as *responsibilities*, even wards, of the state. This paternalistic perspective has contributed to measures like the Indian Act, the reserve system, residential schools, and forced relocation. For instance, during the so-called "Sixties Scoop" that began in the 1960s, many Aboriginal people (often children) were forcibly removed from their homes in a deliberate attempt by government to insulate them against the cultural influences of their communities and assimilate them into mainstream Canadian society. The legacy of this colonialism persists to this day, as Aboriginal people remain largely, though not entirely, excluded from Canadian politics.

Ethnic divisions also persist among Canada's two founding European peoples, the French and English. This is not for lack of effort on the part of politicians to build bridges between them. Indeed, the country's constitutional history is marked by numerous attempts to secure political peace between the two groups. From separate colonies to federal union; from distinct legal systems to common linguistic rights; from forced assimilation to official bilingualism; and from protectionism and marginalization to nationalism and distinct status, the evolution of Canada's political institutions attest to the depth and persistence of cultural difference between its French- and English-speaking communities. The number of French Canadians is much smaller, located primarily but not exclusively in Quebec, with smaller communities in the Maritimes (particularly New Brunswick), Ontario, and elsewhere across the country. Canada's federal system affords provincial governments in these regions the ability to craft laws and institutions to promote the use of the French language, including school systems and commercial regulations. Many credit these laws and programs for the persistence of the French language in Canada, in the face of strong homogenizing forces within the North American and global communities.

Beyond Aboriginal, French, and English Canadians, there exist a host of ethnic communities whose stature in Canadian politics varies from time to time and place to place. In particular, with their distinct political experiences and priorities, ethnic divisions often separate new or second-generation immigrants from broader society. Where they exist in large numbers, like Filipinos in north Winnipeg or Sikhs in Surrey, ethnic groups may exert significant influence on the political system, for example electing candidates to Parliament, the provincial legislature, or city council. Groups that are geographically dispersed, like many Muslims and other religious minorities, face steeper challenges when it comes to representation in Canada's political system, defined as it is along territorial lines.

> **Maritimes** The region of Eastern Canada consisting of New Brunswick, Prince Edward Island, and Nova Scotia.

> ↻ Attempts to bridge the divide between Canada's French and English populations are discussed in Chapter 2, on the constitution.

c) Ideology

Often overwhelmed by the dominance of geography and ethnicity, the third major cleavage in Canadian politics surrounds ideology, or the core beliefs that different groups of citizens hold about the way power should be distributed or exercised. It is sometimes argued that Canadian politics is relatively devoid of ideological debate or conflict, especially in comparison with many European states. While the breadth of the ideological spectrum may be shorter in Canada than elsewhere, meaning that there is more philosophical agreement than discord, there are important nuances that help to distinguish the different ideological "camps" in this country (see Figure 1.3).

> **ideology** A set of ideas that form a coherent political belief system.

In Canada and much of the Western world, the two main competing ideologies are *individualism* and *communitarianism*. Individualism is a "me first" approach to governance. It is a libertarian worldview that supports capitalism, materialism, competition, and freedom from government interference. In Canada, it is commonly associated with the Conservative Party and with political culture in the United States. This contrasts with communitarianism, which is a "society first" mentality. It is a philosophy that prioritizes the community, promotes inclusiveness, and supports government intervention. In Canada, it is commonly associated with the New Democratic Party (NDP), but it also finds adherents among some members of the Conservative Party family.

> **libertarian** Advocating the least possible amount of state intervention in the lives of citizens.

These concepts remain contested by partisans, citizens, and academics alike. The terms predate Canada, and have taken on various meanings over the centuries, and within provincial politics their symbolism can vary somewhat across the country.

Left-Wing and Right-Wing

In politics, ideology is often imagined as a spectrum of views ranging from left to centre to right. In general, people on the left side of this spectrum are more egalitarian than are those on the right. Left-wing thinkers value policies that achieve *equality*

> **left-wing** A political tendency that promotes higher taxes and a bigger role for government while promoting proactive measures to secure social equality.

LEFT-WING	RIGHT-WING

IDEOLOGY

• progressivism	• conservatism
• communitarianism	• individualism
• feminism	• traditionalism
• support for unions and workers	• support for corporations and job-creators
• bigger government: positive view of government role in the economy and society	• smaller government: positive view of individual initiative and competition
• peacekeeping doves	• military hawks

POLICY LEANINGS

economic/fiscal

• government planning and regulation	• privatization and deregulation
• progressive taxation: higher on the wealthy and corporations, to redistribute to the poor	• flatter taxation: lower and more equal tax rates for all
• maintain/expand public services, particularly to improve the lives of the disadvantaged	• trickle-down economics: everyone benefits when the private sector thrives
• environmental protection, even at the expense of economic growth	• economic growth, even at the expense of environmental protection

social/moral

• pro-choice	• pro-life
• support for alternative lifestyles and diversity	• support for traditional lifestyles and conformity
• gun regulation	• gun ownership
• flexible sentencing with a focus on offenders' rights to rehabilitation	• strict sentencing with a focus on victims' rights and retribution

DEMOCRATIC SOCIALISM	LIBERALISM	CONSERVATISM	
traditional democratic socialists • egalitarianism • replacement of capitalism • group rights • challenge traditional institutions **third-way social democrats** • harness capitalism for public good • individual and • collective responsibility • social levelling	**business liberals** • fiscal orthodoxy • free trade • government intervention where necessary **welfare liberals** • social justice • extend the benefits of the market economy to support a strong welfare state • seek a level playing field	**blue tories** • economic nationalism • state support of private business **red tories** • preserve the social fabric • support proven social programs like medicare • reverence for the monarchy	**neoliberals** • libertarian • free markets • fiscal austerity • smaller government through privatization **neoconservatives** • preservation of traditional values • use of military • force to support moral objectives

Note: The colours used in this figure reflect traditional positioning but are not definitive. Political parties constantly refine their ideological positions. For instance, the federal Conservative government under Stephen Harper ran sizeable budget deficits but then brought in balanced-budget legislation. In 2015 the NDP pledged to run a balanced budget whereas in the past it had favoured deficit spending in tough economic times. The current Liberal government purposely plans to run billion-dollar deficits, whereas in the 1990s Liberal governments made major spending cuts to eliminate the deficit.

FIGURE 1.3 | The Canadian Political Spectrum

BRIEFING NOTES

The Political Left and the Political Right in Canada

Overall, four key dimensions separate the left and right in Canada.

- *Fiscally,* left-wing people favour government spending on social programs, while those on the right favour tax or debt reduction.
- *Institutionally,* the left favours reform, while the right favours tradition.
- *Socially,* the left promotes inclusion, while the right promotes conformity.
- *Militarily,* the left tends to be "dovish" (i.e. passive and peace-seeking), while the right tends to be "hawkish" (i.e. aggressive and conflict-seeking).

of result (or *condition*) for all Canadians, and they tend to focus their attention on improving the lives of society's most disadvantaged. They are often regarded by critics on the right-wing side of the spectrum as idealists with a romantic view of the potential and role of government to improve society at home and promote peace abroad. As communitarians, left-wing thinkers tend to value socio-cultural inclusion.

By contrast, **right-wing** thinkers tend to be less averse to hierarchy, whether in terms of government institutions or in society more generally, and favour approaches that promote *equality of right.* In other words, they believe that all Canadians should be allowed to live according to the same laws and that Canadians should compete according to the same set of basic rules. Right-wing people are also less accepting of radical changes: they typically seek to preserve the status quo or, in some cases, revert to more traditional practices. In this sense, people on the right often promote a more limited (if not negative) view of the role of government, opposing institutional or social reforms and promoting individual freedoms over group rights. Right-wing individuals are also often pro-military, and more willing than their counterparts on the left to intervene in foreign conflicts.

Socialism

"Left-wing" and "right-wing" are broad categories that comprise a variety of views ranging from more extreme at the ends of the spectrum to more moderate toward the middle. Beginning on the left side of the spectrum, there are two mainstream branches of socialism in Canadian politics. The first is known as **traditional social democracy**, whose adherents promote democratic reform, the expansion of the welfare state, a more progressive system of taxation (with higher rates imposed on the wealthy), a more inclusive society (through the extension of positive rights), and avoidance of armed conflict to achieve peace on the international stage. Their dedication to replacing capitalism with a more co-operative economic system helps distinguish traditional social democrats (on the far left) from third-way social democrats (in the centre–left).

Third-way social democracy emerged in Canada in the 1990s, as moderates sought to take the radical edge off their left-wing parties and advocacy groups. Third-way social democrats do not believe in displacing capitalism, but rather seek to harness capitalism for the good of a greater number of people. Rather than emphasizing

right-wing A political tendency that promotes lower taxes and a smaller role for government while supporting traditional social hierarchies and those resulting from competition.

traditional social democracy A branch of socialism that remains committed to replacing capitalism with a more co-operative economic system.

third-way social democracy A branch of socialism that accepts capitalism and aims to harness it to achieve equality of result.

the rights of all people to a certain quality of life, they balance this with promotion of individual (as well as collective) responsibility. And they have shifted their focus from pacifism to human security in international relations.

Liberalism

Small-*l* liberalism sits at the centre of the Canadian spectrum, between the equality of result espoused by socialism and the equality of right promoted by conservatism. As with socialism, there are two main branches of Canadian liberalism: business liberalism, which stresses economic matters; and welfare liberalism, which stresses social ones. Business liberals stress fiscal orthodoxy, promoting free trade within Canada and with other states, balanced budgets, debt reduction, and, when necessary, government intervention in the economy to promote growth. Much like third-way social democrats, welfare liberals accept the market economy and seek to extend its benefits to create a more just society (the difference being that liberals are less willing to use the levers of the state to redistribute wealth in order to do so). Welfare liberals also promote individual social rights, both in Canada and abroad. As their name suggests, they also support a strong social welfare state, albeit less expansive than the one social democrats advocate. The differences between third-way social democrats and welfare liberals are more than a matter of degree, however. While their means may appear similar, their ultimate objectives are distinct. Social democrats aim to remake society into a more egalitarian one by engaging in social levelling (equality of result); liberals aim to create not a level society but a level playing field, where everyone has an equal opportunity to compete.

Conservatism

Conservatism is by far the most complex political ideology in Canada, and is best considered along two separate dimensions: the *old right* (consisting of "red" and "blue" tories), and the *new right* (consisting of neoliberals and neoconservatives). Neoliberalism and neoconservatism form the dominant strains of Canadian conservatism today, and while the two terms are often used interchangeably and may be found within the same parties, they carry different meanings. Neoliberals (*not* to be confused with the small-*l* liberals described earlier) tend to focus more on fiscal matters, seeking freer (i.e. more *liberal*) markets and a smaller government through the cutting of government programs, the deregulation of private industry activities, and the privatization of government programs and assets. In contrast to this libertarian approach, neoconservatives are less reluctant to use the levers of the state—though not on economic matters necessarily, but rather on moral ones. Neoconservatives favour government policies and programs that promote or protect traditional values (including the definition of marriage between one man and one woman, or the criminalization of marijuana possession), and often support the expansion of anti-crime and pro-military measures.

Defined by its reverence for the monarchy, hierarchy, and incrementalism, and by its collectivist belief in the social fabric of society, old right toryism not only contrasts with the values of the new right; it is also the main feature distinguishing Canadian and American conservatism.[2] Like welfare liberals and neoconservatives, red tories tend to prioritize social issues ahead of economic ones. Because of their

business liberalism A branch of liberalism that seeks to achieve equality of opportunity in economic terms.

welfare liberalism A branch of liberalism that seeks to achieve equality of opportunity in social terms.

neoliberalism A branch of new right conservatism that favours less government intervention in the economy.

neoconservatism A branch of new right conservatism that promotes the protection of traditional values, and community and national security.

toryism A branch of Canadian conservatism with British, communitarian roots.

red toryism A branch of old right conservatism that promotes the preservation of the social fabric and government institutions.

Opportunities Available

Knowledge of Canadian Politics and Government Preferred!

Coordinator, National Service Desk

Fundraising and Membership Services, Conservative Party of Canada

The Coordinator – National Service Desk is responsible for ensuring that fundraising and membership inquiries are followed up on in a timely manner and that the Customer Service group meets the internal standards of service. This position will participate in recruiting customer service officers, training, documenting procedures and ensuring that there is adequate staff to cover call volumes at various times of day. The Coordinator will strive to continuously improve the level of customer service provided to our members and donors. In addition, the Coordinator is also responsible for providing first tier IT service and support for Conservative Party of Canada software.

Duties and Responsibilities

- Receive queries and comments from the membership and public
- Assists the manager in preparing schedules of work and participates in ensuring adequate levels of staff are available to meet customer needs.
- Ensuring that tax receipt and membership card reprints are handled in a timely manner
- Monitor issues raised by members and donors and identify trends
- Other projects and duties as assigned

Knowledge, Skills and Abilities Required

- Excellent customer service skills—you are positive, professional, courteous and service-oriented
- Experience working with databases and call tracking software
- Thorough knowledge of Party Policies and Constitution
- Possesses strong investigative and problem-solving skills with the ability to follow a problem through to its conclusion
- Ability to clarify inquiries, research issues and respond accordingly
- Must be a team player and have the ability to establish effective interpersonal relationships
- Must demonstrate the ability to multi task in a fast-paced environment
- Excellent organizational skills with compulsive attention to detail
- Works well under tight deadlines and pressure with the ability to be flexible and deal with sudden schedule changes.
- Sound judgment and decision making ability with the resourcefulness and innovation to tackle complex challenges.
- A "do what it takes" work ethic. Possess a high energy level which allows reaction to situations quickly and decisively. Able to work independently and be self-motivated, and to work as a part of or leading a team.

Source: Conservative Party of Canada, "Job description" (2014), www.conservative.ca/media/2013/12/Coordinator-National -Service-Desk.pdf.

communitarian belief that Canadian society is more than a sum of its individuals, and because they have grown to trust and value the welfare state as a proven institution of the Canadian state, red tories are more supportive of programs like medicare and social security than their neoliberal counterparts. They have also tended to support more inclusive moral policies than their neoconservative cousins. **Blue tories**, on the other hand, favour economic matters over social ones, and—in contrast to business liberals and neoliberals—tend to favour government support of private industry (through protectionist policies or subsidies) if it serves the national interest. A defining difference is that red tories lean more towards left-wing political solutions than do blue tories.

Again, these ideological divisions often overlap with the geographic and ethnic divisions discussed earlier. Western Canada is known to many as Canada's bastion of conservatism, while the east features a more receptive audience for greater state intervention in the economy and society. By the same token, different cultural groups, particularly those with devoutly religious members, often adhere more strongly to conservative principles than others. Combined or on its own, the ideological cleavage remains a prominent feature of Canadian politics, shaping everything from the constitution to policy outcomes.

2. Key Institutions

A second maxim underpinning Canadian politics concerns its unique combination of British and American traditions. With its colonial origins as a series of protectorates collectively known as "British North America," Canada has drawn its institutions and practices from both sides of the Atlantic Ocean.

From Britain, Canada has inherited its common-law and Westminster parliamentary traditions, meaning that it is a representative democracy featuring

- a government led by a prime minister and cabinet, supported by a majority of elected legislators;
- an opposition consisting of members outside the governing party;
- a permanent public service, separate from and at the service of the government;
- a judiciary independent from government influence; and
- a constitutional monarch, who exercises power on the advice of the prime minister.

The connection to Britain is significant. Not only does Canada share its monarch with the United Kingdom, but the body of constitutional laws governing Canadian democracy are replete with age-old British statutes and conventions. Moreover, Canadian politics owes its ideological foundations to the British model. Discussed above, the dominance of conservatism, liberalism, and socialism, and the contours of each belief system, draw heavily on the British example.

From the United States, Canada has borrowed the federal principle that, also discussed above, involves dividing power among a common central government and a series of provincial ones. As in the US, this balance between shared and local rule has been precarious from the start, and has shifted continuously over time. On one side stand the forces of *centralization*, bent on ensuring that the federal government has the authority to devise and impose common standards for essential programs like

blue toryism A branch of old right conservatism that promotes economic nationalism.

representative democracy A system in which citizens elect officials to make political decisions on their behalf.

Cultura Creative (RF)/Alamy Stock Photo

Suppose an MP uses the promise of property tax breaks to persuade a large multinational auto parts manufacturer to open a new factory in her riding. The factory promises to revive the struggling local economy by creating jobs. Where does this MP likely fall along the political spectrum, and why? Where on the spectrum will her most vociferous critics come from?

healthcare; to promote harmonization of laws and policies from province to province in order to reduce barriers to trade and mobility; to cultivate a strong, shared identity among Canadians; and so forth. On the other side stand the forces of *decentralization*, aiming to preserve provincial autonomy as a venue for the definition of local priorities, the expression of local interests, and the achievement of local objectives; as a means of fostering policy experimentation and learning among provinces; and as a bulwark against the breakdown of local communities. Proponents on both sides of this spectrum are active on campaign trails and in courtrooms across both the United States and Canada. Notwithstanding variation over time, the former has emerged as one of the world's most centralized federations, and the latter, the most *de*centralized. Canadian provinces now house some of the most powerful subnational governments in the world, active not only in areas of local interest but increasingly on the international stage, as well. This is why provinces feature so prominently in this book.

The American influence is felt elsewhere throughout Canadian politics. For instance, to many observers, the Charter of Rights and Freedoms, established in 1982, imported elements of the American Bill of Rights and a US style of litigiousness and judicial lawmaking that, until the 1980s, had remained foreign to Canadian politics. In a similar vein, Canadian campaign strategists have borrowed heavily from American-style election campaign strategies, including many innovative political marketing techniques. It is easy to overstate the degree of Americanization in Canadian politics, particularly given the Americanization of Canadian popular culture and the integration of the North American economy that has coincided with it. Some critics cite the increased level of negative advertising, the entrenchment of neoliberalism, the president-like concentration of power in the prime minister's office, and other developments as evidence that Canadian politics is becoming increasingly American.

In reality, Canadian politics has *always* featured a heavy American influence, or at least a strong similarity. Attack advertising is not particularly "American," for instance; early Canadian campaign literature suggests that politicos north of the border were every bit as scathing as their American counterparts. Likewise, populists and libertarians have long stood alongside blue tories in many Canadian conservative parties (albeit uneasily), and power has always been concentrated in the hands of the prime minister and the cabinet at the expense of rank-and-file legislators.

This said, it is important to note the extent to which Canadian politics has shifted out of the British orbit and into the American one. Certain notable exceptions notwithstanding, and with due attention to the influence of the party in power at the federal level, when it comes to the fundamental economic, institutional, and ideological underpinnings of its democracy, Canada has become more American and less British throughout its second century as a country. Nestled in between are the remnants of the political influence of France, namely the civil law system that is found in Quebec, and the policy of official bilingualism that requires that all federal government services be available in English and French.

3. Historical Evolution

Throughout this introductory chapter we have attempted to illustrate that Canadian politics has been shaped by centuries of history. Shifting balances of power, the emergence of new policy areas, and various external forces have all contributed to political

Negative (even sexist and xenophobic) political advertising existed in Canada even before this 1891 Conservative campaign poster, which portrayed Canada as a young woman the Liberals were prepared to sell into servitude to Uncle Sam. In what ways is Canada's political culture influenced by American politics? Is it a good or a bad thing?

Library and Archives Canada/Miscellaneous Poster collection/e008748902 change in Canada. Even in elements that have appeared relatively stable, like the persistence of age-old cleavages and institutions, subtle developments have helped send Canadian politics in new directions.

A comprehensive timeline of Canadian politics is beyond the scope or space of this chapter, particularly given the amount of detail found elsewhere in the book. At this opening stage of our journey inside Canadian politics, however, it is useful to take a brief tour of the last five centuries to establish a high-level perspective on the evolution and present state of Canadian politics, or how we got to here. In general, modern Canadian political history can be divided into three main eras, as outlined in Table 1.1.

First Era (late 1800s—early 1900s)

The first modern era spans the late nineteenth and early twentieth centuries, and begins in the 1860s with the negotiation of a federal state in British North America. Amid the American Civil War, colonial leaders from Nova Scotia, New Brunswick, Prince Edward Island, and the Province of Canada (which would become Quebec

TABLE 1.1 | Three Eras of Canadian Politics

	First Era (late 19th to early 20th c.)	Second Era (mid- to late 20th c.)	Third Era (late 20th to early 21st c.)
Central political issues	• federal union • westward expansion • reciprocity (free trade)	• national identity and unity • constitutional amendment • free trade	• fiscal matters • healthcare • terrorism
Deepest cleavages	• east/west • male/female • French Canada/English Canada	• Quebec/rest of Canada	• west/east • rural/urban/suburban • Aboriginal/non-Aboriginal
Principal sites for political conflict	• parliament/legislatures • courts	• parliament/legislatures • intergovernmental conferences • broadcast media	• courts • broadcast media • social media • rallies, protests
Dominant political parties (federal level)	• Liberals • Conservatives	• Liberals • Progressive Conservatives • CCF/New Democrats	• Liberals • Conservatives (and predecessors) • New Democrats • Bloc Québécois • Green
Key events and developments	• Confederation (1867) • Northwest Uprisings (1870, 1885) • World War I (1914-19) • Great Depression (1930s) • World War II (1939-45)	• Quiet Revolution (1960s) • Centennial (1967) • White Paper on Indian Policy (1969) • patriation of the constitution, Charter of Rights and Freedoms (1982) • megaconstitutional negotiations (Meech Lake and Charlottetown Accords) • Quebec referendums (1980, 1995) • North American Free Trade Agreement (NAFTA) (1994)	• September 11 (2001) • Afghanistan War (2001-11) • Great Recession (2008–9)

and Ontario) gathered in a series of high-level conferences to discuss the value and viability of joining together in a new commercial and military union. Newfoundland sent observers, but did not participate. These meetings culminated in a deal known as Confederation, embodied in the British North America Act, 1867. Passed by the British Parliament, the BNA Act became Canada's central constitutional document, establishing the institutional foundations for the new country, including the marriage of British traditions and American-style federalism discussed in the preceding pages of this chapter. The Act fell short of establishing complete sovereignty for Canada, however, as the drafters failed to incorporate an amending formula. In the absence of an agreed formula for changing the constitution, for over a century any changes to Canada's written constitution would require the approval of the British government.

Throughout this period, Canadian politicians were challenged with how to expand the new country's reach into the vast lands known at the time as Rupert's Land and the North-West Territories. Initially, the Canadian federation consisted of just four provinces: Ontario, Quebec, New Brunswick, and Nova Scotia. The constitutional family grew steadily over the course of the next half-century, with Manitoba

Confederation The federal union of provinces and territories forming Canada, originally including Ontario, Quebec, New Brunswick, and Nova Scotia.

amending formula A set of rules governing how the constitution can be changed.

Students and staff of St Barnabas Indian Residential School, Sarcee Reserve, Alberta, c. 1920. How did the treatment of Aboriginal people during the first era of modern Canadian political history develop into one of the deepest political cleavages in Canada today?

Engracia De Jesus Matias Archives and Special Collections, Algoma University

(1870), British Columbia (1871), Prince Edward Island (1873), Alberta (1905), and Saskatchewan (1905) entering the union. All the while, Canadian politics was dominated by the issue of how to assume and maintain control over the vast lands west of the Great Lakes.

This would involve more than negotiating the cession of sovereignty from Britain, establishing a police presence, devolving powers to new provincial governments, and racing the Americans to the West Coast. It also involved colonizing these territories, displacing Aboriginal peoples, and accelerating a long process of assimilation that some critics have associated with cultural genocide. The passage of the federal Indian Act in 1876 came to symbolize the Canadian state's approach to Aboriginal people, labelling them as an area of policy responsibility, marginalizing them with the establishment of reserves, paternalistically rejecting their inherent rights to self-governance with the founding of the band system, and beginning the process of placing their children in residential schools in the custody of white adults, some of whom were abusive.

Thus, Western expansion was far from smooth or uncontroversial. Conflicts erupted between Liberals and Conservatives in Ottawa and provincial capitals across the country, often pushing governments into court to defend their actions against each other and against private interests. The denial of full provincial jurisdiction to the new Western provinces, including control over the language of instruction in schools and natural resource development, sparked alienation and resentment, as did debates over the importance of reciprocity (or free trade) with the United States. The latter pitted Western farmers seeking freer access to American markets for their goods and machinery against central Canadian manufacturers, railway barons, and financiers bent on maintaining their advantages in a closed Canadian market. The federal government's treatment of Aboriginal people on the prairies even resulted in a pair of armed uprisings, led by Métis leader Louis Riel. These issues and developments only served to deepen the ethnic and regional cleavages that marked the first era of Canadian politics.

Amidst all this, women struggled to gain the right to vote and to stand for election. Francophones sought assurances that their dualist role in Confederation would be protected and not pushed aside by Anglophones. Canada suffered great loss during the World Wars, which was also a formative period for nationalism, and hardship during the Great Depression, which spurred the growth of the welfare state.

Second Era (mid-1900s–late 1900s)

The two World Wars and the Great Depression marked a long transition period between the first and second eras of modern Canadian politics. If its first 50 years could be considered its infancy as a country, throughout the ensuing three decades, Canada came of age as a society, as a political culture, and as a democracy. Canadians assumed leadership and an independent stature on the international stage thanks to their participation in the global conflicts. The Depression had the same effect on the country's internal political attitudes, as the Co-operative Commonwealth Federation, later known as the New Democratic Party (NDP), emerged as a competitive third political party. Change to political institutions occurred, as governments collaborated (and often competed) in building one of the world's most comprehensive social welfare states. These calamities—the World Wars and the Depression—forged a sense of common purpose among many Canadians, but not all. Regional, ethnic, and ideological divisions separated Canadians who supported the war efforts (primarily in English Canada) from those who did not (primarily in Quebec), and those who supported the expansion of the state (liberals and socialists) from those who did not (conservatives).

As Canada entered the post-war period, its politics turned toward questions of national identity and unity. Unlike the first era, the epicentre for these debates was not the West but rather Quebec. For decades, Quebecers had railed against the consensus surrounding Canada's involvement in the World Wars. Yet as a voice of the province of Quebec and francophones generally, the Quebec government had taken an inward-looking approach. It seldom engaged meaningfully with the federal and provincial governments on the pan-Canadian stage. At the same time, the ultra-conservative Union Nationale government in Quebec City played only a small role in the everyday lives of Quebecers. Other provincial governments were working with Ottawa to build more expansive health, education, and social programs. But in Quebec, these services continued to be directed largely by the Catholic Church. By the end of the 1950s, Quebec had become an outlier—a predominantly rural, conservative province in a quickly modernizing Canadian society.

This changed rapidly in the decades that followed, as the provincial Liberal Party in Quebec led what became known as the Quiet Revolution. In short order, the Quebec government displaced the Catholic Church as the central institution in Quebec society, building some of Canada's most progressive social programs in the process. The Quebec government also began asserting itself at intergovernmental meetings with the federal government and other provinces, hosting the first annual premiers' conference in 1960. The Quiet Revolution built on, and reinforced, a growing nationalism movement in Quebec—one that, to this day, continues to wax and wane, vacillating between building a stronger province within Canada and establishing an independent Quebec state. Regardless of the status of the nationalist movement, the Quiet Revolution helped to establish Quebec's claim to special status within the Canadian federation. This shaped a national unity discourse that dominated the second era of Canadian politics.

The developments in Quebec coincided with a parallel identity-building exercise in English Canada. In addition to the advent of the civil rights movement, which saw advances for women and other groups that had been traditionally marginalized, the post-war period saw a massive increase in immigration to Canada from Europe and the developing world, literally and figuratively changing the face of Canada in a few short decades. What was once a largely French-Catholic and English-Protestant mainstream was becoming increasingly multicultural, and immigrant and visible-minority communities began asserting themselves in the political arena.

Paradoxically, Aboriginal Canadians experienced more marginalization just as Canada's multicultural mosaic was taking shape. The federal government's *White Paper on Indian Policy* (1969) signalled its intention to dismantle the Indian Act in an effort to assimilate First Nations people into the broader, predominantly European society. The ensuing debate mobilized Aboriginal people as never before, on a regional and national level. In the short term, the federal government pulled back from its assimilationist position; in the longer term, Aboriginal leaders secured a more prominent voice in political discussions around the future of their communities.

Quiet Revolution An early 1960s modernizing movement in Quebec, geared toward a stronger provincial government and outward nationalism.

nationalism A unifying ideology among people who share a common homeland, ancestry, and language or culture.

multicultural Consisting of many culturally distinct groups.

The Centennial celebrations (1967) provided an impetus and backdrop for these various discussions about the nature of Canadian identity. The federal government adopted an official flag and anthem for the country, established Canada as an officially bilingual (if not bicultural) country, and began discussions about patriating the Canadian constitution.

The two identity-building processes collided amid the constitutional negotiations of the 1970s and 1980s. Prime Minister Pierre Trudeau staked his political career on bringing the Canadian constitution under full domestic control, a move that required the incorporation of the elusive amending formula so that the document could be changed without the approval of British Parliament. Trudeau made the patriation process contingent on the entrenchment of a new Charter of Rights and Freedoms. Both the amending formula and the Charter proved points of contention among the federal and provincial governments, and negotiations stretched throughout the 1970s and into the 1980s. At several points, governments found themselves arguing before the Supreme Court of Canada, which insisted that any constitutional consensus must involve substantial provincial consent. In the end, the new constitution—complete with a complex amending formula and circumscribed Charter—received support from nearly all governments before Queen Elizabeth II signed its passage in 1982.

Crucially, the deal did not receive support from the government of Quebec, whose opposition to the new constitution prolonged the high-stakes negotiations for another decade. In 1980, amid the patriation discussions, Quebec held a referendum on separation from Canada, which was defeated, but not without a promise from Pierre Trudeau that Quebec would be accommodated in a new constitution. When this failed to materialize, Prime Minister Brian Mulroney, who formed the government in 1984, renewed the pledge to address Quebec's demands. Among Quebec's proposed amendments to the constitution was the formal recognition of Quebec as a "distinct society." Governments and many leading organizations from across Canada agreed on two complete constitutional reform packages: the Meech Lake Accord (1987) and the Charlottetown Accord (1992). Neither received the necessary legislative or popular support for passage, however, and Canada's written constitution remains largely as it was in 1982. This lack of change produced a new wave of separatist sentiment in Quebec, and in 1995, the newly elected Parti Québécois convened a second sovereignty referendum. This time, the margin of victory for the "non" side was much slimmer: just 50.7 per cent of Quebecers voted to remain in Canada.

The end of the constitutional turmoil and the Quebec referendums brought a tumultuous close to the second era of modern Canadian politics. Questions of national identity and unity, and constitutional preoccupations, overshadowed many other pressing issues. In particular, they distracted many governments and Canadians from the significant economic challenges facing the country, as federal and provincial budgets continued to fall further into deficit while public debts mounted. Much maligned at the time, the Goods and Services Tax (GST) and the Canada–US Free Trade Agreement (FTA)—a precursor to the continent-wide North American Free Trade Agreement (NAFTA)—were among the few notable achievements in this area.

The unpopularity of the constitutional accords, the GST, and NAFTA all contributed to the ultimate downfall of the Progressive Conservative government, which went from a solid majority in 1988 to just two (2) seats in the House of Commons in 1993, making it the largest electoral collapse in Western democratic history. The

patriation The process through which Canadian governments gained the authority to amend the country's main constitutional documents.

Charter of Rights and Freedoms A portion of the Constitution Act, 1982, enshrining Canadians' core liberties and entitlements vis-à-vis their governments.

distinct society A proposed designation for the province of Quebec, recognizing that it features a French-speaking majority, a unique culture, and a civil-law tradition.

Liberal Party resumed its place as Canada's "natural governing party"—a title it held throughout nearly all of the second modern era. However, political fracturing occurred along geographic lines, with the emergence of the Bloc Québécois in Quebec and the conservative Reform Party (succeeded in 2000 by the Canadian Alliance) in the West. This regional fracturing would contribute to the Liberals' winning four straight elections, before Stephen Harper—who was first elected as a Reform MP in 1993—became prime minister in 2006 as leader of the newly minted Conservative Party of Canada.

Third Era (late 1900s–early 2000s)

After the national unity drama climaxed in the early 1990s, governments across Canada turned their attention away from the constitution in earnest, focusing more on their own ballooning budgets and the country's slow economic growth. Upon its return to power, the Liberal Party under Prime Minister Jean Chrétien led the country through one of its most comprehensive rounds of fiscal restructuring since the Second World War, reversing many of the approaches and policies that earlier Liberal governments pursued in growing Canada's welfare state. The federal government launched a series of strict spending cuts, most notably to the transfers it provided to provincial governments for programs and services like healthcare, education, and welfare. Many provinces cut spending in these areas as well, resulting in a noticeable retrenchment in the area of social policy across Canada. By the turn of the century, these reductions placed nearly all federal and provincial governments on firmer fiscal ground, with most posting balanced budgets. In the meantime, the spending cuts hit Canada's universal healthcare system particularly hard, prompting Canadians to identify healthcare as their most important political concern in public opinion polls. This pushed governments to re-invest in the health sector, while seeking to improve the quality of healthcare through collaborative efforts and the sharing of best practices.

balanced budget A budget in which total government revenues equal (or sometimes exceed) total spending.

This firm fiscal focus was disrupted, at least momentarily, by the events of 11 September 2001. The 9/11 terrorist attacks in New York City, Washington, and Pennsylvania reverberated throughout the world. Their immediate impact was felt strongly in Canada. Allegations that the hijackers might have travelled through Canada only heightened attention to North American border security, as both countries enacted sweeping new anti-terrorism legislation that challenged their ability to balance public safety with civil liberties. If the immediate response to the September 11 attacks demonstrated the close relationship between Canada and the United States, its aftermath illustrated the extent to which each government maintained its independence in the area of foreign policy. When the Chrétien administration rejected the Americans' invitation to join coalition forces deployed to remove Saddam Hussein from power in Operation Iraqi Freedom, it became the latest in a series of high-profile differences of opinion over military policy that began, in modern times, with the war in Vietnam. Overall, the two countries seem to see eye-to-eye when their respective governments share a common ideological outlook (as when the Liberals are in power in Ottawa and the Democrats control the White House, or when both the Conservatives and Republicans form governments). Canada contributed to the American-led war on terror by sending troops to Afghanistan, participating in active combat from October 2001 until 2011, when the combat mission transitioned to a training mission prior to troop withdrawal in 2014. More than 150 Canadian soldiers paid the ultimate sacrifice in Afghanistan, as Canadian society's views of its military shifted from an image of underfunded peacekeepers to armed soldiers on the front lines.

Fiscal tensions re-emerged in 2008, when the Great Recession, triggered by the collapse of the poorly regulated American housing market, began to affect markets around the world. As witnessed countless times before, the close integration of the US and Canadian economies exposed Canada to a significant shock, although firmer banking regulations north of the border blunted the blow to a significant extent. In his only two meetings with the premiers of all provinces and territories, Conservative prime minister Stephen Harper orchestrated Canada's response to the recession: a massive, cost-shared stimulus package involving significant, one-time investment in infrastructure across Canada. The joint commitment challenged all Canadian governments to maintain their budget balances, and pushed all but a few into significant and long-term deficits.

The Great Recession also accelerated and highlighted a long-term power shift in Canadian politics. Strong petroleum-based economies in the West weathered the economic storm much better than their neighbours in central and eastern Canada, with British Columbia, Alberta, and Saskatchewan (self-named the New West Partnership) serving as Canada's economic engine throughout the first decade-and-a-half of the twenty-first century. For the first time in Canadian history, the economy of Ontario—home to Canada's largest population and its manufacturing hub—was performing below the national average, and the government was receiving equalization payments from Ottawa. This forced other "have-less" provinces to accept smaller equalization payments, placing further stress on their budgets, while western Canada emerged as the fiscal foundation of Canada's system of federal–provincial transfers. While the long-term effects of the 2014 oil price plunge remain to be seen, the effect of the 2008 recession was clear: economic and political influence had shifted from East to West (if not fully or permanently). This has occurred against a backdrop of greater economic co-operation, as Canadian governments have worked to negotiate a free trade deal with the European Union, as well as to reduce inter-provincial trade barriers.

In addition to the re-emergence of this East–West economic divide, the third modern era of Canadian politics has featured significant social change. Court decisions that enforce the Charter of Rights and Freedoms have facilitated societal change faster than elected or government officials were prepared to advance, in areas ranging from same-sex marriage to the legalization of prostitution. As well, environmentalism has risen as a sustained area of public concern, culminating in the 2011 election to the House of Commons of Green Party leader Elizabeth May, who was re-elected in 2015.

At the same time, the third era has given rise to a new set of geographic divisions and salience to an ages-old ethnic cleavage. On the first count, Canadian elections have come to be fought less on pan-Canadian or broad regional lines (as during the second era), and more along rural–urban–suburban lines. Political scientists have discovered that, more than ever before, Canadians' political attitudes depend on the size of community in which they live. The gradual urbanization of Canadian society has continued over the past century, reinforcing a longstanding political cleavage: rural Canadians continue to be among the most conservative in their outlook on most issues, and urban Canadians more progressive. This division has manifested itself in the success of the federal Conservatives, provincial Progressive Conservatives

Great Recession A decline in the international economy that began in 2008, triggered by the collapse of the US housing market.

equalization A federal transfer program designed to lessen the fiscal disparities among provinces.

INSIDE CANADIAN POLITICS
Are Leaders Afraid of the Media and Political Debate?

No matter who is in power, it seems that opposition leaders routinely seek out media coverage, while the prime ministers and premiers are careful about controlling information. In the late 1800s, John A. Macdonald, Canada's first prime minister, sought to control the media by arranging for friends to buy or launch newspapers that would support his governing Conservative Party and slag his opponents. In the 1970s, Prime Minister Pierre Trudeau regularly battled the press and refused to take their questions, particularly when public attention turned to his failing marriage and away from government business. This seems anti-democratic, yet those who are not careful risk being characterized by the media and opponents as weak and indecisive.

Until recently, trends suggested that the traditional role of the mainstream political media is both evolving and eroding. Former prime minister Stephen Harper refused to participate in scrums organized by the press gallery unless his political staffers got to pick which journalists could ask questions. Mr Harper routinely held media events where a maximum of five questions could be asked; at other times, only photojournalists were permitted to attend. Formal requests for government information sometimes result in journalists' questions being ignored, and details are heavily redacted in access-to-information requests. The prime minister's staffers used to stage an interview of the PM with a friendly moderator before an assembled audience to create the illusion that the leader is being scrutinized. Indeed, armed with new technology, the Prime Minister's Office (PMO) no longer needs the mainstream media to deliver its message. Emails and tweets are regularly sent to supporters and followers, selective information is posted on websites and social media, and a weekly PMO video magazine reveals behind-the-scenes moments in the style of a news report. Meanwhile, the prime minister attends fewer than half of the Question Period sessions in the House of Commons,[3] which already meets far less often than it used to. The ministers and backbenchers who do participate in legislative debates are heavily scripted so that they do not say anything that goes against what the PMO has authorized.

These trends worry observers of Canadian democracy. Prime ministers are derided as friendly dictators and autocrats. Government advertising and communication of its accomplishments are decried as propaganda. The deteriorating role of the legislative branch in the face of the superiority of the executive branch leads to calls from elected officials, even some belonging to the government party, for major changes to the way Parliament works. Things are so worrisome that some academics have labelled Canada a "publicity state," suggesting that everything the government does is driven by a desire to persuade rather than inform.[4] This allows elites to carry out a political agenda regardless of what the public wants, while using public resources to convince Canadians that the government's decisions are good ones.

The governing party, of course, would say that this criticism is overblown. With advances in online communication, the government is far more transparent and reaches far more citizens than at any other time in history. Journalists are working under shorter deadlines and have unrealistic demands for information. Government officials feel the pressure of mistakes that reverberate around social media, so they take longer to scrutinize what is publicly released. Finally, the media thrive on conflict and drama, so it makes sense for the government to seek to limit opportunities for the media to stir instability or opposition. Better to create the perception of a powerful leader than of a weak one, it is reasoned.

VOX POP

Given the promises of change made by Prime Minister Justin Trudeau, has the federal government become more transparent in the way it communicates? What changes could be made to make it more democratic?

(or equivalents—not all provinces have PC parties), and other right-leaning parties in rural areas throughout the country, and the success of Liberals, New Democrats, and other left-leaning parties in most cities. In recent decades, however, suburbanites have emerged as a separate category, motivated by a blend of conservative approaches to fiscal issues and progressive approaches to social and moral ones. Parties across the spectrum at both the federal and provincial levels have taken note, particularly since suburban areas have become true battlegrounds in most elections. This is manifested in their policies, communications, outreach, and fundraising. The targeting of electors is not always obvious in job advertisements for staff to work in political party headquarters, as the employment opportunities box on page 15 shows.

In ethnic terms, the vast socioeconomic and cultural divide between Aboriginal and non-Aboriginal Canadians has persisted throughout Canadian history. Yet it has only recently reached a relatively sustained level of *political* salience, thanks in large part to decades of pressure and advocacy by Aboriginal leaders. From their emergence in response to the 1969 *White Paper on Indian Policy*, to their circumscribed but noticeable participation in the constitutional negotiations of the late twentieth century, to their courtroom victories to protect Aboriginal rights, to their leadership on many pan-Canadian policy issues, National Aboriginal Organizations (NAOs), regional Aboriginal leaders, and grassroots activists have placed the disparities between their communities and broader society closer to the top of the Canadian political agenda. This newfound mobilization has been facilitated, in part, by the ability of social media to connect a geographically disparate political group, epitomized by the Idle No More movement. More frequently than ever before, issues like land claims negotiations, environmental sustainability, economic development, First Nations education, water quality, violence against Aboriginal women and girls, and Aboriginal child welfare are now found as leading news stories, as topics trending on Twitter, in major party platforms, and as full agenda items for federal–provincial–territorial intergovernmental conferences. Whether this increased attention to the disparities between Aboriginal and non-Aboriginal Canadians will result in concrete actions or solutions remains to be seen. For the time being, however, the divide has emerged as a key political cleavage in the third modern era.

Situating Aboriginal Politics

This raises a key consideration when studying Canadian politics: should Aboriginal and non-Aboriginal politics be treated separately, or is it more appropriate to treat them as common elements of the same political system?

Before it reached the relatively high level of salience described above, it had become commonplace to treat Aboriginal politics as a distinct, often subordinate element of Canadian politics. In many Canadian politics textbooks, for example, "Aboriginal people and politics" is a topic confined to a separate chapter. This often allows for a suitably comprehensive discussion of the uniqueness of Aboriginal politics. Yet, in our opinion, it tends to de-emphasize the parallels between Aboriginal and non-Aboriginal politics, particularly on fundamental issues like diversity, representation, activism, and governance. On one hand, treating the two sides separately draws much-needed attention to the deep disparities and divisions between them; on the other, it limits our ability to draw important connections and lessons that remain common and valuable to our understanding of Canadian politics as a whole.

UP FOR DEBATE

Do Aboriginal and non-Aboriginal politics belong in the same political system? The debate supplement at the end of this chapter gives some of the pros and cons, and offers questions and resources to guide a discussion around this important and unsettled topic.

THEY SAID IT
Aboriginal Issues in the Headlines

One of the greatest legacies we can work on together as Indigenous youth for next 7gens is to practice/reclaim our own systems of justice.

—Native Youth Sexual Health Network (@NYSHN)

Ottawa should have consulted First Nations over omnibus bills C-38 and C-45's sweeping legal challenges: Federal Court.

—Russ Diabo (@RussDiabo)

Calling an inquiry into missing & murdered indigenous women and girls will be one of the first priorities of a Liberal government.

—Justin Trudeau (@JustinTrudeau)

This time, I will be respected. The Court decision gave that to me.

—Aboriginal healer known only as "D.H.," after a 2014 Ontario Court ruling defended her constitutional right to withdraw her 11-year-old cancer-stricken daughter from chemotherapy treatments at a Hamilton hospital in favour of traditional medicine administered at a treatment centre in Florida

In this textbook, based on the trajectory of Aboriginal politics noted above, we side with those who treat Aboriginal and non-Aboriginal politics as part of a common Canadian political system. This is why, in lieu of a separate chapter devoted entirely to Aboriginal politics, we have incorporated the discussion of Aboriginal politics throughout the various themes covered in this book. This treatment remains an important and unsettled question among Canadian political scientists, however, so we would challenge our readers to think critically about our approach when engaging in the debate found at the end of this chapter.

Structure of the Book

Armed with these core concepts, maxims, and historical lessons, you are now ready delve more deeply inside Canadian politics. Each chapter's content will provide you with a basis for what we hope will be thriving political conversations, culminating in a debate supplement for use in the classroom, in a seminar group, or on your own time. Here is an overview of what you can expect from the following chapters.

Part I focuses on structures of government and governance in Canada. It begins with Chapter 2, which takes you inside Canada's constitution, examining the democratic principles and institutional components that lie at its core. You will learn about the intricate compromises and delicate nuances involved in crafting the country's highest law, and the perils of constitutional politics in a country challenged by the often competing demands of federalism and human rights. The chapter concludes with a debate as to whether changes to the Canadian constitution should be easier to make than current amending formulas allow.

Chapter 3 examines the structure of Canadian federalism in greater depth, tracing Canada's evolution from one of the most highly centralized to one of the most highly decentralized systems in the world. The discussion also includes the politics of fiscal federalism and the tensions that accompany the distribution of wealth among Canadian governments. This leads to a debate on the proper balance between central and local governance in Canada.

Chapter 4 applies a sharper geographic lens to our understanding of Canadian politics. With a special focus on Quebec, it compares the three main varieties of regionalism in Canada—sectionalism, nationalism, and secessionism—and discusses their impact on the past, present, and future of Canadian unity. The chapter ends by asking whether regionalism remains as dynamic and salient a force in Canada today.

Chapter 5 offers a glimpse inside the seat of power in Canadian politics: the executive. From the Queen and her representatives, to the prime minister and premiers, to the bureaucracy—all elements of Canada's executive branch play leading and interconnected roles. While they provide checks and balances on each other, and while other institutions are designed to hold them democratically accountable, the question at the conclusion of the chapter remains valid: do Canadian first ministers have too much power?

Chapter 6 throws open the doors of Canada's legislatures. The discussion goes beyond the pedantic description of "how a bill becomes a law" to study the dynamics of partisanship on the rules and business surrounding the legislative process. In particular, the topic of debate surrounds the necessity of strict party discipline in parliament and the provincial/territorial legislatures. This leads to a chapter on the third and final branch of the Canadian political system.

Chapter 7 goes beyond the conventional examination of the judiciary to expose the inner workings of Canada's broader justice system as a whole. After examining the core principles of Canadian justice and the specific, interconnected roles of judges, Crown attorneys, the police, and corrections officials, the chapter concludes with a debate on the effectiveness of mandatory minimum sentences for criminal offenders.

Chapter 8 takes us back inside the world of the bureaucracy to address the state of public policy and public administration in Canada. The conversation ranges from the role of ideology in the development of government programs and services—those that are part of the social safety net—to the specific processes and challenges involved in creating or changing elements of public policy. To this end, the chapter closes by questioning the value of political patronage in "getting things done" in governments across Canada.

Chapter 9 opens Part II, on politics and politicking. It kick-starts a series of discussions about electoral politics and representation in Canada, focusing on political parties. The chapter outlines the various types of political parties operating in Canada today, and traces each party's roots to the late eighteenth century. Connecting this conversation to broader issues of democratic diversity, the closing debate surrounds the ability of parties to recruit members of traditionally underrepresented groups, including women, Aboriginal people, and members of visible-minority communities.

Chapter 10 builds on this discussion, focusing more specifically on the fundamental democratic values, ideals, and rules underpinning Canadian elections. The chapter assesses how well the electoral system, redistricting processes, campaign finance regulations, and other laws align with the often high-minded norms of democracy. It also describes how local and national election and referendum campaigns are waged, closing with a debate on whether such campaigns even matter to the functioning of Canadian democracy.

Chapter 11 ties these conversations to the nature of political communication in Canada, with particular attention to the function of the media and the emergence of e-government. Following a rare discussion of the strategies and tactics involved in political marketing today, the capstone debate critiques the place of negative advertising in Canadian campaigns.

Chapter 12 steps outside the conventional realm of electoral politics to address the function of political activism in Canada. The roles of interest groups and social movements are discussed, with a particular focus on their performance in lobbying governments to effect political change. With this in mind, the chapter asks: should election spending by interest groups be regulated in the same manner as political parties and other actors?

Chapter 13 provides a high-level assessment of Canada's ability to promote diversity and representation for all its citizens, taking all of the material in the preceding chapters into account. Specifically, it evaluates the state of Canada's democratic deficit against the backdrop of the country's multicultural mosaic and its constitutional commitment to uphold the inherent right to self-government for Aboriginal people. The concluding debate asks if affirmative action programs are a valuable tool in helping to ensure all Canadians are well represented in the halls of power.

Chapter 14 concludes the book by looking outside the country's borders. It is fitting that a volume devoted to looking *inside* Canadian politics would close with a discussion of Canada's place in the world, as it provides useful perspective on how Canada positions itself in the broader global community and valuable context for the sorts of divisions that define the country's internal politics. The final debate of the book asks a pressing question that strikes at the heart of Canadian identity: should Canada give more money for foreign aid?

Together these chapters provide a high-level glimpse inside the world of Canadian politics. The journey begins with the structural components—the institutions and other building blocks—of Canadian democracy, and gradually works toward the more behavioural aspects of day-to-day Canadian politics. You might prefer a different path, in which case we invite you to jump from chapter to chapter, following the touchstones and guideposts we've provided along the way. We also provide catalytic questions and additional resources throughout each chapter that allow you to dig even more deeply into areas that interest you most. It's now time to get inside Canadian politics.

UP FOR DEBATE

Do Aboriginal and non-Aboriginal politics belong in the same political system?

THE CLAIM: YES, THEY DO!

Both Aboriginal and non-Aboriginal politics are integral to our understanding of the broader Canadian political system to which they belong.

Yes: Argument Summary

It is time to stop treating Aboriginal politics as separate and apart from non-Aboriginal politics in Canada. Far from assimilating Aboriginal perspectives into the broader Canadian society, considering the two worldviews as part of a common political system helps foster a common understanding among both sides of the conventional cleavage. Not only is the continued segregation of Aboriginal and non-Aboriginal politics counterintuitive, given the extent to which both worlds have merged in recent decades; it is also politically counterproductive, as it perpetuates an ages-old division in Canadian society.

Yes: Top 5 Considerations

1. Aboriginal politics has established itself as part of the mainstream discourse and a fundamental component of the institution of Canadian democracy. This is particularly true of the notion of treaty rights and the inherent right to self-government, which have entered the common parlance and become entrenched in common government practice and the constitutional order.
2. As evidenced in each chapter of this book, thanks to advances in scholarship and the progress achieved by Aboriginal leaders, it has become increasingly difficult to discuss the evolution and present state of Canadian politics without explicit and detailed discussion of the influence of Aboriginal people. To leave Aboriginal people out of core discussions about the constitution and core values of representation, or public policy and the courts, would be to miss the major trends and challenges that exist in the system as a whole.
3. Segregating discussions of Aboriginal and non-Aboriginal politics risks ghettoizing the former by perpetuating a sense of difference, or "otherness." Confining Aboriginal politics to a separate chapter in a Canadian politics textbook, for instance, further isolates the two sides of the traditional divide, and misses an important opportunity to build conceptual and political bridges between them.
4. A realistic, pragmatic conceptualization of Aboriginal self-government in the twenty-first century involves finding creative ways of integrating, not partitioning, Aboriginal and non-Aboriginal communities. Successes like the Nisga'a land claims settlement and the establishment of Nunavut provide testament to this, and offer prime examples of how separating discussions of Aboriginal and non-Aboriginal politics fractionalize our understanding and place limits on the evolution of Canadian politics as a whole.
5. Considering Aboriginal and non-Aboriginal politics as part of the same political system does not have to mean assimilating the former into the latter. In fact, only by treating the two traditions as commensurable are we able to integrate Aboriginal understandings of and approaches to power, sovereignty, territory, fairness, and diversity into the mainstream of Canadian politics.

Yes: Other Considerations

- When it comes to the core issues of democracy and representation, Aboriginal and non-Aboriginal politics both rest on a common theoretical foundation. This is why people on both sides of the cleavage find common ground on notions like treaty-making and federalism (the latter owing its origins in large part to the Haudenosaunee, or Six Nations, Confederacy).

- There are many cleavages in Canadian democracy, running along ethnocultural, gender, and geographical lines. Treating Aboriginal politics as separate and apart from non-Aboriginal politics begs the question as to whether other traditionally marginalized groups warrant similar treatment. The worldviews of Canadian women and visible minorities, in particular, differ considerably from the mainstream (white, European, Anglo-Saxon, male) perspective on Canadian politics. So do those of Quebecers or Atlantic Canadians, for that matter. Hosting separate discussions from all of these vantage points fails to capture the complex nature of the Canadian political system as a whole.

- In many ways, segregating our treatment of Aboriginal and non-Aboriginal people means taking the easy way out. Finding ways of integrating the two worldviews under a common political system is not only intellectually stimulating; it is one of the most pressing political challenges facing Aboriginal and non-Aboriginal Canadians today.

THE COUNTERCLAIM: NO, THEY DON'T!

Aboriginal politics are fundamentally distinct from non-Aboriginal politics, and the two ought to be treated as separate political systems.

No: Argument Summary

Aboriginal politics need not, and should not, be integrated into the fundamentally colonial system of Canadian politics. Doing so risks downplaying, if not exacerbating, the unique and profound challenges facing Aboriginal people. Only by recognizing and understanding the differences between the Aboriginal and non-Aboriginal worldviews can we

hope to address the disparities between them and establish true partnerships based on mutual respect.

No: Top 5 Considerations

1. Considering the centrality of the colonial state to our understanding of Canadian politics, any treatment of Aboriginal politics as part of this system would amount to academic assimilation. There are (at least) two broad worldviews on the nature of politics in Canada, and combining them into a single system only serves to further marginalize and downplay these differences.

2. By its very definition, the ultimate achievement of Aboriginal self-government would mean the creation of a separate—albeit integrated and co-dependent—political system parallel to the Canadian one, not within it. Lip service may be paid to the concepts of treaty rights and the inherent right to self-government within Canadian politics, but the true realization of these goals would require a separate political system, entirely.

3. Any parallels drawn between Aboriginal and non-Aboriginal approaches to politics are superficial and due largely to the fact that colonial institutions—band elections, National Aboriginal Organizations (NAOs), land claims settlements, territorial governments, and so on—have been imposed on Aboriginal people. These forms of representation are not based on Indigenous traditions and exist only to allow colonial governments a way to manage their relationships with Aboriginal communities on colonial terms.

4. Indeed, the participation of Aboriginal people in Canadian politics remains extremely limited, both in terms of Aboriginal people's engagement in formal processes like elections, and in terms of the contingent nature of Aboriginal leaders' relationship with colonial governments. NAOs and regional Aboriginal organizations only have a seat at the table when invited by federal, provincial, or territorial governments. Even then, their participation depends on their ability to secure resources to engage meaningfully, and remains confined to being consulted as a stakeholder (not an equal partner) in these governments' decisions.

5. The failure to treat Aboriginal politics as fundamentally distinct from non-Aboriginal politics risks subsuming the unique challenges faced by First Nations, Métis, and Inuit people under broader frameworks or policy approaches that apply solely to other traditionally marginalized groups. Using colonial approaches to addressing the relatively higher rates of poverty and domestic violence confronting Aboriginal people, for example, only perpetuates the same type of paternalistic treatment that contributed to these disparities in the first place.

No: Other Considerations

- The entire notion that there is one form of Aboriginal politics—or one form of non-Aboriginal politics, for that matter—dismisses the diversity that exists among and within the various First Nations, Métis, and Inuit communities.
- By their very definition, colonialism and anti-colonialism are distinct paradigms, meaning that they cannot be combined under a single worldview or political system.

Discussion Questions

- How would you define the boundaries of the "Canadian political system"? Are they broad enough to encompass divergent worldviews, or are some perspectives so far outside the mainstream that they ought to be considered entirely separate from the Canadian system?
- Would the addition of a separate chapter on Aboriginal politics as part of this textbook enhance or hinder your understanding of Canadian politics? Why?
- Should political scientists and students "push the envelope" when it comes to conceptualizing ideal political outcomes, like the full realization of Aboriginal self-government? Or is it better for them to focus their efforts on finding realistic ways to advance causes like social justice?

Where to Learn More about the Traditional Divide between Aboriginal and Non-Aboriginal Politics

Naomi Adelson, "The Embodiment of Inequity: Health Disparities in Aboriginal Canada," *Canadian Journal of Public Health* 96 (2005): pp. S45–61.

Russel L. Barsh and James Youngblood Henderson, *The Road: Indian Tribes and Political Liberty* (Los Angeles: University of California Press, 1980).

Marie Battiste, ed., *Reclaiming Indigenous Voice and Vision* (Vancouver: UBC Press, 2000).

Canada, *Report of the Royal Commission on Aboriginal Peoples* (Ottawa, 1996), www.collectionscanada.gc.ca/webarchives/20071115053257/http://www.ainc-inac.gc.ca/ch/rcap/sg/sgmm_e.html.

Glen S. Coulthard, "Subjects of Empire: Indigenous Peoples and the 'Politics of Recognition' in Canada," *Contemporary Political Theory* 6, no. 4 (2007): pp. 437–60.

Tom Flanagan, *First Nations? Second Thoughts*, 2nd edn (Montreal and Kingston: McGill–Queen's University Press, 2008).

Kiera Ladner, "Treaty Federalism: An Indigenous Vision of Canadian Federalisms," in *New Trends in Canadian Federalism*, 2nd edn, Francois Rocher and Miriam Smith, eds (Peterborough, ON: Broadview, 2003).

John Ralston Saul, *A Fair Country: Telling Truths about Canada* (Toronto: Penguin, 2008).

Annis May Timpson, *First Nations, First Thoughts: The Impact of Indigenous Thought in Canada* (Vancouver: UBC Press, 2010).

Dale Turner, *This Is Not a Peace Pipe: Towards a Critical Indigenous Philosophy* (Toronto: University of Toronto Press, 2006).

PART I

Government
and Governance

2 THE CONSTITUTION

Inside this Chapter

- What are the key democratic principles underpinning Canada's constitution?
- What are the core components of Canada's constitutional order?
- How has the Canadian constitution evolved over time?
- What are the politics surrounding the Charter of Rights and Freedoms?

Inside the Constitution

More than that of most other countries, Canada's history is defined by its constitution. Struggles to form and reform the constitutional order have marked turning points in the country's democratic evolution. At the same time, Canada's constitution is defined by the country's history. This becomes abundantly clear when we try to understand why "Indians and Indian lands" are treated as an area of jurisdiction rather than a separate order of government, why certain powers were granted to provinces and others to the federal government, why Senate seats were distributed unevenly across the country, why the amending formula is so complex, or why the "notwithstanding clause" appears in the Charter of Rights and Freedoms.

Understanding the Canadian constitution requires a deep appreciation for this history. Political actors cannot dabble in constitutional matters. They cannot simply propose formal amendments, or establish laws that either tinker around the edges or push the envelope of the Canadian constitutional order. Doing so raises real opposition from governments, interest groups, businesses, and citizens whose rights and powers may be threatened. Above all, they must be mindful of the following maxims about the constitution.

What the 2015 Election Means for Constitutional Politics

Visit the *Inside Canadian Politics* flipboard for the latest developments relating to Canada's constitution.

Go to
http://flip.it/gblag.

 The constitution consists of both written and unwritten rules. For the sake of ease of reading, we sometimes refer to the constitution as though it were a single document in which all of Canada's governing principles are neatly set down in writing. This is far from the case. In fact, a host of conventions and other unwritten rules underpin the constitutional order, meaning that you will need far more than a copy of the Constitution Act, 1982, to navigate Canadian politics and democracy.

 Minor adjustments are no more feasible than major. It is natural to think that smaller aspects of the constitution could be changed without too much difficulty. However, it is better to think of the Canadian constitution as a package of age-old compromises. Tweaking one element means altering a whole series of historical trade-offs—something prime ministers and premiers have come to know all too well throughout Canadian history.

 The constitution is more than just a government document. Even those who appreciate its significance may believe the constitution to be a largely esoteric body of laws and principles that are of practical importance only to people actively involved in running the country. While this may have been true at Confederation in 1867, when constitutions were all about dividing powers and defining jurisdictions, much has happened over the intervening century-and-a-half. Canadians now have a personal stake in the content of their constitution, and judges have become increasingly important political players, with the embedding of the Charter of Rights and Freedoms in 1982.

Over the course of this chapter, we'll uncover certain misconceptions and learn to tread lightly when it comes to matters respecting Canada's constitutional order.

Overview

A country's constitution is its highest law. But it is much more than that: it is also a record of a country's history, with its evolution marked by the major turning points in the nation's past. A constitution serves as a set of guideposts for normal political behaviour, and a touchstone during times of crisis. In this sense, the constitution sets out the parameters for acceptable and unacceptable conduct; it defines which powers belong to which political actors; and—in Canada's case, since 1982—it codifies the core rights and freedoms enjoyed by the country's citizens.

For these reasons, forming and reforming the constitution of a country is necessarily controversial, as it involves defining the very nature of its democracy. It is not surprising, then, that Canada's constitutional order changed remarkably little over the past century-and-a-half. It remains firmly rooted in British traditions, most of which predate Confederation. This does not mean Canada follows a carbon copy of the United Kingdom's unwritten constitution. The presence of federalism, the recognition of Aboriginal treaty rights, and a codified set of rights and freedoms distinguish the Canadian system from its British model. Nor is this to say that Canada's constitution has remained entirely fixed since 1867. Formal amendments, while few and far between, have resulted in some significant changes, as have several monumental court decisions. Nor is this relative stability due to a lack of efforts at reform: for much of the final quarter of the twentieth century, Canadians openly debated ways of moving away from the Westminster model, whether in the name of modernization or in the vein of Americanization. What it does mean is that, unlike countries whose constitutions are under continual revision, Canada has experienced a comparably calm and incremental constitutional evolution.

This chapter traces the history of Canadian politics through the lens of its constitutional order. Along the way it introduces a number of key concepts and defining moments that are taken up in later chapters. Do not worry if you don't know what an *amending formula* is (it is the way that a constitution is changed), what a *white paper* entails (it is a government planning document), or whether the *Meech Lake Accord* was negotiated at an actual lake (which it was). Instead, read this chapter with the comforting thought that you are simply being introduced to the building blocks of Canadian politics. Some of the material may be a refresher from Canadian history or other social science courses, and a good deal of it is explored in greater detail in subsequent chapters. For the time being, the chapter will provide a legal and historical foundation for Canada's constitutional order, which is important, as it underpins the country's politics and democracy.

UP FOR DEBATE

Should it be easier to amend the Canadian constitution?

Keep this question in mind as you read through the chapter. Consult the end-of-chapter debate supplement for more material to help you engage in an informed discussion of the topic.

Key Constitutional Principles

Canada's constitution is the supreme law of the land, meaning all other laws must be consistent with its principles. These provisions distribute power and constrain the authority of any one politician or institution. A great deal of the constitution is unwritten, so before delving into the precise structure or content, it is important to uncover the broader values embedded in the Canadian constitutional order. Lying at the heart of the constitution are three key principles: *parliamentary democracy*, *federalism*, and *Aboriginal self-government*. This combination of principles, and the way they are defined in terms of the constitution, makes Canada unique.

Parliamentary Democracy

Canada is a parliamentary democracy, distinguished from the many other types of democratic systems found throughout the world. Also known as the "Westminster parliamentary system" (after the Palace of Westminster, the seat of power in the United Kingdom), parliamentary democracy in Canada consists of the following features:

> **parliamentary democracy**
> A democratic system in which government executives must be supported by a majority of elected representatives in a legislature.

- Canada is governed by the rule of law, which means that all Canadians are subject to the same treatment regardless of their status.
- Canada is a constitutional monarchy, meaning that *sovereignty* (or ultimate power) is vested in *the Crown*, the reigning king or queen. The Queen is therefore Canada's head of state and has representatives based in Canada's capital city (the governor general in Ottawa) and in the 10 provincial capitals (lieutenant governors).
- The head of government, also known as the first minister, is the leader of the political party that controls the legislature in Ottawa and in each of the provinces and territories. The first minister who presides over the federal government is the prime minister, and in each of the 10 provinces and 3 territories, there is a premier who presides over the respective provincial or territorial government.
- The first minister and her or his ministers together make up the political executive, also known as *cabinet*. They are in charge of making government decisions, and in this manner they exercise power that has been delegated by the Crown. The Crown typically acts only on the advice of the executive, although not necessarily on all of the executive's advice.
- In Ottawa, the federal Parliament is composed of the Crown and two legislative bodies, commonly known as *chambers* or *houses* of Parliament: a popularly elected lower house (the House of Commons) and an appointed upper house (the Senate). To become a federal law, a bill must be approved by both houses of Parliament and the governor general.
- In the provinces and territories, legislatures are *unicameral*, meaning that they consist of only one house or chamber; there are no provincial or territorial senates. This assembly and the lieutenant governor or territorial commissioner must approve of a bill before it becomes law.
- Under the principle of *responsible government*, the political executive must maintain the confidence of its legislature in order to remain in power. One of the ways a loss of confidence in the government is signified is when a motion that has been put forward is defeated in a critical legislative vote.
- Cabinet ministers remain *individually responsible* for the activities falling within the scope of their separate ministries and *collectively accountable* to the legislature for the activities of government.
- Canada is a *representative democracy*, with members of each legislative assembly (federal, provincial, territorial) elected based on *single-member plurality* electoral systems. In other words, whichever candidate gets the most votes is elected to represent citizens in that electoral district.

- Most Canadian systems are characterised by strong *party discipline*, meaning that members of Parliament are likely to side with the leader of their party on critical legislative votes.
- Canadian legislatures operate on an *adversarial* basis, with the government being held to account by an opposition comprising all members of Parliament who do not belong to the governing party.
- Governments are supported by a non-partisan, *independent civil service*, which helps to develop and implement policy on their behalf.

In this sense, parliamentary democracy in Canada is best understood as a combination of four different facets:

1. liberal democracy
2. representative democracy
3. constitutional monarchy
4. responsible government (see Table 2.1).

a) Liberal Democracy

liberal democracy A system in which equality, rights, and freedoms are preserved through public debate and free and fair elections.

rule of law The principle that no one is above the law, and that any powers granted to elected or non-elected officials must be conferred by legislation.

First and foremost, Canada operates as a democratic system of government. It is a liberal democracy, meaning that those who run the government are elected to do so by the general public, and that certain democratic protections are upheld. Grounded in the rule of law, the Canadian constitution has demonstrated a robust respect for individual and group rights, the protection of minority interests, and the sanctity of the private sphere. The protection of individual rights was not at the forefront when the British North America (BNA) Act was passed in 1867. These rights and freedoms have been protected over time by a combination of parliamentary action and judicial oversight, and have been the subject of great debate over the course of Canadian history. Some view these freedoms in terms of *positive rights* (to be extended *to* individuals and groups *by* the state), while others view them in terms of *negative liberties* (to be kept safe from intrusion *by* the state).

Similar tensions surround the precise definition of *equality*, with many "small-c" conservatives viewing it, from a libertarian perspective, in terms of equality of rights; socialists viewing it, from a more communitarian perspective, in terms of equality of condition; and "small-l" liberals viewing it in terms of equality of opportunity.

In short, equality, rights, and freedoms are integral parts of Canada's system of liberal democracy and key components of its constitutional order. The fact that their

TABLE 2.1 | Characteristics of Westminster Parliamentary Democracy

Liberal Democracy	Representative Democracy	Constitutional Monarchy	Responsible Government
• rule of law • rights, freedoms • equality	• mostly elected legislators • first-past-the-post electoral systems	• sovereignty rests with the Crown • Crown acts on advice of political executive	• fusion of powers • confidence principle • cabinet solidarity • ministerial responsibility

precise definitions remain ambiguous is perhaps as much a product of the openness of Canada's democratic debate as it is a reflection of the depth of disagreement among its citizens.[1] These debates came to a head with the development of the Charter of Rights and Freedoms (1982), discussed later in this chapter.

b) Representative Democracy

Canada is also a representative democracy, meaning that every policy decision is ultimately made by elected representatives, not by fiat or by "the people" themselves. Elected officials collectively make policy decisions on behalf of the citizens they represent. This is an indirect form of democracy, in that the public will is determined and implemented by a group of representatives. This is important to bear in mind when considering the role of initiatives, plebiscites, referendums, and other forms of direct democracy in Canada. Such practices do not technically give Canadians direct authority over the government's actions. In representative democracies like Canada, elected officials make the ultimate decision as to whether or not to follow the public's lead.

representative democracy A system in which citizens elect officials to make political decisions on their behalf.

direct democracy A system in which citizens make political decisions by voting on individual issues.

INSIDE CANADIAN POLITICS
Why Isn't Direct Democracy More Common in Canada?

In constitutional monarchies like Canada, sovereignty rests not with "the people" but with the Crown. This means that authority ultimately resides with the King or Queen of Canada, who almost always acts on the advice of cabinet. In other words, no legislation can be established without a bill first being passed by a government maintaining the confidence of the elected assembly, after which the Crown's representative endorses it to become law.

The Manitoba government learned this first-hand when it tried to pass its Initiative and Referendum Act in 1916. The legislation provided citizens with the opportunity to petition the government for the introduction of a piece of legislation. If the proposal was not enacted immediately, it would be put to voters in the form of a binding referendum;

if a majority of voters was in support, the measure would automatically become law. In 1919, however, the courts ruled the act unconstitutional, because it would have removed the sovereign authority of the Crown's provincial representative, the lieutenant governor, to provide royal assent to all proposed laws.

These constitutional niceties aside, from time to time and for a variety of reasons, Canadian politicians have gone straight to the people to aid in their decisions by adopting certain elements of direct democracy. The Government of Quebec has convened two referendums on whether or not to separate from Canada, and in 1992, the entire country voted on a constitutional reform package known as the Charlottetown Accord.

VOX POP
Should referendums be binding on governments in Canada? Or are there advantages to having elected governments and the Crown make the ultimate decision?

Robin Rowland/The Canadian Press

In an non-binding plebiscite in April 2014, residents of Kitimat, BC, voted against a $6.5 billion project to build a bitumen-carrying pipeline from Alberta to the port town on BC's Douglas Channel. Two months later, the federal government approved the project. What are the advantages of holding a non-binding plebiscite?

↻ The federal referendum on the Charlottetown Accord, Quebec's referendums, and other instances of direct democracy in Canada are detailed in Chapter 10, on democracy and elections.

Depicted in Figure 2.1, Canada's system of representative democracy is shaped by territory, which means that officials are elected to represent specific geographic constituencies. This differs from more functional or corporatist forms of democracy, where representatives are accountable to groups that are not defined by territory (e.g. representing women, indigenous peoples, unions, classes, or specific occupational groups). The Labourites, Progressives, and United Farmers of the early twentieth century held corporatist democracy in high regard, even reforming electoral systems in some provinces for a short period, to reduce the role of territory in defining representation. These experiments were short-lived, however.

With the notable exception of Northwest Territories and Nunavut, which operate based on a consensus (or non-partisan) form of government, Canada's form of representative democracy has also evolved along partisan lines. Indeed, Canadian democracy is virtually unthinkable without political parties.

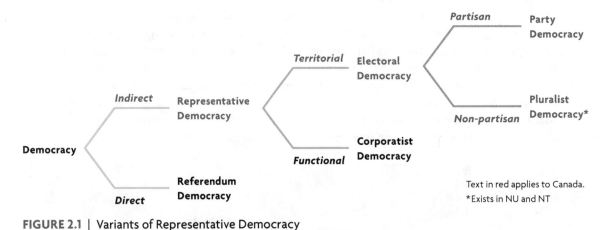

FIGURE 2.1 | Variants of Representative Democracy

Source: Adapted from Kaare Strom (2000), "Parties at the Core of Government," in Russell J. Dalton and Martin P. Wattenberg (eds), *Parties Without Partisans* (Oxford: Oxford University Press): p. 184.

c) Constitutional Monarchy

Third, Canada is a constitutional monarchy, which distinguishes it from republican and presidential systems like the United States. Ultimate sovereignty in Canada rests with the Crown, not "the people" or any single person. The Crown is a timeless concept, embodied in the monarch of the day, whose representatives must approve all government actions before they come into effect.

This makes the reigning king or queen Canada's head of state, represented federally by the governor general and by various lieutenant governors at the provincial level. While they have supreme sovereignty under the constitution, the monarch and her representatives exercise it very rarely. By constitutional convention, the Crown acts only on the advice of the executive, also known as the cabinet or governor-in-council (lieutenant governor-in-council in provincial contexts). The executive, in turn, must act with the full confidence of the legislature, whose members are elected by Canadians. Canada's monarch and her representatives serve primarily as symbolic representatives of Canadians, and they do wield substantive authority when it comes to authorizing government actions. This includes assenting to bills and dissolving legislatures, as well as appointing high-level officials, such as cabinet ministers, senators, and judges. In the words of political scientist David E. Smith, the authority of the Crown is a relatively "invisible" but powerful organizing principle of Canadian democracy.[2] In these ways, Canada's constitutional monarchy is distinct from absolute monarchies, where kings, queens, princes, or other unelected officials preside over their countries as dictators with autocratic control. For more detail, see Chapter 5.

d) Responsible Government

The fourth and final pillar of Canada's system of parliamentary democracy is the principle of responsible government. Responsible government requires that a first minister and the cabinet maintain the "confidence" of the lower house, lest they be stripped of government powers.[3] That is, at all times, a majority of the people's elected representatives present in the legislature must support the government, otherwise the

↻ The connection between representative democracy and Canada's party system is discussed throughout Chapter 9; see especially pages 340–68.

constitutional monarchy A system in which the sovereignty of the Crown is maintained, but exercised by elected officials according to prescribed rules.

Crown The legal concept dictating the supremacy of the monarch over the executive, legislative, and judicial branches of government.

↻ For more detail on the role of the Crown in Canada, see Chapter 5, on the Executive.

responsible government The constitutional principle whereby the executive (cabinet) must be supported by a majority of elected members of the legislature.

BRIEFING NOTES

The Crown, the Monarch, the Queen, and Her Representatives

People often use the terms interchangeably, but there are important distinctions between *the Crown*, *the monarch*, and *the Queen*. *The Crown* is the ultimate seat of power; in Canada's case today, it is filled by the British *monarch*. In the eighteenth century, the French monarch ruled much of what is now Canada, but this changed with the Royal Proclamation of 1763, through which the British monarch staked Crown claim over the territory. Monarchs have various titles; in Canada's case, they go by *king* or *queen*. Today, Queen Elizabeth II is represented in Canada federally by the governor general and provincially by the lieutenant governors, who carry out the day-to-day responsibilities of the Crown on her behalf.

reins of power must be handed over to another party, or the legislature must be dissolved and a general election held.

In Canada, then, there is a fusion of powers between the executive and the legislature, in that cabinet members are drawn from the ranks of the legislature and remain directly accountable to them. In fact, certain members of the Canadian Parliament—namely, senators—are actually selected by the executive, and appointed by the governor general to sit in the Upper House.

This system is very different to that of the United States, which features a *separation of powers*, whereby the executive is *not* directly accountable to the legislature. In fact, the president and cabinet secretaries are frequently in conflict with American congressmen, congresswomen, and senators. Whereas the executive in Canada has near-total control over the legislative process—proposing, drafting, scheduling, and commanding legislators' support for bills and motions—this responsibility is shared in the United States between the president and the two houses of Congress. This makes the Canadian system appear far more streamlined than the American one, which is often given to legislative deadlock, particularly when the executive and houses of the legislature are controlled by opposing parties.

> **fusion of powers** An intimate connection between the authority of the executive and the authority of the legislature.

INSIDE CANADIAN POLITICS

Can Canadians Distinguish between the Canadian and American Constitutions?

Many Canadians confuse their country's constitutional principles with those of the United States. This is not surprising, given the extent to which American politics dominates popular culture on both sides of the border. Yet this confusion has real implications when it comes to Canadians' expectations of their own system of government. Consider the following results of a 2008 opinion poll:

- While three-quarters of Canadian respondents were able to identify the US president as America's head of state, only 21 per cent were able to name Queen Elizabeth II as Canada's.
- Over half of the respondents (59 per cent) knew that Canada was a constitutional monarchy, but 17 per cent believed it was a representative republic, and 25 per cent believed Canada could best be characterized as a co-operative assembly.
- Barely half of Canadians (49 per cent) were able to attribute the slogan "Peace, order, and good government" to their own constitution. One-third (34 per cent) believed that the French slogan "liberty, equality, fraternity" belonged to Canada, and nearly two in ten (17 per cent) believed the American motto "Life, liberty and the pursuit of happiness" was Canada's.[4]

One of the reasons for this confusion may be that Canadians do not recognize the difference between a head of *state* and a head of *government*. The president of the United States is both, whereas the prime minister of Canada is only the head of the federal government, while the monarch is the head of state.

VOX POP

What are some of the negative repercussions for Canadians of having their understanding of democracy so heavily influenced by the United States? What are some means that could be taken to correct Canadians' misperceptions?

Several practices have developed over time to help guide the conduct of responsible government in Canada. In particular, two conventions ensure that executives will act in a coherent and accountable manner: *cabinet solidarity* and *ministerial responsibility*.

According to the convention of cabinet solidarity, all ministers must vote in favour of a government's legislative initiatives, because at all times they must publicly support the decisions made collectively by the executive. This practice ensures that the government speaks with one voice when addressing the legislature and the public. This said, on rare occasions, governments may choose to relax the rules surrounding cabinet solidarity, as sometimes occurs when it announces a free vote on a hot-button issue like same-sex marriage (see Chapter 5).

Cabinet solidarity also imposes collective responsibility on members of the executive, requiring all ministers to resign if the government loses the confidence of the legislature. At the federal level, the government has lost the confidence of the legislature six times in Canadian history. Most often, the government has been defeated on budget votes (1926, 1963, 1974, and 1979), but in recent times governments have fallen after the opposition introduced motions of non-confidence (2005 and 2011).

By virtue of a second convention, ministerial responsibility, each minister must answer for all the actions undertaken in the name of the ministry. This practice means that a minister accepts responsibility for decisions made by the public servants who work under the minister's direction, as well as decisions undertaken by predecessors in that portfolio. This accountability measure typically involves providing responses during Question Period or in various legislative and cabinet committees, as well as to the media.

Ultimately, a minister who fails to live up to either of the principles of cabinet solidarity or ministerial responsibility may cease to be part of the government executive. It is up to the head of government (i.e. the prime minister or premier) to seek consent from the monarch's representative to remove a minister from cabinet. Ministers may choose to resign should they feel unable to support a cabinet decision or should they take responsibility for gross mishandling of affairs in their ministry. In the event that a head of government is planning on sacking a cabinet minister, a senior political staffer will likely communicate, on behalf of the first minister, that there is a window of opportunity for the minister to resign before he or she is fired. Such events are rare in Canadian history, although it is not unusual for ministers to resign their cabinet positions in times of government unpopularity.

Federalism

While its monarchical and Westminster parliamentary traditions may put it at odds with its American counterpart, the Canadian constitution does share some principles in common with the constitution of the United States. In addition to the liberal/representative democratic foundations just described, the Canadian constitution borrowed directly from that of the US in its incorporation of *federalism*—a division of powers between the central (federal) and subnational (provincial) governments. Over time, the founding former British colonies in New Brunswick, Nova Scotia and what is now Ontario and Quebec joined with the rest of Atlantic Canada and the Western territories to form a federation of provinces. They created a central government to govern on behalf of the provinces on matters of pan-Canadian importance, including

cabinet solidarity The understanding that members of the executive remain cohesive and jointly responsible for the government's undertakings.

↻ For a discussion of free votes in relation to same-sex marriage, see the Inside Canadian Politics feature on page 229 of Chapter 6.

ministerial responsibility The understanding that ministers remain individually responsible for the activities undertaken by staff in their respective departments.

↻ Only two federal cabinet ministers have ever resigned over issues of individual ministerial responsibility. To learn about these cases, see the Inside Canadian Politics feature on page 192 of Chapter 5.

administration over the northern territories, while retaining provincial authority over culturally and locally sensitive matters. In doing so, Canada became the world's third modern federation, after the United States and Switzerland. We devote all of Chapter 3 to the concept and inner workings of federalism in Canada. For now, suffice it to say that this combination of shared and self-rule is among the three defining features of Canada's constitution, alongside Canada's status as a parliamentary democracy and its provisions for Aboriginal self-government.

Aboriginal Self-Government

Until very recently, most discussions of Canada's constitutional order would have ended with these two constitutional principles, parliamentary democracy and federalism. The resulting outlook was very limited, reflecting a prevailing and inaccurate belief that Canadian politics and constitutionalism began with the establishment of European institutions. Thanks to increased scholarly scrutiny and the political success of Aboriginal people in Canada in asserting their inherent right to self-government, this colonialism is no longer in the mainstream.

In modern interpretations of Canada's constitutional evolution, Aboriginal people developed a nation-to-nation relationship with European settlers at first contact in the seventeenth century. This mutual respect was codified in the British Royal Proclamation of 1763, which explicitly recognized that Aboriginal people had title to lands in North America unless and until it had been ceded to the Crown through formal treaties or purchase. Over time, First Nations signed several treaties with the British and Canadian Crown. Post-Confederation, these treaties, which were numbered (from Treaty 1 in 1871 to Treaty 11 in 1921), gradually opened up Aboriginal land to new settlement in what is now western Canada. In return, Aboriginal communities were given small tracts of land (*reserves*), annual payments, food aid, and other forms of government assistance (including healthcare and education). Aboriginal people also retained the right to hunt, trap, and fish on their original lands in perpetuity.

Historians and Native studies scholars continue to dispute the terms and legitimacy of these treaties. Many argue that the deals were coerced, negotiated in bad faith, poorly recorded, or struck without respect for traditional forms of Aboriginal leadership (e.g. without approval of hereditary chiefs or the input of women). Many also point to the fact that the treaties never involved ceding sovereignty to the British or Canadian state. While living under the protection of the Crown, as did French and British subjects, Aboriginal people retained their autonomy and never agreed to be subjects of either monarch.

Rather, many Aboriginal people point to the two-row wampum, which is said to have commemorated a treaty between the Mohawk and the Dutch in 1613, as emblematic of the relationship that was forged through treaties. The belt features two rows of purple beads, one representing the First Nations people and one, the European settlers. The two rows run like parallel streams, just as the two peoples were expected to live their lives: together, but in their own respective "boats," each with their own laws and customs. Over time, the two-row wampum has come to symbolize Aboriginal people's understanding of their relationship with the Canadian Crown: while Canadian and Aboriginal societies coexist in peace and friendship, each should respect the right of the other to self-government.

colonialism The imposition, practice, policy, or belief in the supremacy of European settler institutions over those of Aboriginal groups.

Royal Proclamation of 1763 A British document setting out the terms of European settlement in North America following the Seven Years' War.

treaties Agreements between the Crown and Aboriginal peoples establishing mutual duties and obligations.

two-row wampum A ceremonial beaded belt symbolizing the parallel paths and equal-order relationship between the Crown and First Nations people.

self-government The inherent right of a people to sovereignty (or self-determination) over their own affairs.

Andre Forget/SunMedia

The Idle No More movement began as a protest by Indigenous women calling on the federal government to respect the treaty rights of Aboriginal people, particularly concerning environmental protection and indigenous sovereignty. It has since grown to become one of the most influential Aboriginal social movements in recent Canadian history. Why do you think the involvement of women has been instrumental to the success of the movement?

It took over a century of Confederation, but all federal, provincial, and territorial governments eventually arrived at consensus on the inherent right of Aboriginal peoples to self-government. This has by no means resulted in full societal recognition or the functional realization of Aboriginal self-government in Canada. Many barriers remain, as discussed in greater detail in Chapter 13. In the meantime, Aboriginal self-government has become a defining feature of Canada's constitution—albeit more in theory than in practice.

↻ See Aboriginal Representation in Canada, beginning on page 521 of Chapter 13, for a discussion of the barriers to Aboriginal self-government in Canada.

Core Components of the Constitutional Order

Together, the principles of parliamentary democracy, federalism, and Aboriginal self-government are enshrined in various parts of Canada's constitutional order. It is important to use the term *order*, given that not all of Canada's constitution is recorded in a single piece of text. Indeed, much of the constitution is not even recorded on paper. Pause for a moment to consider that concept: the supreme body of rules governing Canada's entire political system is not written down in a single document. These rules are neither recorded nor easily referenced, and, as a result, are often the subject of great debate among people with different perspectives on the principles that underlie them. This sort of ambiguity is often frustrating to students and practitioners of Canadian politics, but as we will discuss, it may be partly responsible for the survival of Canadian democracy. This is because Canada's constitutional order consists

constitutional order
The body of written and unwritten rules that govern all laws in Canada.

Not only is there no single, all-encompassing constitutional document, but both extant copies of the 1982 Proclamation of the Constitution Act, signed by Prime Minister Pierre Trudeau and Queen Elizabeth II, are damaged: one was ruined by rain the day it was signed, while the other was vandalized by a Toronto student, Peter Greyson, while he was viewing it at the national archives in Ottawa, allegedly in protest over American cruise missile testing over Canadian airspace. Restoration specialists were unable to remove the ink and glue mixture without causing damage to the original document, so it remains permanently marked. Greyson pleaded guilty to wilful destruction of public property, and served 89 days in jail. How appropriate was this sentence?

of a series of laws, conventions, and judicial opinions, many of which are constantly evolving to meet the needs and expectations of Canadians and their lawmakers.

Constitutional Laws

Pre-Confederation Laws

When most Canadians think of the Canadian constitution, their minds turn to the document negotiated by John A. Macdonald and the Fathers of Confederation in the 1860s. Others may think of the parchment signed by Queen Elizabeth II on a cold, dreary day in Ottawa in 1982. In reality, several pieces of legislation are considered part of the canon of entrenched constitutional law in Canada. Some of these are listed in Table 2.2, although many scholars contend the list is much lengthier.

Some of these laws predate the formal establishment of Canada in 1867, but their principles remain part of the constitutional order to this day. Take the Royal Proclamation of 1763, for example. A document designed ostensibly to bring an end to the Seven Years' War between Britain and France and their respective Aboriginal

Fathers of Confederation
The colonial leaders who negotiated the terms of union forming the Dominion of Canada.

allies, the text did far more than simply reorganize the two imperial powers' control over lands in North America. According to subsequent court rulings, it also recognized the Crown's obligations to respect Aboriginal rights, including the right to self-government, and to treat Aboriginal peoples as equal nations or orders of government.

The Quebec Act of 1774 placed a considerable amount of this reserved land under the control of the new Province of Quebec. At the same time, it granted government officials in Quebec the right to openly practise their Catholic faith and employ French legal traditions in civil matters; these entitlements made them unique among British colonists, and contributed to the resentment leading up to the American Revolutionary War.

The Constitutional Act of 1791 preserved these rights for French-speaking colonists after the war, creating an asymmetrical political system with one set of laws applying in French Canada and another in English Canada. It also divided the vast Quebec territory into two halves: Upper Canada, which would eventually become Ontario, and Lower Canada, which would become latter-day Quebec. Both colonies were granted representative government, giving colonists increased democratic control over their public affairs.

This division may have fostered peace among French- and English-speaking Canadians, but the lack of autonomy bred resentment in both colonies. Following a pair of brief but jarring armed rebellions, the British government dispatched Lord Durham to investigate ways of meeting the colonists' demands for fully responsible government. In his 1839 report to Britain, Durham described the tension between English and French settlers in Upper and Lower Canada as that of "two nations warring within the bosom of a single state." The symbolism of this phrase continues to resonate centuries later.

Upon Durham's recommendation, the British Parliament passed the Act of Union, 1840, reuniting Upper Canada and Lower Canada under a common legislature and

TABLE 2.2 | Key Components of Constitutional Law in Canada

Legislation	Major Impacts on the Constitutional Order
Royal Proclamation of 1763	• established the inherent right of Aboriginal self-government
Quebec Act of 1774	• established religious, linguistic, legal, and political rights of citizens of the Province of Quebec
Constitutional Act of 1791	• established representative government in Upper and Lower Canada (latter-day Ontario and Quebec)
Act of Union, 1840	• reunited Upper and Lower Canada under a common legislature, and temporarily abolished special rights for French Canadians
British North America Act, 1867 (in 1982 it was renamed the Constitution Act, 1867*)	• established the Confederation of New Brunswick, Nova Scotia, Ontario, and Quebec
Statute of Westminster, 1931	• established the equality of British and Canadian parliaments
Canada Act, 1982	• patriated the Canadian constitution
Constitution Act, 1982*	• established a domestic amending formula, and entrenched the Charter of Rights and Freedoms

*Canadian legislation; all other laws passed by the British Parliament

eventually, in 1848, providing the inhabitants with full-fledged responsible government. Seats in the new Province of Canada legislature were divided evenly between Canada West, whose 450,000 residents were predominantly English-speaking Protestants, and Canada East, whose 650,000 inhabitants were largely French-speaking Catholics.

At the time, this division was viewed as a means of assimilating Quebecers and limiting their political influence in North America. Two facts in particular reinforced this opinion: first, that French was temporarily banned as an official language of government; second, that French-Canadian educational and civil law institutions were abolished. Rapid British immigration soon reversed the population balance between the two sections, and by the 1860s, politicians in Canada West were clamouring for increased influence. In the meantime, deadlock gripped the Canadian legislature, which became governed by coalitions led jointly by premiers from each section and a convention by which major pieces of legislation required the support of majorities in both Canada West and Canada East.

The BNA Act and Legislation since 1867

At around the same time, colonists in Nova Scotia, New Brunswick, and Prince Edward Island also received responsible government, and were considering unifying themselves under a common political system. Leaders in Canada East and Canada West more or less invited themselves to these discussions, which evolved into negotiations of a broader political union. Following a series of constitutional conferences on both sides of the Atlantic Ocean in the 1860s, the Fathers of Confederation and the British government came to terms on the British North America Act, 1867.

The BNA Act, as it is commonly called, created the Dominion of Canada, comprising the provinces of Ontario, Quebec, New Brunswick, and Nova Scotia. This constitution also outlined the powers of the executive and legislative branches of the new central and provincial governments, and detailed the division of jurisdiction in the new country, thereby establishing the initial formal structure of Canadian federalism. While its content was settled upon largely by colonial leaders, the law itself was passed by and remained under the ultimate control of the British Parliament. This meant that if Canadians decided they wanted to revise the terms of Confederation, any changes to the text itself would have to be approved by the British government, and passed only upon the "request and consent" of Canada.

Indeed, the British government passed 20 different BNA Acts between 1867 and 1975, thereby entrenching or altering several key components of Canada's constitutional order. Thus, any time the composition of the Canadian House of Commons or Senate was altered, if a new province was created, or if there was a shift in the jurisdictional responsibilities between the federal and provincial orders, Canadian officials would have to approach the British government to pass a new BNA Act.

This situation persisted throughout much of the twentieth century, as the heads of government across Canada failed to reach agreement on an appropriate amending formula that would allow them to take complete control over this core constitutional document. For its part, the British government showed little interest in maintaining authority over Canada's constitutional affairs. The British Parliament passed the Statute of Westminster, 1931, which affirmed that the legislatures of the various former

amending formula A set of rules governing how the constitution can be changed.

British colonies were of equal status to the British Parliament and could pass their own laws independent of British government oversight. Each of these former colonies, including Canada, Newfoundland (not yet a Canadian province), Ireland, Australia, New Zealand, and South Africa, remained a constitutional monarchy with the British monarch serving as its head of state. The various BNA Acts were explicitly excluded from the Statute of Westminster, however, as the federal and provincial governments continued to disagree on how to make future changes to the constitutional order.

It took until April 1982 for the Canadian governments to negotiate, and for Queen Elizabeth II to sign, the Constitution Act, 1982. In addition to the elusive amending formula, the new law also contained a Charter of Rights and Freedoms, a commitment to uphold Aboriginal treaty rights, formal recognition of the equalization principle, and several other novel constitutional provisions.[5] At the same time, the British North America Act, 1867, was officially renamed the Constitution Act, 1867, thereby commemorating the document's transition from imperial statute to domestic law. Discussed below, the Constitution Act, 1982, commemorated the patriation of the core texts of the Canadian constitutional order, giving Canadians ultimate control over the amendment of these texts without approval of Parliament in the UK.

In addition to these core documents, there are numerous other British, federal, and provincial statutes that form parts of the Canadian constitutional order. Many of these statutes were passed prior to the establishment of the amending formula in 1982; others were passed under provisions of the formula that allow governments to enact changes to their powers unilaterally or with the consent of those jurisdictions directly affected. They include the various acts establishing new provinces, for instance, as well as laws like the Act Respecting Constitutional Amendments, which aimed to establish a series of provincial and regional vetoes over constitutional amendments, and the Clarity Act, which sought to establish federally defined rules for the orderly secession of provinces from Confederation. Other federal laws, like the Supreme Court Act, the Bill of Rights, the Indian Act, and the Canada Elections Act, also form part of the constitutional order, as they directly impact core institutions and principles of Canadian democracy.

Charter of Rights and Freedoms A portion of the Constitution Act, 1982, enshrining Canadians' core liberties and entitlements vis-à-vis their governments.

patriation The process through which Canadian governments gained the authority to amend the country's main constitutional documents.

Constitutional Conventions

As mentioned, not everything in the Canadian constitution is recorded in legislation. A number of entrenched practices that have evolved over time are so fundamental to how the Canadian system of government operates that they are treated as part of the constitution. Canada operates on a series of these constitutional conventions that, together, form an unwritten foundation for all other laws and behaviours.

Many of these practices are so fundamental that Canadians tend to assume they are recorded in law, rather than simply in textbooks. Take, for instance, the principles of the Westminster parliamentary system outlined above. These form the very core of Canada's system of parliamentary democracy. Yet the specific rules are not spelled out in the Constitution Acts or any other piece of legislation. Indeed, the term "prime minister" did not appear in the BNA Act, and was only added as part of the Constitution Act, 1982. The term "premier" remains absent to this day. Nevertheless, the rules establishing first ministers' powers over things like appointments are just as constitutional and real as if they had been set down in writing.

constitutional convention An unwritten rule based on custom that binds political actors to adhere to the traditions of the constitutional order.

As Andrew Heard (2014) explains, constitutional conventions vary in definition, importance, acceptance, and inviolability.[6] The most fundamental conventions govern the very core facets of Canadian democracy and, as such, command the utmost respect and attention. Clear rules like responsible government, ministerial responsibility, cabinet solidarity, and judicial independence must be strictly observed, as breaches would be tantamount to tearing the very fabric of Canada's constitutional order.[7] Other conventions are equally important to the functioning of Canadian democracy, but the way these are defined and applied is more flexible or ambiguous. Consider, for instance, the convention that the prime minister must select people to serve as Supreme Court justices, the convention that all cabinet ministers must have seats in the legislature, or that cabinets must consist of representatives from each major region. Prime ministers may establish—and have established—advisory boards and processes to aid them in judicial selection without altering their constitutional responsibility to send names to the governor general for appointment. Prime Minister Justin Trudeau has pledged to create a similar consultative panel for the appointment of Senators. By the same token, there is no stringent timeline for a non-elected cabinet member to attain a seat in the legislature, nor any hard-and-fast definition of which regions must be represented in cabinet or by how many ministers. Still other conventions lack the same level of consensus or importance, and may be subject to heated debate in times of uncertainty. The obligation of the monarch's representative to dissolve the legislature upon the request of a prime minister or premier, or of a government to resign upon the defeat of a major piece of legislation, remains contestable and subject to definition and application on a case-by-case basis.

The courts typically enforce written, or entrenched, constitutional laws, not constitutional conventions. Exceptions have occurred, however, particularly when judges have been called upon to rule on fundamental constitutional powers or amendments. In these sorts of cases, the judiciary has weighed evidence based on unwritten rules, including the maxim that constitutional powers may lapse if not exercised, known as the *convention of non-use*. They also consider the imperative that governments not attempt to exploit loopholes in order to achieve constitutional reform by bypassing official rules. This situation played out in 1981, when the federal government sought to patriate the constitution without the support of the provinces. The government was not in breach of any written constitutional law. However, in a reference case launched by the provinces and known today as the *Patriation Reference*, the Supreme Court ruled that a convention prevented the federal government from amending fundamental elements of the constitution without substantial consent of the provinces. As a result, the federal government was forced to obtain support from the provinces before patriating the constitution, in negotiations described later in this chapter.

Judicial Opinions

In this way, judicial decisions may become part of the Canadian constitutional order, as well. In a process known as *judicial review*, courts are often asked to rule on the constitutionality of particular pieces of government legislation. This allows citizens, corporations, interest groups, and other Canadian governments to challenge the authority of government decisions.

Many of these cases have involved the division of powers. The courts have settled disputes over which order of government—federal or provincial—has jurisdiction

↻ The process for judicial appointments is explained on pages 273–6 of Chapter 7, on the justice system.

↻ The issue of regional representation and regional ministers is discussed on page 182 of Chapter 5, on the executive.

reference case A proceeding initiated by a government to seek the court's opinion on the constitutionality of legislation.

↻ Reference cases and judicial review are also discussed on page 263 of Chapter 7, on the justice system.

over a particular policy area. The list of legal decisions is too lengthy to itemize here, but the court's opinions on matters like workers' rights (the *Labour Conventions* case), the welfare state (the *Employment Insurance Act* reference), the environment (the *Crown Zellerbach* case), and the economy (the *Securities Act* reference) created important precedents and rules for Canadian federalism.

Other court cases have defined the scope and character of human rights in Canada. Take, for instance, the *Persons* case (1929). That formative ruling saw the court decree that Canadian women were, in fact, "persons" under the British North America Act, 1867. The Supreme Court, which at the time was not the final court of appeal in Canada, had ruled that only men could be senators because the court had interpreted the word "persons" as it was used in the constitution to mean "men." This judgement was overturned upon appeal to the Judicial Committee of the Privy Council, a British body of judges. After this ruling, women were entitled to stand for public office, to vote, and to exercise many other democratic rights and privileges. Similarly, the courts have also helped to define and enforce Aboriginal treaty rights, through rulings including *R. v. Marshall* (1999) and the *Tsilhqot'in Nation* case (2014), and the rights of LGBTT (lesbian, gay, bisexual, transgender, two-spirit) Canadians, through cases like the *Same-Sex Marriage* reference (2004).

Once these rulings and opinions have been released, subject to further legislative or judicial responses, they join formal laws and conventions as part of the Canadian constitutional order. In fact, it was the court that defined Canada's constitution as "a living tree capable of growth and expansion within its natural limits."[8] Viscount Sankey's turn of phrase captures the widely held view that the Canadian constitution must constantly evolve to meet the need of an ever-changing Canadian society. Rather than being grounded in nineteenth-century values, or interpreted word-for-word as an ordinary statute, the constitution must grow and adapt to the times.

The Evolution of the "Living Tree"

The following sections tell the story of the Canadian constitution as a living tree over the country's first century-and-a-half, as leaders struggled to come to the terms of Confederation, and then to perfect it. Important "turning points" are noted in the margins, to draw your attention to the key moments in Canada's constitutional evolution. As you read, keep track of the many trade-offs and compromises that were necessary for the various partners to reach a deal. This will help you to appreciate why any changes to the constitutional order, like redistributing Senate seats or establishing a third order of government for Aboriginal people, tend to upset the delicate balances struck decades before.

The story of Canada's constitution demonstrates the challenges and perils of adjusting the constitutional order. Disputes over the proper place of Quebec in Confederation erupted in a pair of sovereignty referendums in that province, and other constitutional debates tore at the fabric of national unity. It also reveals the unique circumstances that coalesced on several occasions to allow for more significant attempts at constitutional reform. The 1867 and 1982 deals are certainly worthy of attention. Yet, throughout the 1980s and early 1990s, the prime minister, premiers, and Aboriginal leaders from across Canada reached monumental accords that, had they been endorsed by Canadians and ratified in their legislatures, would have forever

THEY SAID IT

John Sankey, Lord Chancellor of Britain, on the "Living Tree"

John Sankey, 1st Viscount Sankey, had only recently been appointed Lord Chancellor of Britain when he famously characterized Canada's constitution as "a living tree" in a landmark ruling in the case of *Edwards v. Canada* (1929), more commonly known as the *Persons* case.

> The British North America Act planted in Canada a living tree capable of growth and expansion within its natural limits. The object of the Act was to grant a Constitution to Canada. Like all written constitutions it has been subject to development through usage and convention.
>
> —*Edwards v. Canada (Attorney General)* (1929)

VOX POP

Many feel that constitutions must evolve to meet the changing needs of society, but not all agree on the best way to guide that evolution. Do you think that judges—who are not elected or otherwise accountable to the electorate—are best positioned to guide the development of Canada's constitution? Should changes be negotiated by politicians? What role should average citizens play?

changed the definition of Canada and its constitutional order. Regardless of their failure, they left a lasting impact on Canadian politics and democracy.

Canadians and their governments have since turned the page on this mega-constitutional chapter, which lasted throughout much of the final quarter of the twentieth century. Yet even though Canada now stands in what many observers call the post-constitutional period, the lessons of the earlier eras remain important for all students and practitioners of Canadian politics. That's because any future efforts to reform the constitution will begin where past efforts left off. According to the old adage, "the maximum demands of today become the minimum demands of tomorrow."

The Road to Confederation

As mentioned earlier, Canada's constitution traces its roots centuries before 1867. The government systems established by the land's Indigenous peoples and then by the French and British colonies continue to hold influence to this day, although the most familiar and prominent features coalesced in the mid-nineteenth century. It was at this point that delegates from the Province of Canada (Canada West and Canada East) joined leaders from the Maritime colonies of Nova Scotia, New Brunswick, and Prince Edward Island to begin serious discussions about a political and economic union. The Maritime colonists had been contemplating union for several decades, notably without the enthusiasm of their Newfoundland neighbours. As deadlock gripped the Canadian legislature following the Act of Union (1840) leaders of Canada West and Canada East (soon to be Ontario and Quebec, respectively) sensed an opportunity to broaden their political institutions and invited themselves to these discussions. A series of constitutional conferences ensued, with each colony's leaders bringing their own unique interests to the table.

Most delegates realized the economic and military benefits of union, and most held a healthy reverence for British parliamentary traditions. United under a common central government, the separate colonies could create a larger common market and begin building a secure economy and society from sea to sea to sea. Central Canadian manufacturing interests would secure captive markets in the Maritimes, while the latter would gain rail access to the interior of the new country. There was great anticipation of the promise held by settling the vast western lands and reaping their natural wealth, particularly given the military and economic threats posed by American encroachment from the south. Most colonists looked forward to the prospect of creating a central government to handle areas of common interest like banking, currency, and national defence, while retaining control over their own local and cultural matters. Leaders from the various colonies differed on the means of achieving this union, however, and on precisely how government powers would be divided.

The most populous region, Canada West, wanted a strong central government—one whose powers would displace those of the British Parliament, and one whose seats would be distributed proportionately according to population (the *representation by population* or *rep by pop* model). Leaders from other regions were understandably less enthusiastic about empowering a national government over which they held relatively little control. While supportive of union, delegates from Canada East sought the sort of cultural protections that they enjoyed under previous constitutional settlements, namely the preservation of the French language, civil law, and Catholic education. The Maritime colonies pushed for a similar level of local autonomy. This would be manifest in a decentralized division of powers, a robust set of subsidies and debt payments, and regional representation in the institutions of the central government, including the Upper House of Parliament.

Given these divergent interests, delegates were drawn to the balance provided by a federal system of government. They opted for a highly centralized form of federalism, one in which the central government obtained overwhelming authority. In fact, the form of government designed by the Fathers was so centralized that some historians doubt Canada's status as a true federation in 1867; it more closely resembled a unitary state like the United Kingdom, where all power is vested in a central government. The newly created federal government was granted

- the dual powers of disallowance and reservation, which offered it a virtual veto over provincial legislation;
- the levers of "peace, order, and good government" (POGG) and the declaratory power that provided the authority to act in the entire nation's interests; and
- residual powers over any policy area not explicitly enumerated as falling under provincial jurisdiction.

↻ See pages 91–4 of Chapter 3, on federalism, for a discussion of six aspects of the BNA Act— including POGG and the powers of disallowance and reservation—designed to ensure that the federal government would have more power than provincial governments.

These centralizing measures were intended to prevent the type of divisive conflict that had erupted in the United States, where strong states had drawn the country into civil war on the eve of Canadian Confederation.

Thus, the Fathers of Confederation chose to meld British parliamentary traditions with a more centralized form of American-style federalism.[10] According to

INSIDE CANADIAN POLITICS

How Does "Peace, Order, and Good Government" (POGG) Differ from "Life, Liberty, and the Pursuit of Happiness"?

Given that the United Kingdom is arguably the United States' strongest ally, it is easy for Canadians to overlook those countries' bloody political separation. The American War of Independence began with Massachusetts locals revolting against British troops in 1775. America's Declaration of Independence (1776) claimed that the King of Great Britain was "a Tyrant [who] is unfit to be the ruler of a free people," one who caused "repeated injuries and usurpations." This provided the 13 founding American colonies with the justification to declare that they would be "absolved from all allegiance to the British Crown".[9] Years of fighting culminated in the withdrawal of British troops, in the British Parliament's supporting peace talks in 1782, and in British loyalists fleeing to Canada and the Caribbean.

By contrast, British troops largely maintained order in the colonies north of the forty-ninth parallel, and the union of the four founding Canadian colonies in 1867 was in part a protectionist effort under the threat of American expansionism. The constitution of Canada expressly maintains a British connection through its name (the British North America Act), its passage (it was enacted by the British Parliament and granted Royal Assent by the Queen), its preamble (signifying an attempt to be similar to Britain), and the formalization of political institutions that range from the supremacy of the British monarch to the use of a parliamentary system of government.

Americans were motivated by the pursuit of libertarianism and individualism, but in Canada a belief system of communitarianism took hold, accompanied by greater deference to the state. The POGG clause has come to represent the defining character of Canada, particularly when contrasted with the mantra of "life, liberty, and the pursuit of happiness" enshrined in the American Declaration of Independence. The two phrases provide sharp contrasts about political life in two highly similar, yet profoundly different, countries. One has a history of civil war and international military action; the other has self-styled itself as a nation of peacekeepers and purveyors of general order. One believes that its citizens should be empowered to solve problems and strive for a happier life; the other promotes the important role that government plays in citizens' lives. Perhaps a defining difference is that Canadians have a far greater awareness of the American motto than they have of their own. The title of the Hollywood movie *The Pursuit of Happyness* (2006), for which actor Will Smith was nominated for an Academy Award, is but one example of how American politics transcends into global popular culture. Conversely, the POGG clause, which also appears in legislation in other Commonwealth countries (it appears in section 51 of the Australian constitution, for example), is largely a matter of importance within the drudgery of Canadian political science.

VOX POP

Considering the power of Americanization, how do you suppose Canada's constitutional motto has survived over a century and a half?

the Westminster model, sovereignty in the new country would remain vested in the Crown, concentrated in legislative assemblies and exercised through the conventions of responsible government. At the same time, legislative authority would be divided between the federal and the provincial orders, albeit unevenly and in favour of the former. As well, regional representation would be built into the upper house, with 24 Senate seats awarded to each of the new provinces of Quebec and Ontario, and to the three Maritime provinces combined. All of these components were incorporated into the British North America Act (1867) passed by the British Parliament and given royal assent by Queen Victoria on 29 March of that year.

This is not to say that British North Americans were unanimously in favour of Confederation. Opponents in Canada West, the Grits, thought the deal gave too much power to commercial and political interests in Montreal, while critics in Canada East, the Rouges, feared the new constitution would consign French Canadians to being a permanent minority in the new Canada. Similarly, provincial autonomists in the Maritimes thought Confederation ceded too much authority to the larger and more economically powerful provinces of Ontario and Quebec. This was a major reason that leaders from PEI and Newfoundland resisted joining Confederation in 1867. And republicans across the new country expressed disappointment at a lost opportunity to shed ties to the British Empire and join a new North American union with the United States. The voices of these opponents were drowned out at the Confederation conferences, however.

<aside>
KEY DATE

1867 The British government passes the British North America Act, establishing Canada's first modern, written constitution.
</aside>

The Path to Patriation

The foundations of this constitutional order remained largely intact throughout much of the next century. In the early years of Confederation, formal constitutional reform was relatively rare and incremental, proceeding through three main means:

1. through formal constitutional amendments to the British North America Act, made by the British Parliament at the request of Canadian governments,
2. through the passage of statutes and orders-in-council in Canada and Britain, and
3. through court decisions.

Between 1867 and 1982, the British Parliament made a series of 19 formal changes to the BNA Act at the request of the Canadian government. These constitutional amendments strengthened the system of federal–provincial transfer payments (1907); redefined the composition of Parliament to incorporate seats in the Senate for the Western provinces, and establish a minimum number of seats for smaller provinces (1915); granted Western provinces the authority over natural resources previously afforded only to the original partners of Confederation (1930); and established Canada's system of social security, including unemployment insurance (1940) and pensions (1951 and 1964).

Canada also added new provinces through a series of formal constitutional amendments. A number of new members entered Confederation via Canadian statute (Manitoba in 1870, and Saskatchewan and Alberta in 1905) and British order-in-council (BC in 1871 and PEI in 1873). Following a pair of referendums in the former colony, Newfoundland joined Confederation in 1949 by way of a new BNA Act. With the noteworthy exception of Manitoba's entry into the union, which followed

<aside>
KEY DATES

1870–1949 New provinces enter Confederation.
</aside>

an armed struggle between John A. Macdonald's government and the Métis provisional government led by Louis Riel, the expansion of provincehood in Canada was relatively orderly. Each of these new provincial constitutions and orders-in-council formed part of the Canadian constitutional order.

Another change to the Canadian constitutional order came via the Supreme Court Act, 1875. This legislation created a domestic high court for the young dominion, which remained subordinate to the British Judicial Committee of the Privy Council (JCPC) until 1949.

Together, the JCPC and Supreme Court have presided over a century-and-a-half of constitutional evolution in Canada. In the beginning, the courts played a relatively limited role, leaving much of the constitutional order intact.[11] By the turn of the twentieth century, however, a series of pivotal JCPC opinions served to subvert the original intent of the Fathers of Confederation to create a centralized federation in Canada. Judicial review minimized the powers granted to the federal government by offering a very limited interpretation of the POGG clause. This restricted the federal government's authority over the economy to international and interprovincial matters, and forced the federal government to obtain the provinces' consent before signing treaties impacting their areas of jurisdiction. At the same time, the JCPC expanded the provinces' purview over property and civil rights, granting them authority over large policy areas like liquor control and labour. While the Supreme Court offered a more balanced view of Canadian federalism after World War II, the early JCPC rulings helped Canada evolve into a highly decentralized federation, notwithstanding the temporary wartime solidarity and enhanced federal powers that came with it.

None of these developments granted Canadians or their domestic governments control over their own constitutional destiny, however. Premiers and prime ministers had attempted on several occasions to patriate Canada's constitution, which is to say that they sought to secure home rule so that the British Parliament was no longer required to approve constitutional amendments. Negotiations among federal and provincial governments repeatedly broke down amid many points of contention, including the establishment of a charter of rights, the division of powers, equalization, the status of the Supreme Court, the legitimacy of the federal spending power, and several others.

Among the points of contention was the constitutional status of Aboriginal peoples. As noted earlier in the chapter, Aboriginal peoples' inherent right to self-government was constitutionally recognized as early as the Proclamation of 1763. This right was all but ignored by the Crown in the intervening centuries, however, as British, colonial, and Canadian governments seized control of Aboriginal lands and, in 1867, placed "Indians and Indian lands" under federal jurisdiction. In the lead-up to patriation, Aboriginal leaders placed significant public and legal pressure on the federal government to rectify this treatment of nations and people as wards of the state. Their efforts culminated in section 35 of the Constitution Act, 1982, which recognized and affirmed existing Aboriginal and treaty rights as enjoyed by all First Nations ("Indian"), Inuit, and Métis peoples. Many critics felt that section 35 fell well short of protecting Aboriginal rights in Canada.

As crucial as Aboriginal rights were to the patriation process, the most significant sticking point was the actual method for changing the constitution. Put simply, in the absence of the British Parliament as an arbiter and in order to bring the constitution "home" to Canada, first ministers would have to agree among themselves how

KEY DATES

1875 The Supreme Court of Canada is established.

1949 The Supreme Court becomes Canada's highest court of appeal, displacing the JCPC.

future changes to the document would be approved. Several amending formulas had been developed over the course of the twentieth century. However, all failed to receive the endorsement of the province of Quebec, whose premiers insisted on a Quebec veto and severe limits on the federal government's ability to intrude on provincial jurisdiction as part of a new constitutional package.

The election of René Lévesque's Parti Québécois (PQ) in Quebec in 1976 made the prospects of agreement on an amending formula and patriation even less likely. A separatist party, the PQ was more committed to negotiating a new sovereignty-association with the rest of Canada than it was concerned with formalizing Quebec's place within Confederation. The PQ resolved to fulfill its promise to hold a province-wide referendum on whether or not to separate from Canada. This was a significant concern to all federalists, but particularly to Prime Minister Pierre Trudeau, a Quebecer who staked his political career on formalizing home rule over the constitution and entrenching in it a new charter of rights.

After nearly a decade in office, Pierre Trudeau had grown impatient over the provinces' lack of agreement with his partition plans. In 1978, the Trudeau government issued a white paper entitled *A Time for Action*, which outlined Ottawa's intention to proceed with patriation with or without the support of the provincial governments. The move prompted opposition across the country, and the governments of Manitoba, Quebec, and Newfoundland referred the federal plans to their respective provincial courts of appeal for judicial review. These cases eventually made their way to the Supreme Court of Canada. In the meantime, all jurisdictions agreed to task their justice ministers to form a new committee to re-engage in patriation negotiations.

In 1980, nearing the end of its mandate, the Lévesque government followed through on its promise to hold a referendum on Quebec sovereignty. The campaign

sovereignty-association A legal arrangement whereby Quebec would be politically independent but maintain economic ties with Canada.

KEY DATES

1976 René Lévesque's separatist Parti Québécois forms a provincial government for the first time.

1978 The Pierre Trudeau government proposes to patriate the constitution unilaterally, prompting court action by Manitoba, Quebec, and Newfoundland.

white paper A document outlining a policy commitment by government.

KEY DATES

1980 The PQ government holds Quebec's first sovereignty referendum, resulting in a 20-point victory for the "non" side.

1981 The Supreme Court of Canada releases its opinion in the Patriation Reference, deciding that fundamental constitutional changes require a substantial degree of provincial consent.

Drew Gragg/The Canadian Press

Canadian prime minister Pierre Trudeau (*left*) appears to get the cold shoulder from Quebec premier René Lévesque (*right*) during constitutional talks in September 1980. Why do you suppose the media ran with a photo like this?

was a tumultuous one, with strategists on both sides aiming to capture the hearts and minds of Quebecers. During the campaign, Prime Minister Pierre Trudeau promised a renewed form of federalism as part of his patriation package. His pledge proved appealing to many Quebecers, 60 per cent of whom voted "non" in the referendum.

Shortly thereafter, the Supreme Court released its opinion in the *Patriation Reference*, concluding that the federal government was required to consult meaningfully with the provinces and obtain their substantial consent before patriating the constitution. This ruling forced the federal government back to the negotiating table.

Emboldened, premiers from all provinces except Ontario and New Brunswick formed the so-called Gang of Eight to deal with the federal government. Their hard-line stance on a 7/50 amending formula and resistance to Pierre Trudeau's proposed Charter of Rights and Freedoms produced a deadlock that was broken only through a creative compromise known as the "Kitchen Accord" (see the Inside Canadian Politics (ICP) box on page 62). The deal granted the Trudeau government the Charter, albeit with a notwithstanding clause that addressed the Gang of Eight's concerns about provincial governments and legislatures needing to retain the power to have the final say over human rights. The Gang of Eight received their 7/50 general amending formula, although significant areas of the constitution remained under the exclusive purview of the federal government.[12]

Quebec was not part of this backroom deal, and in its aftermath, the Lévesque government expressed public consternation over what it called the Night of the Long Knives. On the evening of 4 November 1981, the prime minister and the other nine premiers reached an agreement to patriate the constitution.

The constitutional deal was finalized when Queen Elizabeth II gave royal assent to the Canada Act (UK) and Constitution Act (Canada) in April 1982.[13] Quebec appealed to the courts to have the laws overturned, arguing that by convention the province held a veto over constitutional amendments. The Supreme Court rejected this argument, and the new constitution remained intact.

The new amending procedures were complex, designed to apply different rules to different elements of the Canadian constitution. While often referred to as a single formula, there are actually five separate amending rules requiring at least the consent of the jurisdictions affected and at most the consent of Parliament and all 10 provincial legislatures (see Table 2.3).

Many critics claim that the amending formula sets too high a threshold for constitutional change, with the result that it slows progress in the modernizing of Canadian democracy. Others feel the formula is appropriately rigid, requiring would-be reformers to engage in the same level of debate and negotiation that went into forging its original terms.

The method by which each jurisdiction would provide its consent to constitutional amendments was just as important as the formula itself. Rather than holding a referendum on an issue, as the Pierre Trudeau government had proposed early in the patriation negotiations, first ministers decided to preserve the principle of legislative supremacy by requiring all amendments to pass through their legislatures as identical resolutions. This allowed the prime minister and premiers to negotiate constitutional amendments before returning home to introduce them for ratification in their own legislatures.

First ministers also agreed to place a three-year time limit on the 7/50 rule, meaning that all resolutions falling under section 38 would have to be passed within 36

Gang of Eight The group of provinces united in opposing the federal government's plans to patriate and centralize the Canadian constitution.

7/50 amending formula A rule for passing most amendments to the constitution, requiring the consent of Parliament and the legislatures of seven provinces representing 50 per cent of Canada's population.

KEY DATES

1981 On 4 November, a deal is reached to patriate the constitution. Quebec officials are not present, and not supportive.

1982 In April, the Canadian constitution is patriated.

Night of the Long Knives An incident in November 1981 in which the federal government and 9 of 10 provincial governments reached a deal to patriate the constitution, without the presence of Quebec government officials.

UP FOR DEBATE

Should it be easier to amend the Canadian constitution? The debate supplement at the end of the chapter gives some of the pros and cons, and offers questions and resources to guide a discussion around this unsettled topic.

TABLE 2.3 | The Amending Formula

Formula	Consent Required	Matters Covered by the Formula
Unanimity formula (section 41)	Parliament plus all 10 provincial legislatures	• the office of the Queen and her representatives • the minimum number of senators per province • the use of French and English • the composition of the Supreme Court • the amending formula itself
General formula (section 38)	Parliament plus the legislatures of at least 7 provinces comprising at least 50 per cent of the population of the provinces combined (the "7/50" formula)	• the principle of representation by population in the House of Commons • the number and residency requirements of senators for each province • the powers of the Senate and method of selecting senators • the Supreme Court of Canada in general • the creation of new provinces or extension of provinces into existing territories
Parliament-only formula (section 44)	Parliament alone	• any matters not outlined in sections 41 and 42 that address the federal legislative and executive branches
Province-only formula (section 45)	Provincial legislature affected	• any matters confined to the province's own constitution (e.g. the Manitoba Act, 1870)
Province-specific formula (section 43)	Parliament plus the legislature(s) of the province(s) to which the amendment applies	• changes to provincial boundaries and the use of English and French

months. Described below, these processes proved problematic in the passage of the Meech Lake and Charlottetown Accords, as the three-year window for negotiations allowed consensus to break down and prompted many citizens to demand direct input into the final decision.

The Mega-constitutional Period

Patriation was an uncertain victory for the first ministers involved in the deal. Several constitutional shortcomings soon became apparent, most notably the failure to fully address Aboriginal people's right to self-government or to incorporate Quebec's interests into the new constitutional framework.

As part of the Constitution Act, 1982, first ministers agreed to hold a series of constitutional conferences with Aboriginal groups to discuss the appropriateness of further amendments to address their concerns. While these conferences received less fanfare than those surrounding Quebec's status in Confederation, and while the meetings fell short of establishing a separate order of government for Aboriginal people, they did generate some notable results. For one, reforms were made to section 35 to clarify that the term "treaty rights" encompasses those rights that exist at present through land claims agreements as well as those rights that may be acquired in the future. Second, and as a result of pressure from the Native Women's Association of Canada, treaty rights were guaranteed for both men and women. Aside from these important amendments, the 1983–4 constitutional conferences, themselves, set an important precedent for future rounds of negotiation: Aboriginal people, represented

INSIDE CANADIAN POLITICS
Why Was the 1981 Kitchen Accord So Significant?

Debates over the amending formula hinged on the level of federal–provincial agreement required to make changes to the various parts of the Canadian constitution. Throughout history, would-be reformers have proposed a variety of rules, such as the 1927 Lapointe formula, the 1965 Fulton-Favreau formula, and the Victoria Charter of 1971. None of these formulas achieved consensus across Canada, however.

This proved possible only when the amending formula was packaged with a unique combination of other constitutional compromises, in what became known as the "Kitchen Accord"—so named because it was reportedly negotiated by three justice ministers in the kitchen of the Government Conference Centre in Ottawa, late in the evening on 4 November 1981. Through it, all jurisdictions except Quebec agreed to entrench a new *Charter of Rights and Freedoms* in the constitution, including a notwithstanding clause that would allow legislators to override certain provisions; and to incorporate the 7/50 amending formula, under which ordinary changes to the constitution could be made with agreement of Parliament plus two-thirds of provincial legislatures representing 50 percent of Canadians. This "general amending formula" would apply to most parts of the constitution. More fundamental changes to the constitution would require unanimity among Parliament and provincial legislatures. Remaining amendments could be made by Parliament alone, or by Parliament and the province(s) directly affected by the proposed changes.

VOX POP

Why do you think it was so difficult for Canada's first ministers to reach an agreement on an amending formula? Why do you think the governments involved felt they should proceed without Quebec?

by national Aboriginal organizations, would need to be involved in any new mega-constitutional deals.

Changes in government marked the beginning of a new era, with Progressive Conservative prime minister Brian Mulroney and Liberal premier Robert Bourassa coming to power in Ottawa (1984) and Quebec City (1985), respectively. Both governments were committed to bringing Quebec back into the constitutional family with "honour and enthusiasm," as Mulroney put it.[14] Bourassa made the first move in May 1986, releasing five conditions for Quebec to agree to engage in amendment negotiations:

KEY DATE

1986 Quebec Liberal premier Robert Bourassa releases his "five conditions" for Quebec to engage in constitutional negotiations.

1. constitutional recognition of Quebec as a "distinct society"
2. a Quebec veto over all constitutional amendments
3. total control for Quebec over immigration to the province
4. Quebec input into Supreme Court appointments and a guaranteed three seats on the nine-person bench
5. strict limits on the federal spending power, achieved by allowing provinces to opt out of national programs with full compensation.

Premier Bourassa's conditions were built on the notion that Canada consisted of two founding nations: French Canada, represented by the Government of Quebec, and English Canada, represented by the federal and other provincial and territorial governments. This conceptualization did not align with that of Aboriginal Canadians or of those who viewed Canada as comprising 10 equal provinces.

Nonetheless, seizing the opportunity to negotiate with a non-separatist government in Quebec, other first ministers pulled onside with Bourassa's vision of federalism, endorsing his five demands at the Annual Premiers Conference in August 1986. Prime Minister Mulroney also agreed to Bourassa's terms as a basis for discussion. So began the intense bargaining surrounding the so-called "Quebec Round" of constitutional negotiations.

On 30 April 1987, first ministers meeting at Meech Lake, Quebec, reached an agreement in principle that would become known as the Meech Lake Accord. The package addressed all five of Bourassa's conditions, although most of the requests for Quebec autonomy were broadened to apply to all provinces who wished to exert those powers. Quebec's request for input into Supreme Court of Canada appointments, for example, was extended to include *provincial* input in general. In addition, the Meech Lake Accord promised to establish annual first ministers' meetings among the prime minister and premiers. Given that several of these proposed reforms would have fundamentally altered the constitutional order, the package as a whole tripped the unanimity provisions of the amending formula. This meant parliament and the legislatures of all provinces would have to pass the Accord.

After a marathon negotiating session, all 10 provincial premiers and the prime minister signed the Meech Lake Accord on 3 June 1987. The Quebec National Assembly became the first legislature to pass the Accord later that month, with all first ministers committing to have their respective legislatures approve the deal within three years. Within just over a year, the Accord passed in Parliament and all but the legislatures of New Brunswick, Newfoundland, and Manitoba.

That is when the amendment process stalled. Opposition mounted amid concerns over the awarding of federal contracts to Quebec, the formation of new federal political parties, and the Quebec government's passage of restrictive new language laws. Critics worried that the new "distinct society" clause provided Quebec with too much autonomy, and feared that this status would be used to marginalize linguistic minorities in the province and francophones throughout the rest of Canada. Others saw restrictions on the federal spending power as limiting the development of strong national programs, and increased use of provincial vetoes as preventing any hope of future constitutional amendments. And Aboriginal groups opposed the exclusion of more comprehensive self-government reforms from the constitutional package. Above all else, however, opposition to the Meech Lake Accord centred on the process by which it was reached: through a series of backroom negotiations by "11 white men in suits" (i.e. the prime minister and the 10 provincial premiers), involving little to no public input. These developments and changes in government in Manitoba and Newfoundland forced first ministers back to the negotiating table in an effort to save the deal.

These last-ditch efforts came to naught. A companion deal was struck to address New Brunswick's concerns over language issues, but the ratification process remained at a standstill in the remaining two holdout provinces. Procedural rules in Manitoba required unanimous support of all members of the legislative assembly to fast-track

Meech Lake Accord
A failed constitutional amendment package in the late 1980s that would have recognized Quebec as a "distinct society."

KEY DATE

1987 On 3 June, all first ministers sign the Meech Lake Accord, an amendment package designed to bring Quebec fully into the constitutional family.

passage of the Accord before the three-year deadline expired. Manitoba MLA Elijah Harper, a member of the province's New Democratic Party and member of the Oji-Cree community of Red Sucker Lake, refused to support the Accord, citing its failure to accommodate Aboriginal concerns. Meanwhile, Clyde Wells, a vocal critic of the Accord, was elected premier of Newfoundland and Labrador. After revoking his government's approval of the Accord, he refused to convene the province's House of Assembly for another vote. To the chagrin of the other governments, the Meech Lake Accord officially died on 23 June 1990.[15]

The Bourassa government responded swiftly, introducing a bill establishing that Quebecers would hold a referendum in October 1992. It would be up to the rest of Canada to decide whether this would be a referendum on separating from Canada or a referendum on a new constitutional amendment package. In other words, unlike the previous "Quebec Round" of negotiations, the prime minister and premiers in the rest of the country would have to initiate the "Canada Round" and entice Quebec to the bargaining table with the opening offer.

The other governments did so in July 1992, building their proposal on the foundations of the Meech Lake Accord. This included familiar terms regarding provincial input on federal appointments; limits on federal spending and an increased number of constitutional areas covered by the unanimity formula. The English-Canadian proposal also included a series of new provisions raised by other provinces and groups.

Chief among these innovations was the entrenchment of a "Canada clause" at the beginning of the Constitution Act, 1982, which would have defined the fundamental qualities of Canadian democracy. These terms included not only Quebec's status as a "distinct society" but also commitments to parliamentary democracy, the equality of peoples and provinces, and Aboriginal rights. The new constitutional package also recognized the inherent right of self-government for Aboriginal peoples, creating a third constitutional order autonomous from the federal and provincial governments. At the same time, the new package provided for the creation of a new "triple-E" Senate. This would require that Senators be *elected*, not appointed; that the Senate seats be divided *equally* among provinces, not among regions; and that the Senate's powers be *effective*, not ornamental. The new deal would also extend exclusive provincial jurisdiction over natural resources (forestry and mining), culture (tourism and recreation), and urban affairs (including housing). Lastly, the accord included a "social charter," committing governments to pursue common objectives in healthcare, education, environmental protection, and other policy areas, as well as a commitment to enhancing internal trade.

All of these elements were incorporated into a new amendment package, dubbed the Charlottetown Accord. By 28 August 1992, all first ministers and leaders of major Aboriginal organizations had signed the new accord. However, the deal did not only require the unanimous support of all provincial legislatures and Parliament: it would also have to pass a nationwide series of provincial referendums, scheduled for 26 October 1992. This was a crucial difference between the Meech Lake and Charlottetown processes, as the former was never put directly to the public for a vote. While the results of these referendums were not constitutionally binding on the various governments, politically it would be very challenging for first ministers to introduce and pass the Accord in their home legislatures if the majority of their constituents were opposed.[16]

KEY DATE

1990 The Meech Lake Accord expires, having failed to pass in the legislatures of Manitoba and Newfoundland.

Charlottetown Accord A failed accord in the early 1990s that proposed to renew the constitution, but was defeated in a national referendum.

KEY DATE

1992 On 28 August, first ministers and Aboriginal leaders sign the Charlottetown Accord, a second amendment package designed to meet a broader set of constitutional demands.

Meech Lake Accord (1987 proposed constitutional amendment)					
"distinct society" clause	provincial input on Senate and Supreme Court of Canada (SCC) appointments	limits on federal spending power	provincial vetoes	provincial control over immigration	annual First Ministers' Conferences (FMCs)

Charlottetown Accord (1992 proposed constitutional amendment)							
"Canada Clause"	provincial input on SCC appointments	triple-E Senate	limits on federal spending power	provincial vetoes	enhanced exclusive provincial jurisdiction	economic and social union	Aboriginal self-government

FIGURE 2.2 | Comparing the Proposed Meech Lake and Charlottetown Accords

In an unusual show of unity, the three largest federal political parties, all provincial premiers, and many First Nations and business leaders campaigned in favour of the Accord. In an odd historical twist, Quebec sovereigntists, alienated western Canadians, and supporters of Prime Minister Pierre Trudeau and his original constitutional vision joined forces to oppose the Accord.

In the end, the Charlottetown Accord was defeated on a pan-Canadian basis by a margin of 55 per cent to 45 per cent, having failed in seven provinces to achieve majority support.[17] The only provinces where it passed were New Brunswick, Newfoundland and Labrador, and PEI; it also passed in Northwest Territories. Research suggests that Canadians found a variety of flaws in the Accord, viewing it as too generous to others and not generous enough to themselves. Many also associated the Accord with its principal architect—Prime Minister Mulroney—whose popularity had plummeted following a series of unpopular political initiatives. This included his government's establishment of the Goods and Services Tax and the Free Trade Agreement with the United States.

The public's rejection of the Charlottetown Accord marked the beginning of the end of the mega-constitutional period. The failure of the two constitutional accords aggravated regional grievances, and Canadians had become disdainful of political elites. Changes in government in Ottawa (from the Progressive Conservative Party to the Liberals) and in Quebec (from the Liberals to the PQ) once again reduced appetites for further negotiations. Premiers and Canadians across the country appeared fatigued and discouraged at the prospects of achieving comprehensive constitutional reform.

Within three years, Quebecers participated in a second referendum on sovereignty, with barely half (50.6 per cent) voting to stay in Confederation. The 1995 Quebec sovereignty referendum ushered in a new era of non-constitutional renewal of the Canadian federation, with few Canadians interested in engaging in the sort of heightened debates that had torn at the threads of national unity for almost three decades.

KEY DATE

1992 On 26 October, the Charlottetown Accord is defeated in a nationwide referendum.

KEY DATE

1995 The "non" side wins the second Quebec sovereignty referendum, this time by just over 50,000 votes.

The Post-constitutional Period

Canadians could be forgiven if they suffered from political fatigue in the mid-1990s, as could politicians and senior-level officials who subsequently declared the constitution off limits. The routine first ministers' conferences of the 1980s were gradually phased out, giving way to occasional bilateral meetings between the prime minister and individual premiers. Other major issues had fallen down the political agenda for over two decades, and the economy and healthcare were showing signs of neglect.

Yet first ministers could not entirely ignore the constitutional fissures that remained exposed following the Charlottetown and Quebec referendums. Rather than reopen formal amendment discussions, however, they opted to proceed through non-constitutional, incremental reforms that, when taken as a whole, went some distance toward addressing many of the grievances that led to the divisive debates in the first place.

Most of these measures were taken in a symmetrical way, extending new authority to all provinces equally, and not to Quebec alone. In 1996, for instance, the federal

Fred Chartrand/The Canadian Press

Demonstrators show their support for the Meech Lake Accord, with signs noting that Canadian unity depends on the inclusion of all 10 provinces. The accord, which was never put to a public vote, was scuttled by two provinces: Manitoba and Newfoundland. The Charlottetown Accord, in contrast, was supported by all first ministers before being defeated in a nationwide referendum. What do you think is the best way to ratify a change to the Canadian constitution?

government passed An Act Respecting Constitutional Amendments, which gave Quebec, Ontario, BC, and Alberta effective vetoes over future changes to the constitution. The act established regional vetoes by stipulating that Parliament would not endorse constitutional amendments unless they had the support of a majority of provinces including:

- Quebec;
- Ontario;
- British Columbia;
- at least two Atlantic provinces (totalling more than 50 per cent of the region's population); and
- at least two Prairie provinces (totalling more than 50 per cent of the region's population).

Debates persist as to the constitutionality of the 1996 act, as it could be seen as revising the amending formula—a change that would require more than a simple federal law to effect. Nonetheless, as a political document, the regional veto law did acknowledge provinces' concerns over unilateral federal actions to amend the constitution without their consent.

The federal Liberal government, under Prime Minister Jean Chrétien, also granted provinces increased control over immigration. The Liberals also signed on to the Social Union Framework Agreement, which placed limits on the federal spending power by requiring majority provincial consent for any new national programs in areas of provincial jurisdiction and allowing dissenting provinces to opt out with full compensation.

These restrictions on the spending power were echoed in the federal Conservative government's later promise of "open federalism." Furthermore, in 2006, the Conservative government led by Stephen Harper introduced and secured passage of a House of Commons motion declaring "that the Québécois form a nation within a united Canada."[19] The government also took steps toward addressing other regional grievances as expressed during the mega-constitutional era—again, though, without engaging the provinces in formal negotiations over constitutional amendments. The Harper government introduced several pieces of legislation to effect Senate reform, one of which formed the foundation of a reference case heard by the Supreme Court of Canada over the proper constitutional and non-constitutional routes to modernizing the Upper House. The Conservatives also devolved authority to the territorial governments and engaged National Aboriginal Organization leaders on issues of major concern, meeting multilaterally with those leaders more often than with the premiers.

Granted, none of these changes have been formally enshrined in the constitution. First ministers remain reluctant to engage in the sort of mega-constitutional negotiations of the late twentieth century. Yet this latest chapter does demonstrate the extent to which successive federal governments have gone to achieve workable changes to the political order, if not the constitutional one. And some political observers feel that these incremental changes may help pave the way for eventual constitutional reforms.

KEY DATE

1996 The federal government passes a regional veto law, placing constraints on its own ability to amend the constitution.

↻ For more on the Social Union Framework Agreement, particularly as it was received in Quebec, see the ICP box on pages 106–7 of Chapter 3, on federalism.

KEY DATE

2006 The House of Commons passes a symbolic resolution declaring the Québécois "a nation within a united Canada."

Opportunities Available

Knowledge of Canadian Politics and Government Preferred!

Summer Student Positions

Centre for Constitutional Studies

The Centre for Constitutional Studies is seeking summer students (May-August) to research and write articles for our website, to assist with constitutional research and to work on Public Legal Education projects.

Qualifications

- effective research and writing skills
- ability to write in plain language
- interest in constitutional issues
- ability to work independently and with a team
- current status as a 1st- or 2nd-year J.D. student at the University of Alberta

Hours

- 35 hours per week for 12 weeks between May 11 – August 7, 2015

To apply, please email the following documents to the Executive Director:

- a cover letter
- C.V. (including contact information for at least one reference)
- a scanned copy of all official, post-secondary transcripts

Shortlisted candidates will be asked to submit a writing sample and partake in a writing evaluation.

The Charter of Rights and Freedoms

If the amending formula was the lynchpin of the patriation deal, the Charter of Rights and Freedoms was its catalyst. Prime Minister Pierre Trudeau made it his personal mission not only to bring the British North America Act fully under Canadian control but also to entrench certain fundamental liberties in an expanded constitution. On the surface, and with decades of hindsight, Trudeau's objective was hardly controversial. After all, how could any Canadian, let alone a provincial premier, be opposed to protecting human rights and freedoms? The answer to that question is more complex than at first appears, however, and requires a deeper understanding of how rights are preserved in parliamentary democracies like Canada.

There is a thin line between rights and freedoms, on one hand, and needs and desires, on the other. What is a fundamental liberty to one person may be a luxury or privilege to another. Consider the issue of housing, or clean water. Should every Canadian be entitled to shelter and safe drinking water? In other words, should governments provide these things for all Canadians, or take steps to ensure that everyone has access to them? What about healthcare? Marriage? Gun ownership? Wearing a kirpan? There are no easy answers to these questions, which is part of the reason Pierre Trudeau's proposal met so much resistance.

In general, rights may be divided into two kinds: those granted to individuals, like the right to vote, and those belonging to groups, like the right to self-government for Aboriginal peoples. Similarly, freedoms come in one of two forms: *negative liberties*, which protect people from interference by government or other people, like the freedom of religion, and *positive entitlements*, which empower people to exercise their autonomy, like the right to a fair trial. Taken together, rights and freedoms come in a wide variety of forms, from political and legal, to moral and rational, to economic and social.

Some but not all of these rights and freedoms are found in the predecessor to the Canadian Charter, the Canadian Bill of Rights, 1960. At the time the Bill of Rights was passed by John Diefenbaker's Progressive Conservative government in 1960, Canadians were not only witnesses to but active participants in a global human rights movement. While their constitution had been founded on the liberal-democratic principles of equality and protection of minorities, these notions were broadened and elevated to greater salience amid civil rights campaigns elsewhere in the world, most notably in the United States. These events coincided with the centennial of Confederation, prompting many leaders, including prime ministers Diefenbaker, Pearson, and Pierre Trudeau, to promote pan-Canadian visions of citizenship.

Given all of these developments, Canadians and their leaders were primed for a debate over whether to entrench a more comprehensive set of rights and freedoms in the constitution. Crucially, constitutionalizing these rights would mean affording the judiciary a greater role in defining and protecting them. Much as the courts had become arbiters in disputes over the federal–provincial division of powers in the BNA Act, 1867, so, too, would they be asked to adjudicate between varying views of entitlements and liberties if they were entrenched in the constitution.

This prospect did not sit well with supporters of parliamentary supremacy, particularly those in provincial governments, who feared a new federally defined charter interpreted by federally appointed judges would disturb their constitutional jurisdiction over human rights in Canada. Manitoba premier Sterling Lyon and other old-right Tories resisted patriation for this very reason.

In the end, those wanting to entrench rights in the written constitution and those wanting to preserve the power of legislatures reached a compromise: they would embed a set of rights and freedoms in the newly patriated constitution but allow legislatures to override certain provisions under specific conditions. The notwithstanding clause, as it came to be known, was a key component in the Kitchen Accord, and came with a strict set of rules for its use. Federal, provincial, and territorial governments could pass laws that violated a particular set of rights and freedoms in the Charter (those in section 2 or sections 7–15). Such rights included "fundamental freedoms" like freedom of conscience and association, legal rights, and equality rights. Democratic rights, mobility rights, and language rights were excluded from the scope of the notwithstanding clause, however, meaning that no legislature could pass laws contravening them. The same was true of other core rights found elsewhere in the constitution, like Aboriginal treaty rights in section 35.

If a government chose to pass a law that violated certain rights, it would have to publicly declare this by inserting a clause in the act stating that the law exists

rights Legal claims or entitlements to have something or to act in a particular manner.

freedoms The autonomy to live and act without external restraint.

Bill of Rights, 1960 A federal law detailing Canadians' rights and freedoms vis-à-vis the federal government.

↻ Attempts to re-imagine Canadian citizenship were part of a "new nationalism" that occurred during the 1960s. For more information, see Chapter 14, on Canada's place in the world.

parliamentary supremacy A doctrine under which legislatures and executives, not courts, define key elements of public policy.

notwithstanding clause Section 33 of the Constitution Act, 1982, which permits legislatures to pass laws that breach certain rights and freedoms.

Pierre Roussel Images Distribution

A defaced STOP sign serves as a reminder of the contentious debate over Quebec's Bill 101, also known as the Charter of the French Language, 1977. The provincial law made French the principal language of both politics and business within the province, but its ban on the use of English on commercial signs failed a Charter challenge in 1988, when the Supreme Court ruled the law violated freedom of expression. The Quebec government responded by invoking the notwithstanding clause to preserve its so-called "sign law." Is it appropriate to have such a limitation on the reach of the Charter? In what other circumstances might it be used?

reasonable limits clause Section 1 of the Charter, which allows governments to pass laws that would otherwise contravene rights and freedoms but which are deemed necessary to protect other democratic norms.

"notwithstanding" the Charter. Moreover, such laws would not be permanent; they would expire, or "sunset," after five years. If a government wished to maintain the new law, it would have to re-enact the legislation once every election cycle, which would allow the public an opportunity to evaluate the government's choice.

Charter advocates, including Trudeau himself, believed that the notwithstanding clause marked a major deficiency in the new constitution. It created a hierarchy of rights, some of which were violable by government and others that were not, and it allowed for the development of different regimes in various provinces across the country. To Charter critics, the notwithstanding clause did not go far enough to protect the concept of parliamentary supremacy. They felt the entire scope of the Charter of Rights and Freedoms should be subject to its provisions, and felt that the five-year sunset requirement placed undue burdens on duly elected legislators. In the end, the compromise satisfied neither side entirely.

The notwithstanding clause was not the only limitation placed on the rights and freedoms in the Charter. Section 1 established that these terms were guaranteed "subject only to such reasonable limits prescribed by law as can be demonstrably justified in a free and democratic society." In other words, it may be justifiable to limit certain Charter rights in exceptional cases. The courts have used this reasonable limits clause as a filter when deciding cases involving alleged violations of Charter rights. Indeed, section 1 forms a key element of the Supreme Court's Oakes test, which judges apply to determine whether the purported democratic objectives of the law outweigh the negative impacts it would have on Canadians' rights and freedoms (see Figure 2.3). Once the court has determined that a law has violated a Charter right, the judges ask themselves whether the overall objective of the law is sufficiently important —that is, whether it addresses problems that are so pressing—as to justify that breach. If the answer is yes, the court then asks whether the measures the law takes are suitable and proportionate to achieve those objectives and, ultimately, whether the means justify the ends.

The Oakes test derives from a 1986 Supreme Court decision in the case of David Edwin Oakes, who was arrested in London, Ontario, in 1981 on suspicion of narcotics trafficking. The basis for his arrest was the possession of small amounts of hashish oil and cash, which, under section 8 of the Narcotic Control Act, constituted reasonable grounds for the presumption of guilt. The Supreme Court ruled that section 8 of the NCA violated section 11(d) of the Charter, and that such a violation could *not* be justified according to the terms set out in section 1 of the Charter, the reasonable limits clause. Contrast this with the case of Alberta teacher Jim Keegstra, who was charged with wilfully promoting hatred under the Criminal Code for making anti-Semitic statements in class. Keegstra argued that the ruling violated his Charter right to freedom of expression. However, the Supreme Court upheld the charge, arguing that a reasonable limitation on the right to freedom of expression was justifiable under the circumstances.

As entrenched in the Constitution Act, 1982, the Charter contained a defined set of rights and freedoms, but these were by no means set in stone. Indeed, the list of

Oakes test A model employed by the court to weigh the democratic benefits and assess the constitutionality of a law that breaches certain Charter rights.

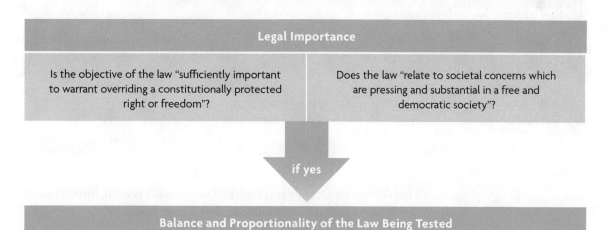

FIGURE 2.3 | The Oakes Test

The Oakes test was established by the Supreme Court of Canada in the case of *R v. Oakes* (1986). The test is used to assess the constitutionality of a law that breaches Charter rights.

INSIDE CANADIAN POLITICS

Testing the Limits on Charter Rights: English-only Signs and the *Ford* Case

The *Ford* case (1988) provides a good example of the notwithstanding clause and the Oakes test in practice. A group of Montreal merchants taken the Government of Quebec to court over the province's language laws, which at the time prohibited the use of English-only signs in their businesses. Lower courts in Quebec found in favour of the merchants, declaring the law unconstitutional. The Quebec government appealed the case to the Supreme Court of Canada. In its ruling, the Supreme Court also found in favour of the business owners, deciding that the part of Quebec's language law prohibiting English-only signage contravened Quebecers' constitutional right to freedom of expression. While deciding that the purpose behind the sign law met the "importance" standard in its goal to preserve French language and culture, the justices found that the precise means through which the Quebec

government went about achieving that objective were too heavy-handed. The Court thus struck down the law as unconstitutional.

The Quebec government, under Premier Robert Bourassa, responded by making very minor changes to the law in 1989, and invoking the notwithstanding clause to protect it from further judicial scrutiny. It was able to do so as all governments are permitted to violate Canadians' freedom of expression, provided they explicitly invoke the notwithstanding clause. Four years later, the Quebec government made the changes necessary to conform with the Supreme Court opinion, amending the law to include a more proportionate means of meeting its objective. In this case, it required that French be the predominant, but not exclusive, language on all signage in the province. The notwithstanding clause was not invoked on this new law.

THE LESSON

Canadian governments are permitted to violate certain rights and freedoms, but such decisions are subject to judicial review.

VOX POP

Sections 1 and 33 established real limits on rights and freedoms found in the Charter. How effective and justified are these limits? Who should have the final say on the limits of rights and freedoms in the Charter: appointed judges or elected politicians?

rights and freedoms is continually revisited, and occasionally revised, through court interpretations. At the time it was established, the Charter protected:

- *fundamental freedoms*, including those of conscience, religion, thought, belief, opinion, expression, the press, peaceful assembly, and association;
- *democratic freedoms*, including the right to vote, to hold office, and to participate in elections at least once every five years;
- *mobility rights*, to move and pursue a livelihood in any province;
- *legal rights*, namely to life, liberty, security of the person, access to timely justice, and freedom from unreasonable search and seizure (*habeas corpus*);
- *equality rights*, such as the rule of law and freedom from discrimination;

- *language rights* when interacting with governments; and
- *minority language education rights.*

While extensive, this list of rights was by no means exhaustive. The Charter did not set out social rights, such as the right to education, housing, or healthcare. It did not protect economic rights, like the right to employment or private property, or the right to strike. The Charter itself did not include Aboriginal rights, although these are entrenched elsewhere in the constitution. Nor did the written document enumerate constitutional protections for Canadians on the basis of their sexual orientation; this was later "read into" the document by the courts. It is also important to note that the Charter applies only to Canadian governments, not to private disputes involving individual Canadians, businesses, and other organizations; those rights issues remain under the purview of provincial human rights legislation. This said, the advent of the Charter of Rights and Freedoms marked a major innovation in Canada's constitutional order—one that established Canada as a constitutional model for other common-law countries.[19]

↻ The individual rights of Canadians are discussed in Chapter 7, on the justice system.

Charter Politics

In the decades before 1982, Canadians' rights and freedoms were protected by a combination of unwritten British common law and recorded legislation. Passed in 1960, the Bill of Rights was one of several similar laws in place across Canada, many of which remain in force to this day. Together, these pieces of legislation were built on the principle of parliamentary supremacy, under which elected legislators and governments would define and protect Canadians' rights with minimal interference from the courts.

Prime Minister Pierre Trudeau and other critics of this model pointed to a plethora of human rights abuses by Canadian governments acting under the guise of parliamentary supremacy. The forced displacement and oppression of Aboriginal peoples, the residential schools system, the sterilization of mentally disabled people, the lack of a universal franchise, the suppression of the press, the internment of Japanese Canadians during World War II . . . there was no shortage of high-profile cases of governments violating Canadians' rights and freedoms. Furthermore, the centrepiece of the Canadian human rights regime, the Bill of Rights, lacked the necessary scope or force to prevent future abuses from occurring. It did not apply to governments beyond the federal level, it did not hold *primacy* (or *precedence*) over other federal laws, it contained no prescribed remedies in the event it was violated, and its rights remained defined as they were at the time of passage. Moreover, as an ordinary federal statute, it could be amended at the sole discretion of the federal government.

The Charter changed all of this by entrenching rights and freedoms in the constitution, thus requiring the consent of provincial governments to alter it and making all other laws—federal and provincial—subject to its provisions. The Charter also established the judiciary as a key actor in the politics of rights and freedoms in Canada. Whereas the courts played a relatively passive role vis-à-vis federal and provincial legislatures prior to 1982, the new regime assigned the judiciary a role not only to interpret human rights and freedoms in Canada but also to define them. As with most other elements of the constitution, the Charter contains broad, sometimes intentionally ambiguous language, forcing judges to use discretion when offering their opinions on cases that come before the bench.

And as with other parts of the constitution, judges are empowered to use the Charter to *strike down* (or *nullify*) laws that contravene it. The Supreme Court struck down a ban on tobacco advertising, for example, as the prohibition ran contrary to the freedom of expression (the 1995 *RJR-MacDonald* case). Alternatively, judges may strike down parts of a law, grant an exemption to particular groups or individuals, or postpone the nullification until the government is able to respond. This was the case in the 2013 *Bedford* decision, where the Supreme Court served the federal government one year's notice that major elements of its prostitution laws were unconstitutional. Judges are also permitted to "read in" new rights, supplementing those that were originally included in the Charter. The Supreme Court did this when extending equality rights to homosexuals in several landmark cases, culminating in the *Same-Sex Marriage* reference.

These instances of judicial review may make it appear, and even make it more likely, that judges have the final say when it comes to the rights and freedoms Canadians enjoy. But this is not necessarily the case. According to the dialogue model, judicial review is only one side of the democratic conversation. The other half is spoken by the legislature and the executive, who have the opportunity to respond to judicial rulings by amending or abandoning legislation. If the rights in question fall under sections 2 or 7–15 of the Charter, governments may also opt to re-pass the law by invoking the notwithstanding clause, as discussed earlier.

Critics of parliamentary supremacy and proponents of judicial review feared that this latter option would become commonplace in the years following the Charter. Their predictions of federal or provincial governments passing laws infringing on Charter rights proved to be overstated, however, as the only effective use of the notwithstanding clause has occurred in Quebec. As a signal of the provincial government's opposition to patriation, Premier Lévesque inserted a notwithstanding clause in each and every statute passed by the Quebec National Assembly from 1982 to 1985, a practice that ended when his government left office. Lévesque also attempted to extend this principle retroactively, passing a law stating that all Quebec statutes passed before 1982 existed notwithstanding the Charter; in the *Ford* case, the Supreme Court later ruled that this blanket, retroactive exemption of Quebec laws from the Charter was invalid (*Ford v. A.G. Quebec*, [1988] 2 S.C.R. 712). Premier Robert Bourassa subsequently used the notwithstanding clause to briefly shield Quebec's sign law from judicial review, as noted in the Inside Canadian Politics box on page 72. No other governments have successfully invoked the notwithstanding clause.

Several governments have threatened to do so, though. The very first invocation of the notwithstanding clause occurred in Yukon in 1982; however, its Land Planning and Development Act was never brought into force. Threats to invoke section 33 occurred in Alberta in the 1990s, when Progressive Conservative Premier Ralph Klein openly mused about using the notwithstanding clause to protect the government against costly lawsuits over the province's eugenics program, which had sterilized over 2,800 disabled Albertans from 1928 to 1972. The Klein government abandoned that idea, but later inserted a notwithstanding clause in a bill that would have defined marriage in Alberta as a union between a man and woman. The Supreme Court later ruled that the definition of marriage fell under federal jurisdiction, however, making the Alberta government's use of section 33 invalid. A similar situation

dialogue model The notion that the definition of rights and freedoms is reached through the interaction of judges, legislatures, and executives.

had unfolded in Saskatchewan a dozen years earlier, when, in 1988, the government of Grant Devine attempted to "Charter-proof" its back-to-work legislation by wording it in such a way as to withstand legal challenges. In the *Alberta Labour* reference, the Supreme Court ruled that the Charter did not contain a right to strike, rendering the Saskatchewan government's pre-emptive measures unnecessary. The Supreme Court corrected its earlier interpretation in 2015, declaring the Saskatchewan government's new back-to-work legislation unconstitutional. This placed Premier Brad Wall in a similar position, forcing him to weigh the merits of invoking the notwithstanding clause to prevent the ability of certain public sector workers to strike.

Observers have interpreted this dearth of section 33 activity in a number of ways. Parliamentary supremacists view it as the result of the chill being placed on legislative responses to court decisions. Legislators, they argue, are wary of invoking the clause for fear of public backlash, given the results of opinion research that indicates Canadians trust judges and courts more than they trust politicians and legislators. From the opposite side, judicial supremacists view this as evidence of the success of the Charter, as it demonstrates the important check-and-balance served by the courts in protecting Canadians' rights and freedoms from government overreach.

All told, we can group proponents and opponents of the post-1982 Canadian rights regime into two camps, *charterphiles* and *charterphobes*.[20] Charterphiles value the fact that the system offers a new access point for Canadians seeking to defend or expand rights protections. Rather than having to lobby governments or field candidates for office, which can be difficult for minority or traditionally disadvantaged Canadians, rights-based interest groups have made use of the alternative route provided by the courts. In this sense, Charterphiles view judges as independent, objective, expert arbiters of human rights issues, more distanced from the ideological, partisan, and majoritarian world of traditional electoral politics.

Charterphobes sit on the opposite side of the rights debate. While not fearing the Charter (as certain interpretations of their label may suggest), Charterphobes disagree with the direction in which it has steered rights-based discourse in Canada. Many view the rise of judicial supremacy and litigiousness (or "jurocracy") as an unfortunate departure from Canada's parliamentary and democratic traditions. Charterphobes lament the fact that, rather than having duly elected officials defining and adjudicating rights disputes, it is appointed and unaccountable judges who now appear to have the greatest lawmaking powers.

Contrary to popular conceptions and general patterns, not all Charterphiles sit on the left side of the political spectrum, and not all Charterphobes are conservative. Consider several high-profile Charter cases. Left-leaning proponents of the Charter system were pleased with the outcome of the *Keegstra* case, where a high school teacher was found guilty of inciting hatred against Jewish Canadians by teaching anti-Semitic lessons in his high school classroom. The ruling placed limits on freedom of expression in the interests of preventing hate speech against identifiable groups in Canada. Yet other cases can shake progressives' faith in the judicial process, particularly when judges reject positive rights claims—as occurred when the right to strike was denied in the *Alberta Labour* reference—or provide Canadians with certain negative liberties. The latter resulted from the *Chaoulli* decision, when the Court established that the right to security of person could extend to the freedom to seek private healthcare alternatives if the public system did not meet certain standards.

Charter-proof Pre-emptive steps taken by a government to ensure that its proposed legislation withstands judicial review.

Charterphiles Supporters of the enhanced role of judges in the Canadian rights regime.

↻ For a discussion of diversity and the courts, see pages 516–20 of Chapter 13, on diversity and representation.

Charterphobes Opponents and skeptics of the enhanced role of judges in the Canadian rights regime.

The same type of moral conflict occurs on the other side of the spectrum from time to time. The *Same-Sex Marriage* reference drew the ire of right-wing Charterphobes, who viewed it as the result of judicial overreach in defining group entitlements. Yet decisions like *Chaoulli* and the *Alberta Labour* reference can turn otherwise staunch opponents of the judiciary into proponents of the judges' decisions.

Concluding Thoughts

Notwithstanding the advent of the Charter in 1982 (pun intended!), Canada's constitutional order has remained remarkably constant over the past two centuries. The country's supreme law remains rooted in the same principles of parliamentary democracy and federalism that predated its colonies' entry into Confederation. And while the recognition of Aboriginal rights to self-government and the advent of the Charter marked significant innovations in Canada's constitutional order, these changes remain dwarfed in volume and consequence compared to events in the United States, which has undertaken 14 separate constitutional amendments; in France, which has undertaken two complete re-writes of its constitution; and in the numerous countries that have undergone civil wars or revolutions over the same period.

Canada's constitutional stability is not for lack of effort on the part of reformers. Premiers, prime ministers, Aboriginal leaders, and activists in the last quarter of the twentieth century invested a great deal of political capital in attempting to patriate and perfect the Canadian constitutional order. For better or worse, their efforts left a lasting mark on Canadian politics and democracy, prompting their successors to invest just as much energy avoiding the constitutional quagmire that had consumed the country for over three decades. Canada is now in a post-constitutional era, but many of the same constitutional questions remain unanswered. The next generation of leaders must decide whether to leave these issues in abeyance, or address them in a new round of constitutional negotiations. History reveals the challenges and opportunities that lie in either approach. Insiders heed these lessons.

For More Information

Looking for the cornerstone of Canada's constitutional monarchy? David E. Smith writes about it in *The Invisible Crown: The First Principle of Canadian Government* (University of Toronto Press, 1995).

Just how difficult is it to amend the constitution in the 21st century? Ask Emmett Macfarlane and his contributors to *Constitutional Amendment in Canada* (University of Toronto Press, 2016).

Wonder which values underlie the Canadian constitutional order? So did Janet Ajzenstat and Peter Smith in their edited volume *Canada's Origins: Liberal, Tory or Republican?* (Carleton University Press, 1995).

Want to learn more about the inner workings of Westminster traditions in Canada? Read insights in *Responsible Government: Clarifying Essentials, Dispelling Myths and Exploring Change*, by Peter

Aucoin, Jennifer Smith, and Geoff Dinsdale (Canadian Centre for Management Development, 2004).

Ever consider what role bureaucrats play in responsible government? Donald Savoie examines the relationship between the political and permanent executive in *Breaking the Bargain: Public Servants, Ministers and Parliament* (University of Toronto Press, 2003).

Considering ways of reforming the constitutional order? You're not alone: Peter Aucoin, Mark Jarvis, and Lori Turnbull contemplate constitutional reform in *Democratizing the Constitution: Reforming Responsible Government* (Emond Montgomery, 2011).

Want to read the actual words of the Fathers of Confederation, and learn more about how they reached the deal? Consult *Canada's Founding Debates* (Janet Ajzenstat et al.; University of Toronto Press, 1999) and *1867: How the Fathers Made a Deal* (Christopher Moore; McClelland and Stewart, 1997).

Want first-hand accounts of what *really* happened behind the scenes of the various rounds of mega-constitutional negotiations? See *And No One Cheered: Federalism, Democracy and the Constitution Act* (Keith Banting and Richard Simeon, eds; Methuen, 1983); *Meech Lake: The Inside Story* (Patrick Monahan; University of Toronto Press, 1991);

and *The Charlottetown Accord, the Referendum, and the Future of Canada* (Kenneth McRoberts and Patrick Monahan, eds; University of Toronto Press, 1993).

Curious about the democratic trajectory of Canada's constitutional evolution? Peter Russell examines the issue in *Constitutional Odyssey: Can Canadians Become a Sovereign People?* (University of Toronto Press, 1993).

Ever thought that first ministers ought to just leave the constitution alone? Read David Thomas's *Whistling Past the Graveyard: Constitutional Abeyances, Quebec, and the Future of Canada* (Oxford University Press, 1997).

Skeptical of the impact of judges in Canada's constitutional order? Read John T. Saywell's *The Lawmakers: Judicial Power and the Shaping of Canadian Federalism* (University of Toronto Press, 2002).

Want access to all of the key constitutional documents? Canadiana.ca has assembled an annotated constitutional history. Go to www.canadiana.ca/citm/themes/constitution1_e.html, or search: Canada in the Making constitution.

Looking to view behind-the-scenes footage of the mega-constitutional era? The CBC has ample news coverage in its online archives: www.cbc.ca/archives.

Deeper Inside Canadian Politics

1. Is the Canadian system of governance more or less democratic than the American system of governance? In your answer, ensure you provide a concrete definition of the term *democracy*, and provide substantial evidence to support your position. Your response should also address potential criticism from the opposing side of the debate.

2. Identify the three most important ways in which

Canada's system of parliamentary democracy ought to be reformed. In your answer, ensure you clearly state the problem(s) with the way parliamentary democracy functions in Canada, and the specific means by which you would address these shortcomings. In defending your choices, you should address why you rejected other leading problems and solutions.

UP FOR DEBATE

Should it be easier to amend the Canadian constitution?

THE CLAIM: YES, IT SHOULD!

Constitutional amendment is too difficult to achieve in Canada, to the detriment of meaningful and necessary democratic reform.

Yes: Argument Summary

The amending formula has placed the Canadian constitution in concrete shoes. The level of elite accommodation required to reach the necessary federal–provincial agreement sets a high enough bar. Add to that the necessity of engaging special interest groups and securing the support of the judiciary and the public, and the threshold is all but insurmountable. As a result, the Canadian constitution remains mired in the regional and governmental conflicts of the nineteenth century, and Canadians remain stuck with many of the same institutions they had in that foregone era.

Yes: Top 5 Considerations

1. The rigidity of the amending formula has left several fundamental issues unresolved. For instance, while bound by the terms of the Constitution Act, 1982, Quebec remains outside of the Confederation family. The appointed Senate remains a relic of the Victorian era, and an embarrassment for a modern democratic country.
2. Leaving certain constitutional questions unaddressed for generations results in pent-up frustrations, which boil over from time to time in full-blown national unity crises. The 1995 Quebec referendum demonstrates how the failure to achieve constitutional reform can have the perverse effect of destroying the constitutional order entirely.
3. The nature and history of constitutional reform in Canada make piecemeal reforms all but impossible. Achieving the necessary level of consensus around any one area of the constitution cannot be accomplished without making trade-offs involving other parts of the constitution. This time-consuming process of linkage and packaging necessarily pushes negotiations behind closed doors, waters down any attempts at meaningful reform, and draws attention and political capital away from other important areas of public policy (like healthcare or the economy).
4. Constitutional deals almost inevitably end up before two courts: the judiciary, and the court of public opinion. The former is an independent, but ultimately unaccountable, arbiter. The latter has demonstrated little appreciation for the value of grand constitutional compromises that may appear to favour "them" over "us."
5. The original amending formula made constitutional reform arduous enough. The federal regional veto law (An Act Respecting Constitutional Amendments, 1996) added an extra layer of difficulty.

Yes: Other Considerations

- The strict nature of the amending formula provides governments with incentives to push the envelope when attempting democratic reform. Pierre Trudeau's plans to unilaterally patriate the constitution and impose a Charter of Rights and Freedoms, and the Harper government's abortive attempts to effect Senate reform without the input or consent of provincial governments, amounted to playing politics with the supreme law of the land.
- The political fallout for the Mulroney government stemming from the failure of the Meech

Lake and Charlottetown Accords has become a warning to future prime ministers: re-open the constitutional debate at your peril!

- Proposing any fundamental change to the constitution immediately prompts other political interests to lobby against that change unless their concerns are also addressed.

THE COUNTERCLAIM: NO, IT SHOULDN'T!

The amending formula is appropriately rigid, protecting the core elements of Canadian democracy from whimsical change.

No: Argument Summary

Constitutional reform should not be easy. As the supreme law of the country, the constitution forms the foundation of Canadian democracy, and it should not be uprooted on an occasional basis. The amending formula is built on the premise that fundamental changes to the constitution should be made only with the substantial consent of the partners of Confederation. Building this level of consensus takes time and effort, as it should. The deals struck in 1867 and 1982 involved a highly complex series of trade-offs and compromises. These bargains did not coalesce overnight, and they should not be altered or broken without a similar level of consideration.

No: Top 5 Considerations

1. Plenty of flexibility exists in the Canadian constitutional order to allow for Canadian democracy to evolve with the times. Look no further than the expansion of the franchise and other rights and freedoms that took place throughout the twentieth century, and the continued extension of rights that persists to this day.
2. Not all constitutional change occurs through formal amendments to the Constitution acts. A combination of conventions and judicial review continue to keep Canada's constitution in line with evolving democratic norms.
3. In particular, the emerging convention that the public must be consulted prior to any fundamental constitutional change should not be seen as a weakness. It is a strength of Canadian democracy, and a sign that Canadians view the Constitution Act as *their* document—not simply one that belongs to governments and political elites.
4. The high threshold set by the amending formula has forced governments to consider alternative means of democratic reform, through non-constitutional channels. This has resulted in fruitful experimentation, like the advent of Senate nominee elections in Alberta.
5. The tendency for amendment negotiations to result in mega-constitutional accords reflects the highly complex, interconnected nature of the grand bargains that emerged in 1867 and 1982. Altering the terms of Confederation should be just as complicated, considering changes to any one element of those original deals amounts to reneging on the bottom-line terms of some partners.

No: Other Considerations

- The mega-constitutional era was not entirely fruitless in terms of democratic reform. Whether by convention, by law, or by common practice, many of the Bourassa government's five conditions for Quebec have become widely accepted as facts of Canadian political life. And the closed-door, closed-off nature of executive federalism has given way to a more transparent brand of intergovernmental relations.
- Decades of constitutional strife contributed to placing Canada in a perpetual state of crisis. By refraining from re-opening constitutional debates, successive prime ministers have avoided aggravating regional and other political tensions.

Discussion Questions

- There are serious flaws with the design of the Canadian constitution; conversely, changing the constitution risks splitting the country apart. Do you think it is better to put up with the constitution the way it is, or time to start a new round of constitutional negotiations? Why?
- In your opinion, what is the best way to engage Canadians in a debate about how to reform the constitution?

- To what extent is it a problem that the Government of Quebec did not support the passage of the Constitution Act, 1982? Is getting Quebec's signature on the constitution viable?
- Considering the thresholds imposed by the amending formula, combined with the emergence of regional vetoes, how likely is the constitution to be amended in your lifetime?

Where to Learn More about the Canadian Constitution

Peter Aucoin, Mark Jarvis, and Lori Turnbull, *Democratizing the Constitution: Reforming Responsible Government* (Toronto: Emond Montgomery, 2011).

Adam Dodek, *The Canadian Constitution* (Toronto: Dundurn, 2013).

Peter Hogg, *Constitutional Law of Canada* (Toronto: Carswell, 2013).

Peter Russell, *Constitutional Odyssey: Can Canadians Become a Sovereign People?* (Toronto: University of Toronto Press, 1993).

David E. Smith, *Federalism and the Constitution of Canada* (Toronto: University of Toronto Press, 2010).

David E. Smith, *The Invisible Crown: The First Principle of Canadian Government* (Toronto: University of Toronto Press, 2013).

David Thomas, *Whistling Past the Graveyard: Constitutional Abeyances, Quebec, and the Future of Canada* (Toronto: Oxford University Press, 1997).

3 FEDERALISM IN CANADA

Inside this Chapter

- What is federalism, and why was it chosen as a foundation of Canadian democracy?
- How does federalism function in Canada, and who are the major actors?
- How has Canadian federalism evolved over time?

Inside Canadian Federalism

Where you stand on Canadian federalism really depends on where you sit. If you live in a large, comparatively affluent region, your perception of the way federalism functions will be different from what it would be if you lived in a smaller, poorer

What the 2015 Election Means for Canadian Federalism

Visit the *Inside Canadian Politics* flipboard to learn about the latest developments in the area of Canadian federalism.

Go to
http://flip.it/gblag.

community. By the same token, your status as a member of a minority group could have a positive or negative effect on your attitudes toward Confederation. Your age can also play a factor: Canadians who lived through the mega-constitutional debates of the late twentieth century view the divisiveness of Canadian federalism very differently from the generation that has followed them. In short, how you feel about the distribution of power in Canada depends on your political values and your expectations of government, which are shaped by your social situation.

In this sense, peering inside Canadian federalism requires each of us to examine our own frame of reference. As we do so, we need to bear in mind certain maxims of federalism in Canada.

 Federalism is about more than just the constitution. Many people who have grown up learning in school about the importance of Canada's constitution believe it determines the way power is distributed today, just as it did 150 years ago. However, while providing a necessary legal foundation for Canadian federalism, sections 91 and 92 of the Constitution Act, 1867, do not paint a comprehensive or contemporary picture of the balance of power today. By virtue of court decisions and major economic and demographic shifts, Canadian federalism has evolved considerably over the century-and-a-half since Confederation, and in fact, as we shall see, it continues to evolve with every global crisis, every leadership change, and other major developments.

 Federalism is about more than just the premiers and prime minister. At the close of the twentieth century, first ministers' meetings still served as the focal point for Canadian federalism, as they had for close to a century. To the general public, these highly publicized conferences are the clearest form of what we call inter-state federalism, providing evidence that the premiers and prime minister are working together. Since the failure of the 1992 Charlottetown Accord, however, first ministers' meetings have been few and far between, and a great deal of Canadian federalism now takes place at the bureaucratic level. New actors, including city and Aboriginal governments, have also joined in the fray.

 It's about more than just money. It sometimes appears that Canada's provinces are constantly at odds with the federal government over money: over health and social transfers and the equalization formula. While it is true that fiscal arrangements dominate debates in Canadian federalism as much today as they have throughout the country's history, they do not consume the entire intergovernmental agenda. Canadian governments have come together to forge not only an economic union but social and environmental ones as well.

The following insider's look examines these and other topics in Canadian federalism.

Overview

Federalism is a system of government that enables public policy to be responsive to local concerns while being unified by a set of common, overarching objectives. In this sense, federalism helps keep diverse countries like Canada together—despite regular conflict and competitiveness between regions (see Chapter 4). It is one of the defining features of Canadian democracy, and one of the biggest sources of confusion for outsiders, newcomers, and long-time residents alike. Consider the following facts:

- With one of the world's strongest and most productive economies, Canada is one of the few developed countries without a national department of education.
- Canada's "national" healthcare system—itself a symbol of what it means to be Canadian—is, in fact, a network of at least 14 separate healthcare systems.
- The central government spends more money on areas that fall *outside* its own jurisdiction than it spends on areas *within* its constitutional purview.
- Finding ways to address pan-Canadian challenges such as climate change and economic development requires that over a dozen governments collaborate and reach a consensus.
- Major concerns like Aboriginal poverty and labour force development often fall through the cracks of constitutional jurisdiction.

Federalism is as much a political mentality as it is a system of rules. It is as much an element of Canada's political life as it is a core dimension of its constitution. This chapter explores these various dimensions in greater detail.

The Story of Federalism in Canada

Federalism in Context

Canada's system of government remains an amalgam of those of the United Kingdom and the United States. When the United States of America was formed, it brought 13 colonies together into a single federation. A national government would be responsible for policy matters that required central coordination, such as military defence, while individual states such as New York and South Carolina would have the authority to respond to local policy concerns. The federal system therefore constitutionally divided powers between a central government based in Washington, DC, and state governments based in the capitals of various states, now numbering 50.

This differed from the unitary system of government in place in the United Kingdom, where political decisions were foremost made out of London, and where there was no written constitution to devolve powers to local authorities. Over time, Britain has had to confront serious regional tensions in Northern Ireland, Wales, and Scotland, which have led to the gradual devolution of central authority. Governments in the US and Canada have managed to broker such regional tensions under relatively stable systems of federal government, America's Civil War and Quebec's sovereignist referendums notwithstanding.

In formal terms, federalism is a system of governance featuring at least two orders of government. Each of these types of government derives

- its authority from a distinct electorate;
- its sovereignty from a separate basis; and
- its jurisdiction from a common constitution.

unitary system A political system featuring a central government that chooses what powers to devolve to regional bodies.

devolution The act of transferring (*devolving*) powers from a central government to regional or local governments that remain under its constitutional purview.

federalism A constitution-based division of powers between two or more orders of government.

BRIEFING NOTES

Confederation

Don't confuse the terms *federation* and *confederation*. When the original colonies came together to form the Dominion of Canada, they labelled their union
"Confederation." Their choice of terms is misleading today, as political scientists
distinguish between federations like Canada, on one hand, and confederations
like the European Union, on the other.

Crucially, neither order can alter or revoke the powers of the other. In this sense,
federations lie somewhere between unitary states and confederal alliances on a spectrum of political systems. The most centralized federations, like the United States,
where the federal government has considerable authority, tend to resemble the most
decentralized unitary states, like the United Kingdom, where Parliament has granted
regional governments a considerable degree of home rule. Conversely, decentralized
federations like Canada, where the provincial governments have considerable authority, share much in common with rather centralized confederations of states, such as
the European Union, where member nation-states retain considerable autonomy.

In true federations, regional governments retain sovereignty in some areas while
surrendering some sovereignty to a central government to act on behalf of all members. That is, each of these orders of government has the legal authority to govern and
to control state resources over geographical areas and topics that are prescribed in the
constitution. In confederations like the European Union, member states retain full
sovereignty, though they may delegate some decision-making to a central institution.
Just as central governments in unitary states may remove any powers they delegate to
regional governments, so, too, may member states in a confederation withdraw their
support from common decisions made by a central authority. By contrast, in federations like Canada, powers cannot be revoked by either order without permission of
the other. This is a key distinction between federations, which have *divided* sovereignty among different orders, and confederations, whose member states have *pooled*
sovereignty in order to meet common objectives.

sovereignty The power
to exercise government
authority over a polity
within a defined
geographical area.

The Origins of Canadian Federalism

Canadian federalism has never developed in isolation, nor has it been viewed from
the same perspective across the country. The conventional view of Canadian history holds that the Fathers of Confederation drew their greatest inspiration from
the United States—the Western world's first modern federation. The United States
was in the midst of its Civil War just as the Canadian colonial leaders were drafting
the terms of their own union. The strife afflicting their southern neighbour gave the
Canadians reason for pause when considering the merits of federalism, and they took
great pains to prevent similar developments by granting Parliament greater authority vis-à-vis the provincial legislatures than the American Congress enjoyed over the

state assemblies. This centralized balance of power would not last long in Canada, but the influence of the American model was evident nonetheless.

Recent scholarship challenges this historical understanding.[1] Some American historians have uncovered evidence suggesting the US Founding Fathers, and Benjamin Franklin and Thomas Jefferson in particular, based their constitutional architecture at least partly on the Six Nations (Iroquois) Confederacy, which is a decentralized form of governance developed by the Haudenosaunee. Evidence of the Haudenosaunee's *direct* influence on Canadian drafters of the constitution has yet to be established. Nevertheless, the presence of a federation of First Nations in such close proximity to the Canadian colonies would suggest that there was at least some familiarity with that form of governance among the British political elite.

INSIDE CANADIAN POLITICS
Why Was Federalism the Preferred Model for Canada?

The Fathers of Confederation had many options at their disposal as they crafted the terms of union for Canada. Out of practicality and urgency as much as principle and necessity, they decided to adopt a federal system of government. Numerous factors supported their choice.

Militarily, the mighty Union Army was wrapping up an ultimately successful campaign against the Southern Confederacy, and many Canadian colonists feared that these American troops, already mobilized, would turn northward in pursuit of more territory. The nineteenth-century American belief system known as "manifest destiny" held that the United States was destined to rule the entire continent of North America. The possibility of American expansion, along with threats posed by Fenian raids, made some form of central military force very attractive in the northern British colonies.

By the same token, the colonies saw great value in some sort of economic and monetary union. The ramping down of favourable British import policies and the end of *reciprocity* (or free trade) with the United States persuaded the British North

Americans to forge a common market. Looking westward, Canadian leaders also saw the potential benefit in admitting new territories (and, eventually, provinces) as the circumstances allowed. In this sense, federation would provide an "alternative to empire," as William Riker once said of the American union.[2] Combined with provincial control over language, education, and other cultural issues, the federal option appeared to strike a suitable balance between areas of shared rule and self-rule.

Domestically, federation would help break the sort of deadlocks experienced by the joint legislature in the United Canadian legislature (of Canada West, now Ontario, and Canada East, now Quebec). A bicameral parliament, in particular, seemed to strike the right balance between representation by population (in the lower house, which became the House of Commons) and regional representation (in the upper house, which became the Senate of Canada). In sum: for economic and military reasons, the Fathers preferred federalism to a looser confederal alliance; for democratic and political ones, they favoured federalism to a unitary form of government.

VOX POP
Given what you've read thus far in this book, do you think the Fathers of Confederation made the right choice in adopting federalism as a core institution for Canada? Why or why not?

THEY SAID IT

John A. Macdonald on Canadian Federalism

In 1865, John A. Macdonald participated in several debates about the merits of negotiating a federation of British colonies in the present-day regions of Ontario, Quebec, and Atlantic Canada. His reflections on the experience illustrate his philosophical approach to a process that would formally create the Dominion of Canada in 1867.

> …[All] the great questions which affect the general interests of the Confederacy as a whole, are confided to the federal parliament, while the local interests and local laws of each section are preserved intact, and entrusted to the care of the local bodies. As a matter of course, the general parliament must have the power of dealing with the public debt and property of the confederation. Of course, too, it must have the regulation of trade and commerce, of customs and excise. The federal parliament must have the sovereign power of raising money from such sources and by such means as the representatives of the people will allow. It will be seen that the local legislatures have the control of all local works; and it is a matter of great importance, and one of the chief advantages of the federal union and of local legislatures, that each province will have the power and means of developing its own resources and aiding its own progress after its own fashion and in its own way. Therefore all the local improvements, all local enterprises or undertakings of any kind, have been left to the care and management of the local legislatures of each province. . . ."[3]

VOX POP

Given what you know about Canadian federalism today, to what extent have Macdonald's plans for Confederation come to fruition?

Distinguishing Features of Canadian Federalism

Federalism within a Constitutional Monarchy

A distinguishing feature of Canadian federalism is that it operates within a constitutional monarchy, as we saw in the last chapter. In Commonwealth federations like Canada and Australia, separate orders of government share their monarch, in a situation known as a **divided crown**. In Canada, sovereignty is divided between the federal and provincial orders of government, each of which has equal status to act on behalf of the Crown (see Table 3.1). Thus, the sovereignty of the provinces is conferred not by the federal government but by the Crown itself, and the power of

divided crown A monarchy whose sovereignty is split among different orders of government.

TABLE 3.1 | Federal and Provincial Powers in Canada

Federal Jurisdiction	Provincial Jurisdiction	Concurrent Jurisdiction
• any mode of taxation	• admnistration of justice	• agriculture
• census and statistics	• direct taxation	• immigration
• criminal law	• education	
• currency and banking	• hospitals	
• fisheries	• incorporations and	
• Indians and Indian lands*	commercial licensing	
• marriage and divorce	• local works	
• military and defence	• municipalities	
• navigation and shipping	• natural resources	
• postal service	• property and civil rights	
• trade and commerce	• public lands	
• treaties	• solemnization of marriage	
• weights and measures		

* The use of the term "Indian" here for First Nations people preserves the language used in the relevant legislation.

the federal government is derived from the permission not of the provinces but of the Crown.

While we commonly refer to different "levels" of government, it is important to note that neither provincial nor federal order is subordinate to the other. There is theoretically no hierarchy in Canadian federalism. In constitutional, if not political terms, both orders are equally entitled to govern within their defined areas of jurisdiction. This relationship was unclear in the early years of Confederation until the Judicial Committee of the Privy Council (JCPC) ruled in 1892 that "a Lieutenant-Governor . . . is as much a representative of Her Majesty for all purposes of provincial government as the Governor General himself is, for all purposes of Dominion government."[4] This does *not* mean that each has an equal amount of responsibility, nor does it mean that each has an equal ability to fulfill its obligations. It simply means that each is equally authoritative in the exercise of its sovereignty.

This division of powers is constitutionally entrenched, primarily in sections 91 and 92 of the Constitution Act, 1867. Matters of common, pan-Canadian interest are reserved for the federal government, while matters of a more local or regionally sensitive nature fall under provincial jurisdiction. Among the constitutional responsibilities of the federal government are banking, money, and trade; international and Aboriginal treaties; most taxation; the postal service; the census; military defence; penitentiaries; offshore fisheries; interprovincial ferries; and unemployment insurance. Provincial governments exercise authority over local matters including hospitals, education, municipalities, licences (e.g. shops, bars, auctions, marriage), some taxation (e.g. property), and natural resources. The constitution also defines areas of *concurrent* (or shared) jurisdiction, including agriculture and immigration. Crucially, should federal and provincial laws conflict in these areas, federal laws are deemed authoritative. This reflects the original intent of the Canadian constitution, which sought to provide a strong central government. Over time, however, the federation has become decentralized as areas of provincial jurisdiction have increased in public importance and cost.

The three Northern territories and the thousands of municipalities across Canada do not have the constitutional status that is accorded to provinces. In many ways, governments in Yukon, Northwest Territories, and Nunavut govern in the same manner as provinces. They have control over their own healthcare and education systems, and they are gaining increased control over their natural resources. Ultimately, however, territorial governments' authority is devolved from the federal government; it can be rescinded or altered at any time without the permission of the territorial governments. A similar power relationship exists between municipalities (i.e., cities, towns) and provincial governments. Municipalities are to provinces as territories are to the federal government. While most municipal governments have the ability to levy property taxes, carry out infrastructure projects, and establish bylaws to govern our behaviour, their powers exist at the discretion of their respective provincial governments.

Photo courtesy of The Journey: the Blog of Marine Atlantic

A view from the Marine Atlantic ferry *MV Blue Puttees*, as it is led by the coast guard icebreaker *Louis S. St-Laurent* into Sydney Harbour after being stuck in heavy pack ice for three days in March 2015. Interprovincial ferry service is vitally important to residents of coastal communities in Atlantic Canada, who depend on ferry traffic not just for travel but for shipping of goods and produce. In optimal conditions, the 180 km sea voyage from Port aux Basques, NL, to North Sydney, NS, takes about six hours. Marine Atlantic, which provides ferry service between Nova Scotia and Newfoundland, is a federal Crown corporation. The federal budget allocates millions of dollars annually to subsidize a higher quality and more affordable service than if left to the private sector or provincial governments. However, complaints about Marine Atlantic—over such issues as pricing, departure delays, booking problems, and other customer service problems—are a constant source of news for local media. What do you think are the advantages and disadvantages of having interprovincial ferry service be a responsibility of the federal government?

INSIDE CANADIAN POLITICS

Should the Government of Ontario Have Removed Toronto Mayor Rob Ford from Office?

Why didn't the Government of Ontario remove Toronto mayor Rob Ford from office after his erratic behaviour made an international mockery of Toronto?

Section 92(8) of the Canadian constitution states: "In each province the legislature may exclusively make laws in relation to . . . municipal institutions in the province." So when questionable behaviour by Mayor Ford led to a police investigation, a media firestorm, and attempts by Toronto City Council to curtail his authority, there were calls for Ontario premier Kathleen Wynne to intervene. Why, then, was she so hesitant to exercise her constitutional powers to do so?

Rob Ford is a populist whose anti-elite messaging resonated with Torontonians in the 2010 municipal election campaign. His tenure as mayor was marked by controversy from the moment he took office, when, at his inauguration ceremony, he was introduced by hockey personality Don Cherry, who took the opportunity to deride "left-wing pinkos." Subsequent controversies grew in both number and gravity, from Ford's use of office letterhead in a fundraising letter for a football foundation he supported to his eventual admission to having smoked crack cocaine, likely in one of his self-described "drunken stupors."

By the fall of 2013, national media were routinely covering Ford's escapades. The following months provided evidence of the mayor's indiscretions too sensational for international news outlets to ignore. These included video of an intoxicated Ford in a profanity-filled tirade, vowing to commit "first-degree murder"[5] against an unknown opponent, and his subsequent confession to City Council that he had purchased illegal drugs in the past two years, and that he "really effed up."[6] All of this was topped when, in a media scrum, a defiant Ford made vulgar remarks about oral sex and his wife—remarks that, he would later acknowledge, featured "unforgivable language."

During this time, the calls for Ford's resignation from councillors and protesters intensified, and the mayor responded by repeatedly vowing not just to stay on but to seek re-election. Councillors were not empowered to eject him from office and so passed motions that would curtail the mayor's powers. Meanwhile, the developments made news around the world, including CNN, *The Economist*, *The New York Times*, the BBC, *The Independent* (UK), and *The New Zealand Herald*. Ford's antics were fodder for American late-night talk shows and comedy programs, including *The Daily Show* and *Saturday Night Live*. The Canadian media began to report that Torontonians were worried that the negative publicity had damaged their city's reputation and would harm their economy. A report by Cormex Research found that while only 3 per cent of global news coverage of Toronto had been negative in early 2011, the figure soared to 22 per cent in 2013.[7] For his part, Ford declared: "I'm going to continue to fight for the little guy, I'm going to continue to save taxpayers' money, and if the councillors want to strip all my powers, that's up to them, but the people haven't spoken yet."[8]

The matter thus became a provincial issue. Should the premier intervene and remove Ford from office? If so, could this be interpreted as anti-democratic? After all, Ford had been elected to the position and had not been convicted of any crime. Electors would have the opportunity to hold him accountable in the 2014 mayoral election. On the other hand, if the premier chose not to intervene, Ford's behaviour could immobilize City Council, prevent normal operations from proceeding, and turn Canada's largest city into an international laughingstock.

On 14 November, Premier Wynne addressed the matter at a news conference where she did not take any questions from reporters. In a statement, she hinted that the government was willing to amend provincial legislation to allow municipal councils to immobilize a mayor. However, she said, she would pursue such a course of action only on the following conditions:

continued

- that she had been formally invited to do so by City Council
- that it was clear that City Council was unable to function
- that she had the support of the province's other major political parties.

As Wynne explained,

> The things we are seeing and hearing about Mayor Rob Ford are truly disturbing. The City of Toronto has a mayor and council that were elected by the residents of Toronto and must be accountable to them. It is up to the municipal level of government to address the issues they face. . . . If council were to clearly indicate that they lack the ability to function as a result of this matter, the province would respond

to a request from council to be provided new tools, depending on what that request might be."[9]

This position reflects a general deference to the will of the electorate, who have the democratic right to formally express their judgement in an election. If the premier of Ontario had chosen to get involved in municipal politics, this would likely have escalated the matter and caused civil unrest. The many people who voted for the mayor, and even some who opposed him, would have been upset by the intervention. It likely would have been characterized as heavy-handed and authoritarian, and would possibly have caused Torontonians to rally around their embattled mayor against the premier. Wynne's decision not to intervene recognizes the relative autonomy of municipalities in modern society, despite their non-status in Canada's constitution.

THE LESSON

Provincial governments may have constitutional jurisdiction over municipal matters, but intervening in municipal governance invokes concerns of over-reaching.

VOX POP

Why do you think provincial leaders would be so reluctant to intervene in matters of municipal governance? What would be the political risk of overturning the will of the electorate?

Opportunities Available

Knowledge of Canadian Politics and Government Preferred!

Policy Analyst

Department of Environment, Government of Nunavut

Under the direction of the Senior Policy Analyst, the Policy Analyst provides support to the department in conducting research, assisting in legislation/policy development, tracking of ongoing departmental initiatives, preparing ministerial briefing materials, reviewing draft correspondence, coordinating statutory appointments, and tracking and coordinating responses to questions taken in the Legislative Assembly. The Analyst assists in the department's strategic/business planning initiatives and from time to time may coordinate preparations for federal/provincial/territorial activities and other one-time projects.

Ideally, the successful candidate will have postsecondary training in areas such as political science, public administration, law, or a related field, and experience working within government administration, policy development/analysis, and/or strategic planning. The applicant will have knowledge of current Nunavut environmental issues; environment-related legislation, policies, and guidelines; the Nunavut Land Claims Agreement; and public policy and legislation development. The applicant will also have strong research skills, excellent communications skills, and the ability to work effectively while largely unsupervised. The ability to speak Inuktitut will be considered an asset.

Note: The Government of Nunavut is committed to creating a more representative workforce so it can better understand and serve the needs of Nunavummiut. Priority will be given to Nunavut Land Claims Beneficiaries.

Source: Government of Nunavut, "Government of Nunavut Employment Opportunity" (2014), www.finance.gov.nu.ca/apps/UPLOADS/fck/file/14%2002%2007/13-501502_JA_Policy_Analyst.pdf.

Centralization and Decentralization

Canada's division and balance of powers is unique. Canadian federalism is among the world's most decentralized. Collectively, Canadian provinces have more revenue-generating capacity and a greater scope of responsibility than constituent units in other federations, such as the United States and Switzerland. This is ironic, given the original intentions of the Fathers of Confederation. Macdonald and his fellow constitutional framers wished to create a highly centralized version of federalism. In fact, so many elements of centralization were incorporated into the British North America Act that many political scientists and historians have questioned Canada's status as a true federation, at least in the beginning. In six specific ways the BNA Act makes it clear that the original intent was to treat the federal government, rather than the provinces, as the primary decision-maker:

1. Section 55 of the Act identified the power of reservation. This allowed a province's lieutenant governor to "reserve" a piece of provincial legislation for review by the governor general. As the governor general acts only on the advice of the prime minister and the cabinet, effectively, reservation meant that the federal government could prevent a bill that had been passed by a provincial legislature from becoming law. Section 55 states: "Where a bill passed by the houses of the Parliament is presented to the governor general for the Queen's assent, he shall declare, according to his discretion, but subject to the provisions of this Act and to her majesty's instructions, either that he assents thereto in the Queen's name, or that he withholds the Queen's assent, or that he reserves the bill for the signification of the Queen's pleasure." The federal government has not exercised its power of reservation since 1961, when the lieutenant governor of Saskatchewan withheld passage of legislation concerning a corporation's access to minerals.

2. Section 56 gave the federal government the power of disallowance, which permitted it to nullify any provincial statute within two years of passage. The actual wording of section 56 is as follows: "Where the governor general assents to a bill in the Queen's name, he shall by the first convenient opportunity send an authentic copy of the Act to one of her majesty's principal secretaries of state, and if the Queen in council within two years after receipt thereof by the secretary of state thinks fit to disallow the Act, such disallowance (with a certificate of the secretary of state of the day on which the Act was received by him) being signified by the

decentralized federalism A federal system of government where the regional units have considerable power.

centralized federalism A federal system of government where the national government has considerable power.

reservation The constitutional power of the federal government to withhold the passage of provincial legislation, so as to cause short-term or permanent delay.

↻ See Constitutional Monarchy on page 43 of Chapter 2 for an explanation of the Crown's role in Canadian politics.

disallowance The constitutional power of the federal government to veto provincial legislation and cause its termination.

governor general, by speech or message to each of the houses of the Parliament or by proclamation, shall annul the Act from and after the day of such signification." Disallowance was often used in the nineteenth century to protect the federal government's commercial interests, such as ensuring the development of the Canadian Pacific Railway, but it has not been used since 1943. In that case, during World War II, the government of Alberta attempted to introduce legislation that would have made it illegal to sell land to a Hutterite, or to any "enemy alien"; the federal government disallowed the law, deeming that it extended beyond provincial authority because provinces do not have the power to identify military enemies.

POGG The acronym for the constitutional objective of "peace, order, and good government."

3. The "peace, order, and good government" (POGG) clause in section 91 of the constitution states that "It shall be lawful for the Queen, by and with the advice and consent of the Senate and House of Commons, to make laws for the peace, order, and good government of Canada." The POGG clause established the principles on which the country was founded, and confirmed that the interests of federal institutions shall preside over provincial or local arms of government. In effect, the POGG clause was designed to give the federal government overwhelming

INSIDE CANADIAN POLITICS

How Can the Federal Government Overturn a Law Passed by a Provincial Legislature?

Enshrined in the British North America Act, 1867, the dual powers of reservation and disallowance established a quasi-colonial relationship between Ottawa and the various provincial capitals. In the early years of Confederation, the federal minister of justice routinely reviewed provincial laws to determine whether they were in the best interests of the young country.[10] Lieutenant governors reserved a total of 70 provincial bills up to 1961, and the federal government disallowed a total of 112 provincial acts up to 1943. The federal government justified its actions on a host of grounds, deeming the provincial legislation to be contrary to the constitution, the federal government's priorities, the national interest, or fundamental standards of justice. While the federal government reserved or disallowed acts from all provincial legislatures except Newfoundland, which did not join confederation until 1949, the vast majority of cases involved the Western provinces.

Some provincial governments deliberately provoked the federal response, including feigned attempts by Social Credit governments in Alberta to legislate in areas of federal jurisdiction (namely monetary policy and currency). The ultimate effect of the federal government's actions, however, was to foster a heightened sense of Western alienation (see Chapter 4).

During constitutional bargaining, Prime Minister Pierre Trudeau sought to have these powers removed from the constitution, but wrangling over the failed Victoria Charter (1971) led to the issue's being dropped. Thus, when the Constitution Act, 1982, was passed, it preserved the federal government's supremacy, though invoking either reservation or disallowance would put the prime minister in serious political peril. In recent decades, the only serious mention of disallowance and reservation has concerned the federal government's ability to prevent a province's unilateral secession from Canada.

VOX POP

Under what conditions would it be acceptable for a federal government to reserve or disallow a provincial law today?

Kinder Morgan Canada, Trans Mountain

Environmental and Aboriginal groups in British Columbia have called on their provincial government to oppose the building of more pipelines across the province from Alberta's oil sands. The federal government favours pipeline construction for economic reasons, and can invoke its declaratory power to approve new projects in spite of any objections that might be raised by the BC premier. Is declaratory power a practical means of settling disputes between provinces, or does it give the federal government too much power? See the ICP box beginning on page 99 for more on this topic.

authority in defining the national interest, and extraordinary powers in times of national emergency.

4. Section 92, which enumerates most of the powers accorded to provincial governments, includes a reference to declaratory power: the federal government's ability to control any public works or undertakings deemed to be in the best interests of Canada or at least two provinces. Specifically, section 92(10c) states: "Such works as, although wholly situate within the province, are before or after their execution declared by the Parliament of Canada to be for the general advantage of Canada or for the advantage of two or more of the provinces." Most recently, the use of the declaratory power has been considered in the building of national infrastructure projects, including pipelines, pitting national priorities and federal government prerogatives against local interests and provincial preferences.

5. Some sections of the constitution stipulate that federal laws would prevail in the event of conflict with provincial laws. This is known as *federal paramountcy*. For instance, section 92A grants authority over non-renewable natural resources to the provinces, but with the caveat that if "such a law of Parliament and a law of a province conflict, the law of Parliament prevails to the extent of the conflict." Another example is section 95, which allows provinces to make laws regarding agriculture and immigration, "as long and as far only as it is not repugnant to any Act of the Parliament of Canada."

6. These clauses, along with the POGG principle, aimed to provide Parliament, not the provincial legislatures, with all residual powers, that is, those powers not explicitly outlined in the constitution. This meant that any policy area that

declaratory power The authority of the federal government to decide that an issue falls within its jurisdiction.

residual powers Any powers not specifically identified in the constitution, which default to the federal government.

developed subsequent to 1867—for instance, aviation or telecommunications—would, by default, fall under federal jurisdiction.

While having constitutional authority to be the final authority in a political debate may seem like an advantage, there are times when it has placed federal leaders in a quagmire. As described in Chapter 12, on political activism, the provision in section 93(4) for the federal cabinet to "make remedial laws" on matters of education presented a serious problem for five Conservative prime ministers during the Manitoba schools crisis in the late 1880s and early 1890s.

INSIDE CANADIAN POLITICS
How Do Governments Balance Economic and Environmental Interests?

Getting oil sands products to tidewater has long been a shared priority for the government of Alberta and the federal government. This is why both have supported the $8 billion Northern Gateway Pipeline project as proposed by Enbridge. Transporting oil products from northern Alberta to Pacific ports would allow Alberta producers to earn higher value for their commodities in burgeoning markets like Asia, generating economic growth and increased government revenue in the process. At the same time, moving crude oil to market poses environmental risks, in addition to questions about Aboriginal rights.

This raises the question: precisely whose approval is required before a project like Northern Gateway can be initiated?

Provincial governments like those of Alberta and British Columbia may conduct environmental and regulatory assessments of the leg of the pipeline that runs through their respective jurisdictions. At the same time, the Canadian government is constitutionally responsible for reviewing and approving all such interprovincial projects through two federal agencies, the National Energy Board and Canadian Environmental Assessment Agency. Jointly, the two bodies held dozens of public hearings and received thousands of submissions from citizens, interest groups, corporations, Aboriginal communities and organizations, and governments. In the end, federal regulatory bodies endorsed the project, subject to Enbridge's meeting over 200 environmental

conditions, including those related to species protection and to spill prevention and cleanup. The federal government reviewed this report and, in 2014, provided its approval.

The joint panel's recommendation and the federal decision based upon it are being challenged in court by several groups. Among them are groups representing environmentalists and First Nations, who have raised concerns over the real and potential ecological impact of the pipeline and the increased oil sands activity it could spur. Together, these parties insist that neither the federal government nor the Alberta government has the so-called "social licence" to endorse the pipeline, which is to say the necessary level of public and moral support.

Aboriginal communities along the proposed route have questioned whether industry and governments are fulfilling their constitutional duty to consult and their political commitment to ensure Aboriginal peoples share in the economic benefits of the project. In the case of the former, they rely on Supreme Court of Canada rulings that suggest Aboriginal communities must consent to development projects that have significant impacts on their traditional lands.

For its part, the British Columbia government highlighted these Aboriginal concerns, while also seeking a series of environmental and economic assurances before giving its blessing to the Northern Gateway initiative. On the eve of the 2013 provincial election, BC premier Christy Clark issued five conditions for her government's endorsement of the Northern Gateway project, including a positive environmental assessment, a world-leading oil-spill prevention and response system to protect BC lands and coastlines, respect for Aboriginal treaty rights, and assurances that BC would receive its "fair share of the fiscal and economic benefits" of the project.[11] While the first four conditions were placed squarely on the shoulders of industry and the federal government, the last stipulation was seen by many observers as a requirement that the government of Alberta cede some of its revenue to British Columbia. Alberta Premier Alison Redford immediately took this issue off the table, refusing to share resource royalties with another provincial government.

The two sides remained deadlocked until after the 2013 provincial election in BC, at which point, armed with a new mandate from voters, Premier Clark agreed to form a joint Alberta–BC working group to resolve any outstanding issues barring the way of a pipeline. In the end, the two sides agreed that BC's "fair share" condition should be met through direct dealings with the pipeline owner, Enbridge, and that the remaining conditions would be dealt with in collaboration with industry and the federal government.

Questions remain as to whether any provincial government could prevent an interprovincial pipeline being constructed in its territory. Had its conditions not been met, there would have been little to prevent the BC government from waging a public relations battle against Enbridge and its government supporters. It could also have sought to deny the BC-based leg of the project through its own environmental review process, or it could have imposed an array of regulations and taxes that would have delayed the project or destroyed its economic viability.

For its part, Alberta's government would have been unlikely to impose such barriers in its own jurisdiction, given its view of the economic benefits of the project to the province. Instead, Alberta's role was one of persuasion—seeking to build public, Aboriginal, and intergovernmental support for the pipeline through a combination of advocacy, diplomacy, and energy literacy. These were the driving factors behind Alberta's leadership of the Canadian Energy Strategy at the Council of the Federation table, and resemble the same sort of strategies used to persuade governments in the United States to approve the north–south Keystone XL pipeline. The 2015 election of an NDP government in the province has raised new questions, as Premier Rachel Notley has not declared unequivocal commitment to the Keystone project.

Should the federal government wish to remove any provincially imposed barriers to the Northern Gateway project, Ottawa could, as a last resort, attempt to invoke its declaratory power. This would involve declaring the pipeline to be in the national interest and stripping provincial governments of any authority to stand in the way of its construction. The use of declaratory power would amount to drastic action, however, and such a measure would not be taken lightly.

THE LESSON

Major national infrastructure projects involve a number of governmental and nongovernmental actors, but ultimately the federal government has the final say.

VOX POP

Despite its explicit support for the Northern Gateway project, the federal government was reluctant to intervene in the dispute between Alberta and BC. With so much at stake for the entire country, why would the federal government have been unwilling to get involved in a dispute between provinces?

The Tools of Federal Power

In addition to these constitutional provisions, the government of Canada has historically exercised its clout through its federal spending power. With far greater fiscal capacity than any one province, the federal government has, over time, gained the ability to spend in any area where it has seen fit to do so. While this spending power is not specifically enumerated in the constitution, it has furnished the federal cabinet with the means to develop policy in areas under exclusive provincial jurisdiction. By spending federal funds directly on Canadians, their businesses, or their local institutions, or by offering money to the provinces, the federal government can set the terms determining how those monies can be spent. The conditions that the federal government attaches to funds transferred to provinces for spending on healthcare is a good example. This has steered the provinces toward following pan-Canadian standards on policy matters that, according to section 92 of the constitution, are under provincial control. Quebec in particular has pushed back, demanding that it alone should decide how best to respond to local needs. Other provinces, such as those in Atlantic Canada, have tended to tacitly endorse the use of federal spending power because they recognize that their citizens will benefit from funds designed to raise services up to national standards. Nevertheless, the federal spending power remains a bone of contention between Ottawa and the provinces.

A further means by which federal politicians are able to exercise their influence is through the appointment power, the authority of the first minister to fill senior government jobs. For example, the positions of governor general and lieutenant governor are filled upon a recommendation from the prime minister to the monarch. The federal government has exclusive jurisdiction over the selection of provincial representatives to national institutions, including senators, Supreme Court justices, and other judges. Members of the federal cabinet, including regional ministers, are selected by, and are loyal to, the prime minister. Less noticeably, the federal government appoints the members of the board of directors of a considerable number of federal bodies. This ranges from organizations that have a significant national presence, such as VIA Rail, to those with a focused local role, such as Enterprise Cape Breton Corporation.

Together, these powers were intended to produce a highly centralized federation in Canada. The evolution of Canadian federalism has revealed the fragility of even the best-laid constitutional plans, however. The federal powers of disallowance and reservation have fallen into disuse—a status that, according to convention, limits the federal government's ability to invoke them in the future. Constitutionally, both are considered lapsed powers, despite being retained in the text of the Constitution Act, 1982. Politically, the use of either power rests on the willingness of the federal government to disrupt the activities of a democratically elected provincial legislature.

Moreover, over time the courts have placed strict limits on Parliament's ability to legislate in the interests of "peace, order, and good government," leaving the federal government with authority to make laws only in emergencies, in cases of provincial inability or incapacity, and in areas of national concern. Since the late 1960s, some provinces have attempted to place restrictions on the declaratory and federal spending powers. As we saw last chapter, efforts at amending the constitution to this effect during the patriation, Meech Lake, and Charlottetown rounds of negotiation

INSIDE CANADIAN POLITICS

Should the Federal Government Help Fund Provincial Social Programs?

The federal spending power has been one of the leading irritants among provinces in the Canadian federation over the past half-century. Tensions surface whenever Ottawa threatens to enforce federal standards through legislation like the Canada Health Act (which ties federal funding to five conditions defined by Parliament) or new national programs like the Millennium Scholarship Fund (which funded post-secondary students according to federal stipulations) and the Canada Job Grant (which aimed to better align Canadian skills with labour market needs).

For the most part, the federal government has defended its use of the federal spending power as a necessary element in forging Canada's social union. Without the ability to spend in areas of provincial jurisdiction, Ottawa and its (left-leaning) ideological and (less-affluent) provincial compatriots fear the loss of national standards in social programs, resulting in an uneven "patchwork" of provincial services.

Some provinces, particularly Quebec and Alberta, have sought to limit Ottawa's ability to spend in areas of provincial jurisdiction. They cite the value and constitutionality of having governments that are more sensitive to local needs determining the proper policy direction in matters like education and healthcare, and they insist on the ability to "opt out" of any federal initiatives with full compensation so that they can initiate their own comparable programs and services. Historically, there have been several compromises negotiated on the use of the federal spending power, beginning with the ill-fated Victoria Charter in 1971 and the Meech Lake and Charlottetown Accords, and most recently through the Social Union Framework Agreement in 1999. However, comprehensive, constitutional agreement on the federal spending power has eluded Canadian governments.

VOX POP

To what extent should the federal government be able to expend funds however it sees fit, even in areas of provincial jurisdiction? What sort of restrictions could or should be placed on this spending power?

were unsuccessful, but federal governments have made a political commitment to consult provinces in advance of introducing any new national programs involving provincial jurisdiction.

Interpretations of Canadian Federalism

Major Models of Federalism

As we mentioned in the introduction to this chapter, where you stand on Canadian federalism depends on where you sit. The definition, nature, merits, and even the terms of Confederation differ widely across the country (see Table 3.2).

Confederation can be interpreted as a system in which the roles and responsibilities of each order of government are clearly delineated. According to the classical federalism perspective, the Canadian constitution created a series of impermeable "watertight

classical federalism A model of federalism in which federal and provincial governments operate independently of each other in their own respective areas of jurisdiction.

TABLE 3.2 | Models of Federalism in Canada

Federalism	Defining Characteristic	Example
Classical	Federal and provincial governments look after their separate jurisdictions	The federal government does not meddle in healthcare or education
Co-operative	Federal and provincial governments work together	The federal government creates national programs supported by the provinces
Collaborative	Provincial and territorial governments collaborate to provide leadership	The Council of the Federation, created in 2003, provides a forum for premiers and various working groups to collaborate with each other
Emergency	The federal government takes the lead in a national crisis	The federal government initiates spending programs to stimulate the economy after the global recession
Symmetrical	All provinces are treated equally	Every province has equal powers when it comes to designing and implementing their respective healthcare systems
Asymmetrical	Some provinces receive special powers, especially with respect to Quebec	Quebec is granted unprecedented jurisdiction over immigration
Treaty	First Nations enjoy equal status with the federal and provincial governments representing the Canadian Crown	First Nations maintain sovereignty over education

compartments." This view of federalism maintains that the jurisdiction of the provinces was distinct and protected from that of the federal government, and vice-versa. In other words, each level of government minds its own affairs. This characterized Canadian politics roughly from when Wilfrid Laurier took office in 1896 to the onset of World War I. In modern times, the compartment model is espoused by those who wish to disentangle federal and provincial jurisdictions by having Ottawa withdraw from matters of provincial responsibility, including healthcare and social programs.

The reverse of classical federalism is co-operative federalism, where federal and provincial governments operate in partnership to solve common policy challenges through consensus. The golden era of co-operative federalism occurred after World War II, when Ottawa sought to finance the expansion of the welfare state. Federal Liberal governments sponsored the growth of social programming that adhered to national standards. The provinces were willing to accept federal funds, even though strings were attached to ensure the monies were spent in ways that aligned with Ottawa's priorities. This spirit of co-operative federalism is responsible for the establishment of a variety of cost-shared programs, including medicare, which will be discussed later on in this chapter.

Today, the co-operative model has been replaced by a province-driven model of collaborative federalism. Coined by political scientists David Cameron and Richard Simeon, the term reflects the realities of governance in a globalized and interconnected modern society.[12] The important role that provincial and territorial governments play in public life means that they no longer can risk being dependent on the federal government, especially with the threat of cuts to fiscal transfers. Rather,

co-operative federalism
A model of federalism in which federal and provincial governments work together to solve public-policy problems.

collaborative federalism
A model of federalism in which provincial governments take the lead to solve common public policy problems together.

they may proceed to seek to resolve policy issues amongst themselves. The Council of the Federation was formed in 2003 with this objective in mind. It supports regular meetings among provincial and territorial leaders and has, since its inception, spawned working groups to pursue common goals in the economic, health, energy, seniors, and even Aboriginal affairs sectors. Pan-Canadian policy thus no longer needs to be championed by the federal government, nor does it need to depend on the federal spending power, because when the provinces and territories work together, they can advance a common agenda.

In times of calamity, all of the approaches mentioned so far give way to emergency federalism. In periods of war, terrorism, natural disaster, pandemics, national unity crises, or global economic strife, all eyes turn to the government of Canada to take the lead. The federal government's constitutional powers ensure that it is the primary political actor on matters of national importance. Furthermore, it can invoke emergency powers, engage the country in national endeavours, and negotiate with leaders of other countries.

There are other ways to categorize Canadian federalism, beyond these intergovernmental relationships. One perspective involves assessing the balance of power

Council of the Federation
An organization that supports regular meetings among provincial and territorial premiers.

emergency federalism
A model of federalism in which the federal government assumes control in a national crisis.

The Canadian Press/AP, HO-Nav Canada

On 11 September 2001, the town of Gander, Newfoundland and Labrador, became a surprise destination for thousands of international air travellers after the federal government shut down Canadian air space, and the minister of transport ordered planes to land in areas away from densely populated centres. Even so, the federal government on that day acted without having to override provincial authority, meaning that emergency federalism has not been invoked since the October Crisis of 1970. Under what sort of circumstances can you envision Ottawa invoking emergency federalism in the twenty-first century?

among the members of Confederation. We spoke earlier about centralized versus decentralized forms of federalism, which depend on which order of government (federal or provincial) holds sway. Another viewpoint considers the balance of power among the provinces themselves. In this vein, some observers see Canada's federation as consisting of a compact of 10 equal units. All came together as equal partners to form a common union; therefore, each province is deserving of the same powers and authorities under the constitution. This sets up a form of symmetrical federalism, wherein the powers granted to one province must be available to all provinces. This perspective treats all provinces as equals, irrespective of their geographic size, population, economic capacity, history, or political identity.

Others view Canada from a two-nations perspective (also known as the concept of *deux nations*). This view considers Confederation as an agreement between French Canada (represented by Quebec) and English Canada (represented by Ottawa and/or all other provinces). Accordingly, two-nations proponents view Quebec as possessing a unique constitutional status among all provinces, requiring an asymmetrical distribution of powers that favours *La Belle Province*. Typically, then, an asymmetrical style of federalism refers to Canada treating Quebec as a founding partner, rather than just one of 10 equal provinces. More broadly, this approach to federalism posits that some provinces in some situations deserve unique treatment or status. Indeed, provinces other than Quebec have at times argued that their own situation is unique and that a particular policy matter warrants special treatment. This produces a competitive dynamic and inevitable conflict as other provinces jostle for more power and resources.[13]

Others reject both the symmetrical and two-nations views, preferring to recognize the sovereignty of Aboriginal peoples. Known as treaty federalism, this model treats Aboriginal sovereignty on par with the Canadian Crown, such that there are not simply two orders of government in Canada (federal and provincial), but three.

As we observed in Chapter 2, the ambiguities of the constitution allow all of these views to co-exist in Canada. Indeed, somewhat ironically, the strength of the federal culture in Canada may actually contribute to the development of these diverging perspectives.

Assessing Fairness in Canadian Federalism

In his seminal book *The Federal Condition* (1987), Canadian political scientist Donald Smiley demonstrated just how closely one's own interests are tied to one's perceptions of fairness in federal systems like Canada. Smiley challenged readers to imagine a series of situations in which an electorate was asked to decide upon matters of local and country-wide importance. The outcome of these hypothetical decisions depends upon whether the system is unitary or federal, and the fairness of the result hinges on the vantage point of the observer. Drawing on Smiley's examples, consider the following hypothetical scenarios in which voters are asked to weigh in on the decriminalization of marijuana.

In the first scenario, there are 500,000 total voters in our fictional country. All five of the constituent units (regions A to E) are the same size (100,000 voters). All voters were asked if they favoured the decriminalization of personal marijuana use ("for") or opposed it ("against"). The results are summarized in Table 3.3. If the decision were

---

symmetrical federalism A model of federalism in which provincial governments are entitled to equal powers.

asymmetrical federalism A model of federalism in which jurisdictional powers are distributed unequally among provinces.

treaty federalism A model of federalism recognizing the equal-order relationship between First Nations and the Crown.

↻ Treaty federalism is discussed in detail on pages 532–6 of Chapter 13, on diversity and representation.

TABLE 3.3 | Referendum Scenario 1: Changing Policy in a Unitary System and a Decentralized Federalist System

Region	Total Voters	Votes For New Policy	Votes Against New Policy	Result	
				Unitary System	Decentralized Federalism
A	100,000	**60,000**	40,000	No policy change	**New policy**
B	100,000	30,000	**70,000**	No policy change	No policy change
C	100,000	**80,000**	20,000	No policy change	**New policy**
D	100,000	**65,000**	35,000	No policy change	**New policy**
E	100,000	10,000	**90,000**	No policy change	No policy change
Total	500,000	245,000	**255,000**		

being made on a nationwide basis using the rules of a unitary system, the likely outcome would be "against" decriminalization (255,000 to 245,000). Provided the government abided by the results of the referendum, there would be no change to the existing policy: the personal use of marijuana would remain a criminal activity. This outcome would be welcomed in two of the five regions (regions B and E), but would be unpopular in the other three. Place yourself in the shoes of folks in these various regions.

Now imagine the same scenario in a state with a *decentralized* federal system, where criminal law powers belonged to the regional (or provincial) governments and not the federal government. In that event, decriminalization would be implemented in regions A, C, and D, but not in regions B and E. While voters in regions B and E may be upset about the policy developments in other parts of the country, they would have the freedom to make their own policy, and would therefore not be subject to the same reforms. This leads us to ask: which outcome is more desirable in Scenario 1: the one governed by unitary system rules that ensures conformity across the country, or the one governed by decentralized federalism that allows regional variances?

Now consider the second scenario (see Table 3.4). Once again, under a unitary system, the outcome would still preclude the decriminalization of marijuana use. And again, were the decision left up to individual regions under a federal system of government, the same provinces would move toward decriminalization. In this scenario,

TABLE 3.4 | Referendum Scenario 2: Changing Policy in a Unitary System and a Centralized Federalist System

Region	Total Voters	Votes For New Policy	Votes Against New Policy	Result	
				Unitary System	Centralized Federalism
A	250,000	**165,000**	85,000	No policy change	No policy change
B	125,000	25,000	**100,000**	No policy change	No policy change
C	75,000	**40,000**	35,000	No policy change	No policy change
D	25,000	**13,000**	12,000	No policy change	No policy change
E	25,000	2,000	**23,000**	No policy change	No policy change
Total	500,000	245,000	**255,000**		

however, imagine that a system of *centralized* federalism were in place, and that the federation's central government were empowered to legislate on criminal matters. Also imagine that, in contrast to our first example, the constituent units in Scenario 2 are not the same size. Region A makes up half the country: it has twice the population of the next largest region (region B) and 10 times the population of each of regions D and E. If the central government were to follow the will of the nationwide majority, it would not decriminalize marijuana use. This decision would likely upset a sizeable majority in the largest region (Region A), however, which would set up a dilemma should the national governing party wish to maintain popularity in that area of the country.

The dilemma of balancing the national interest against regional preferences is exacerbated in the third scenario (see Table 3.5). In this case, voters in four of the five regions were overwhelmingly opposed to decriminalizing marijuana use, but the most populous region was in favour. As before, in a unitary system and in a system of centralized federalism, the national government would follow the will of the overall majority, and it would therefore not change the status quo. But it would do so against the overwhelming majority of voters in the country's largest province, who would be outraged. Conversely, if the central government were to move forward with reform, the smaller regions would clamour that this would be tantamount to allowing the will of one province to trump the interests of all others. This is a scenario where decentralized federalism could broker regional tensions. If the regions, and not the central government, had the authority to decide, then the government of region A would change the policy, whereas the governments of regions B, C, D, and E would not. This flexibility solves a predicament. However, over time, this elasticity creates a culture of regional governments cultivating local identities, possibly inhibiting national unity and even provoking political fissures (see Chapter 2).

These three scenarios may be hypothetical, but they have real-life application and illustrate the types of tensions that exist across Canada. Federal governments are challenged to choose between policies or programs that have broad, country-wide appeal but cause deep resentment in certain parts of the country. For instance, the long-gun registry was a national program that required gun owners to register their firearms with the federal government. The policy was popular in many urban parts of Ontario and Quebec, but it was intensely unpopular in western Canada and ultimately disbanded by the Harper Conservative government. By the same token, provincial governments may be pressured, even induced, to adopt policies or programs with broad country-wide

TABLE 3.5 | Referendum Scenario 3: Changing Policy in a Unitary System and Federalist Systems

Region	Total Voters	Votes For	Votes Against	Unitary System	Centralized Federalism	Decentralized Federalism
A	250,000	**225,000**	25,000	No policy change	No policy change	**New policy**
B	125,000	5,000	**120,000**	No policy change	No policy change	No policy change
C	75,000	5,000	**70,000**	No policy change	No policy change	No policy change
D	25,000	3,000	**22,000**	No policy change	No policy change	No policy change
E	25,000	2,000	**23,000**	No policy change	No policy change	No policy change
Total	500,000	245,000	**255,000**			

Saskatchewan Archives Board R-A12109-4

Canada already had a system of universal, publicly funded hospital care in July 1962, when the government of Saskatchewan extended health coverage to primary physician care. The move sparked province-wide protests—led by the province's college of physicians and surgeons—and a national debate on the merits of universal healthcare. The federal government, under Liberal prime minister Lester Pearson, followed Saskatchewan's lead in 1966, when it established the modern system of medicare via the Medical Care Act.

appeal despite any misalignment with their own interests and objectives. Manitoba and Alberta were longstanding holdouts from Canada's national system of hospital insurance and medicare, for instance. Those provincial governments eventually yielded to popular pressure from within their borders amid sizeable federal funding promises. Again, the adage applies: where you stand on Canadian federalism depends on where you sit on the issues at hand, and in your region of the country.

VOX POP

To what degree does Canada's brand of decentralized federalism represent the interests of all Canadians? In what areas is it most successful? In what areas is it not? Consider such topics as healthcare, education, criminal justice, environmental protection, and the management of natural resources, like minerals.

The Politics of Fiscal Federalism

The regional tensions mentioned in the last section are no more acute than when it comes to money and social programs. Over time, the importance that the general public has attached to social welfare programs has meant that provincial governments have become more powerful than the Fathers of Confederation anticipated. This growth is largely attributable to the lead role provincial governments play in maintaining Canada's social safety net. The term *social safety net* suggests that the

social safety net
Government-funded social welfare programs designed to assist citizens in their time of need.

government will catch people before they fall on hard times, through publicly funded programs that help those in need and improve society. Of the various support networks the social safety net comprises, some are exclusively the federal government's responsibility (e.g. employment insurance, old age security, family allowance), some are exclusively the provincial government's domain (e.g. healthcare, childcare services, social assistance), and some have become intergovernmental (e.g. pensions).

The social safety net is an impressive enterprise undertaken jointly by governments and nongovernmental actors. It includes areas of provincial responsibility that the federal government helps to finance, such as health insurance, student loans, social assistance, and housing subsidies. There are also financing agreements in place between federal, provincial, and municipal levels of government, as well as not-for-profit organizations, to provide services such as food banks and emergency shelters. Establishing which level of government should pay and be accountable for what type of service is a constant source of dispute.

Gaps in the System

In this sense, the constitutional division of powers is only one component of the "rules" of Canadian federalism. Fiscal resources are just as important in determining the shape of Canadian politics. Fiscal federalism refers to the system of funding transfers that have been established to redistribute revenue between the two orders of government. Normally this involves the federal government distributing funds to provincial and territorial governments, but it may include federal–municipal or federal–citizen grants as well. Fiscal transfers are designed to balance the capacities of the various governments to deliver programs and services to Canadians in different parts of the country. In this vein, federalism has two dimensions: one horizontal (among provinces) and one vertical (between the federal and provincial orders).

Every federation has so-called *fiscal gaps* between their various governments; that is, some governments have more revenue at their disposal than others do. Horizontal fiscal gaps exist when certain regional governments enjoy greater revenue-generating capacities than others. In Canada, regional disparities are due almost entirely to differential access to natural resources like oil and gas. Those provinces that enjoy bountiful resource bases—like BC, Alberta, Saskatchewan, and Newfoundland and Labrador—are deemed to be more affluent than their counterparts in other parts of the country.

In and of themselves, these horizontal fiscal gaps do not automatically create problems in Confederation. If the distribution of population aligned with these revenues—such that provinces with greater wealth also had larger populations, and those provinces with less wealth faced fewer demands in terms of spending—there would be little reason for concern. This ideal alignment does not exist in Canada, however. Instead, Canada has a horizontal fiscal imbalance, whereby provinces have varying abilities to raise revenues, which affects their ability to deliver comparable public services. Take, for example, Alberta and Newfoundland and Labrador. Alberta is home to over 3.8 million residents; Newfoundland and Labrador's population is just 513,000. Alberta's oil and gas wealth spans decades, such that the province was debt-free from 2004 to 2013, and it has set aside billions of dollars for future generations in its Alberta Heritage Savings Trust Fund. Conversely, Newfoundland and Labrador has accumulated substantial debt, reflecting the fact the province has some of Canada's highest rates

fiscal federalism The manner in which revenues and responsibilities are distributed among various orders and governments.

horizontal fiscal gap Inter-provincial revenue disparities.

horizontal fiscal imbalance A situation in which some provinces have greater capacity to fund their constitutional responsibilities than others.

of unemployment and underemployment, some of the country's lowest income levels, and significant reliance on government assistance. Its offshore oil and gas revenues are a recent phenomenon. Governments in both of those provinces enjoy a windfall of revenues that are envied by others, but they must respond to different local circumstances. They are also faced with the reality that the value of these resources is subject to the ups and downs of prices set on international commodity markets, and that once these natural resources are exhausted, the non-renewable revenue streams will dry up without considerable investment in other sectors. Indeed, faced with massive revenue declines due to the low price of oil, both provinces have been grappling with spending restraint and have registered significant budget shortfalls. Thus, even provinces with generous resource bases have dissimilar policy priorities and spending pressures.

At the same time, vertical fiscal gaps exist wherever the revenue-generating abilities of the central government are different from the (collective) fiscal capacities of the regional governments. In other words, one order of government is able to generate more revenue than another. We might assume that in Canada the federal government is at a significant fiscal advantage because of the federal spending power. However, Canada is the only federation in the world in which the vertical fiscal gap actually favours the provinces. That is, as a group, the provincial governments enjoy more "own-source" revenue than the federal government. This gap exists even *before* federal transfers are counted, and is once again attributable to the fact that the provinces have exclusive access to natural resource revenues.

vertical fiscal gap A revenue disparity between the federal and provincial orders of government.

At first blush, this vertical fiscal gap might suggest the Canadian provinces should be contributing money to the federal government, and not vice versa. Revenues are only one half of the fiscal equation, however. On the expenditure side, provinces are collectively responsible for a larger proportion of public programs and services than the federal government—and increasingly so. Since the advent of the modern welfare state in the aftermath of World War II, the provinces have inherited responsibility for the fastest-growing areas of government spending, most notably healthcare and education. Under these circumstances, the provinces may enjoy a higher level of revenue, collectively, than the federal government, yet they remain challenged to provide the scope and quality of public services that Canadians demand. This has given rise to the vertical fiscal imbalance—a situation in which the federal government has more revenue than it can spend in its own areas of jurisdiction, while the provincial governments have more constitutional responsibilities than they can afford. In many instances, the vertical fiscal imbalance has forced provincial governments to raise taxes, cut services, and/or run budget deficits and accumulate debt (see Chapter 8).

vertical fiscal imbalance The federal government has an excess of revenue, and the provinces an excess of responsibilities, with respect to their constitutional obligations and fiscal capacities.

Addressing Imbalances

Political parties have different approaches to addressing fiscal gaps. When the Conservative Party, led by Stephen Harper, assumed office in early 2006, it advocated what it called "open federalism." On the surface, and with regard to the social safety net, this approach marked a return to classical federalism. It espoused

taking advantage of the experience and expertise that the provinces and territories can contribute to the national dialogue; respecting areas of provincial jurisdiction; keeping the federal government's spending power within bounds; [and]

full cooperation by the Government of Canada with all other levels of government, while clarifying the roles and responsibilities of each.[14]

In particular, Prime Minister Harper's approach to federalism involved addressing complaints about the fiscal imbalance in a manner that "combines the advancement of Quebec with the development of Canada." It will take some time for Prime Minister Justin Trudeau's style of federal–provincial relations to materialize in fiscal federalism.

INSIDE CANADIAN POLITICS
How Do Federal and Provincial Budgets Intersect?

In the early 1990s, the government of Canada was in a precarious fiscal position, running budget deficits of over $30 billion annually. Canada's international credit rating was downgraded, and its debt reached 68 per cent of the country's gross domestic product in 1995. A notorious *Wall Street Journal* editorial referred to Canada as "an honorary member of the Third World" and to the Canadian dollar as the "northern peso."[15]

To bring public spending under control, the federal Liberal government reduced department budgets, cut programs, laid off workers, introduced tax increases, reduced employment insurance spending, and slashed fiscal transfer payments to the provinces. All of these changes were announced, without consulting the provinces, as part of the historic 1995–6 federal budget.

As a result largely of the federal government's cuts to transfer payments, the provincial governments, which themselves were attempting to rein in spending, were unable to sustain their social programming. Citizens complained about the declining quality of healthcare services, and students were upset about rising tuition fees. In turn, provincial premiers laid blame on the federal government for balancing its budget on the backs of the provinces, and pressed for a reinstatement of transfers.

By 1997, the federal government was running a moderate budget surplus of $2.9 billion, and by 2000, the surplus peaked at $19.9 billion. This allowed the Liberal governments of Jean Chrétien and Paul Martin to increase spending, reduce taxes, and pay down the federal debt. A significant portion of the federal government's surplus strategy involved the use of the federal spending power—something the government of Quebec, in particular, resented.

Under Premier Lucien Bouchard, Quebec marshalled provincial support behind a new Social Union Framework Agreement. This accord was designed to prevent the federal government from taking unilateral action to establish new national programs, or dismantle existing federal–provincial funding programs, without provincial consultation. In 1999, the agreement was signed by the federal government and all provinces and territories—except Quebec. The federal government's insistence on including a clause that promoted the federal spending power as "essential to building Canada's social union" drove Quebec away from the table.

In 2001, the Parti Québécois government in Quebec announced the formation of the Commission on the Fiscal Imbalance. There was little surprise when the Commission concluded that Quebec should receive $2 billion of the $8 billion that was projected as an immediate need for the provinces, and that these monies should be granted by the federal government without any conditions attached to them. The Quebec political class latched onto the matter, and nationalists began citing the fiscal imbalance as evidence that federalism wasn't working. Other provinces rallied behind the notion of the vertical fiscal imbalance, and addressing it became a central objective of the newly formed Council of the Federation (see page 99). The federal Liberal government countered that under the constitutional division of powers, each government was responsible for its own priorities.

In 2007, one year after assuming power in Ottawa, the federal Conservative government responded by committing $39 billion in transfers to the provinces and territories over seven years. In his budget speech, federal finance minister Jim Flaherty proclaimed:

There's been a lot of talk about fiscal balance. . . . But what is it really all about? It's about better roads and renewed public transit. Better healthcare. Better-equipped universities. Cleaner oceans, rivers, lakes and air. Training to help Canadians get the skills they need. It's about building a better

future for our country. And that means getting adequate funding to provincial and territorial governments.[16]

Talk of the fiscal imbalance fizzled after that, but for an unexpected reason: the global economic recession of 2008, and the resulting pressure on governments to spend to stimulate the economy, marked an end to federal government surpluses. Since then, the federal government has returned to deficit financing, including a budget deficit of $55.6 billion in 2009. As the government of Canada returns to balanced budgets or even surpluses, we should anticipate that the provinces will resume pressuring it for more funding.

VOX POP

How do you think governments should address Canada's vertical fiscal imbalance?

Since Confederation, a series of transfer programs have been established to address these horizontal and vertical fiscal imbalances (Table 3.6). Three of these deserve the bulk of attention, as they are by far the largest and most contested: equalization, the Canada Health Transfer (CHT), and the Canada Social Transfer (CST).

TABLE 3.6 | What Each Province and Territory Will Get From Major Federal Transfers 2015-16 ($M)

Province	Equalization/ Territorial Formula Financing	Canada Health Transfer (CHT)	Canada Social Transfer (CST)	Total
Newfoundland and Labrador	0	501	191	692
Prince Edward Island	361	140	53	554
Nova Scotia	1,690	897	342	2,929
New Brunswick	1,669	718	273	2,660
Quebec	9,521	7,852	2,990	20,363
Ontario	2,363	13,091	4,986	20,440
Manitoba	1,738	1,230	468	3,436
Saskatchewan	0	1,081	412	1,493
Alberta	0	3,966	1,511	5,477
British Columbia	0	4,439	1,690	6,129
Yukon	874	35	13	922
Northwest Territories	1,233	42	16	1,291
Nunavut	1,454	35	13	1,502

Source: Reproduced with the permission of the Department of Finance, 2015 from www.fin.gc.ca/fedprov/mtp-eng.asp.

Equalization

equalization A federal
transfer program that is
designed to lessen the fiscal
disparities among provinces.

Alongside regional development initiatives and differential formulas built into other federal programs (like employment insurance), equalization is the primary transfer program designed to address the horizontal imbalance in Canada. The equalization program was established in 1957 as a mechanism of distributing federal funds to those provinces deemed to be in greatest need. The program's principles were subsequently enshrined in section 36(2) of the Constitution Act, 1982, to ensure that "provincial governments have sufficient revenues to provide reasonably comparable levels of public services at reasonably comparable levels of taxation." Equalization payments are paid to the most disadvantaged provinces out of the federal government's general revenues, and the formula by which they have been distributed has varied considerably over time. The most recent set of changes to the equalization formula came between 2007 and 2009, when the federal government moved to simplify and, at least initially, enrich the size of the program. In 2013–14, the federal government paid just over $16 billon to the six recipients, plus an additional $335 million to compensate Nova Scotia as part of a deal to offset offshore oil and gas revenues.

The federal government typically consults with provinces every five years regarding the funding formula for the program; however, the distribution of equalization funds is ultimately determined by Ottawa. Since 2007, the equalization formula has been based on a 10-province standard, meaning that all jurisdictions are included in the calculation of the country's average revenue-generating capacity. Provinces that fall below the national average receive equalization payments based on their population size, while those above that average do not. Not all revenue sources are included in this calculation, however. Four tax-base indicators are incorporated—personal income taxes, corporate taxes, sales taxes, and property taxes—and provinces are assessed according to how much they *could* generate if all provinces had the same tax rate. A fifth indicator—50 per cent of natural resource revenues—is also included in the calculation of each province's fiscal capacity.

Needless to say, some premiers attempt to use media pressure to persuade the federal government to devise a formula that will benefit their province the most.[17] This can lead to divisive politicking, pitting so-called "have" provinces (the wealthier provinces who are ineligible for equalization) against so-called "have-not" provinces (those whose financial capacity is below the national average, qualifying them for equalization). The term "have-not" has become so pejorative in Canadian politics that some now use the nomenclature "have-less" and "have-more" to distinguish the provinces that do and do not qualify for equalization funding.

BRIEFING NOTES

Canada's Equalization Program

There are a number of persistent myths about Canada's equalization program. The following misconceptions often cloud our understanding of fiscal federalism.

- *Myth 1: There are perennial "takers" and "makers" in Canada.* It is sometimes believed that certain provinces are always dependent on transfers from Ottawa while others never benefit. In fact, every province has received equalization at one point or another in Canadian history. Alberta was among the first set of "have-not" or "have-less" provinces, even though it has not received payments from the program since 1962. Until recently, Ontario had never received equalization payments, but began doing so in 2009. At the same time, Newfoundland and Labrador moved into the "have" or "have-more" category for the first time. Several provinces have moved in and out of the "have-more" category several times, notably BC and Saskatchewan.

- *Myth 2: Equalization payments flow directly from have-more provinces to have-less provinces.* Critics claim that equalization funds flow from more affluent to less affluent provinces, but this is inaccurate. Unlike the German *lander*, equalization funds are not transferred among the Canadian provinces. Rather, the transfers flow from the general revenues of the federal government to provincial governments with lower-than-average fiscal capacities. This said, compared to their counterparts in have-less provinces, individuals and corporations in Canada's richer provinces contribute more to the federal government in terms of tax dollars than their provinces receive in federal transfers or program spending.

- *Myth 3: It is possible to trace, and judge, how provinces spend their "equalization" funds.* Some critics of the equalization program argue that recipient provinces squander their transfers, using their equalization moneys to lower taxes, depress electricity prices, or create lavish public service programs. Such judgements are simply speculation. Equalization is an unconditional transfer that flows into the general revenues of each recipient province. As such, it is not possible to determine how each province spends its equalization allotment.

Graeme MacKay

In 2006, Alberta premier Ralph Klein threatened to withdraw from Canada's equalization program rather than have his province's oil and gas revenues go to other provinces. This cartoon is typical of the era, showing the premiers of other provinces seeking a share of Alberta's wealth. Which of the three myths highlighted in the box above does this kind of thinking reflect?

Vertical Transfers: The CHT and CST

In contrast to equalization, the other two major funding mechanisms—the Canada Health Transfer (CHT) and Canada Social Transfer (CST)—serve to diminish the vertical fiscal imbalance. As its name suggests, the CHT flows from Ottawa to all provinces to help cover the costs of healthcare. Conversely, the CST is intended to assist with the costs of maintaining a host of other social programs, ranging from education and universities to civil legal aid and welfare. All provinces receive both the CHT and CST, with each transfer being distributed based on each province's population (per capita).

Initially, Ottawa transferred funds to the provinces on a shared-cost basis for health, post-secondary education, and welfare programs (Figure 3.1). In some instances, Ottawa provided matching funds as a means of facilitating the growth of provincial welfare states. These came to be known as "fifty-cent dollars" because they came with the stipulation that a province must pay half. Popular if not sustainable in the immediate post-war period, these shared-cost models strained federal and provincial budgets.

In the late 1970s, the federal government began transitioning these early unconditional (or block) transfers toward conditional grants, placing tighter restrictions on how provinces could spend them. If a province accepted these funds, it was obliged to spend them as per the conditions set by the federal government. For example, the Canada Health and Social Transfer (CHST), in place from 1996 until 2003, prohibited provinces from imposing residency requirements on Canadians receiving welfare services. This meant that a provincial government could not turn away clients based on the fact they had not lived in the province for a specified period of time, ensuring that all Canadians had access to services across the country. It also forced provinces to abide by the five conditions of the Canada Health Act, namely that provincial health services be:

1. publicly administered,
2. portable across the country,
3. comprehensive in terms of medically necessary services,
4. universally available, and
5. accessible to all.

Provinces that failed to live up to these conditions—for instance, by allowing certain types of private health services for insurance—were subject to clawbacks in the form of reductions in federal transfers. These mobility conditions continue to apply to the CST and CHT, just as the Canada Health Act continues to apply to the latter. Ottawa imposes similar conditions on dozens of other federal–provincial transfer programs related to justice, infrastructure, labour market development, immigration, environmental sustainability, cultural development, and many other sectors.

Recent developments have challenged the foundations of Canada's system of federal–provincial fiscal transfers. As of 2014, both the CHT and CST involve per capita transfers. This means that these federal funds are distributed to provinces based on the size of their populations rather than on other, needs-based factors, as they had been previously. In an effort to prevent less affluent provinces from losing out as a result of this shift to per capita funding, the federal government promised that no province would lose CHT or CST funding year-over-year. In establishing a series of so-called

conditional grants Federal transfers to the provinces that may only be used for a specific purpose, and are subject to federal government restrictions or standards.

Canada Health Act Federal legislation imposing conditions on provincial governments for the expenditure of funds from health transfers.

↻ For more on medicare and the Canada Health Act see page 323–6 of Chapter 8.

per capita transfers Funds distributed to provinces based on how many people live in their jurisdictions.

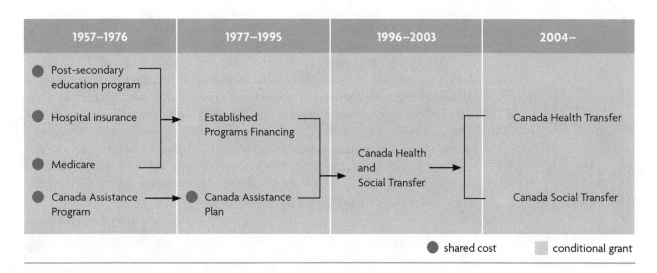

| 1957–1976 | 1977–1995 | 1996–2003 | 2004– |

FIGURE 3.1 | The Evolution of Vertical Transfers

"escalators," Ottawa also guaranteed that all three major transfers would grow at a predictable rate, eventually in line with the growth in Canada's gross domestic product (GDP) or 3 per cent, whichever is higher. These federal reforms were designed to encourage provincial governments to rationalize their spending over time, but they may result in adverse policy implications for areas with declining populations.

The sudden, unforeseen economic downturn in the fall of 2008 prompted a second look at this fiscal framework. While retaining its commitment to move the CHT and CST to per capita formulas, the federal government placed a ceiling on the growth of the equalization program. The so-called "GDP cap" made any increase in Ottawa's

THEY SAID IT

The Canada Health Act

How about a new Canada Health Act that includes Evidence, Cost Effectiveness and Patient Safety as key priorities? Yes to key fed role.

—Dr Brian Goldman, ER physician at Mount Sinai Hospital (@NightShiftMD)

Should hospital parking be free? BC Medical Assoc. says pay parking contravenes Canada Health Act.

—CTV British Columbia (@CTVBC)

RT @liberal_wire: Harper talks abt investing in health care—but in 1997 he said "It's past time feds scrapped the Canada Health Act."

—Liberal Party of Canada (@liberal_party)

Cdn gov't should call "time out" on Canada Health Act so provinces can experiment with new ways to fund health care.

—The Fraser Institute (@FraserInstitute)

Today in question period I re-iterated the long-standing #NDP support for the Canada Health Act and pressed the government on its position.

—NDP leader Jack Layton (@jacklayton)

contribution to equalization contingent upon Canada's economic growth. Critics in have-less provinces claimed the federal government had reneged on the earlier CHT/CST/ equalization deal, eroding the principles of adequacy, stability, and predictability upon which it was based. The change also came at an inopportune time, pushing equalization-receiving provinces into even more difficult fiscal positions at a time of recession.

Making matters worse, for the first time in history, the recession had driven Ontario into have-less status. Canada's largest province drawing funds from equalization left less revenue for the remaining recipients, further challenging them to provide comparable services at comparable rates of taxation. This is the state of Canada's system of fiscal federalism as Ottawa contemplates reforming the equalization formula and perhaps the entire interconnected transfer system.

Other Transfers

In addition to the big three (equalization, CHT, and CST), the federal government provides a series of other transfers to the provinces. Among them are the following:

- infrastructure funds (to build roads and bridges, for example);
- devolved services agreements (e.g. to provide services on behalf of the federal government, such as education or policing services in First Nations communities);
- one-off grants to provincially run universities and hospitals; and
- shared-cost programs like legal aid.

Every year, the federal government enters into hundreds of these sorts of fiscal arrangements with each province. Federal funding to the three territorial governments is

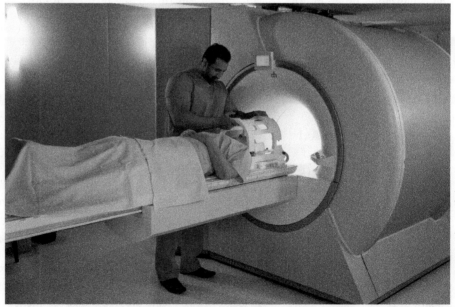

© Hero Images Inc./Alamy Stock Photo

After allowing several private MRI clinics to open in the province's lower mainland, the British Columbia government has incurred penalties in the form of clawbacks to its transfer payments from the federal government. Do you agree that a provincial government should pass on the opportunity to receive federal dollars for health care? Why or why not?

covered under an entirely separate set of arrangements, with the block Territorial Formula Financing grants making up the vast majority of each territory's budget.

Fiscal Federalism: Is It Working?

Critics of Canada's system of fiscal federalism allege that it disrupts market forces. They argue that it keeps weaker provincial economies alive, provides incentives for Canadians to remain in slow-growth regions, dampens inter-provincial economic competition, and fosters a sense of dependency on federal funding. This prompts calls for the reform (if not abolition) of the equalization program in particular. Some also disparage vertical transfers like the CST and CHT for blurring the lines of democratic accountability: with federal dollars flowing into provincial programs and services, critics find it challenging to assign credit or blame for policy outcomes.

Others see numerous strengths and advantages in Canada's system of fiscal federalism. Some view equalization as akin to a national system of revenue sharing, not unlike similar models in use in professional sports leagues. For instance, the National Hockey League redistributes some of its revenues to the smallest markets for the good of the league as a whole. Wealthy teams that contribute the most to the league's success, like the New York Rangers and the Toronto Maple Leafs, do not qualify for revenue sharing like less profitable teams operating in small markets, such as the Columbus Blue Jackets and the Nashville Predators. The analogy points to the advantages of creating a stronger national economy (or league) by contributing to the growth of smaller provincial economies (or teams). Just as sports leagues generate more revenue and build their market shares by building their brand in smaller markets, federations, too, are stronger when their weaker members are more economically viable. This economic union is stronger both internally (by creating domestic markets for Canadian goods and services) and externally (in the eyes of international investors).

David Stobbe/Reuters

An inspector examines a pile of potash at the Mosaic Potash mine storage facility in Colonsay, Saskatchewan. Potash mining, along with rising commodity prices, has helped Saskatchewan emerge as a "have-more" province after decades as a "have-less."

Proponents of Canada's fiscal federalism also look at the equalization program as a sort of governmental safety net, allowing provinces to take risks in developing their own-source revenue streams without fear of insolvency. As evidence of this success, they point to the experience of formerly have-less provinces that became have-more, notably Saskatchewan, which achieved marked success in developing its potash industry. Proponents also argue that the equalization program and CST/CHT strengthen Canada's social union by fostering the equality of all Canadians regardless of where they live, and by helping long-term communities of interest to survive (and thrive).

Inter-state and Intra-state Federalism in Canada

executive federalism A system in which the elected leaders of federal and provincial governments make public policy decisions.

When it comes to negotiations over Canada's social and economic union, Canadian politics has been dominated by what is known as executive federalism. The term refers to instances where intergovernmental bargaining, deal-brokering, and policy decisions take place among leaders of the various federal, provincial, and territorial governments. Executive federalism was epitomized during so-called "mega-constitutional" period discussed in Chapter 2. This elite-driven set of negotiations produced a series of real and tentative constitutional accords; however, the outcomes were widely panned for reflecting the aims of 11 white men in suits behind closed doors, and for not sufficiently reflecting the priorities of the broader public and special interests. Executive federalism persists today through meetings of premiers and ministers, and private one-on-one meetings between the prime minister and first minister colleagues.

functional federalism A system in which civil servants conduct the bulk of intergovernmental activity.

While the summit-style meetings that characterize executive federalism garner more media attention, the day-to-day relationships among Canadian governments are maintained at the bureaucratic level in what is known as functional federalism. In the most active and expansive sectors, like health and social services, provincial and territorial civil servants hold weekly teleconferences to collaborate on matters of mutual interest. This sort of intergovernmental dialogue occurs behind the scenes, but it is crucial to maintaining Canada's social and economic union. In the aftermath of the mega-constitutional era, first ministers and citizens alike had become wary of grand political negotiations and summits. In this atmosphere of constitutional fatigue, most activity in Canadian federalism shifted away from the high-stakes political level.

inter-state federalism A system of formal interactions among government officials and leaders.

first ministers' meetings Formal gatherings of the premiers, sometimes hosted by the prime minister.

Whether executive or functional, there are two main sets of actors in Canadian federalism: those who work in *inter-state institutions* (like the Council of the Federation) and those who work within *intra-state institutions* (like the Canadian Senate). As its name suggests, inter-state federalism takes place *between* governments, their leaders, and their officials. Meetings between prime ministers, premiers, and various ministers are by far the most visible forms of inter-state federalism, but they are by no means the most frequent. In fact, first ministers' meetings between the prime minister and all 13 provincial and territorial premiers have become increasingly rare since the mega-constitutional period. Prime Minister Harper convened only two first ministers' meetings between 2006 and 2014, and they took place in a brief two-month period, in December 2008 and January 2009, amid the so-called "Great Recession." During the 2015 federal election campaign, Justin Trudeau committed to hosting annual first ministers' meetings, including one on climate change just one month into his prime ministership.

THEY SAID IT

The Council of the Federation

Premiers will discuss affordable and social housing issues at this week's Council of the Federation meeting.

—Co-operative Housing Federation of Canada (@CHFCanada)

Council of the Federation: Three days of less than nothing. Premiers posture, ignore reality while guzzling tax dollars.

—Calgary Beacon (@CalgaryBeacon)

Health care rally knocks on Council of the Federation's door!

—Canadian Health Coalition (@HealthCoalition)

Council of the Federation announces news for pharmacists: read all about it!

—Canadian Pharmacists Association (@CPhA/APhC)

VOX POP

In 2014, the Council of the Federation rebranded itself as "Canada's Premiers" for all public news releases. Why do you think they made the shift?

Meetings among premiers, without the prime minister, are far more frequent. Since being created in 2003 to replace the Annual Premiers Conference, the Council of the Federation brings together all 13 premiers, face to face, at least twice per year. They engage in periodic conference calls on a regular basis, as well. Provincial leaders also gather each summer around regional tables like the Western Premiers' Conference, the Council of Atlantic Premiers, and the Northern Premiers' Forum, and join their American counterparts around tables like the Western Governors' Association and the New England Governors' meetings. While generally productive, these meetings rarely garner the same level of national attention paid to a full forum comprising all first ministers. As PEI premier Robert Ghiz lamented after the 2013 Council of the Federation meetings, "Federal and provincial governments are equal partners in Canada. . . . We need to make sure we're working together, and unfortunately, right now, that's not happening."[18] This may be changing. One of Prime Minister Justin Trudeau's first acts was to invite premiers to accompany him to a Paris climate summit.

Provincial ministers of various sectors also meet on an annual basis. Justice ministers gather once per year to discuss common challenges, just as ministers of finance, health, culture, infrastructure, agriculture, energy, and other sectors do. Some of these meetings feature federal, provincial, and territorial representatives, while others are composed of only provincial or provincial and territorial members. Some are regional, and some are pan-Canadian.

In contrast to inter-state federalism, intra-state federalism takes place *within* the bounds of the central government. In Canada, regional and provincial interests are built into several federal government institutions. A prime example is the Senate, where seats are distributed on a regional basis (see Chapter 6). Compared to other federations, like the United States, Canada's intra-state institutions are far weaker than its inter-state ones are. Whereas federal US senators tend to wield more power

intra-state federalism
A system in which regional interests are represented within the institutions of the central government.

in relation to state governors when it comes to national policy-making, Canadian senators are dwarfed by provincial/territorial premiers.

Yet regional representation is found in other institutions, as well. By convention, the federal cabinet contains ministers from each province, with lead ministers from each jurisdiction called "lieutenants" or "regional ministers." Federal political parties are also structured around regional lines, with provincial executives and campaign managers (see Chapter 9). Justices of the Supreme Court are selected from various provinces; Quebec perennially receives three seats on the bench, and the other six spots are distributed among the remaining provinces on a rotating basis. At the functional level, the federal government maintains offices in various regions of the country, although recent budget cutbacks have resulted in the closure of many. Combined, these intra-state institutions are designed to integrate regional interests within the confines of the central government.

↻ The distribution of Supreme Court judges is explained on page 270 of Chapter 7, on the judiciary.

The Evolution of Canadian Federalism

We have maintained from the outset of this chapter that one's view of Canadian federalism depends on where one sits. It depends, too, on *when* one is looking. The following brief history (supported by Figure 3.2) serves to summarize the lessons from this chapter while giving structure to the evolution of Canadian federalism:

- The Fathers of Confederation sought to create a highly centralized form of government in Canada, one in which power tipped largely in favour of Ottawa and away from the provincial capitals. However, a series of factors coincided to *decentralize* the Canadian federation.
- A strong provincial rights movement—led initially by Ontario premier Oliver Mowat, his Maritime colleagues, and his partners in the corporate sector—helped

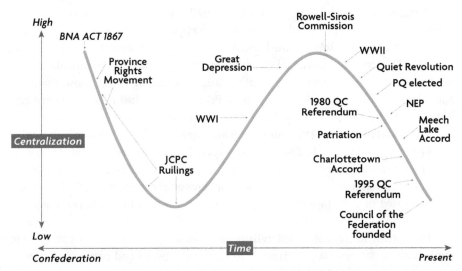

FIGURE 3.2 | The Centralization and Decentralization of the Canadian Federation

Source: Adapted from Robert J. Jackson and Doreen Jackson, *Politics in Canada: Culture, Behaviour and Public Policy*, 7th edn (Toronto: Pearson Education, 2009): p. 202.

to shift the balance of power through a combination of politics, lobbying, and litigation. The last of these approaches, litigation, found supporters in London, where the Judicial Committee of the Privy Council released several province-friendly rulings that helped weaken section 91 (federal powers) and bolster section 92 (provincial powers) of the BNA Act.

- A combination of war and economic calamity led to a period of emergency federalism, which shifted power back to Ottawa once more, as provincial governments welcomed—even insisted upon—federal intervention in the interests of national security.

- Struck by the federal government in 1937, the Rowell-Sirois Commission released its report amid this tumultuous period. Among other findings, the Commissioners recommended that the federal government assume control over unemployment insurance and pensions, and establish a more robust system of federal-provincial transfers (including equalization). Governments heeded this advice in the decades to come.

- The beginning of Quebec's Quiet Revolution in the 1960s, and the subsequent election of the Parti Québécois government in 1976, accelerated the post-war decentralization of Canadian federalism (see Chapter 4).

- The Pierre Trudeau government's introduction of the controversial National Energy Program galvanized decentralist sentiments in western Canada, where governments and citizens railed against the federal Liberal government's attempts to redistribute the natural resource wealth of the Western provinces (particularly Alberta) to the weaker economies in central and eastern Canada. Western Canadians saw the federal program as an intervention in areas of provincial jurisdiction.

- Together with the 1980 Quebec referendum, these events set the stage for the mega-constitutional period of Canadian federalism: an era in which first ministers would come to agreement on no fewer than three constitutional reform packages.

- The failure to satisfy the Quebec government during the patriation of the constitution and the failure of provincial legislatures to ratify the Meech Lake and Charlottetown Accords paved the way to Quebec's second referendum on sovereignty in 1995 (Chapters 2 and 4).

- In the aftermath of that vote, the federal government took several steps to assuage those who wanted to see a more decentralized Canadian federation. The Clarity Act, through which Parliament gave itself the authority to determine what constituted a clear question and clear majority upon which to negotiate any potential secession following a future referendum on provincial sovereignty, was not among them. However, Ottawa would grant the provinces increased control over immigration and labour market development, and place certain limits on the federal spending power. These moves did not go as far as many provincial governments would have liked, and they went only so far in addressing the vertical fiscal imbalance that had been growing since the 1995–6 federal budget. Combined with a reinvestment in fiscal transfers, the federal government's approach eventually served to decentralize control over health and social programs in Canada.

- This process was complemented by the formation of the Council of the Federation in 2003, through which provincial and territorial premiers have asserted their authority and prominence in national policymaking in Canada.

Concluding Thoughts

Federalism is one of the most fundamental, yet most challenging, elements of Canadian democracy. In this chapter we have covered the *what, where, why, how, who,* and *when* of Canadian federalism. We have defined it, contextualized it, explained its origins, identified its actors, and described its evolution. How it functions is the topic of entire textbooks and university courses, however, and how *well* it functions is truly in the eyes of the beholder. There are those who yearn for the "classic" days of Canadian federalism, when for a very brief period areas of federal and provincial jurisdiction were contained in "watertight compartments." Others see Canadian federalism in terms more of "interlocking" compartments, espousing a view that recognizes the importance of governments working together to address national policy issues. Some seek a more centralized form of federalism, while others see virtue in enhancing provincial powers. Some view Canadian federalism in symmetrical terms, with all provinces entitled to the same powers, while others see certain provinces as exercising (and/or deserving) different sets of powers because of their unique status. All of these views have been accommodated to a greater or lesser extent at different points in the history of Canadian federalism, and the system is bound to undergo transformations of equal magnitude in the future.

It is also worth noting that as an organizing principle of Canada's constitutional order and political life, federalism serves to define the country's politics along territorial and regional lines. Unlike countries where political debates feature ideological or gendered fault lines, the major cleavages of political conflict in Canada tend to emerge among geographically defined communities, as we will see in the next chapter, on regionalism.

For More Information

How democratic is Canadian federalism? Jennifer Smith assesses this as part of the Democratic Audit series in her book, *Federalism* (UBC Press, 2004), as do Herman Bakvis and Grace Skogstad in *Canadian Federalism: Performance, Effectiveness and Legitimacy* (Oxford University Press, 2012).

How does inter-state federalism really work in Canada? Bakvis, Baier and Brown take us inside the world of intergovernmental relations in *Contested Federalism: Certainty and Ambiguity in the Canadian Federation* (Oxford University Press, 2009).

What really happened during the "mega-constitutional" negotiations of the 1990s? For insiders' accounts of the debates, see Banting and Simeon's *And No One Cheered: Federalism, Democracy and* the Constitution Act (Methuen, 1983); Monahan's *Meech Lake: The Inside Story* (University of Toronto Press, 1991); and McRoberts and Monahan's *The Charlottetown Accord, the Referendum, and the Future of Canada* (University of Toronto Press, 1993).

What did the Fathers of Confederation really think about federalism? Return to the foundations of our democracy with *Canada's Founding Debates*, edited by Janet Ajzenstat et al. (University of Toronto Press, 1999) and Christopher Moore's *1867: How the Fathers Made a Deal* (McClelland and Stewart, 1997).

What role have the courts played in the evolution of Canadian federalism? John T. Saywell examines this in *The Lawmakers: Judicial Power and* *the Shaping of Canadian Federalism* (University of Toronto Press, 2002), as does Alan Cairns in "The Judicial Committee and Its Critics" (*Canadian Journal of Political Science*, 1971).

How does "functional federalism" really function? Gregory Inwood, Carolyn Johns, and Patricia L. O'Reilly take us *Inside the Worlds of Finance, Environment, Trade, and Health* to examine *Intergovernmental Policy Capacity in Canada* (McGill–Queen's University Press, 2011).

How does Canadian federalism compare to other forms of federalism? The former president of the Forum of Federations, George Anderson, has written a pair of concise primers that introduce students to the world of federalism: *Federalism: An Introduction* (Oxford University Press, 2007) and *Fiscal Federalism: A Comparative Introduction* (Oxford University Press, 2009).

What are the normative underpinnings of Canadian federalism? Samuel V. LaSelva has written the seminal account, in *The Moral Foundations of Canadian Federalism: Paradoxes, Achievements, and Tragedies of Nationhood* (McGill–Queen's University Press, 1996).

What are the prospects for future constitutional amendments to redefine Canadian federalism? Ask David Thomas, whose book *Whistling Past the Graveyard: Constitutional Abeyances, Quebec, and the Future of Canada* (Oxford University Press, 1997) addresses many of the implications.

Which came first: Canada's federal institutions or our federal society? Alan Cairns was the first political scientist to tackle this question, in his seminal piece "The Governments and Societies of Canadian Federalism" (*Canadian Journal of Political Science*, 1977).

How does federalism affect the development of public policy in Canada? Kathryn Harrison critically examines this question in her book *Passing the Buck: Federalism and Environmental Policy* (UBC Press, 1997).

What is "open federalism" and the "fiscal imbalance"? Graham Fox explored these questions in a summary piece he prepared for *Policy Options*. See "Harper's 'Open Federalism': From the Fiscal Imbalance to 'Effective Collaborative Management of the Federation" (March 2007: pp. 44–7).

Want to see what happens at intergovernmental meetings? The Canadian Intergovernmental Conference Secretariat has been supporting and documenting meetings of various federal, provincial, and territorial officials since 1973. To view press releases from these hundreds of meetings, visit: www.scics.ca.

Need more information on how federal-provincial transfers are distributed in Canada? The federal Department of Finance maintains an updated database here: http://tinyurl.com/fedprov.

Looking for academic literature on Canadian federalism? The Institute of Intergovernmental Relations is a prime resource: www.queensu.ca/iigr.

Deeper Inside Canadian Politics

1. Criticisms of the federal form of governance have evolved throughout Canadian history. Compare and contrast the opposition to Confederation in the 1860s with the criticisms of mega-constitutionalism a century later. What are the similarities between these two sets of critiques? What are the differences?

2. Identify three elements that distinguish Canadian federalism from federalism in other countries. For each element, discuss whether it represents an advantage or a disadvantage over other forms of federalism.

UP FOR DEBATE

Is federalism working in Canada?

THE CLAIM: YES, IT IS!

The concentration of power in Canada's political system strikes just the right balance between the federal and provincial orders of government.

Yes: Argument Summary

Canada has become one of the world's most decentralized federations. It is true that the Fathers of Confederation dreamed of a much stronger federal government, assigning glorified municipal powers to the provinces in 1867. The federation has evolved considerably since then, adapting to the new and increasing demands that Canadians have placed on their governments. Most of these new responsibilities have fallen to the provinces and territories and, with notable financial assistance from the federal government, they have built and maintained some of the strongest health, education, and welfare systems in the world. Canadian federalism has become a model for other countries, allowing the provinces to wield an effective amount of authority over matters of regional importance, and the federal government to retain a considerable amount of power to govern on behalf of all Canadians.

Yes: Top 5 Considerations

1. Canadian federalism must be sufficiently flexible to accommodate the country's varying political cultures and regional characteristics. Policy designed in government offices in Ottawa may not be suitable for implementation across the country, where there are varying socioeconomic and socio-political considerations. Regional federal ministers, premiers, and provincial ministers are the conduits for local perspectives that national policymakers may otherwise overlook.

2. No less of a centralist than Pierre Trudeau once referred to the provinces as important "laboratories" of social experimentation. Indeed, federalism has allowed provinces and territories to experiment with different models of public policy and service delivery, then share best practices to spread innovations across the country. Universal healthcare, which began in Saskatchewan, is a prime example.

3. Federalism fosters healthy competition among provincial governments, while providing for a minimum standard of performance. For instance, while provinces and regions continually compete to create the most attractive climate for business investment, federal transfers ensure that every government is able to deliver comparable rates of social services at comparable rates of taxation.

4. The federal government is not nearly as weak as centralists would have you believe. Above all, Ottawa wields the federal spending power, which allows it to fund (and thereby shape) activities that fall within provincial jurisdiction. If Ottawa chooses not to implement national standards or schemes, that is their choice; they are free to do so, but are often reluctant for fear of disrupting effective, and popular, provincial programs and services.

5. The persistence of the vertical fiscal imbalance ensures that the federal government will always hold the purse strings in Confederation. This means they will continue to set the overall economic and social agenda in Canada, funding (or defunding) programs that meet Ottawa's objectives and thereby influencing provincial governments' own priorities.

Yes: Other Considerations

- Centralists may criticize Canada's patchwork of social programs, but such critiques overlook the reality that federalism responds effectively to the unique needs and tastes found among people of different regions. Just as not everyone loves plaid, not everyone loves private automobile insurance, and some prefer a government-run insurance program.

- Where provinces feel that the federation is too decentralized, they have bound together in pan-Canadian or regional alliances. Consider the Council of the Federation's energy strategy and healthcare innovation working groups, the New West Partnership, or harmonization in Atlantic Canada.

- Regardless of the party in power, the federal government has not been shy in introducing new, pan-Canadian initiatives, often without consulting the provinces and territories. Consider, most recently, the introduction of the Canada Job Grant.

THE COUNTERCLAIM: NO, IT ISN'T!

Provincial governments have far too much power and their quest for local control is watering down what it means to be Canadian.

No: Argument Summary

A defining characteristic of the federal system of government is that it allows public policy to be responsive to local needs. But this overlooks that provincial politicians continually push for more power and resources. This search for more authority can pit them against national political actors and/or those in other provinces. The stakes in this intergovernmental power struggle have been growing with the importance of the welfare state and have inhibited constitutional renewal. Over time, the federal government loses the ability to unite citizens, and the sum of localized decisions erodes what it means to be Canadian.

No: Top 5 Considerations

1. The special status accorded to Quebec ensures that it will be forever different from the rest of Canada. For instance, the Quebec Pension Plan is managed by the Quebec government, whereas all other workers in Canada are required to pay into the Canada Pension Plan. This type of policy distinctiveness only serves to aggravate regional tensions, to treat people differently, and to blur our ability to define what it means to be Canadian.

2. When premiers are successful in securing special treatment for their provinces in Confederation, this only motivates other premiers to table their own list of grievances. The spate of side deals over natural resources sparked by the Atlantic Accords is a great example. Continual spats over the perceived unfairness of the equalization formula (e.g. pundits asserting that Alberta is subsidizing the Maritimes) are an example of a recurring source of controversy that pits provinces against each other.

3. Provincial politicians' appetite for more power can never be satisfied. Their bickering and grandstanding is so upsetting to the national fabric that prime ministers dare not reopen constitutional debates. As a result, Canada has a constitution that is deeply flawed and inequitable, yet consensus on even minor constitutional changes remains elusive.

4. When the constitution was signed in 1867, it was not possible to predict the pervasiveness of the modern welfare state. The provincial governments' authority over healthcare and education are two constitutional responsibilities that warrant significant national standards. While the federal government has used its spending power to promote common healthcare standards, there is no such national standard for education; there isn't even a federal department of education, limiting our ability to develop and train Canadians to compete in the international economy.

5. Provincial government services play an integral role in the lives of Canadians. However, the unicameral legislature, unbridled authority of the premier's office, the often limited resources of

opposition parties, and the smaller news bureaus of local media mean that provincial government decisions are not subject to sufficient scrutiny. The intensity of the federal arena of politics means that federal government policy, election candidates, and journalism all tend to be of a higher standard than at the provincial level of government.

No: Other Considerations

- As the importance of the provincial government has grown, so has the perceived influence and power of premiers, including their personification of local political culture.
- Premiers may resort to extreme measures to pressure federal politicians to meet their demands. The well-known examples of Quebec sovereignty referendums are interspersed with more episodic events such as Newfoundland Premier Danny Williams ordering all Canadian flags removed from provincial government buildings in 2004, Quebec Premier Pauline Marois's challenging of federal Senate reform legislation and Supreme Court appointments, and BC Premier Christy Clark's five conditions for pipeline development.

Discussion Questions

- Do you believe that Canada should have a strong national government, or that powers should be devolved to the provincial and territorial governments? Why?
- At various points in time Canadians have the opportunity to elect a member of Parliament, a provincial representative (MLA, MPP, MNA, or MHA), and municipal representatives. They also have an appointed representative in the Senate. Does federalism mean that we have too many politicians?
- In your opinion, does federalism keep this country together because it allows provincial governments to respond to the varied policy preferences of Canadians, or does it result in stronger regional tensions?
- Does federalism give too much power to large provinces at the cost of small provinces, or do small provinces receive more than their fair share?
- Does it make sense that Canadian social programs (such as medicare and employment insurance) follow some common principles, but nevertheless Canadians receive different types of service depending on where they live? Or should service be identical across the country?

Where to Learn More about Federalism in Canada

Herman Bakvis, Gerald Baier, and Douglas Brown, *Contested Federalism: Certainty and Ambiguity in the Canadian Federation* (Don Mills, ON: Oxford University Press, 2009).

Loleen Berdahl, "(Sub)national Economic Union: Institutions, Ideas, and Internal Trade Policy in Canada," *Publius: The Journal of Federalism* 43, no. 2 (2013): pp. 275–96.

Alain-G. Gagnon, *Contemporary Canadian Federalism: Foundations, Traditions, Institutions* (Toronto: University of Toronto Press, 2009).

John Kincaid and Richard L. Cole, "Citizen Attitudes toward Issues of Federalism in Canada, Mexico, and the United States," *Publius: The Journal of Federalism* 41, no. 1 (2011): pp. 53–75.

Hamish Telford, "The Federal Spending Power in Canada: Nation-Building or Nation Destroying?," *Publius: The Journal of Federalism* 33, no. 1 (2003): pp. 23–44.

Linda A. White, "Federalism and Equality Rights Implementation in Canada," *Publius: The Journal of Federalism* 44, no. 1 (2014): pp. 157–82.

4 REGIONALISM IN CANADA

Inside this Chapter

- What is regionalism, and why is it so strong in Canada?
- What are the three main varieties of regionalism in Canada?
- What are the sources and consequences of regionalism in Canadian politics?

Inside Regionalism in Canada

Even before Confederation, Canadian democracy was grounded in territorial notions of identity and sovereignty. The four provinces that came together in 1867 defined their common institutions along regional lines and protected regional autonomy over matters of local interest. Over time, the highly regionalized political culture

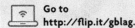
that spawned the Canadian constitution came to be reinforced by it. To this day, talk of pan-Canadian government programs and other forms of centralized federalism draws calls for improved regional representation in Ottawa—and the ire of those seeking to maintain their home communities' way of life.

Perhaps not surprisingly given its pervasiveness, regionalism in Canada is the subject of a few popular misconceptions. Be mindful of the following maxims as you read through the chapter.

 Regionalism means different things to Canadians across the country. While Canadians in all parts of the country identify with the culture, history, geography, and political interests of their local territory, there are several distinct varieties of regionalism in Canada—some bent on wielding greater influence within the central government, others on achieving local autonomy, and still others on establishing new, independent states.

 Regionalism is not necessarily a divisive force. Regionalism is often portrayed as a threat to national unity. When managed effectively, however, it can act as a safety valve of sorts, helping to preserve union through diversity.

 Regionalism is far from a natural part of the Canadian political order. There are those who believe that differences along regional lines are inevitable in a country the size of Canada. In reality, no mystical forces were involved in establishing regionalism in Canada; rather, a combination of socioeconomic and historical factors were involved. And no invisible forces help to sustain it: schools, constitutional architects, and politicians do. Regionalism is not and never was inevitable.

Peering inside Canadian regionalism requires us to look into and beyond these tenets.

Overview

This chapter illustrates that how Canadians think about politics is related to their sense of place. For many Canadians, the way they identify with politics is rooted in where they live. Do they consider themselves foremost Canadian, do they foremost identify with their province, or do they think about both equally? While many citizens feel a patriotic connection with Canada, the reality is that the country's national identity is a work in progress, and there are varying political cultures from coast to coast to coast. The common way of looking at these variances is to divide Canada along provincial, territorial, or regional lines. Geographic barriers; economic realities; ethnic, cultural, and social forces; the diversity of political institutions; and varying emotional attachments are among the many factors that contribute to how Canadians perceive their political selves so differently. As a result, the variety of national and regional identities in Canada is as broad as the landscape itself.

While often viewed as divisive, regionalism may be seen as a unifying force that brings together people who have shared political concerns, such as farmers on the Prairies who feel alienated from Ottawa, or frustrated francophones in Quebec. The different outlooks in regions are reflected in distinct political cultures within the country's main regions, normally considered to be Atlantic Canada, Quebec, Ontario, the Prairies, the Pacific region, and the North. This localized political perspective is propagated by popular political leaders who cite how their region of the country is being treated poorly by its neighbours or by the federal government.

UP FOR DEBATE

Is regionalism still a dynamic force in Canadian politics?

Keep this question in mind as you read through the chapter. Consult the end-of-chapter debate supplement for more material to help you engage in an informed discussion of the topic.

Regionalism and National Identity in Canada

Defining Regionalism and Canada's Regions

At its core, regionalism is a form of subnational identity. If a *region* is a territory with its own unique political characteristics, regionalism is a socio-psychological connection to that territory—an identification with it, and a commitment to it.[1] In other words, if a region is a matter of terrain, regionalism is a state of mind: a shared sense of purpose and identity among people within a particular geographic community. At least that's how insiders define it.

Regionalism is perhaps the most salient and enduring characteristic of Canadian politics. Yet, Canadians' sense of self and their political state of mind are by no means uniform. At any given time, regions may comprise multiple provinces, such as western Canada or the three Maritime provinces; individual provinces or territories; and even areas within a province, such as Cape Breton, or a capital city. Regionalism is as much an inward expression of group cohesion as an outward expression of identity, frustration with the political system, and demands for improvements. Among the timeworn regional grievances in Canada are ideological clashes, class and identity struggles, and the geographic imbalance of power in Ottawa.[2] Canada's political history is marked with instances of one region becoming frustrated not only with the federal government but with other regions, a situation that has often led to the fracturing of national unity.

Among Canadians, regionalism is in many ways like the proverbial elephant in the room: everyone knows it is there, few want to draw attention to it, and even fewer know how to define it (aside from saying, "it's an elephant!"). In 1979, as part of the Canadian National Election Study, researchers posed the following statement to respondents:

> People often think of Canada as being divided into regions, but they don't always agree on what the appropriate regional divisions are. We would like to know if you think of Canada as being divided into regions.[3]

The vast majority that answered that, yes, they did think of Canada as being divided into regions. They were then asked to identify which region they lived in, and what the other regions in Canada were. In total, respondents gave over 3000 unique responses,

regionalism An allegiance or psychological connection to a territory with its own unique political characteristics.

ranging from the West and the East to the country and the city; from the forgotten region and the most powerful region to the industrial heartland and the grain belt; from the Canadian Shield and the Arctic to Atlantic Canada and the Pacific Coast; and so on. The sheer number and variety of the responses were staggering.

Researchers also asked participants to engage in the following exercise:

> *Here is a blank map of Canada. It has no writing on it at all. We would like you to write in five words or phrases that you think best describe politics in Canada. You can put down anything you want and write anywhere on the map, but you can only put down five things.*[4]

This time, respondents offered over 2000 separate responses, many of which involved personal judgements about the rest of the country. Some labelled central Canada as privileged, favoured, having lower taxes, and having better roads, for instance. Others drew borders along linguistic and ethnic lines, or made reference to dominant parties and personalities. Still others labelled certain regions as parochial, self-centred, arrogant, inward-looking, or a number of other pejorative terms. In short, Canadians had little trouble looking at politics through a regional lens, although they disagreed when it came to naming or defining the borders around Canada's various regions.

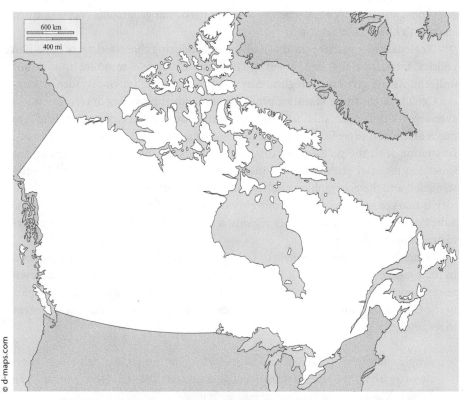

© d-maps.com

How would you draw a regional map of Canada? Complete the exercise described above by writing in five words or phrases you think best describe politics in Canada. You can put down anything you want and write anywhere on the map.

Approaches to the Study of Regionalism

Regionalism continues to be a fundamental element of Canadian politics nearly three decades later. It also remains one of the most contested, almost mysterious subjects of political science research. Just like their survey respondents, Canadian political scientists are far from consensus when it comes to defining the terms *region* and *regionalism*. Garth Stevenson's definition of *region* is among the most pervasive: "a territorial entity having some natural and organic unity or community of interest that is independent of political and administrative boundaries."[5] According to this view, a region is

- primarily defined by *territory*, distinguishing it from other forms of community rooted in gender, ethnicity, language, or other non-geographic variables; and
- *innate*, meaning it is not artificially constructed by politicians or map-makers, but grounded in an almost primordial set of common values and mutual needs.

From this naturalist perspective, regions are grounded in a combination of geography and socioeconomic political community—"the product of historical experience, human organization, and social interaction," in Janine Brodie's words.[6] Naturalists see regions not as artificial constructs but as organic, natural elements of political reality.

Others, like Richard Simeon, consider regions as "simply containers. . . . How we draw the boundaries around them depends entirely on what our purposes are. . . ."[7] In the positivist worldview of scholars like Simeon, regions are purely academic devices—frames applied by observers to make sense of patterns of political attitudes and behaviour. From this perspective, regional lines could be drawn around political borders (creating 10 provincial and 3 territorial "regions"), topographic regions (the Maritimes, the Prairies), historical regions (Old Canada in the east and New Canada to the west), or transprovincial regions (the West, the North, central Canada, Atlantic Canada), or even within individual provinces.

In other words, where naturalists see regional boundaries as inherent parts of the political environment (to be discovered, not imposed), positivists view regional boundaries as flexible and contingent on the purposes of the observer.

Regional Political Cultures

Whether organic or imposed, regional divisions are among the deepest, most enduring political cleavages in Canada. Canadians living in a geographic area tend to share common expectations of government that, collectively, are slightly different from the views of Canadians residing in other areas of the country.

In this sense, much is often made of the distinct political cultures that exist across the country: those common sets of values that underpin each political system and distinguish it from its neighbours. Often stereotypical and unstated, each political community has its own, unique political culture—a guiding ethos, a constellation of political values that is bound up in its symbols and reflected in the attitudes of its mainstream members. For instance, why is it that the residents of St John's identify so passionately with the seal hunt, but their neighbours in Halifax are less enthusiastic and Torontonians are vehemently opposed, even though few residents in any of these

political culture A society's innate political characteristics, embodied in the structure of its institutions and beliefs of its members.

Ian Smith/Vancouver Sun

Why do you think the introduction of a harmonized sales tax (HST) sparked protests, petitions, a constitutional challenge, and a referendum on one coast (in BC) while passing with barely a raised eyebrow on the other (in PEI)?

capital cities have participated in the annual hunt? Why is Canada Day such an enormous national celebration in some areas of the country, but to others July 1 is a solemn day to remember World War I (in Newfoundland), is marked as "Fête du déménagement" because apartment leases expire (in Quebec), or merely a day off work?

In Chapter 14, we discuss the distinctions between political culture and national identity in Canada and the United States. Just as Canadian political culture is distinct from America's, so, too, are Canada's regional cultures distinct from one another. This is why many scholars view Canada as comprising multiple political *cultures*, as much as a single, overarching political culture.

Western Canadians are often viewed as being more populist, individualist, and "right-wing" than their Eastern neighbours, for instance. Alberta, notwithstanding recent NDP gains in the province, is often portrayed as the cradle of Canadian conservatism: home to the country's lowest taxes and labour standards, and highest support for traditional marriage and the federal Conservative Party. Compared to this Wild West image, politics in Atlantic Canada reserves a space for government intervention in the economy. There, social assistance and regional development programs are favoured over the laissez-faire, small-government ethos that appears to pervade the West. Quebec maintains a polarized political culture unto itself, defined at times by a left–right ideological divide and a cleavage between federalist and nationalist forces. Meanwhile, central Canada—Ontario and, at times, Manitoba—maintains its own middling political culture, a microcosm of the broader Canadian ethos described above. Canadian provinces have sufficiently diverse attributes that each has its own political culture and yet shares commonalities with other provinces (see Table 4.1).

TABLE 4.1 | The Varied Characteristics of Canadian Provinces and Territories

Region	Characteristics
West Coast region	
British Columbia 	British Columbia is Canada's westernmost province, and Vancouver is Canada's gateway to the Asia–Pacific. About one-half of all the goods produced in BC are forestry products; it is also known for mining, fishing, and agriculture. The province's large East and South Asian communities have made Chinese and Punjabi the most spoken languages in its cities after English. The capital, Victoria, is a tourist centre and headquarters of the navy's Pacific fleet. Year of entry into Confederation: 1871 Population (2014 data): 4,631,300 Seats in the federal Parliament in Ottawa: 48 (42 MPs, 6 senators) Seats in the provincial Legislative Assembly in Victoria: 85 MLAs
Prairie region	
Alberta 	Alberta is the most populous Prairie province. It is Canada's largest producer of oil and gas, and the oil sands in the province's north are being developed as a major energy source. Alberta is also renowned for agriculture, especially for its vast cattle ranches. Year of entry into Confederation: 1905 Population (2014 data): 4,121,700 Seats in the federal Parliament in Ottawa: 40 (34 MPs, 6 senators) Seats in the provincial Legislative Assembly in Edmonton: 87 MLAs
Saskatchewan 	Saskatchewan is the country's largest producer of grains and oilseeds. It also boasts the world's richest deposits of uranium and potash, used in fertilizer, and produces oil and natural gas. Regina is home to the training academy of the Royal Canadian Mounted Police, while Saskatoon, the largest city, is the headquarters of the provincial mining industry. Year of entry into Confederation: 1905 Population (2014 data): 1,125,400 Seats in the federal Parliament in Ottawa: 20 (14 MPs, 6 senators) Seats in the provincial Legislative Assembly in Regina: 58 MLAs
Manitoba 	Manitoba's economy is based on agriculture, mining, and hydroelectric power generation. The province's most populous city is Winnipeg, which is home to western Canada's largest francophone community. Manitoba is also an important centre of Ukrainian culture and has the largest proportion of Aboriginal people of any province. Year of entry into Confederation: 1870 Population (2014 data): 1,282,000 Seats in the federal Parliament in Ottawa: 20 (14 MPs, 6 senators) Seats in the provincial Legislative Assembly in Winnipeg: 57 MLAs
Ontario region	
Ontario 	More than one-third of Canadians live in Ontario. Toronto is Canada's largest city and its main financial centre. Many Ontarians work in the service, manufacturing, or agriculture industries. Founded by United Empire Loyalists, Ontario also has the largest French-speaking population outside of Quebec. Year of entry into Confederation: 1867 Population (2014 data): 13,678,700 Seats in the federal Parliament in Ottawa: 145 (121 MPs, 24 senators) Seats in the provincial Legislative Assembly in Toronto: 107 MPPs

continued

Quebec region

Quebec

More than three-quarters of Quebecers speak French as their first language. Quebec industries include forestry, energy, and mining, as well as cutting-edge industries such as pharmaceuticals and aeronautics. Quebec films, music, literary works, and cuisine have international stature. Montreal, Canada's second-largest city, has considerable cultural diversity.

Year of entry into Confederation: 1867

Population (2014 data): 8,214,700

Seats in the federal Parliament in Ottawa: 102 (78 MPs, 24 senators)

Seats in the provincial National Assembly in Quebec City: 125 MNAs

Atlantic Canada region

New Brunswick

New Brunswick was founded by the United Empire Loyalists and has a vibrant French cultural heritage. It is the only officially bilingual province. Forestry, agriculture, fisheries, mining, food processing, and tourism are the principal industries.

Year of entry into Confederation: 1867

Population (2014 data): 753,900

Seats in the federal Parliament in Ottawa: 20 (10 MPs, 10 senators)

Seats in the provincial Legislative Assembly in Fredericton: 49 MLAs

Nova Scotia

Nova Scotia's identity is linked to its Celtic and Gaelic traditions. Its economy features shipbuilding, fisheries, and shipping, as well as offshore oil and gas exploration, and has a history of coal mining, forestry, and agriculture. The capital of Halifax has played an important role in Atlantic trade and defence, and is home to Canada's largest naval base.

Year of entry into Confederation: 1867

Population (2014 data): 942,700

Seats in the federal Parliament in Ottawa: 21 (11 MPs, 10 senators)

Seats in the provincial House of Assembly in Halifax: 51 MLAs

Prince Edward Island

Prince Edward Island is the smallest province, known for its beaches, red soil, tourism, and agriculture, especially potatoes. It is connected to mainland Canada by the Confederation Bridge. The provincial capital is Charlottetown, where parts of the 1867 British North America Act and the 1992 Charlottetown Accord were negotiated.

Year of entry into Confederation: 1873

Population (2014 data): 146,300

Seats in the federal Parliament in Ottawa: 8 (4 MPs, 4 senators)

Seats in the provincial Legislative Assembly in Charlottetown: 27 MLAs

Newfoundland and Labrador

Newfoundland and Labrador is oldest colony of the British Empire and is known for its fisheries, coastal fishing villages, and distinct culture. Today, offshore oil and gas extraction contributes a substantial part of the provincial economy, as do the immense hydroelectric resources in Labrador.

Year of entry into Confederation: 1949

Population (2014 data): 527,000

Seats in the federal Parliament in Ottawa: 13 (7 MPs, 6 senators)

Seats in the provincial House of Assembly in St John's: 40 MHAs

The North	
Yukon 	Mining has been a significant part of the Yukon economy ever since thousands of miners arrived during the Gold Rush of the 1890s. Yukon holds the record for the coldest temperature ever recorded in Canada (-63°C). It is the only territory to use a political party system. Year of entry into Confederation: 1898 Population (2014 data): 36,500 Seats in the federal Parliament in Ottawa: 2 (1 MP, 1 senator) Seats in the territorial Legislative Assembly in Whitehorse: 19 MLAs
Northwest Territories 	The capital of Northwest Territories, Yellowknife, is called the "diamond capital of North America." More than half the population is Aboriginal (Dene, Inuit, and Métis). Year of entry into Confederation: 1870 Population (2014 data): 43,600 Seats in the federal Parliament in Ottawa: 2 (1 MP, 1 senator) Seats in the territorial Legislative Assembly in Yellowknife: 19 MLAs
Nunavut 	Nunavut was established in 1999 from the eastern part of Northwest Territories. The population is about 85 per cent Inuit, and Inuktitut is an official language and the first language in schools. Year of entry into Confederation: 1999 Population (2014 data): 33,600 Seats in the federal Parliament in Ottawa: 2 (1 MP, 1 senator) Seats in the territorial Legislative Assembly in Iqaluit: 19 MLAs

Source: Modified from: Government of Canada. "Discover Canada: The Rights and Responsibilities of Citizenship" (2013), www.cic.gc.ca/english/resources/publications/discover/section-13.asp. Flags: © iStock/mstay.

These regional images are grounded in our historical view, with the differences among them starker in stereotype than in reality. Indeed, when political scientists remove the regional lens from their analyses and examine Canadians without first dividing them by province of residence, other patterns emerge. Ailsa Henderson's study found that when it comes to their attitudes, voting behaviour, party preferences, political activity, and ideology, Canadians live in nine distinct communities. Many of these defy our traditional conception of regions as contiguous and provincially defined. According to her research, people in each of the following nine groups have more in common with each other than with members of the other eight communities:

1. Cosmopolitan Quebec
2. Suburban Toronto and Vancouver
3. Urban Canada
4. Rural and Mid-Northern Canada
5. Manufacturing Belt (including parts of Atlantic Canada, Quebec, and Ontario)
6. New France (including Quebec and parts of the Maritimes)
7. British North America (including parts of Atlantic Canada and Ontario)
8. Far North
9. Metropolitan Toronto

In recent years, federal political parties have similarly been moving away from approaching Canada as a collection of regions. Instead, the development of campaign

INSIDE CANADIAN POLITICS
How Does the Federal Government Define "Regions" in Canada?

There are many ways to identify Canadian regions, and even the federal government does not use a single definition. The federal public service routinely groups provinces together to assist with service delivery, policymaking, and resource distribution. Historically, the Government of Canada was guided by the constitution's model of allocating seats in the Senate. That organized provinces into four regions: the West (British Columbia, Alberta, Saskatchewan, Manitoba), Ontario, Quebec, and the Maritimes (New Brunswick, Prince Edward Island, Nova Scotia). The last of these regions was modified to become known as Atlantic Canada when Newfoundland joined Canada in 1949.

Over time, the growth of British Columbia (and the natural barrier of the Rocky Mountains) gave many an impression that it deserved to be distinguished from the Prairies. This crystalized in the mid-1990s, when the federal government made a commitment that it would veto any proposed constitutional amendment that did not have the support of each of *five* regions in Canada, namely British Columbia, the Prairies, Ontario, Quebec, and the Atlantic region. This unofficial regional grouping is a mechanism to achieve greater population symmetry and aligns provinces with similar political cultures. Since the territories lack provincial status, they are alternately grouped together as the North or else clustered with the region that is situated closest to them (e.g. BC and Yukon are sometimes known as the Pacific region).

Moreover, portfolios in the federal cabinet formally recognize a variety of regions. In late 2013, a number of federal ministers had regions of the country in their formal titles, including the minister of the Economic Development Agency of Canada for the regions of Quebec; the minister of the Canadian Northern Economic Development Agency; and the minister for the Arctic Council. There were also four ministers of state who were tasked with overseeing the Atlantic Canada Opportunities Agency, the Federal Economic Development Initiative for Northern Ontario, the Federal Economic Development Agency for Southern Ontario, and Western Economic Diversification. All such categorizations may be commonplace for federal politicians, public administration, and political science, and their meanings are likely familiar to most Canadians.

↻ The Act Respecting Constitutional Amendments (1996), which established five regions in Canada, is discussed on page 67 of Chapter 2, on the constitution.

THE LESSON
There is more than one way to define regional political boundaries in Canada.

VOX POP
Why do you think the federal government employs so many different definitions of "region"? What are the advantages and disadvantages of this approach?

promises and political communication has treated voters on the basis of whether they live in a city, in the suburbs, or in a rural area.

Politicking aside, the reality is that most Canadians identify most closely with their home community, in whatever manner they choose to define home. For some, it is their hometown, for others wherever they currently live. For still others, it is their province, or perhaps Canada as a whole. A survey commissioned by the Mowat Centre in 2010 found that the majority of Canadians thought of themselves foremost

TABLE 4.2 | National and Provincial Identity in Canada

Question: *People have different ways of defining themselves. Do you consider yourself to be . . .*	All	Atlantic	QC	ON	MB & SK	AB	BC & Territories
Canadian only	28%	20%	9%	43%	25%	29%	23%
Canadian first, but also province	31	34	17	32	42	39	37
Equally Canadian and province	21	30	19	19	22	20	27
Province first, but also Canadian	16	13	42	4	8	12	10
Province only	3	<1	11	<1	<1	<1	3
Don't know/no reply	2	2	2	3	3	2	2
(n)	(2697)	(300)	(407)	(1482)	(179)	(164)	(165)

Note: May not add to 100% due to rounding. Margins of error vary with sample sizes.

Source: Mowat Centre, "Canadians' Attitudes toward the Federation" (22 Feb. 2010), www.mowatcentre.ca/general/MCpoll_Attitudes_02-2010.pdf.

as Canadian, or else identified with Canada and their province (see Table 4.2). Few citizens identified exclusively with their province. Nevertheless, a sizeable number of Quebecers did say that they defined themselves only with their province, or first with Quebec and second with Canada. This contrasts sharply with neighbouring Ontario, where a majority of respondents said that they identified themselves as a Canadian only, or as Canadian first. And Atlantic Canada is not a monolith, given that the strength of nationalism and regional attachment fluctuates between and within provinces. To be certain, identification with one's region does not preclude identification with one's country, just as having many regional political cultures does not necessarily detract from Canada's having a broader political culture.

↻ The targeting of electors based on shared interests that transcend regional boundaries is discussed on page 347 of Chapter 9, on Canadian political parties.

VOX POP

How would you define the Canadian region you live in, or the Canadian region you're from? What distinguishes it from neighbouring regions? How would you describe its political culture?

THEY SAID IT

Prime Ministers on Canadian Identity

I am branded in Quebec as a traitor to the French, and in Ontario as a traitor to the English. . . . In Quebec I am attacked as an Imperialist, and in Ontario as an anti-Imperialist. I am neither. I am a Canadian.

—Prime Minister Wilfrid Laurier (1911)[8]

When Canadians are asked what difference there is between their country and the United States, they should answer in French.

—Prime Minister Lester B. Pearson (1967)[9]

Patrick Corrigan/Cagle.com

Do you think the political divide between urban and rural/suburban Canadians is now greater than differences between, say, eastern and western Canadians? What other prominent regional cleavages divide Canadians?

Types of Canadian Regionalism

Sectionalism, Nationalism, and Secessionism

Even if the evidence of unique regional political cultures is weaker than one might expect, the concept of regionalism remains strong in Canada. Regionalism is a form of ideology—a consistent set of beliefs involving a significant obstacle, primary agent, and overarching goal.[10] Led by people from their own territory, regionalists seek to gain greater influence over their own political affairs by dismantling or reforming institutions that subject them to rule by leaders from other parts of the country. In this way, it is common for regional leaders to make demands for more political power and resources, either in an effort to protect what they already have, or in an attempt to enhance their influence. Politicians often tap into citizens' feelings of economic and political inferiority when they attempt to mobilize these regional grievances. Inward protectionism and outward growth are commonplace in a federal system, because whenever one region advances an argument for favoured status, other regions are prompted to respond with their own demands.

Many shades of regionalism have existed throughout Canadian history, ranging from general forms of geographic solidarity to militant independence movements. The latter have been relatively rare and short-lived, including nineteenth-century movements like the Métis uprisings in Manitoba and Saskatchewan, and radical twentieth-century terrorist organizations like the Front de Libération du Québec (FLQ). Today, mainstream Canadian regionalism comes in three general strains, namely *sectionalism*, *nationalism*, and *secessionism* (Table 4.3).

Sectionalism

The first category is **sectionalism**: a strong sense of territorial cohesion combined with a significant sense of alienation from the rest of the country and/or the central government. Sectionalism often manifests itself in a desire for increased input into

> **sectionalism** An emotional connection with one's regional homeland, rather than with one's country.

TABLE 4.3 | Strains of Canadian Regionalism

Type of Regionalism	Political Grievances	Prominent Political Actors	Objectives
Western Canada			
Western alienation (sectionalism)	• limited control over natural resources • lack of free trade • preferential treatment of "Old Canada" • low representation in Parliament	Louis Riel William Aberhart Peter Lougheed Preston Manning Ralph Klein	• symmetrical federalism • Senate reform • free trade (internal and international)
Ontario			
sectionalism	• federal–provincial transfers • shift of influence to western Canada	Dalton McGuinty Kathleen Wynne	• reforms to equalization • per capita transfer formulas • representation by population in national institutions
Quebec			
autonomism, federalism (sectionalism, nationalism)	• centralization of the federation • federal unilateralism • vertical fiscal imbalance • dominance of English Canada	Jean Lesage Robert Bourassa Jean Charest	• decentralization • asymmetrical federalism • "distinct society"
separatism (nationalism, secessionism)	• lack of self-determination • lack of constitutional status for Quebec nation • federal unilateralism	René Lévesque Jacques Parizeau Lucien Bouchard	• "sovereignty–association" • secession from Canada
Atlantic Canada			
sectionalism	• representation by population • marginalization	Richard Hatfield Brian Tobin	• constitutional protections • harmonization
Newfoundland nationalism (nationalism, sectionalism)	• loss of distinctiveness in Confederation • lack of control over off-shore oil resources	Brian Peckford Danny Williams	• Atlantic Accord
The North			
sectionalism	• lack of political and economic control • marginalization	Dennis Fentie Stephen Kakfwi Floyd Roland Paul Okalik	• devolution • creation of Nunavut

BRIEFING NOTES

Regionalism and Populism

Regionalism is especially prominent when the people rally behind a populist leader who champions the cause. *Populism* is a grassroots political movement that aims to wrest power from government elites and bring it closer to the people.[11] Followers put enormous trust in populist leaders who may use rhetoric to stir sectionalist or nationalist sentiments, and advocate radical change in order to protect regional values. Populists typically promote nostalgia, criticize the system that has kept their "people" on the political periphery, and pledge an end to corruption among the political elites they seek to unseat. Some of Canada's most prominent premiers have been populists who have been fierce defenders of provincial interests, such as Alberta's Ralph Klein, Quebec's René Lévesque, and Newfoundland's Danny Williams.

national policymaking processes, for local autonomy, or for both. It may manifest itself as inward-looking and defensive, or outward-looking and proactive. Over time, sectionalism has taken different forms in different parts of the country. An example is the idea of "Atlantica," which would foster greater economic ties between Atlantic Canadian provinces and New England states.

Western alienation
Political discontent in areas west of Ontario, normally encompassing frustration with perceived political favouritism to areas east of Manitoba.

Sectionalism is perhaps strongest in the West, at least historically. Western alienation traces its roots to the nineteenth century, driven by a persistent sense of economic and political marginalization. Prominent economic disputes have erupted over John A. Macdonald's National Policy (1879), and the corresponding protectionist measures that erected tariffs and imposed higher business costs on Western farmers, and the National Energy Program (1980), which proposed to redistribute oil revenues from Alberta to the Eastern provinces. More recently, the sentiment behind Western alienation was captured in a 1990s Reform Party bumper sticker that read, "NO Kyoto, NO wheat board, NO gun registry," with reference to restrictive environmental, agricultural, and firearms policies established by the federal government that went against more conservative public opinion in the West.[12] Such policies reflected a central Canadian perception of what constitutes the Canadian interest, and have informed Westerners' frustrations with the federal system. These have included outrage over the federal government's awarding a multimillion-dollar contract for the maintenance of CF-18 aircraft to a Montreal firm in 1986, and thereby rejecting a superior bid from a Winnipeg firm, in a blatant example of favouring of Quebec interests.

Periodically, Westerners respond to such grievances by rejecting traditional parties. Federal–provincial disputes have spawned Western-based protest parties like the Progressives, Social Credit, and the Co-operative Commonwealth Federation (CCF). The most recent political movement led to the birth of the Reform Party of Canada. Under the slogan "the West wants in," Reformers opposed unique treatment for any regions or provinces, and pushed for Senate reform and other changes to ensure Western voices were more adequately represented in Ottawa. Eventually, like the

The Canadian Press/Ryan Remiorz

Most political observers would agree that the Conservative Party's victory in 2006, and subsequent majority government in 2011, marked the culmination of a decades-long push to incorporate Western voices and priorities in the federal government. What do you make of the future of Western alienation in Canada?

other political movements before it, Reform became shackled by the very system that it sought to change. In an effort to broaden its appeal beyond its Western base and form an alternative government, the party rebranded itself as the Canadian Alliance, before eventually merging with the PC Party in 2003 to form the Conservative Party of Canada. Among its lasting successes, Reform pressured the federal government to get deficit spending under control, and remodelled Canadian conservative politics as a pan-Canadian force. Most significantly, Stephen Harper, one of Reform's original senior members, went on to lead the new Conservative Party that replaced the Liberal government in 2006.

↺ Chapter 9 provides a summary of Western protest parties. See especially page 365.

The West is not uniformly or permanently disaffected, of course. The Reform Party was more popular in Alberta and BC than it was Saskatchewan and Manitoba, and Western alienation waned after the Conservative Party and Harper assumed power. Although born in Ontario, Prime Minister Harper represented an Alberta riding, and a large proportion of his caucus, if not cabinet, was from western Canada. Whether the 2015 election of a Liberal government headed by a prime minister from Quebec brings a return of Western alienation is a matter worth watching in the years to come.

And alienation is no longer the monopoly of the West, if it ever was. In Quebec, federalists have pushed for more autonomy and unique status for the province within Confederation. Atlantic Canadians have long advocated for protections to ensure that, despite their declining share of the national population, they remain well represented in federal institutions. This has included constitutionally entrenching the so-called "Senate floor rule," which ensures each province has no fewer MPs than it has senators, and the grandfather clause, which guarantees each province no fewer seats than it had in 1985. Atlantic Canadian sectionalism has also manifested itself, periodically, in calls for a formal Maritime Union—the kind originally contemplated by the Atlantic Fathers of Confederation. Formal merger of the three Maritime (or the four Atlantic) provinces remains conceptual given the political obstacles involved (e.g. where would the capital city be located, and how would provincial governments retain autonomy over important local matters like education and healthcare). Yet, through co-operation at the Council of Atlantic Premiers, the governments of New Brunswick, Nova Scotia, PEI, and Newfoundland and Labrador have taken significant steps toward harmonizing areas of public policy, including apprenticeship training. By combining forces, governments aim to remain economically competitive in the face of steep competition from neighbouring regions in Canada and the United States.

Meanwhile, for decades, Northerners pressured Ottawa for increased control over their own political and economic affairs. Their efforts culminated in the creation of a new territory (Nunavut, in 1999) and the transference of province-like powers through devolution. Yukon became the first northern territory to gain greater control over lands and resource management in 2003. A similar agreement-in-principle was signed between Ottawa and Northwest Territories a decade later. Long-term negotiations are in the early stages in Nunavut.

A form of sectionalism has also developed in Ontario, as political leaders there have begun to dispute the province's unequal treatment in Confederation, particularly in terms of federal–provincial fiscal transfers. Historically, Ontario-based regionalism has been among the weakest in Canada, with most Ontarians identifying themselves as part of the broader Canadian community. This was understandable, considering the province's dominant position in Confederation. Its economy was Canada's economic engine; its population dwarfed all others; and—as a consequence—its political influence in Ottawa was unparalleled. This sentiment has changed somewhat since 2008, when the province began its slight but perceptible economic, demographic, and political decline vis-à-vis western Canada. That year, Premier Dalton McGuinty promoted a so-called "fairness campaign" in an effort to focus the federal government's attention on Ontario's economic interests.

Nationalism

nationalism A unifying ideology among people who share a common homeland, ancestry, and language or culture.

Nationalism constitutes a second brand of regionalism in Canada. It is a highly politicized identity, often grounded in a romanticized ideal community. Citizens' nationalist sentiments are based on a palpable regional grievance, and a powerful connection with their homeland. These emotions are hardened by exposure to media and through personal experiences, and can be exploited by politicians. People identifying with a nation share a sense of political culture that is developed and reinforced through an often selective recall of history. This myth-building means that nationalism tends to involve invented traditions, exaggerated grievances, and an ignorance of self-culpabilities. It can exacerbate feelings of economic oppression and may identify scapegoats who are to blame for holding the nation back from reaching its full and rightful potential. This can

THEY SAID IT

Ontario Premier Dalton McGuinty's "Fairness Campaign"

Ontario premier Dalton McGuinty's media remarks during the 2008 federal election campaign were typical of what premiers in other provinces might say, but was quite unusual for an Ontarian:

> Where do you stand on fairness for Ontario? Are you going to address employment insurance for Ontarians? Are you going to give us the same amount of money for healthcare that other Canadians get? Are you going to give us the same amount of money for our infrastructure? How about a regional economic development plan? . . . The manufacturing sector of Ontario is having the stuffing kicked out of it. This is an opportunity for Ontarians to come together and stand together on this issue.[13]

lead to in-group and out-group dynamics, where those belonging to the nation share a sense of togetherness and unity against a common foe. The cause of nationalism is often championed by charismatic leaders who citizens feel epitomize their identity and concerns. This sense of pride can motivate the oppressed to rise up and achieve political gains. However, public emotions can also be manipulated through propaganda, leading to an exaggerated sense of victimhood, irrational anger, and civic unrest.

BRIEFING NOTES

Nationalism in Canada

Outsiders can be forgiven for mistakenly conflating the terms *nation* and *country*, or *nationality* and *citizenship*, when it comes to describing Canadian politics. Globally, most nations are nation-states, with the dominant ethnic community commanding sovereignty over its own territory. Countries like Germany, France, and Spain may be poly-ethnic, containing a variety of different ethnic communities, but political power within these countries is wielded by a single, predominant ethnic group (Germans, the French, and Spaniards, respectively). Even in highly multicultural countries like the United States, patriotism is strong enough to forge a solid sense of nationalism.

By contrast, Canada is both a poly-ethnic and a multi-national state. This means there is no pan-Canadian form of nationalism, but rather several different forms of nationalism within a single state. It is improper, then, to refer to a Canadian nation-state or even a Canadian nationality. Such references confuse political nationalism with economic nationalism, which is the activation of a national identity foremost to advance an economic, rather than ethnic, agenda. Instead, nations in Canada refer to a select group of regional factions, chiefly in Quebec and Aboriginal communities, but also in Newfoundland and Labrador. As discussed in Chapter 14, on Canada's place in the world, the appropriate term for pride in being Canadian is *patriotism*.

Unlike other forms of group identity, the members of a nation are considered to share a common ethnic background, to have ties to an ancestral homeland, and to possess a strong sense of self-determination. Nationalists may work together to achieve more political autonomy and even outright independence. Within Canada, at least three groups have staked claim to being nations: the Québécois, Newfoundlanders, and First Nations.

While, by definition, nationalism requires a homeland, its reach is not necessarily confined to a geographic area. First Nations members reside throughout the country, which is one of the reasons they have experienced difficulties mobilizing. Similarly, Quebecers or Newfoundlanders who leave their home provinces may still self-identify as such. Residents within those provinces may claim that such labels are reserved for those who are born on provincial soil and embody a political culture that can only be inherited, not learned.[14] This sense of ethnic nationalism can marginalize outsiders, reinforced with mildly derogatory terms such as "Anglos," "mainlanders," or "come from away."

Secessionism

secessionism A widely held sentiment that a province or territory should leave the Canadian federation.

The third form of Canadian regionalism is secessionism. As its name suggests, the concept entails a desire to secede, or separate, from Canada entirely. Separatists have existed throughout Canada, notably forming political parties in the West (e.g. Western Canada Concept and Alberta First) and governments in Quebec under the Parti Québécois. In that province, separatists may be motivated by a combination of rationalist, economic, political, or ethnic/nationalist arguments. Secessionism tends to flare up when there is a regional grievance that is interpreted as an affront to a national or regional identity; in response to other provinces gaining more power; and/or in the presence of a populist leader.

Regionalism in Quebec

↺ The rise of Western alienation during the mega-constitutional period contributed to the failure of the Charlottetown Accord. See pages 64–5 of Chapter 2, on the constitution.

These three forms of regionalism—sectionalism, nationalism, and secessionism—interact with one another. During the mega-constitutional period, Western alienation increased in response to the success of Quebec nationalism. By the same token, the political and economic rise of the West has created room for regional resentment in other parts of the country, including Ontario. Quebec is an excellent case study of all three variants of regionalism in Canada. The province's history illustrates the tensions that often develop between provincial and federal governments when it comes to defining and meeting the demands of regionalists across the country.

The Growth of Quebec Nationalism from Confederation to the Quiet Revolution

Quebec has always enjoyed a distinct character within Canada. Since Quebec's earliest days as a French colony, its politics has featured a unique legal structure, the *Code Civil* as opposed to English common law. Its dominant linguistic, cultural, and religious community stands in sharp contrast to the mainstream Canadian cultural community outside the province. Indeed, the differences between Lower Canada

THEY SAID IT

Canadian Prime Ministers on Regionalism

If some countries have too much history, we have too much geography.

—Prime Minister William Lyon Mackenzie King (1936)[15]

The politics of federalism are the politics of accommodation on the part of the governments and, it needs to be said, of people. . . . "Unity" exists in so far as we are inspired by like ideals, and pursue these in common and in concert. "Unity," for us in Canada, cannot mean "sameness."

—Prime Minister Pierre Elliott Trudeau (1976)[16]

(now Quebec) and Upper Canada (now Ontario) were so stark that early British North American institutions were developed to accommodate the diversity, through divided legislatures and special majority voting rules. This approach to treating Canada as having been formed by two founding nations is often resurrected as a basis for giving Quebec unique treatment within Confederation.

Throughout most of the first century of Confederation, Quebec's distinct nature manifested itself in an inward-looking, protectionist brand of sectionalism. The ultra-conservative Union Nationale provincial governments of Maurice Duplessis (1936–9, 1944–59) embodied this image. Premier Duplessis sought to protect Quebec's autonomy and that of the Catholic Church from encroachment by Ottawa and the rest of Canada. Like most of his predecessors, Duplessis was a champion of the province's rights within Confederation, and he had little interest in expanding Quebec's influence on the pan-Canadian stage. However, it soon became evident that a province could not insulate itself from global economic and cultural forces. Evidence that French culture needed protection from English continentalism began to mount.

BRIEFING NOTES

Quebecers and the Québécois

Outsiders often struggle to find the correct terms to refer to the people of Quebec. The term *Quebecer* is used to describe a resident of the province, regardless of the individual's language of choice. French-speaking residents of Quebec are often referred to as Québécois or Québécoise, depending on their gender. When used collectively, the term Québécois has also referred to the cultural nation of self-identifying individuals based in Quebec.

For many French-speaking Canadians, the conscription crisis of 1917–18 was the defining moment of World War I. It culminated in the Easter riots of 1918, when thousands of anti-war protesters occupied the streets of Quebec City for four days, prompting Prime Minister Borden to invoke the War Measures Act to deploy soldiers—mostly from Ontario—to disperse the crowds. As many as five of the rioters were killed. Since that time, Quebecers have remained among the least supportive Canadians when it comes to armed conflict, most recently with respect to joining the US-led invasion of Iraq and Canada's frontline engagement in Afghanistan and in the fight against ISIL. What do you think explains Quebecers' relatively high level of opposition toward war—historically and today—and what impact does this level of opposition have on Canadian foreign policy?

Amid the global nation-building era immediately following World War II, some francophones in Quebec began adopting the term *Québécois* to express their unique cultural and political position—not just within Canada, but within the world at large. By the 1960s, the movement had become known as the Quiet Revolution, with Quebec nationalists elevating the newly named National Assembly above the traditionally dominant Catholic Church as the primary source of power and influence within the province. Until that time, Quebec's identity struggle was defensive and protectionist, and coloured by the conservative nature of the church. The Quiet Revolution marked the dawn of a new era in which Quebec would take active measures to strengthen its identity and position within Confederation. Quebec politicians began demanding more local political and economic control over government affairs so that Quebec could become *maîtres chez nous*, "masters of our own house." Both secessionists and nationalists united under a common "sovereignist" (or "separatist") banner, seeking to establish an autonomous state for Quebec. The separatist movement was marred by the radicalism of the Front de Libération du Québec (FLQ), which mounted a campaign of terror in Quebec in the 1960s, culminating in the October Crisis of 1970.

Thus, two branches of the nationalist movement evolved in Quebec, with federalists (seeking greater autonomy for the provincial government within Confederation) on one side and sovereignists (bent on achieving independence from Canada) on the other. Under premiers like Jean Lesage (1960–6) and Robert Bourassa (1970–6; 1985–94), the Quebec Liberal Party emerged as a champion of the federalist cause. Mainstream sovereignists rallied behind the upstart Parti Québécois (PQ), which eventually formed the provincial government in 1976 under Premier René Lévesque (1976–85).

As mentioned in Chapter 2, one of the legacies of the Lévesque government was the passage of Bill 101, the Charter of the French Language, which detailed ways

Quiet Revolution An early 1960s modernizing movement in Quebec, geared toward a stronger provincial government and outward nationalism.

↻ See pages 560–61 of Chapter 14, on Canada's place in the world, for a description of the October Crisis. The crisis is discussed in the context of the War Measures Act on page 258 of Chapter 7, on the justice system.

BRIEFING NOTES

The Charters in Quebec

Outsiders often confuse the many "charters" that exist in Quebec politics, many of which have proven controversial.

There is the Charter of the French Language (*La charte de la langue française*, or Bill 101), which was passed by the Lévesque government in 1977 as a legislative expression of the province's language policies. The provincial government also has its own Charter of Human Rights and Freedoms (*Charte des droits et libertés de la personne*). Passed by the Bourassa government in 1976, this statute serves as the province's bill of rights. Lastly, former PQ premier Pauline Marois introduced a Charter of Quebec Values (*Charte de la laïcité* or *Charte des valeurs québécoises*) in 2013—a bill that would have created a Quebec-specific definition of reasonable accommodation and secular multiculturalism. It died on the order paper with the PQ's loss in the spring 2014 provincial election, but not before stirring up considerable debate about Quebec's position regarding immigration and multiculturalism.

Each of these charters is distinct from the Canadian Charter of Rights and Freedoms (part of the Constitution Act, 1982), and all of them of them are subject to its provisions.

that the state would use its resources to protect and promote the French language in Quebec. This included enforcing French as the normal language of instruction in schools, commerce, and government. For instance, the Quebec government has reminded businesses that it is their responsibility to ensure that workers in the service industry greet shop visitors in French, not English. Not surprisingly, Bill 101 has led to controversies. Court challenges regarding the portion of the law prohibiting English-only signs contributed to the use of the notwithstanding clause and, in part, to the failure of the Meech Lake Accord. Since that time, businesses using English names have been forced to comply with the revised legislation, such as the international restaurant chain McDonald's being required to remove the apostrophe from its signage in Quebec.

Federalists and Sovereignists during the Mega-constitutional Era

Between 1980 and 1995, PQ governments held two provincial referendums that pitted federalists against separatists. The first referendum, held in 1980, sought a mandate to negotiate sovereignty–association with Canada, promising another referendum on the resulting agreement. During the referendum campaign, Prime Minister Pierre Trudeau promised Quebec nationalists a renewed place for Quebec in Confederation, provided they voted against the referendum's proposal. The pledge proved to be part of a victory for the Non side, as 59.6 per cent of Quebecers voted against the notion of sovereignty–association. But this win was tainted by the reality that four in ten Quebecers voted to take steps toward withdrawing from Confederation.

Few nationalists viewed the subsequent constitutional negotiations as securing sufficient autonomy for Quebec, however. Premier Lévesque objected to the final terms of the patriation bargain, which was forged without his input in what became known as "the Night of the Long Knives." Despite Quebec's disapproval, the Constitution Act, 1982, was given Royal Assent, and the Supreme Court ruled that the constitutional settlement was valid and applied to Quebec.

The constitutional protections accorded to English and French languages in the new Charter of Rights and Freedoms, along with the federal government policy of official bilingualism, went some way to addressing concerns that francophones were marginalized in Canadian society. Henceforth, Quebec politicians could no longer claim that they were the only defenders of the French identity in Canada. As Prime Minister Trudeau put it, "Quebec cannot say it alone speaks for French Canadians. . . . Nobody will be able to say, 'I need more power because I speak for the French-Canadian nation."[17] This was, however, of little value to Quebec nationalists, who viewed the Quebec government as the only legitimate representative of French-speaking Quebecers.

After the constitution was patriated against the Quebec government's wishes in 1982, a changing of the guard in Ottawa (1984) and in Quebec City (1985) brought Progressive Conservative prime minister Brian Mulroney and Liberal premier Robert Bourassa to power. The two men found common ground in seeking to keep Quebec's soft nationalists within the federalist camp. Together, they set about crafting a constitutional amendment package that culminated in the Meech Lake Accord. As detailed in Chapter 2, the Accord was signed by all 11 first ministers in 1987, and passed first by the Quebec National Assembly in June of that year. It proposed to

↺ Quebec's use of the notwithstanding clause in response to a constitutional challenge of Bill 101 is discussed in the ICP box on page 72 of Chapter 2, on the constitution.

sovereignty–association A proposed legal arrangement whereby Quebec would be politically independent but maintain economic ties with Canada.

↺ The Night of the Long Knives is discussed on page 60 of Chapter 2, on the Constitution.

Meech Lake Accord A failed constitutional accord in the late 1980s that would have recognized Quebec as a "distinct society."

BEFORE...   APRÈS...

Graeme MacKay

Quebecers' support (or tolerance) for the province's so-called "language police" was tested in 2013, when an Italian restaurant complained that it had been advised to translate the word "pasta" into French on its menus. The incident attracted international attention and led to the resignation of the head of the Office Québécois de la Langue Française. Many businesses go along with Bill 101, including Tim Hortons, which removed the apostrophe from its signage across the country to comply with the Quebec law. Why do you think some people thought the "language police" were going too far when they required the Italian restaurant to change its menus? Why do you suppose some people thought it was a good idea in the first place?

---

constitutionally recognize Quebec as a "distinct society," while securing for all provinces greater autonomy and input into federal appointments. The amendment process foundered, however. Changes in government and rising public opposition transpired to keep legislatures in Manitoba and Newfoundland from passing the accord within the three-year deadline. The legal fuzziness of those two polarizing words—*distinct society*—became both a compelling reason to support the Accord, and ultimately its undoing.

Prominent Quebec nationalists interpreted the failure of the Meech Lake Accord as a sign of English Canada's rejection of Quebec's distinct status within Confederation. Popular support for the Bourassa government waned; disaffected nationalists in the Mulroney government, led by the prime minister's Quebec lieutenant, Lucien Bouchard, aligned with some opposition Liberal MPs to form their own party, the Bloc Québécois. These events, plus the rise of the Reform Party in western Canada, helped stall passage of a second constitutional reform package, the Charlottetown Accord, in 1992. The Charlottetown Accord, too, would have recognized Quebec's distinctiveness. However, the provision was couched in a much

Charlottetown Accord
A failed accord in the early 1990s that proposed to renew the constitution, but was defeated in a national referendum.

↻ The Bloc Québécois is discussed in the context of protest parties, on page 365 of Chapter 9.

broader framework that included a variety of other democratic principles, among them gender equality and Aboriginal self-government. Once again, all first ministers endorsed the accord. Yet it failed to receive a majority of popular support in the Canada-wide referendum, endorsed by voters in only 5 of the 12 provinces and territories (New Brunswick, Newfoundland, Ontario, PEI, and Northwest Territories). For their part, Quebecers voted 57 per cent to 43 per cent in opposition to the Charlottetown Accord. This second failed attempt was interpreted as a rejection of political elites and a warning to future prime ministers not to reopen the constitutional debate.

Changes in government once again ensued in Ottawa (1993) and Quebec City (1994), bringing Liberal Jean Chrétien and PQ member Jacques Parizeau to power as prime minister and Quebec premier, respectively. The latter moved swiftly to hold Quebec's second sovereignty referendum, in October 1995. Early polls demonstrated a substantial lead for the federalist side, but momentum shifted quickly toward the sovereignists once Bloc Québécois leader Lucien Bouchard assumed full leadership of the "oui" campaign. Some federalists worried that the PQ government was intentionally using a murky question that included a reference to an offer "for a new Economic and Political Partnership" with Canada. Moreover, Quebecers who were concerned about the economic implications of an independent Quebec were assured by some that they would continue to have access to a Canadian passport, would use Canadian currency, and would be protected by the Canadian military. Meanwhile, Prime Minister Chrétien and the federal Liberals kept their distance, not wanting to be seen to meddle in provincial affairs. In the closing days, opinion polls revealed a slim lead for the sovereignists, prompting an estimated 100,000 Canadians from outside Quebec to converge on Montreal to take part in a unity rally. With all ballots counted, the "non" side won by just over 50,000 votes (50.6 percent against sovereignty-association, but 49.4 percent for).

After the Referendums: Quebec Nationalism since 1995

In the aftermath of the second referendum vote, Premier Parizeau blamed federal money and "the ethnic vote" for the referendum's defeat. He stepped down as PQ leader and premier, and was succeeded by Bouchard, who vacated the leadership of the Bloc to take the position. While the PQ won the subsequent provincial election in 1998, support for sovereignty waned and the party avoided holding another referendum until so-called "winning conditions" re-emerged. By this point, political observers tended to no longer exclusively contrast the ambitions of federalists with those of sovereignists, the term preferred by Quebec nationalists. Instead, sovereignists were now understood to comprise a coalition of hardline secessionists and soft nationalists, just as federalists comprised people loyal to the status quo and sectionalists who identified as Canadian but wanted more for Quebec within Confederation. Sovereignists continued to push for another referendum, while federalists argued that Quebecers were tired of the secession question. Both continued to joust for the hearts and minds of the soft nationalists who felt that Quebec deserved unique status, but one that did not necessarily warrant separating from the Canadian federation.

In Ottawa, the Chrétien Liberals pursued a two-pronged, non-constitutional response to the 1995 referendum results. "Plan A" involved reaching out to Quebecers in an attempt to convince soft nationalists (and soft federalists, for that matter) that Canada was stronger with Quebec and vice versa. This carrot approach included providing Quebec with a veto over future constitutional amendments (the Act Respecting Constitutional Amendments), and was supported by the creation of the Sponsorship Program, an advertising campaign designed to increase the salience and popularity of the federal government in Quebec. While "Plan A" was designed to appease Quebecers, "Plan B" was a concurrent policy that was developed to address the frustrations of federalists throughout the country.

"Plan B" (the stick) involved clarifying the terms and conditions under which a province could leave Confederation. Through the *Secession* reference (1998), the federal government asked the Supreme Court its opinion on the issue. The Court concluded that provinces could not unilaterally secede under Canadian or international law, and that Parliament did have the power to determine what constituted a clear referendum question. On the other hand, the Court found that the Government of Canada would be obligated to enter into negotiations with any province should a clear majority of its electorate vote in favour of independence. Based partly on this ruling, the federal government passed the Clarity Act in 2000, through which Parliament gave itself the authority to determine what constituted a clear majority and clear question in any secession referendum, as well as the terms of any subsequent negotiations on separation. In particular, the Clarity Act empowers Parliament to vote on whether a question is sufficiently clear before the referendum vote is held.

Clarity Act Federal legislation passed in 2000 that sets out the terms for the federal government to deal with a province proposing to secede.

The Government of Quebec responded with its own legislation. In 2000, the province's National Assembly passed Bill 99, An Act Respecting the Exercise of the Fundamental Rights and Prerogatives of the Québec People and the Québec State. Predictably, its terms proclaimed Quebec's right to declare self-determination, stating that "No other parliament or government may reduce the powers, authority, sovereignty or legitimacy of the National Assembly, or impose constraint on the democratic will of the Quebec people to determine its own future." Whereas the Clarity Act authorizes the House of Commons to decide what constitutes a sufficient majority of Quebecers voting to support a sovereignty proposal, Bill 99 states that a majority vote of "fifty per cent of the valid votes cast plus one" in a referendum is sufficient to identify which side is the winner. Since then, intergovernmental wrangling over secession has been mostly dormant, though it has periodically flared up. For instance, while the national media was paying attention to the 2013 Speech from the Throne, the attorney general of Canada quietly filed an intervention in Quebec Superior Court to participate in a legal case that challenges the legality of Bill 99. This court case is still ongoing at the time of writing.

The next significant flash of Quebec nationalism ignited in 2006, when the Bloc Québécois took steps to recognize "Quebecers as a nation" in the House of Commons. If passed, the draft Bloc resolution would likely have had no legal force, though we cannot be certain. Instead, the move was intended to provoke federalist parties to vote against it, giving sovereignists a reason to reignite their calls for independence. Federalist parties were put in a difficult position, as voting in favour of the motion could have sparked regionalist reactions in the rest of the country, while voting against it could have been viewed as yet another rejection of Quebec's unique status in Confederation.

In what has come to be seen as a smart tactical move, then prime minister Stephen Harper introduced his own motion before the Bloc resolution reached the floor,

INSIDE CANADIAN POLITICS
Was the Wording of the Quebec Sovereignty Referendum Questions Appropriate?

The wording of the 1980 and 1995 Quebec sovereignty referendum questions has been a source of much debate, particularly regarding whether or not the questions are sufficiently clear to produce a response that accurately represents the will of the voter.

1980 Referendum Question
The Government of Quebec has made public its proposal to negotiate a new agreement with the rest of Canada, based on the equality of nations; this agreement would enable Quebec to acquire the exclusive power to make its laws, levy its taxes and establish relations abroad—in other words, sovereignty—and at the same time to maintain with Canada an economic association including a common currency; any change in political status resulting from these negotiations will only be implemented with popular approval through another referendum; on these terms, do you give the Government of Quebec the mandate to negotiate the proposed agreement between Quebec and Canada?

1995 Referendum Question
Do you agree that Quebec should become sovereign after having made a formal offer to Canada for a new economic and political partnership within the scope of the bill respecting the future of Quebec and of the agreement signed on June 12, 1995?

VOX POP

Do you think the questions are clear enough to allow Quebecers to make an informed choice between the status quo and a new state of affairs? In what way (if any) could they be improved? How do they compare with the referendum question put before Scottish voters in 2014, which asked: "Should Scotland be an independent country?"

Quebec nation motion
A non-binding federal motion passed in 2006 that recognized the unique character of the Québécois.

sponsorship scandal
An affair in which Liberal advertising agencies received public funds for work that was never performed.

calling upon the House of Commons to recognize "that the Québécois form a nation within a united Canada." The Quebec nation motion passed the minority legislature with the unanimous support of Conservative, Bloc Québécois, and NDP members in attendance; the Liberals were divided on the motion. Several western Canadian Conservative MPs abstained, and the vote cost the Conservative government their intergovernmental affairs minister, who also abstained and resigned on the principle of cabinet solidarity. The political symbolism of recognizing the Québécois as an ethnic community in this manner has muted calls for unique status.

Since reaching 49 per cent in 1995, and 55 per cent during the sponsorship scandal a decade later, support for Quebec sovereignty was mired at 34 per cent in May 2013. While the PQ returned to power in 2012, it did so without immediate plans for a referendum on the issue—the first time sovereignty was not an explicit part of the party's agenda while in power. The Parti Québécois was ousted by the Liberals in 2014, and many insiders attributed the loss in part to the fiery, separatist rhetoric of PQ star candidate Pierre Karl Péladeau, whose fist-pumping, unscripted promise to make Quebec a country was unpopular among a Quebec electorate weary of the separation debate. Nevertheless, support for sovereignty stood at 41 percent in April 2015.[18]

Over the course of these three, relatively tumultuous decades, institutions have been developed to solidify the unique status of Quebec within Confederation. At the same time, consensus has built, both within and outside the province, that Quebec warrants special treatment. Although *not* enshrined in the constitution, and while falling short of some nationalists' ambitions, a number of advancements have been made on all five demands originally articulated by Premier Bourassa in the leadup to the Meech Lake Accord (see Table 4.4).

Many of these advancements were made in a *symmetrical* fashion, such that guarantees to Quebec were also offered to other provinces. This, in itself, raised criticism among some Quebec nationalists, who have sought *asymmetrical* treatment of Quebec as a unique province (and nation) within Confederation. This final point illustrates the tensions that often develop between competing types of regionalism in Canada: whereas nationalists may seek a unique status for their province or region within Canada, sectionalists may rally against such treatment, evoking principles of provincial equality. The result may see some nationalists pursuing secessionism as the only means to achieve sufficient control over their own affairs.

Today, four-fifths of Quebecers speak French as a first language (see Table 4.5), but the focus of the national identity debate has shifted. Allophones (Canadians who speak neither official language) comprise a growing proportion of the Canadian population, including Quebec's. Canada's constitutional protections and multiculturalism policies have afforded these political minorities the freedom to maintain their own ethnic and political cultures, and they are changing the fabric of Canadian society.

allophones Canadians whose dominant language is neither French nor English.

TABLE 4.4 | Progress on Quebec's Five Demands for Constitutional Renewal

Bourassa's Five Demands (1985)	Advancements Since 1985
Recognition of Quebec as a distinct society	• 1997 – all premiers outside Quebec endorse the Calgary Declaration, a non-binding accord recognizing that "the unique character of Quebec society, including its French-speaking majority, its culture and its tradition of civil law, is fundamental to the well-being of Canada. Consequently, the legislature and Government of Quebec have a role to protect and develop the unique character of Quebec society within Canada." • 2006 – the House of Commons votes overwhelmingly in favour of a motion recognizing "that the Québécois form a nation within a united Canada."
Right of veto for Quebec over constitutional amendments	• 1996 – the federal government passes An Act Respecting Constitutional Amendments, giving Quebec (and other regions) vetoes over most changes to the Canadian constitution.
Limits on the federal spending power	• 1999 – the federal government signs on to the Social Union Framework Agreement, which, with other provisions, places limits on the use of the federal spending power. • 2006–10 – under the mantra of "open federalism," the federal government promises legislation to restrict the use of the federal spending power and allow provinces to opt out of new federal programs with compensation. (At the time of writing, this legislation had not been introduced.)
Quebec input into appointing senators and Supreme Court justices	• 2014 – the Supreme Court rejects efforts by Ottawa to initiate Senate reform without following the 7/50 amendment formula.
Increased provincial powers over immigration	• 1991 – the Canada–Quebec Accord enhances the Quebec government's control over immigration to the province.

TABLE 4.5 | Canadians' Home Language, by Province and Territory (percentage of total population)

	Language Spoken Most Often at Home		
	English	French	Other
British Columbia	80.5	0.4	1.5
Alberta	80.5	0.6	1.1
Saskatchewan	92.1	0.4	5.8
Manitoba	84.4	1.5	10.5
Ontario	78.9	2.2	14.3
Quebec	9.8	79.9	7.1
Nova Scotia	95.4	1.8	2.1
New Brunswick	69.2	28.4	1.3
Prince Edward Island	95.5	1.7	2.1
Newfoundland and Labrador	98.5	0.2	0.9
Yukon	92.2	3.7	2.4
Northwest Territories	88.9	1.3	8.8
Nunavut	45.4	0.7	5.3

Note: Percentages do not add up to 100 because some Canadians speak more than one language at home. Figures are rounded.

Source: Statistics Canada, "Population by home language, by province and territory" (2011 Census), www.statcan .gc.ca/tables-tableaux/sum-som/l01/cst01/demo61a-eng.htm.

↻ The policy of reasonable accommodation is discussed at length in Chapter 13, on diversity and representation. See especially pages 511–16.

In 2013, the Parti Québécois government, led by Premier Pauline Marois, responded to concerns about the changing ethnic demographics of Quebec society by proposing a Charter of Quebec Values. If adopted, such legislation would have banned provincial public servants from wearing visible religious symbols, including burkas, hijabs, kirpans, turbans, and large crucifixes. This followed the internal debate prompted by the "Consultation Commission on Accommodation Practices Related to Cultural Differences" that explored the topic of reasonable accommodation of allophones in Quebec society (see Chapter 13). Ultimately, the Charter of Quebec Values was never passed into law, as the PQ government was defeated and the Liberals returned to power in 2014. Subsequently, the Quebec Liberal government introduced a watered-down version of the PQ's cultural neutrality policy, preserving some room for accommodation of religious freedoms.

The Evolution of Regionalism in Canada

As with most political phenomena, understanding regionalism in Canada today requires an in-depth understanding of the country's history. The roots of regionalism run deep, grounded in a series of structural factors and nurtured over time by a series of key political actors and patterns of behaviour. Geography is, obviously, one of the structural factors contributing to regionalism. The placement of a particular region at the *core* (centre) or *periphery* (outskirts) of the country, and its endowment with either abundant or scarce natural resources, may explain a lot in terms of its level of alienation. Demography also plays a large role in determining the shape of regionalism in Canada. Each region features its own cultural (linguistic, religious, ethnic) makeup, not to mention the size of its Aboriginal, immigrant, senior, or youth constituencies. This diversity helps define the level of internal unity and external uniqueness among Canada's various regions. Formal political institutions like federalism, the constitution, the first-past-the-post electoral system, regional premiers' forums, and so on also provide the structural foundations for Canadian regionalism. At the same time, patterns of socialization, political competition, and elite (non)accommodation all contribute to the intensity and longevity of regionalism in Canada. In this vein, it is important to distinguish between the forces that contributed to the *origins* of regionalism in Canada (see Figure 4.1) and the forces that have helped to *sustain* it over the past century-and-a-half.

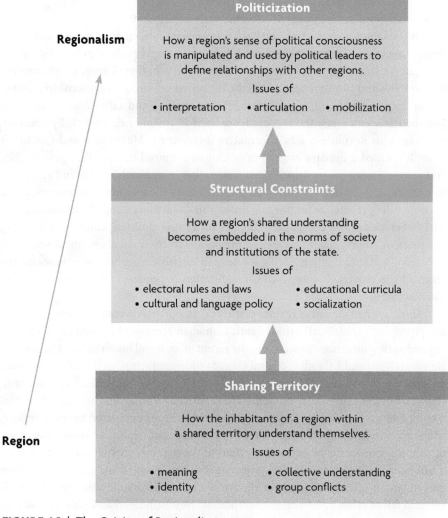

FIGURE 4.1 | The Origins of Regionalism

Source: Adapted from Figure 2.1 in Harry Hiller, "Region as a Social Construction," in *Regionalism and Party Politics in Canada*, ed. Lisa Young and Keith Archer (Don Mills, ON: Oxford University Press, 2002), 36.

Origins of Regionalism

Nelson Wiseman (2007) points to *settlement patterns*, *formative events*, and *economic staples* as three interrelated factors that laid the foundations of regionalism in Canada.

In the first instance, each region in Canada has been shaped by its own unique pattern of immigration. Earlier settlers have had a particularly strong impact on the political cultures of their new communities. They are fragments of their native countries, bringing with them the ideologies and institutions of their old homelands. The first immigrant wave, from France up to 1760, helped establish a quasi-feudal conservative culture in Quebec and Acadia. Decades later, United Empire Loyalists from the United States arrived in the Maritimes and Ontario, cementing the regions' penchant for British political institutions and outlook. British immigration would continue throughout the next two centuries, first imprinting Ontario and the Maritimes with a liberal bent, then fostering labour–socialist leanings on the Prairies. Western American settlers pushed northward in the early twentieth century, making liberal-populists a founding fragment of Alberta's early population.

By the same token, each region has undergone its own set of formative and transformative events that have helped send it down a unique path of political development. In Newfoundland and Labrador, debates over whether to enter Confederation (in the 1860s and 1940s) reflect and shape the province's unique relationship with the rest of Canada. For them, Confederation was a choice—and a divisive one, at that—and their late entry sets them apart from their Maritime neighbours. By contrast, the American Revolution was a formative moment for Maritimers and Ontarians alike: it sparked a massive migration of United Empire Loyalists that gave the liberal democracies of these two regions a so-called "tory touch" not found elsewhere in Canada. This "touch" involved a more collectivist vision of conservatism, and a corresponding reverence for law and order, the social fabric, and the monarchy. The Riel Rebellions had a comparable impact on Prairie political culture, embedding the roots of Aboriginal and Western alienation in the region's political soil. And the arrival of the Canadian Pacific Railway to British Columbia not only sealed the terms of the province's entry into Confederation but opened BC as the gateway to Canada's west.

↻ See the discussion of ideology on page 14 of Chapter 1 for an explanation of toryism.

Third, each of Canada's regions features a unique endowment of natural resources, or *staples*.[19] Historically, the Atlantic Canadian economy has been based on fishing and agriculture, notwithstanding the recent offshore oil boom in Nova Scotia and Newfoundland and Labrador; central Canada on manufacturing; that of the Prairies, on agriculture and energy; and that of BC, on forests and minerals.[20] According to staples theory, regions whose economies have thrived on boom and bust commodities, like oil and gas, tend to develop more capitalist cultures compared to those regions whose economies are built on less lucrative and more vulnerable resources, like wheat or fish. Regions in the latter category tend to develop a higher level of expectation, if not penchant or reverence, for government intervention in the economy, because government is often seen as one of the few sources of economic security. The recent rise and fall of offshore oil and gas revenues in Newfoundland and Labrador, and to a lesser extent in Nova Scotia, will test the lasting impact of the region's historically insecure staples on its regional culture. To date, spending demands by residents have outstripped the revenues generated from those non-renewable resources.

BRIEFING NOTES

When Natural Resource Disputes Aggravate Canadian Regionalism

From time to time, rivalries can develop within regions. This is particularly evident when neighbouring provinces have competing ambitions in the energy sector. The ongoing feud between Newfoundland and Quebec is a case in point. While bad blood between the provinces began with territorial disputes over Labrador, their energy animosity dates back to a 1969 agreement that allowed Quebec to acquire power from a new Churchill Falls hydroelectricity station at cut-rate prices. Attempts by Newfoundland to reopen the deal have failed, meaning that the province is obligated to continue to sell power to Quebec at well under market value through 2041.[21] So sour is the relationship that, as Newfoundland continues to develop new hydro projects, the two provinces remain unable to come to terms on an agreement to route energy exports through Quebec to the United States, and Quebec challenges any federal government investment in Newfoundland hydro as preferential treatment. A similar, though far briefer and less heated, dispute erupted between Alberta and British Columbia in 2013, as discussed in the ICP box in Chapter 3 (pages 94–5).

VOX POP

Why do you suppose energy politics are particularly divisive in Canada?

Persistence of Regionalism

These historical factors go only so far in explaining the persistence of regionalism in Canada today. Regions do not simply freeze into place following settlement, though this was the prevailing theory of regionalism, presented by American political scientist Louis Hartz in the mid-twentieth century. How is it that events, institutions, and economics that originated with settlers over a century ago continue to exert influence on Canadian politics? How does regionalism continue to define Canadian politics, given that innovations in transportation and communication have broken down many of the geographical barriers that separate Canadians? How can regionalism be so intense if most citizens today were either not born or not living in this country when these original forces were at play? The reason for the persistence lies in a combination of *socialization*, *institutionalization*, and *politicization*.

Socialization

Through a process known as *socialization*, regionalism is passed down from generation to generation and from residents to newcomers. A host of actors—from families, churches, schools, and peer groups to artists, academics, bureaucrats, and the media—all play leading roles in instilling foundational beliefs. Most experts on socialization agree that the process is cumulative, so that things we are taught to believe early on tend to act as a filter for later learning.[22] As children, many Canadians are exposed to politics in the home. Parents often act as role models in this regard, helping to pass regional views from generation to generation.[23] Peers have a similar impact. Schools are important venues for socialization, as "the myths and legends from the past, the policies and programs of the present, and the goals and aspirations of the future are taught selectively. Consciously or not, textbooks and other teaching materials justify and rationalize political practices."[24] In the same way, academic discourses help to reinforce existing political cultures by sanctifying certain historical narratives. The artistic community and the media play similar roles in popularizing views about regional cultures in Canada.

Barry Cooper's (2002) observations regarding the impact of the Laurentian myth are particularly insightful. According to this view, Quebec and Ontario were granted preeminent status among all provinces at the time of Confederation and in the century that followed. Their dominance and the related power of white, British, English speakers, we would add, was enshrined in the constitution, which granted them full regional status in and of themselves, including a full complement of 24 Senate seats. The outlying jurisdictions were considered subordinate, particularly as new provinces were added in the West. Whereas the two founding Maritime provinces were granted 10 senators each and full control over their natural resources, the Western provinces were granted six Senate seats and lacked jurisdiction over resources until 1930.

The persistence of the Laurentian thesis has been challenged over time, most recently by *Globe and Mail* columnist John Ibbitson and pollster Darrell Bricker in their book *The Big Shift* (2013). They argue that immigration patterns have fundamentally transformed Canadian society such that political power is shifting westward and toward electoral districts that are populated predominantly by allophones. The worldview of Canada as a fragile state that needs the federal government to bind Canadians through the welfare state and through special favours for Quebec no longer holds, the thesis argues.

Institutionalization

In addition to these forces of socialization, regional divisions also become *institutionalized*. Federal economic development programs, organizations, structures, laws, and other systems develop in ways that further entrench geographic differences in Canada. Federalism is the most important of these institutions. As discussed in Chapter 3, the Fathers of Confederation chose federalism as a means of forging a pan-Canadian union that respected regional differences. The institutions of federalism—the division of powers, intra-state bodies like the Senate, inter-state bodies like first ministers' meetings, and so on—certainly did not predate the existence of Canada's regional communities. Yet federalism has served to reinforce those differences over time, by empowering provincial governments to legislate in a wide range of socio-political areas and emboldening premiers to act as spokespeople for and defenders of provincial interests.

In Canada, this division of powers has allowed provincial governments to establish systems of taxation, healthcare, social services, and education that meet the needs of their residents and align with their own unique political cultures. Quebec has developed Canada's most comprehensive public daycare system, for example. The province's extensive government programs and relatively high rates of taxation align well

Laurentian myth A theory that historic perceptions of central Canadian dominance have spawned regionalist resentment in peripheral parts of the country.

INSIDE CANADIAN POLITICS
Are Regions Like Monkey Cages?

To appreciate the power and nature of socialization, consider the following popular story, based loosely on the research of primatologist G.R. Stephenson:

> Five monkeys were placed in the centre of a cage, along with a ladder at the top of which sat a banana. Every time a monkey started up the ladder, scientists would douse the entire cage with cold water. After a few times, the monkeys began threatening those who would approach the ladder, such that no monkey dared consider capturing the banana. Once this context had been established, scientists began replacing each of the monkeys in the cage, one by one. Not having witnessed the cold-water implications of climbing the ladder, each new monkey was tempted to go after the banana. But, one by one, each was dissuaded by the other monkeys in the cage. By the end

of the experiment, none of the five original monkeys was left in the cage. And, yet, none of the new monkeys would attempt to climb the ladder.

Some psychologists and business scholars use this research as evidence of how culture is passed "naturally" to newcomers. While the initial conditions and actors that fostered the culture have disappeared, the culture persists. The same process could be said to be at play in transmitting political culture. While few Canadians today personally experienced events like the Great Depression and Newfoundland's entry into Confederation, and while today's youth and recent immigrants were not present during the FLQ crisis or the controversy surrounding the National Energy Program, these events continue to shape politics in various regions because the lessons are passed down from generation to generation and from native-born residents to new arrivals.

VOX POP

What socializing forces are at play in transmitting the political culture of the Canadian region in which you now live, from generation to generation and from longtime residents to newcomers?

with its social-democratic political culture, just as Crown corporations may be attributed to, and contribute to, that province's social-democratic tradition. The same is true, to a lesser degree, in Manitoba and the Atlantic provinces. By the same token, Alberta's low-tax environment—a luxury derived from its endowment of natural resources—both matches and strengthens its laissez-faire conservative political culture. To a lesser extent, the same pattern holds true in British Columbia. Federalism encourages such diversity in public policy and helps to reinforce regional cleavages in Canada.

When debates erupt over the distribution of wealth from one region to another, for example through changes to the equalization program or other major transfers, such regional divisions are often laid bare on the editorial pages of major newspapers and at major federal, provincial, and territorial (FPT) meetings. The grand constitutional conferences that brought together the prime minister and all premiers used to provide a national forum for premiers to bargain and, in some cases, grandstand. The prime minister has withdrawn from such meetings, but ministers, premiers, and public servants continue to gather (see Table 4.6). Indeed, institutions like the Council

TABLE 4.6 | Major Provincial and Territorial Meetings

Institution	Established	Members	Meeting Dates
Northern Premiers' Forum	2003	YT, NWT, NU	April/May
New West Partnership	2010	BC, AB, SK	variable
Western Premiers' Conference	1973	BC, AB, SK, MB, YT, NWT, NU	early June
Council of Maritime Premiers	1972	NB, NS, PEI	variable
Council of Atlantic Premiers	2000	NB, NS, PEI, NL	early June
Council of the Federation	2003	All provinces and territories	late July and January

of Atlantic Premiers, the Western Premiers' Conference, the New West Partnership, and the Northern Premiers' Forum often serve to strengthen regional tendencies, and deepen regional cleavages, in Canada. Premiers meet on a regional basis several times per year, often in advance of pan-Canadian meetings of the Council of the Federation. They use these regional meetings as opportunities to forge regional consensus, advance joint priorities, explore opportunities for collaboration, and promote common positions on the national and international stage. On the last of these points, premiers often travel together abroad and work with their counterparts in other countries. In addition to various regional trade missions to countries like China and India, eastern Canadian premiers (from the Atlantic provinces and Quebec) have met with New England governors on an almost annual basis since 1973, and Western premiers have met with Western US governors since 1990. This has resulted in the development of transnational regions, held together by coalitions of subnational governments.

↻ See the discussion of inter-state federalism in Chapter 3 for more on first ministers' meetings.

Opportunities Available

Knowledge of Canadian Politics and Government Preferred!
Intergovernmental Policy Analyst

Alberta Environment and Sustainable Resource Development

Under the general direction of the Section Head, Intergovernmental Relations, the Policy Analyst plays an essential role in furthering effective intergovernmental relations that support departmental and government-wide priorities. Intergovernmental relationships are critical to the success of departmental priorities, including Integrated Resource Management and establishing Alberta as an environmental leader.

Responsibilities and Activities

1. Further Alberta's integrated resource management and broader intergovernmental objectives.
2. Ensure effective departmental participation in other intergovernmental forums and relationships.
3. Develop and maintain effective intergovernmental relationships to support Alberta Environment and Sustainable Resource Development and Alberta Government objectives.

4. Track and coordinate intergovernmental relations activities.

Knowledge

- Strong understanding of principles and challenges associated with intergovernmental relations and integrated resource management.
- Understanding of the roles, responsibilities and programs of the department and across the Government of Alberta.
- Knowledge of the department acts, regulations, policies and decision-making documents and processes.
- Understanding of the department and Government of Alberta priorities.
- Understanding of government roles and responsibilities.
- University degree, with at least 2 years of related experience. Equivalencies may be considered.

Skills

- Strong analytical and research skills.
- Excellent written and oral communications skills.
- Strong interpersonal skills.
- Strong coordination and organizational skills.
- Project management skills.
- Time management.

Abilities

- Ability to work independently and to work as part of a team, as the situation requires.
- Ability to work collaboratively.
- Ability to build and maintain relationships.
- Ability to think creatively.
- Ability to respond to rapidly changing priorities and timelines and to multi-task.

Source: www.jobs.alberta.ca/pprofile/pp1028085.htm.

Politicization

Lastly, regionalism persists in Canada because it is continually *politicized* by Canadian politicians. For it to enter and remain a part of the political discourse in Canada, regional consciousness must first be interpreted, articulated, and mobilized by political elites (see Figure 4.1).[25] Successful politicians take advantage of code politics, campaigning on the core beliefs that prevail within their province or region, and that reinforce a sense of otherness in comparison with the rest of Canada. At times, these codes cultivate a type of siege mentality, presenting a leader as the great guardian of the province or region against outside influence (normally the federal government). This type of rhetoric is especially evident in peripheral regions like the West and Atlantic Canada, but it can be found in the campaign platforms of leaders throughout the country, throughout history.[26]

Code politics and regionalism are heightened by the tones of public discourse and political communication. Take, for example, the politics of Saint-Jean-Baptiste Day. The French tradition of celebrating St John the Baptist on 24 June was brought to the New World by French colonists, and in 1908 he was named the patron saint of Canadian francophones. Since 1977, Saint-Jean-Baptiste Day has been a statutory holiday in Quebec, where it is a celebration of French and Québécois culture, and is known both as the Fête Nationale du Québec and colloquially as "la Saint-Jean." We can peek into the code politics by looking at the choice of words used by federal party leaders to acknowledge the holiday. As we would expect, the leader of the Bloc Québécois uses it as an opportunity to defend the vibrancy of Quebec identity, whereas the prime minister typically finds a way to reinforce that Quebec is an important part of Canada.

Canada's political system is rife with incentives that encourage politicians to engage in this brand of regionalized politics. Beyond federalism and the regional premiers' conferences discussed above, the single-member plurality (SMP) electoral system exerts a powerful influence over the behaviour of Canadian elites and voters. Unlike many forms of proportional representation, the single-member districts in Canada's SMP system are explicitly organized along geographic lines. Just as premiers and senators represent their respective provinces on the national stage, all members of Parliament represent their own territorial districts. While party discipline remains strong in Canada, and while advances in communication and transportation have allowed for nationwide campaigns, these constituency boundaries exert a powerful influence on the structure of Canadian elections. Each general election consists of hundreds of constituency-level campaigns, with candidates appealing to local interests and issues in the process. National leaders are encouraged to appeal to the same dynamics, often releasing specific platforms or agendas for each region, and appointing provincial or regional lieutenants to conduct the campaign in different parts of the country. In some federal elections, a federal party's chief lieutenant in a province is the premier—or, alternatively, a premier may be its greatest local adversary.

↻ See pages 83–4 of Chapter 3 for the differences between federal and unitary systems of government.

Regionalism and National Unity

All of this discussion of regionalism raises a question: if Canadians are so divided, what holds them together? Similar regional conflicts—particularly those that overlap with deep cleavages like language, ethnicity, and resource wealth—have resulted in instability and even civil war in other countries, including in the United States. And yet, regionalism in Canada has thrived within the bosom of the Canadian state for nearly 150 years. What makes Canada so unique in this regard?

Part of the answer can be found in the structure of Canada's political institutions. These not only allow for but actively promote unity through diversity. Federalism and our electoral system act as safety valves of sorts, allowing for the legitimate expression of regional differences within the boundaries of Canadian democracy. The Canadian constitution also entrenches regional protections. Minority rights are provincially guarded and nationally guaranteed against both global forces and domestic governments. Residents of all provinces, large and small, are guaranteed representation in Parliament. A combination of convention and electoral necessity ensure that all regions have influence during election campaigns and in the course of national policymaking.

Moreover, regional and pan-Canadian institutions like premiers' conferences have become more powerful and institutionalized over time. This has occurred despite the propensity of premiers to act in their jurisdictions' own self-interest. The quest for collective provincial clout has helped to foster broader consensus among provinces and territories. In the face of globalization, rather than champion protectionism, we are seeing evidence of provincial and territorial governments perceiving and demonstrating the value of working together to promote common interests on the domestic and international stage.

Perhaps most importantly, however, regionalism has always been part of the Canadian condition. It has been socialized and politicized into our culture for generations—with few exceptions—as a fundamental, if not positive, feature of Canadian society. It is not that Canadians fail to see the depth of our regional cleavages. A

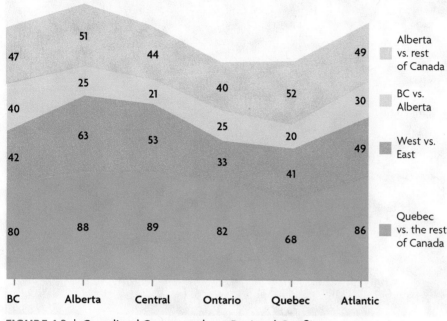

% viewing conflicts as serious and very serious threats to national unity

	BC	Alberta	Central	Ontario	Quebec	Atlantic	
Alberta vs. rest of Canada	47	51	44			49	
BC vs. Alberta	40	25	21	40	52	30	
West vs. East	42	63	53	25 / 33	20 / 41	49	
Quebec vs. the rest of Canada	80	88	89	82	68	86	

FIGURE 4.2 | Canadians' Concerns about Regional Conflicts

Source: Based on data from Abacus National Poll (7–8 Dec. 2012), http://abacusdata.ca/wp-content/uploads/2012/12/AlbertaFederalism-and-Jealosy_dec2012.pdf.

2012 Abacus Data poll revealed that a vast majority of Canadians perceived the division between Quebec and the rest of Canada as a serious or very serious threat to national unity, for instance (see Figure 4.2). Large proportions were also concerned with the cleavages between Alberta and the rest of Canada. Yet, with the notable and periodic exception of Quebec separatism, few of these have posed real threats to Canada's existence.

Nevertheless, most forms of Canadian regionalism are of the sectionalist variety. This means that their adherents are looking for a better deal *within* Canada, not outside it. This continual search for improvement does not always result in reforms, especially when the calls for change are at odds with each other. And no country is forever safe from secessionism, especially when its Supreme Court has been asked to provide a road map in case of that eventuality. Nonetheless, history to this point does suggest that Canadians—from various parties and backgrounds—have come to accept, if not embrace, regionalism as a prominent fixture of the country's politics. It would appear that, as has been the case throughout history, Canadians view regionalism as a fact of life, not a threat to it.

Concluding Thoughts

Notwithstanding the ebbs and flows of Western sectionalism, or the presence of nationalism among some groups, the strength of local identity and unique political culture is most pervasive in Quebec. In that region, secessionism is a legitimate threat to national unity and the continued viability of the current political structure of the

© Gari Wyn Williams/Alamy Stock Photo

If you were travelling abroad, how would you define yourself—by country? By region? Province or city? What, if anything, does your answer tell you about the strength of regionalist sentiment in the part of the country you're from?

country. Efforts to accommodate Quebec and other regions in the constitution, notably the Meech Lake and Charlottetown Accords, have failed and are a warning signal to other prime ministers not to reopen the constitutional debate. Instead, in the face of a referendum that was nearly won by sovereignists, federalists countered by setting the terms of a future debate on separation under the controversial Clarity Act. Some of Quebec's regional grievances have been addressed, though others—such as the call for formal recognition as a nation—periodically emerge. By and large, provincial and territorial political executives have been soldiering on with the business of running their governments, and the Canadian identity continues to take shape. However, history suggests that it is only a matter of time until the next eruption of regionalist hostility. What form could it take?

A concomitant problem with the regionalization of Canadian politics is that it suppresses other forms of political conflict. Political matters concerning class, gender, Aboriginal, post-material, and other non-territorially defined concerns have been less successful at getting on the national agenda. Unlike other countries, Canada has never featured a robust left–right political discourse or strong far left- or far right-wing parties, for instance—not, at least, at the federal level. Vocal critics of regionalized politics make up the so-called "creative politics school," which alleges that Canadian political elites have conspired to marginalize the interests and proponents of disadvantaged groups in favour of regionally based ethnic and linguistic communities. That populists championing regional grievances have tended to be English-speaking white, Anglo-Saxon, Protestant (WASP) men is certainly an outcome of the system, a contributing factor, or both.

↻ The creative politics school is critical of Canada's democratic deficit, which is explained in Chapter 13, on diversity and representation. See especially pages 498–9.

For More Information

Is there a common Canadian identity? It is a question with no clear answer, and though medicare has long featured prominently in ways that Canadians distinguish themselves from Americans, the advent of "Obamacare" in the US may lessen that gap. Hockey, the CBC, the monarchy, Quebec, and Tim Hortons may also make the list. Read more in works such as Philip Resnick's *The European Roots of Canadian Identity* (Broadview Press, 2005) and *Desiring Canada: CBC Contests, Hockey Violence and Other Stately Pleasures*, by Patricia Cormack and James F. Cosgrove (University of Toronto Press, 2013).

Are there really regional cleavages in Canadian public opinion today? Yes and no. Christopher Cochrane and Andrea Perrella suggest there is some evidence, in their 2012 *Canadian Journal of Political Science* article "Regions, Regionalism and Regional Differences in Canada" (45: 829–53). Ailsa Henderson takes a revolutionary view of "Regional Political Cultures in Canada" in her 2004 article found in the same journal (37: 595–615).

How do newcomers adapt to regionalism in Canada? Antoine Bilodeau and colleagues analyze "The Development of Dual Loyalties: Immigrants' Integration to Regional Canadian Dynamics" (*Canadian Journal of Political Science* 43: 515–44).

What are the historical foundations of Canadian regionalism? David Bell traced *The Roots of Disunity* in 1992 (Oxford University Press), while Nelson Wiseman went *In Search of Canadian Political Culture* in 2007 (UBC Press). Mildred A. Schwartz wrote the seminal work on the topic in her 1974 book *Politics and Territory: The Sociology of Regional Persistence in Canada* (McGill–Queen's University Press).

What is the "creative politics school"? Janine Brodie outlines many of the main tenets in *The Political Economy of Canadian Regionalism* (Harcourt Brace, 1990). For the genesis of the school, see John Porter's *The Vertical Mosaic: An Analysis of Social Class and Power in Canada* (University of Toronto Press, 1965).

How do regional premiers' conferences work? J. Peter Meekison, Hamish Telford, and Harvey Lazar edited the volume *Reconsidering the Institutions of Canadian Federalism* as part of the annual "Canada: The State of the Federation" series (McGill–Queen's University Press, 2004).

How does the federal party system affect regionalism in Canada? Lisa Young and Keith Archer and their contributors present a series of responses in *Regionalism and Party Politics in Canada* (Oxford University Press, 2001).

How have successful federal politicians built regional coalitions in Canada? John Duffy explores over a century of electioneering in *Fights of Our Lives: Elections, Leadership, and the Making of Canada* (Harper Collins, 2002).

How have provincial politicians constructed unique political cultures? Jared Wesley explores the development of *Code Politics: Campaigns and Cultures on the Canadian Prairies* (UBC Press, 2011). An example of how code politics is entwined with regionalism, populism, and ideology can be found in "Masters of Our Own Destiny: The Nationalist Evolution of Newfoundland Premier Danny Williams," by Alex Marland (*International Journal of Canadian Studies* 42 [2010]: 155–81).

What is the state of "Western alienation" in the twenty-first century? Roger Gibbins and Loleen Berdahl offer a retrospective and prospective look at regionalism in *New West, New Canada* (University of Toronto Press, 2014).

What was the atmosphere really like around the 1995 Referendum? CBC News produced a three-hour documentary, *Breaking Point*, to commemorate the tenth anniversary of the campaign, interviewing all of the key players—Jean Chrétien, Lucien Bouchard, Jacques Parizeau, Daniel Johnson, Jean Charest, Brian Tobin, and others.

Want to ensure you're up to date on news and current events across Canada? Access the online magazine *Ottawa and Beyond*. Simply download the free Flipboard app, and subscribe.

Deeper Inside Canadian Politics

1. There are a lot of ghosts in the graveyard of Canadian regionalism. Examine one of the following issues and explain how it continues to influence politics in Canada:

    a)   the National Energy Program
    b)   the sponsorship scandal
    c)   the Atlantic accords
    d)   the changes to the equalization formula

2. Premiers meet several times each year on a regional and national basis. Drawing on the communiques (press releases) from the most recent meetings of the Western, Atlantic, and Northern premiers' forums, describe the sorts of activities that governments commit to undertaking on a regional basis. Is there any correlation with the outcomes of Council of the Federation meetings?

3. In recent years, there have been heated debates concerning the abolition of the Canadian Senate. How would abolishing the Senate affect regionalism in Canada?

4. According to Roger Gibbins, senior fellow at the Canada West Foundation:

Regional differences and hence regional conflict are inevitable in a country of Canada's size and complexity. The regions—be they provinces, the northern territories, or more abstract amalgamations such as the West and Atlantic Canada—differ substantially in their economic foundations, socio-demographic composition, and political cultures. Therefore regionalism—the intrusion of territorially based interests, values, and identities into national public life—is unavoidable. . . . However, we can and should ask to what extent our political institutions *moderate* or *exacerbate* regional conflict and regional alienation.[27]

Has Canadian federalism been successful in handling and containing regional conflict? Or have its institutions and practices intensified such conflict? In short, when it comes to regionalism in Canada, has federalism been part of the solution or part of the problem?

UP FOR DEBATE

Is regionalism a dynamic force in Canadian politics?

THE CLAIM: YES, IT IS!

Regionalism is as strong as ever in Canada; you just might not recognize its more positive tone.

Yes: Argument Summary

Canadian regionalism has evolved considerably, taking on a distinctly constructive tone in recent decades. Gone are the days of blind reactionary provincialism. Calls like "Quebec wants out" and the "West wants in" have been replaced by a more proactive, collaborative approach on the part of provincial and territorial governments toward meeting the needs of their residents. They have forged stronger intergovernmental bodies, built their own domestic and international agendas, and successfully harmonized regulations in a number of important sectors. At the same time, the federal government continues to operate along regional lines, recognizing and reinforcing Canada's regionalized brand of federalism. In short, while regionalism was once measured by the amount of dysfunction in Canada's political system, today, it is best gauged by how well provinces and territories are working together to break down province-based barriers and address areas of common interest.

Yes: Top 5 Considerations

1. Provinces and territories have expanded, empowered, and further institutionalized bodies like the New West Partnership, the Council of Atlantic Premiers, and the Northern Premiers' Forum. Each of these groups is increasingly active, and serves to regionalize the Council of the Federation agenda by convening in the leadup to each meeting.
2. Regions are increasingly thinking about harmonization and globalization. In addition to collaborating on domestic issues like healthcare and post-secondary education and training, these regional bodies have also undertaken a considerable amount of international work. They continue to build stronger cross-border regional alliances with their counterparts in the United States and have undertaken international trade missions.
3. Provincial and territorial governments continue to harmonize a lot of their regulations, reducing mobility barriers for Canadians and businesses, and creating a series of regional economies and subnational freer trade zones.
4. The federal government continues to operate on a regional basis, appointing regional ministers (e.g. a Quebec lieutenant) and staffing regional offices in major departments (like Aboriginal Affairs).
5. The more traditional brand of regionalism is alive and well in Quebec, evidenced by the provincial government's numerous constitutional challenges of the federal government.

Yes: Other Considerations

- The fact that Western alienation and support for Quebec sovereignty are at all-time lows does not signal a decline in regionalism. Rather, it reflects the fact that Canada's institutions of interstate federalism—including the Council of the Federation and various regional bodies—have given new voice and power to regional interests.
- Western premiers meet annually with the Western Governors' Association, just as Atlantic and Quebec premiers meet with New England governors.
- The New West Partnership Trade Agreement has improved credential recognition across the three westernmost provinces; Atlantic harmonization projects such as the Atlantic Workforce Partnership and the Atlantic Procurement Partnership have streamlined transportation systems in the region; and the Pan-Territorial

Adaptation Strategy is helping Nunavut, Northwest Territories, and Yukon to coordinate their actions on climate change.

• The Quebec government has launched constitutional challenges to the federal government's authority to unilaterally reform the Canadian Senate, change the rules of royal secession in Canada, and appoint a justice to the Supreme Court.

THE COUNTERCLAIM: NO, IT ISN'T!

Regionalism has been dying in Canada ever since the sovereignists were defeated in the 1995 Quebec referendum.

No: Argument Summary

The divisive tone of Canadian politics that has characterized much of its history may have climaxed with the 1995 Quebec sovereignty referendum. Up until then, Canada was a parade of political spectacles, as premiers and aggrieved nationalists used national first ministers' conferences (FMCs) as forums for vocalizing regional grievances. As soon as one premier expressed outrage over alleged unfair treatment, the others stood up to defend the status quo, or to go on the attack themselves. Prime ministers who sought to negotiate the jurisdiction over national programs, to seek compromise on federal–provincial funding agreements, and to find ways to "fix" the Canadian constitution were inevitably greeted with indignation and squabbling. The perilous nature of the 1995 Quebec referendum that brought the country to the brink of division remains seared in the national consciousness. Canadian federal politicians now understand that those who dare aggravate regional tensions do so at their peril.

No: Top 5 Considerations

1. The period from the mid-1960s through to the mid-1990s was the golden era of constitutional reform and attempts to accommodate Quebec's demands for different status. The Quiet Revolution, punctuated by the FLQ crisis, forced Ottawa to respond to Quebec's outward nationalism. A series of efforts beginning with the Bilingualism and Biculturalism Commission in the 1960s transitioned into constitutional wrangling that included the failed Victoria Charter (1971), the passage of the Constitution Act (1982), the failed Meech Lake Accord (1987), and the failed Charlottetown Accord (1992)—but nothing since.

2. Provincial governments have turned inward. In Quebec, outrage directed at the federal government and the rest of Canada has gradually receded. Although nationalism flames up periodically, for the most part it has been replaced by localized concerns such as the reasonable accommodation of allophones.

3. As in the early and mid-twentieth century, regionalist parties have once again folded back into the larger brokerage organizations. The Western-based Reform Party rebranded itself twice before merging with the Progressive Conservative Party, and with the election of one of Reform's former top officials, Stephen Harper, to the prime minister's office, the West officially was "in." Likewise, the Bloc Québécois lost momentum, failing to win official party status (12 seats) in the 2011 and 2015 federal elections. The resounding defeat of the Parti Québécois in the 2014 provincial election signalled Quebecers' loss of appetite for any discussion of sovereignty or referendums.

4. The productive tone of provincial intergovernmental meetings has kept regionalism under the radar for a reason: it simply isn't as relevant in today's society. In the past, premiers were guardians of insulated communities, the unchallenged spokespeople for provincial interests. But today, provinces are competing in a global economy, citizens are exposed to news media from around the world, interest groups have grown in power, and social media facilitate community activism.

5. The national debates about renewing the Canadian constitution that dominated headlines in the late twentieth century were a lesson for future prime ministers: avoid national media forums that can inflame regional tensions. As prime minister, Stephen Harper did just that, preferring to meet privately with premiers

one-on-one, and reportedly threatening to cancel such meetings if the media were informed beforehand. Depriving premiers of a national media platform appears to have succeeded in hiding, if not dissuading, regional tensions.

No: Other Considerations

- For a number of years, healthcare and the economy have topped the list of concerns among Canadians, even those within Quebec. The perpetual state of political crisis that characterized the pre-1995 era is unrecognizable for new Canadians and Canadian youth.

- The bread-and-butter of the Liberal Party of Canada was arguably that it was best positioned as the defender of national unity. The erosion in support for that party is evidence of shifting public concerns from national unity to the more pressing issues noted above.
- With the strength of the Bloc Québécois greatly diminished and with the PQ out of office, the separatist movement in Quebec is as weak as it has ever been. The public appetite for separation appears to have been replaced by concerns shared by other Canadians, such as improvements to healthcare, stable jobs, and sound management of the government's finances.

Discussion Questions

- Do you identify most with your home community, your province, or your country? Why?
- How can Canadians amend their constitution without aggravating regional identities and straining national unity? Is it better just to put up with the status quo?
- In an increasingly globalized world, does it make sense for provincial governments to be

protecting their turf, or should they be finding ways to co-operate with each other?
- Do you think Quebec will ever separate from Canada? Why or why not?
- To what extent do you think that the growing number of allophones in Canada, particularly in urban centres, is causing politicians to think in multicultural terms rather than regional terms?

Where to Learn More about Regionalism in Canadian Politics

David Cameron and Richard Simeon, "Intergovernmental Relations in Canada: The Emergence of Collaborative Federalism," *Publius: The Journal of Federalism* 32, no. 2 (2002): pp. 49–72.

Christopher Cochrane and Andrea Perrella, "Regions, Regionalism and Regional Differences in Canada," *Canadian Journal of Political Science* 45, no. 4 (2012): pp. 829–53.

Charles Conteh, *Policy Governance in Multi-Level Systems: Economic Development and Policy Implementation in Canada* (Montreal and Kingston: McGill–Queen's University Press, 2013).

David McGrane and Loleen Berdahl, "'Small Worlds' No More: Reconsidering Provincial Political Cultures in Canada," *Regional & Federal Studies* 23, no. 4 (2013): pp. 479–93.

Michael D. Ornstein, H. Michael Stevenson, and A. Paul Williams, "Region, Class and Political Culture in Canada," *Canadian Journal of Political Science* 13, no. 2 (1980): pp. 227–71.

R.A. Young, Philippe Faucher, and André Blais, "The Concept of Province-Building: A Critique," *Canadian Journal of Political Science* 17, no. 4 (1984): pp. 783–818.

5 THE EXECUTIVE

Inside this Chapter

- What are the main components of the executive branch in Canada?
- How does the executive function?
- How are political executives held accountable to the legislature, and to Canadians?

Inside the Executive

Power concentrates at the top of most organizations, and Canadian governments are no different. Sovereignty is vested in the Crown and exercised by the government, not the people. Cabinet ministers are not directly accountable to citizens; in fact, as leaders chosen by their local constituents and appointed by their political parties, many are *twice* removed from direct accountability to Canadians.

This does not mean that executive power in Canada remains entirely unchecked, however. In Chapter 2, we saw that Westminster parliamentary traditions, including the principle of responsible government, do place great powers in the hands of premiers, prime ministers, and their cabinets, yet they also impose accountability on these executives, for the vast majority of their actions are subject to the endorsement of the legislature, the Crown, or both.

Thus, peering inside the Canadian executive, we find a delicate balance of powers and responsibilities, and a complex network of checks and balances—not to mention the following maxims.

 The prime minister and the cabinet are not the only members of the executive. While the prime minister and the cabinet are indeed important players in the executive, we must not overlook the important role played by the Crown (the *formal executive*) and the civil service (the *permanent executive*), not to mention the various provincial and territorial premiers, their cabinets, and bureaucracies.

 The prime minister does not wield absolute control over Canadian politics. Popular accounts—especially recent ones—treat the prime minister's role as akin to that of a dictator, an autocrat who single-handedly directs policy while crafting and controlling the political message. Friendly or not, these comparisons to Second or Third World despots misjudge the very real constraints that exist on the Canadian prime minister's power.

 Executives today hold no more power than they did in the past. The belief in growing executive power assumes there was once a time when Canadian legislators enjoyed a golden age of influence over their counterparts in the executive. In fact, remarkably little has changed by way of the formal rules of parliamentary democracy in Canada. While party discipline may have grown stronger over time, a variety of new constraints have developed to keep executives accountable to their respective legislatures.

In addressing these tenets, this chapter pulls back the curtain on the executive, revealing the complex set of institutions, actors, and relationships that drive governments in Canada.

Overview

Atop the Canadian political system sits *the executive*: the political elites and decision-makers who preside over the direction of their respective governments. The executive is, most often, the strongest of three interconnected branches of government in Canada, with the others being the legislative branch (Chapter 6) and the judicial branch (Chapter 7).

Executives are the leaders who have supreme authority and responsibility for decision-making in their organizations. Just as the chief executive officer of a corporation is its most senior manager, in politics there are presiding officers who head up various aspects of government, and who are the chief decision-makers. Depicted in Figure 5.1, there are three types of government executives:

What the 2015 Election Means for the Executive

Visit the *Inside Canadian Politics* flipboard to learn about the latest developments affecting the executive.

 Go to http://flip.it/gblag.

government The body consisting of all cabinet ministers, who remain responsible to the legislature for state decision-making.

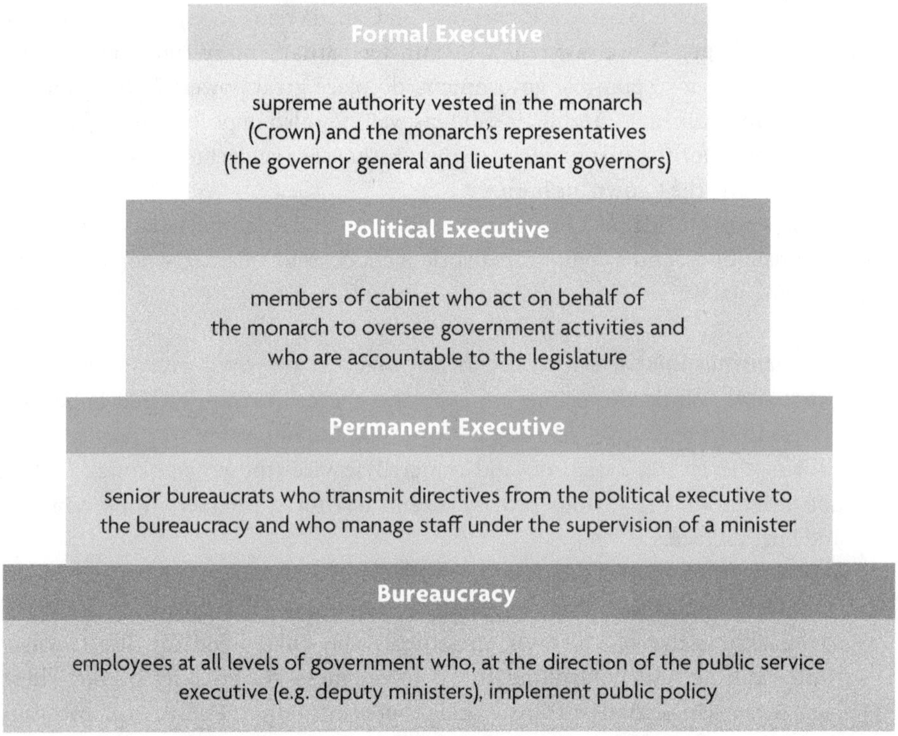

Formal Executive

supreme authority vested in the monarch
(Crown) and the monarch's representatives
(the governor general and lieutenant governors)

Political Executive

members of cabinet who act on behalf of
the monarch to oversee government activities and
who are accountable to the legislature

Permanent Executive

senior bureaucrats who transmit directives from the political executive to
the bureaucracy and who manage staff under the supervision of a minister

Bureaucracy

employees at all levels of government who, at the direction of the public service
executive (e.g. deputy ministers), implement public policy

FIGURE 5.1 | Distribution of Power in the Canadian System of Government

1. the *formal executive*, comprising the figureheads who hold ceremonial, mostly symbolic positions of authority;
2. the *political executive*, made up of the elected power-brokers who make the broad policy decisions; and
3. the *permanent executive*, consisting of the appointed senior bureaucrats who advise the political executive and who oversee the bureaucracy as it implements those policy decisions.

The concentration of power in the formal, political, and permanent executive is sometimes criticized, because the broad authority of a small group of political elites appears to be at odds with grassroots notions of democracy. On the other hand, the Canadian executive has the ability to be very decisive and affords political elites the benefit of a strong network of expertise when formulating and implementing policy. Generally speaking, the interaction between the different executives normally, but not always, produces a smooth system of governance.

UP FOR DEBATE
Do Canadian first ministers have too much power?

Keep this question in mind as you read through the chapter. Consult the end-of-chapter debate supplement for more material to help you engage in an informed discussion of the topic.

The Formal Executive

The figurehead with supreme power in a political system is known as the head of state. The role and official title of a head of state vary from country to country. For instance, the system of absolute monarchy that throughout much of history gave the heads of royal families the divine right to rule has all but vanished, though still exists as a form of authoritarianism in a handful of countries, notably Saudi Arabia. In sovereign republics, such as France and the United States, the formal executive is embodied by the president. In constitutional monarchies like Australia and the United Kingdom, the head of state is a king or queen whose powers have been reduced to ceremonial duties. The head of state therefore has enormous executive authority that may or may not be exercised, depending on the political system.

> **head of state** The highest-ranking figure in a sovereign state, serving as its foremost ceremonial representative.

Canada's head of state is the king or queen holding the hereditary position of monarch. Since 1952, the monarch has been Queen Elizabeth II, the head of the royal family in the United Kingdom. In all likelihood, the position will one day be assumed by her first-born child, Charles, just as Elizabeth II was the heir to the throne under her father, King George VI. Unless circumstances change, Charles will become King of Canada; his first-born child, Prince William, will eventually inherit the crown; and one day, Prince George of Cambridge, the first-born child of Prince William and Princess Kate, will become King. Thus, for over six decades, Commonwealth countries including Canada have been presided over by a queen, but future generations seem destined to be ruled by kings.

> **monarch** The absolute head of a monarchy, whose power is typically derived by birth.

The supreme authority of the monarch is clearly stated in the Canadian constitution. Article III of the Constitution Act, 1867, frames the organization of the formal and political executive in Canada, declaring that "The Executive Government and Authority of and over Canada is hereby declared to continue and be vested in the Queen." While the monarch technically has supreme power, in practice the position involves ceremonial duties as the face of the Crown in Canada. The Crown and its representative, the monarch, are non-partisan symbols of all government institutions. This is one of the reasons why Queen Elizabeth appears on Canadian currency, for example. Ceremonial duties include touring, attending special events, being a patron of select charities, granting honours, and sending anniversary messages as well as words of condolence. The monarch is also the symbolic head of the Canadian military, by virtue of section 15 of the Constitution Act, 1867 ("The Command-in-Chief

> **Crown** The legal concept dictating the supremacy of the monarch over the executive, legislative, and judicial branches of government.

BRIEFING NOTES

Heads of State and Heads of Government

In many presidential systems—like that of the United States—the head of *government* is also the head of *state*. These two roles are kept separate in constitutional monarchies like Canada, however. The Canadian head of state is the monarch (a king or queen), who is represented by the governor general at the federal level and a series of lieutenant governors at the provincial level. First ministers serve as the heads of government—the prime minister at the federal level and premiers at the provincial level.

George Pimentel

Canadians' support for the monarchy tends to vary depending on which Royal is the focus of attention. Queen Elizabeth is popular, as are William and Kate, the duke and duchess of Cambridge, and their two children. Prince Charles, the heir to the throne, and his wife Camilla are not as popular. What does it say about the monarchy in Canada that our attitudes are so contingent on our impressions of individual personalities?

of the Land and Naval Militia, and of all Naval and Military Forces, of and in Canada, is hereby declared to continue to be vested in the Queen").

The constitutional monarch who presides over the United Kingdom is simultaneously the monarch for 15 other Commonwealth realms around the world, including Australia, Barbados, Canada, Jamaica, and New Zealand. She maintains several official residences in the UK, including Windsor Castle and Buckingham Palace in southeastern England. Since she does not reside in Canada, her executive authority is delegated to a local resident, as per section 10 of the Constitution Act, 1867.

governor general The monarch's representative at the federal level in Canada.

The governor general (GG) carries out tasks on behalf of the monarch and is likewise responsible for the constitutional operations of the Canadian state. Governors general are selected by the monarch on the advice of the Canadian prime minister, and typically serve for a term of four to six years. Increasingly, GGs have come to represent a broader cross-section of Canadian society, with appointments alternating between anglophones and francophones since the 1950s. In recent years, members of socio-demographic groups that rarely if ever hold elected positions have been appointed to the positions of governor general and lieutenant governor, including women, non-whites, non-Anglophones and persons with disabilities.

The GG's primary responsibility is to ensure that Canada has a functioning, constitutional government. The governor general's routine duties include the symbolism of signing bills into law, thereby granting royal assent; appointing and swearing in key government officials, including the prime minister, cabinet ministers, senators, and justices of the Supreme Court; and fulfilling more episodic duties that include reading the Speech from the Throne, opening and closing Parliament, and signing writs of election. The governor general is also responsible for traditional ceremonial work, such as serving as Canada's commander-in-chief, presenting honours and awards on behalf of all Canadians, representing Canada abroad, and promoting national unity

INSIDE CANADIAN POLITICS
What Happened When Byng Refused King?

Only twice at the federal level has the governor general unilaterally switched which party holds power without requiring a general election: first, following the Pacific Scandal of the 1870s; then, during the King–Byng affair of 1926.

The episode began in 1925, when Liberal prime minister Mackenzie King asked Governor General Viscount Byng to dissolve the House of Commons so that a general election could be held. At the conclusion of the election, the Conservative Party had 115 seats, the Liberals 100, and the Progressive Party 22 seats. We might therefore assume that the leader of the Conservatives, Arthur Meighen, would be appointed prime minister.

Not so. King could remain prime minister as long as he could demonstrate that he had control of the House of Commons. Senior Liberals entered into negotiations with the Progressives and secured their support. King now controlled 122 seats to Meighen's 115, so there was no need for the governor general to intervene.

A year later, however, having lost the support of Progressive MPs, Prime Minister King again asked Governor General Byng to sign a writ of election. In an unprecedented move, Byng refused, on the basis that Canadians had only recently gone to the polls. Instead, he asked Meighen to form a government, the Conservatives holding the greatest number of seats in the legislature. Prime Minister Meighen and the Conservatives assumed control of the government but avoided reconvening the legislature, recognizing that they would be defeated. Sure enough, just two months after the head of state's representative had appointed a head of government, the Conservative government fell, and a general election was called. During the ensuing 1926 election campaign, King made an issue out of the matter, and his Liberal Party was returned to power.

THE LESSON
The King–Byng affair is a warning that a Canadian head of government must not assume that an executive request will be approved by the Crown's representative.

VOX POP
How have times changed since 1925–6? Under what circumstances could we expect a governor general to deny a prime minister a request for an election in the twenty-first century?

and identity. In recent decades, governors general have also undertaken promotional duties in support of special causes. For instance, Canada's twenty-eighth governor general, David Johnston, has placed philanthropy and volunteerism, learning and innovation, and family and children at the forefront of his public agenda.

As discussed in Chapter 3, the Crown is divided in Canada, meaning that the monarch is represented in Ottawa by the governor general and in the provinces by **lieutenant governors** (LGs), who perform similar duties with respect to provincial matters. Each lieutenant governor is appointed by the governor general on the advice of the prime minister (*not* the premier's advice) and serves for an average of five years. Similar positions, called *commissioners*, exist in the three territories, although each commissioner serves as a representative of the federal government, not of the monarch. In 2012, the federal government created an Advisory Committee on Vice-Regal Appointments to provide recommendations to the prime minister on the selection of governors general, lieutenant governors, and commissioners.

As representatives of the head of state, the governor general and lieutenant governors have a variety of formal executive powers. The most significant is **prerogative authority**, which grants final say to the head of state on any matter not explicitly addressed in the constitution. Section 91 of the Constitution Act, 1867, which identifies federal powers, begins by remarking that the Crown may "make laws for the Peace, Order, and good Government of Canada" (POGG) for any matter that is not specifically allocated to the federal or provincial governments in the Act. In 1947 the Letters Patent were passed, granting the governor general more authority to act on behalf of

lieutenant governor The monarch's representative in each province.

prerogative authority Powers that are not explicitly granted to the political executives, and that remain vested in the Crown.

THEY SAID IT
Canada's Navy and Air Force Get the Royal Treatment

Canadians were variously delighted, bemused, outraged, and disinterested in 2011, when Canada's defence minister, Peter MacKay, announced his Conservative government's decision to change the names of the Maritime Command and Air Command back to the Royal Canadian Navy and Royal Canadian Air Force, respectively. The Land Force Command was renamed the Canadian Army.

Our Conservative government believes that an important element of the Canadian military heritage was lost when these three former services were required to relinquish their historic titles.

—Minister of National Defence Peter MacKay[2]

It smacks of the days when Canada was an Anglo society, which it is not anymore. And when our armed forces followed British models, which they do not anymore.

—historian Jack Granatstein[3]

In our military, it is often tradition and a sense of place in history that sustains us, especially when life is under threat. To reinstate the long-established names of our armed services supports the Canadians serving in harm's way around the world, is respectful of our veterans, and is good for our nation.

—Ret. Colonel Chris Hadfield[4]

We've had gradual, incremental changes toward putting our colonialist symbols into the dustbin of history, and this is the first time a government has taken steps to restore it.

—Tom Freda, director of Citizens for a Canadian Republic[5]

the monarch, particularly if the monarch should become incapacitated. Over time, the scope of this prerogative authority has been narrowed, as legislatures have assumed increasing responsibility and have demanded more accountability from the Crown. Today, the GG and LGs normally behave almost exclusively in a ceremonial manner.

There is varying consternation in Canada about the continued relevance of the monarchy and its representatives. Historically, the issue has galvanized tories and members of the (Progressive) Conservative Party, who tend to revere the monarchy, its stability, and its traditions. Conversely, progressives and members of the Liberal and New Democratic parties have viewed the monarchy as anti-democratic, un-Canadian, and too expensive. Neither group of partisans has placed high priority on the issue, however, and abolishing the monarchy has not been a serious topic of constitutional debate since the 1840s.

Public opinion surveys in Canada tend to show divided support for remaining a constitutional monarchy or becoming a republic with an elected head of state. Support for the latter is much more pronounced in Quebec,[1] where the monarchy is seen as a symbol of colonial dominance. In 2009, for instance, some Quebec nationalists threw eggs at Prince Charles when he visited Montreal, claiming a cultural genocide had been committed and waving signs that said "Majesty go home!"

Nevertheless, the idea of Canada's becoming a sovereign republic like the United States does not tend to be part of the political discourse. In fact, in recent years the federal Conservative government has taken steps to increase the presence of the monarchy in Canada. Most notably, in 2011 it reversed a decision taken by a Liberal government in 1968, changing the name of the Maritime Command back to the Royal Canadian Navy, and the Air Command back to the Royal Canadian Air Force. By comparison, in Australia, criticism of the monarchy culminated in a 1999 referendum on becoming a republic, a proposal that was ultimately defeated after considerable public debate.

> **republic** A system of government in which sovereignty is vested in "the people," not "the Crown."

The Canadian Press/Andrew Vaughan

Is restoring "Royal" to the formal titles of the Canadian air force and the Canadian navy a fitting tribute to Canada's veterans and its military history? An affront to new Canadians from post-colonial countries? An act of tokenism designed to curry favour among Canadian monarchists? Or much ado about nothing?

The Political Executive

first ministers The heads of government in Canada, namely the prime minister and the premiers.

head of government The highest-ranking elected official in a jurisdiction, appointed by the Crown to lead the executive.

In practice, Canada's monarch *reigns* but does not *rule*, while first ministers *rule* but do not *reign*. This transfer of executive authority from the head of state to the heads of government sees the monarch's representatives routinely act on the advice of the leader of the party that controls the legislature (i.e. the prime minister or premier). However, the governor general or lieutenant governor always reserves the right to refuse a first minister's advice. In this way, the monarch reflects the concerns of subjects while upholding the Canadian constitution. These relationships are depicted in Figure 5.2.

Interestingly, the original Canadian constitution made no explicit mention of a prime minister or premier. Rather, section 11 of the BNA Act, 1867 stated:

> There shall be a Council to aid and advise in the Government of Canada, to be styled the Queen's Privy Council for Canada; and the Persons who are to be Members of that Council shall be from Time to Time chosen and summoned by the Governor General and sworn in as Privy Councillors, and Members thereof may be from Time to Time removed by the Governor General.

Privy Council The body of prominent federal politicians and officials that typically advise the governor general.

This provision stipulates that members of an executive body known as the Privy Council serve at the pleasure of the governor general and assume responsibility for the daily management of the federal government. The governor general appoints members to the Privy Council on advice of the prime minister. Chief justices, retired governors

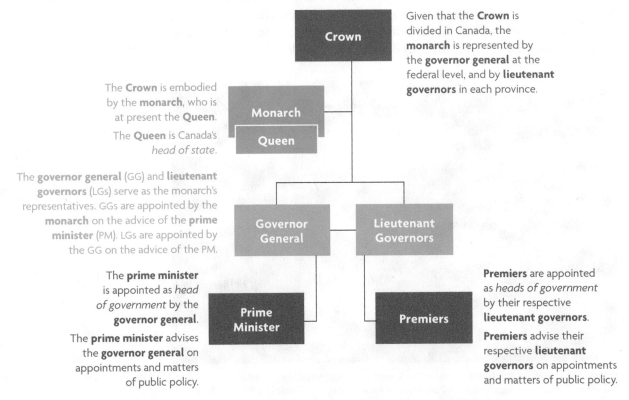

The **Crown** is embodied by the **monarch**, who is at present the **Queen**.
The **Queen** is Canada's *head of state*.

The **governor general** (GG) and **lieutenant governors** (LGs) serve as the monarch's representatives. GGs are appointed by the **monarch** on the advice of the **prime minister** (PM). LGs are appointed by the GG on the advice of the PM.

The **prime minister** is appointed as *head of government* by the **governor general**.
The **prime minister** advises the **governor general** on appointments and matters of public policy.

Given that the **Crown** is divided in Canada, the **monarch** is represented by the **governor general** at the federal level, and by **lieutenant governors** in each province.

Premiers are appointed as *heads of government* by their respective **lieutenant governors**.
Premiers advise their respective **lieutenant governors** on appointments and matters of public policy.

FIGURE 5.2 | The Formal and Political Executive in Canada

general, and anyone who was ever appointed to the federal cabinet are all permanent, lifetime members of the Privy Council. The term *privy* means "private," signifying the Privy Council's origins as a formal body of the monarch's closest advisers. In order to be granted access to top-secret information, all members of the Security Intelligence Review Committee are also appointed to the Privy Council, as are leaders of opposition parties on some occasions. Section 12 of the Constitution Act, 1982, makes a similar stipulation for each lieutenant governor, who is likewise to be advised by a provincial executive council that oversees the relevant provincial government.

↻ The functions of the Security Intelligence Review Committee are discussed on page 563 of Chapter 14, on Canada in the world.

Historically, the Privy Council was created to guide the decisions of the head of state. In practice, the full Privy Council is a ceremonial group that seldom meets, nor does it advise the GG or LGs. Instead, executive powers are conferred upon only those members of the Privy Council who are current members of the government cabinet, which is headed by the current prime minister or premier (see Table 5.1). Since the heads of government and members of cabinet ordinarily have seats in the legislature (whereas the majority of Privy Council members do not), this arrangement ensures greater accountability to the electorate.

cabinet The leaders of the political executive, consisting of the sitting prime minister and ministers. Ministers of state and associate ministers may attend upon invitation.

Thus, at the federal, provincial, or territorial level, the political executive consists of the first minister and the cabinet. The political executive is responsible for ensuring that the government functions effectively within the jurisdiction, by:

- maintaining solidarity and secrecy;
- organizing legislative votes;
- advising the heads of state on key appointments;
- controlling the public purse by initiating all money bills;
- initiating legislation and regulations; and
- executing intergovernmental and international agreements.

BRIEFING NOTES

Who Is "Honourable"?

An appointment to the Privy Council is a lifetime membership. Its members are permanently referred to as "honourable" and have the honorifics "P.C." (for "Privy Council") after their name. This means federal cabinet ministers, senators, and speakers of the House of Commons and the Senate are known as "honourable," even after retirement. Ministers of state are inducted into the Privy Council, but parliamentary secretaries are typically not. As members of the Privy Council, lieutenant governors also retain the term honourable for life. However, other provincial dignitaries (including premiers and ministers) are not members of the Privy Council,

and are referred to as honourable only during their term in office. From time to time, specific premiers may be selected to become members of the Privy Council, as occurred around the time of the patriation debates discussed in Chapter 2. Superior Court judges, chief judges of provincial courts, and judges of the federal Tax Court are also known as honourable, although they, too, are not members of the Privy Council.

For the record, prime ministers and chief justices of the Supreme Court are known as "the Right Honourable" for life, and governors general are known as "His" or "Her Excellency."

TABLE 5.1 | Structure of the Executive Council in Federal and Provincial Governments

	Federal Government	Provincial Government	Territorial Government
Head of State	Monarch (head of the British royal family, determined by line of succession to the throne)		
Head of State's representative	**Governor General** (appointed by the monarch on recommendation of the PM)	**Lieutenant Governor** (appointed by the monarch on recommendation of the PM)	**Commissioner** (appointed by the PM)
Head of Government	**Prime Minister** (leader of the political party that controls the House of Commons)	**Premier** (leader of the political party that controls the provincial legislature)	**Premier** (in Yukon, leader of the political party that controls the legislature; in Nunavut and NWT, leader selected by members of the legislature)
Executive Body	**The Privy Council** (all current and former members of the federal cabinet, and select others)	**The Executive Council** (all current members of the provincial cabinet)	**The Executive Council** (all current members of the territorial cabinet)
Cabinet	**Prime minister + federal ministers** (appointed by the governor general)	**Premier + provincial ministers** (appointed by the lieutenant governor)	**Premier + territorial ministers** (in Yukon, appointed by the commissioner; in Nunavut and NWT, selected by the members of the legislature and appointed by the commissioner, with portfolios assigned by the premier)
Unique cabinet portfolios	Defence, Foreign Affairs, International Trade, Veterans Affairs, etc.	Education, Municipal Affairs, Social Services, etc.	
Common cabinet portfolios	Indigenous Affairs, Environment, Finance, Health, House Leader, Intergovernmental Affairs, Justice, Labour, Natural Resources, Treasury Board, etc.		

Heads of Government

prime minister The head of government at the federal level.

In Canada, the head of government, unlike the head of state, is a politician. The prime minister (PM) is the leader of the party that controls the House of Commons and oversees the people who administer the Government of Canada. The PM is only *indirectly* elected as the federal head of government. Canadians in various constituencies elect their respective members of parliament (MPs), and the party with the most MPs is typically asked by the governor general to form a government. The leader of that group—as chosen by the party's members—becomes prime minister.

premier The head of government in a provincial or territorial government.

Likewise, a premier is the head of the political party that controls a provincial legislature, is the chief executive who presides over the administration of the provincial government, and is appointed by a lieutenant governor. Heads of territorial governments are also called premiers. In Nunavut and Northwest Territories, which do not have party systems, premiers are chosen by a vote of the legislature and appointed by the commissioner.

This relationship between the head of government and head of state is unique to constitutional monarchies like Canada. In republics, each position is filled by a separate, democratically elected individual like France's prime minister—the head of government—and president—the head of state, or both roles may be fulfilled by a single individual, like the president of the United States. Another feature that sets Canada's constitutional monarchy apart from republican systems is that Canadian first ministers need not be elected. While convention holds that premiers and prime ministers should seek a seat as soon as possible, GGs and LGs may appoint heads of government who do not sit in the legislature. For instance, premiers Christy Clark (BC, 2013), Clyde Wells (Newfoundland, 1989), Don Getty (Alberta, 1989), and Robert Bourassa (Quebec, 1985), and Prime Minister Mackenzie King (1925) all led their respective parties to victory in general elections, yet failed to win races in their own constituencies. Each was appointed head of government, however, and went on to win a seat in a subsequent by-election, joining their government colleagues in the legislature.

In contrast to their counterparts in republics, Canadian heads of government wield considerable executive power. The prime minister and premiers decide how their governments should be structured, how to deal with policy issues, and what legislation to introduce. A first minister is the face of the government, commanding media attention at home and representing constituents internationally. The routine responsibilities of a first minister include managing cabinet, making policy decisions, publicly explaining the government's positions, and attending public events. The head of government will meet with international and domestic counterparts in private and during summits. When the legislature is in session, there is the added duty of leading legislative business and fielding inquiries during Question Period. A first minister also has the ability to advise the GG or LG on the adjournment, proroguing, and dissolution of the legislature. During an election campaign, these responsibilities are replaced with touring, participating in leaders' debates, and posing for photo-ops.

Sean Malley/CBC Licensing

Nunavut MLAs vote unanimously to expel one of their members from the legislature (October 2014). In Nuvavut and Northwest Territories, the premier and cabinet ministers are selected by members of the legislature. In what ways might this approach to selecting the political executive be superior to the process used at the federal level and the provinces? What would it take to make such an approach work at the provincial or federal level?

↻ Adjournment, prorogation, and dissolution are discussed in The Life of the Legislature, in Chapter 6 on page 233. Party leaders' responsibilities in an election campaign are explained in Chapter 10, on elections—see pages 413–17 in particular.

patronage The awarding of government jobs, contracts and/or other financial benefits to friends of the government party.

prime minister's office (PMO) Partisan staff appointed by the prime minister to advance the political interests of the federal cabinet, in particular those of the first minister.

premier's office Partisan staff appointed by the premier to advance the political interests of the provincial cabinet, in particular those of the first minister.

One of the perks of office is the ability to dispense public goods. As heads of government, first ministers hold an appointment power that involves advising the monarch's representative on who should be a member of cabinet, who should preside over various courts, who should head up government departments, and who should fill a myriad of other public posts, from members of boards to heads of agencies. The prime minister, unlike a premier, has the added perk of advising who should be appointed to the Senate and to diplomatic positions abroad. There is, however, a gradual movement toward reducing the PM's appointment power, with some patronage positions becoming elected posts, being opened up to public competition, or being eliminated altogether. The authority to call elections has also been circumscribed somewhat because most legislatures have passed fixed-date election legislation. However, these laws must respect the constitutional authority of the monarch's representative to decide when to dissolve the legislature, and first ministers retain the ability to request an early election.

All significant decisions in the federal government flow through the prime minister's office (PMO). The PMO encompasses the prime minister's chief of staff, director of communications, press secretary, caucus adviser, and other advisers and support personnel. The PMO is not to be confused with the Privy Council Office (or PCO), which provides *policy* advice (not *political* advice) to the government. Discussed below, the PCO is now part of the *permanent executive*. Dispensing both political and policy advice was part of the mandate of the PCO for the first century of Confederation, and these twin functions remain fused in many premiers' offices to this day.

The PMO employs the government's most powerful political staff, all of whom are loyal to the prime minister. They offer strategic advice, recommend people for some patronage positions, and coordinate the PM's busy schedule. PMO staff handle media relations and speechwriting, while providing logistical support for communication events, such as news conferences, public speaking engagements, and tours. They play an active role in ensuring that the major policy initiatives prioritized by the prime minister are implemented by ministers and officials throughout the government. The preeminent PMO employee is the chief of staff, who is in charge of PMO employees, is in daily contact with the prime minister, and speaks privately for the prime minister. A chief of staff tends to act discreetly and maintain a low public profile, despite having considerable authority and political clout. The position involves a combination of political smarts and human resource skills. Percy Downe, a chief of staff to Prime Minister Jean Chrétien, once remarked: "I tell people I don't need a degree in political science to do this job—I need one in marriage counselling."[6] Chiefs of staff also work closely with the government whip to ensure that caucus members remain aligned with the government's priorities. For Ian Brodie, a chief of staff to Prime Minister Stephen Harper, this involved convincing MPs that his "most important common priority is getting you re-elected."[7]

The influence of the prime minister's office and premiers' offices over members of the governing party, including ministers, has been growing as government operations centralize. The clout of the political executive is some cause for concern because only members of the legislature are held publicly accountable for their decisions, while staff of the PMO and premiers' offices seldom are. Recently the media and political scientists have raised concerns that first ministers, acting through the PMO or premiers' offices, wield too much power. One *Globe and Mail* columnist dubbed Jean Chrétien the "friendly dictator," while another chronicled Stephen Harper's despotic reign over

"Harperland."[8] Political science, while taking a more measured approach to studying these themes, has likewise proffered the thesis that Canadians should be concerned that too much power is concentrated in what is sometimes called "the centre" of government.[9] This reflects perceptions that a head of government has significant control with few constraints.

It is true: members of the governing party, including ministers, routinely support the leader, and the presence of cabinet members in the legislature inhibits the checks and balances found in presidential systems of government.[10] Conventions surrounding cabinet responsibility mean it can be no other way: cabinet ministers are bound to support the agenda of their government. In Canada, the head of government is also supported by considerable central agency resources, including policy expertise, budgetary resources, and information control—none of which are available to the government's opposition. As political scientist Donald Savoie observed close to two decades ago, "The prime minister, much more often than not, now embodies political authority within the federal government rather than cabinet or individual cabinet ministers."[11]

VOX POP

Thinking about current media characterizations of the prime minister, to what extent does Savoie's remark hold true today? Do you think it needs updating?

This gives rise to the notion of the **presidentialization** of politics, which suggests that Canada's heads of government are becoming akin to presidents but with fewer constraints.[12] One of the ways this manifests itself is when the head of government chooses to designate a member of cabinet as the top lieutenant in the fashion of a vice-president. The honorary title "deputy prime minister" or "deputy premier" has no force of law and it is not always conferred. Nevertheless it signifies that there is a second-in-command to a supreme leader in the style of a president. References to Canadian governments as "administrations" also draw parallels with the republican system south of the border.

While there is some truth to perceptions of the presidentialization of Canadian politics, it is arguably more present at the provincial level of government. The ability to push an agenda forward is related to the degree of constraint placed by other heads of government, members of opposition parties, interest group mobilization, and the media, all of which are much more intense at the federal level.

It is important not to overstate the power enjoyed by Canadian first ministers. Despite comparisons with dictatorships in other parts of the world, constitutions do place significant constraints on the prime minister and premiers, vesting all sovereignty in the Crown. Although party leaders tend to control their parties, they may face internal pressure as others manoeuvre for their job. They must also balance preferences within their party, caucus, and cabinet with what their own constituents and the broader general public want. Prime ministers and premiers are encumbered by federalism, the economy, globalization, the bureaucracy, the courts, and other governments (international, Aboriginal, and local), which limit their ability to take unilateral action on policy issues. In recent times and in several jurisdictions, first ministers are also bound by legislation, like reform acts, balanced budget laws, or fixed election dates.

presidentialization The concentration of executive power in the office of the prime minister or premier, at the expense of broader cabinet authority.

First ministers who try to operate outside these laws do so at their peril, as former Alberta PC premier Jim Prentice can attest. In the wake of his party's loss to the NDP in the 2015 provincial election, several pundits suggested he angered voters by calling them to the polls ahead of the fixed election date. Indeed, the media and public opinion also place constraints on a first minister's power, particularly when opposing interest groups are at their most effective. In reality, a modern head of government is faced with a deluge of complaints and conflicts with limited options for moving forward.

First ministers also act as checks on each other. Observers have often remarked that the most effective brake on the prime minister's authority lies not across the aisle in the House of Commons but in the unofficial opposition located in premiers' offices across the country. Premiers have, both individually and collectively, halted or altered federal plans for pan-Canadian initiatives, including Senate reform and international trade agreements. With the expanded role assumed by the Council of the Federation, premiers have found strength in numbers, witnessed by their resistance to unilateral federal initiatives like the Canada Job Grant. By the same token, a prime minister can act to thwart premiers' agendas, and fellow premiers can often act as checks on one another. Alberta premiers' plans for developing the province's petroleum industry were slowed by Prime Minister Chrétien's signing of the Kyoto Protocol (1997) and, not quite 20 years later, by BC Premier Christy Clark's issuing of five conditions for pipeline development in BC. Episodes like these serve as reminders about the importance of first minister diplomacy in Canada. The term was coined by political scientist Richard Simeon to describe intergovernmental relations among premiers and prime ministers in Canada.

first minister diplomacy The characterization of Canadian premiers and prime ministers as the primary spokesperson of their government's interests.

BRIEFING NOTES
The "Five Ps" of Power

When considering the source of first ministers' power in Canada, remember the so-called "five Ps":

- *prerogative*, meaning they possess significant decision-making authority when advising the Crown on matters including the opening and closing of the legislature and the appointment of allies to key roles in government;
- *parliament*, in that first ministers have control over the legislative process and agenda;
- *party*, as they sit atop their political party apparatus, and have authority over election strategy, campaign slates, and election platforms;
- *patronage*, in that they control access to plum political appointments and may direct government resources toward favoured projects and initiatives; and
- the *press*, as they are focal points of most media attention.

Together, these five sources of power grant first ministers a massive advantage over their fellow legislators, cabinet members, opposition leaders, and opponents.

VOX POP
What are the benefits of having so much power concentrated in the hands of Canada's first ministers? What are the dangers?

Cabinets

By convention, the government is run by a committee of active members of the political executive (or cabinet), who develop policies and oversee day-to-day administrative matters. The cabinet is typically made up of members of the legislature who are appointed by the monarch's representative on the advice of the first minister. Ministers of the Crown occupy most of the positions within cabinet, which often also includes the House and Senate leaders and a host of so-called "junior ministers." Collectively, these members are accountable to both the monarch's representative and, more importantly, to the legislature.

> **minister of the Crown** The political head of a government ministry, responsible for directing and overseeing the activities of its departments and agencies, boards, and commissions.

At the federal level, cabinet typically consists of between 35 and 40 members, whereas provincial cabinets tend to operate with roughly half as many. In rare circumstances, an individual without a seat in the legislature is appointed to cabinet. Prime ministers have often selected at least one senator to serve in cabinet, to serve as the government's representative in the Upper House and to ensure each province is represented, should the governing party's complement of MPs not contain members from all 10 jurisdictions.

Members of cabinet meet frequently to make government policy decisions, address issues of the day, and review proposed legislation. While BC has held portions of cabinet meetings in public, and while western Canadian governments have held joint cabinet meetings on occasion, for the most part, cabinet meetings take place behind closed doors. Details of these meetings are treated as cabinet confidences, meaning that information such as when a meeting was held, who was present, what background materials were prepared, and who said what is not made public. Normally, the only non-politician present is the government's top civil servant, the clerk (or chief deputy minister). Cabinet meetings are chaired by the first minister, whose style may range from command and control to collegial and collaborative.

Most members of cabinet become ministers of the Crown. Ministers are held accountable for their respective portfolios by fielding questions in the legislature and from media. The minister is in regular contact with senior public servants who relay directions to other bureaucrats, provide the minister with information, and present recommendations. For instance, Scott Brison was first elected as a Progressive Conservative member of Parliament for the Nova Scotia riding of Kings-Hants in 1997. In 2003, he crossed the floor to sit as a Liberal MP. He was re-elected as a Liberal in 2004, and Prime Minister Martin recommended to the governor general that Brison be appointed to the Privy Council as minister of public works. Brison became the first openly gay member of a federal cabinet. However, when the Conservative Party won the most seats in the 2006 election, the governor general called upon that party's leader, Stephen Harper, to form a government. Although Brison continued to be re-elected in Kings-Hants, for nearly a decade he sat as a member of the Liberal opposition. In 2015, the Liberal Party once again won the most seats, and leader Justin Trudeau recommended that the governor general appoint Brison as president of the Treasury Board. Minister Brison therefore holds a seat among the front benches of the House of Commons (the back benches are reserved for non-cabinet ministers), has a duty to attend cabinet meetings, oversees the Treasury Board Secretariat, and simultaneously represents the approximately 83,000 constituents living in his Nova Scotia electoral district.

> **portfolio** An office or area of responsibility for a minister of the Crown.

Sometimes ministers are assigned additional duties, serving as regional representatives or leading in specific priority areas. In 2013, for instance, Prime Minister

Harper named Finance Minister Jim Flaherty as minister responsible for the greater Toronto area (GTA), while assigning Minister of Labour Kellie Leitch responsibilities for the status of women portfolio. At the provincial level, many premiers, themselves, assume responsibilities as ministers responsible for Aboriginal, intergovernmental, or international relations.

regional minister A minister whose portfolio includes additional responsibility for government in a broad geographic area.

Regional ministers are designated as cabinet representatives of large geographic regions. Whether or not the designation is formal and publicly stated, the duties of a regional minister entail being the government's go-to person for a large city or for an area within a province. At the federal level, a regional minster may become responsible for an entire province. Typically all political decisions affecting a given region

INSIDE CANADIAN POLITICS
Why Was C.D. Howe Known as the "Minister of Everything"?

Occasionally an experienced, high-profile minister who wins the trust of the prime minister or premier will rise to become the *de facto* head of government, assuming greater control of key government decisions. The situation develops over time, as the minister's capable handling of important portfolios, sage advice at the cabinet table, and influence among other ministers is noticed. As sensitive issues emerge, the minister may be asked to lead the file; as other ministers exit cabinet, the minister may assume their portfolios in an acting capacity. Eventually, the minister may be asked to head up a "super ministry" of combined departments.

The most prevalent case of a "minister of everything" is surely that of C.D. Howe, a member of the federal cabinet for 22 consecutive years under Liberal prime ministers Mackenzie King (1935–48) and Louis St Laurent (1948–57). Howe was minister of munitions and supply during World War II. During the post-war years, he was minister of reconstruction, and then minister of trade and commerce, guiding Canada through a transformative period

that saw its economy less and less dependent on agriculture and more and more on manufacturing. His autocratic style of decision-making, combined with the fact he held the confidence of the prime minister, ensured that the things Howe championed were achieved.

Howe's impatience with parliamentary procedure contributed to his political downfall during the pipeline debate of 1956. Minister Howe wanted the government to fund a pipeline that would transport natural gas from Alberta to central Canada. The pipeline was to be built by an American company. To expedite approval of the pipeline and limit criticism from the opposition parties, the Liberals invoked closure to cut off parliamentary debate. The boldness of the move attracted the censure of political critics, who saw the government as taking the legislature for granted after nearly two consecutive decades in power. Following a month of heated exchanges the pipeline bill was approved, but within a year the Liberal Party's reign, and Howe's political career, would be over.

THE LESSON
A minister who gains the trust of the premier or prime minister can wield considerable power within cabinet, at times rivalling the authority of the first minister.

VOX POP
What are the advantages and dangers of having a "minister of everything" in cabinet?

BRIEFING NOTES

Ministries and Departments

While the terms are often used interchangeably, there is an important distinction between a *ministry* and a *department*.

Departments are administrative units, typically assigned to a deputy minister who reports to a minister responsible for that policy area. The deputy minister of education heads the Department of Education, for example, and reports to the minister of education for the administration of all public servants who work in the department.

Ministries are broader units that include not only departments, but also any ministers of state, parliamentary secretaries, and agencies, boards, and commissions (ABCs) that fall under that minister's authority. Unlike departments, these other bodies typically report directly to the minister, and are not accountable to any department or deputy. In this sense, ministers may be responsible for more than one department, and have more than one deputy.

For example, prior to 2015, the federal minister of Employment and Social Development Canada oversaw the entire ministry, which also included departments (Labour, Service Canada), ministers of state (for the status of women, for social development, for seniors), and numerous ABCs (including those related to seniors, persons with disabilities, and pensions). By the same token, provincial ministers of justice typically hold responsibility for the departments of Justice (courts) and Public Safety (law enforcement). Ministers of health often have separate ministers of state and deputy ministers devoted to acute care (hospitals and clinics) and wellness (health promotion and prevention), in addition to chief executive officers who report to them on the operations of individual regional health authorities. Similarly, ministers responsible for post-secondary education may have separate departments devoted to universities and colleges as well as labour market development.

have to flow through the regional minister's office, which increases that minister's clout.[13] Beyond the symbolism of such representation, there is the practical need to direct the flow of information and communication. For instance, a regional minister can be delegated duties to be the prime minister's chief liaison with a premier, with mayors, and with other regional political actors. He or she may also have special influence over the party's election strategy.

Ensuring that all regions are represented in cabinet is so important that first ministers will sometimes get creative to guarantee proper geographic representation. For instance, at times the federal Conservative government of Stephen Harper was without an MP from Vancouver, Montreal, Prince Edward Island, and Newfoundland and Labrador. The PM ensured those regions had cabinet representation by (1) encouraging a Liberal MP to cross the floor to take up a Tory cabinet position; (2) appointing a Montreal-based party fundraiser as a Quebec senator, who was then brought into cabinet; and (3) tapping a Nova Scotia minister to assume responsibility for PEI and, later, Newfoundland and Labrador. With a broader complement of Liberal MPs from across Canada, Prime Minister Justin Trudeau did not have to draw on such creativity when forming his first cabinet in 2015.

To execute their responsibilities, ministers are supported by a team of political staff. Like the PMO or premier's office, but on a much smaller scale, ministerial teams include a chief of staff within the department, an executive assistant, legislative assistants, and constituency assistants. These partisans may have been involved in the governing party's election campaign, may have personal ties with the minister, or may have been planted in a department at the prerogative of the first minister's office. There are also communications personnel, who in some jurisdictions are political staff, whereas in others they are apolitical members of the bureaucracy. The chief of staff and executive assistant provide issues management support, interact with central agencies, and communicate political decisions to public servants. Legislative assistants participate in the drafting of bills, while constituency assistants handle inquiries from citizens in the minister's electoral district. These types of positions are often filled by young people, except the chief of staff position, which requires broader experience. Not all of these positions exist in smaller provinces and territories.

In addition to full ministers of the Crown, the political executive often features a pair of junior positions that exist outside the formal cabinet: *ministers of state* and *parliamentary secretaries*. Ministers of state (also known as *associate ministers* in some cases) are not always members of the cabinet, but they demonstrate political and policy leadership and are bound by the same rules of collective responsibility and confidentiality. They provide cabinet or individual ministers of the Crown with support in specific policy areas, often acting on behalf of full ministers by responding to questions in the legislature, serving on committees, and meeting with stakeholders in their particular areas of responsibility. Typically reporting to a specific minister of the Crown, a minister of state has a narrow policy responsibility and is supported by a small staff. He or she does not tend to advance files or deal with issues that require cabinet's attention. For instance, until recently, the Government of Canada did not have a department of democratic reform but rather had a minister of state responsible for that policy area. Prime Minister Justin Trudeau changed this approach in his first cabinet, creating a stand-alone Minister of Democratic Institutions. A minister of state may also be assigned a policy area that mirrors a department, such as a minister of state for finance. Finally, a minister of state may have no designated area of responsibility whatsoever; a person in this position used to be known as a *minister without portfolio*, whose presence in cabinet usually involved some symbolic, representational, or partisan objective.

Parliamentary secretaries (also known as *parliamentary assistants* or *secretaries of state*) fulfill many of the same roles as ministers of state. Both perform duties on behalf of a minister of the Crown, such as delivering speeches, giving interviews, representing the minister in the legislature, and attending special events. Both positions help to link their minister to the legislative branch; however, neither has significant power or decision-making authority. Where parliamentary secretaries differ from ministers of state is in the fact they are not formally a part of their respective ministries. This means parliamentary secretaries do not have policymaking or leadership authority, do not introduce their own bills or motions, do not have automatic or full membership in cabinet committees, do not have control over departmental resources, and generally possess less authority and autonomy than ministers of state. Rather than providing policy leadership, a parliamentary secretary's primary role is to link the minister to the legislative branch. This means serving as a liaison between the minister and colleagues in the legislature, committees, and caucus, ensuring that the minister's legislative agenda is communicated, understood, and supported. While parliamentary secretaries may respond on behalf of ministers to policy-related questions during Question Period, the more sensitive matters are assigned to ministers of state.

minister of state A member of the legislature assigned by the first minister to provide support to Cabinet by exerting leadership over a particular policy area.

parliamentary secretary A member of the legislature assigned by the first minister to assist a minister in the performance of ministerial duties.

Ministers of state and parliamentary secretaries are generally considered patronage positions, used as signals to young and sometimes restless backbenchers that they are in training to become a full minister. Ultimately, full ministers of the Crown are responsible for everything that happens under their portfolio, including the actions of ministers of state and parliamentary secretaries.

Just as the governing party assembles its cabinet to develop policy initiatives and oversee the day-to-day administration of government, each opposition party maintains its own shadow cabinet, consisting of critics assigned to each of the major government portfolios. As their title suggests, these critics are responsible for scrutinizing the work of their assigned minister of the Crown, acting as the chief party spokesperson in the legislature, committees, and the media. They are also responsible for leading their party's own policy development in that subject area.

Deciding whom to appoint to cabinet is a complex proposition for a number of reasons.[14] First and foremost, prime ministers and premiers are generally limited by having to select from among those candidates who have won seats in the general election. Although it is possible to appoint members of cabinet who do not serve in the legislature, the practice is used sparingly. Next, there is an imperative to balance geography and socio-demographic considerations. Finally, there are other factors to consider, such as a member's diverse skills and experience, loyalty to the leader, and prospects for re-election. The cabinet appointment process has been described by political scientist Matthew Kerby as a "witch's cauldron" due to the many personal and political factors at play.[15] He found that a member of a governing party stood

backbencher A rank-and-file member of the legislative assembly without cabinet responsibilities or other special legislative titles or duties.

shadow cabinet A group of opposition party members responsible for holding ministers of the Crown to account for their actions.

critic An opposition party member assigned to scrutinize the activities of a particular minister of the Crown.

the greatest chance of being recommended by the prime minister for appointment to cabinet if he or she had past experience as a minister and/or was considered a legitimate challenger for the party leadership. Women, lawyers, and regional representatives were also more likely to be appointed—provided, of course, they were present in the government's caucus in the first place. Like Sylvia Bashevkin before them, Linda Trimble and Manon Tremblay refer to the "higher the fewer" principle: compared with men and once elected, female politicians have as good, or better, chances of making it to cabinet.[16] However, women tend to be appointed as ministers of social matters such as education, environment, and health, whereas the so-called "power positions" of defence, finance, justice, treasury board, and natural resources tend to be allocated to men. Nevertheless, in

David Kawai

Conservative Party MP Steven Fletcher became the first quadriplegic to serve in the House of Commons in 2004, and was later appointed to cabinet, first as minister of state for democratic reform (2008), then as minister of state for transport (2011). Under Prime Minister Justin Trudeau, Calgarian Kent Hehr, victim of a 1991 drive-by shooting that left him paraplegic, was named minister of veterans' affairs. What kinds of challenges is a person who uses a wheelchair likely to face when campaigning for office, when serving as a member of Parliament, or when holding a cabinet position?

recent years, the presence of women at the cabinet table has increased, beginning at the provincial level, where, since 2008, women have chaired cabinet as first minister of six provinces and territories: Nunavut, Newfoundland and Labrador, British Columbia, Alberta, Quebec, and Ontario. In 2015, Alberta and the federal government joined Quebec (2007) as the only jurisdictions in Canada to have featured gender parity in cabinet.

The membership of cabinet obviously changes over time. Cabinet shuffles occur regularly, and range from innocuous mini-shuffles to major events. The biggest turnover occurs after a general election, when ministers who have not sought re-election or have been defeated must be replaced, and when, potentially, a different party forms the government. Major change also occurs when the government party selects a new leader, who often decides to use a shuffle to reward supporters and demote opponents. Periodically, a head of government will tinker with the composition of cabinet to fill gaps that emerge due to resignations and the demotion of underachievers, which creates room to promote competent performers or inject new blood.

In Canada, cabinet shuffles are a regular occurrence. Politically, they are used to place a fresh face on portfolios that have gotten out of hand, to remind ministers that they serve at the pleasure of a higher authority, and to limit grumbling among

cabinet shuffle A change in the composition of a government's political executive between elections.

Council of the Federation

In July 2013, 6 of the 13 first ministers attending the Council of the Federation meeting at Niagara-on-the-Lake, Ontario, were women. Since that time, the number of women at the premiers' table has fluctuated, but there remain more women party leaders and premiers than ever before. Why is this shift taking place at the provincial/territorial level but not happening at the federal level?

INSIDE CANADIAN POLITICS

Who Are the Women Who Cracked Glass Ceilings in Canadian Politics?

Over time, the proportion of non-white heterosexual males in the political executive has been declining. But it took a number of firsts to set this change in motion. The first woman to be appointed to a provincial cabinet is believed to be Mary Ellen Smith, who became minister without portfolio in the 1921 British Columbia government. Canada's first female federal cabinet minister was Ellen Fairclough of Hamilton, who was appointed secretary of state in 1957, and then minister of citizenship and immigration in 1958. The first woman to become a lieutenant governor was Pauline Mills McGibbon of Ontario in 1974, and Quebec's Jeanne Sauvé was appointed as the first female governor general in 1984. The first female premier was Rita Johnson, who briefly led the BC Social Credit government in 1991. The first female prime minister was Kim Campbell in 1993, the same year that PEI Liberal premier Catherine Callbeck became the first woman to lead a provincial party to election victory. In 1999, Adrienne Clarkson, whose family emigrated from Hong Kong, became the first non-white female governor general. In 2013, premier of Ontario Kathleen Wynne become the first openly homosexual politician to head a Canadian government.

VOX POP

What factors do you think contributed most to the achievement of these "firsts"? In what ways are the factors contributing to elected and appointed positions for women the same as for men? How are the factors different?

backbenchers who hope one day to be appointed. Shuffled ministers are exempted from having to answer questions about previous departments they headed; aside from the first minister, only the current minister or designate can speak officially on behalf of a government department. Administratively, many shuffles also involve the creation of new ministries and departments, or a redefinition of portfolios depending upon the government's priorities of the day.

BRIEFING NOTES

Kitchen Cabinets

The most influential people in government are part of the so-called "kitchen cabinet," which is an unofficial term used to describe the handful of elected and non-elected advisers within a first minister's inner circle. In Canada we know very little about these people, but a kitchen cabinet likely includes key ministers, top party personnel, select political staff, political consultants, long-time friends, and certain family members, including a spouse. Given the (unknown) influence of such people, who are often not accountable to the legislature, some critics view them as potential cause for concern, while others see them merely as trusted sources of advice.

Being part of cabinet does not necessarily mean that power is distributed equally. The head of government is meant to be *primus inter pares* (Latin for "first among equals"), meaning that ministers are led by one of their own. In reality, by virtue of their position, prime ministers and premiers are superiors among their hand-picked followers. Some ministers are part of the inner cabinet, which is an unofficial term to describe the handful of members of cabinet who are closest to the head of government. Members of the inner cabinet typically hold the most powerful cabinet portfolios, tend to be regional ministers, and are often members if not chairs of the most influential cabinet committees. These ministers tend to be the power brokers who hold the most sway around the cabinet table.

Compared to political executives in other countries around the world, Canadian cabinets tend to:

- be unusually large for the size of their electorates, given the need to accommodate a more diverse constituent base;
- be highly institutionalized, meaning that ministers have access to a larger amount of resources and are bound by a more complex series of rules, checks, and balances;
- consist of cabinet members from only one political party;
- feature more democratically selected members; and
- exercise greater authority over the legislative branch.

Cabinet Processes

Ministers are given an abundance of information to help them prepare for cabinet meetings. This includes memorandums to cabinet authored by public servants and brought forward to cabinet by a minister seeking a decision on a particular matter. But the size of cabinet membership, considerable time constraints, and the volume of government issues means that it is impossible for every matter to be examined in detail in full cabinet meetings. Cabinet therefore makes considerable use of small subgroups of ministers, known as cabinet committees. These should not be confused with legislative committees, which are the all-party committees that scrutinize government business and are usually open to the public. Cabinet committees hold closed-door meetings to examine issues and report back in private to the full cabinet for a government decision. At the federal level, there are three major cabinet committees that have become institutionalized (see Table 5.2), as well as a handful of other committees that are subject to change.

⟳ The function and composition of legislative committees are discussed on pages 241–2 of Chapter 6, on the legislature.

The most powerful cabinet committee is agenda and results (formerly priorities and planning), whose members are among the government's most capable and trusted ministers. It is chaired by the prime minister and meets to strategize longer-term issues, to develop and maintain a consistent government narrative and message, and to review cabinet recommendations. The parliamentary affairs (formerly operations) committee deals with shorter-term issues management, including the government's legislative agenda. The Treasury Board is the nucleus of fiscal decisions, particularly those dealing with the budget. Other cabinet committees reflect priorities of the government of the day. For instance, after a major cabinet shuffle in mid-2013, Prime Minister Harper designed three core cabinet committees (priorities

TABLE 5.2 | Main Cabinet Committees, Government of Canada*

Committee Name	Committee Chair	Committee Priorities
Agenda and Results	prime minister	• strategic direction on government priorities and expenditure management • ratification of committee recommendations • approval of routine government appointments
Parliamentary Affairs	senior minister	• day-to-day coordination of the government's agenda • issues management • legislation and house planning • communication
Treasury Board	president of the Treasury Board	• accountability and ethics • financial, personnel, and administrative management • comptrollership • approval of regulations and most orders-in-council

*2015 data. All cabinet committees are supported by staff in the PMO and PCO; however, the Treasury Board receives further assistance from staff in the Treasury Board Secretariat.

Source: Prime Minister of Canada, "Cabinet committee mandate and membership" (2015), www.pm.gc.ca.

and planning, operations, and Treasury Board), and four additional ones devoted to government administration, social affairs, economic prosperity, and foreign affairs and security. Prime Minister Justin Trudeau renamed two of these core committees (agenda and results, and parliamentary affairs), and reorganized the remainder (creating cabinet committees on inclusive growth, opportunities and innovation; diversity and inclusion; Canada in the world and public security; intelligence and emergency management; open and transparent government; and environment, climate change and energy).

Similar main committee structures exist at the provincial level of government, though not all provinces have an operations committee. Indeed, there is a considerable variety of provincial cabinet committee structures. In 2013, for instance, the British Columbia cabinet had six specialist committees to focus on specific policy initiatives (core review; environment and land use; legislative review; secure tomorrow; strong economy; liquefied natural gas), but next door in Alberta, there were no specialist committees.

When the full cabinet considers a recommendation from a minister or a cabinet committee, its role is to collectively make a decision based on all of the available information at hand. A decision made by cabinet is recorded as a Minute of Council. At the federal level, this written decision is understood to reflect the views of the full Privy Council, including those who are not members of cabinet, and is submitted to the monarch's representative. A Minute of Council either directs whether information, such as a government report, should be shared with the governor general (or lieutenant governor) or seeks authorization for a course of action, such as appointing someone to a government board.

Given the volume of decisions within government, not all matters requiring the signature of the GG or LG need to be vetted by cabinet. A minister may submit a routine request directly to the monarch's representative in the form of a Governor in Council (GIC) submission. It is prepared by public servants and signed by the minister. These are required for a variety of matters, and drafts of a GIC are vetted by analysts in the Treasury Board Secretariat, Department of Justice, and the Privy Council

Office before the minister signs. To authorize the government to act on the cabinet's request, whether communicated in the form of a Minute of Council or Governor in Council, the governor general or lieutenant governor signs an Order in Council. An Order in Council has the force of law, and permits the political executive and the public service to proceed with implementation.

Executive Accountability

Holding the executive branch accountable remains one of the common challenges facing all fully functioning democracies. In Canada, political elites are held to account through the concept and conventions of responsible government. As discussed in Chapter 2, this principle holds that those appointed to govern must be supported by the people's elected representatives. That is to say, the political executive must maintain the confidence of the legislature. This is how members of cabinet, as well as the bureaucracy that serves them, are indirectly accountable to the electorate while governing. To ensure that the government reflects the public will, the governing party must face the Canadian electorate at least once every five years and, in the interim, cannot lose a major vote in the legislature. In practice, the main restraint in the legislature is the confidence con-vention (also known as a confidence vote). This principle holds that when the public's elected representatives vote in the legislature on a major decision of cabinet, a minimum of half of those present must vote in favour of the government's position. Otherwise, if a majority votes against it, then the legislature is deemed to have lost confidence in the government, and the legislature must be dissolved. A general election must then be held or, under extremely rare circumstances, the monarch's representative may call directly on an opposition party leader to form government. The latter has occurred only twice in Canadian history: once after the Pacific Scandal of 1873 and the other after the King–Byng affair of 1926. In both cases an election followed soon afterwards.

Matters of confidence vary, but traditionally they include votes on the budget and on the government's reply to the Speech from the Throne. Governments, themselves, may declare any vote a matter of confidence, and opposition parties may put forward motions of non-confidence, or propose amendments to any piece of legislation to that effect. Crucially, this means that not all legislature votes are measures of confidence in the government. The government may lose many minor motions and parliamentary issues without fear of losing power.

Most governments fall of their own volition, either by asking the GG or LG to dissolve the legislature and call an election, or by orchestrating their own defeat on a confidence vote. It is rare for governments to be defeated on matters of confidence, but it does happen on occasion. In these instances, the governing party may be dis-patched in favour of a new government in the subsequent election (as in the 2006 federal election that saw the reigning Liberals ousted by the Conservatives), or the governing party may be returned to office with a larger number of seats than before (as with the 2011 federal election, which saw a Conservative minority replaced with a Conservative majority).

In systems of responsible government like Canada's, two conventions of account-ability apply to cabinet ministers. The first is *cabinet solidarity*, which holds that, as a group, cabinet ministers are accountable for all government decisions. Even if a minister privately disagrees with a course of action or has played no direct role in it whatsoever,

confidence convention
The practice under which a government must relinquish power when it loses a critical legislative vote.

↻ Only twice in Canadian history has the monarch's representative invited an opposition party leader to form government following a government's loss of a confidence motion. See the ICP box on page 171 of this chapter for an account of one case, the King–Byng affair.

he or she is obliged to support the cabinet's decision (or, at least, refrain from opposing it) in legislative votes and public statements. In public, all ministers must vocalize their support for cabinet and government policy, and the public comments of one minister must reflect the public position of cabinet as a whole. Ministers take a lifetime oath of secrecy and therefore do not tend to speak about cabinet debates even after they have left office. If a minister disagrees with a cabinet decision, there are two options: carry on or resign. This solidarity promotes strength, trust-building, and efficiency. It also means that ministers must always vote together with the head of government. This can frustrate constituents, when their member of the legislature votes in support of a policy decision that will have negative implications in their riding. By the same token, cabinet solidarity in Ottawa can upset premiers who decry that a federal minister's position is at odds with provincial interests (despite the fact that premiers themselves command unwavering solidarity from their own cabinets). Such conflict is fodder for political media, and raises an interesting question: does a minister exist foremost to promote the government's position to constituents or to promote constituents' position to the government? The latter does occur, but typically behind closed cabinet meeting doors.

Cabinet is collectively responsible for government actions, but individual ministers remain personally accountable to the legislature. Under the second principle, that of *ministerial responsibility*, a minister is directly accountable for decisions taken in her or his portfolio. As the public face of a department, a minister accepts credit for good news and policy initiatives but must also shoulder the blame in the event of problems—even if the minister had no personal knowledge of what transpired until after the fact. Thus, ministers are responsible for their own actions, for department policies, for misspending, and for bureaucratic errors, even those that occurred before the minister assumed responsibility for the portfolio. The minister must answer to the legislature, which routinely involves fielding questions. If there is sufficient controversy, this can trigger a cabinet shuffle or, at the extreme, the minister's resignation from cabinet entirely. Contrary to opposition rhetoric and popular opinion, the convention of ministerial responsibility in Canada has never required members of government to resign automatically.

The concentration of power in the cabinet and the party hierarchy generally, and in the head of government specifically, has led to concerns about the limited role of backbenchers in the legislature. Stifling party discipline, feelings of disempowerment among legislators, the politicization of legislative committees, and a public service that is fearful of engaging with Canadians have contributed to perceptions of a *democratic deficit* in Canada. The term refers to the disconnect between people's expectations of how democratic institutions should function and the actual performance of those institutions. In a major speech delivered by Paul Martin in 2002, prior to his becoming prime minister, he lamented that average MPs do not have enough power, and that what mattered most to having any policy influence was "who you know in the PMO."[18] Martin advocated six reforms to address the democratic deficit: (1) loosening party discipline, (2) consulting MPs after first reading of a bill, (3) providing private members with more opportunities to introduce bills, (4) giving standing legislative committees more autonomy, (5) giving MPs the opportunity to review partisan appointments, and (6) creating an independent ethics officer. The changes were never implemented.

In 2015, Conservative MP Michael Chong surprised many when his private member's bill, designed to put more power in the hands of MPs, passed. Bill C-586,

↺ The principles of cabinet solidarity and ministerial responsibility are introduced on page 45 of Chapter 2, on the constitution.

↺ For more about democratic deficit see page 498 of Chapter 14.

commonly known as the Reform Act, amended the Elections Act and the Parliament Act. There are two main elements. First, it shifts responsibility for approving candidate nominations away from party leaders to designated individuals other than the leader. Second, it requires each party's newly elected caucus to vote on whether they will follow the new caucus parameters during the life of that Parliament. What this means is that should the party leader decide to remove an MP from the caucus, or to recruit an MP from another party, caucuses that have "opted in" will be given the chance to vote on the move. Party caucuses that have voted to follow the new parameters will enjoy other powers as well: the power to decide when a party leader should be removed from the position, or whether to remove the caucus chair. These moves can be initiated by a written request that must be signed by at least 20 per cent of the party's MPs, followed by an internal secret ballot vote that must receive the support of a majority of the party's MPs. According to Chong, "The passage of the Reform Act

INSIDE CANADIAN POLITICS

Is It True that Ministers Must Resign in the Face of Controversy?

Some observers mistakenly believe that ministerial responsibility requires cabinet ministers to resign for the misconduct or poor performance of their employees. This is not, and has never been, the case under the conventions of responsible government. Only two federal cabinet ministers have ever resigned over issues of individual ministerial responsibility, which is to say that they accepted accountability for ill-administration of their departments.[17]

Henry Stevens, federal minister of trade and commerce, resigned in 1934 after being publicly rebuked by Conservative prime minister R.B. Bennett for shaming the business community through his chairmanship of a royal commission examining corruption. Stevens went on to form his own (short-lived) political party before returning to the Conservative caucus in 1939. Fifty years later, John Fraser, as minister of fisheries and oceans in the Mulroney government, resigned from cabinet after intervening directly to approve the release of tuna that his department officials deemed unfit for human consumption. A far greater number of ministers have resigned over refusal to support cabinet decisions.

It is also a myth that ministerial responsibility shields civil servants from being held accountable for their actions. Non-partisan deputy ministers are accountable to their ministers, and all department staff are accountable to their deputies for the performance of their duties. Ministers and deputies who discover malfeasance in their departments are often swift to discipline individual staff. In recent years, however, bureaucrats have been called to appear before parliamentary committees examining their decisions and performance. Several federal civil servants were called before the Public Accounts Committee in 2004, for example, to testify about the sponsorship scandal. The Privy Council Office explained this approach as maintaining the *accountability* of bureaucrats to their respective ministers, while allowing them to be *answerable* to Parliament.

VOX POP

Do you think ministers should take more responsibility for the actions of their staff, resigning when major problems occur under their watch? Or should unelected public servants themselves be more accountable?

Gary Clement, National Post

Backbench MPs are often characterized in the media as trained seals or puppets of the prime minister. Should a backbencher be able to challenge the head of government's stance on an incendiary issue? Or should backbenchers just toe the party line?

is a victory for democracy . . . [and] addresses a long-standing problem in Ottawa: the concentration of power in party leaders, including the prime minister. It will give individual Members of Parliament more power to represent their constituents and Canadians."[19] The full implications of the Reform Act remain to be seen. It presents a significant opportunity for dramatic power struggles as well as a mechanism for a leader to potentially exercise further control over a loyal caucus.

During the 2015 federal election campaign, Liberal leader and future prime minister, Justin Trudeau, promised a host of democratic reforms aimed at limiting the power of the executive, including: establishing a special "Prime Minister's Question Period"; increasing the number of free votes, limiting the use of omnibus bills and prorogation, and strengthening the role of legislative committees; respecting the role of parliamentary watchdogs (particularly the Parliamentary Budget Officer); and increasing the transparency of government appointments, budgeting, and national security.

The Permanent Executive

The formal and political executives sit at the apex of Canada's democratic system, as Figure 5.1 showed, but they are dwarfed in size and complexity by the bureaucratic structure supporting them. The **permanent executive**, as it is known, encompasses non-partisan government employees holding a wide variety of high-level positions in the government. Otherwise known as the *public service executives*, they are considered permanent because, unlike their formal political counterparts, they typically remain in place regardless of the election cycle.

permanent executive
Non-partisan bureaucratic officials serving at the pleasure of the Crown and its ministers.

clerk of the Privy (or Executive) Council The highest-ranking public servant in the federal (or provincial/territorial) bureaucracy.

deputy minister Reporting to the minister, the highest-ranking public servant in a given government department.

↻ The functions of the public service are discussed throughout Chapter 8, on public policy and administration.

central agencies Coordinating bodies that steer government business across all departments.

The most senior federal bureaucrat is the clerk of the Privy Council, who serves as the deputy minister to the prime minister and leader of the council of deputy ministers. The position is filled by the clerk of the Executive Council in the provinces and territories. Just as the first minister's chief of staff is head of political staff, the clerk is the head of the public service, and both positions are in regular contact with the head of government (i.e. the prime minister or premier). As the secretary to cabinet, the clerk is the only civil servant to attend cabinet meetings, and is on hand to clarify questions about government process, ensuring that cabinet receives information and effective oversight of the implementation of its directives. In addition to overseeing the Privy (or Executive) Council Office, the clerk works with leaders of the public service commission to encourage the professional development of the public service.

Not to be confused with elected officials like ministers of state and parliamentary secretaries, deputy ministers (DMs) occupy a key role within the senior ranks of the non-partisan public service. Typically appointed by the clerk and serving at the pleasure of the minister responsible for the portfolio, the DM is the top bureaucrat and functional head of a department. Under the minister's instruction, a deputy minister manages departmental business, including the budget, and follows directives received from the clerk. DMs are non-partisan appointees who may have worked their way up through the public service, or may have been recruited from the outside. They provide policy advice to the minister, ensure that the minister's directives are implemented, and occasionally perform duties on behalf of the minister, such as meeting with stakeholders.

As the integration between departments and central agencies has grown, so have the interactions between DMs and deputy minister equivalents, like presidents of key government agencies and crown corporations. They regularly consult with each other on policy issues, participate on interdepartmental committees, and, at the federal level, attend weekly deputy minister breakfast meetings chaired by the clerk. Each department also employs several assistant, or associate, deputy ministers (ADMs), who work under the direction of the deputy. An ADM often has specialized knowledge or skills, and oversees staff in a division of the department.

In general, the permanent executive consists of three main bodies:

1. *central agencies* that coordinate policy across government
2. *line departments* that focus on program and service delivery under specific policy portfolios, and
3. *agencies, boards, and commissions* that provide programs and services at arm's length from government.

While their names may vary, all three types of bodies exist in federal, provincial, and territorial governments.

Central Agencies

Generally speaking, the four central agencies in the federal government are the PMO, the Privy Council Office, the Treasury Board Secretariat, and the Department of Finance. Only the PMO, described earlier in the chapter, employs exclusively political staff; the other three central agencies are staffed by non-partisan public servants. Premiers' offices often contain a combination of political and policy staff. In both cases, this concentration of power has, as mentioned, been dubbed simply "the centre."[19]

Headed by the federal clerk, the Privy Council Office (PCO) is the bureaucratic equivalent of the partisan PMO. The PCO employs policy research and analysis experts who provide high-level expertise to the prime minister and cabinet. Their central function is to act on the wishes of cabinet, to assist in coordinating cabinet submissions and cross-ministry initiatives, and to provide impartial advice. Specifically, the primary tasks of the PCO are to

- "provide unbiased advice to the prime minister, cabinet, and cabinet committees on matters of national and international importance;
- ensure the smooth functioning of the cabinet decision-making process and facilitate the implementation of the government's agenda; and
- foster a high-performing and accountable public service."[20]

As government employees, staffers in the Privy Council Office are politically neutral professionals. Yet they are politically astute and among the most influential public servants in the system. Among the many employees in the PCO are

- a national security adviser, who briefs the prime minister about security intelligence;
- an associate secretary to cabinet, who acts on behalf of the clerk where necessary and who is deputy minister of intergovernmental affairs;
- ADMs, who deal with intergovernmental policy and federal, provincial, and territorial (FPT) relations;
- deputy and assistant secretaries to cabinet, who coordinate policy between departments and manage issues;
- various directors, who assist with the preparation of cabinet documents, communications, and intergovernmental matters; and
- staff who assist cabinet committees.

There can also be PCO positions created to deal with special topics, such as the deputy minister who led a 26-member Afghanistan task force to advise Prime Minister Harper about Canada's evolving military presence in that country. The PMO's chief of staff interacts regularly with the PCO and normally attends the weekly meetings of its senior staff. In the provinces, PCO functions are typically performed by office staff of the Executive Council.

The Treasury Board Secretariat (TBS) employs public servants to support the financial management work of the Treasury Board cabinet committee. This support includes information and advice based on their scrutiny of existing and proposed government spending. The TBS enforces policies and guidelines with an eye toward cost-efficiencies and standardization across government. As a central agency, the TBS has responsibility for encouraging effective management of a variety of government-wide activities, including:

- information and information technology;
- the management and accountability of deputy ministers;
- risk management; and
- human resources, including remuneration, pensions, and benefits.

Privy Council Office (PCO) The central agency responsible for coordinating the federal government's overall implementation of policy.

Treasury Board Secretariat The central agency responsible for coordinating government spending, as well as human and technical resources.

Within the federal TBS is the Office of the Comptroller General of Canada, which provides internal government advice on financial accounting such as audits, contracting, and property management. An example of the type of career opportunities that exist within the TBS is presented in the Opportunities Available box on page 197.

The fourth central agency is the Department of Finance. Its primary coordination role is the preparation of the government's annual budget and any related economic updates or reports. It is responsible for articulating taxation, borrowing, and tariffs policies, as well as fiscal transfers to the provinces and territories. At the federal level, the department also has jurisdiction over financial institutions such as the banking industry. Its staffing follows the normal model for a department, in that the minister is supported by a management team comprising a DM and ADMs, as well as possibly a minister of state or a parliamentary secretary. However, the finance department may have a smaller complement of staff than departments involved in the delivery of public services.

Department of Finance The central agency responsible for setting and monitoring the government's fiscal and economic policy, including overseeing the budget process.

Line Departments

Aside from these central agencies, the bureaucracy also contains a host of line departments (or *line ministries*), each of which falls under the political direction of a minister of the Crown and the bureaucratic direction of a deputy minister. Their existence tends to be closely related to areas of jurisdiction that are enumerated in sections 91 to 95 of the Constitution Act, 1867. Section 91 identifies over 30 areas of exclusive federal authority, such as "militia, military and naval service, and defence"; section 92 lists over a dozen areas of provincial responsibility, such as "municipal institutions in the province"; section 92A assigns natural resources to the provinces, as does section 93 with respect to education; section 94A assigns old age pensions and benefits to the federal government; and section 95 establishes concurrent powers for agriculture and immigration. Flowing from this, we find that there is a federal department of national defence; there are provincial departments of municipal affairs, of natural resources, and of education; and there are federal and provincial departments of agriculture and of immigration, though in some provinces these matters are subsumed into broader departments. Each line department is headed by a minister who is a member of cabinet and who issues directives to a deputy minister.

line departments Units responsible for the development and delivery of policy, programs, or services under a particular portfolio.

Agencies, Boards, and Commissions

Lastly, the permanent executive also consists of the leaders of a host of agencies, boards, and commissions (ABCs). These bodies exist at an arm's length from the rest of the executive, meaning that their day-to-day business is not overseen or conducted by central agency or line department officials. Agencies, boards, and commissions are established by statute, regulation, or incorporation (see examples in Table 5.3). These advisory, operational, and regulatory organizations, which are ostensibly depoliticized, have more of a direct daily impact on Canadians' lives than most other government actors.[21] As the Government of Manitoba explains it, ABCs are "entities established by government to carry out a range of functions and services, and include councils, authorities, advisory bodies, funding bodies, professional organizations, and

ABC An agency, board or commission responsible for delivering a program or service, or producing goods, at arm's length from government.

Opportunities Available

Knowledge of Canadian Politics and Government Preferred!

Executive Director

Treasury Board (Secretariat), Office of the Comptroller General, Government of Canada

Official language proficiency: Bilingual

Education

- University degree from a recognized university in a field related to the position (e.g. accounting, finance or business).
- A valid and recognized Canadian professional accounting designation.

Experience

- Significant experience in leading the preparation of, and/or auditing of, audited financial statements for large complex organizations.
- Experience in the provision of financial analysis, financial management advice, and problem resolution at the executive (or equivalent) level.
- Significant experience in the briefing of senior management or boards of administration (or equivalent) on matters pertaining to the financial management of the organization or the preparation of its audited financial statements.

Knowledge

- Knowledge of the role of Treasury Board Secretariat.
- Knowledge of the Canadian Public Sector Accounting Standards and their application to government organizations.
- Knowledge of managerial theory and practices in the areas of financial and human resources management.
- Knowledge of government priorities, trends, and developments in public sector management.

Abilities and skills

- Values and ethics; integrity and respect
- Strategic thinking; analysis and ideas
- Engagement; mobilizing people, organizations, partners
- Management excellence; action management, people management, financial management

Security and reliability: Secret security clearance

The Public Service of Canada is committed to building a skilled, diverse workforce reflective of Canadian society. As a result, it promotes employment equity and encourages candidates to indicate voluntarily on their application if they are a woman, an Aboriginal person, a person with a disability, or a member of a visible minority group.

Source: Abridged from Public Service Resourcing System, "Executive Director" (2014), https://emploisfp-psjobs.cfp-psc.gc.ca/psrs-srfp/applicant/page1800. Accessed March 2, 2014.

quasi-judicial tribunals."[22] The Government of Nova Scotia differentiates between *adjudicative* and *non-adjudicative* ABCs. An adjudicative agency, board, or commission performs quasi-judicial functions; it is expected to "consider evidence, make findings of fact and law, and issue decisions affecting a person's liberty, security, or legal rights."[23] Conversely, the function of a non-adjudicative ABC is to "make financial, regulatory, business, or policy decisions or recommendations to government that have far-reaching implications." In considering the important function of agencies, boards, and commissions we must bear in mind that the executive branch, which is accountable to the legislative branch, is the one with ultimate authority to steer government policy and to set budgets. Some ABCs are permanent, while others are discontinued when their original purpose is deemed to have run its course. To provide an idea of the scope of ABCs, consider that the government of Ontario alone has over 560 agencies, boards, commissions, councils, authorities, and foundations.[24] These are distinct from agents of the legislature, such as the auditor general and chief electoral officer.

↻ Offices and agents of the legislature, including the Office of the Auditor General, are discussed on pages 228 and 230 of Chapter 6, on the legislature.

TABLE 5.3 | Examples of Government Departments and ABCs

Name (Government)	Mandate	Reports to
Departments		
Transport Canada (Canada)	Promotes a safe, efficient, and environmentally responsible transportation network in Canada.	Federal minister of transport
Department of Agriculture, Fisheries and Food (Quebec)	Regulates and supports the province's food industry, with an emphasis on sustainable development.	Quebec's minister of agriculture, fisheries and food
Agencies		
Canada Revenue Agency (Canada)	Administers tax, benefits, and related programs. Ensures compliance with such regulations on behalf of federal, provincial, and territorial governments across Canada.	Federal minister of national revenue
Ontario Clean Water Agency (Ontario)	Responsible for water and sewer services, with an objective of delivering safe, reliable, and cost-effective clean water.	Ontario's minister of the environment
Boards		
National Energy Board (Canada)	Regulates the international and interprovincial aspects of pipelines, energy development, and trade in the oil, gas, and electric utility industries.	Federal minister of natural resources
Disaster Assistance Appeals Board (Manitoba)	Reviews appeals submitted by applicants for disaster financial assistance who were dissatisfied with their assessment.	Manitoba's minister responsible for emergency measures
Commissions		
Canadian Human Rights Commission (Canada)	Promotes equal opportunity and protects human rights by administering the Canadian Human Rights Act and ensuring compliance with the Employment Equity Act, such as dealing with discrimination complaints.	Speaker of the House of Commons
Financial and Consumer Services Commission (New Brunswick)	Crown corporation that protects consumer interests by administering and enforcing provincial legislation concerning co-operatives, credit unions, insurance, pensions, securities, trust and loan companies, and other consumer matters.	New Brunswick's minister of justice

Source: © Privy Council Office, Orders in Council Division (2015)

An **agency** of government is a specialist organization that is tasked with overseeing the administration of specific legislation. The nature of an agency's scope of work is generally considered to require a depoliticized environment. Its operations are therefore narrower and more autonomous than those of a government department. Whereas ministers steer the daily business of a department, their oversight of the agencies in their portfolio tends to be in an arm's-length, formal reporting capacity. Examples of federal government agencies include the Atlantic Canada Opportunities Agency, the Canadian Food Inspection Agency, and the Canadian Space Agency.

A subtype of government agency is a **board**, made up of appointed citizens who bear responsibility for reviewing potentially contentious issues, including decisions made by a government agency. This includes advisory councils and marketing boards. Members are appointed by the relevant minister or by the Queen's representative at the recommendation of cabinet. Examples of federal boards include the Copyright Board of Canada, the National Film Board, and the Parole Board of Canada.

A further subtype is a **government commission**, which is set up to provide detailed policy recommendations on a specific issue to government. Its recommendations are not necessarily binding. Commissions, task forces, and tribunals conduct research to investigate an issue and may hold public hearings to ensure that the public has an opportunity to voice their concerns. Examples of federal commissions include the Canada Employment Insurance Commission, the Canadian Nuclear Safety Commission, and the Commission for Public Complaints Against the RCMP.

The highest-profile type of commission is a **royal commission**, also known as a **commission of inquiry**. Royal commissions are occasionally struck by cabinet to investigate an issue that is deemed to be of significant public interest; they are equally a mechanism for the political executive to defer contentious policy decisions.[25] A commission is overseen by an appointed commissioner, usually someone who is distinguished in the field such as a judge or retired politician, and is commonly referred to by the commissioner's last name (e.g. the Royal Commission on the Future of Health Care in Canada, otherwise known as the Romanow Commission, because it was headed by former Saskatchewan Premier Roy Romanow). The terms of reference establish its scope of work, and the final report includes a variety of submissions, evidence, working papers, and other documents. The recommendations may or may not lead to significant policy changes, depending on the findings and the political will of the government.

Crown corporations are among the most well-known ABCs in Canada. A Crown corporation is set up by the government in an area of the economy that it feels is in the public interest but that the private sector has deemed unprofitable and/or fit only for the state's involvement. Unlike a profit-motivated business, the government offers services with a primary goal of sustainability, although there is growing pressure on Crown corporations not to be a drain on the public purse and even to be profitable. They tend to be managed by a board of directors and report to the legislature through a minister. Examples of federal Crown corporations include the Canada Mortgage and Housing Corporation, the Canada Post Corporation, and the Canadian Broadcasting Corporation. Periodically the government sells some or all of the assets, as the federal government did with Air Canada, Petro-Canada, and Atomic Energy of Canada. Others include regulatory agencies, like the liquor control boards and gaming commissions, or quasi-governmental bodies like correctional systems, police forces, universities, hospitals, and school boards. ABCs are typically created to establish some

government agency An arm's-length corporate body operating on behalf of a government.

government board A public advisory committee made up of appointed citizens.

government commission An agency of government that provides specialized policy expertise and oversight.

royal commission / commission of inquiry A special research investigation of a contentious area of public policy.

Crown corporations Enterprises owned by a federal or provincial government.

distance between the functions they provide and the political or bureaucratic control that comes with the business of line departments. This may add a sense of non-partisanship, objectivity, and longer-term thinking to the work they do.

While a government entity whose name includes the word "corporation" is a giveaway that it is a Crown corporation, the ability to differentiate among ABCs is not always easy. There is such a growing and "bewildering variety of organizations and procedures, as well as names" that ABCs are often lumped together under the umbrella term "agencies."[26] One of many examples is the Canadian Dairy Commission, which is accountable to the federal minister of agriculture and agri-food. Its name indicates that it is a commission, but it is also a Crown corporation. Moreover, it chairs the Canadian Milk Supply Management Committee, which is a permanent board of provincial members of the National Milk Marketing Plan. Given that there can be such a variety of non-governmental organizations, the most prudent way to differentiate them is as either a department or an ABC.

In working for ABCs many civil service workers (professors, nurses, physicians, teachers, and so on) do not consider themselves public servants in the broader sense of the term, nor do many government workers or citizens often view them as part of the formal public service. Depending on the organization, the legislature, the cabinet, or an individual minister may be responsible for appointing an ABC's leaders, defining its mandate, approving its budget, reviewing its annual reports, or otherwise directing its business. Otherwise, however, the day-to-day functioning of an ABC is shielded from political interference and bureaucratic oversight.

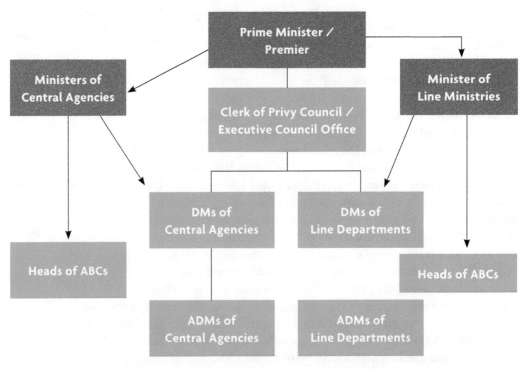

FIGURE 5.3 | The Permanent Executive in Canada

Source: Privy Council Office, Decision-making processes and central agencies in Canada: Federal, Provincial and Territorial Practices—Canada, Annex 2, Retrieved from archived content: http://www.pco-bcp.gc.ca/index.asp?lang=eng&page=information&sub=publications&doc=aarchives/decision/canada-eng.htm

Sam Koerbrich

In December 2013, Canada Post announced plans to phase out door-to-door mail delivery in urban neighbourhoods in an effort to stem millions of dollars in losses annually; residents would have instead obtained their mail from community mailboxes. The Crown corporation reasoned that the home delivery model is unsustainable given that mail is no longer used as a primary source of communication. Citizens' groups objected, arguing that seniors, especially, would be inconvenienced by the move, and the Liberal Party under Justin Trudeau vowed to stop plans to end door-to-door delivery and undertake a review of Canada Post's operations. How do we decide whether profitability or convenience is the greater good when it comes to a Crown corporation?

It is important to remember: the permanent executive, as a whole, is not politically accountable for the functioning of government. This responsibility rests with cabinet, meaning that—until very recently—senior bureaucrats were protected from being investigated by legislative committees. This has changed recently, particularly at the federal level.

Concluding Thoughts

Some prevailing wisdoms about the executive branch of Canadian government have merit. These include perceptions that a post in the formal executive is little more than a patronage position to rubber-stamp the will of the cabinet; that the coordination function of central agencies is cause for concern because it adds to the already significant power of the prime minister or premier; and that senior public servants who have significant input into public policy are not held to public account. Conversely, the head of state performs important ceremonial duties that are welcomed by many Canadians; central agencies significantly improve the quality of government organization, accountability, efficiency, and service delivery; and our system of government holds that only members of the cabinet and legislature are directly accountable to the electorate. Perhaps what matters most is the recognition that due to the complexity of government, there is a need for competent executives who are kept accountable to Canadians.

For More Information

How is power concentrated in the PMO?
Donald Savoie examines the evolution of the prime minister's office in *Governing from the Centre: The Concentration of Power in Canadian Politics* (University of Toronto Press, 1999).

How do first ministers interact? Richard Simeon explains the intricate processes involved in *First Minister Diplomacy: The Making of Recent Policy in Canada* (University of Toronto Press, 2006).

What about cabinets? Loleen Berdahl explores the emergence of a new brand of executive federalism in "Region-building: Western Canadian Joint Cabinet Meetings in the 21st Century" (*Canadian Public Administration* 54 [June 2011]: pp. 255–75).

How democratic are Canada's political executives? Graham White explores *Cabinets and First Ministers* in his contribution to the Canadian Democratic Audit series (UBC Press, 2005).

Just how malevolent is Canada's political executive? Jeffrey Simpson peers behind the prime ministerial curtain in *The Friendly Dictatorship* (McClelland and Stewart, 2002).

Where is authority truly concentrated in democracies like Canada's? Donald Savoie expands his scope beyond *Governing from the Centre* (University of Toronto Press, 1999) to ask *Power: Where Is It?* (McGill–Queen's University Press, 2010).

How have provincial executives evolved over time? Christopher Dunn explains the development of *The Institutionalized Cabinet: Governing in the Western Provinces* (McGill–Queen's University Press, 1995).

Seeking to learn more about your ABCs? Read about how they are evolving in Peter Aucoin and Elizabeth Goodyear-Grant's 2002 article "Designing a Merit-Based Process for Appointing Boards of ABCs: Lessons from the Nova Scotia Reform Experience" (*Canadian Public Administration* 45: pp. 301–27). See also Donald C. MacDonald's earlier (1993) piece "Ontario's Agencies, Boards, and Commissions Come of Age" (*Canadian Public Administration* 36: pp. 349–63).

Want to see what the Governor General does, day-to-day? Subscribe to the GG's YouTube channel: www.youtube.com/user/CanadaGG/.

Want the Web's most vigorous defence of the monarchy in Canada? Visit the Monarchist League's website: www.monarchist.ca/.

Looking to track the popularity of first ministers? Angus Reid conducts quarterly public opinion polls on the topic. Visit their website (www.angusreidglobal.com/) and search: premiers approval. For a historical look on the prime minister's approval rating, visit: www.queensu.ca/cora/_trends/PM_Approve.htm.

Deeper Inside Canadian Politics

1. Critics argue that the monarchy has outlived its usefulness in Canadian democracy. Do you agree? What sorts of changes would be required to abolish the monarchy in Canada?

2. Who do you think wields more power relative to the rest of the actors in their political system: a premier or a prime minister? Why?

3. In response to a reporter's question as to why he placed so much emphasis on gender parity in his first cabinet, Prime Minister Justin Trudeau replied, "Because it's 2015." Why do you suppose it took so long to achieve this milestone at the federal level, and why have all but two provinces failed to reach gender parity in cabinet?

UP FOR DEBATE

Do Canadian first ministers have too much power?

THE CLAIM: YES, THEY DO!

Prime ministers and premiers are too powerful in Canadian politics.

Yes: Argument Summary

There is good reason for the conventional wisdom that Canada's prime ministers and premiers are too powerful. Never before has a leader's public persona been as important as it is today, and Canada's first ministers are now the focus of a permanent, tightly controlled marketing campaign, making their names synonymous with not just the parties but the governments they represent. Simultaneously, the need for government departments to operate in unison has increased the authority of political staff and central agencies, which have assumed greater coordination and direction roles. The presidentialization and centralization of Canadian government is an unrelenting reality that the parliamentary system of government was not designed to handle. As a result, the power and autonomy of the legislative branch and most parliamentarians has correspondingly declined, and the ability of anyone other than the courts to hold first ministers to account is sometimes suspect. This is especially evident in provinces, particularly if the premier is a populist or nationalist who faces a weak opposition.

Yes: Top 5 Considerations

1. The power of the Canadian first minister is increasing, in a trend that has been described as the "presidentialization" of the parliamentary system. Yet Canadians do not directly elect prime ministers or premiers, and the system is not designed to hold the head of government directly accountable. In the presidential system, the executive branch is *separate* from a more independent legislative branch, providing an effective check on executive authority, but in the parliamentary system, the first minister exercises control over *both* branches.

2. Governments worldwide are becoming centralized, regardless of which political party is in power. In Canada the increasing clout of central agencies—namely, the prime minister's office or premier's office, the Privy Council Office or Executive Council, the Department of Finance, and the Treasury Board—is reducing ministerial and departmental autonomy.

3. The first minister enjoys a number of perks of office that can be used to solidify her/his position. This includes the power to appoint people to government positions, to chair cabinet and key cabinet committees, and to steer government policy.

4. The power of a Canadian first minister over her/his political party is significant, particularly if the position was earned by securing the broad support needed to win a leadership campaign.

5. Premiers are especially powerful due to the smaller nature of provincial politics, the propensity for weak opposition, and reduced media scrutiny. The power of a populist or nationalist who epitomizes a political community and who pursues politics that disrupt national unity is particularly worrisome.

Yes: Other Considerations

- First ministers who have a majority of seats in the legislature wield even more power than those who govern with a minority.
- The strength of party discipline in Canada augments the clout of a first minister.
- Political parties routinely emphasize leadership, as do the media. This results in portrayals of the Canadian system of government being a "friendly dictatorship," as *The Globe and Mail*'s Jeffrey Simpson put it in a book of that title.

- The power of a first minister is such that unelected political staffers working in the prime minister's office or the premier's office issue instructions to members of cabinet and especially to backbenchers.

THE COUNTERCLAIM: NO, THEY DON'T!

Prime ministers and premiers have an appropriate amount of power.

No: Argument Summary

There is no trend toward presidentialization; on the contrary, our parliamentary system has always been designed to concentrate power in the hands of the few. Someone has to lead in any organization, democratic or not. Our system ensures there is balance between giving leaders the latitude they need to carry out their democratic mandate, and the constraints they need to prevent abuse. First ministers exercise their power responsibly and according to constitutional standards; statements to the contrary (e.g. that they are dictators) are based on hyperbole and a lack of appreciation for real dictatorships than on a true understanding of Canadian democracy. Premiers and prime ministers are formally accountable not only to their respective legislatures, cabinets, and caucus, but also to each other, and they are held to account by a growing number of watchdogs, both inside and outside government.

No: Top 5 Considerations

1. Critics hold misconceptions about Canada's system of government, basing their views on a populist style of democracy that has never existed in this country. The Westminster system is designed to vest ultimate sovereignty in the Crown, and to concentrate power in an accountable political executive. Logic (some would say, nature) suggests that power within that legislature and cabinet will be concentrated in one form or another. In Canada, this concentration is guided by the constitution, traditions, and our political culture.

2. Federalism plus responsible government equals executive federalism. To the outsider, this system of first minister diplomacy appears to grant unlimited powers to each head of government. In reality, each first minister acts as a check on the others thanks to the institutionalization of provincial–territorial relations, the rules spelled out in our constitution, and the guidelines established through successive court rulings.

3. If anything, their authority is waning, with first ministers taking it upon themselves to place constraints on their own power. Nearly all have passed fixed election date legislation to limit their ability to manipulate the parliamentary life cycle; many have passed balanced budget legislation to bind themselves to fiscal discipline; they have created a plethora of arm's-length watchdogs; and they have institutionalized the appointments process to provide transparency and democratic input.

4. Indeed, the exercise of power by first ministers has never been more transparent. Their day-to-day business is in plain public view thanks to the 24/7 news cycle, access to information legislation, and party members' access to social media.

5. Most formal studies of the concentration of power are based on evidence and anecdotes collected from people on the periphery. This includes bureaucrats in line departments, disgruntled backbenchers, jaded journalists, and the like. This is akin to asking an accountant whether she feels the CEO has too much control over the company, or an intern whether he feels powerless in an international NGO.

No: Other Considerations

- Citizens who complain about the concentration of power in the PMO or premier's office should join a political party and help choose the next leader.
- Think first ministers are predominant in their own spheres of authority? Ask former Alberta premier Alison Redford about BC premier Christy Clark's influence over Alberta's access to oil markets. Ask former premier of Quebec Jacques Parizeau about Jean Chrétien's role in the

1995 Quebec referendum campaign. Consider what Pierre Trudeau and Brian Mulroney might have to say about how their PM-led initiatives for renewing the constitution were variously thwarted, stalled, derailed, and hijacked by provincial first ministers.

Discussion Questions

- To what extent should we be concerned that the current prime minister has too much power? What about the current premier of your province?
- First ministers portrayed in some media circles as authoritarian are viewed in others as delivering strong leadership; those who change their minds in response to political pressure are portrayed by the media as more democratic but weak. If you were a prime minister or premier, which public image would you prefer?
- What does the term "presidentialization" imply?

Can it accurately be applied to parliamentary government? If yes, is the presidentialization of the parliamentary system of government a positive or negative development? Why?
- Is it possible that the concentration of decision-making leads to better government? How?
- Suppose there is a very unpopular prime minister or premier. What options do Canadians have if they feel that the first minister should be removed from office before the next scheduled general election?

Where to Learn More about Executive Power in Canadian Politics

Herman Bakvis and Steven B. Wolinetz, "Canada: Executive Dominance and Presidentialization," in *The Presidentialization of Politics: A Comparative Study of Modern Democracies*, ed. Thomas Poguntke and Paul Webb (Oxford: Oxford University Press, 2005).

Luc Bernier, Keith Brownsey, and Michael Hollett, eds, *Executive Styles in Canada: Cabinet Structures and Leadership Practices in Canadian Government* (Toronto: University of Toronto Press, 2005).

Jonathan Malloy, "The Executive and Parliament in Canada," *The Journal of Legislative Studies* 10, no. 2 (2004): pp. 206–17.

Thomas Poguntke and Paul D. Webb, eds, *The Presidentialization of Politics: A Comparative Study of Modern Democracies* (Oxford: Oxford University Press, 2005).

Donald J. Savoie, *Governing from the Centre: The Concentration of Power in Canadian Politics* (Toronto: University of Toronto Press, 1999).

Richard Simeon, *Federal–Provincial Diplomacy: The Making of Recent Policy in Canada* (Toronto: University of Toronto Press, 2006).

Jeffrey Simpson, *The Friendly Dictatorship* (Toronto: McClelland and Stewart, 2001).

Paul G. Thomas, "Governing from the Centre," *Policy Options* (December 2003): pp. 79–85.

Graham White, *Cabinets and First Ministers* (Vancouver: UBC Press, 2005).

6 THE LEGISLATURE

Inside this Chapter

- How are legislatures structured and organized in Canada?
- How do legislatures conduct routine business?
- How do legislatures differ across Canada?

Inside the Legislature

Field trips and 30-second news clips of Question Period: these are often the only times that Canadians have an opportunity to view their legislators in action. They can be forgiven for not liking what they see. Raucous exchanges between the opposition and government, loud heckling and sarcastic catcalls, chaotic yet somehow scripted post-session scrums—none of these breed confidence in the legislative process.

Peering inside the legislature means moving beyond these surface observations and recognizing certain maxims about legislative politics in Canada.

 Media coverage of Question Period does not capture the essence of the legislative process. You may have stumbled upon live House of Commons or provincial legislature proceedings on television and thought to yourself, so *this* is how our elected officials spend their days. In reality, the vast majority of legislators' work takes place outside the legislative chamber, in committees and in their home constituencies.

 Parliament is not the heart of legislative activity in Canada. Do you think Parliament is the nexus of lawmaking and policymaking in Canada? Far from it. An increasing amount of public policy—particularly on matters of highest priority to Canadians, like healthcare and education—is taking place in provincial and territorial capitals across the country. No insider's view of the legislative branch would be complete without examining these thirteen assemblies.

 Majority governments and absolute party discipline are not the norm in Canadian politics. Many people believe that government stalls or stops unless there is a majority government with a strong leader who commands the confidence of legislature. A related belief is that legislatures themselves hold very little value in terms of the policymaking process, as power remains concentrated in the hands of the executive, in general, and the prime minister, in particular. These beliefs are false. Minority governments are more common, and individual legislators play a more powerful role, than conventional wisdom suggests.

This chapter throws open the doors of Canada's legislatures to explore these ideas and demonstrate how governments are held to account and Canadians are represented in the twenty-first century.

Overview

Since the beginning of democracy as we know it, people have formed legislatures as houses for their representatives to assemble and debate the political issues of the day. Over time, legislatures have become forums for these representatives to make laws and approve government spending, for the governing party to advance an agenda, and for critics to scrutinize government activities. Canada has a total of 14 legislatures, the most recognized of which—Parliament—is located in Ottawa. Each of the provinces and territories has a legislature, located in its capital city, whose practices generally follow those of the federal House of Commons.

What the 2015 Election Means for the Legislature

Visit the *Inside Canadian Politics* flipboard to learn about the latest developments affecting the legislature.

 Go to http://flip.it/gblag.

UP FOR DEBATE

Is strict party discipline necessary in Canadian legislatures?

Keep this question in mind as you read through the chapter. Consult the end-of-chapter debate supplement for more material to help you engage in an informed discussion of the topic.

The Structure of Legislatures

Before delving more deeply into the inner workings of Canadian legislatures, it is important to review some of the key concepts raised in earlier chapters. At its core, Canada is a parliamentary democracy based on the federal model. This means that Canada is a *liberal democracy* (built on a system of rights, preserved by free and fair elections), a *representative democracy* (in which elected officials make decisions on behalf of the citizenry), and a *constitutional monarchy* (rooted in Westminster parliamentary traditions, and with a divided Crown whose sovereignty rests with both the federal and the provincial orders of government). Perhaps most important to our discussion here, Canada operates on the principles of responsible government, which require executives to maintain the confidence of their respective assemblies in order to continue ruling. This constitutional framework establishes the role of Canadian legislatures.

As Canada is a representative democracy, its constitution grants Canadians the opportunity to elect members of each legislature at least once every five years, allowing voters to hold their representatives accountable for their actions and to renew their political mandates on a regular basis. In practice, elections occur more often than that, particularly in minority government circumstances, and in jurisdictions that have passed fixed-date election laws defining the election cycle as four years. Nothing in these laws prevents elections from occurring more frequently, of course. A by-election can be held in an electoral district when an elected representative vacates the seat. There can also be a snap general election, such as when the governor general or lieutenant governor grants the government a dissolution of parliament, or if a majority of elected representatives no longer support the government.

Should the latter occur, the principle of responsible government requires that the first minister and the cabinet resign, or request that a general election be held. This ensures that executives who have the power to make government decisions must maintain the support (or confidence) of a majority of all elected representatives. By convention, this includes voting on the budget, the throne speech, motions of non-confidence, and anything that the government declares in advance will be a confidence matter. If the governing party does not carry a majority of legislators' support on these votes, then the government falls. This is typically followed by a general election allowing citizens to render their own judgement.

Federalism also helps structure Canadian legislatures. At the federal level, Parliament is a bicameral legislature, meaning that it consists of two separate houses: the House of Commons and the Senate. By contrast, provincial and territorial legislatures are unicameral, many having abolished their upper houses decades ago in favour of a single chamber of elected officials.

The House of Commons and the Senate

As its name suggests, the federal House of Commons is meant to represent the interests of the common people—the citizens of Canada. Located in Ottawa, the House of Commons is responsible for

- supervising, authorizing, and otherwise holding to account the executive;
- passing laws and resolutions to govern the country; and
- representing Canadians when debating the pressing political issues of the day.

---

fixed-date election law Legislation prescribing that general elections be held on a particular date, or range of dates, typically every four years.

by-election A district-level election held between general elections.

↺ By-elections are discussed in greater detail on page 445 of Chapter 10.

confidence convention The practice under which a government must relinquish power when it loses a critical legislative vote.

bicameral legislature A legislative body consisting of two chambers (or "houses").

unicameral legislature A legislative body consisting of one chamber (or "house").

House of Commons The lower house of the Canadian Parliament, consisting of elected members from across the country.

Provincial and territorial legislatures, located in capital cities, perform the same function within their respective jurisdictions.

The Senate, like its prototype, the British House of Lords, was designed as a chamber of "sober second thought." The Senate was originally designed as a counterweight to the Commons by providing Canada's upper class with representation in Parliament. This is one of the reasons property requirements were placed on membership in the Senate: to ensure that the better-off in Canadian society retained political power in the face of a popularly elected House of Commons. With its members appointed, not elected, the Senate is intended to be shielded from the whims of public opinion, and better equipped to provide detailed, long-term analysis of proposed laws and public policy. The Senate is located next to the House of Commons, on Parliament Hill in Ottawa.

Senators are summoned to Parliament by the governor general, on advice of the prime minister of the day. This makes Canada's Senate, alongside the British House of Lords, one of the few remaining non-elected legislative bodies in Western democracy, and a source of much consternation among democratic reformers. Senators must be at least 30 years old and own property in the province that they were appointed to represent. They may stay in the position without facing election until they turn 75, at which point they are required to retire. Conscientious senators who can ignore the histrionics of the media can take a longer-term view to public policy. Their years of experience afford them a sense of perspective that is less common among elected representatives.

In addition to serving as a check on the House of Commons, the Senate is also structured to provide for regional representation in Parliament. In all jurisdictions but Quebec, where separate senatorial districts exist, a senator is viewed as representing

Senate Also known as the Red Chamber, the upper house of the Canadian Parliament, consisting of members chosen by the executive.

senator One of the appointed members of the upper house of the Canadian Parliament.

The Canadian Press/Brian Gable

Politicians and academics have devoted entire careers to the project of Senate reform. Considering what you learned in Chapter 2, on the constitution, why do you suppose Senate reform has remained elusive?

INSIDE CANADIAN POLITICS

Why Does the Senate Need Reform—and What's Taking So Long?

People constantly say that the Canadian Senate needs to be reformed, or even abolished. Since Confederation, would-be reformers have focused on improving the Canadian Senate in four main ways: through its composition and its powers, and through the selection and the tenure of its members.

- *Composition:* Senate seats are distributed on a re-gion-wide basis, meaning that some provinces (like Ontario and Quebec) receive a full complement of 24 senators, while others (like those in western Canada) receive one-quarter of that number. Many reformers have aimed to address this discrepancy by dividing seats equally among all provinces, re-gardless of their size.
- *Powers:* Reformers have also sought to create a more "effective" Senate—one possessing a number of new tools that would empower senators to conduct more than routine legislative business. Suggestions included providing the Senate with veto powers over federal appointments, language legislation, treaties, and other matters. At the same time, reformers have been careful to balance any new powers against the possibility of deadlock with the House of Commons. Most proposals have given the House of Commons primacy in case of conflict (e.g. by making any Senate vetoes temporary).

- *Selection:* Along with the British House of Lords, the Canadian Senate remains one of the only non-elected legislative chambers in the democratic world. Reformers have sought to end the process of appointment, replacing it with a system of direct or indirect elections, or supplementing it through the creation of a non-partisan advisory panel on appointments.
- *Tenure:* Prior to a 1965 constitutional amendment, senators were appointed for life. Since 1965, senators have served until a mandatory retirement age of 75. Viewing this as virtually a lifetime appointment, reformers have sought fixed terms, on a renewable or non-renewable basis. This would help make sen-ators democratically accountable to Canadians.

During the mega-constitutional period and driven by the Alberta government and federal Reform Party, all four of these elements were incorporated into a ser-ies of proposed constitutional amendment packages, most notably in the ill-fated Charlottetown Accord.

Since that time, Senate reform has taken on a more incrementalist tone. Upon reaching office, the Conservative government of Prime Minister Stephen Harper introduced no fewer than seven pieces of Senate reform legislation. All dealt with the selection and tenure of senators, and none passed Parliament.

her or his entire province. While seats in the Commons are distributed based on population (such that larger provinces receive greater representation), Senate seats are based on a regional formula, which grants some smaller provinces a relatively greater say in national decision-making than their population size would otherwise allow.

The basis for appointing senators is normally loyalty to the party in power. Historically, the prime minister has rewarded party loyalists with Senate seats. Pessimists would suggest the Senate merely employs party fundraisers (sometimes known as "bagmen") and a party's election campaign organizers. At times, it has been a soft landing spot for candidates who have failed to win an election, and for former ministers. Optimists would remark that sometimes high-profile Canadians are appointed, such as athletes and journalists, as well as community activists. Prime ministers are careful about the strategic calculations of making appointments because Senate appointments tend to attract negative media coverage. On rare occasions, the prime minister has recommended that the governor general appoint a supporter of a

Crucially, none of the Harper government's proposed reforms involved engaging the provinces in full-blown constitutional negotiations.

In 2012, the Quebec government challenged the federal government's most recent legislation (Bill C-7) in court, referring the law to its provincial Court of Appeal. Quebec argued that the proposed reforms involved fundamental changes to the constitution and, as such, could not be accomplished by the federal government alone. The Court of Appeal agreed, finding that the federal government's plans required the consent of the provinces.

In an unsuccessful effort to pre-empt the Quebec Court of Appeal case, the federal government referred a series of questions to the Supreme Court of Canada. These asked for the Court's opinion on the constitutional approach required to effect changes to the tenure, selection, and property qualifications of senators, as well as the process required to abolish the Senate entirely. The Supreme Court responded that all significant reforms would require meaningful consent from the provinces, thus ending the federal government's plans to modernize the institution unilaterally. Considering that no first minister appeared interested in re-opening constitutional negotiations, the momentum behind Senate reform stalled with the Supreme Court's ruling.

The Supreme Court reference came at the height of scandals surrounding the expense reports of several senators. In response to these, the Senate took the unprecedented step of suspending three of its members without pay, forcing (ex-Conservative) senators Mike Duffy, Pamela Wallin, and Patrick Brazeau out of the Upper Chamber for the remainder of the parliamentary session. Liberal leader Justin Trudeau also took the unprecedented step of expelling all Liberal senators from caucus in a move viewed by proponents as a means of distancing elected from unelected officials, and by opponents as an act of political opportunism. Trudeau also promised to establish a "non-partisan, merit-based process" to advise the prime minister on Senatorial appointments.

VOX POP

Do you think the Senate should be reformed, preserved as is, or abolished altogether? Why do you think change is so difficult? Defend your position.

different political party. Conservative prime minister Stephen Harper's approach to the Senate was unusual in that he went extended periods without filling seats, to the point that the Senate experienced difficulty operating. When he resigned as prime minister, Harper left 22 vacant seats, and the new Trudeau government promised to fill them by considering advice from an advisory board.

As a result of these factors, Senate reform is a recurring theme in Canadian politics. The Senate suffers from a terrible image problem because it is widely seen as an anti-democratic relic of the past. Many critics view it as little more than a way for the prime minister to reward friends with lucrative patronage appointments. This is the impetus behind Prime Minister Justin Trudeau's efforts to remove Senators from caucus and cabinet, and to establish an arms-length appointment process. It has been difficult to expunge members who have behaved poorly—including a senator who retained the appointment despite having moved to Mexico—and this fact can generate public outrage. The lack of public accountability of its members has led some critics to call for significant reforms or for the Senate's outright abolition. The Conservative and Liberal parties as well as the provinces of Ontario and Quebec have long enjoyed disproportionate representation in the Senate; by comparison, complaints from opposition parties like the New Democratic Party and upstart organizations like the former Reform Party of Canada have tapped into western Canadian populist sentiments. The Reform Party was an advocate of "triple-E" Senate reform, which would provide each province with an *equal* number of seats, make senators' work more *effective*, and require that senators be *elected*. This was championed as a panacea to Westerners' frustrations with Ottawa, but in reality even if an American-style triple-E senate had been implemented it would not have solved many longstanding grievances about the federal government.[1] Despite Canadians' frustrations, the likelihood of meaningful Senate reform seems very low.

In contrast with senators, representatives in the House of Commons, known as members of Parliament (MPs), are elected to represent a particular electoral riding. At the federal level, Canada is divided into hundreds of defined areas known as *ridings* or *electoral districts*, and residents in each area elect a member of Parliament to represent them. The House of Commons has more power than the Senate because of the public legitimacy it enjoys and because, as per section 53 of the Constitution Act, 1867, only MPs can initiate bills that would require the government to spend money. Moreover, by convention, the House is where the prime minister and almost all cabinet ministers hold their seats. Other than these important distinctions the Senate and the House of Commons are remarkably similar institutions.

As Table 6.1 shows, one of the problems with representation is developing a formula for a fair distribution of *seats*, which is to say electoral districts that are

member of Parliament (MP) One of the over 300 representatives elected by Canadians to serve in the House of Commons.

THEY SAID IT

Saskatchewan Premier Brad Wall on Senate Reform

All provinces and territories are represented in the Senate. But as Saskatchewan premier Brad Wall asks, how important is regional representation if a senator's party affiliation puts it at odds with the governing party of the province that the senator represents?

At this point in the life of the province, given what we've been battling: Reform it, abolish it, paint it pink. I don't really care at this point. We need to ask a few more questions on the reform front from a provincial perspective. . . . If all the senators, elected or otherwise, are still whipped, if they are all part of their respective whipped parliamentary caucus, . . . are they free to speak on behalf of the province they come from or are they toeing a party line?

—Brad Wall, commenting on the Conservative government's Senate reform proposal in a telephone interview, June 2011[2]

VOX POP

Why do you think that most senators tend to vote the way that their Senate leadership wants, rather than voting how the premier of their province wants?

TABLE 6.1 | Distribution of Canadian Senators and Members of Parliament

Region	Population*	Land Area (km²)	Senators	MPs	Average # of Electors per riding
British Columbia	4,650,000	925,186	6	42	110,714
Alberta	3,965,340	642,317	6	34	116,628
Saskatchewan	1,093,880	591,670	6	14	78,134
Manitoba	1,277,340	553,556	6	14	91,239
Ontario	13,583,710	917,741	24	121	112,262
Quebec	8,099,100	1,365,128	24	78	103,835
New Brunswick	754,040	71,450	10	10	75,404
Nova Scotia	945,020	53,338	10	11	85,911
Prince Edward Island	145,760	5,660	4	4	36,440
Newfoundland & Labrador	513,570	373,872	6	7	73,367
Yukon	34,020	474,391	1	1	34,020
Northwest Territories	43,350	1,183,085	1	1	43,350
Nunavut	36,420	1,936,113	1	1	36,420
Canada (total)	35,141,540	9,093,507	105	338	103,969

*2013 population statistics. Rounded figures.

represented in the legislature. The rule of thumb is that representation in the Senate is based on geography and fixed, whereas representation in the House is based on population and constantly growing. The composition of the Senate is prescribed in sections 21 to 22 of the Constitution Act, 1867, which organize representation around four regions of the country, before the territories and Newfoundland are factored in:

- the Maritimes (24 senators)
- Quebec (24)
- Ontario (24)
- the West (24).

The seat allocation is rounded out by the addition of the territories (1 senator each) and, in 1949, of Newfoundland (6 senators). This formula disproportionately rewards the four original signatories of Confederation and creates odd dynamics that disadvantage the Western provinces in particular. Quebec and Ontario each have four times as many Senate seats as any Western province; even Atlantic Canada collectively has more seats than the West. Little wonder that a sign spotted outside a Saskatoon sports bar proclaimed: "The only Senators the West cares about are the ones that play hockey!"

The distribution of seats in the Senate is both balanced and distorted by the representation formula in the House of Commons. For the lower chamber, the Representation Act, 1985, prescribes a formula that considers the total Canadian population and how many seats should be allocated per province. It then makes some adjustments, following the "Senate floor" rule that a province cannot have fewer MPs than it has senators, and the "grandfather clause," which says that no province can have fewer MPs than it had in 1985. As well, the geographic areas that MPs represent

BRIEFING NOTES

When Does the Number of Senators Change?

Because Canada's geography is not growing, the total number of senators is reasonably static; the last time it increased was when Nunavut was allocated a seat upon its creation in 1999. Yet although it is widely assumed that the total of 105 senators is a fixed number, this could nevertheless change quickly. Sections 26 to 28 of the Constitution Act allow for the special appointment of one or two senators for each of the four regions. If this provision were to be triggered, the total number of Senate seats would increase to either 109 or 113—the maximum allowed—and would return to 105 as senators retired.

The purpose of this obscure provision is to help ensure that the unelected upper house does not stymie the business of the elected lower house. The last time it was used was in 1990, when the Liberal majority in the Senate vowed to block the bill passed by the Progressive Conservative majority in the House of Commons to create the Goods and Services Tax (GST). Amid considerable uproar, Prime Minister Brian Mulroney secured the governor general's approval to invoke the constitutional clause. Eight Conservative senators (two per region) were appointed to ensure the bill's passage.

THE LESSON

The Senate may stall debate over a particular government bill, but the prime minister has the ability to override most obstruction.

shift as the boundaries of electoral districts are adjusted to reflect population movement. The result is that Quebec and Ontario retain the greatest number of seats in the House of Commons; however, representation from the West has been growing, while the presence of the Atlantic region has been proportionately shrinking.

Provincial and territorial representatives who meet in a local capital city are called members of the Legislative Assembly (MLAs), except in Newfoundland and Labrador, Quebec, and Ontario, where slightly different titles are used (see Figure 6.1). The political interests of every Canadian are therefore represented by a number of appointed senators, one elected MP, one elected provincial or territorial politician, and, usually, at least one municipal councillor. In addition, Canadians may also be represented by school board trustees, union representatives, and special interest groups. Post-secondary students for example tend to be represented by a students union at their school, and in many cases also by a national students' association like the Canadian Federation of Students (CFS) or the provincial Association pour une solidarité syndicale étudiante (ASSÉ).

VOX POP

It may seem as though Canadians have a lot of elected political representation, until you consider that in the United States, many citizens elect all manner of public officials, from judges to senators to dog catchers. What would be the advantages and disadvantages of electing senators in Canada? What about judges? How about dog catchers?

NUNAVUT (IQALUIT)

LEGISLATIVE ASSEMBLY (19 MLAs)

HOUSE OF COMMONS (1 MP)

SENATE (1 senator)

NORTHWEST TERRITORIES (YELLOWKNIFE)

LEGISLATIVE ASSEMBLY (19 MLAs)

HOUSE OF COMMONS (1 MP)

SENATE (1 senators)

YUKON (WHITEHORSE)

LEGISLATIVE ASSEMBLY (19 MLAs)

HOUSE OF COMMONS (1 MP)

SENATE (1 senator)

NEWFOUNDLAND AND LABRADOR (ST. JOHN'S)

HOUSE OF ASSEMBLY (40 MHAs)

HOUSE OF COMMONS (7 MPs)

SENATE (6 senators)

PRINCE EDWARD ISLAND (CHARLOTTETOWN)

LEGISLATIVE ASSEMBLY (27 MLAs)

HOUSE OF COMMONS (4 MPs)

SENATE (4 senators)

NEW BRUNSWICK (FREDERICTON)

LEGISLATIVE ASSEMBLY (49 MLAs)

HOUSE OF COMMONS (10 MPs)

SENATE (10 senators)

NOVA SCOTIA (HALIFAX)

HOUSE OF ASSEMBLY (51 MLAs)

HOUSE OF COMMONS (11 MPs)

SENATE (10 senators)

BC (VICTORIA)

LEGISLATIVE ASSEMBLY (85 MLAS)

HOUSE OF COMMONS (42 MPs)

SENATE (6 senators)

ALBERTA (EDMONTON)

LEGISLATIVE ASSEMBLY (87 MLAs)

HOUSE OF COMMONS (34 MPs)

SENATE (6 senators)

MANITOBA (WINNIPEG)

LEGISLATIVE ASSEMBLY (57 MLAs)

HOUSE OF COMMONS (14 MPs)

SENATE (6 senators)

SASKATCHEWAN (REGINA)

LEGISLATIVE ASSEMBLY (58 MLAs)

HOUSE OF COMMONS (14 MPs)

SENATE (6 senators)

ONTARIO (TORONTO)

LEGISLATIVE ASSEMBLY (107 MPPs)

HOUSE OF COMMONS (121 MPs)

SENATE (24 senators)

QUEBEC (QUEBEC CITY)

NATIONAL ASSEMBLY (125 MLAs)

HOUSE OF COMMONS (78 MPs)

SENATE (24 senators)

CANADA (OTTAWA)

HOUSE OF COMMONS (338 MPs)

SENATE (105 Senators)

FIGURE 6.1 | Characteristics of Federal, Provincial, and Territorial Legislatures

The Partisan Composition of Legislatures

Any discussion about a federal or provincial/territorial legislature in Canada must consider how its seats are distributed among various parties, and how much control the governing party wields over its members. The routines of formal legislative business are consistent regardless of the partisan composition of the assembly. However, the way members behave changes somewhat depending on the relative size of each **party caucus**. As a result, some governments (executives) have more power to impose their will than others, and the relative influence of elected representatives varies.

The number of members in a legislature who are affiliated with a political party is subject to fluctuation between general elections. Numbers decrease when a seat becomes vacant when an individual resigns or dies, or leaves the party caucus to sit as an independent. The number changes again whenever the party wins a by-election. Occasionally, one party's loss is another's gain. This happens in dramatic fashion when a member of a legislature decides to leave one party to join another. This act is known as **crossing the floor**, and refers to the idea that the seat of a member on one side of the chamber is literally moved to another area of the chamber. It is a controversial action, because the member's constituents may not support the move, and normally have no say in the matter.

In general, there are two main ways a legislature may be organized: as a majority government, or as a hung parliament, though in Canadian politics it is more common to distinguish between *majority government* and *minority government* (see Figure 6.2).

Majority Governments

Majority governments exist wherever one political party holds 50 per cent or more of the seats in the legislature. In the case of the federal government, this means a

party caucus All the members of a political party who hold a seat in the legislature.

crossing the floor A situation in which a member of the legislature leaves one political party to join another party.

majority government A government in which the governing party controls at least half of the seats in the legislature.

INSIDE CANADIAN POLITICS

Why Did Nine Alberta MLAs Cross the Floor?

In December 2014, in a move unprecedented in Canadian history, nine opposition members of the Alberta legislative assembly crossed the floor to join the government caucus. The group included the leader of the official opposition, Wildrose Party leader Danielle Smith, who explained the defections as the product of having "aligned principles and values" with the province's governing Progressive Conservatives. Alberta premier Jim Prentice defended the move as "not a merger of parties, [but] a unification of conservatives as Progressive Conservatives."

In the ensuing provincial election just six months later, none of the nine floor-crossing MLAs was elected to serve in the legislature. Some chose not to run or lost a PC nomination race, while others were defeated in the general election. The governing PCs also went down to defeat.

VOX POP

What lessons about floor-crossing can be drawn from this historic episode?

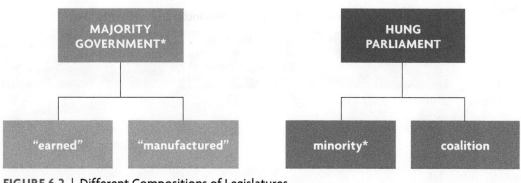

FIGURE 6.2 | Different Compositions of Legislatures

* *Majority government* and *minority government* are the terms most commonly used to describe the organization of Canadian legislatures.

majority of seats in the House of Commons. In majority government situations, the business of the assembly is reasonably efficient, because the opposition parties do not have enough members to explicitly obstruct or otherwise impede the government's plans. Thus, any vote will result in a win for the government—provided enough members of the governing party are present for the vote, and provided they all respect the convention of party discipline. Under these circumstances, the prime minister or premier can be confident that proposals to introduce new legislation, and to change or repeal existing laws, will be carried. However, because a majority government is not compelled to act on the wishes of its opponents, legislation may be rushed through without considering an array of perspectives. This can result in one-sided policy that disadvantages certain segments of society or that lacks the benefit of deeper scrutiny. This is particularly likely at the provincial level, where majority governments have been more common and more lopsided.[3] Such a situation is rare at the federal level; there is so much diversity across Canada, and so many more seats in Parliament, that the prime minister typically faces a more vibrant opposition.

Majority governments are seldom built on the support of half of the voting population. There have been only three of these so-called earned majorities since World War I: the King government of 1940, the Diefenbaker government of 1958, and the Mulroney government of 1984. The last of these cases marked the only time a governing party has received a majority of the popular vote in every single province. Landslide victories and true majorities are far more common at the provincial level, as Table 6.2 shows.

At the federal level, Canada's "first-past-the-post" electoral system and multi-party environment have combined to produce more manufactured majorities than earned majorities. Manufactured majority governments are those in which the governing party enjoys more than half of the seats in the legislature, but less than half of the popular vote in the preceding election. Sometimes, the electoral system may even produce a so-called "wrong winner," awarding control of government to a party whose candidates received fewer votes, overall, than one of its opponents.

Hung Parliaments and Minority Governments

Other times, no party wins a majority of seats in an election, resulting in what's known as a hung parliament. The term "hung" refers to the fact that the electorate,

party discipline
Legislators' strict adherence to the directives of their party leadership.

earned majority A majority government in which the governing party's share of the popular vote is at least 50 per cent.

manufactured majority A majority government in which the governing party's share of the popular vote is less than 50 per cent.

↻ Earned and manufactured majorities are discussed again on pages 422–23 of Chapter 10, in the context of Canada's single-member plurality (or "first-past-the-post") electoral system.

hung parliament A government in which no single party controls at least half of the seats in the legislature.

TABLE 6.2 | Composition of Federal and Provincial Governments, 1965–2015

Jurisdiction	Earned majority governments	Manufactured majority governments	Minority governments	Coalition governments
Federal	1	10	6	
BC	1	11		
AB	6	7		
SK	5	7	1	1
MB		12	1	
ON		10	3	1
QC	2	9	2	
NB	4	9		
PE	12	2		
NS	2	8	4	
NL	10	5		

like a hung jury, has failed to produce a decisive verdict on which party should control the legislature. Logic dictates that hung parliaments are more likely to occur in party systems with more than two strong contenders: without a third party to draw support away from the top two, a majority government (true or manufactured) is all but assured. This is why Canada's first hung parliaments did not occur until the rise of the Progressives and other third parties in the early twentieth century. Under these circumstances, the party with the most seats usually, but not necessarily, forms a government. The governing party's grip on power is more tenuous than in a majority situation. Hung parliaments usually last about half the duration of majority governments, for this reason.

There are two types of hung parliaments, depending upon how cabinet is structured. In Canada, governing parties are most likely to form a minority government, with cabinet ministers selected from their own party, alone. The governing party can either take its chances that opposition members in the legislature will support their initiatives on a vote-by-vote basis, or alternatively it can negotiate the temporary support of another party. In the former case, it risks being defeated in the legislature; in the latter, it must make policy concessions. In either case, cabinet continues to comprise only members affiliated with the governing party.

Regardless of all of this political science terminology, the two common ways of looking at Canadian governments is whether the governing party has a majority or a minority of seats. More explicitly than majority governments, minority governments ensure that competing perspectives are considered by political elites. It can lead to pragmatic solutions to difficult problems, it reduces the power of the political executive, and it increases the relevance of the public's elected representatives.[4] However, a minority government can also produce high-stakes brinksmanship, overspending, an aversion to long-term planning, and constant campaigning.[5] As a result, minority governments often feature some of the tensest times in the life of a legislature. Perhaps fortunately, these periods are often short-lived. On average, hung parliaments in

minority government A hung parliament in which the cabinet consists of members from one political party.

Canada last approximately 20 months. As the government is in near-constant jeopardy of losing a confidence vote, parties are in permanent campaign mode, often paralyzing the legislative process until the legislature is dissolved.

Yet it is often said that minority governments produce some of the most dynamic environments for public policy innovation. Given the closeness of prospective votes, backbench MPs are often given newfound influence over the direction of their party leaders. Successful minority governments demand collaboration between parties on both sides of the aisle, forcing compromises and accommodation. Critics may label the results watered down or question the ability of Canadians to hold their MPs accountable for joint decisions made by multiple parties. Yet, history demonstrates that some of Canada's most enduring and significant policy milestones were, in fact, developed in minority government situations:

↻ The events that led to the adoption of the Canadian flag are chronicled in Chapter 14, on pages 574–5.

- Mackenzie King's Liberal governments (1925–6, 1926–30), supported by the Progressives, increased immigration, developed Canada's first pension plan, and transferred control over natural resources to the Western provinces.
- John Diefenbaker's PC government (1957–8) and Lester B. Pearson's Liberal governments (1963–8), supported by the CCF/NDP, forged Canada's country-wide system of universal healthcare.
- Pearson's minority governments were also responsible for adopting a new Canadian flag and anthem.
- Pierre Trudeau's minority government (1972–4), supported by the NDP, revamped Canada's social security, election financing, and foreign investment systems.
- Stephen Harper's minority governments (2006–11), supported at times by various parties, passed significant reforms to Canada's childcare and employment insurance systems; established a new accountability regime; declared Quebec a "nation"; and apologized for, and launched a commission of inquiry into, the treatment of Aboriginal people in residential schools.

A second form of hung parliament is less common in Canada than in other parts of the world: the coalition government. Coalitions occur when two or more political parties collectively have enough seats to form a government. Unlike a majority or minority government scenario, in this circumstance party elites divide the spoils of power, and cabinet is formed of representatives from at least two different political parties. The Conservative–Liberal Democrat coalition that governed Britain from 2010 to 2015 broadened awareness of the viability of this option in Canada.

coalition government A hung parliament in which the cabinet consists of members from more than one political party.

For a variety of reasons, however, coalitions remain exceedingly rare in Canadian politics, at both the federal and the provincial level. For one, Canada's institutions foster more adversarial competition than inter-party collaboration. Westminster parliamentary traditions dictate that parties oppose each other in the legislature, mitigating the formation of multiparty alliances. This can translate into animosity outside the chamber. Unlike some forms of proportional representation that encourage parties to reach out to their opponents' supporters, Canada's electoral system promotes dog-eat-dog competition at the constituency and the national level. A century's worth of this dynamic, both inside and outside the legislature, has conditioned Canadians and their leaders to believe that cut-throat competition is the political norm, and that collaborative politics including coalition government is an aberration.

INSIDE CANADIAN POLITICS

What Happened with the Coalition Crisis of 2008?

The plausibility of coalition government rocketed to Canadians' attention after the 2008 federal election, which returned the Conservative Party to office with a larger minority of seats. To everyone's surprise, the leaders of the Liberal Party and the NDP signed a pact to form a coalition government that would be supported in the legislature by the separatist Bloc Québécois. This led to the so-called "coalition crisis" that brought the governor general back from an international trip so that she could weigh options: should she acquiesce to Prime Minister Harper's request to prorogue Parliament, thereby forestalling a non-confidence vote that would create the conditions for the opposition-led coalition to form the government, or should she turn down his request and let the government fall even though an election was just held? The GG eventually agreed to the prime minister's request to prorogue Parliament, and the coalition plan fizzled. Had the coalition come to fruition, the Liberal leader would have become prime minister, and there would have been a Liberal cabinet with some NDP members. However, had that occurred, the Conservative Party might have mobilized political and public opposition to the institution of the governor general itself.

↻ A fuller summary of the coalition crisis is given in Chapter 11, on pages 456–61.

Chris Mikula/The Ottawa Citizen

Protesters on Parliament Hill express their opposition to the proposed Liberal–NDP–Bloc coalition. Rallies were also held in favour of the coalition. Read some media commentary from the time of the crisis: why was the proposed coalition so polarizing? What do you think was the biggest reason?

THE LESSON

The term "coalition" carries a negative tone in Canada, thanks largely to a political culture that has conditioned Canadians to prize inter-party competition over collaboration.

BRIEFING NOTES

Coalitions vs Legislative Alliances

Many observers mistake Liberal premier David Peterson's minority government in Ontario (1985–7) for a coalition government. As his cabinet contained only Liberals, however, it was not a coalition. The Ontario Liberals did strike a formal accord with Bob Rae's NDP, guaranteeing the New Democrats certain legislative victories in return for a pledge not to defeat the government for two years. These types of pacts are not uncommon in minority government situations. The Manitoba PCs and Manitoba New Democrats signed a similar, albeit secret, accord in 1988. But it is crucial to note that no matter how formalized the arrangement, a hung parliament becomes a coalition *only* if its cabinet contains ministers from more than one party.

Indeed, coalition government has only occurred once at the federal level in Canada, when Prime Minister Borden formed the so-called Union Government during World War I. At the time, the conscription issue (i.e. mandatory military service) divided the Liberal and Conservative parties, and Western Liberals decided to join with like-minded Conservatives to form a pro-conscription coalition government following the 1917 election. The cabinet contained 12 Conservatives (including Borden as prime minister), 9 Liberals (led by future Progressive leader Thomas Crerar), and 1 member of the Labour Party (to this day, the only non-Liberal, non-Conservative minister at the federal level in Canada). The Union Government was short-lived, with Borden retiring in 1920 and Crerar leading his Western Liberals out of the government to form a new political party, the Progressives. Mackenzie King's Liberal Party went on to form a majority government in 1921, with Crerar's Progressives placing second in terms of seats in Parliament.

There have been three coalition governments at the provincial level in Canada. The first two took place during World War II: one in Manitoba from 1940 to 1950, when Premier John Bracken led a wartime cabinet that, at one stage, contained members from six different parties; and one in BC, where premiers John Hart and Byron "Boss" Johnson led Liberal–Progressive Conservative coalitions from 1941 to 1952. The third occurred in Saskatchewan from 1999 to 2000, when NDP premier Roy Romanow welcomed two dissident Liberals across the aisle and into cabinet.

Legislative Institutions

While the partisan composition of an assembly naturally changes over time, and distinguishes one Canadian assembly from another, the federal and provincial legislatures share a number of common features.

The Chamber

The chamber of the legislature is the forum where elected officials convene to discuss the issues of the day, to debate motions, and to vote. Generally speaking, members of the government party caucus sit on one side of the chamber, and opposition members sit on the other side. This seating arrangement is not out of convenience or happenstance. It reflects centuries of Westminster parliamentary tradition in which the best public policy is seen to derive from adversarial debate between the government of the day and Her Majesty's Loyal Opposition. Seating these forces on opposite sides of the chamber forces the government to face its opponents, literally and figuratively, and makes for high drama when exchanges during Question Period feature shouting across the aisle.

Not all legislative assemblies in Canada are arranged in this way. For one, depending on the size of each party caucus, it may be necessary to physically seat opposition party members or independents on the government side, or vice versa. More fundamentally, assemblies in Northwest Territories and Nunavut are arranged in a circle, reflecting the presence of consensus government in those jurisdictions. Many municipal and city councils also arrange their members in this circular pattern, not simply because of the lack of political parties around which to organize seats, but also because of a conscientious desire to avoid the adversarial style of politics embedded in the Westminster system. A further reason that this is feasible is due to the low number of members.

In the middle of the chamber floor sits a table where staff from the office of the speaker of the House of Commons are ready to provide advice on parliamentary rules and procedures. In front of the table is a large speaker's chair whose size and design serves as a reminder of the moderator's authority. On the floor above is the public gallery, from which citizens can observe members. A press gallery reserves seats and provides technical accommodations for accredited political journalists.

↻ The consensus government of Canada's territorial legislatures is explained later in this chapter, on pages 247–8.

speaker The member of the legislature responsible for presiding over its rules and general decorum.

Roles in the Legislature

Not all legislatures or members are guided by partisanship. Aside from independents, who sit as legislators without being members of any political party caucus, the one member of a legislature who attempts to behave in a non-partisan manner is the *speaker*. Dressed in traditional black and white robes and seated in a ceremonial chair at the front of the chamber, the speaker is the designated moderator of debate in the chamber, and is responsible for overseeing the legislature's operations. The position entails enforcing rules, monitoring votes, and following established customs. This includes limiting the time that members can speak, ordering that "strangers" (i.e. non-members watching from the public galleries) be removed from time to time, and ensuring that there are no disturbances during voting. The speaker does not take part in debate and casts a vote only in the event of a tie. Rulings by the speaker cannot be appealed.

The speaker is selected in a secret ballot by other members, which is usually the first order of business after a general election. Typically, the choice is based on the candidate's parliamentary experience, fair-mindedness, and appreciation for the rules of parliamentary procedure. The speaker continues to represent constituents, and is typically affiliated with a political party, but must be careful to put party affiliation on hold. By tradition, the speaker, once selected, is literally dragged into the designated position at the front of the chamber by the first minister and leader of the opposition, signifying that the individual has not sought the position for partisan or personal gain.

The Canadian Press/Adrian Wyld

As part of parliamentary tradition, each newly selected speaker is escorted to the chair by the first minister and leader of the official opposition. The speaker is expected to feign reluctance and be "dragged" up the aisle—a custom dating back to the early days of the position in Britain, when speakers who ruled against the Crown were subject to punishment by the monarch. In 2011, 32-year-old Conservative MP Andrew Scheer (*left*) became the youngest ever speaker of the House of Commons. What qualities do you think MPs look for when choosing a Speaker?

There are a number of other positions affiliated with the speaker's office. The deputy speaker serves when the speaker is unavailable, and also bears the title "Chair of Committees of the Whole." At the federal level, this person must be fluent in the official language not ordinarily used by the speaker (i.e. French, if the speaker's first language is English). The speaker's office also employs a number of public servants who assist with coordinating documents, managing members' expense claims, and overseeing the production of televised proceedings. Some positions, like the sergeant-at-arms and the usher of the black rod, are largely ceremonial; other staff, such as the clerk of the legislature, provide essential support, such as advising on rules of order. Among the services rendered is the transcription of debate known as *Hansard*, which is the official record of proceedings. The financial affairs of the House of Commons are monitored by the all-party Board of Internal Economy.

Maintaining decorum in a highly charged atmosphere is a difficult proposition for most speakers. The intense nature of differences of opinion between members on opposing sides often results in loud heckling that can drown out debate. The speaker is also responsible for ruling on the exceptional protection of free speech, known as **parliamentary privilege**, that protects members from the possibility of being sued for defamation or other libel because of something said in the legislature. This is why members often dare opponents to repeat their remarks outside the chamber where normal free speech limitations exist. That does not preclude the possibility of a breach of privilege. In such a case, the speaker threatens to "name" a member who has been

parliamentary privilege
The legal immunity enjoyed by members of a legislature for things done or said in the course of their duties in the chamber.

deemed to have behaved poorly, and to temporarily expel that person from the legislature. By the same token, legislatures may also suspend their own members for set periods of time, as the Senate did in 2013. Such escalations are unusual, and while much routine business is quite mundane, the tone of political debate is not always civilized.

Perhaps more significant, but thankfully rare, is when a an individual member or a government as a whole is found to be in contempt. This formal censure declares that some action has occurred that is an affront to the legislature, such as disobeying accepted practices, ignoring a ruling of the speaker, or obstructing the business of the legislative assembly.

In addition to the speaker, a number of other members of a legislature have positions that are over and above their duties to represent their constituents. In recognition of their special status, these members occupy the front benches, which is to say the chairs in the front row. Chief among these is the prime minister (or premier) and cabinet. But for the purposes of organizing activity in the legislature, arguably the most important position is that of the house leaders. Each party appoints a member to be its house leader, who must then communicate upcoming business. Ordinarily an expert in parliamentary procedure, this person maintains timetables of events, prepares a list of speakers, and rises on points of order. At the federal level, parties also appoint senate leaders to fulfill similar roles in the upper house. These positions are so integral to the government's agenda that the governing party's house and senate leaders are members of cabinet.

Like the government party, opposition parties assign a variety of other duties to their members. Tasked with monitoring the government's performance, these people must attempt to project an image of being ready to assume power. Chief among them

contempt A formal denunciation of a member's or government's unparliamentary behaviour by the speaker.

house leader A member of the legislature responsible for the overall performance of her or his party in the legislative process.

INSIDE CANADIAN POLITICS
Do Canadians Care about Contempt and Confidence?

In 2011, a House of Commons committee recommended that the governing Conservatives be found in contempt of Parliament because they refused to provide members with requested information about government spending. Not providing financial details to the people's elected representatives strikes at the heart of the principle of responsible government. This prompted the official opposition Liberal Party to introduce a motion that "the House agrees with the finding of the standing committee on procedure and House affairs that the government is in contempt of Parliament, which is unprecedented in Canadian parliamentary history, and consequently, the House has lost confidence in the government."

The motion of non-confidence passed by a vote of 156 to 145, and the Conservative prime minister, Stephen Harper, promptly asked the governor general to dissolve the legislature and sign a writ of election. However, in the ensuing general election, the Conservative Party increased its seat count and formed a majority government, while the Liberal party was reduced to third-place status for the first time in its history.

THE LESSON
What matters to parliamentarians in terms of process is not necessarily what matters to Canadians at the ballot box.

BRIEFING NOTES

Her Majesty's Loyal Opposition

One of the hallmarks of Westminster parliamentary democracy is the adversarial roles it assigns to the government and Her Majesty's Loyal Opposition. The latter term reflects both the value of injecting opposing views into parliamentary debates and the necessity of having a government-in-waiting that, while vigorous in its criticism of government actions, remains loyal to the Crown and the constitution.

We say usually because some leaders and parties eschew the role and title of official opposition. When they formed the second-largest party in the House of Commons following the 1921 election, the Progressives declined to serve as the official opposition, mostly based on their opposition to the old-style, adversarial partisan politics that the role implied. In that case, the Conservatives—whose caucus was third-largest—served as Her Majesty's Loyal Opposition.

On the other hand, when the Bloc Québécois elected enough members to sit as the second-largest caucus in Parliament following the 1993 federal election, the party *did* choose to serve as official opposition. This established a unique and somewhat ironic situation in which a party dedicated to removing Quebec from Confederation and to dissolving the Canadian state as we know it was officially obliged to serve as "Her Majesty's Loyal Opposition."

---

is the leader of the official opposition, who is typically the head of the party with the second-highest number of seats in the legislature. The leader of the official opposition has the privilege of starting off Question Period. Collectively, non-government party leaders are known as *opposition leaders*. Discussed in Chapter 5, opposition leaders create *shadow cabinets* by assigning critic positions to select members. By virtue of their caucus size, critics in smaller parties are responsible for scrutinizing multiple portfolios. This is particularly true in the provinces, though the situation also occurs in the House of Commons.

> **leader of the official opposition** Typically, the leader of the party with the second-most seats in the legislature.

The Rank and File: Backbenchers

Most members of a legislature do not have extra powers or responsibilities. These regular members are called backbenchers, because they are literally assigned chairs located in the rear of the legislative chamber. Their primary focus tends to be on assisting constituents with obtaining government services. For example, David McGuinty, a Liberal member of Parliament for Ottawa South, published newspaper advertisements encouraging constituents to contact his office for information about Government of Canada services including social security programs, citizenship inquiries, Canadian passports, immigration matters, business opportunities, grants and funding, student loans, and taxation issues. A backbencher and support staff may work on behalf of a constituent to solve problems dealing with government service and policy. Backbenchers routinely attend community events ranging from official openings to funerals; send congratulatory messages to constituents to mark a notable achievement ranging from wedding anniversaries to winning a talent competition; and deliver petitions in the house. While these are the sorts of activities undertaken

> **backbenchers** Rank-and-file legislators without cabinet responsibilities or other special legislative titles or duties.

by all elected officials, including cabinet ministers, backbenchers have more time to attend to constituency matters.

Behind the scenes, the work of elected officials is supported by political staff, including the constituency assistants who busily manage phone calls, emails, letters, and office visits from citizens, politicians, reporters, interest group leaders, party officials, and others. An example of the many duties of an MP's constituency assistant is presented in the Opportunities Available box on page 227. As this suggests, MPs place a high priority on meeting the demands of constituency work.

Maintaining Party Discipline

The limited clout of backbenchers is related to the ferocity of party discipline in Canadian politics. The leaders of political parties expect that elected officials will vote as the leader instructs, and will stay "on message." If the member does otherwise, he or she faces escalating sanctions. These punishments may include being scolded in private, being admonished in front of caucus, having various privileges revoked (for example, committee memberships), being denied party resources during an election campaign, or ultimately being kicked out of the party caucus or denied the party's nomination in the ensuing election. To ensure control, each party designates one of its members a party whip, whose responsibilities are to inform fellow members of their tasks and to ensure unison.

Party discipline extends far beyond the public remarks a member is or is not permitted to make. In addition to the formal powers identified in the party's constitution, a party leader controls what partisans can speak about publicly, while also exercising the authority to:

- choose which parliamentarians may ask questions in the legislature;
- appoint parliamentarians to legislative committees and indicate what strategy they should deploy;
- promote members of the parliamentary wing of the party through the assignment of official positions, seating arrangements in the chamber, and extra privileges;
- instruct parliamentarians how to vote in the legislature and in committees, regardless of their constituents' wishes or their personal preference;
- sanction, demote, or eject a caucus member from the party;
- choose whether to deploy party resources to a candidate's riding during an election campaign; and
- refuse to approve a candidate's nomination to represent the party in an election (although this power has been circumscribed at the federal level, by the new Reform Act).

Party discipline helps strengthen the leader's control over the legislative process, which increases the party's ability to accomplish its agenda and become more attractive to voters. When functioning well, it also inhibits party instability and infighting. While government ministers must always vote together by virtue of cabinet responsibility, nonetheless, a high level of party discipline is required to maintain backbench loyalty. A similar level of caucus cohesiveness is required if opposition parties hope to be effective in holding the government to account and maintaining the image of a true government-in-waiting.

party whip Individual member of the legislature responsible for ensuring caucus members toe the party line.

This level of control can make some backbenchers feel and behave like so-called "trained seals"—or "sheeple", as one former government member[6] put it. They may also feel as though they sit between a rock—their party leadership's position on a

Opportunities Available

Knowledge of Canadian Politics and Government Preferred!

Constituency Assistant (Casework)

NDP Member of Parliament, Windsor West

Responsibilities

- Manage and respond to constituent casework with an emphasis on immigration including intake, outreach and correspondence
- Administer and log incoming phone calls, emails, faxes and walk-in traffic
- Liaise with various federal government departments and community organizations
- Assist with Member's constituent- and critic-related correspondence
- General administrative and reception duties
- Maintain database lists and direct mail to constituents in coordination with Ottawa parliamentary office
- Represent Member at events and meetings as required
- Monitor events in constituency and advise Member on issues in the constituency
- In consultation with Parliament Hill office, coordinate and manage outreach opportunities relating to the Member's work in the riding
- Liaise with House of Commons department and Member's Ottawa office to ensure smooth coordination of constituency office including office logistics and overseeing expenses as required
- Other duties as required

Qualifications

- Proven communication skills (verbal and written)
- Multilingual an asset
- Strong organizational skills, ability to work under pressure and to meet deadlines
- Proven research and case work skills
- Knowledge of government departments, community organizations and the labour movement
- Knowledge of Windsor West riding and riding priorities
- Knowledge of the New Democratic Party and sound political judgement
- Experience with database management an asset
- Media relations skills an asset

Source: New Democratic Party of Canada, "Job Opportunities" (2014), www.ndp.ca/job/brian-masse-constituency-assistant-casework-permanent-part-time-30-hoursweek.

particular issue—and a hard place—their constituents' opposing views. From this perspective, party discipline conflicts with the principle that members of a legislature are meant to represent the views of the people who elected them. On the other hand, it forces members to pick their battles, to lobby for change in private, and to achieve compromise. And, by providing a set of partisan cues and a broader election platform by which to judge performance, this discipline allows voters to better predict the behaviour of their elected representatives and hold them accountable. In the end, the right of a party leader to withhold support in an election usually triumphs, given the immense benefits of partisanship (resources, branding, and recognition) during campaigns.

Yet a leader's power over caucus is not unlimited. The leader must maintain the respect and loyalty of fellow party members. For these reasons, on certain controversial, divisive issues, the leader may allow a free vote, which permits members to vote their conscience, without penalty, regardless of the party (leader's) position. When used judiciously and without pretense, free votes may allow a party to promote a democratic image while helping the leader to avoid a caucus revolt.

Offices of the Legislature

Just as bureaucrats support the government by forming a permanent executive, a number of employees assist with the considerable activities that take place within a legislature. These activities range in pace from frenetic in the early months of the year to considerably calmer when the assembly is not sitting.

Each legislature has a number of appointed officers who report to it rather than to the government. Chief among these is the auditor general, whose office employs accountants tasked with examining public-sector spending. Auditors question the value for money and accounting practices of government departments. The auditor general regularly issues reports that draw public attention to government misspending and offer recommendations for improvement.

Over the years, other offices of the legislature have been created (see Table 6.3). One such independent body is the Office of the Chief Electoral Officer, which is responsible for the administration of free and fair elections. The list of officers also includes the privacy commissioner, who advocates for the privacy rights of Canadians, and the access-to-information commissioner, who assists citizens with concerns about the government's freedom-of-information practices. Positions that are unique to the House of Commons include the official languages commissioner and the commissioner of lobbying. Other legislatures may use different titles, may combine titles, or may have other offices that do not exist at the federal level. For instance, in Ottawa there is a conflict of interest and ethics commissioner as well as a public sector integrity commissioner; in Quebec there is simply an ethics commissioner; and in Ontario the position is known as the Office of the Integrity Commissioner. Whereas at the federal level there is a privacy commissioner and an access-to-information commissioner, at the provincial level these positions are fused into a single office, such as BC's Office of the Information and Privacy Commissioner. As well, some provincial legislatures have different offices entirely, such as an ombudsman and/or a child and youth advocate. Although they all perform important functions, in reality most Canadians do not avail of their services, though they may indirectly benefit from the efforts of these government watchdogs.

↻ The "delegate" view of representation, also known as substantive representation, is described on page 524 of Chapter 13.

free vote A bill or motion in the legislature on which party members, except members of cabinet, are allowed to vote however they choose without sanction.

auditor general An independent officer responsible for auditing and reporting to the legislature regarding a government's spending and operations.

INSIDE CANADIAN POLITICS

How Were Free Votes Used to Deal with the Hot-Button Issue of Same-Sex Marriage?

Free votes are rare in Canadian legislatures, although a pair occurred on the divisive issue of same-sex marriage. In 2005, several leaders released their members from the requirement to toe the party line on Bill C-38, which became known as the Civil Marriage Act. While his ministers remained bound to support the bill by virtue of cabinet solidarity, and facing a minority government situation, Prime Minister Paul Martin allowed Liberal backbenchers a free vote on the issue. So, too, did Conservative Party leader Stephen Harper and Bloc Québécois leader Gilles Duceppe. Jack Layton chose to whip his caucus, however, obliging New Democrats to vote in favour of legalizing same-sex marriage.

The Liberal cabinet voted nearly unanimously in support of same-sex marriage; none opposed, and one member abstained. Yet the Liberals' backbench was the most divided on the same-sex marriage vote. While 59 backbench members voted in favour of the bill, 32 opposed, with 3 abstaining. Despite the free vote, members of the other parties ended up voting predictably along party lines. Even in the absence of party discipline, the Bloc was remarkably unified in its support of the bill with 43 of 54 voting in support. By the same token, the Conservative caucus was almost entirely unified in opposing the bill with 93 of 98 members voting nay, 3 yea, and 2 abstaining. Conversely, despite the requirements of party discipline, one member of the NDP—Manitoba MP Bev Desjarlais—voted against the motion, citing personal religious convictions. Desjarlais was stripped of her position in Layton's shadow cabinet as a result,

and lost a subsequent nomination race in her home constituency before resigning from the NDP caucus to sit as an independent. She ran, but finished third, in the subsequent federal election.

Bill 38 passed by a final tally of 158 to 133, with 15 not voting, and by 47–21–3 in the Senate, becoming the Civil Marriage Act with Royal Assent on 20 July 2005.

The law re-emerged as a focal point in the 2006 federal election, when Stephen Harper announced his party's intention to hold another free vote, this time on whether or not to revisit the issue. The electorate granted Harper's Conservatives a minority government, and as one of the prime minister's first acts, he introduced a motion to "restore the traditional definition of marriage without affecting civil unions and while respecting existing same-sex marriages." The motion was defeated 175 to 123, with notable divisions occurring in the Conservative and Liberal caucuses. Citing a precedent set by PC prime minister Brian Mulroney during the free vote over capital punishment, Harper released all of his members—including cabinet ministers—to vote their conscience on the motion. As a result, 6 of the 25 ministers chose to vote against the motion, joining 7 of their backbench Conservative colleagues, 85 Liberals, and all 47 Bloc and 29 NDP members. By contrast, the remaining 110 Conservative MPs voted in favour of restoring the traditional definition of marriage; only 13 opposition members, all Liberal, supported the motion. Following the vote, Prime Minister Harper pledged not to re-open the same-sex marriage issue.

THE LESSON

Leaders may publicly release their members from the constraints of party discipline, yet the results of free votes almost always break down along traditional party lines.

VOX POP

Why do you suppose that members of the legislature tend to support their party leader's position during free votes?

TABLE 6.3 | Statutory Offices of Canadian Legislatures

	Auditor General	Chief Electoral Officer	Languages Commissioner	Information /Privacy Commissioner	Conflict of Interest / Ethics Commissioner	Commissioner of Public Sector Integrity	Commissioner of Lobbying	Ombudsman	Representative / Advocate for Children /Youth	Public Interest (Disclosure) Commissioner	Other
CAN	✓	✓	✓	✓[1]	✓	✓					
BC	✓	✓		✓	✓	✓[2]		✓	✓		✓[3]
AB	✓	✓		✓	✓			✓	✓	✓	
SK	✓	✓		✓	✓			✓	✓	✓	
MB	✓	✓		✓	✓			✓	✓		
ON	✓	✓		✓				✓	✓		✓[4]
QC	✓	✓			✓		✓	✓[5]	6		
NB	✓	✓	✓	✓	✓			✓			✓[7]
NS	✓	✓			✓			✓			
NL	✓	✓		✓				✓[8]	✓	✓[9]	
PE	✓	✓		✓	✓						
YT	10	✓		✓				✓			
NT	10	✓	✓	✓	✓						
NU	10	✓	✓	✓		✓					

Note: As of May 2015, this list includes independent officers that report to each legislature, but does not include legislative services, including offices of the clerk, records management, Hansard, legislative library, and so on.

[1] Two positions: Privacy Commissioner and Access to Information Commissioner; [2] Merit Commissioner; [3] Police Complaint Commissioner; [4] Environment Commissioner; [5] Public Protector; [6] Commission des droits de la personne et des droits de la jeunesse is independent from government, and does not report to the National Assembly; [7] Consumer Advocate for Insurance; [8] Citizens' Representative; [9] Commissioner for Legislative Standards; [10] Role fulfilled by federal Auditor General

Sources. Canada: www.parl.gc.ca/Parlinfo/compilations/OfficersAndOfficials/OfficersOfParliament.aspx; BC: https://dir.gov.bc.ca/gtds. cgi?showPage=lass&subPageTitle=Legislative+Assembly; Alberta: www.assembly.ab.ca/links.htm; Saskatchewan: www.legassembly.sk.ca/about/officers/; Manitoba: www.gov.mb.ca/legislature/about/officers.html; Ontario: www.auditor.on.ca/en/resources_en.htm; Quebec: www.assnat.qc.ca/en/abc-assemblee/ assemblee-nationale/personnes-designees-assemblee.html; New Brunswick: www.gnb.ca/legis/index-e.asp; Nova Scotia: http://nslegislature.ca/index.php/ people/offices/; Newfoundland and Labrador: www.assembly.nl.ca/offices/default.htm; PEI: www.assembly.pe.ca/index.php3?number=1024556&lang=E; Yukon: no list available; Northwest Territories: www.assembly.gov.nt.ca/about/statutory-officers; Nunavut: www.assembly.nu.ca/faq#n1906.

VOX POP

Take a look at Table 6.3. What are the likely reasons why some provinces have a child and youth advocate position, and others do not? Why would Quebec have its own commissioner of lobbying? Why does Ontario have no ethics commissioner? Do any other positions on this list surprise you?

Legislator Remuneration

A source of constant debate is how much the people's representatives should be paid for their work. The concept of parliamentary indemnity holds that to attract top-quality representatives, there must be an attractive pay package. Otherwise, lawyers, business-people, and other relatively well-paid professionals with lucrative occupations will not put their careers on hold to enter the political realm. Moreover, if representatives are poorly paid, they are more susceptible to accepting bribes from people who want political favours. A third consideration is that being a public figure, especially a member of cabinet, is a stressful and demanding job that can involve long hours when the legislature is sitting. Members spend a lot of time travelling and may have to live in the capital city away from family, attend community events on the weekends, and be constantly be on call. Members of the government who make unpopular but important decisions are berated by constituents in the mass media, on social media, through contact with the member's office, and in person. Even backbenchers forgo their ability to venture into public places for fear of being intercepted by citizens anxious to chat, banter, and complain. The worst aspect of life for a public official may the teasing or bullying a member's children are subjected to at school because of the parent's political career, a cruelty for which higher pay is seldom seen as an appropriate form of compensation.

For these reasons, the remuneration and perks afforded to elected officials remain generous. It is common for base salaries to be in the $100,000 range, and there are extra stipends for supplementary duties ranging from being a minister to being the chair of a committee. Salaries for public officials are subject to frequent scrutiny and review, and they change regularly, increasing over time but also decreasing periodically when a government is forced to cut its operating budget. Table 6.4 provides a snapshot of federal, provincial, and territorial remuneration, to give you an idea of

TABLE 6.4 | Snapshot of Legislator Remuneration by Jurisdiction, 2012

Jurisdiction	Annual Base (Indemnity)	Member Non-taxable Expense Allowance	Total with Grossed-Up Non-taxable Allowance*	Supplements	
				First Minister (i.e. Prime Minister or Premier)	Minister with Portfolio
House of Commons MP	$157,731		**$157,731**	$157,731	$75,516
British Columbia MLA	101,859		**101,859**	91,673	50,930
Alberta MLA	52,092		**90,708**	81,312	63,912
Saskatchewan MLA	89,300		**89,300**	64,947	45,465
Manitoba MLA	85,564		**85,564**	55,944	36,745
Ontario MPP	116,550		**116,550**	92,424	49,301
Quebec MNA	85,388	15,538	**108,418**	89,657	64,041
New Brunswick MLA	85,000		**85,000**	79,000	52,614
Nova Scotia MLA	86,619		**86,619**	109,485	47,609
Prince Edward Island MLA	65,344		**65,344**	71,094	45,688
Newfoundland & Labrador MHA	95,357		**95,357**	74,824	54,072
Yukon MLA	69,531	13,371	**88,571**	53,485	37,439
Northwest Territories MLA	96,615	$6,962	**106,574**	73,482	51,709
Nunavut MLA	90,396		**90,396**	83,287	70,109

* Non-taxable expense allowance grossed up based on the combined federal and provincial marginal income tax rate. For Alberta, amount as provided by the Legislative Assembly of Alberta.

Source: Hay Group, Alberta MLA Compensation Review (2012), p. 219: www.mlacompensationreview-alberta.ca/PDF/MCR_Report2012_WEBFinal2.pdf.

how these vary among jurisdictions. Note that these figures will have changed since 2012; they are provided for illustrative purposes only. Elected members participate in pension and supplementary health plans well above the private sector standard. They receive travel, housing, and meal allowances; they have access to support staff in their office; they can go on international junkets; and they are invited to innumerable social events. If they are defeated in an election, they receive a substantial severance package; and when they retire, most enjoy supplementary pension and health benefits. Members of the legislature also receive non-monetary incentives such as the psychological benefits of influencing public policy and the ego boost of being in the public eye.

Even with the stresses of office, there are good reasons to be critical of the extravagance of these rewards. Despite the fact that many jurisdictions assign the review of legislators' pay to committees or commissions, members are collectively and ultimately responsible for setting their own remuneration schemes. In particular, their pension plan may be viewed as unjustifiably rich, with some long-time MPs eligible to be paid over $100,000 a year when they retire from politics, which may be on top of another pension that they have earned in a career outside of politics. Given the generous rewards and benefits of public life, it's a wonder some elected and appointed officials see the need to take advantage of the system. And yet there have been numerous scandals about unethical and/or illegal spending behaviour. Cases include a Nova Scotia MLA being reimbursed for a generator stored in his garage, members in various legislatures claiming tens of thousands of dollars in housing allowances by lying about the location of their primary residence, and a senator using his staff to clear wood on his personal property. This does not even begin to touch on the financial issues uncovered in a recent review of Senators' expense claims. Increasingly there is public scrutiny of such behaviour and auditors general and ethics commissioners are granted permission to review expense claims.

As the attentive public becomes more aware of the perks of office, it is prone to contrast this with the declining number of sitting days of most legislatures, which they may interpret to mean that politicians are working less than they did in the past. A legislature tends to sit roughly at the same times of year when children are in school and adjourns for lengthy breaks around Thanksgiving, Remembrance Day, Christmas, Easter, and for the summer. The number of sitting days varies depending on the jurisdiction. Yet most legislatures are often closed for long stretches, and some members, particularly provincial backbenchers, may see little need to come into the office every day. The competitiveness of the party system, the proximity to an election, the presence of a majority versus a minority government, the activist nature of a government's agenda, the level of public unrest—these are all things that can increase or reduce how often members assemble. The higher number of sitting days in Parliament reflects the diversity of competing perspectives, the volume of bills, the vitality of the committee system, and the extra-parliamentary scrutiny from the media and elsewhere. The general trend is that the number of sitting days is in decline (see Table 6.5). Canada has also not been plunged into great national political debates in recent years. The 1970s and 1980s featured deep constitutional discussions, which have been noticeably absent since the mid-1990s. As well, technological innovations have sped up transportation, communication, and research, enabling MPs to make decisions and carry out business outside the chamber. It also means that MPs' working hours have expanded in concert

TABLE 6.5 | Number of Sitting Days in Canadian Legislatures, 1987–8 vs 2010–11

Region	1987	1988	2010	2011
Government of Canada Legislatures				
Senate	91	90	79	64
House of Commons	183	165	119	98
Provincial/Territorial Legislatures				
British Columbia, Legislative Assembly	115	69	46	48
Alberta, Legislative Assembly	81	72	50	47
Saskatchewan, Legislative Assembly	97	69	65	48
Manitoba, Legislative Assembly	91	121	67	50
Ontario, Legislative Assembly	66	91	93	57
Quebec, National Assembly	77	86	81	82
New Brunswick, Legislative Assembly	44	38	65	41
Nova Scotia, House of Assembly	59	56	62	68
Prince Edward Island, Legislative Assembly	42	48	40	28
Newfoundland and Labrador, House of Assembly	65	71	51	33
Yukon, Legislative Assembly	50	36	60	30
Northwest Territories, Council	51	59	51	48
Nunavut, Legislative Assembly	n/a	n/a	33	31
Mean (all)	79.4	76.5	64.1	51.5

Source: Reproduced with permission from the Parliament of Canada. (2013). At: http://www.parl.gc.ca/Parlinfo/compilations/ProvinceTerritory/SittingDays.aspx

with the public's increasing expectations of prompt service, even as the public assumes that MPs are working less because the assembly meets less often.[7]

VOX POP

Why would a lawyer, businessperson, union leader, physician, or anyone else earning a high salary take a pay cut to enter the rough-and-tumble world of politics?

The Life of the Legislature

Regardless of the jurisdiction, all legislatures in Canada follow a common rhythm. Discussed below, each session of each legislature begins with a throne speech, includes a presentation of the budget and the budget estimates, and ends with prorogation or dissolution (see Figure 6.3). Other business is conducted in the interim, such as the government party advancing legislation, the opposition attempting its own initiatives, and private members introducing motions.

The lifespan of the legislature is like that of a hockey season. Just as each season consists of individual games, which consist of periods separated by intermissions, so, too, does each parliament (or legislature or assembly) consist of individual sessions, which consist of sittings separated by periods of recess. A parliament usually lasts

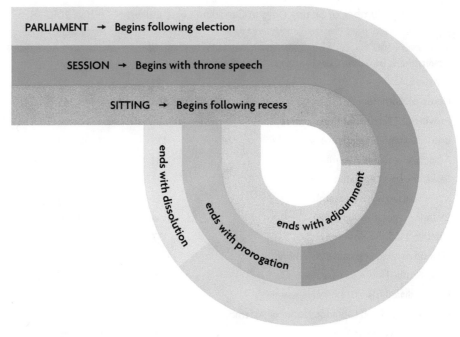

PARLIAMENT → Begins following election

SESSION → Begins with throne speech

SITTING → Begins following recess

ends with dissolution

ends with prorogation

ends with adjournment

FIGURE 6.3 | The Parliamentary Life Cycle

four years. The typical session lasts one to three years, and can contain hundreds of individual sittings.

Every parliament, legislature, or assembly is named chronologically, and—except in cases of resignations and by-elections—contains a relatively static group of legislators. Canada's 41st Parliament convened for the first time in 2011, and the 42nd Parliament convened after the 2015 federal election. Each of these groups of legislators is officially sworn in following an election, with oaths administered by the governor general or lieutenant governor.

Most parliaments consist of two to five legislative sessions, which are also numbered. Each session begins with the reading of the speech from the throne (or *throne speech*), which offers the governing party an opportunity to outline its legislative agenda for the life of that session, and which typically contains items drawn from the party's most recent election platform. The red carpet is rolled out for the monarch's representative, who arrives at the legislature to great fanfare. The pageantry and formal rituals, such as inspecting the guards, are reminders of the supreme executive authority of the Crown in Canada's parliamentary system of government. When a throne speech is delivered in Ottawa, the governor general proceeds to sit in the speaker's chair in the Senate and is flanked by his or her spouse (the *viceregal consort*) and the prime minister. Supreme Court justices, parliamentarians, and other distinguished guests fill the chamber to listen to the monarch's representative formally enunciate the government's priorities and planned initiatives. The speech is written by partisans in the prime minister's office, who integrate election campaign commitments, input from government departments, and recent events that are deemed to warrant government attention. By repeatedly saying, "My government will . . ." the governor general gives public notice from the Crown what initiatives the appointed cabinet intends to pursue. The same

speech from the throne Document read by the governor general or lieutenant governor, officially opening a new session of the legislature and detailing the government's plans.

custom is carried out in provincial and territorial legislatures, with the corresponding roles being filled by the lieutenant governor or commissioner, the premier, provincial justices, and staff in the premier's office.

Once read, the speech from the throne is put to a vote in the legislature, offering members the opportunity to debate, and in rare cases reject, the government's legislative agenda. If the speech is rejected, the government is denied the confidence of the house and must resign.

Each session consists of hundreds of sittings, which are scheduled to coincide with the legislative agenda and seasonal calendar. At the conclusion of a sitting, the speaker announces that the legislature is closed for the day, which is known as adjournment. Business is put on hold until the next meeting, which can begin as early as the next morning or else many weeks later, after a scheduled break, or *recess*.

The business of the legislature grinds to a halt when a session comes to an end. In an effort to reset the legislative agenda, every year to three years the first minister approaches the governor general or lieutenant governor for a prorogation of the legislature. All work, including legislation, that is currently before the legislature ceases and must be re-introduced in the next session should the government wish to advance it. Such bills are said to have "died on the order paper." First ministers may request prorogation for a host of reasons. Some may decide that their legislative agenda, announced in the throne speech, has been completed and that the legislature needs to establish a new mandate. Others may seek prorogation to begin a cooling-off period amid tense parliamentary debates or even scandal. By convention and on the advice of constitutional advisers, the monarch's representative is granted very little discretion when it comes to assessing the merits or viability of the first minister's request for prorogation. Historically, these requests have almost always been granted, and—contrary to recent popular conceptions—prorogation occurs on a regular basis in the life of every parliament, legislature, and assembly in Canada.

Eventually, the composition of the legislature needs to be renewed via a general election. Constitutionally, this renewal must occur at least every five years, except in the event of "real or apprehended war, invasion, or insurrection." In such cases, an election can be postponed, as long as no more than a third of members are opposed. The only time the federal Parliament sat for more than five years was during Robert Borden's Conservative government, when a one-year stay was granted in 1916, during World War I.

On a more practical level, governments' agendas often wrap up or expire over the life of a legislature; counterproductive animosity among legislators may build; and public support may need to be obtained for new policy proposals. Political parties, even the governing party, may have a new leader who has not yet faced the electorate in that capacity. In any of these cases, the first minister may wish to seek a new batch of legislators and a fresh mandate from the electorate before proceeding with new legislation. To accomplish this, he or she must request dissolution, which occurs when the governor general (or lieutenant governor) declares the end of a parliament (or legislature) and signs the writs for a new general election.

In the past, the prime minister or premier sought an election when the chances of seeking a new mandate were greatest—either when the governing party was enjoying a high public approval rating or when the opposition parties were especially weak or disorganized. Nowadays, all jurisdictions except Nova Scotia, Nunavut, and Yukon

adjournment The temporary suspension of a legislative sitting until it reconvenes.

prorogation The process by which a legislative session is closed.

dissolution The process by which a Parliament or legislature is closed, resulting in a general election of new members.

have fixed-date election legislation stipulating when the next election is to be held. Regardless of these laws, and particularly in minority government situations, a government may lose the confidence of the House, triggering dissolution before the end of the parliamentary term. Moreover, the possibility remains that the first minister will seek to time the election call to the governing party's advantage.

Each year, typically but not always after the Christmas break, the government introduces its budget. In essence, the budget proposes how the government intends to raise and spend money, and includes the government's forecast for how the economy will fare in the year ahead. Most budgets contain the government's plans for day-to-day operational expenses; investments in things like roads, schools, or infrastructure (capital expenses); and savings or debt retirement. Each budget reflects months of work by public servants and political staff who are guided by the throne speech and election promises. It therefore strikes a balance between departmental and political priorities, as it is the minister who acts as the intermediary with central agencies like the Treasury Board.

budget A document containing the government's projected revenue, expenditures, and economic forecasts.

↻ Budgets are discussed in the section on financial administration in Chapter 8, on public policy.

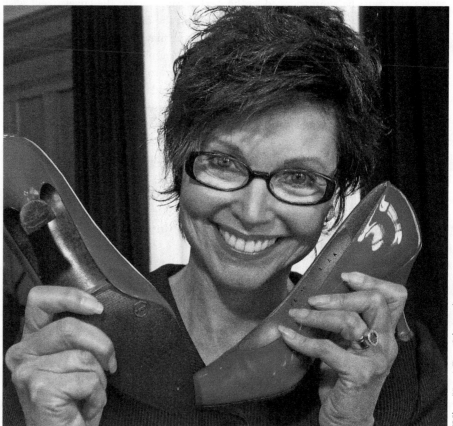

CP Photo/Victoria Times Colonist–John McKay

BC finance minister Carole Taylor was criticized when she wore a $600 pair of Gucci shoes on budget day in 2006. In 2007, she wore these resoled red pumps. A finance minister's purchase—or resoling—of shoes before budget day has become an important media event, with political commentators analyzing the symbolism of the minister's choice. Are we attaching too much significance to a quirky Canadian tradition? Did critics exhibit a gender bias when reporting the Taylor story, or should the minister's staff have known better when planning the Gucci shoes photo-op?

The budget is tabled in the legislature by the minister of finance amidst much secrecy and hoopla. Key representatives of the opposition parties, other governments, industry, civil society, and the media may be given advance copies of the budget on the day it is released, but only under the condition of strict confidentiality. These people are placed in what's known as "lock-up": herded behind closed doors with no ability to communicate with the outside world, they are allowed to review the budget and to ask government officials any questions. A set period after the budget speech has commenced, these individuals are free to report and brief their colleagues on the details of the budget. It is essential that details not be leaked, not only because of the formality of informing members first, but because speculators could profit from advance notice of the government's financial plans. There is also the matter of ensuring that the finance minister is the one who announces the information, which he or she does by way of the budget speech. Considerable effort is invested in preparing a speech, briefing the media, and even selecting the minister's shoes.

> **lock-up** The process through which invited individuals are given confidential advance access to budget documents.

After the finance minister has delivered the budget in the legislature, the budget is debated, usually for a period of four days. At this time, a formal vote is held to determine whether or not a majority of the members in the legislature approve of the government's broad fiscal plans. This is a central tenet of responsible government, wherein the appointed members of the government executive must have the confidence of the people's elected representatives. If a political party controls a majority of the seats, the budget vote is a foregone conclusion, and the budget will pass. However, in a minority government situation, there is considerable drama. If the governing party does not persuade members of another party to vote in favour of the budget, then the government falls and there is usually an election.

The budget debate is followed by budget estimates. This ensures that members from different parties have an opportunity to scrutinize line-by-line spending plans for the upcoming fiscal year (1 April to 31 March). Typically, representatives from the department concerned, namely the minister and deputy minister, are expected to answer committee members' questions about the estimates. Issues that emerge can inform future lines of government critique for the opposition and areas of investigative inquiry for journalists.

> **budget estimates** The more detailed, line-by-line statements of how each department will treat revenues and expenditures.

Governments are not always correct in their budget projections. Economic circumstances may shift over the course of the year, so governments typically announce adjustments to their revenue and spending projections in quarterly fiscal updates. The most acrimonious fiscal update occurred during the 2008 economic crisis, which led to the coalition crisis described in the Inside Canadian Politics box earlier in this chapter and at length in Chapter 11.

> **fiscal update** Semi-annual announcement of the state of the government's economic, revenue, and spending projections.

Daily Business

There is more to governance than grand speeches, of course. The routine business of the legislature is governed by standing orders. These formal rules differ from legislature to legislature, and are non-partisan but nevertheless favour the government party over the opposition. The procedures specify the length of time a member may speak or a motion may be debated, and stipulate the need for members to address each other by titles as opposed to their given names. Standing orders also prescribe the meeting times for each sitting, which for the House of Commons are presented in Figure 6.4. These

> **standing orders** The body of rules governing the conduct of the legislature.

adjournment times are subject to change if a motion is passed to continue the sitting so that some specific business can carry on without interruption. In some cases, however, rules are put in place to prevent debate extending outside extraordinary circumstances. In Manitoba, for instance, standing orders are in place to allow MLAs to spend time with their families in the evening. The various activities identified in the standing orders of the House of Commons are identified in Table 6.6.

In preparation for proceedings, the government house leader identifies a priority list of items that the governing party wishes to advance. The *order paper* is presented at the start of each day to members for their collective approval. Once it is approved, it will guide the day's business, and staff in the speaker's office can proceed to prepare supporting materials, such as the circulation of photocopied documents.

<table>
<tr><th>Hours</th><th>Monday</th><th>Tuesday</th><th>Wednesday</th><th>Thursday</th><th>Friday</th><th>Hours</th></tr>
<tr><td>10:00–11:00</td><td></td><td rowspan="6">ROUTINE PROCEEDINGS
....
Government Orders</td><td rowspan="6">Review of Delegated Legislation*</td><td rowspan="6">ROUTINE PROCEEDINGS
....
Government Orders</td><td>Government Orders</td><td>10:00–11:00</td></tr>
<tr><td>11:00–11:15</td><td rowspan="2">Private Members' Business</td><td>Statements by Members</td><td>11:00–11:15</td></tr>
<tr><td>11:15–12:00</td><td>Oral Questions</td><td>11:15–12:00</td></tr>
<tr><td>12:00–1:00</td><td rowspan="3">Government Orders</td><td rowspan="3">ROUTINE PROCEEDINGS
....
Government Orders</td><td>12:00–1:00</td></tr>
<tr><td>1:00–1:30</td><td>1:00–1:30</td></tr>
<tr><td>1:30–2:00</td><td>1:30–2:00</td></tr>
<tr><td>2:00–2:15</td><td>Statements by Members</td><td>Statements by Members</td><td>Statements by Members</td><td>Statements by Members</td><td rowspan="2">Private Members' Business</td><td>2:00–2:15</td></tr>
<tr><td>2:15–2:30</td><td rowspan="2">Oral Questions</td><td rowspan="2">Oral Questions</td><td rowspan="2">Oral Questions</td><td rowspan="2">Oral Questions</td><td>2:15–2:30</td></tr>
<tr><td>2:30–3:00</td><td rowspan="4"></td><td>2:30–3:00</td></tr>
<tr><td>3:00–5:30</td><td rowspan="2">ROUTINE PROCEEDINGS
....
Government Orders</td><td>Government Orders</td><td>ROUTINE PROCEEDINGS
....
Notices of Motions for the Production of Papers
....
Government Orders</td><td>Government Orders</td><td>3:00–5:30</td></tr>
<tr><td>5:30–6:30</td><td>Private Members' Business</td><td>Private Members' Business</td><td>Private Members' Business</td><td>5:30–6:30</td></tr>
<tr><td>6:30–7:00</td><td>Adjournment Proceedings</td><td>Adjournment Proceedings</td><td>Adjournment Proceedings</td><td>Adjournment Proceedings</td><td>6:30–7:00</td></tr>
</table>

FIGURE 6.4 | Weekly House of Commons Timetable

Source: Reproduced with permission from the Parliament of Canada.

The daily activity that unquestionably attracts the most attention is oral questions, commonly known as question period (or QP). This is the scheduled time for opposition members to question the head of government and cabinet members. On the opposition side, preparation involves researching, drafting, and rehearsing questions, as well as jostling for who gets to speak. On the government side, ministers attempt to anticipate what questions will be lobbed their way, and review the briefing notes prepared by public servants in their department. Bureaucrats prepare lengthy briefing binders for their respective ministers' use and are on call in the event that the opposition raises an issue with which the minister is unfamiliar. Internally, the various parties also identify key message themes that they want to repeat so that their main points are consistent and conveyed to onlookers in the press gallery.

question period The time allotted for members to ask oral questions of the government in the legislature.

TABLE 6.6 | Summary of Routine Events in the House of Commons

Event	What Is It?
Private members' business	Members are given a 60-second opportunity to share uplifting news, such as an accomplishment by a constituent. Motions concerning government policy can also be raised.
Public bills, private bills, notices of motions	Notice is given for future discussion about proposed legislation (i.e. the motion to introduce a bill known as "first reading").
Government orders	Time is allotted for any business that was proposed by a minister for discussion, such as debate on a bill. This makes up a considerable amount of daily activity.
Tabling of documents	Reports and other papers are formally presented to the house, ranging from annual reports to special requests for written information.
Statements by ministers	Short information or policy announcements are made by ministers, with opportunities for the opposition to briefly respond.
Oral questions	A period of time is given to opposition members to ask questions of government members.
Presentation of reports from interparliamentary delegations	The head of a group that has included at least one member of the legislature and that has recently returned to Canada must report on its activities.
Presentation of reports from committees	A designated member gives a brief summary of a committee's report.
First reading of Senate public bills	A bill that has been approved by the Senate must also be introduced for review in the House of Commons.
Motions	As most motions are dealt with in other orders of business, this has become a catch-all for remaining motions, such as seeking approval of a committee report or a motion concerning house proceedings/sittings.
Presenting petitions	A member presents a list of constituent signatures in support of a plea for government action. These must have been inspected in advance by the clerk of petitions. No debate in the house ensues after a petition's presentation, and the matter is referred to the relevant ministry for a written response.
Questions on the order paper	A member can submit a written question about public affairs to a minister for response.

Source: Adapted from the Parliament of Canada, Standing Orders of the House of Commons (2013). Not intended to be an exhaustive list.

In these ways, question period remains an integral part of Canada's system of responsible government, allowing opposition and even government backbenchers to hold the executive to account. This is done in the public eye, as official records of legislative proceedings are transcribed and, for the House of Commons and most provincial/territorial legislatures, broadcast live or on tape delay. Critics point out that *question* period is seldom *answer* period, in that participants do not reasonably expect to secure information from the government. Rather, the opposition often uses QP to embarrass the government and draw public attention to an issue, while cabinet members attempt to respond earnestly while also deflecting criticism. This often conditions members to focus on witty remarks, sharp questions, and theatrics in an attempt to secure the short sound bites that make the news. Consider the following exchange from November 2013 when Justin Trudeau was the leader of the Liberal Party opposition, which is one of countless similar examples of the back-and-forth that occurs, wherein the opposition tries to embarrass the government, and the government's representative tries to turn the tables:

Mr Justin Trudeau (Papineau, Lib): Canadians are worried that the Prime Minister is paying little attention to the integrity of the electoral process. Why does the Prime Minister, time after time, put the interests of his party ahead of the interests of Canadians? Why does he consistently show an obvious lack of respect for the investigators who work to support the democratic process?

Right Hon. Stephen Harper (Prime Minister, Conservative): Mr Speaker, that statement is completely untrue. The hon. member could take lessons on accountability on a whole bunch of things. For instance, I know he opposes any kind of mandatory prison sentences for those who commit violent crime in this country. He should believe in some accountability on that. Of course, when it comes to terrorism, we saw his first reaction to terrorists: to make excuses for them, that it is all social exclusion. It is time the Liberal Party learned that our justice system is based on accountability.[8]

At the federal level, the parliamentary calendar stipulates that 20 days be allocated to the opposition parties so that they have time for debate about their own motions. These opposition days, also known as *supply days*, are opportunities for non-government parties to advance their own agendas. While this includes debate about new policy ideas, it also invariably is seen as an opportunity to critique the government. Scheduled opposition days take on greater significance in a minority government situation because they can be used to introduce a motion of non-confidence that, by convention, will trigger an election if passed. Depending on the standing orders governing a particular legislature, the government may have more or less control over the scheduling of opposition days.

opposition days Time allotted to opposition parties to raise their own motions and legislation.

legislative committee A small group of legislators assigned to deliberate and report back to the legislature.

Legislative Committees

Question period gets all of the attention, but the real business of the legislature tends to occur in legislative committees. These are small groups of members of the legislature, belonging to different political parties, who meet to discuss government activities and call expert witnesses to testify. They typically take a closer look at a bill or an issue and subject it to scrutiny before it is voted on by the committee of the whole or the entire legislature. Committees are typically more active at the federal level, as the smaller number of members in provincial and territorial legislatures may allow for efficient and effective work by the committee of the whole. In all jurisdictions, the committee of the whole provides an opportunity for special debate.

Committee chairs fulfill similar duties as the speaker does for the committee of the whole, and are selected according to rules that vary from legislature to legislature. In the House of Commons, recent changes now grant committee members the power to select their own chairs, meaning that, particularly in minority governments, it is possible for opposition parties to chair committees. In other jurisdictions, chairs are selected by party leadership. While committee chairs do possess considerable power over the group's agenda and decorum, legislative committees provide backbenchers with an opportunity to gain experience and to influence government policy. This work takes time, of course, and the engagement of committees slows down the passage of proposed legislation.

Not to be confused with the cabinet committees discussed in Chapter 5 are a variety of legislative committees that differ from one another in terms of their membership, focus, and duration. The main point of distinction is between *standing* and *ad hoc* committees. A standing committee is permanent since it is designated in the standing orders as playing such an essential role in the business of the legislature that it must operate regardless of the party in power. Typically a standing committee deals with matters concerning a particular department like the standing committee on health, or a body of government, such as the standing committee on procedures and house affairs. By comparison, an ad hoc committee is created with a special mandate that may eventually be completed, such as a special committee tasked with drafting or scrutinizing legislation. In Ottawa, where there are two legislative chambers, many standing and ad hoc committees are made up of members exclusively from either the House of Commons or the Senate. However, some joint committees feature representation from MPs and senators, such as the standing joint committee on the library of Parliament.

The Legislative Process

Laws are created, changed, and repealed after public debate and scrutiny. They begin as ideas, perhaps based on a political ideology, on pressure from special interests, and/or as a response to an emerging situation. Often, but not always, these ideas are included in a political party's election platform and are mentioned in the throne speech. Some ideas for laws are fast-tracked, whereas others linger for years. For instance, the September 11 terrorist attacks in the United States caused governments worldwide to urgently revise laws designed to ensure domestic security. Ideas to introduce laws that will protect the environment, however, often languish. If polls or election results are any indication, many people do not consider climate change an issue that warrants immediate action, nor would they accept the tradeoffs that would result from meaningful action.

An idea for a law is formalized when it is written out as a bill. Federally, bills may be introduced in either chamber of Parliament, although those involving government spending must be initiated in the House of Commons by a member of cabinet. Each

committee of the whole Another name for the body of all legislators.

standing committee Also known as a permanent legislative committee, whose existence is defined by standing orders.

ad hoc committees Also known as a working legislative committee, whose mandate is time-limited.

bill A piece of draft legislation tabled in the legislature.

RealWorldImage.com

Environmental issues like global warming are a serious problem that rarely generate radical action. Conversely, the threat of terrorist attacks since 11 September 2001 prompted the federal government to pass several anti-terror laws. Why do you suppose terrorism garners such swift and decisive political response, while issues like climate change do not?

bill is numbered sequentially depending on the order in which it is introduced during a particular session. Bills initiated in the House of Commons are given names beginning with "C" such as the Senate Reform Act which was labelled Bill C-7 when it was introduced in the first session of the 41st Parliament, while bills originating in the Senate are labelled with an "S." Once passed, a bill may be called a law, an act, or a statute.

There are several different types of bills, distinguished by their targets, sponsors, and structure. The first dichotomy divides *private bills*, which deal with matters that apply to a small subset of the Canadian population, and *public bills*, which apply to society as a whole. The classic example of the former existed prior to 1968, when couples were required to petition Parliament for a divorce. Following an investigation, these were granted by means of a vote in the Senate. Private bills are far less common today, but they are used to guide the activities of corporate entities governed by Parliament such as Scouts Canada.

Public bills are far more common, and may be divided into two main categories: *government bills*, which are introduced by cabinet, and *private members' bills*, which are introduced by backbenchers of any party and which are not to be confused with the *private bills* noted earlier. A government bill is proposed legislation that has been endorsed by the governing party, and only a minister can move for its introduction to the assembly. A private member's bill is a proposal from a member who is not part of cabinet; while this is an important practice, particularly for raising attention to matters of concern to a member's constituents or drawing focus to issues not on the government's agenda, in reality, private members' bills are rarely passed.

In turn, government bills may be subdivided into those that involve spending and revenue (*money bills*) and those that do not. Money bills cannot be introduced by private members or senators. Only cabinet members may introduce legislation to that effect.

Lastly, bills may be categorized as stand-alone legislation, addressing one particular area of public policy, or omnibus legislation, which addresses a wide range of issues. For example, a bill on cyber-crime may be considered stand-alone in that it focuses solely on one topic. By contrast, budget implementation bills, passed shortly after the budget is approved, are often omnibus bills containing amendments to a host of existing laws adjusted by the new fiscal plan. Opposition parties often criticize governments for over-using omnibus bills as a means of obfuscating issues or precluding sufficient debate on topics that deserve individual attention which is why Justin Trudeau's Liberal Party has promised to amend the standing orders to end their use.

The process for passing a government bill into law varies somewhat among jurisdictions. It normally begins with a policy idea being pitched by a minister in cabinet. In Ottawa, this requires a formal policy proposal that has been drafted by departmental staff so that it can be referred to a cabinet committee for review. To prepare a proposal, public servants research the subject matter, review legislation in other jurisdictions, revise multiple drafts, consult with other departments, and potentially seek input from stakeholders and partners, namely other orders of government, Aboriginal communities, interest groups, industry, or the public. If the cabinet committee endorses the proposal, then staff in the minister's department begin to draft legislation. They submit this to the department of justice, where government lawyers scrutinize and tweak the draft bill. That draft is submitted back to a cabinet committee for review, and if it approves the draft, then the draft is submitted to the full cabinet for approval. If cabinet consents, the draft bill is signed by the first minister or the house leader in preparation for its presentation to the legislature.

The draft bill is introduced to the legislature by the sponsoring minister. This verbal introduction is known as *first reading*. This permits the legislature's staff to circulate printed copies to other members, and the bill is scheduled for debate through its inclusion on the order paper. First reading therefore serves to give advance notice of an upcoming discussion about a bill. A bill introduced by a minister stands a good chance of being passed, particularly during a majority government; however, a bill introduced by an opposition MP or a private member is likely to be defeated. Nevertheless, non-ministers can have some success. Consider the following record of the first reading of a private member's bill by New Democrat MP Pat Martin, who for years called on the Canadian Mint to stop producing the one-cent coin:

41:1 Hansard - 77 (2012/2/9)
[Bill C-391. Introduction and first reading]
Mr Pat Martin (Winnipeg Centre, NDP) moved for leave to introduce Bill C-391, An Act to amend the Currency Act and the Royal Canadian Mint Act (calling in of the cent).

He said: "Mr. Speaker, it is my pleasure to re-introduce this bill and I, again, thank my seconder. There are over 30 billion pennies in circulation in Canada today, many of which are underneath my bed in an old cookie jar. I believe everyone here has a similar jar underneath their bed. In spite of this silliness, one billion pennies are produced by the Royal Canadian Mint every year. Each penny costs more to produce than it is worth and nobody wants them. We are spending a fortune producing something nobody wants and nobody needs, and that

> **omnibus legislation** Bills or laws that address a wide variety of public policy issues in a single document.

provides no functional service to the public anymore. If any evidence is needed, it is the freebie jar at every cash register that says "Take one or leave one." We do not see jars full of loonies there because loonies are worth something and pennies are not. I am urging the minister of finance, perhaps in the budget or by the introduction of this bill, to eliminate the penny. I ask that he do us all a favour. I hope this receives broad support from my colleagues."

(Motion deemed adopted, bill read the first time and printed)[9]

MP Martin's core argument, which he repeated for years, was that the penny cost more to manufacture than it was worth. His bills were never passed in the legislature, but the government was listening. The 2012 federal budget contained a provision to phase out production of the penny from Canada's coinage system. While the Conservative government and Finance Minister Jim Flaherty took credit for the decision, the origins of the announcement can be traced to an individual opposition MP's efforts.

The Canadian Press/Ryan Remiorz

In 2012, the federal government introduced a 425-page budget bill (Bill C-38) that introduced, amended, or repealed 70 separate federal laws relating to matters including environmental protection, Old Age Security, and new rules concerning employment insurance. When it comes to promoting a fair and functional democratic system in Canada, what are the benefits and downsides of omnibus legislation?

At a future point, the schedule of events identified on the order paper indicates that the time has arrived for debate on the bill. The minister motions that debate may begin, which is known as *second reading*. It is at this stage that the government outlines the purpose behind the legislation. Members debate the draft bill, and in most but not all Canadian legislatures, the bill is referred to the appropriate legislative committee for clause-by-clause scrutiny and possible amendments. This may take some time, particularly if expert witnesses are called. Once these amendments are accepted, the bill moves to *third reading*, which is a vote on the amended bill by the committee of the whole, or the entire legislature. The speaker asks members to rise to indicate if they support the bill and wish to have their vote of assent ("yea") recorded, or if they are opposed and wish to have their vote against ("nay") documented. Members can also abstain, in which case they are treated as though they were not present to vote.

In the Canadian Parliament, where there are two chambers, a bill that has passed through either the House of Commons or the Senate must then pass through the other chamber via the same process. A bill that does not make it through both chambers during a legislative session because the legislature is prorogued or dissolved "dies on the order paper" and must be re-started from the beginning in a future session.

Several steps remain after a bill is supported by a majority of members present for third reading. The endorsed bill must be signed by the Queen's representative—the governor general for bills that were passed in Parliament, or the lieutenant governor for bills that were approved in a provincial legislature. This formal signing of the bill into law is called *royal assent* and affirms the consent of Canada's formal executive, where sovereignty ultimately rests. Bills that are sent for royal assent typically contain a *proclamation date* indicating when their provisions come into force. This allows governments to delay the implementation of an act to permit Canadians time to adjust. Lastly, cabinet or individual ministers may be called upon to pass regulations to implement the terms of the legislation. Often, the true meat of a law is found in how it is to be administered, making regulations which are published in the Gazette an important source of information for those affected.

Passing bills may be the most familiar legislative activity, but it is by no means the only set of tasks assigned to legislators. They are often called upon to pass motions of various kinds, binding Parliament to a particular course of action. Among other things, motions may be used to censor, suspend, or even expel members; to officially support or condemn the actions of other governments; or to apologize on behalf of the government.

This legislative process sounds orderly and straightforward, but both the government party and the opposition deploy a variety of tactics in a bid to achieve their objectives. The governing party can stipulate a maximum length of time a bill can be debated. It can also invoke closure on a bill, which cuts off debate and permits one day to complete that stage of the three reading process. But the opposition has its own repertoire of strategic manoeuvres. Chief among these is the filibuster, which is a coordinated effort among non-government members to protest a bill by delaying its passage. In a filibuster, members take turns speaking over and over again, sometimes about nonsense, purely to avoid ceding the floor to the government. In Canada, during a filibuster, members may talk all through the night and may schedule rotations so that members can take naps in their offices before returning to the chamber. As with any activity in the legislature, filibusters are governed by different rules in different jurisdictions.

regulation A directive passed by the executive specifying how the primary legislation is to be administered.

Gazette The official journal listing government appointments, changes to laws and regulations, and other notices.

motion A proposed parliamentary action.

filibuster The extension of parliamentary debate, typically by opposition members, to delay the passage of a bill.

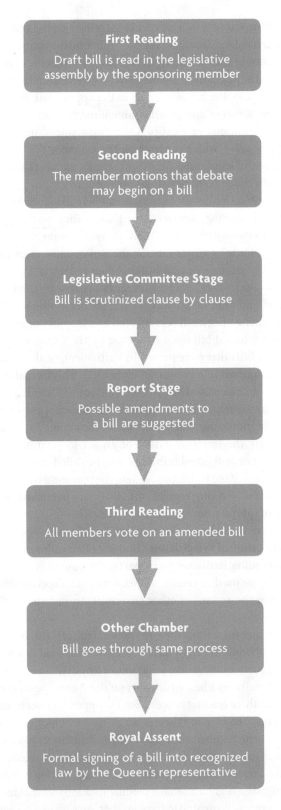

FIGURE 6.5 | How a Federal Bill Becomes Law in Canada

BRIEFING NOTES

Three Readings

A bill must pass through three separate stages before becoming a law.

- At first reading, the bill is simply introduced to the legislature to signal its sponsor's intention to legislate.
- At second reading, the bill's main purpose is outlined, and it is shepherded off to committee.
- At third reading, the bill—including any amendments that may have been attached at the committee stage—is submitted for the approval of the entire legislature.

Territorial Legislatures

So far, our discussion has focused on how legislatures operate at the federal and provincial level. Most of these lessons apply also to Yukon, but not all of them are applicable to Northwest Territories (NWT) and Nunavut. Unlike Yukon and its Southern neighbours, these two territorial jurisdictions operate consensus government systems without political parties.

In Parliament and the provincial legislatures, the monarch's representatives select first ministers based almost always on their position as leaders of the party with the most seats in the legislature. Prime ministers and premiers then select their cabinet ministers from among members of their own party caucus. In the absence of parties, executives in Nunavut and NWT are chosen by the committee of the whole, which is to say by a vote of all members of their respective territorial assemblies. Territorial representatives select the premier and members of the cabinet, after which the premier assigns individual ministers portfolios at her or his own discretion.[10]

The simplest way to conceive of consensus government is to consider how Canadian legislatures operated before the advent of the modern political party system. This is not to say that consensus systems are in any way more primitive than partisan ones. Indeed, the case could be made that consensus governments take us closer to the democratic ideal by empowering individual members of the legislature and removing the constraints of party discipline. Nor is this to suggest that NWT and Nunavut will evolve and adopt party politics at some later stage of development. The territories were granted responsible government amid the patriation debates of the late 1970s, meaning that federally appointed commissioners no longer served as heads of government; today, premiers do. Northwest Territories has maintained consensus government since then, and shows few signs of moving toward a partisan form of government. Yet consensus legislatures do share many characteristics in common with those that developed in pre-Confederation colonies before political parties were formed.

In this sense, legislatures in Nunavut and NWT encounter many of the challenges that led to the development of political parties in the South. Parties evolved as a solution to the so-called "loose fish" (or "shaky fellow") problem: in the absence of

consensus government
A system of governance that operates without political parties.

BRIEFING NOTES

Consensus Government in Nunavut and Northwest Territories

There are several misconceptions about consensus government in Canada. First, despite its name, consensus government does not involve the complete absence of opposition, conflict, or debate. Legislatures in Nunavut and Northwest Territories operate on the same Westminster parliamentary traditions as those in other jurisdictions: they contain executives that are responsible to the legislature, and opposition members who hold governments to account; decisions are made based on majority rules (not unanimity); and the principles of ministerial responsibility and cabinet solidarity apply. This said, as noted earlier, the Nunavut and NWT legislative chambers have seats arranged in a circular pattern, reflecting the preference for collaboration over conflict.

Second, political parties are not formally banned from practising in Nunavut and NWT. Doing so would constitute a breach of the Charter right to assembly, discussed in Chapter 2. Rather, the political culture in these jurisdictions, grounded in Aboriginal traditions of collaborative governance, militates against the development of political parties. Those candidates who do appear aligned with parties, or who appear to be forming them, face stiff resistance. This said, the single MP in each territory represents a federal party. Nunavut's Leona Aglukkaq served as a high-ranking member of the Harper government, for example and Justin Trudeau named Hunter Tootoo, also from Nunavut, to serve as minister of fisheries and oceans in his first cabinet.

VOX POP

What are the prospects of introducing consensus principles to other legislatures in Canada? What opportunities and challenges would it present to the way politics is conducted in the provinces and Parliament?

parties, government leaders were repeatedly challenged to marshal votes in favour of their individual legislative initiatives because of the unpredictability of backbenchers' actions and demands. Party discipline emerged as a solution to this challenge, creating a more orderly, albeit hierarchical, means of structuring parliamentary votes. For better or worse, consensus systems like those in Nunavut and Northwest Territories neither enjoy the benefits nor suffer the downsides of party discipline.

Concluding Thoughts

Canadian legislatures have a long history steeped in traditions inherited from the United Kingdom. Certainly, Parliament and provincial assemblies have evolved over time. In general, party discipline has strengthened, and legislative institutions have evolved to suit new democratic norms. At the federal level, committee chairs are now elected, and the speaker is chosen by secret ballot. Many jurisdictions now televise their debates. Free votes are not infrequent, particularly on contentious issues like same-sex marriage. And there is considerable variation in the conduct of legislative business from order to order, east to west, and north to south.

Yet, for the most part, Canadian legislatures operate according to many of the same broad principles and general rules that they did in the nineteenth century.

For More Information

How democratic are Canadian legislatures, really? David Docherty audits the various federal, provincial, and territorial assemblies in *Legislatures* (UBC Press, 2004).

Are hung parliaments underappreciated in Canada? Peter Russell lays out his case in *Two Cheers for Minority Government: The Evolution of Canadian Democracy* (Emond Montgomery, 2008).

Is it possible to renew Canada's unelected upper house? Contributors to Jennifer Smith's *The Democratic Dilemma: Reforming the Canadian Senate* (McGill–Queen's University Press, 2009) lay out the obstacles and opportunities facing would-be reformers.

How does the Red Chamber compare to similar upper houses elsewhere? David E. Smith examines *The Canadian Senate in Bicameral Perspective* (University of Toronto Press, 2006).

Party discipline is exceptionally strong in Canada—but why? Consider the perspectives of Jonathan Malloy in "High Discipline, Low Cohesion? The Uncertain Patterns of Canadian Parliamentary Party Groups," in Reuven Y. Hazan's *Cohesion and Discipline in Legislatures* (New York: Routledge, 2006). See also Christopher J. Kam's 2009 book *Party Discipline and Parliamentary Politics* (New York: Cambridge University Press).

Can one backbencher really make a difference? Ian Stewart shows how pivotal a role a single member of the legislative assembly can play in the course of Canadian history, in his book *Just One Vote: From Jim Walding's Nomination to Constitutional Defeat* (University of Manitoba Press, 2009).

How does consensus government work in the North? Ailsa Henderson "Rethinks Political Culture" in her book *Nunavut* (UBC Press, 2007).

Want to review throne speeches and budget speeches, and even compare them to political party platforms? The Poltext Project has compiled hundreds of these documents: http://poltext.org.

Looking for a law? The Canadian Legal Information Institute (CanLII) maintains a database of all existing and inactive legislation from all orders of government: www.canlii.org.

Want to read bills currently before a legislature, or what is said during the debates? The Bora Laskin Law Library at the University of Toronto has created a portal for access to all bills, statutes, debates, and regulations across Canada. Go to www.law-lib.utoronto.ca/canleg.htm or search: Bora Laskin canleg.

Deeper Inside Canadian Politics

1. Want to learn more about legislatures? There are plenty of ways for people to learn more about the business of a legislature:
   - Canadian legislatures offer guided tours of the building and the chamber.
   - When the legislature is sitting, the proceedings are usually broadcast on television and online, and the public is allowed to sit in the gallery to watch in person. Committee meetings are somewhat less accessible but, depending on the situation, may be open to the public.
   - Senators and elected representatives may be available to meet with constituents.
   - A popular job for many students is as a legislative page. A page is hired by the office of the speaker to provide assistance with proceedings, such as distributing official documents to members, filling water glasses, and attending to special requests.
   - Students are often hired to act as tour guides, particularly on Parliament Hill.
   - Finally, across Canada there are many Model Parliament organizations, where students get the opportunity to role-play in the legislature.

2. Some people argue that backbenchers have more power in minority government situations than in majority governments. Do you agree? Why or why not?

3. Is there a role for appointed senators in a twenty-first–century Canadian Senate? If so, what is it?

UP FOR DEBATE

Is strict party discipline necessary in Canadian legislatures?

THE CLAIM: YES, IT IS!

Party discipline is a necessary element of a healthy democracy in Canada.

Yes: Argument Summary

Party discipline has a poor reputation because it is viewed as anti-democratic and callous. The romanticists who espouse a greater role for backbenchers and free votes are blind to the repercussions of an undisciplined political party. Ensuring that parliamentarians vote as a cohesive group, deliver the same public messages, and support each other are among the many benefits of party discipline. In particular, it ensures that a majority government does not risk defeat and removes the opportunity for critics to attack. Most importantly, it forces the people's representatives to reach compromises on political issues. In the end, like all forms of democratic authority, party discipline carries with it as many benefits as burdens.

Yes: Top 5 Considerations

1. Party discipline emerged as the cure for the so-called "shaky fellow" syndrome that characterizes most non-partisan legislatures. By providing order and predictability to voting, the mechanisms of party discipline prevent the legislative process from devolving into a series of inefficient, one-off negotiations on every bill or motion. It also allows the monarch's representative to select a viable, stable political executive to lead the country.

2. Party discipline provides accountability. Canadians know what they're voting for in an election, and can hold all members of that party to account for their performance toward meeting the objectives stated in their platforms. In the absence of parties, representatives would travel to the legislature armed with very narrow and often conflicting mandates, making it difficult to make gains on behalf of their constituents, let alone achieve consensus on issues of importance to all citizens.

3. By concentrating power in the party leadership, party discipline prevents manipulation of the legislative process by small groups of legislators. As campaign finance rules place the heaviest responsibility and restrictions on party leaders, discipline also prevents legislator-level manipulation of the system by lobbyists and special interests. In a parliamentary system of government, this is especially important for the government party and ministers' bills because they risk defeat if the confidence of the legislature is not maintained.

4. Most Canadians have never been behind the closed doors of caucus meetings, which is where most insiders agree the real conflict in Canadian democracy takes place. Every week that the legislature sits, party leaders will meet with caucus to receive their endorsement of the leadership's plans. If the leader's pitch falls flat, the idea is unlikely to proceed. More often, competing ideas are brokered, and the resulting policy or decision reflects a broad consensus among the party's elected representatives.

5. Should their actions be viewed as draconian or against the best interests of their followers, leaders can be overthrown by members of their party through a formal leadership review, and caucuses can force the resignation of party leaders, including first ministers. If these incidents are rarer than

critics expect, it is only because fear of revolt deters leaders from over-exerting their power.

Other Considerations

- Simply because members emerge united from cabinet, caucus, or constituency meetings doesn't mean that they didn't disagree vehemently behind closed doors.
- Publicizing internal grievances only provides opposition parties, pundits, and the media with ammunition to critique the party, its members, and their ideals. History has shown that only political parties that show strength and stability through unity are trusted by Canadians to form and manage government.
- Party discipline is the antidote to chaos, inefficiency, and narrow-mindedness in Canadian legislatures. It provides predictability for Canadians seeking a strong but accountable political executive, and real authority for party members both within caucus and in the grassroots.
- Party discipline is not a straitjacket. Politicians leave caucus voluntarily almost as frequently as they are expelled, and many cases of expulsion result from a conscious choice on the part of the member. When they leave, these politicians serve or even campaign as independents. Some are successful in these roles, wielding the balance of power in the legislature and successfully defending their seats.
- Critics of strong party discipline in Canada should be careful what they wish for: systems with weaker party discipline, like that of the United States, may feature an even higher level of hyper-partisanship, and are prone to individual or small groups of legislator(s) hijacking the political process to extort gains in the interests of their narrow constituencies.
- Sitting premiers (e.g. Ralph Klein in Alberta) and prime ministers (e.g. Jean Chrétien) have stepped down from office amid pressure from their membership and/or caucus. And they led some of the most stable, popular governments in Canadian history!

THE COUNTERCLAIM: NO, IT ISN'T!

Party discipline is a significant impediment to rigorous political debate in Canada.

No: Argument Summary

Members of Canadian legislatures almost always vote with their party. They are unlikely to speak out against the party's position and invariably vote in favour of motions that may harm the interests of their constituents. The power of party officials to control perks such as whether a member can speak in the legislature means that parliamentarians are incentivized to follow the instructions of the party whip or risk being sanctioned. The idealized notion of free speech and pluralistic debate in a democracy is therefore contravened by Canada's rigid party discipline. Conformity, command, and control are prized above openness, transparency, and accountability—all to the detriment of constructive democratic debate.

No: Top 5 Considerations

1. Strong party discipline undermines the principles of responsible government, which state that the political executive must maintain the confidence of a majority of members of the legislature. Party discipline makes government MPs accountable to the premier or prime minister, not vice versa.
2. Every party designates a parliamentarian as a party whip, tasked with ensuring that members fall in line with what the party leadership decrees. In Britain, there are different types of whip votes to signify to parliamentarians the degree of freedom to break ranks, but in Canada even insignificant votes are treated as important. Those who behave independently are punished in ways that include being socially ostracized, having perks removed or withheld, and potentially being pushed out of the party.
3. Those who hold senior positions within a political party, such as the party leader and the

house leader, decide which members of their party should be authorized to speak in the legislature and which ones should be appointed to parliamentary committees. One consequence is that the legislative branch is more likely to descend into partisan theatrics at the cost of honest debate.

4. Party discipline stifles democratic debate, or—at the very least—pushes it behind closed caucus and cabinet doors. This is contrary to the principle of transparency, and prevents Canadians from holding their duly elected representatives to account for their actions.

5. There are means of relaxing party discipline without abolishing it entirely. Elsewhere and at earlier points in Canadian history, caucuses held greater control over the selection and removal of leaders, for instance, and parliamentarians were allowed to speak their conscience through a greater number of free votes.

No: Other Considerations

- In the Westminster system, political parties are incentivized to promote cohesion so that they alone can control the government. Elected representatives are prevented by their parties from speaking off-message (or even at all) for fear of losing public favour. The centralization of power in the leader's office means that communication is scripted and parliamentarians are rarely able to pass private members' bills.

- Party discipline can be so stifling that sometimes parliamentarians exit their parties to sit as independents, or they cross the floor to join another party. This is, in itself, anti-democratic because there is no requirement for a by-election to provide constituents with an opportunity to have their say. The person who was elected on the basis of her or his affiliation with a party may end up working to oppose it.

- Partisan identities and party loyalties run so deep that coalition governments where more than one political party has representation in cabinet are very rare in Canada. Revolts against the leader of a Canadian political party are also rare.

- Party discipline means that there is less likelihood of holding the government to account. Questions asked in the legislature are met with responses that stick to party messaging.

- Strong party discipline is not a necessary component of a fully functioning democracy. Discipline is weaker in the United States and United Kingdom—two of the most stable and effective democracies in the world. Party discipline does not exist at all in Northwest Territories, Nunavut, and the vast majority of municipalities across Canada.

Discussion Questions

- To what extent is party discipline anti-democratic?
- Suppose that you were a member of Parliament, and an issue arose in the House of Commons that you had been a passionate supporter of since childhood. Now suppose that your political party as well as the majority of your constituents were strongly opposed to that very issue. What do you do?

- Why do you think party discipline is so strong in Canada compared with other countries that use the parliamentary system of government?
- What kinds of reforms could solve the alleged problem of strict party discipline?
- Under what circumstances would you be inclined to vote for an independent candidate over one running with a major political party?

Where to Learn More about Legislative Party Discipline in Canada

Sylvia B. Bashevkin, *Toeing the Lines: Women and Party Politics in English Canada*, 2nd edn (Oxford University Press, 2003).

Kenneth R. Carty, William Cross, and Lisa Young, *Rebuilding Canadian Party Politics* (UBC Press, 2000).

Sam Depauw and Shane Martin, "Legislative Party Discipline and Cohesion in Comparative Perspective," in *Intra-Party Politics and Coalition Governments*, ed. Daniela Giannetti and Kenneth Benoit (Routledge, 2009).

David Docherty, *Legislatures* (UBC Press, 2005).

Monique Guay, "Party Discipline, Representation of Voters and Personal Beliefs," *Canadian Parliamentary Review* 25, no. 2 (2002): pp. 7–9.

Christopher J. Kam, *Party Discipline and Parliamentary Politics* (Cambridge University Press, 2009).

Matthew Kerby and Kelly Blidook, "It's Not You, It's Me: Determinants of Voluntary Legislative Turnover in Canada," *Legislative Studies Quarterly* 36, no. 4 (2011): pp. 621–43.

Jonathan Lemco, "The Fusion of Powers, Party Discipline, and the Canadian Parliament: A Critical Assessment," *Presidential Studies Quarterly* 18, no. 2 (1988): pp. 283–302.

Jonathan Malloy, "High Discipline, Low Cohesion? The Uncertain Patterns of Canadian Parliamentary Party Groups," *Journal of Legislative Studies* 9, no. 4 (2003): pp. 116–29.

L. Marvin Overby, Christopher Raymond, and Zeynep Taydas, "Free Votes, MPs, and Constituents: The Case of Same-Sex Marriage in Canada," *American Review of Canadian Studies* 41, no. 4 (2011): pp. 465–78.

Parliament of Canada, "House of Commons Procedure and Practice," 2nd edn (2009), www.parl.gc.ca.

7 THE JUSTICE SYSTEM

Inside this Chapter

- What are Canada's legal foundations?
- Who plays the various roles in Canada's justice system?
- How is the justice system structured in Canada?

Inside the Justice System

Most examinations of Canadian democracy begin by separating governance into three distinct branches: the executive branch, the legislative branch, and the judiciary. The last of these categories is almost always confined to a discussion of judges and the courts over which they preside. This approach neglects the important role played by a host of other actors involved in the broader *justice system*. After all, Canadian justice is more than a set of courts; it is a complex world, consisting of a patchwork of provincial, territorial, and federal systems, knitted together by strong allegiance to the rule of law. It consists of a host of actors, from judges and lawyers, to ministers and bureaucrats, to police and corrections officers.

Peering inside the Canadian justice system reveals the complicated nature of these networks, and uncovers a few key maxims.

- **There are no clear lines separating the political and judicial realms.** Canada's judges are protected by the principle of judicial independence, which is designed to prevent politicians from interfering with the affairs of the courts. Nevertheless, the line becomes very blurry considering the politicized nature of judicial appointments and the increasing role of judges in crafting public policy.
- **There is much more to the justice system than courtrooms and judges.** When you think of the justice system, your first thoughts may evoke judges presiding over courtrooms, where witnesses are called and cross-examined, and decisions are handed down. However, the vast majority of activity in the Canadian justice system takes place outside the courtroom, and increasingly so.
- **Constitutional responsibility for justice is shared—and the federal government does not always hold the upper hand.** The Canadian justice system is complex, with many parts falling under federal, provincial/territorial, or municipal authority. Yet it is also highly integrated, meaning that even if one order has jurisdiction over a particular area as the federal government does over criminal justice, for example, it needs to work very closely with its partners to ensure consistency and effectiveness.

Without duplicating material found in a first-year law school textbook, this chapter examines certain misconceptions, and offers a comprehensive and accurate insider's perspective on Canadian justice.

Overview

Laws are a pervasive part of Canadian democracy. They govern everything in society: the way Canadians drive and hunt; whom they are allowed to marry and bequeath property to; the content provided by their television and Internet providers; the way they rent apartments and buy houses; the way they use credit and debit cards; the way they raise their children and pets; how they treat the environment and each other; and so on. Laws are best understood as imparting a set of legal rights and responsibilities. They permit Canadians to live in a free and fair society—provided they live up to certain obligations to the state and to each other.

While various governments establish these laws, the responsibility for determining how laws should be interpreted, applied, and enforced falls to the judiciary and the broader justice system. In Canada, justice is an area of shared federal and provincial jurisdiction, with the provinces devolving some authority to municipalities and Aboriginal governments playing an increasingly prominent role. All governments must work closely to ensure that the definition and administration of justice remain aligned and coherent.

In this chapter, we look beyond the judiciary to examine the entire justice system as a whole. In addition to judges and justices, our discussion includes the important roles played by ministers of justice, Crown attorneys, clerks, magistrates, police officers, prison guards, lawyers, bar associations, public servants, and a host of other actors who support judges in upholding Canadian justice maintaining law and order.

UP FOR DEBATE

Do mandatory minimum prison sentences go too far?

Keep this question in mind as you read through the chapter. Consult the end-of-chapter debate supplement for more material to help you engage in an informed discussion of the topic.

Principles of Canadian Justice

People employed throughout Canada's justice system are subject to three core principles:

1. the rule of law;
2. the rule of judicial impartiality; and
3. the rule of judicial independence.

rule of law A basic legal principle that holds no one is above the law.

The first of these applies to all Canadians, whether or not they are employed in the justice system. To say that Canadians are protected by the rule of law means that all citizens are subject to the same treatment under the justice system regardless of their status or position in society. Everyone is governed by the same set of laws, and not subject to arbitrary treatment by those in positions of power. No one in Canada wields any special powers unless conferred on them by law, which helps to establish a sense of accountability and orderliness by ensuring that all government actions must be authorized by democratic processes.

Enshrined in English law since King John signed the Magna Carta in 1215, the rule of law is so fundamental to Canadian justice that it is entrenched in the preamble of the Charter of Rights and Freedoms. Over time, the principle has come to embody the notion that all laws be made transparently and publicly accessible, that they be applied consistently and without discrimination, and that they provide affordable access to justice for all Canadians.

habeas corpus The right not to be detained without cause or due process.

Several rights flow from the rule of law, including the right not to be unlawfully detained, otherwise known as *habeas corpus*. A writ (or court order) of *habeas corpus* requires the government to bring a prisoner before the court to determine whether the individual is being detained constitutionally. This right forms a core element of the British common-law traditions inherited by Canada, and is entrenched in section 10(c) of the Charter of Rights and Freedoms, which states: "Everyone has the right on arrest or detention . . . to have the validity of the detention determined by way of *habeas corpus* and to be released if the detention is not lawful."

Prior to the introduction of the Charter in 1982, the federal government suspended Canadians' *habeas corpus* rights on three occasions under the War Measures Act:

- during World War I, when Ukrainian Canadians, suspected communists, and other so-called "enemy aliens" were detained;
- during World War II, when Canadians of Japanese, German, and Italian ethnicity, as well as those suspected of having fascist or communist sympathies, were detained; and
- in 1970, during the October Crisis, when those suspected of domestic terrorism were detained.

↻ The October Crisis is discussed on pages 560–62 of Chapter 14, on Canada's place in the world.

Wayne Cuddington/Postmedia News

Since the October Crisis, Canadians' *habeas corpus* rights have not been suspended, even in the aftermath of the September 11 terrorist attacks or the 2014 attack on Parliament Hill. Under what circumstances might it be reasonable for the government to suspend Canadians' *habeas corpus* rights? What are the dangers of taking such a step? Should non-Canadians be treated any differently on Canadian soil?

The October Crisis remains the only occasion on which Canadian's *habeas corpus* rights were suspended in peacetime, and the events of that period prompted much reflection by Canadians and their leaders on the nature of the rule of law. In 1988, the federal government repealed the War Measures Act, replacing it with a new Emergencies Act, which subjected cabinet's authority to declare an emergency to parliamentary review and ensured that any temporary laws put in place must respect the Charter of Rights and Freedoms. This includes the rule of law, but is also subject to the notwithstanding clause, meaning that there are still extraordinary circumstances under which governments could suspend such rights.

The two remaining core principles of Canada's justice system concern the role of judges. Under the rule of judicial impartiality, protected by section 11(d) of the Charter, judges are expected to preside over courts to ensure Canadians are "presumed innocent until proven guilty according to law in a fair and public hearing by an independent and

judicial impartiality The principle by which judges decide cases based on evidence and an objective interpretation of the law.

THEY SAID IT

Pierre Trudeau, the War Measures Act, and the October Crisis

Excerpts from CBC reporter Tim Ralfe's interview with Prime Minister Pierre Trudeau, 13 October 1970, moments after the federal government invoked the War Measures Act to quell terrorist activity by the Front de Libération du Québec:

Prime Minister (Pierre Trudeau): Well, there are a lot of bleeding hearts around who just don't like to see people with helmets and guns. All I can say is, go on and bleed, but it is more important to keep law and order in this society than to be worried about weak-kneed people who don't like the looks of a soldier's helmet.

Interviewer (Tim Ralfe): At any cost? How far would you go with that? How far would you extend that?

Trudeau: Well, just watch me.

Ralfe: At reducing civil liberties? To that extent? . . . [Does] this include wire-tapping, reducing other civil liberties in some way?

Trudeau: Yes, I think the society must take every means at its disposal to defend itself against the emergence of a parallel power which defies the elected power in this country and I think that goes to any distance. So long as there is a power in here which is challenging the elected representative of the people I think that power must be stopped and I think it's only, I repeat, weak-kneed bleeding hearts who are afraid to take these measures.[1]

VOX POP

- Do you think the circumstances of the October Crisis warranted the suspension of *habeas corpus* rights? Why or why not?

- Do you find it surprising that the only prime minister to suspend *habeas corpus* rights in peacetime is also the one responsible for introducing Canada's Charter of Rights and Freedoms? What does it tell you about the perceived gravity of the situation that Pierre Trudeau was willing to take such a measure?

impartial tribunal." This means that each side in a court dispute has the opportunity to present evidence, that the case must be based solely on that evidence, and that neither side has an inherent advantage over the other. It also means that judges must leave their personal opinions and values aside when presiding over these cases, and base their decisions on the laws in question and the facts presented. To guard against the possibility of impartiality, Canadians are afforded the right to appeal lower-court judgements, provided they have reasonable grounds to believe that the judge acted in a biased fashion. At the same time, judges are barred from engaging in public debate about any ongoing or previous cases, expressing any political opinions that could lead Canadians to view their decisions as biased, or undertaking business outside of their judicial duties.

Under the final principle, that of judicial independence, judges remain free from the influence of the legislative and executive branches, allowing them to decide cases without fear of intrusion or retribution by governments. This is particularly important in Canada, given judges' authority to undertake judicial review of governments' actions and jurisdiction. To preserve judicial independence in Canada, judges are afforded (1) political immunity, which includes guaranteed tenure and salaries that are not directly determined by government, and (2) control over the administration of their courts, which allows judges to decide which cases to hear and how to manage them at trial.

> **judicial independence**
> The principle by which judges are free from political interference when deciding cases.

THEY SAID IT

Chief Justice McLachlin on Judicial Impartiality

In 1995, before becoming chief justice of Canada's Supreme Court, then-Justice Beverley McLachlin offered the following thoughts on judicial impartiality:

> What mental practices will lead judges to impartiality? . . . One, as old as judging itself, is the injunction that the judge should proceed on the basis of the facts, the submissions and the law in the record before the court. . . .
>
> A second injunction, almost equally well-recognized, is that the judge should hold the decision in abeyance until she has thoroughly considered all sides of the issue. . . .
>
> But patience alone will not bring us to understanding. And understanding what is really happening and really significant in the case requires an active effort to appreciate how each party sees the matter. . . . In an act of imagination, the judge should attempt to see life through each litigant's eyes. . . .
>
> A final and indispensable judicial practice in the search for impartial justice is a conscious commitment to rationality. . . .
>
> The end result of these practices—the putting aside of personal views, the preserving of an open mind, the mental act of placing oneself in the position of each of the parties, and finally, the use of reason to draw inferences from carefully considered facts instead of stereotypical assumptions—might be called the art of judging. . . . It is a professional process which has been used by the most respected judicial and quasi-judicial decision-makers for centuries to attain the degree of objectivity required for good judging. It is, I believe, the final and best guarantee of judicial impartiality.[2]

Judicial independence also imparts rules on politicians, who are barred both from interfering in judicial appointments and from publicly commenting on, or privately intervening in, cases before the courts. Without these safeguards, judges could become beholden to political masters, who could withhold or reduce judges' livelihoods if they disagreed with the outcome of a particular case, or else micro-manage judges' dockets and procedures. In this sense, judicial independence is key to maintaining the rule of law and preserving judicial impartiality.

The Foundations of Canadian Law

public laws Rules governing individuals' relationships to the state and society.

private laws Rules governing the relationships among citizens and organizations.

All laws in Canada fall into two general categories. Public laws are legal rules that impact society as a whole. They serve to define the relationships between citizens and organizations, on one hand, and their governments, on the other. Criminal, constitutional, and administrative laws all fall under the public category. By contrast, private laws concern the narrower relationships among individuals and organizations. To illustrate, if someone has committed murder, we might at first assume that it would be dealt with under private law because it involved two individuals. Not so: murder is a punishable crime that is an affront to society at large, and so it is dealt with under public law. Conversely, if two people are in a dispute but no laws that concern the state are broken, then this falls under private law. A disagreement between a landlord and a tenant that escalates to small claims court is an example of private law being used to resolve a matter that is essentially of concern only to those directly involved.

common-law system A legal order based on customs, usage, and precedent.

Private law—again, law that governs the relationships among individuals and organizations in matters that do not have broader public concern—is built on two distinct legal systems in Canada. The first is the British-style common-law system, which applies throughout the nine English-speaking provinces, the three territories, and much of the British Commonwealth and United States. It is grounded in the rulings passed down over centuries of court decisions known as *case law*, because the outcomes of past legal cases are consulted, in addition to any statutes that may have been passed. Common law is based on the notion that judicial decisions represent the common customs of the community. Hence, certain unwritten rules—like the definition of common-law marriage—exist without having been recorded in statutes. In

BRIEFING NOTES

Civil Law in Canada

Many observers are confused by the dual meaning of the term *civil law* in Canada. On one hand, it contrasts with *public law*. In this sense, civil law is synonymous with *private law* which applies to all matters strictly among individuals and organizations. On the other hand, civil law is also a specific, codified legal system employed to handle private matters in the province of Quebec. This second definition distinguishes civil law from the common-law traditions found in the rest of Canada. Thus, depending on the context, the term *civil law* may deal with private matters more broadly throughout Canada or private matters within Quebec more specifically.

common-law systems, judges are bound to consider previous court rulings as authoritative, using them as precedents on which to base their own decisions. This principle is known as *stare decisis*, according to which similar cases are treated consistently. Judges may set new precedents in cases involving novel circumstances, and governments may pass laws to either overrule these precedents or codify them.

The second form of private law is based on Roman civil law, which applies in Quebec, the state of Louisiana, France, and most of Europe. In the civil-law system, legal traditions are grounded in a written civil code, which serves as a foundation for all other laws concerning civil (non-criminal) matters. The preservation of Quebec's civil-law system has been a point of contention since the French relinquished control over their North American colonies in the eighteenth century. Quebec's civil code traces its roots to the 1804 Napoleonic Code (or *Code Napoléon*), which covered such matters as family, property, and commercial business. Since that time, Quebec's code has undergone several rounds of revision, and—since 1994—now contains 10 books relating to areas including the following:

civil-law system A legal order based on a written code.

- basic individual rights;
- family law;
- wills and estates;
- property rights;
- contract law;
- mortgages; and
- legal rights.

Many of these elements align with common-law traditions in the rest of Canada, and they remain subordinate to those entrenched in the Charter of Rights and Freedoms. The uniqueness of the Quebec code requires that lawyers and judges be versed in the civil-law tradition before engaging in cases involving it. For this reason, the Supreme Court of Canada must have at least three justices from Quebec, all of whom must have experience with civil law in the province.

It is important to note that while Quebec and the rest of Canada have distinct legal systems governing private laws, all public laws—including criminal, constitutional, and administrative laws—apply throughout the country. All public law in Canada is rooted in the common-law system, meaning that the province of Quebec has a *bijuridical system*, with its private laws based on the civil code, and its public laws based on common law.

Broadly speaking, in Canada, the federal government has authority over the definition of criminal law, while civil law and the administration of justice are matters of provincial jurisdiction. All other matters, including constitutional law and administrative law, are shared between the two orders. More detail on these various branches of public law is provided below.

Functions and Roles in the Justice System

The basic objective of the Canadian justice system is to foster safe and secure communities. It does this by administering a fair and independent process to decide disputes among citizens, their governments, and their various organizations. A number of different actors from a variety of different governments must work together to achieve this goal, including cabinet ministers, judges, lawyers, law enforcement officers, and correctional services workers.

Ministers of Justice and Public Safety

Political responsibility for the Canadian justice system is spread across the country, and can be divided internally within a given jurisdiction. Duties and obligations typically fall under two separate categories: the *justice portfolio* which includes the court system and the *public safety portfolio* which involves all matters of community security. At the federal level, these portfolios are usually assigned to two separate ministers—the minister of justice and the minister of public safety. In most provinces and territories, these responsibilities are divided into separate departments but fall under the same minister, the minister of justice (see Figure 7.1).

Regardless of the jurisdiction, the minister of justice is one of the highest-ranking members of a provincial/territorial or federal cabinet. In particular, he or she is responsible for overseeing the court system and justice department. In this capacity, most ministers of justice also serve as their jurisdiction's attorney general, whose responsibilities include recommending judicial nominees to cabinet, administering the criminal justice system, representing the Crown in civil-law matters involving the government, providing legal advice to the rest of the government, and overseeing Canada's systems of legal aid.

While attorneys general are responsible for the administration of justice, solicitors general carry out duties related to law enforcement, corrections, emergency management, and overall community security. As of 2005, the federal government no longer has a solicitor general, with those duties passing to the minister of public safety and emergency preparedness. Most provinces and territories have solicitors general, some with stand-alone portfolios, others with an expanded set of responsibilities including those of the attorney general's portfolio under the minister of justice. This means that a province or territory's minister of justice could serve as both attorney general and solicitor general, and often does.

minister of justice The member of the government responsible for the administration of the justice system within a given jurisdiction.

attorney general A cabinet member and the highest-ranking elected legal officer in a jurisdiction.

solicitor general A cabinet member typically responsible for the penal and policing aspects of the justice system.

Justice Portfolio	Public Safety Portfolio
Administered by **Minister of Justice** and/or **Attorney General** Responsible for • recommending judicial nominees • administering the criminal justice system • representing the Crown in court cases involving the government • overseeing legal aid	Administered by **Minister of Public Safety** (and **Emergency Preparedness**) and/or **Solicitor General** Responsible for • law enforcement • corrections • emergency management • community security

FIGURE 7.1 | Federal Justice and Public Safety Portfolios

Ministers responsible for justice and public safety (including both attorneys general and solicitors general) meet face to face once a year to discuss areas of shared concern, including challenges of common interest such as access to justice, crime prevention, rehabilitation, and justice system efficiencies. These meetings are among the most highly structured involving ministerial groups, reflecting the highly integrated nature of the Canadian justice system.

The Judiciary

The judiciary sits at the heart of the Canadian justice system. It serves as an umpire of sorts with respect to interpreting and applying the laws passed by governments across the country. Judges are often called upon to decide winners and losers in disagreements over property, disputes over constitutional jurisdiction, conflicts over rights and freedoms, and criminal charges laid by governments against their people.

The judiciary encompasses the entire system of courts across Canada. According to conventional wisdom, the judiciary interprets and applies laws developed by the executive and passed by the legislature. This model is mostly accurate, although Canadian courts have also maintained considerable authority to shape and re-shape the legal landscape, particularly through opinions related to the constitution.

The courts have always held a prominent place in Canadian democracy, fulfilling three major functions:

- *guardianship* over the legal system and order through judicial review;
- *adjudication* of disputes between Canadians, their governments, their businesses, and other organizations through court cases; and
- *guidance* of our democratic system through commissions of inquiry.

Among its primary responsibilities, the judiciary is charged with upholding the supreme law of the land, the Canadian constitution. Through a process known as judicial review, the courts assess the actions and laws of Canadian governments to ensure they are consistent with the constitution. These constitutional law cases typically involve deciding which order of government, federal or provincial, has jurisdiction over a particular policy area, or whether Canadians' rights and freedoms have been breached by government. These cases may arrive at the courts through the traditional route, as citizens and governments challenge each other through criminal or civil court action. Or they may be referred to the courts by the governments themselves, in what are known as reference cases. Thus, the Canadian judicial system is structured on the ability of appointed judges to interpret the constitution and to exercise the power to overrule laws passed by the legislators who were elected by the people.

Courts may also be called upon to adjudicate cases based on administrative law, which involve determining whether government actors perform their duties in an authorized and fair manner. Typically, administrative law cases require judges to decide whether a government official or body has acted within its mandate or statutory authority, or whether it has applied legal rules in an unbiased manner. Most administrative law cases are heard by administrative tribunals, meaning that a number of disputes are resolved without resorting to the courts. Governments have established administrative tribunals, for instance, to hear disputes over the application

judicial review The authority of the courts to adjudicate matters of constitutional law.

constitutional law The branch of public law dealing with the authority of the state.

reference cases Proceedings initiated by governments asking for the court's opinion on the constitutionality of legislation.

administrative law The branch of public law involving the review of government decisions and disputes between citizens and state agencies.

administrative tribunals Quasi-judicial bodies empowered to decide administrative law cases, and whose decisions may be appealed to the court system.

of regulations concerning property, human rights, and government benefits. These tribunals operate parallel to the court system, and may have their decisions reviewed by superior or federal courts.

The courts also fulfill a broader adjudication role, ensuring that private disputes over property and contracts are settled in a fair and just manner, and that charges, regulatory decisions, or other disputes between citizens and their government are resolved. These cases come in one of two varieties, involving either criminal or civil law.

Criminal law, which falls within the realm of public law, involves activities that, while often harming individuals, have a broader effect on society as a whole. When someone acts violently toward another person—for example, committing sexual assault or robbery—this is seen not only as an offence against the victim involved but as a crime against the entire community: it offends society's core values of civility and violates everyone's sense of security. The definition of crimes falls under federal jurisdiction, with the criminal law power being defined in section 91 of the Constitution

criminal law Body of statutory rules governing misconduct affecting not only the victims, but society as a whole.

The Canadian Press/Sean Kilpatrick

Plaintiff Lee Carter (*left*) and Grace Pastine, litigation director of the BC Civil Liberties Association, meet the media inside the Supreme Court after the Court unanimously declared the ban on doctor-assisted suicide unconstitutional in February 2015. The ruling gave governments 12 months to develop appropriate "right to die" legislation. Is this a case of the Supreme Court forcing the government's hand—as it had done previously on abortion and prostitution—or a case of the government letting the Court do the heavy lifting on a politically sensitive issue that all parties had been unwilling to raise? Either way, what are the upsides and downsides of having unelected judges, rather than elected members of the legislature, weigh in on social policy in Canada?

Amanda Todd Legacy Society / amandatoddlegacy.org

The very tragic cases of Amanda Todd (*above*) and Rehtaeh Parsons brought the issue of cyberbullying to national—and international—attention in 2012–13, and helped the Conservatives pass Bill C-13, designed to protect Canadians from online criminal activity in 2014. What makes a crime like cyberbullying an affront to society as a whole?

Act, 1867. The Criminal Code of Canada contains hundreds of criminal offences, and lists the range of penalties that judges may impose, including jail time, probation, community service, fines, and other sanctions. Also under federal jurisdiction, the Youth Criminal Justice Act contains a similar catalogue of offences and sentences for individuals aged 12 to 17. In cases involving crimes punishable by five years' imprisonment or more, citizens have the right to choose trial by jury or trial by judge alone. Judges or juries in criminal cases must render verdicts based on proof beyond a reasonable doubt, and the burden of that proof falls to the Crown, as accused persons are deemed innocent until proven guilty.

It is important to note that criminal laws apply to private parties in Canada—not simply individual citizens, but also businesses, unions, interest groups, and other organizations. The federal criminal law power extends to areas like environmental protection, for instance, meaning that companies can be charged for polluting. Criminal law in Canada is part of a broader category of penal laws that make certain acts or behaviours illegal. Provincial/territorial laws and municipal bylaws may impose penalties, including fines for speeding and public drunkenness.

It is also worth noting that governments have established alternative dispute resolution processes, like out-of-court negotiation, mediation, and arbitration, to help settle cases outside the traditional courtroom. Aboriginal justice initiatives exist in several provinces and territories, which aim to establish culturally sensitive alternatives and supplements to the criminal justice system. Sentencing circles are one such innovation, with judges inviting the offender, victims, elders, social services, lawyers, family, and supporters to discuss possible sentencing outcomes. While the judge is not bound by the circle's recommendations, this style of restorative justice does allow for community input into the decision.

restorative justice Drawn from Aboriginal traditions, a set of principles that emphasizes repairing relationships between criminal offenders, their victims, and the community.

civil law The body of rules governing disputes between or among private parties.

↻ The Royal Commission on Equality in Employment is discussed in the context of pay equity in Chapter 13, on diversity and representation: see the section Diversity in the Civil Service.

commission of inquiry An independent body of experts created by a government to investigate an issue of great importance.

↺ Commissions of inquiry, or royal commissions, are discussed on page 199 of Chapter 5, on the executive.

Discussed above, civil law, which is otherwise known as *private law*, deals with issues of a more private nature, involving harm to individuals but not necessarily to the broader community. When someone feels wronged, that individual may launch a lawsuit asking the court to adjudicate a dispute over matters like contracts, property sales, child support, negligence, or others. The state has no role in civil proceedings unless the government is the *plaintiff* (the suing party) or the *defendant* (the *respondent*), or its officials are called to testify as social workers might be. The court must decide whether the case has merit and, if so, what sort of corrective action is required of the losing party. This typically involves the paying of restitution to cover damages. Judges and juries decide civil-law cases on a balance of probabilities, meaning that they must weigh whether it is more or less likely that the defendant caused harm to the plaintiff. This standard of proof is considerably lower than that required for a finding of guilt in criminal proceedings.

Lastly, the judiciary may be called upon to lead task forces, inquests, and commissions of inquiry into matters of public policy or public sector misconduct. These panels are often empowered to call witnesses under oath, hold public hearings, and otherwise collect evidence to support a final report to the government. Depending on the mandate given to them by the government, these commissions may consult broadly and offer a set of wide-ranging recommendations, or report back on a narrower set of questions.

Not all commissions of inquiry are led by judges; some are led by academics, former politicians, or other experts. Among the various actors in Canada's political system, however, judges are among the best respected for their independence, fairness, and skills in inquisition. For these reasons, they are often trusted to investigate controversial issues confronting governments or communities. Twenty years before her appointment as a Supreme Court justice in 2004, for instance, Judge Rosalie Abella led the Royal Commission on Equality in Employment. Over the course of his career, and into retirement, Justice Thomas Berger led a series of commissions into a variety of matters including child and family law, the construction of the Mackenzie Valley Pipeline, Aboriginal healthcare, and electoral reform in Vancouver. Similarly, Judge Ted Hughes has led several inquiries in various jurisdictions into matters including conflict of interest laws in British Columbia and Northwest Territories, and separate incidents involving a prison riot and the tragic death of an Aboriginal girl in state care in Manitoba. Judge James Igloliorte was one of three commissioners appointed by the Government of Newfoundland and Labrador in 2002 to lead the province's Royal Commission on Renewing and Strengthening Our Place in Canada.

The highest-profile commissions of inquiry typically focus on government scandals. In 2011, the Quebec government appointed Superior Court justice France Charbonneau to investigate corruption in the province's construction industry. Seven years earlier, the Government of Canada selected her former colleague, Justice John Gomery, to lead the Commission of Inquiry into the Sponsorship Program and Advertising Activities (see Chapter 7). Many of these justices have played such prominent roles in the proceedings that their names have become synonymous with their investigations (e.g. the Charbonneau Commission, the Gomery Commission).

All told, hundreds of judges have led thousands of independent inquiries in Canadian history. Commissioners' reports are not binding on the government of the day, although their recommendations often influence public opinion and form the basis of public policy debate and development.

INSIDE CANADIAN POLITICS
Who Should Determine Canada's Prostitution Laws?

In 2013, the Supreme Court of Canada struck down several elements of Canada's prostitution laws as unconstitutional, deciding that prohibiting the sale of sex and the running of brothels breached prostitutes' right to security of person. The Court left all parts of the laws in force and provided the federal government with one year to revise them. As the issue not only involved the definition of criminal law which falls under federal jurisdiction but also impacted the enforcement and administration of justice provincial jurisdiction, the federal government committed to working with the provinces to develop this new legislation.

In the meantime, however, provincial governments were left to decide how to handle new and ongoing prostitution cases. As overseers of Crown attorneys in their respective jurisdictions, attorneys general had the authority to issue directives on whether or how to prosecute these cases. Some provinces decided to halt all prosecutions until the new federal legislation could be implemented. Other provinces decided not to prosecute cases involving the parts of the law struck down by the courts, but to continue to pursue offences under the remaining parts of the law left intact, including assault, human trafficking, and sexual interference with minors. Still other provinces elected to pursue prosecutions involving all aspects of the law, including those that had been struck down.

VOX POP

Do you think individual provinces should have the ability to determine how to handle the prosecution of criminal cases? Or should such decisions fall to the federal government to ensure uniformity across Canada?

Peace Officers

Canada's police and prison systems are under civilian control, unlike those of certain other countries, where the responsibility for law enforcement and incarceration falls to the military or private firms. In Canada, most peace officers—police; sheriffs; customs, corrections, parole, and conservation officers, and so on—are specially trained employees of provincial/territorial governments, and have responsibility for enforcing a whole host of laws within their respective jurisdictions. The laws that they administer range from those found in the Criminal Code to those in provincial/territorial statutes, meaning that provincial peace officers are empowered to enforce many federal and provincial/territorial laws. Peace officers in Canada are separate and apart from private security personnel, often referred to as *special constables*, who are employed by universities, hospitals, and private businesses. Special constables do not have the authority to enforce provincial/territorial or federal laws and are highly regulated by Canadian governments.

peace officer A specially trained individual granted government authority to enforce laws.

Crown Attorneys

Once peace officers have uncovered evidence of a crime, the state investigates and decides whether to prosecute the alleged offender on behalf of the victim and community as a whole. As the alleged offence is considered a crime against society, the individuals directly affected are not required to press charges in order for the case to proceed to court. That decision rests with government employees. These Crown attorneys work with victims and police and are responsible for determining whether criminal cases proceed to court, and under which specific charges and proposed penalties. Crown attorneys are appointed and directed by attorneys general across Canada and fall under their direction. This illustrates the complexities of Canada's justice system, which divides authority over the definition and administration of criminal law between the federal and provincial orders, respectively.

Crown attorney A lawyer who acts on behalf of the government when deciding how to pursue criminal cases.

The Structure of the Justice System

As discussed above and illustrated in Figure 7.1, Canada's justice system is divided into two main portfolios, with the courts on one side and public safety on the other. Each component is highly federalized, dividing responsibilities among the federal and provincial orders, with provincial governments devolving a number of duties to their respective municipalities. The Canadian justice system is also highly integrated, requiring federal–provincial/territorial coordination to ensure an appropriate level of consistency across the country.

The Courts

Canada's system of courts is both *hierarchical* and *federal*: hierarchical in terms of allowing more serious cases, and appeals from lower levels, to proceed to higher courts; and federal in terms of its division of jurisdiction and responsibilities between the two orders of government. Judges for some courts are appointed by the federal government; for others, by provincial governments. At the same time, certain courts hear cases related to areas of federal jurisdiction alone such as, the Tax Court of Canada and the military courts, while others hear cases involving provincial/territorial legislation such as family or traffic courts. Table 7.1 lists the functions of these various courts, and an illustration of the hierarchical organization of the Canadian court system is provided in Figure 7.2.

In each province and territory, except Nunavut, there are two levels of courts: *provincial/territorial courts*, whose judges are appointed by the provincial/territorial justice minister; and *superior courts*, whose judges are appointed by the federal justice minister.

Typically referred to as *section 92 courts* since they were created under the provincial powers portion of the Constitution Act, 1867, *provincial and territorial courts* exist in every jurisdiction except Nunavut. Otherwise known as magistrates, the judges in these courts hear cases on a wide variety of subjects in both public and private law. These so-called "lower courts" are the true workhorses of the Canadian justice system, handling the vast majority of cases. To deal more efficiently with caseloads, most jurisdictions have developed specialized court streams to deal with particular areas of the law, routing cases through small claims, criminal, family, and youth divisions. Municipal bylaw courts have also been established to deal with matters like traffic violations.

Superior courts exist in every jurisdiction, although their names vary across the country. Known as *section 96 courts* because they fall under the federal powers listed in the Constitution Act, 1867, they have inherent jurisdiction, meaning that they are empowered to hear any case that is brought before them unless that authority is granted to another court explicitly by legislation. In addition to reviewing decisions of some provincial ABCs (agencies, boards, and commissions) and administrative tribunals, superior courts typically deal with the most serious criminal and civil cases, preside over divorce proceedings, and hear appeals from provincial courts.

Courts of appeal exist in every jurisdiction as well. As the name suggests, they review decisions from lower courts at both the provincial and the superior level. They also hear constitutional cases referred to them by their respective provincial and territorial governments. Unlike lower courts, appeals courts typically feature panels of three judges who, together, preside over cases. While superior court and appeals court judges are appointed by the federal government, the courts themselves are administered and paid for by the provincial and territorial governments.

With hearings held across the country, *federal courts* deal with matters involving federal law (e.g. citizenship and immigration), which may include reviewing the decisions of federal ABCs and tribunals. Specialized federal courts exist to deal with matters like taxes and military justice. Appeals from the former are heard by the federal court of appeal, while those from the latter are heard by the court martial appeal court. Judges for all of these federal courts are appointed by the federal government.

The **Supreme Court of Canada** is the country's highest court, holding jurisdiction over all laws in Canada. While first established by the federal government in

Supreme Court of Canada
Canada's final court of appeal.

TABLE 7.1 | Courts of Law in Canada

Court	Court Administration	Areas of Jurisdiction
Provincial/ Territorial Courts	Province/ Territory	• matters specifically designated by the province/territory
Superior Courts*	Province/ Territory	• all matters not specifically assigned to other courts • serious cases • divorce • appeals from lower courts • review of decisions made by provincial ABCs and tribunals
Courts of Appeal	Province/ Territory	• appeals arising from provincial/territorial and superior courts • references from provincial/territorial governments
Federal Courts	Federal	• matters specifically designated by the federal government • review of decisions made by federal ABCs and tribunals
Tax Court of Canada	Federal	• matters relating to federal tax laws
Federal Court of Appeal	Federal	• matters of constitutional and administrative law • appeals arising from the Federal Court and Tax Court of Canada
Military Courts	Federal	• matters relating to military justice (including those under the National Defence Act and Code of Service Discipline)
Court Martial Appeal Court	Federal	• appeals arising from military courts
Supreme Court of Canada	Federal	• appeals arising from all other courts • reference cases from the federal government

*Known as Court of Queen's Bench (AB, SK, MB, NB); Provincial Supreme Court (BC, NS, NL, PE, YT, NWT); Superior Court (ON, QC); or Court of Justice (NU).

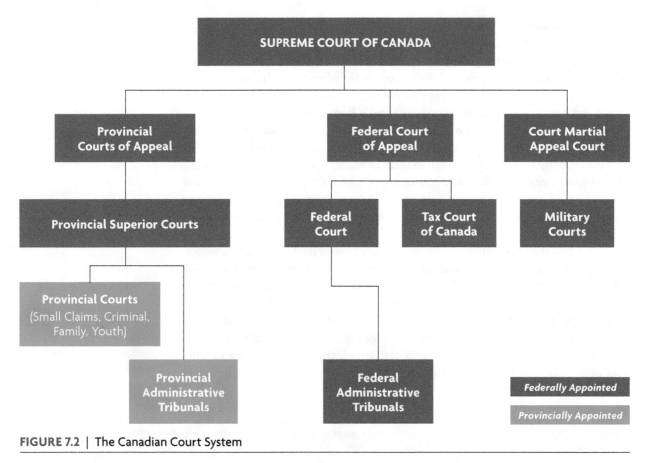

FIGURE 7.2 | The Canadian Court System

Note: While similar to provincial courts, territorial courts are distinct in ways not represented in this figure.

1875, the Supreme Court did not assume its status as the highest judicial authority in Canada until 1949, when it displaced the British-based Judicial Committee of the Privy Council (JCPC) as Canada's highest court.

The Supreme Court consists of eight justices and one chief justice, all of whom are appointed by the federal government through the following process. According to the Supreme Court Act, at least three of the nine justices must be appointed from the province of Quebec. This provision ensures that the court has enough justices who are qualified to preside over cases involving Quebec's civil code. By convention, the remaining seats on the bench are distributed among the western provinces (two), Ontario (three), and the Atlantic provinces (one). By practice, one of the justices is selected directly from among lawyers, while the remainder are elevated from other judicial positions. A candidate for the Supreme Court must have been a member of her or his respective provincial/territorial law society for at least 10 years or have served as a superior court judge. From time to time, federal court judges are also elevated to the Supreme Court. No fewer than five justices may review a particular case, which number one hundred per year, on average.

Whenever someone asserts, "We're going to appeal this all the way to the Supreme Court!" they presume that the court has the time and interest to consider

The Canadian Press/Jesse Johnston

Leighton Hay walks out of a Toronto court house in November 2014 after the Crown withdrew charges against him, overturning a decade-old wrongful conviction for first-degree murder. The list of wrongly convicted Canadians who served prison time for crimes they did not commit includes James Driskell, Donald Marshall, David Milgaard, Guy Paul Morin, and Steven Truscott, to name just a few. Some see these cases as stains on the courts that sent innocent men to prison, while to others they represent the strengths of a criminal justice system that allowed these cases to be reopened and that ultimately got the right result. What safeguards exist to prevent the innocent from being imprisoned and the guilty from being set free in Canada?

the appeal. This is not always possible. For the most part, the Supreme Court selects which cases it will hear, and prioritizes matters that are in the national interest. It may choose to grant **leave** to appellants who have exhausted all levels of appeal in lower courts and whose cases involve a matter of public importance and/or warrant reconsideration by the highest court on a question of law or fact. Other cases proceed directly to the Supreme Court as *appeals of right*, including criminal cases where one of the appeals court judges dissents on a point of law. The Supreme Court also hears reference cases submitted to it by the federal government, and may grant leave to hear appeals of provincial/territorial references once they have been adjudicated by courts of appeal.

Lastly, it is important to note that the Canadian judiciary is supported at its foundation by a large number of **justices of the peace**. Appointed by the lieutenant governor on the advice of provincial cabinet, these judicial officers operate at the provincial level, and have varying responsibilities from jurisdiction to jurisdiction. Most are empowered to conduct hearings outside or before formal court proceedings. This includes mediation and settlement conferences as well as routine business, including presiding over marriages, administering oaths, issuing warrants, and witnessing affidavits. In larger provinces, justices of the peace may preside over bail hearings and cases involving minor offences.

leave Permission granted by a court to hear a case.

justice of the peace An individual appointed to provide routine, administrative judicial services.

Opportunities Available

Knowledge of Canadian Politics and Government Preferred!

Executive Assistant

Fredericton, NB

Description

The Law Office of Kelly Lamrock, Q.C., seeks an Executive Assistant to help build our growing practice in administrative & immigration law and public policy consulting.

The Executive Assistant shall:

- Assist in the drafting and organizing of documents in complex files
- Ensure documentation of hours, invoicing of clients, and financial records
- Provide for the scheduling of meetings and travel
- Undertake research into public policy issues and co-ordinate Right to Information requests
- Develop a marketing strategy for the practice, with a special focus on multicultural communities and new Canadians
- Manage client communications and intake, and provide support to the lawyer when dealing with culturally diverse files

The position offers participation in health and insurance plans, as well as allowances for professional development and generous vacation time.

Qualifications

The successful applicant shall:

- Have a Bachelor's Degree, preferably in Political Science, Communications, or related fields
- Have experience working in communications and media relations, preferably in a public policy field
- Have excellent written communication skills
- Have experience working in public policy or government, preferably in the New Brunswick context
- Have experience working with a culturally diverse clientele in a multicultural environment, preferably with connections to communities in Fredericton
- Have experience in file management and financial reporting
- Have a demonstrated understanding of issues of social justice, equality and diversity
- Be fluent in English and French

Source: Courtesy Kelly Lamrock

BRIEFING NOTES

Reference Cases

Governments may refer cases only to the highest court in their respective jurisdictions. This means that while the federal government may refer questions, bills, or laws to the Supreme Court of Canada, provincial and territorial governments cannot. Rather, they may refer cases to their respective courts of appeal. Governments are not limited to referring their own laws for judicial review; they may choose to refer other governments', as well. Consider the pair of references concerning the federal government's proposed reforms to the Senate, as discussed in Chapter 6. The Quebec government referred federal Bill C-7 to the Quebec Court of Appeal, while the federal government referred a set of broader questions to the Supreme Court of Canada.

Judicial Appointments

Provincial and Territorial Court Appointments

The appointment process for provincial/territorial court judges varies from jurisdiction to jurisdiction. For the most part, lawyers who would be judges apply for appointment to the bench and have their applications vetted by a judicial appointments council. In British Columbia, for example, the Judicial Council consists of three judges and a justice of the peace, two lawyers, and three members of the public. After investigating each applicant, the council compiles a list of suitable judges for consideration by the provincial minister of justice, who then forwards her or his selection to the provincial cabinet for approval. If the candidate is endorsed, the premier advances the person's name to the lieutenant governor, who makes the final appointment on the advice of the government.

Many superior court judges are appointed by the federal government through a similar application and vetting process. To be eligible for appointment, candidates must have at least 10 years' experience practising law in the jurisdiction for which they are being appointed, and must meet qualifications listed in section 3 of the Judges Act. Judicial advisory committees are empanelled in each jurisdiction, comprising a representative selected by the provincial/territorial government, lawyers from the Canadian Bar Association and provincial/territorial law society, a senior judge, and members of the public and law enforcement community as selected by the federal government. These committees actively investigate the candidate's personal and professional history before assessing each candidate as suitable ("recommended") or not for appointment. The federal minister of justice reviews the list of recommended applicants and presents a recommendation to the federal cabinet for approval. Should the person be considered for the chief justice position in a given province or territory, the prime minister advances the nominee's name to the federal cabinet for consideration. If approved, the prime minister offers this advice to the governor general, who makes the ultimate appointment on behalf of the Crown.

Judges who have been elevated from lower courts do not have to undergo the first part of this screening process. The minister of justice may conduct the investigation herself or himself before submitting the person for cabinet consideration. A similar

BRIEFING NOTES

The Bar and the Bench

Lawyers are called to the bar before they may practise as barristers in court. In figurative terms, "the bar" is used to refer to all lawyers who have passed their bar examination, who are deemed qualified to represent others in court, and who are members of their provincial/territorial law society. In literal terms, the bar is the barrier that separates the public area at the rear of a courtroom from the front area where the judge, lawyers, parties, and court workers sit. Lawyers selected to serve as judges are summoned to the bench—the raised platform and desk from behind which they will hear cases.

process exists for all federal courts, as well, with a single judicial advisory committee serving the entire country.

Supreme Court Appointments

Appointments to the Supreme Court of Canada follow a unique process, which has become more transparent over time, particularly as recent prime ministers Paul Martin and Stephen Harper have subjected most of their nominees to some form of public scrutiny. Indeed, while featuring similar, internal screening procedures to establish a short list of potential candidates, the process for selecting appointees to the Supreme Court has changed considerably since the turn of the twenty-first century, and continues to evolve in the absence of any legislated or codified rules.

In general, the federal minister of justice, as attorney general, consults with senior members of the judicial, legal, and law enforcement communities, as well as the respective provincial government, in creating a pool of candidates. This pool is then vetted by an all-party selection panel, which narrows the list even further, typically to three. The federal minister of justice selects one person from this short list, recommending an individual nominee for the prime minister's consideration. Once selected by the prime minister, most nominees for the Supreme Court of Canada undergo a variety of public screening processes, which in recent years have sometimes included answering questions before ad hoc parliamentary committees and in televised interviews. These questions are confined to the nominee's professional career and credentials, and typically do not focus on her or his personal life. These ad hoc committees act in a purely advisory capacity; they do not have the power to confirm or veto the prime minister's choice of nominees, but they do promote public awareness about the process. At times, the federal government forgoes this final screening process in the interests of expediency. As with other federal appointments, the governor general makes the ultimate choice, on advice of the prime minister.

Criticisms of the Appointment Process

At all levels of the judiciary, these screening and vetting procedures are designed to select the most competent judges to serve on Canada's courts. Critics note that they have not helped to ensure gender balance. In 2014, women made up barely one-third of all federally appointed judges on the Supreme Court, the Federal Court of Appeal, the Federal Court, the Tax Court, and various provincial courts of appeal and the Queen's Bench.[3] This disparity persists despite the fact that women make up the majority of law students and nearly 4 in 10 lawyers in Canada. Explanations for the lack of gender balance range from the lack of women applicants to judicial positions to systemic discrimination in the appointments process.

These screening procedures are also designed to prevent flagrant patronage appointments to the bench, and to protect judges' political independence. Gradually, these processes have been made more transparent, amid accusations that provincial and federal governments were selecting candidates with close party ties. Some critics argue that this vetting process falls short of placing any sort of constraint on governments. Initial pools and short lists are ultimately determined by ministers of justice and their officials, and the final recommendation to the Crown lies solely with the first minister. Other critics feel that the public screening process for Supreme Court justices is too politicized. By subjecting judicial nominees to parliamentary review, these new processes disturb the independence of the judiciary and give Parliament undue influence over the composition of the Supreme Court. While far from perfect in terms of insulating the judiciary from political influence, the Canadian judicial appointments system is a far cry from the American one, where judges in some states run as partisans for election, and nominees for the US Supreme Court are subject to a more highly politicized confirmation process.

As you have read, judges in Canada are appointed by governments, not elected by voters. So, too, are the Crown attorneys that prosecute crimes on behalf of the government. This also helps to distinguish the Canadian legal system from the American one, where many judges and prosecutors are elected alongside politicians. The American system holds judges and prosecutors accountable to the public for their decisions; discussed above, the Canadian system—modelled on British tradition—maintains the judiciary's distance and independence from public opinion.

Once appointed, judges serve until a mandatory retirement age (75 for federal appointees and 70 for some provincial/territorial judges), free from the possibility of dismissal for any reason short of gross personal or professional misconduct. It is not as though Canadian judges are entirely unaccountable for their actions, however. In addition to appealing a federally-appointed judge's decision to a higher court, Canadians and governments may lodge a formal complaint with the Canadian Judicial Council about a judge's conduct in presiding over their case. The council consists of a panel of 39 high-ranking judges, who, after investigating the complaint, may recommend to the government that one of their peers be removed from the bench. This

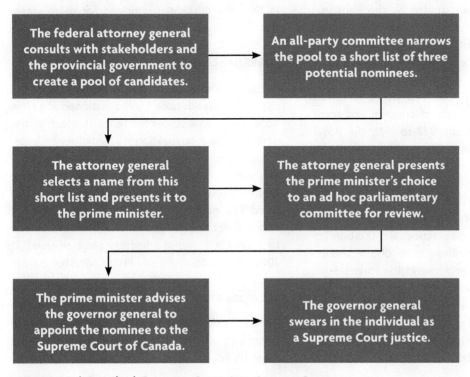

FIGURE 7.3 | Standard Supreme Court Appointment Process

decision would be based on the judge's failure to live up to the expected ethical standards, including remaining diligent, independent, and impartial, while respecting the importance of integrity and equality in decision-making. Similar judicial councils exist for judges appointed by provincial and territorial governments.

Judicial investigations are exceedingly rare, and when they do occur, typically result in the resignation of the accused judge. Removal of a federally appointed judge would require a joint resolution by the House of Commons and the Senate—something that has never occurred in Canadian history. In other words, judges enjoy tremendous security of tenure and remain in their positions regardless of whether the government of the day disagrees with their decisions.

Law Enforcement

Federal Law Enforcement Agencies and the RCMP

Law enforcement in Canada is an equally complex and expensive component of the justice system, with various orders of government establishing police services to oversee compliance with their own legislation and regulations. All told, policing costs governments over $6 billion per year, and encompasses nearly 70,000 officers across

INSIDE CANADIAN POLITICS
Why Has Public Trust in the RCMP Been Declining?

The RCMP's operations are guided by the core values of integrity, honesty, professionalism, compassion, respect, and accountability.[4] Over the years, the organization and its officers have been celebrated for their dedication, service excellence, and work ethic. Nevertheless, the country's national police force has occasionally been the subject of criticism and scandal. Most significantly, from 1977 to 1981, the Royal Commission of Inquiry into Certain Activities of the RCMP (known as the McDonald Commission) explored a variety of allegations that security officers had overstretched their mandate. Revelations about the exuberant monitoring of Parti Québécois members, including illegal surveillance practices and the burning down of a barn owned by the mother of a separatist, led the commission to recommend the force's espionage division be separated into a new federal civilian spy agency; consequently, the Canadian Security Intelligence Service (CSIS) was established in 1984.

More recently, the RCMP has been embroiled in a number of highly publicized controversies:

- In 1997, the RCMP was criticized for using excessive force against protesters at the Asia–Pacific Economic Cooperation (APEC) summit in Vancouver in 1997 (see Chapter 14).

- In 2002, Maher Arar, of dual Canadian and Syrian citizenship, was detained and questioned at a New York airport as a suspected terrorist. Much of the basis for the interrogation was intelligence information supplied by the RCMP. The American government deported Arar not to Canada but to Syria, where he was imprisoned for nearly a year and tortured. The incident led to a Commission of Inquiry into the Actions of Canadian Officials in Relation to Maher Arar, whose findings were released in 2006. The following year, Prime Minister Harper apologized to Arar on behalf of the Government of Canada and offered a $10.5 million settlement.

- Robert Dziekański, a Polish immigrant arriving in Canada to visit his mother, was tasered multiple times by RCMP officers at Vancouver International

Canada. These figures may sound enormous, but Canada's police force is actually smaller per capita than those of many other Western democracies, including the United States.

Constitutionally, most policing falls under provincial responsibility in Canada, as provinces are responsible for establishing police forces and setting policing standards within their borders. In practical terms, most provinces have devolved authority over city policing to municipal governments, allowing city councils to hire and maintain their own forces. At the same time, most provinces contract the federal government to provide rural and remote police services through the Royal Canadian Mounted Police (RCMP). The RCMP was originally founded as the North-West Mounted Police in 1873. The establishment of a federal police presence in the northwestern regions of the continent militated against the lawlessness of the American Wild West and fulfilled the Canadian constitutional principle of "peace, order, and good government." Since that time, the RCMP has evolved to play a formidable role in policing the country, and the Canadian Mountie has become one of the most recognizable articles of Canadiana.

The RCMP falls under the direction of the federal minister of public safety and emergency preparedness. It is an agency that operates through local detachments located throughout Canada, in some cases as the nominal provincial police force,

RCMP A pan-Canadian police force commissioned by the federal government.

↻ The principle of peace, order, and good government is discussed in Chapter 2, on the constitution. See especially the ICP box on page 56.

Airport and died. The disturbing incident was captured on video by a bystander. An inquiry found that officers had acted inappropriately in dealing with Dziekański, who could not speak English, and that they later misled investigators about key aspects of the incident.

- Catherine Galliford, a former RCMP corporal, alleged that during her career she was subjected to sexual harassment by male colleagues.

These are by no means the only controversies associated with law enforcement in Canada. Intelligence officers failed to detect preparations for the Air India bombing (see Chapter 14), and police forces took years to catch Vancouver-area serial killer Robert Pickton. Across the country, citizens' videos of peace officers allegedly using excessive force periodically emerge and attract media coverage. Consequently, Canadians' confidence in their police has been plummeting: in 1997, over 80 per cent trusted the RCMP, provincial forces, and municipal officers, but in 2012, only about 40 per cent felt this way.[5] Even the many members of policing service organizations who epitomize professionalism must confront the reality that their occupation is under scrutiny as never before. At the same time, it is worth noting that over the same 15-year span, 31 RCMP officers were killed in the line of duty. This includes four officers killed in 2005 in an ambush in Mayerthorpe, Alberta, but does not include three officers who were targeted in a shooting spree in Moncton, New Brunswick, in 2014. Both incidents highlight the dangers of working in Canada's highest-profile law enforcement agency.

VOX POP

Can you think of ways to improve the accountability and ethical conduct of police forces in Canada, such as the RCMP? Do you think the public concern about policing is fair or overblown?

and in all cases in close connection with local forces. The RCMP provides a host of services to police forces across Canada, either free of charge or through cost-sharing or cost-recovery arrangements with provincial and territorial governments. For instance, to assist police in conducting investigations, the RCMP maintains the National Police Services (which provides forensics, intelligence, and training) and several national databases, including the National DNA Data Bank and the Canadian Police Information Centre.

The RCMP enforces federal laws through six different sections:

1. commercial crime, including so-called "white-collar" crimes involving fraud and counterfeiting;
2. criminal intelligence, particularly concerning organized crime like gangs and the Mafia;
3. customs and excise, including smuggling;
4. drugs, including domestic and international trafficking;
5. immigration and passports; and
6. federal law enforcement, including consumer and environmental protection.

The RCMP is also responsible for the country's protective policing service, which provides security details for the prime minister, governor general, visiting dignitaries, parliamentarians, federal judges, Supreme Court justices, and others designated by the minister of public safety. As discussed in Chapter 14, the RCMP works in close connection with other federal security agencies to preserve national security.

In addition to the RCMP, the federal government maintains law enforcement agencies to police its borders, prisons, parks, and oceans, and has compliance officers, inspectors, investigators, and other peace officers to protect its staff and enforce its laws in areas like the military, the environment, health, food inspection, railways, consumer protection, national buildings (including Parliament), and the postal service.

Law Enforcement in the Provinces and Territories

While provinces have jurisdiction over most areas of law enforcement within their borders, all but three sign contracts with the federal government making the RCMP their official provincial police force. These contracts are subject to renewal, and can be revoked with appropriate notice. Ontario maintains its own province-wide police force, known as the Ontario Provincial Police. Likewise, the Sûreté du Québec polices the province of Quebec. In Canada's easternmost province, the Royal Newfoundland Constabulary operates in the most populous regions, while the policing of rural and remote parts of Newfoundland and Labrador are contracted to the RCMP.

Provincial police—whether the RCMP, on contract, or one of the three stand-alone police forces—are responsible for everything from traffic enforcement on highways and maintaining provincial firearms registries to conducting province-wide criminal investigations and assisting in inter-provincial investigations. Depending on the matter under investigation, provincial police officers may be empowered to arrest and charge a suspect, or turn the accused and any evidence over to the federal government.

Local law enforcement duties—including crime prevention, apprehending suspects, providing victim services, executing warrants, participating in prosecutions

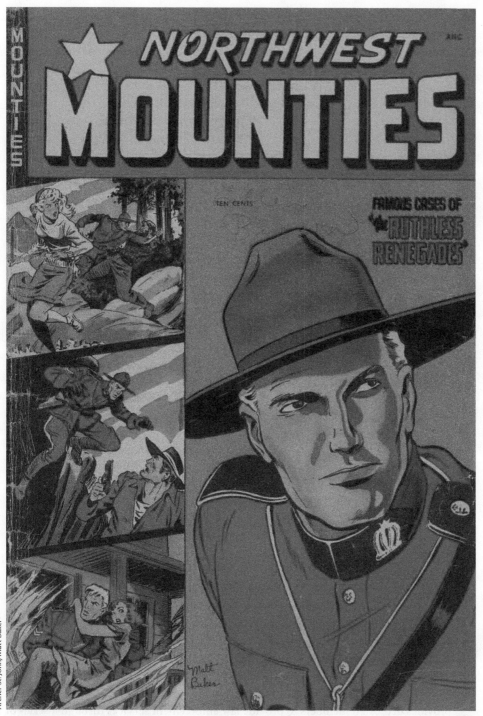

Archer St. John/Matt Baker

The Mountie is more than a national icon. In the nineteenth century, RCMP members played a key role in the establishment of Canadian legal institutions in the West. Throughout the twentieth, the RCMP expanded its role as the country's only pan-Canadian police force. Today, alongside other national and international agencies, the RCMP is at the forefront of preserving public security in rural and urban communities alike. How has the RCMP's role changed over time, and how has it stayed the same? Is the RCMP for you a symbol of Canadian diversity? Of Canadian law enforcement?

of offenders, and otherwise enforcing municipal bylaws to preserve the peace of the community—are typically devolved from the province to its larger municipalities. These larger communities maintain city police forces, like the Brandon Police Service or the Halifax Regional Police. Smaller municipalities unable to afford their own police forces rely on the provincial government to provide law enforcement through either the provincial police force or the RCMP. Each province also maintains a host of sheriffs who may handle security for the premier and lieutenant governor, transfer prisoners, issue subpoenas, and oversee traffic enforcement; bailiffs who often deal with courtroom security, repossessions, and evictions; wardens who patrol parks and jails; and other peace officers.

In northern Canada, the federal government has devolved authority over policing to territorial governments, all of which then contract the RCMP to deliver services within their jurisdictions. Since the 1970s, the federal government has also reached a number of tripartite agreements with First Nations bands and provincial governments to empower First Nations police officers to deliver services on reserve. These officers may act as part of a stand-alone Aboriginal police force or as dedicated personnel within existing provincial or federal forces.

To gain a better sense of policing in Canada, consider how law enforcement agencies operate in one particular province. There are no fewer than 12 police services operating in Alberta. In its largest communities, the provincial government has devolved law enforcement powers to municipal governments including Calgary, Edmonton, Lethbridge, Medicine Hat, Taber, and Lacombe. Other provinces do likewise, permitting city and town governments to set up their own local police forces, which operate under provincial authority and according to provincial standards.

For rural policing, the Alberta government has signed a Provincial Police Services Agreement with the federal government, which contracts the RCMP to enforce laws in towns, villages, Métis settlements, and other municipal districts with populations under 5000. The RCMP has signed separate contracts with larger municipalities to provide policing services in their communities. The Alberta government pays 70 per cent of the costs associated with this rural and remote policing; the federal government pays the remaining 30 per cent. Again, similar arrangements exist in all other provinces except Ontario and Quebec, where provincial governments operate their own provincial police services and do not contract the RCMP.

Together, the Alberta and federal governments have signed a series of tripartite agreements with some of the largest Aboriginal communities in the province, establishing independent First Nations police services operating exclusively on those reserves, and funded jointly by the federal and provincial governments. For example, on the Blood Indian Reserve, Canada's largest, the First Nation manages its own police service in accordance with provincial legislation and regulations, with constables being trained according to provincial standards. In other First Nations, the RCMP provides dedicated members to provide law enforcement services through a series of cost-sharing arrangements with the Alberta government. Similar tripartite arrangements exist throughout Canada as part of the federal First Nations Policing Program.

In addition to these police forces, and like all other provinces, Alberta maintains corps of conservation officers and investigators, as well as a provincial sheriff's department.

The "K" Division of the RCMP maintains over 100 detachments throughout Alberta, employing more than 2500 officers—over 2000 of whom are on contract to the province and municipalities. The RCMP works collaboratively with other police forces in the province to suppress organized crime, halt the drug trade, address terrorist threats, combat economic crimes, protect VIPs travelling throughout the province, and protect Canada's border with the United States.

Lastly, law enforcement officers and provincial justice officials work in close co-operation with the RCMP and CSIS to monitor and address any threats to critical infrastructure and public security in the province.

The Correctional System

Much like its court and law enforcement systems, Canada's correctional system is highly federalized, with responsibilities divided among various orders of government. The greater part of Canada's correctional system is run by provincial governments through their solicitors general, who are responsible for overseeing the detainment of people awaiting trial and those found guilty of minor offences, the administration of youth detention centres, and the conduct of those serving community-based sentences like parole or probation. The federal government operates federal prisons to house Canada's most serious offenders, along with a limited number of institutions to deal with people who have broken federal laws, including those awaiting deportation for immigration offences.

Canada's correctional system includes institutions to hold people in custody including remand centres, provincial jails, federal penitentiaries, and other facilities as well as community supervision programs for people on parole, on probation, in community service, or facing fines. Over three-quarters of the correctional population fall into the latter category, with the remaining 25 per cent incarcerated in institutional settings. This balance reflects the overall priority of the correctional system

> **correctional system** The network of community-based and institutional programs designed to detain, rehabilitate, and deter those involved in illegal activity.

BRIEFING NOTES

Prisons in Canada

There are four main types of prisons, or correctional facilities, in Canada:

- provincial remand centres;
- provincial youth detention centres (juvenile detention centres, known informally as "juvies");
- provincial jails; and
- federal penitentiaries.

Note the terminology: there are no *federal jails* or *provincial penitentiaries*.

Note also that the distinction between provincial and federal prisons depends on the length of the sentence, not the jurisdiction responsible for the law that was broken: adults sentenced for more than two years serve their time in federal prisons, while all others are sent to provincial ones. Federal facilities come in a variety of forms, including minimum-, medium-, and maximum-security prisons.

According to Canada's correctional investigator, Aboriginal men and women, who make up less than 4 per cent of Canada's population, account for 23 per cent of the country's federal prison inmate population.[7] What impacts does this have on Aboriginal communities? What do you think are the root causes of this relatively high level of incarceration?

in Canada, which is designed to reform or rehabilitate offenders as opposed to simply punishing or detaining them.

As mentioned, Canada operates a separate system of justice for youth aged 12 to 17. The Youth Criminal Justice Act and similar federal and provincial statutes treat young offenders differently, subjecting them to lesser sentences and incarcerating them in separate provincially run youth detention centres.

Canada's adult prison population is divided roughly equally among those temporarily detained awaiting trial and those sentenced to serve time in provincial and federal facilities. Accused offenders awaiting trial are held in remand, most of the time in provincial remand facilities or jails. Offenders who have been sentenced to serve time are incarcerated in either provincial/territorial jails (for sentences of less than two years) or federal penitentiaries (for sentences of two years or more).

All told, for every 1000 Canadians, roughly 6 are under some sort of state supervision in Canada, whether in institutional facilities or in the community. This number has declined from a high point of 7 of every 1000 in the 1990s, driven mostly by a decrease in the number of Canadians on probation, on parole, or under other forms of community supervision. The rate of adults in custody has risen slightly over time, owing mostly to an increase in the number of people in remand—that is, detained while awaiting trial.

remand Court-ordered, temporary detention for accused offenders awaiting trial.

incarceration Court-ordered confinement in a provincial, territorial, or federal prison.

This increase in Canada's remand population has been cause for concern, particularly for provincial governments, whose remand facilities and jails are used to house individuals awaiting trial. The remand challenges are driven mostly by a backlog of cases in the court system. Recent efforts to hire more Crown attorneys and court staff, streamline court processes, develop alternative routes to justice (including drug treatment courts), and find other efficiencies in the justice system have helped stem the rise in the remand population. So, too, has the removal of the so-called "two-for-one" credit for time served in remand, under which offenders in remand received two years credit on their sentences for every one year spent in pre-trial detention; the credit created a disincentive to speed up proceedings, as those in custody awaiting trial would obtain shorter prison sentences in the long run. Critics warn that the advent of mandatory minimum sentences may offset many of these gains, however, as judges no longer have discretion to divert certain criminals out of the institutional setting.

Rates of adult incarceration vary from jurisdiction to jurisdiction in Canada, with Quebec featuring the country's lowest rate, and Manitoba, Saskatchewan, and the three territories featuring the highest. The entire correctional system costs Canadians over $4 billion per year, with the costs of prisons and their personnel accounting for the lion's share. Because of the higher level of security and more specialized forms of rehabilitative programming, it costs almost twice as much to incarcerate an individual in a federal penitentiary as in a provincial or territorial jail.

This said, adult incarceration rates in Canada are among the lowest in the Western world. At just over 1 in 1000, the number of adults in state custody in Canada is seven times lower than in the United States, and half of what it is in Mexico. Scandinavian incarceration rates are somewhat lower than Canada's.[8]

mandatory minimum sentence The shortest allowable prison term a judge may impose upon a person convicted of certain crimes (such as firearms and drug offences) or under certain conditions (e.g. a repeat offence).

↻ Do mandatory minimum prison sentences go too far? The debate supplement at the end of this chapter gives some of the arguments on both sides, and offers questions and resources to guide a discussion around this pressing topic.

Concluding Thoughts

Canada's justice system is very complex, designed to divide responsibility over the creation, interpretation, and enforcement of Canada's laws among a variety of political players. This division of power not only helps to distribute an immense amount of labour and resources across a broader set of actors; it also prevents any single authority from exerting complete control over law and order, as is the case in other countries.

All of the actors in Canada's justice system are subject to a core set of democratic principles, most importantly the rule of law, which helps to ensure Canadians, regardless of where they live, are subject to roughly the same treatment. At the same time, Canada's justice system is highly federalized, meaning that, notwithstanding federal jurisdiction over higher-level judicial appointments and the definition of criminal law, provincial governments maintain control over the administration of justice within their respective jurisdictions. This creates many challenges in terms of coordination, but also many opportunities in terms both of tailoring justice to local customs and needs and of sharing best practices developed in certain jurisdictions.

For More Information

Eager to peer behind the bench? Using interviews with current and former Supreme Court justices and their staff, Emmett Macfarlane delves deeply into the role of the court in Canadian democracy, as well as the norms that guide its justices, in *Governing from the Bench: The Supreme Court of Canada and the Judicial Role* (UBC Press, 2012).

Want an insider's look into Canadian policing? Long-serving officer Robert Chrismas shares his views on the fast-paced evolution of *Canadian Policing in the Twenty-First Century* (McGill–Queen's University Press, 2013).

Seeking to delve more deeply into the correctional system in Canada? Curt Griffiths explores *Canadian Corrections* (Nelson, 2010), peering behind the critical issues facing the system today.

Wonder how Canada's justice system stacks up against those in other Western democracies? Try *The New Punitiveness: Trends, Theories, Perspectives*, edited by John Pratt and associates (Willan Publishing, 2005).

Want to explore the realities and possibilities of Aboriginal justice in Canada? See David Milward's *Aboriginal Justice and the Charter: Realizing a Culturally Sensitive Interpretation of Legal Rights* (UBC Press, 2013).

Curious about the role of race in Canada's criminal justice system? Editors Wendy Chan and Kiran Mirchandani explore the intersection of ethnicity and justice in *Crimes of Colour: Racialization and the Criminal Justice System in Canada* (University of Toronto Press, 2001).

Worried about the implications of biology casework and your civil liberties? Neil Gerlach explores the implications of biological testing and banking in *The Genetic Imaginary: DNA and the Canadian Criminal Justice System* (University of Toronto Press, 2004).

Looking for a primer on Canadian law? Jessie Horner provides an entry-level textbook: *Canadian Law and the Canadian Legal System* (Pearson, 2006).

Want to learn more about youth justice in Canada? See John A. Winterdyk and Russell Smandych's edited collection, *Youth at Risk and Youth Justice: A Canadian Overview*, 2nd edn (Oxford University Press, 2016).

Want to examine the full text of any Canadian law or judicial ruling? The Canadian Legal Information Institute (CanLII) maintains a comprehensive, fully-searchable database. Go to: www.canlii.org.

Seeking the basics on the rule of law and other core concepts in Canadian jurisprudence? The Centre for Public Legal Education in Alberta has put together several online presentations as part of their LawCentral Schools project. Search: "The Law that Rules."

Curious about how Supreme Court justice appointment hearings proceed? Justice Nadon's appearance is available online. Go to: http://tinyurl.com/SCCappointments.

Deeper Inside Canadian Politics

1. On the campaign trail in 2015, the federal Liberals pledged to "legalize, regulate, and restrict access to marijuana" in Canada. What are the key elements of this pledge that require meaningful engagement with provincial/territorial governments?

2. Research the transfer of Omar Khadr from US custody in Guantanamo Bay to Canadian custody in Alberta. Given the nature of his offences and the age at which he committed them, was he transferred to the appropriate facilities in Canada? Why or why not?

UP FOR DEBATE

Do mandatory minimum prison sentences go too far?

THE CLAIM: YES, THEY DO!

Mandatory minimum sentences are a regressive means of treating offenders in Canada's justice system.

Yes: Argument Summary

Repeat and violent offenders should be kept behind bars; however, mandatory minimum sentences are in many cases arbitrary, racist, and unconstitutional. They remove the ability of Crown attorneys and judges to apply their own constitutionally prescribed discretion when approaching criminal cases, and may result in cruel and unusual punishment for first-time, non-violent offenders. The judiciary and Crown attorneys—not elected politicians without a direct connection to the case—should have discretion to decide whether the circumstances behind a particular conviction warrant a lighter punishment.

Yes: Top 5 Considerations

1. The Canadian criminal justice system has always been built on a delicate balance between denunciation and deterrence, on one hand, and rehabilitation and restitution, on the other. Mandatory minimums disrupt this balance by removing the ability of Crown attorneys and judges to weigh the benefits of the latter.

2. Mandatory minimums don't work. There is no evidence that they deter crime or reduce recidivism rates. Justice Canada has commissioned a number of reports on this, and research in the United States continues to challenge the misconception that mandatory minimums reduce crime rates.

3. Not all people subject to mandatory minimums are violent or repeat offenders. Consider the case of Leroy Smickle, a Canadian who posted a picture of himself on Facebook wielding a loaded handgun. The offence carried a mandatory minimum three-year sentence, which the superior court judge refused to impose on the grounds that Mr Smickle was not using the gun in an intimidating manner.

4. Mandatory minimums are typically applied to crimes that are disproportionately committed by people of lower socioeconomic status, including Aboriginal people and ethnic minority groups. They are not applied to white-collar crimes such as fraud and embezzlement, for instance.

5. Faced with the prospect of unfairly sentencing an individual to a lengthy prison term, Crown attorneys and judges may opt to drop some cases entirely. This could result in more cases slipping through the cracks of the justice system.

Yes: Other Considerations

- Even without mandatory minimums, Crown attorneys and judges are free to pursue lengthy prison terms for violent, repeat offenders. In fact, the average sentence for some crimes now subject to mandatory minimums was actually *longer* than the one imposed by the government. Over time, this could mean that sentences for these crimes are actually lighter than they were before mandatory minimums were imposed.

- Many US states are presently reviewing their approach to mandatory minimums, after decades of evidence demonstrate it is a failed policy leading to unequal treatment and overcrowded prisons.

- Mandatory minimums cause prison rates to rise, leading to overcrowded prisons and huge costs to taxpayers.

- In 2014, BC judge Joseph Galati refused to issue the mandatory minimum sentence of one year to a man convicted of three counts of drug possession, on the grounds that such a sentence would constitute cruel and unusual punishment, thereby violating section 12 of the Charter of Rights and Freedoms.

- In 2015, the Supreme Court of Canada struck down a federal law containing mandatory minimum sentences for gun possession, finding the penalties to be cruel and unusual punishment.

THE COUNTERCLAIM: NO, THEY DON'T!

Mandatory minimum sentences are necessary to preserve and promote community safety.

No: Argument Summary

People convicted of the most heinous offences—including violent crimes, drug offences, sexual assault, child abuse, gang activity, drinking and driving, and others—deserve to be sentenced to prison. They would pose a danger to society if judges were allowed to impose community-based sentences. It is in the best interest of the community at large if these criminals are placed behind bars.

No: Top 5 Considerations

1. Put simply, some people pose such a high level of danger to society that they should face mandatory prison sentences. The most dangerous among them may be held under preventive detention for an indefinite period if they are designated with the "dangerous offender" label.
2. Whether or not these convicted offenders are capable of rehabilitation is beside the point. Victims deserve to see their offenders duly punished for their crimes with prison time and a criminal record.
3. Democratically elected governments make laws, and appointed judges interpret them. It is well within the government's authority to dictate which sentences should be imposed for which crimes, and it is up to judges to follow the guidelines provided to them by law, regardless of how stringent those guidelines may be.
4. By establishing a common sentence for all crimes of a certain nature, governments can ensure that offenders are treated equally and according to standards developed by democratically elected representatives of the community and are not subject to arbitrary treatment by judges.
5. Mandatory minimum sentences do not create new criminals; they simply punish existing criminals more appropriately by placing them behind bars instead of putting them under house arrest, probation, or community service. If anything, in fact, mandatory minimums may create fewer criminals by deterring people from considering criminal activity in the first place.

No: Other Considerations

- Mandatory minimums are nothing new in Canada, and they are not a Conservative idea. The Pierre Trudeau government established them for gun-related crimes in 1977, and these were later stiffened under the Chrétien government in 1997.
- There is no way of pinpointing whether *any* particular measure, including mandatory minimums, leads to a lower crime rate. Rates of crime are driven by a host of factors.
- Comparisons between mandatory minimums in Canada and the United States are misleading. Penalties south of the border are far harsher and are applied to far more offences.
- Mandatory minimums do not remove judicial or prosecutorial discretion entirely. Crown attorneys may still choose which offences to pursue, and judges may still determine whether or not to convict the individuals based on their assessment of the accused's guilt. In addition, governments have developed many alternative justice mechanisms, including drug treatment courts and restorative justice processes, to deal with cases outside the traditional criminal system.

Discussion Questions

- In your opinion, do mandatory prison sentences act as a deterrent to would-be criminals?
- The federal government used to award two-for-one credit for time served while the accused awaits trial. Do you agree or disagree with the decision to end that policy? Why?
- What do you feel is a better use of public funds: creating longer incarceration sentences and spending more money on the penitentiaries that keep criminals off the streets, or reducing incarceration sentences and spending more money on rehabilitation programs?
- Is it time to re-open the capital punishment debate? Do you feel that the state should execute perpetrators of the most heinous crimes when there is overwhelming evidence that that person is undisputedly guilty?
- What would be the advantages and disadvantages of requiring that some judicial positions in the system be filled through a general election rather than by appointment?

Where to Learn More about Mandatory Minimum Sentences

Anthony N. Doob and Carla Cesaroni, "The Political Attractiveness of Mandatory Minimum Sentences," *Osgoode Hall Law Journal* 39, no. 287 (2001): pp. 288–305.

Thomas Gabor, "Mandatory Minimum Penalties: Their Effects on Crime, Sentencing Disparities, and Justice System Expenditures" (Ottawa: Department of Justice Canada, 2002).

Jeffrey Mayer and Pat O'Malley, "Missing the Punitive Turn? Canadian Criminal Justice, 'Balance' and Penal Modernism," in *The New Punitiveness: Trends, Theories, Perspectives*, ed. John Pratt, David Brown, Mark Brown, Simon Hallsworth, and Wayne Morrison (Willan Publishing, 2005).

Julian V. Roberts, Nicole Crutcher, and Paul Verbrugge, "Public Attitudes to Sentencing in Canada: Exploring Recent Findings," *Canadian Journal of Criminology and Criminal Justice* 49, no. 1 (2007): pp. 75–107.

8 PUBLIC POLICY AND PUBLIC ADMINISTRATION

Inside this Chapter

- What is public policy?
- What do we mean by governance and public administration?
- How and to what extent do ideologies underpin public policy in Canada?
- What are the major budgeting, taxation, and spending considerations in Canadian government?
- What are the components of Canada's social safety net?

Inside Public Policy and Public Administration

It takes more than reading the constitution or tracing how a bill becomes a law to understand policymaking in Canada. The process is as much about connections and ideas as it is about guidelines and rules. Politicians and bureaucrats interact with each other through a series of complex networks, most of which remain behind closed doors or, more often, beyond the interest of the average Canadian. Those with an inside view of public administration are aware of certain maxims about Canadian policymaking.

- **Government decisions aren't just made by politicians and their political staffers.** It's tempting to imagine our elected officials single-handedly drafting legislation, or sitting around a boardroom brainstorming innovative policy ideas with a handful of staffers. In reality, much of the legwork is done by civil servants, so that public policymaking involves a close interaction between elected and non-elected officials.

- **Public policy is neither based entirely on ideology nor is it bereft of any guiding principle beyond re-electing the government.** Many civil servants lament the amount of the facetiously labelled "decision-based evidence-making" they are required to do to find justifications for policy directions that have already been chosen. For the most part, though, public policy development in Canada follows the evidence-based decision-making model, which is apolitical. In this way, public policy is generated in the broad middle ground between the two poles of ideology and evidence.

- **There is no truth to the maxim that absolute power corrupts absolutely.** Certainly, Canadian politics is by no means devoid of corruption and scandal. Yet, more than ever before, the increasing transparency and accountability brought by open government and e-government initiatives have helped to expose, if not deter, this type of dishonesty.

Peering inside public policy and public administration in Canada means shedding light on these and other factors.

> ### UP FOR DEBATE
> **Is political patronage still necessary in today's Canada?**
>
> Keep this question in mind as you read through the chapter. Consult the end-of-chapter debate supplement for more material to help you engage in an informed discussion of the topic.

Overview

Public policy has been defined as "debate, recommendations, laws, and regulations relating to any course of action that may be undertaken by a level of government, and that affects the public."[1] It's a broad concept that is really about determining the kind of role a government will play in the lives of its citizens. In essence, public

What the 2015 Election Means for Public Policy

Visit the *Inside Canadian Politics* flipboard to learn about the latest developments affecting public policy and public administration.

 Go to http://flip.it/gblag.

policy is a set of principles, rules, and guidelines used to translate political direction into government action. Those who believe in a strong role for government in society believe that government should devote more attention and resources to reducing the gap between the rich and the poor, for instance. On the other side are those who worry about government overreach and overspending, who believe that the social safety net discourages ingenuity. Should it be easier or more difficult for laid-off workers to access employment insurance? Should the government acquiesce to healthcare professionals' demands for more money, or should it hold the line on costs and risk a strike? Should taxpayers subsidize post-secondary tuition further, or should students have to pay their way through college or university? If government intervention is appropriate, which level should intervene—federal, provincial, territorial, municipal, Aboriginal, or some combination of these? And what sorts of tools should they employ? These are some of the many sources of chronic debate about public policy and how government officials should manage the public purse.

Public Policy and Governance

Resolving Difficult Public Issues

Governments attempt to resolve difficult public policy issues every day. Before getting into the theory behind public administration and governance, consider this topical example that illustrates one of the many kinds of issues that falls within the realm of public policy.

Research and common wisdom suggest that the recreational use of heroin is dangerous. The drug is highly addictive and brings many health risks to users; it affects the health of the broader population through the spread of HIV and hepatitis through the sharing of needles; and the drug trade generates profits for organized crime. The question of how to address drug abuse is an ongoing challenge in Canada, one that often pits federal and provincial governments against local health authorities, academics, and advocacy groups, and legislators against judges. In particular, the debate places proponents of rehabilitation and harm reduction on one side, against proponents of punishment and deterrence on the other. The former often support treatment programs, while the latter support harsher criminal sentences for trafficking and drug use.

In an attempt to find a solution, the federal Liberal government in 2003 granted the province of British Columbia a temporary exemption from section 56 of the Controlled Drugs and Substances Act to undertake an innovative pilot project. The exemption, justified on the grounds of science and research, allowed the provincial government to provide users of heroin and other illegal intravenous drugs a safe place to inject. The BC government funded a building in Vancouver's Downtown Eastside, one of the poorest neighbourhoods in Canada, where heroin use is rampant. Aside from destroying lives, the drug has had a damaging effect on the area as a whole.

The result of this initiative was InSite, a supervised injection site in downtown Vancouver that is equipped with healthcare workers who can supervise injections while providing medical and counselling assistance. Addicts are provided with clean needles to limit the spread of disease, and information about how to inject in a safe manner; they are not provided with the drug itself. Addicts also receive medical attention onsite in the event they should overdose. To some, this is a pragmatic and compassionate way to keep addicts safe and off the street; to others, the notion of the government sanctioning illegal drug use is unconscionable and a poor use of tax dollars.

In 2006, after campaigning on a tough-on-crime agenda, the newly elected federal Conservative government chose to allow the section 56 exemption to lapse, thus slating an end to the three-year InSite pilot project. InSite and its supporters challenged the federal government's decision in court, arguing that closing the clinic would violate its patients' section 7 Charter of Rights and Freedoms rights to security of person. Lower courts found in favour of the clinic. The federal government appealed those decisions to the Supreme Court of Canada, arguing that it no longer wanted to facilitate, condone, or promote illegal drug use, and that the public policy decision as to whether to grant safe injection sites an exemption under the Controlled Drugs and Substances Act should fall to the government of the day. The Supreme Court found against the government, however, forcing it to issue an exception and extend the clinic's exemption under Canadian drug laws.

The courts' actions in the InSite case presented real questions about the role of judges in determining public policy in Canada. In reaching their decisions, the judges

Dan Toulgoet/Vancouver Courier

In spite of the Supreme Court's decision in the InSite case, and the broad support of medical experts across the country, the clinic remains the only legally operating supervised injection facility in Canada. A second facility in Vancouver, located at the Dr Peter Centre for long-term care of AIDS patients, has been quietly supervising injections for years, and has filed an application for a section 56 exemption to make its service legal. The application was stalled pending the passage of federal legislation, Bill C-2, which would have made it much more difficult for facilities like the Dr Peter Centre to gain the exemption to the Controlled Drugs and Substances Act. What role do you think the courts should play when it comes to determining public policy, like the provision of safe injection sites?

often weighed the impact the clinic was having on Vancouver's population of addicts, in particular by reducing the rate of death due to overdose. Critics argued that such assessments amounted to public policy evaluations—a task belonging to legislators and beyond the purview of the courts. They argued that judges had used the Charter as a pretext for supporting a particular public policy, rather than deciding the case on its legal or constitutional merits. For its part, the federal government questioned the value of the clinic from both a public health and a public safety perspective. Yet the courts sided with the clinic's supporters, whose evidence they found more convincing. There has since been some discussion about opening facilities like InSite in downtown Montreal, Toronto, and Ottawa.

This case raises important questions about how Canadians are governed. What should be done when complicated issues need resolving? Should the courts decide the merits of government programs? Or should policy decisions be left up to elected governments alone? To answer such questions we need to understand what government is.

Government and Public Policy

In *Leviathan* (1651), British philosopher Thomas Hobbes theorized that society would exist in a "state of nature" without government. Without social order, people would be in a constant state of war with each other, and life would be "nasty, brutish, and short." Hobbes's mid-seventeenth–century musings are a reminder that government exists to improve our lives. People throughout the world struggle to satisfy their basic needs, protect themselves from harm, advance their personal priorities, and achieve their communities' priorities; this prompts competition with others to shape government decisions. Life with good government has a better chance of being pleasant, fulfilling, and long—but even in a prosperous country like Canada with its constitutional objective of "peace, order, and good government," there are no guarantees.

welfare state A suite of government programs, services, and financial supports designed to assist the least fortunate in society.

Others since Hobbes have observed the important role government plays in people's lives, especially in countries with an expansive welfare state. Government is a system by which a state or community is ruled or controlled. It comprises institutions that legitimately make collective rules for society. Through the creation and enforcement of laws, the government attempts to regulate human behaviour to achieve a civilized society. Government maintains order and public security; administers public revenues and public expenditures; and implements public programs and services. Funds are raised largely through taxation, and those resources are deployed in ways that policymakers deem appropriate.

public administration The study and delivery of public policy by government.

The civil servants who oversee and implement government business are engaged in public administration. As discussed in Chapter 5, bureaucrats are obliged to follow the directives of their respective ministers, as long as the instructions are within the boundaries of the rule of law. This does not mean that permanent government employees are blind followers of the partisans who temporarily occupy seats at the cabinet table, or servants of those ministers' political staff. Senior bureaucrats are guided by a principle of speaking truth to power and the mantra of "fearless advice and loyal implementation." This means that clerks, deputy ministers, and others provide prudent counsel to prime ministers, premiers, and ministers, and that whatever political decision is made by the executive will be acted upon faithfully. In other words, elected officials decide and direct, while bureaucrats advise and implement.

Government follows a chain of command whereby those with a higher rank issue directives to those with a lower rank. In this way, the government is organized very much like a military operation, with clearly defined roles and positions of authority. German sociologist Max Weber concluded as much in his posthumous treatise *Economy and Society* (1922).[2] He identified a number of characteristics of a functioning government that continue to apply to bureaucracy in Western societies, including Canada. For instance:

- There must be rules within the civil service.
- Government must employ skilled experts.
- These experts must operate within an organized hierarchy.
- There must be employee training so as to encourage uniform performance.
- When bureaucrats take action, they must follow written rules and preserve their actions as files for others' reference.
- People must be treated equally, including through standardized hiring and firing.

These formalities that Weber identified are intended to ensure the smooth running of a non-partisan civil service that will help develop and implement public policy on the direction of elected leaders.

At the simplest level, **public policy** is anything that a government chooses to do or not to do, as Thomas Dye explained in *Understanding Public Policy* (1972). A more recent variation is that public policy constitutes "what government ought or ought not do, and does or does not do."[3] Public policy therefore encompasses government laws, rules, regulations, and decisions designed to define obligations, prohibitions, and rights enjoyed by Canadians. In this way, public policy sets the boundaries of acceptable conduct in society, with objectives being met through any combination of public education, financial incentives, guidelines or standards, and sanctions. Public policy is often the outcome of an ideological competition among political actors who seek to influence the distribution of finite public resources. Political parties, the media, and special interests all seek to influence public policy by identifying problems and pitching solutions. Politicking results when there is disagreement about the urgency of the policy problem and/or the most appropriate policy solution.

public policy A plan or course of action chosen by a government to respond to an identified problem.

Connecting the Public to Policymaking

Governments often struggle to connect the public to the policymaking process. Plebiscites, referendums, initiatives, and other forms of direct democracy are rarely used; in any event, they are technically non-binding on the government of the day, though public pressure may dictate otherwise. The Westminster traditions discussed in Chapter 2 offer Canadians only indirect access. First ministers and their cabinets are accountable to legislatures, whose members, in turn, must answer to their constituents through elections held at least once every five years. From time to time, governments will launch public consultations on matters of particular interest, and designated officials will visit communities to listen to local concerns.

Historically, these have been the main formal institutions and mechanisms for directly engaging citizens in the policymaking process. Advances in communication technology offer new opportunities for the government to engage with the public it

↻ See Chapter 10 and the section Direct Democracy in Canada (pages 422–5) for more information about referendums and plebiscites, and why they're rarely used in Canada; also see the section on representative democracy in Chapter 2, beginning on page 41.

↻ See the discussion of e-democracy on pages 444–5 of Chapter 11 for information on how governments are using information communication technologies (ICTs) to engage citizens.

green paper A government document released to explore policy options, without any commitment to the outcome.

white paper A document outlining a proposed policy commitment by government.

↻ See page 41 of Chapter 2, on the constitution, for an explanation of representative democracy.

pluralism The presence of diverse socioeconomic groups participating in public affairs.

serves. Governments can gather information from polling their constituents, or monitoring social media. They can host policy discussions online and supplement consultation processes with information received electronically. Citizens and the media, for their part, can obtain more information about government than at any point in history, faster than ever and at any time of day, from almost anywhere. This includes identifying what consultations are currently ongoing. The federal government's *Consulting with Canadians* website (www.canada.ca/consultingcanadians) maintains a chronology of past and ongoing consultations. This area of public administration involves myriad consultation tools, including draft documents, special reviews, consultation papers, invitations for public comment, updates on policy initiatives, and opinion surveys.

On matters of varying public importance, a government may initiate a green paper to stimulate public discussion on a particular policy issue. These documents typically provide background on the issue at hand and a broad set of possible strategies to address it. Green papers are designed to inform a ministerial response. For example, the Mackenzie King government issued a series of green papers on universal healthcare at the close of the Second World War; these would prove to be the early formal stages of the Medical Care Act (1966) that was passed over two decades later. The federal government has produced over 30 green papers since 2000, on topics ranging from Internet piracy and voyeurism to same-sex marriage and official bilingualism.

By contrast, white papers are more direct and specific, outlining a government's proposed course of action. White papers are usually released prior to the drafting of legislation, allowing the government to adjust its approach after hearing from the public. While both green papers and white papers are used in public consultations, the former are far more open-ended, while the latter are sanctioned by cabinet before being tabled in the legislature. For instance, the 1970 *White Paper on Metric Conversion* was initiated by the federal Liberal government, but it was a PC government that passed legislation introducing metric as the national standard of measurement in 1985. The federal government has released over 20 white papers since 2000, most dealing with issues of national defence and private-sector regulation.

From time to time, governments may also launch public consultations to review the effectiveness of public programs and services, or to solicit input on constitutional or intergovernmental positions. The Government of Manitoba held public consultations on bilingualism and the Meech Lake Accord in the 1980s, for example, and convened similar community forums on its role in the Social Union Framework Agreement and the prospect of Senate nominee elections in the province.

These sorts of public consultations are few and far between at both the federal and the provincial/territorial level, however, disappointing many proponents of grassroots democracy. According to the delegate model of democratic representation, public policies ought to consider citizens' preferences, and these should have primacy over the preferences of the political executive. Pluralism holds that the diversity of perspectives in a society should be reflected in the shaping of public policy. It is a belief that government power should not be concentrated in political elites, namely politicians, interest group leaders, business owners, and labour union bosses.[4] Democracy is theoretically stronger when decision-makers consider different points of view. However, the problem with pluralism is that the pressure of many competing voices does not necessarily result in good public policy, and may even result in decision paralysis.

To this end, when crafting public policy, the political executive considers its election platform and resolutions passed at its party convention, which are supplemented with public opinion data, news coverage and editorials, the positions of special interest groups, and counsel from the public service. Other sources of input include debate in the legislature and legal decisions, in addition to any public forums, petitions, and formal consultations. In Canada, pluralism is most vibrant at the federal level, where there is a vigorous struggle to influence government. Conversely, there is greater homogeneity in smaller provinces that are more likely to feature government information control and weaker opposition parties; influential special interests operating without much competition; many reporters but few muckraking journalists; and the fear of sanctions for speaking out against government.

The Public Policy Cycle

Beyond these sorts of public consultations, under Canada's system of parliamentary democracy, it is elected officials who make the ultimate policy decisions. They are aided in their duties by civil servants, who provide options based on evidence and analysis.

The design of public policy may follow many different paths but generally proceeds through what is known as the public policy cycle (see Figure 8.1). A number of variations of the policy cycle model exist. The stages are not always ordered and linear; they merely give shape to an often chaotic process involving a host of different actors.

The first stage in most models is known as agenda setting. This is the stage where a matter of public policy gains such prominence that it comes to the attention of decision-makers. Agenda setting involves what is often the most challenging part of the policy cycle: defining the problem and identifying its root causes. The government's response to the problem can enter the public policy cycle in countless ways. The response might originate as a resolution at a party convention, end up in an election campaign platform, and be promoted by cabinet. It could come about as a result of a judicial ruling that forces the government to respond. It might be a solution proposed by an opposition party after having chastised the government on the issue during Question Period. It might be put forward by an interest group, or the media jumping on a sensationalist issue. It might be a solution prepared by civil servants to address concerns raised by the auditor general. Whatever the details, people seeking to influence public policy during the agenda setting stage must achieve media coverage, influence public opinion, and apply public pressure.[5]

Once the problem has been identified, officials must assess the most viable policy responses; this is typically the next stage in the public policy cycle. An increasingly popular occupation for graduates of political science programs is the role of a policy adviser, or policy analyst. Policy advisers are research specialists who examine the feasibility of potential policy responses and who evaluate existing, revised, or new policies. They engage in objective analysis by using social science methods to collect and analyze data. This includes the manipulation of statistics such as census data to inform cost–benefit analysis and risk assessment. Policy advisers also engage in subjective analysis: for instance, they may formulate options in response to protests, media coverage, and inbound correspondence. An example of the type of career opportunities that exist for those who are interested in public policy is presented in the Opportunities Available box on page 298.

public policy cycle The common stages in public decision-making, from conception to implementation and modification.

agenda setting The use of strategies and tactics to generate public and government support for a proposed public policy.

policy adviser An occupation that involves analysis of data to assess and recommend possible courses of ongoing action.

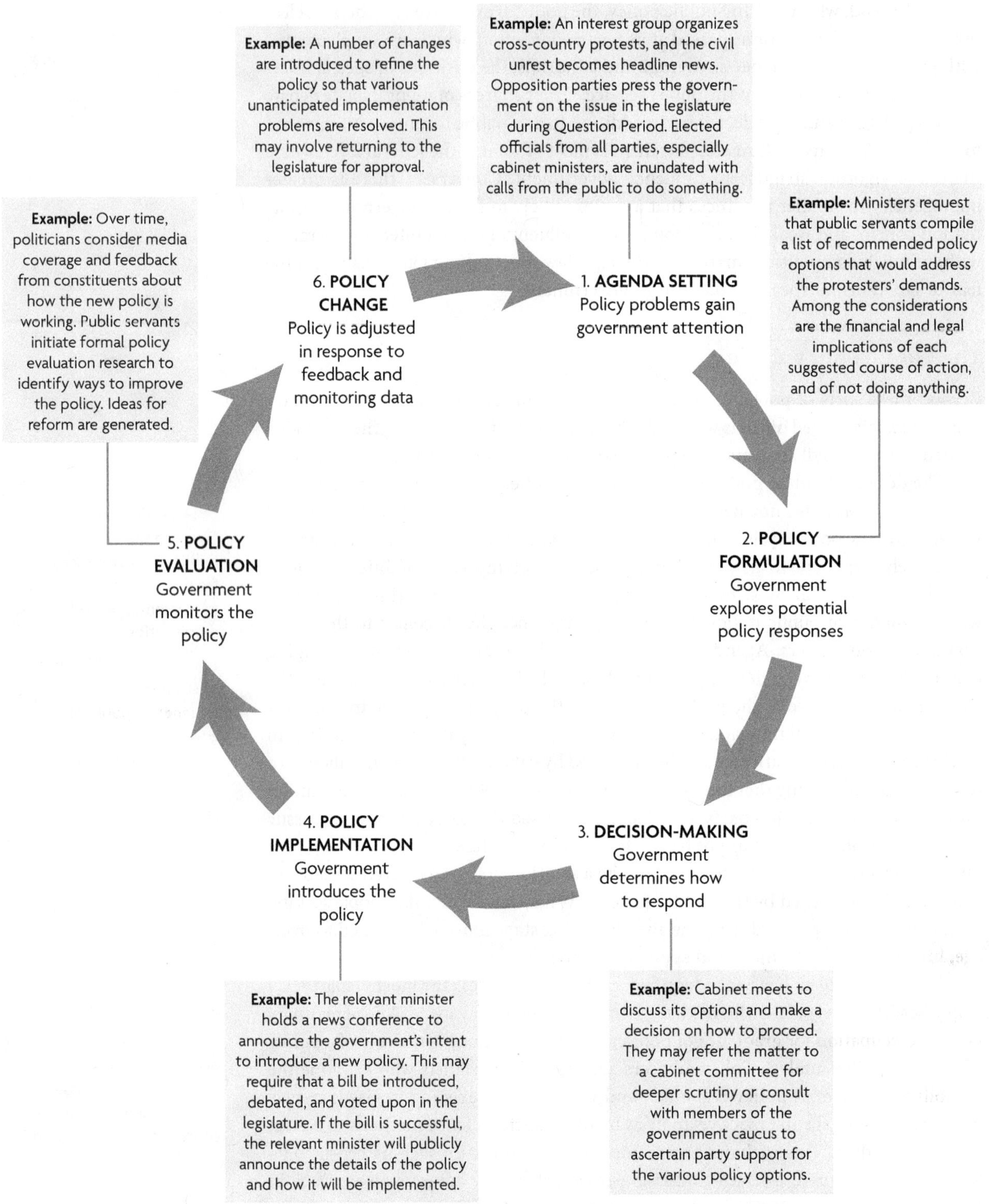

Example: A number of changes are introduced to refine the policy so that various unanticipated implementation problems are resolved. This may involve returning to the legislature for approval.

Example: An interest group organizes cross-country protests, and the civil unrest becomes headline news. Opposition parties press the government on the issue in the legislature during Question Period. Elected officials from all parties, especially cabinet ministers, are inundated with calls from the public to do something.

Example: Ministers request that public servants compile a list of recommended policy options that would address the protesters' demands. Among the considerations are the financial and legal implications of each suggested course of action, and of not doing anything.

Example: Over time, politicians consider media coverage and feedback from constituents about how the new policy is working. Public servants initiate formal policy evaluation research to identify ways to improve the policy. Ideas for reform are generated.

6. **POLICY CHANGE**
Policy is adjusted in response to feedback and monitoring data

1. **AGENDA SETTING**
Policy problems gain government attention

5. **POLICY EVALUATION**
Government monitors the policy

2. **POLICY FORMULATION**
Government explores potential policy responses

4. **POLICY IMPLEMENTATION**
Government introduces the policy

3. **DECISION-MAKING**
Government determines how to respond

Example: The relevant minister holds a news conference to announce the government's intent to introduce a new policy. This may require that a bill be introduced, debated, and voted upon in the legislature. If the bill is successful, the relevant minister will publicly announce the details of the policy and how it will be implemented.

Example: Cabinet meets to discuss its options and make a decision on how to proceed. They may refer the matter to a cabinet committee for deeper scrutiny or consult with members of the government caucus to ascertain party support for the various policy options.

FIGURE 8.1 | The Public Policy Cycle

INSIDE CANADIAN POLITICS

Why Is There so Much Fuss Over Changes to the Census?

Section 91(6) of the constitution assigns responsibility for "the census and statistics" to the federal government. The census is the official collection and recording of information about citizens through the administration of a nationwide questionnaire every five years. It compiles data about Canadians and their communities, and informs public policy decisions by providing a detailed account of Canada's citizens in terms of age, education, ethnicity, immigration status, language, housing situation, family composition, marital status, occupation, place of work, and income. Governments rely on census data when distributing grants or transfer funds to different sized communities, when drawing electoral boundaries, or when deciding how and whether to deliver certain public services in different regions. The census is so important for policy-makers that the Statistics Act stipulates that the federal government must conduct it, and that it is against the law for citizens not to complete it.

From 1971 to 2006, Canada used two census questionnaires: the standard form, distributed to all households and consisting of eight questions about basic household composition, and the long-form questionnaire, distributed to a sample of the population and consisting of around fifty additional questions on topics including religion, ethnicity, and education. Response rates for both parts of the census typically fell over 80 percent. In 2010, the Harper government announced the cancellation of the mandatory long-form census questionnaire. It was replaced with the voluntary National Household Survey, on the grounds that in a free society, participating in the more detailed and personal portions of the census should be a citizen's choice. This libertarian approach was publicly supported by members of the Conservative Party of Canada and by a handful of interest groups, including the right-wing think tank the Fraser Institute. Critics argued that the optional census form would produce a lower response rate while increasing the sampling error and what researchers call *non-response bias*, particularly among such groups such as single parents, renters, and low-income Canadians. The result, they argued, would be less reliable data that would be far less useful in identifying and achieving policy objectives. Such criticism came from the opposition parties, medical and religious groups, arts organizations, municipalities, some provincial governments, numerous members of the academic community, and public policy and statistical associations. The controversy culminated with the resignation in July 2010 of the chief statistician of Canada. The cabinet did not bend, however, and the mandatory long-form questionnaire was discontinued in favour of the optional household survey. In 2015, one of the first policy announcements of the Justin Trudeau government was to re-establish the long-form questionnaire.

VOX POP

- Why does a country need a census? How much information is reasonable to ask?

- In what ways does the new, voluntary approach toward the long-form census affect governments' ability to develop and implement public policy? How likely are future governments to shift back to a mandatory long-form census?

Policy advisers must be familiar with a variety of tools and analytical methods. The tools an analyst considers are the various ways of addressing the policy issue in question. These include the following:

- new, amended, or repealed legislation;
- new, revised, or eliminated taxes;
- regulations;
- subsidies and grants;
- new or improved service provision;
- budget changes;
- information campaigns;
- public education and consultation; and
- bureaucratic and political reforms.[6]

Opportunities Available

Knowledge of Canadian Politics and Government Preferred!
Administrative Officer (Various Classifications)

**Manitoba Civil Service Commission
(Various Departments/Various Locations)**

The Manitoba government is recruiting applicants for the **Career Gateway Program** inventory. The **Career Gateway Program** is intended to attract Aboriginal people, persons with a disability, and visible minorities who are interested in a career with the Manitoba government. We are one of Canada's Top 100 Diversity employers. We have a substantial benefits package which includes extended health, health spending, dental, vision, long-term disability, supportive employment, maternity and parental leave, and a defined pension plan.

Applicants with backgrounds in any of the following job categories—finance, human resources, law, corrections, information technology, health, social services, engineering, policy, administration, management, transportation, education, trades, science, and other fields—are encouraged to apply. If candidates would like to be considered for specific categories, they are encouraged to indicate the applicable categories on their covering letter or resume.

Qualifications

- Education, training and/or experience relevant to field of expertise
- Good communication skills
- Strong interpersonal skills
- Values diversity
- Experience using Word, Excel, and Outlook is desired
- Ability to speak an Aboriginal language (Cree, Ojibway, etc.) and/or French is desired

Conditions of employment vary from position to position, but may include one or more of the following:

- Ability to travel
- Ability to work overtime
- Manitoba Driver's Licence
- Criminal Records Check
- Child Abuse Registry Check
- Adult Abuse Registry Check
- Security Check

Duties

Successful candidates will be hired on a term basis and introduced to the systems and processes of the Manitoba government. Depending on the position, candidates will gain directly relevant experience which will assist them in applying for future positions within the Manitoba government.

Source: http://jobsearch.gov.mb.ca/, Advertisement Number 28652

It is the analyst's job to assess the merits of the various courses of action. For instance, an analyst might attempt to predict the anticipated economic value of a possible policy, a common approach known as a *cost–benefit analysis*. Or the analyst might consider the benefits of the policy minus all of its possible financial implications. An *embedded cost–benefit analysis* combines these two approaches, by considering all of the possible costs and benefits to society. This approach is widely used in Government of Canada policy analysis.[7] These sorts of fiscal assessments are particularly important when the government's budget is under constraint, and the goal is to identify the most cost-efficient policy.

The research techniques a policy analyst will use in carrying out this assessment of the various policy options include media monitoring, literature and Internet searches, and public consultations. For large projects, the government outsources public opinion research, including surveys, polls, and focus groups. Increasingly, policy analysts are expected to gather such data themselves, by designing and administering online surveys, hosting group discussions, and conducting depth interviews. An increasingly common method of conducting public opinion research is *crowdsourcing*, whereby online discussion forums are set up and different perspectives are compiled from contributors with little effort or expense.

BRIEFING NOTES

Nudging

Policymakers often struggle when it comes to striking a balance between establishing incentives and establishing disincentives to shape citizens' behaviour. A policy that provides too generous an inducement in the form of, say, tax deductions or grants, may be criticized for wasting taxpayers' money; a policy that carries too hefty a sanction in the form of fines or regulations, may be criticized for being too coercive.

In response to this dilemma, policymakers have begun drawing lessons from academic studies that suggest citizens may be "nudged" into complying with the government's direction.[8] This means designing policy tools that *encourage* the desired behaviour, but that do not provide direct incentives or disincentives to ensure compliance. In their book *Nudge:*
Improving Decisions about Health, Wealth, and Happiness, Richard Thaler and Cass Sunstein cite the example of governments mandating grocery stores to display healthier foods at eye level as a means of encouraging individuals to shop and eat more responsibly, as opposed to subsidizing farmers or banning junk foods. In Canada, governments have taken similar steps when it comes to discouraging tobacco use, by requiring cigarette companies to print graphic images of the effects of smoking on peoples' health or by requiring retailers to keep cigarettes behind the counter out of sight. Neither of these nudge policies provides a direct incentive or disincentive to Canadians in the way that removing tax from smoking cessation aids or increasing cigarette taxes did.

VOX POP

What are some other instances of governments "nudging" citizens toward desired behaviour? What sorts of "nudges" do you think would be effective in encouraging more Canadians to take public transit or support the arts community, for example?

It is important to note that despite the care involved in carrying out these methods of analysis, public policy is not created in an ideological vacuum: policymakers—both elected and non-elected—are also influenced by their own opinions and underlying value systems. Once the agenda is set, policy advisers may consider any number of public policy theories as they identify the optimal course of action (see Table 8.1). Whether used alone or in combination, these theories provide means of determining and rationalizing the existence of a given policy. In this vein, the rational choice theory of how people behave has a profound effect on the study of politics and public policy. Initially expressed by American economist Anthony Downs in his landmark work *An Economic Theory of Democracy* (1957), the model supposes that humans routinely evaluate costs and benefits when making a decision, and are rational actors who seek to optimize their own personal situation. Though it is not without its critics, the theory can be used to explain a variety of political behaviours, and can help policymakers determine appropriate courses of action to address public issues. For instance, given the exceedingly low odds that a single vote will change the outcome of a national election, the costs of voting, including the effort exerted researching choices, the gasoline used to drive to the polling station, the time spent in line to vote, normally exceed the expected benefits. Through this lens, people who do not vote are more rational that those who do, a perspective that can help elections agencies figure out what, if anything, they can do to increase election turnout. This may involve highlighting additional incentives for voters (e.g., emphasizing the value of fulfilling one's civic duty), or creating disincentives for not voting (e.g., implementing a fine for failure to visit the polls).

This is just one theoretical approach, and is unsettling to many, because it discounts the value of the broad social benefits of living in a vibrant participatory democracy. In the end, public policy rarely, if ever, fits a single theoretical model. The application of many philosophical approaches by different participants tends to result in public policy that has integrated the perspectives of a variety of competing interests—though that approach in itself describes pluralism theory.

Given the vast array of information and considerations, how can a policy adviser possibly narrow down the available options and make the best possible recommendation (the next stage of the public policy cycle)? Public policy scholar Eugene Bardach points out that policy analysis is not an exact science and is not nearly as rigid as textbooks would have us believe. With experience, and through trial and error, policy analysts learn ways to apply less structure on problem-solving. He recommends that analysts follow the simplistic approach below.[9] He is careful to advise that it is only a guide and subject to interpretation; these are not instructions that must all be followed in sequence:

- Define the policy problem.
- Assemble some evidence.
- Construct the alternatives.
- Select the criteria to be used to assess the options.
- Project the outcomes of a policy decision.
- Confront the tradeoffs of the decision.
- Make a decision.
- Tell the story when communicating the decision.

rational choice theory
A theory that citizens are self-interested actors whose decisions fulfill their own needs and wants.

Bardach's approach illustrates the path that public policy follows, from problem definition through to communication. Its similarities with the public policy cycle outlined in Figure 8.1 suggest that, behind the scenes, policy analysts are present at each stage, from identifying the problem to analyzing its resolution.

Communicating policy advice (the next stage of the public policy cycle) requires careful consideration of the inherent biases of the policy adviser and the adviser's

TABLE 8.1 | Public Policy Concepts

Concept	Description and Example
derived externalities	The free market is prevented from addressing the side effects of government policy. **Example:** Medicare governs healthcare services and prevents the private sector from responding to public needs.
destructive competition	Too many businesses operating within an industry will damage the industry through intense market rivalry that deflates prices, lowers working conditions, and reduces profit margins. **Example:** The government issues too many liquor licences for the bar and nightclub industry.
elite theory	Policies are made by a handful of powerful people, particularly members of the political executive. **Example:** A premier unilaterally announces a policy decision without consulting the relevant minister or civil service.
imperfect information	Government, political actors, and the general public do not have sufficient information to make rational policy decisions. **Example:** We cannot be certain if unusual weather patterns are a result of climate change caused by humans.
institutional	The political system shapes policy outcomes. **Example:** The bicameral nature of Parliament normally produces deeper scrutiny of government policy than occurs in a unicameral provincial legislature.
natural monopoly	A large-capacity organization has the exclusive ability to develop infrastructure; however, it operates amid a lack of competition and market regulation of prices. **Example:** Government-funded hydroelectric megaprojects may lack the cost efficiencies that would occur if they operated in a free market.
pluralism	Interest groups attract volunteers who are in competition to influence public policy; sometimes the government funds groups to ensure sufficient diversity. **Example:** Economic and professional associations compete to shape public policy in a political arena that includes broader public interest groups receiving government grants.
political	Public policy is an imperfect outcome of political struggle. **Example:** The variation in post-secondary tuition fees across Canada is a result of localized political debates about policy choices.
rational choice	Citizens are self-interested and behave rationally to maximize their personal gains. **Example:** The government uses a variety of policy tools to discourage smoking, but some smokers are willing to put up with these inconveniences because to them the value of smoking outweighs the costs of quitting.
tragedy of the commons	There is no short-term requirement to sustain a common pool of resources for long-term benefit. **Example:** Atlantic fish stocks are fished to extinction.

superiors. For instance, partisans may interpret the viability of a policy option differently than permanent civil servants do, and their recommended approach is subject to change with evolving circumstances. This gives rise to what is known as the principal–agent problem. Only the principal decision-maker—normally the first minister or another member of cabinet—has the true authority to set public policy on behalf of the government. However, given the sheer volume of decisions confronting prime ministers, premiers, and ministers, some of these responsibilities must be delegated to employees. Political staff and the permanent civil service thus become agents for the principal decision-maker. This is a problem, because agents may arrive at different interpretations of policy than the principal might. This is a weakness of the democratic system of government and tends not to be appreciated by the general public, although it is often satirized, such as in the BBC TV programs *Yes, Minister* and *The Thick of It.*

Once developed and implemented, policies must be evaluated for their effectiveness (the next stage of the public policy cycle). Most public servants use the familiar "input–output–outcome" logic model to accomplish this evaluation, and it continues to form the foundation of most professional and master's programs in public administration. Program investments (*inputs*) are weighed against the participation of, and activities undertaken by, those who are targeted (*outputs*) and the short-, medium-, and long-term impacts on society of these activities (*outcomes*). For example, provincial and territorial governments all maintain policies when it comes to immunizing their residents against the seasonal flu. The desired outcome of these policies is to

principal–agent problem
A problem arising from the fact that someone (an agent) working on behalf of a decision-maker (the principal) may not take the course of action the principal intended.

© John Mitchell/Alamy Stock Photo

Public policy concepts can be used to predict how citizens might respond to a policy decision. Suppose the government is considering a policy response to a study showing that adult Canadians are, on average, more obese than they were 10 years ago. Among the policy options are (a) a tax on junk food, (b) a tax credit for adult fitness activities, (c) a new website providing information on fitness and nutrition, and (d) a new law requiring a larger display of nutritional information on food packaging. Assess each of these options from a rational choice perspective. Which would be most effective?

produce a healthier population. To achieve this, policymakers must assemble resources, including vaccination supplies, sites, and healthcare professionals to administer the vaccines, as well as public relations specialists to design promotional campaigns, and so on. These resources are used to produce concrete outputs, including a certain number of vaccinations per week or the launching of a province- or territory-wide television advertisement. Policymakers hope that these outputs will help to achieve the desired outcome: a healthier, flu-resistant population.

The policy cycle is closely linked to the election cycle (see Figure 8.2). Once elected, or re-elected, a government needs time to orient itself to power. During this start-up phase, ministers receive direction from their prime minister or premier, and public servants brief their respective ministers on the top issues in their portfolios. Once this onboarding stage is complete, the government enters the action phase of the election cycle. Typically beginning with the government's second budget, this period features an activist agenda designed to address many of the governing party's election promises and, if necessary, initiate any tough and potentially unpopular policy measures (e.g. increasing taxes or cutting programs). This action phase continues until late in year three, when the government begins taking steps to fix any remaining policy problems before the next election. The final six months of the election cycle are known as the red zone—a period in which the government announces or re-publicizes popular government initiatives in an effort to gain momentum in the upcoming campaign.

INSIDE CANADIAN POLITICS

How Can Policymakers Encourage Individuals to Fulfill Their Civic Duty?

Two policy examples reveal the challenges many governments and their agencies face when it comes to persuading citizens to perform their civic duty. Most political scientists agree that high voter turn-out signals a healthy democracy, just as most medical experts agree that a high vaccination rate is key to maintaining the benefits of herd immunity (i.e. insulating the most vulnerable people in society from preventable diseases by ensuring that those who can be immunized receive their shots). Most government officials would agree, although politicians often avoid public commitments to increasing either turnout or immunization rates, often for fear of alienating citizens averse to state intervention in these issues.

The question facing policymakers becomes, how do we persuade individuals to fulfill their civic duty to vote or to get vaccinated? One approach would be to encourage the behaviour through positive rewards, such as tax credits offered to citizens who show up to the polls or deductions on health premiums to citizens who receive a vaccination. Another would be to discourage undesirable behaviour—for instance, by making voting or getting vaccinated mandatory and imposing fines or other penalties for non-compliance.

VOX POP

Why do you think Canadian politicians have avoided taking more substantive steps to increasing voting and vaccination rates? Which approach do you think would be most effective when it comes to ensuring people vote or vaccinate? Would any "nudges" be more appropriate?

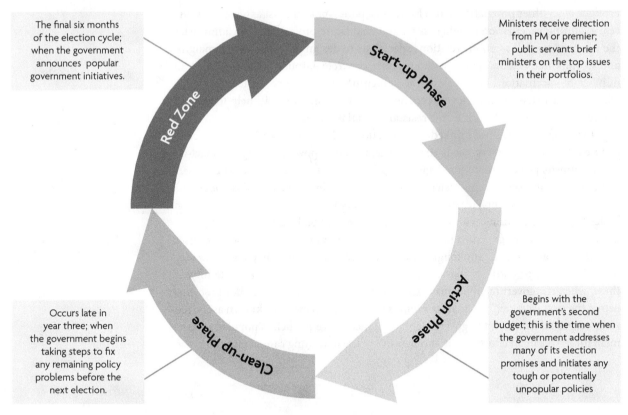

The final six months of the election cycle; when the government announces popular government initiatives.

Red Zone

Start-up Phase

Ministers receive direction from PM or premier; public servants brief ministers on the top issues in their portfolios.

Action Phase

Begins with the government's second budget; this is the time when the government addresses many of its election promises and initiates any tough or potentially unpopular policies

Clean-up Phase

Occurs late in year three; when the government begins taking steps to fix any remaining policy problems before the next election.

FIGURE 8.2 | Public Policy and the Election Cycle

Policy Options

Financial Administration

The ability of a government to make public policy decisions is highly dependent on its fiscal situation. The fiscal capacity of a government is enormous and is as varied as its population. To illustrate, in the 2012–13 fiscal year, the federal government generated $254.2 billion in revenues, $251 billion in program expenses, and $29 billion in public debt charges. To put this in perspective, the budget of the United States federal government is measured in trillions of dollars, while Prince Edward Island's entire budget is less than $1 billion.

The finances of the federal government, including Crown corporations, are governed by the Financial Administration Act. It establishes that the Treasury Board (a central agency that is supported by the Treasury Board Secretariat) shall preside over the government's financial decisions. The Treasury Board is a committee of five ministers, including the president of the Treasury Board, who is the chair. The scope of its authority is impressive: according to section 7 of the Act, it may take action on behalf of cabinet "on all matters" concerning the following:

- general administrative policy in the federal public administration;
- the organization of the federal public administration and how it is controlled;

Treasury Board The cabinet committee that is tasked with reviewing and authorizing government revenue and expenditure policies.

↻ The role of the Treasury Board Secretariat is discussed in Chapter 5, on the executive: see page 195.

- financial management (including "estimates, expenditures, financial commitments, accounts, fees or charges for the provision of services or the use of facilities, rentals, licences, leases, revenues from the disposition of property, and procedures by which departments manage, record and account for revenues received or receivable from any source whatever");
- determining the priorities of departmental spending and reviewing spending plans;
- the management of human resources in the federal public administration, including terms and conditions of employment, such as group insurance and benefit programs; and
- internal audits.

At both the federal and the provincial levels, the president of the Treasury Board is normally also the minister of finance. Section 15 of the Financial Administration Act stipulates that the federal department of finance is responsible for "the supervision, control and direction of all matters relating to the financial affairs of Canada not by law assigned to the Treasury Board or to any other minister." It further states that estimated expenditures by the government must be presented to Parliament. As per section 64 of the Act, by December 31, the president of the Treasury Board must submit the annual report of the government's accounts, comprising its expenditures, revenues, assets, and liabilities, to the House of Commons. Furthermore, every three months, departments must prepare financial statements and identify any "significant changes to operations, personnel and programs," which the department's minister must release to the public within 60 days (section 65.1). Provincial governments have their own treasury boards that generally follow the same processes as their federal counterpart.

As discussed in Chapter 6, each year the minister of finance delivers a budget to the legislature, in order to obtain approval from the people's representatives for the government's planned revenues and expenditures. Is the government spending beyond its means, requiring it to borrow money? If so, it is running a budget deficit and is said to be "in the red." Many view this as sensible fiscal policy during an economic downturn, when society may benefit from government spending to provide stimulus for job growth or to bolster social support programs, but getting out of deficit and balancing the budget then becomes a major political challenge. What if the government has been running an annual deficit for many years and is under pressure

> **budget deficit** A situation in which spending exceeds revenues during a given period.
>
> **stimulus** Increased government spending to encourage job growth amid an economic downturn.

BRIEFING NOTES

In the Black and In the Red

The expressions "in the black" and "in the red" originate in ages-old accounting practices, when operating expenses were recorded using red ink, and revenues in black. If revenues exceed expenditures once the ledger is tallied, the organization is running a surplus and is said to be in the black. If not, the organization is running a deficit and is in the red.

public debt The accumulated amount borrowed by a government to finance budgets and considered owing.

interest rate The percentage rate of money charged by lenders to borrowers.

↻ See the ICP box How Do Federal and Provincial Budgets Intersect?, beginning on page 106 of Chapter 3, for more information on how cuts to the federal budget affected the provinces.

budget surplus A situation in which revenues exceed spending during a given period.

to make spending cuts? In this situation, the government is concerned not only about getting its spending under control but about the implications of years of overspending. Paying down the public debt, which is the sum of money borrowed to finance the government's budget deficits plus any interest charges incurred, moves up the public agenda. Public debt mounts as budget deficits accumulate, and as governments borrow funds to spend on things like roads, bridges, schools, and other infrastructure projects. Given these constraints, promoting a public policy that will cost money is more likely to be successful when the government is in a spending mode, especially in an election year, than it is in an environment of spending cuts, particularly in the post-election period.

A large public debt is a problem when the prospects of repayment diminish and when interest rates are high. The same is true of private debts, as accumulated by corporations and individuals in Canada. The Bank of Canada, which is an independent federal Crown corporation that works closely with the federal department of finance, sets the minimum national interest rate that is followed by lending institutions like banks that loan money to Canadians and their businesses. The central bank's interest rate policy is influenced by a multitude of domestic and international economic considerations. A low rate encourages borrowing and spending. As a monetary policy tool, it contributes to devaluing the national currency in international markets. This increases the price of imports, but in turn a cheaper currency improves the attractiveness of goods and services offered by domestic manufacturers. This may stimulate economic growth; however, economic growth can cause inflation, which erodes Canadians' buying power, and the risk of bankruptcies rises. A higher interest rate is then introduced to cool the economy; however, one outcome is that interest payments on the public debt increase, which decreases the availability of funds for other policy initiatives.

In the early 1990s, after nearly three decades of annual deficits combined with high interest rates, the federal government amassed a debt of over $550 billion. At one point, 37 per cent of its debt repayment went simply to meeting the interest payments. To get the debt under control, the Chrétien government introduced significant spending cuts to the civil service, the military, employment insurance, provincial transfers, and other national departments and programs. By 1997, the deficit was gone and debt repayment began. However, the spending cuts created other policy problems by forcing a number of programs, in particular social programs administered by provincial governments, to operate with greatly reduced budgets.

What if the government finds itself with extra money? By the 2000s, the federal government's balance sheet was so strong that it was able to pay down debt, and it found itself with money to fund new policy options. In such a scenario, the government operates a budget surplus and is "in the black." Surpluses often invite questions as to whether the government is over-taxing or under-spending, the answer to which depends on the ideological perspective of the observer (see Table 8.2). Those on the political left in Canada believe that surpluses should be used to support or enhance public programs and services, while those on the right believe they should be reduced through tax relief and debt repayment. In the case of federal government surpluses, advocates for provincial governments often call for an increase in federal–provincial transfers to address the fiscal imbalances discussed in Chapter 3.

TABLE 8.2 | General Ideological Approaches to Budgeting

Left-Wing Ideology	Right-Wing Ideology
In times of budget deficit	
Increase: • spending • borrowing • taxes	**Maintain:** • taxes **Decrease:** • spending • borrowing • programs and services
Maintain: • programs and services	
Delay: • debt repayment • spending reductions	**Delay:** • debt repayment • tax increases
In times of budget surplus	
Increase: • spending • programs and services	**Increase:** • debt repayment **Maintain:** • programs and services
Maintain: • revenues • taxes	**Decrease:** • revenues • taxes
Delay: • debt repayment	**Delay:** • spending increases

Economic downturns, like the Great Recession that began in 2008, often bring an end to budget surpluses, encouraging governments to engage in deficit financing and borrow money to fund infrastructure projects in an attempt to stimulate economic growth. This approach forms the foundation of the Justin Trudeau government's approach to budget management. In this way, the government follows a budget cycle, with periods of expansion and growth followed by retrenchment and cutbacks.

BRIEFING NOTES

Public Debts in Canada

Unlike countries with weaker economies, which borrow directly from international lenders and banks, Canadian governments borrow most of their money from domestic and foreign investors by issuing securities and selling government bonds through capital markets. It is also worth noting that some of Canada's more prosperous provinces—including BC, Alberta, and Saskatchewan—have established long-term savings and investment accounts. These funds may be counted as government assets, and weighed against any debts the governments owe to lenders.

Funding the Public Service

collective bargaining
The formal negotiation of the terms of an employment contract between the representatives of a group of employees and their employer.

labour union An organization of workers that represents its members' interests, especially in bargaining with their employer.

A significant component of a government's financial administration is its ability to maintain a suitable level of pay and benefits for its employees. The collective bargaining process is a source of considerable pressure on political executives. They are tasked with the difficult proposition of simultaneously controlling public spending, paying competitive wages to retain and attract public servants, and ensuring that optimal levels of government services are offered with minimal interruption. Conversely, a labour union (or *trade union*) seeks to optimize contract matters for its members, including wages and benefits, hours of work, workplace conditions, job classifications and duties, and human resource matters such as terms of hiring, promotion, and dismissal. Unions are funded through membership dues that must be paid by all members of a unionized workforce. When a labour agreement is reached, the terms of employment are detailed in a collective bargaining agreement that is in effect for a specified period, such as four years; upon its expiry, a new deal must be negotiated. The collective bargaining process is partly funded by the trade union's membership, who have mandatory deductions on their paychecks that finance union personnel salaries and operational costs.

Collective bargaining presents two challenges for government. First, some of the most powerful unions in the country work on behalf of public servants. Unions representing civil servants include the country's largest union, the Canadian Union

Politicians and journalists are fond of comparing public finances with household budgets. Rhetoric during recent election campaigns encourages Canadians to think about public spending around the kitchen table, as opposed to around the boardroom tables of Canada's financial districts. Most economists and political scientists question the wisdom of comparing public and private finances, however. What are some of the major differences between the way Canadians handle their personal or family budgets and the way governments do? What lessons could governments take from the way households maintain their budgets?

wong yu liang/Shutterstock.com

INSIDE CANADIAN POLITICS
Why Aren't Governments Required to Balance their Budgets?

After years of budget deficits, the Harper Conservative government promised to introduce balanced budget legislation to help guide its approach to revenues and expenditures. Passed in 2015, the Federal Balanced Budget Act made Parliament the eighth Canadian legislature to have a balanced budget law, which has existed in various forms in every province except Newfoundland and Labrador, Nova Scotia, and PEI. Overall, these laws are designed to require governments to balance their revenues with expenditures; individually, each includes its own provisions to regulate spending growth and the use of surpluses, restrict tax increases, and set aside rainy day, or contingency, funds. Some laws have gone so far as to impose reductions on ministers' salaries in the event of a budget deficit; most rely on transparency provisions to hold the government publicly accountable for failing to balance its books.

Much like the fixed-date election laws described in Chapter 11, balanced budget legislation can be amended or repealed at any time. On the campaign trail in 2015, Justin Trudeau pledged to scrap the Harper government's balanced budget law, for instance, in favour of running deficits to finance infrastructure investments. The Liberals' stance separated them from the Conservatives and NDP, who pledged to run balanced budgets. Notwithstanding Trudeau's victory, proponents of the laws have held them up as tools to allow politicians to say no to special interests seeking increased public spending, and as security against increased debt loads. Critics see them as tying governments' hands during economic downturns—the precise occasions when increased government spending is required to support the most vulnerable and stimulate the economy.

Research is mixed when it comes to the effectiveness of balanced budget legislation in Canada. While jurisdictions with balanced budget laws have, nonetheless, run deficits and amended their legislation to permit them to do so, it is impossible to determine whether those deficits would have been larger had the legislation not been in place.

VOX POP

Is balanced budget legislation worthwhile? What would the implications be if balanced budget requirements were enshrined in the Canadian constitution, as has been proposed in the United States? Why do you suppose that the only three provinces without balanced budget legislation are on Canada's east coast?

of Public Employees (CUPE), and the Public Service Alliance of Canada (PSAC). Unifor Canada is the country's largest private-sector union, formed through the 2013 merger of the Canadian Auto Workers and the Communications, Energy and Paperworkers unions. In addition to collective bargaining, these interest groups engage in political activism to achieve their members' policy objectives. Labour union support for left-wing political parties, including formal alliances with the New Democratic Party, adds a pressure dynamic no matter which party is in power.

Provincial governments must navigate particularly challenging contract demands from civil servants, doctors, nurses, homecare workers, police officers, teachers, professors, road maintenance workers, administrative staff, and a variety of other public-sector employees. Those workers' unions often argue that their members are underpaid compared with workers in other jurisdictions, and they may balk at the terms of employment being offered. To apply pressure, unions may urge their members to take up work-to-rule tactics, that is, to refuse to perform any extra services beyond those that are required under the bargained agreement, or they may threaten to or go on strike. This can cause civil unrest if services are interrupted, especially at peak demand, for example, if teachers or snowplow operators are off the job in January as opposed to July. In some cases, the sector may have been deemed an essential service to remove the threat of job action, and in other instances the government may impose the terms of an agreement by introducing back-to-work legislation. These tensions often end in court action, with the Supreme Court of Canada ruling at various times in favour and against the notion that the Charter of Rights and Freedoms encompasses the right to strike.

The second challenge presented by collective bargaining concerns the private—not the public—sector. Because the government is interested in the smooth running of the state and the economy, it has an interest in ensuring labour peace in the private sector, as well. The unionization rate varies across the country (see Figure 8.3), and unionized employees generally enjoy a better quality of life than non-unionized workers do. However, work disruptions and stoppages can grow from an internal matter to a broader public policy problem. Polarized negotiations and the breaking off of contract talks can lead to tense situations: both sides may run advertising campaigns to generate public sympathy for their cause; picketers may attempt to prevent access to buildings; unions become irate when replacement workers (pejoratively known as "scabs") are brought in by employers; workers may be under financial duress as their strike pay dries up; and businesses may threaten to relocate or shut down permanently. Moreover, unionized employees in one sector may support their so-called

↻ See page 75 in Chapter 2 for a discussion of the Alberta Labour reference, in which the Supreme Court determined the right to strike is not guaranteed under the Charter of Rights and Freedoms.

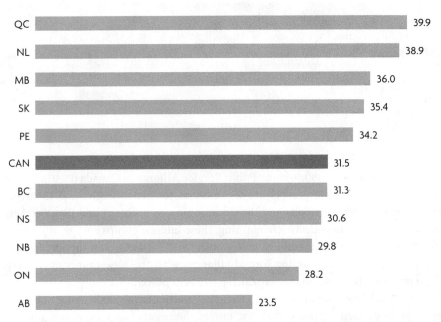

FIGURE 8.3 | Unionization Rates, Canada and its Provinces (% of employees)

Source: Statistics Canada, Labour Force Survey, 1997 to 2012.

THEY SAID IT

Labour Unions in Canada

#CAUT poll says 70 per cent of Canadians say unions #canlab are still needed despite years of Tory union bashing.

—Canadian Labour (@CanadianLabour)

Quebec corruption inquiry turns focus to unions.

—CBC Top Stories (@CBCNews)

As unions lose power, Canada gets the blue-collar blues.

—Globe and Mail (@globeandmail)

A strike began today at the Univ of Windsor which involves #CUPE1393 professional, trade and technical employees.

—CUPE 129 (@CUPE129)

We're proud to have been a part of creating a change in the federal gov. Now we're expecting @JustinTrudeau to live up to it.

—Unifor Canada (@UniforTheUnion)

In January 2015, the Supreme Court of Canada struck down a Saskatchewan law that would have prevented some public-sector employees from striking. The law would have applied to public employees in certain "essential services," including healthcare, policing, and education. Are there some government sectors where employees should not be permitted to walk off the job?

union "brothers and sisters" by refusing to cross the picket line. All of this civil unrest is fodder for media coverage and, as the situation escalates or negotiations reach a standstill, calls for government involvement. To this end, most federal and provincial governments have ministries of labour that offer mediation and conciliation services, with provinces also enforcing employment standards and workplace safety.

In general, as discussed above, people and parties on the left side of Canada's political spectrum tend to support the rights of workers and the actions of unions. People and parties on the right tend to side with private and public-sector employers, as did the Harper government when it passed Bill C-377 in 2015, requiring unions to take extraordinary measures to publicly report their expenditures.

Government Revenues

The federal (Figure 8.4) and provincial (Figure 8.5) governments raise money through a number of major recurring revenue sources. The most universal method of generating government revenues is through taxes. Canada's public bodies all raise funds through taxation. Taxation policy details the requirements for citizens and corporate bodies to pay money to the public treasury, and this money is used to finance government spending. Individuals and businesses are taxed in a plethora of ways, including income tax, sales tax, property tax, licences and fees, gas taxes, and payroll taxes, among others. This is in addition to payments citizens make into mandatory benefit programs, notably the Canada Pension Plan and employment insurance, and some dedicated levies, fees, or premiums for services like education and healthcare. Such policies normally originate as bills in the corresponding elected legislature.

There are two broad ways of collecting taxes in Canada. Direct taxation occurs when the taxpayer pays the government without the involvement of any other body. Examples of direct taxation include fees charged by a government department for a liquor licence or a driver's licence. Another example is a property tax. The provinces delegate that authority to municipalities, which collect funds from property owners, normally using a mill rate that calculates a percentage of the estimated value of the property. In some communities, local government is financed through a poll tax, which is a fixed amount paid by all residents regardless of whether or not they own property.

The second way of collecting taxes is through indirect taxation, whereby the taxpayer gives funds to an intermediary, who then transmits the funds to the government. Examples of indirect taxation include income tax, if the employee allows the employer to make paycheque deductions, and sales tax. The federal, provincial, and territorial governments all have income tax policies. To streamline the process, the Canada Revenue Agency collects personal income tax on behalf of all governments except for that of Quebec, which does so itself, and corporate income tax on behalf of all governments, except for those of Alberta and Quebec.

The most recognizable form of indirect taxation is a sales tax, which is a levy applied to the final sale of a good or service. The seller collects the tax from the buyer, and the seller transmits the money to the government on the buyer's behalf. For example, if the price of a can of pop is advertised at a convenience store as $1.00, and the sales tax is 5 per cent, then by law the store will charge $1.05 and remit 5 cents to the government. The federal government requires a sales tax, the goods and services tax (GST), throughout Canada, and all provinces except Alberta have some form of a

taxation policy The regulations, mechanisms, and rates set by government to generate revenues from people and businesses in its jurisdiction.

direct taxation The collection of taxes by government without using an intermediary.

indirect taxation The collection of taxes by an intermediate body on behalf of the government.

sales tax A revenue-generating tax charged by a government on the sale of applicable goods and services.

GST A federal value-added tax applied to the sale of most goods and services in Canada.

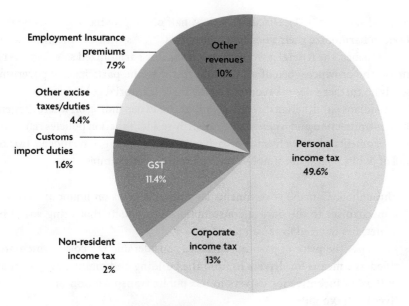

FIGURE 8.4 | Federal Government Revenues

Note: Rounded figures, using 2013–14 data. Percentages calculated by authors.

Source: Modified with percentages calculated from Government of Canada. 2013. Budget Plan, Table 4.2.5. http://www
.budget.gc.ca/2013/doc/plan/chap4-2-eng.html#a0-Chapter-4.2:-Fiscal-Planning-Framework.

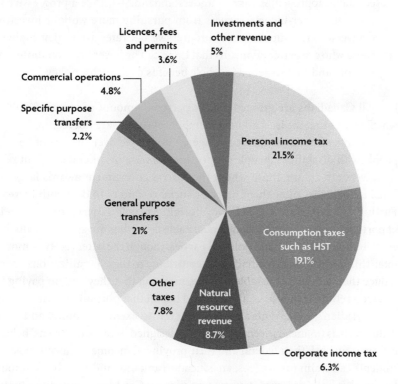

FIGURE 8.5 | Consolidated Provincial Government Revenues, All Provinces

Source: Data from provincial ministries of finance, mean of budget estimates and plans, 2013–14.

provincial sales tax (PST). Discussed below, half of the provincial governments have chosen to harmonize their sales taxes with the GST. As with the income tax system outside Quebec, the federal government collects this harmonized sales tax (HST) revenue on the provinces' behalf and reimburses it to the participating governments. There is no further sales tax required by the three territorial governments.

Canadians pay different direct and indirect taxes depending on where they engage in a sales transaction and where they ordinarily reside. Taxation policies reflect different governments' philosophical approaches and financial capacity. Indeed, taxation is a tool of public policy, not simply a revenue source. For example:

- Throughout Canada, governments levy sizeable taxes on liquor and tobacco as a mechanism to discourage consumption of products that bring social harm, sometimes referred to as "sin taxes".
- Likewise, the price of gasoline includes considerable tax costs, which are justified as a means for drivers to fund the building and maintenance of roads as well as an incentive for drivers to use public transportation or other alternatives to automobiles.
- Perspectives on income tax rates also vary by province and territory. A *flat tax* policy, as existed in Alberta from 1999 to 2015, taxes all income above a certain threshold at a single rate. Conversely, a *progressive tax* policy, which is the norm across Canada, is an incremental scale so that those with the highest incomes pay the highest tax rate. The proponents of a flat tax maintain that it is the most equitable approach, is easy to understand, and—unlike a progressive tax—does not deter upper-income earners from pursuing more work or investing locally. Conversely, the supporters of progressive tax rates argue that higher taxes on those who are better off means that there can be lower taxes on those who are less well off, and that society as a whole benefits from such a policy.

All Canadians are granted a basic personal amount of at least $11,000 tax-free, which means that the least affluent members of society are not required to pay income tax. Parents of children under the age of 18, people over the age of 65, pensioners, people with disabilities, people supporting a spouse or other dependent relative, and caregivers are among those whom the federal government awards larger basic personal amounts to allow them more financial resources to deal with increased costs. Further deductions are available for Aboriginal people living on reserves and residents of northern areas. A proportion of charitable donations are also tax-deductible, as are contributions to unions and political parties, though the latter receive a more generous rate. This means that Canadians who contribute to these organizations are entitled to reduce their amount of taxable income, meaning that they end up paying less tax or receive a refund if they have already paid tax on that portion of their income.

tax credits A tax exemption on money spent on a specific activity, up to a specified limit.

Canadian governments also offer tax credits, exempt amounts, and various other deductions as financial incentives that are designed to reward citizens' behaviour. For instance, on both their federal and their provincial income tax forms, post-secondary students can claim tuition fees, an education amount, and a textbook amount, which tells us that both orders of government support Canadians' pursuit of higher education. Provincial and territorial governments may supplement federal tax credits with their own tax credits. For example, New Brunswick is one of a number of jurisdictions that offers a small business investor tax credit and a venture capital tax credit, which are designed to encourage investment in provincial businesses and stimulate economic growth. Such tax incentives are an important policy tool and yet the practice invites questions about social engineering.

It is noteworthy that governments pay for tax credits and deductions by giving up revenues they would have otherwise collected. The federal Conservative Party prioritized the use of tax credits and deductions as a policy initiative and a campaign tool. They identified segments of the electorate who they believed were likely to vote Tory and campaigned on micro-policy pledges to create tax breaks for those voters. Families were targeted through the creation of the Children's Fitness Tax Credit, the Children's Arts Tax Credit, the Family Caregiver Tax Credit, and the First-Time Home Buyers' Tax Credit. Other credits targeted at specific constituencies have included the Volunteer Firefighter Tax Credit, the Tradesperson's Tools deduction, and the Tax Credit for Public Transit. Supporters claim that this is smart public policy that puts money back in the pockets of taxpayers, whereas critics lament the millions of dollars in forgone revenues that could be used to finance government programs. Moreover, this approach to tax policy reduced the future ability of opposition parties to propose grandiose government programs without also proposing to increase taxes, wrap up tax credit programs, cut other spending, and/or go into deficit, as the 2015 Liberal Party of Canada platform attested.

Governments do more than tax income, of course; they also tax Canadians as they consume goods and services. In this vein, the GST is a sales tax added to the price

Michael Stuparyk/GetStock.com

Liberal and Conservative governments vowed to repeal or reduce the goods and services tax after it was introduced in 1991. Yet the Harper government's decision to lower the GST by 2 percentage points was not universally embraced. Critics lamented the loss of $15 billion in revenue that could be used to finance social programs, lower the debt, or reduce income taxes. Following the federal government's decision to lower the GST, provincial NDP governments in Nova Scotia and Manitoba took advantage of this new tax room by increasing their respective sales taxes. What are the implications of lowering consumption taxes like the GST? What arguments could governments use to sell a tax increase to the electorate?

of most products and services in Canada, with some exceptions, such as groceries and medical services. Because the intent is to apply the tax only to the finished product and not to any goods and services used in the manufacturing process, the GST is

INSIDE CANADIAN POLITICS

What Happens When Direct Democracy Meets Tax Policy?

Harmonizing sales taxes is not as straightforward as it may seem. It involves melding together two sets of tax rules, meaning that overall rates on certain goods and services may increase or decrease depending on the details of the federal-provincial agreement. These changes can spark public unrest, which is magnified in provinces that have strongly populist political cultures and institutions, like BC.

British Columbia's Recall and Initiative Act is unique in Canada. If a sufficient number of eligible voters sign a petition to remove a sitting MLA from office, the province's citizens can force a by-election. Likewise, a petition can be used to force the government to reconsider existing public policy or introduce new policy. Both of these elements of BC's direct democracy system came into play in July 2009, when the BC government announced an agreement to harmonize the 7 per cent provincial sales tax with the 5 per cent GST.

According to the provincial government's deal with Ottawa, the province would receive a $1.6 billion HST transition payment from the federal government, and BC would save $30 million annually in administration costs. While the sales tax would be lowered on some goods and services—in particular, on new homes—it would go up on a suite of routine consumer purchases such as haircuts, magazines, dry cleaning, taxi rides, movie tickets, phone and cable bills, and restaurant meals.

Not everyone was in favour of the change, and a petition campaign was launched to recall certain

government MLAs and trigger an initiative vote. In September 2010, after reviewing the petition application, the province's Select Standing Committee on Legislative Initiatives recommended that an initiative vote be held. In March 2011, the government announced instead that a province-wide referendum would be held by mail-in ballot. To pass, the referendum would require a simple majority (50 percent plus 1), whereas the initiative vote would have also required majorities in each of at least two-thirds of electoral districts. Unlike the complex questions used in Quebec sovereignty referendums (see Chapter 4), the question wording was straightforward: "Are you in favour of extinguishing the HST (harmonized sales tax) and reinstating the PST (provincial sales tax) in conjunction with the GST (goods and services tax)?"

Throughout the summer of 2011, the Fight HST Society advocacy group spearheaded the "yes" campaign and the Smart Tax Alliance group urged electors to vote no. Over 3 million voting packages were sent, and 1.6 million voters sent in a vote, for a turnout rate of 49.4 per cent. The results were 54.7 per cent in favour of the petition and 45.3 per cent against. Consequently, the government chose to repeal the HST, and the province had to return the $1.6 billion transition payment. The total cost of the referendum to Elections BC was over $8 million.

It is noteworthy that, at various points in time, laws in some provinces have required governments to hold elections or referendums before introducing major tax increases.

VOX POP

What are the advantages and downsides of deciding taxation policy through popular vote? Why do you think that voters rejected adopting the HST in referendums in Ontario and BC, but in the Atlantic provinces the conversion to a harmonized sales tax was met with general acceptance and was passed smoothly?

known as a value-added tax. This means businesses can claim a GST rebate on certain eligible expenses incurred in the creation of the final product or service. As well, low-income Canadians can apply for a GST rebate, in recognition that higher proportions of their incomes are being used to pay for taxable goods and services. The introduction of the GST in 1991 was designed to assuage concerns voiced by businesses that they were unable to compete internationally with the application of a manufacturers' tax of 13.5 per cent that was hidden, built into the sticker price of a product. Brian Mulroney's Progressive Conservative government proposed to replace that sales tax with a visible sales tax of 7 per cent. The public outrage was so significant that three Tory MPs quit the party. The Liberal-dominated Senate refused to pass the bill, and so, quite unusually, Mulroney invoked section 26 of the Constitution Act, 1867, which allows the government to appoint four or eight additional senators under special circumstances. As mentioned in one of the briefing notes in Chapter 6, the appointment of eight PC senators brought more controversy but ensured the passage of the bill. This debate over the federal government's monetary policy coincided with intense public debate over free trade.

In 1996, Jean Chrétien's Liberal government negotiated the fusion of the GST with the provincial sales tax (PST) in three provinces: New Brunswick, Nova Scotia, and Newfoundland and Labrador. The rationale for the new harmonized sales tax (HST) was that by streamlining operations, this would produce major cost savings for both orders of government and would reduce the administrative burden on business. But when the premiers of Ontario and British Columbia negotiated deals to transition to an HST policy effective July 2010, the plans were met with organized protests. The harmonized tax proceeded in Ontario but had to be repealed after its introduction in BC. In 2013, Prince Edward Island became the fifth province to adopt the HST, while four others retain both the GST and PST. Alberta remains the only province without a PST or HST.

In 2006 and again in 2008, the Harper government cut the GST by a percentage point, reducing it from 7 per cent to 5 per cent. This move allowed some provinces to increase their provincial sales tax rates commensurately, occupying the tax room vacated by the federal reduction.

Government Spending

As with its approach to revenue-raising, government spending intersects with our lives in many ways. The state's mix of taxing and spending ensures that society's wealth is shared through the redistribution of funds from the well-off to the less-fortunate, and that all Canadians enjoy a baseline quality of life through the provision of public services. Above all else, government seeks to ensure that citizens are safe and have the basic necessities of life, namely access to water and food, clothing and shelter. Public safety is a significant policy priority, but the bulk of government spending is focused on helping young families and seniors; those who fall on hard times when they lose their job, get sick, or experience some other type of crisis; and citizens who are perpetually homeless, unemployed, and/or poor. Examples of the many programs and services that are available include the following:

- *Feeling unwell?* Citizens who require medical attention and who meet residency status are eligible for healthcare services within Canada. Residents of northern

↻ The debate over free trade is discussed on pages 571–3 of Chapter 14, on Canada in the World.

harmonized sales tax (HST) In Atlantic Canada and Ontario, a value-added consumption tax that combines both federal and provincial rates.

↻ See pages 262–3 of Chapter 7 for a description of the public safety portfolio.

areas who are required to travel a long distance for specialized medical services may qualify for travel grants. Residents who have travelled outside the country may be eligible for some of the costs of emergency health services. Non-essential services such as cosmetic surgery are seldom covered. Provinces may provide additional services; for instance, Ontario covers annual eye examinations for youth and seniors, and for people with medical conditions.

- *Don't have food or shelter?* Meals, lodging, clothing, and counselling are available on an emergency basis in male-only and female-only shelters. For instance, in the city of Peterborough, Ontario, men may stay for up to six months in a local mission, depending on their circumstances; women may be eligible for both short-stay services and subsidized housing. Other temporary housing is available for youths 16–24 years old and for young families. Occupants may stay in an emergency shelter for up to six weeks before moving into transitional housing, where up to 12 young people live together while paying rent. They may also receive a monthly supply of food from an emergency food bank. During emergencies, such as the Toronto ice storm in 2013 and southern Alberta floods in 2014, the provincial government may distribute debit cards to affected residents.

- *Having a child?* The federal government provides parental leave through the Employment Insurance program. The federal government also provides subsidies to Canadians to help defray the costs of whatever childcare services the parents deem appropriate. In Quebec, a subsidized system allows parents to choose between childcare, daycare, and home childcare services for a cost of $7 to $20 per day, depending on their income. In addition to paying for their primary and secondary schooling, governments also provide a series of tax credits to offset the costs of enrolling children in sports and cultural activities.

- *Need career-related training?* Many government programs exist to encourage Canadians to obtain the education they need to find and maintain employment. Federal and provincial governments offer student loans and grants for post-secondary education. Specialized training incentives exist for students, Aboriginal people, people with disabilities, older workers, and people who are illiterate. Provinces offer employment services that assist new Canadians with transitioning into the workforce; literacy, math, official language, and basic skills training; employment counselling services; and labour market information, such as job postings and career profiles. Also, the federal government maintains a series of labour market agreements with the provinces, which ensure that training for recipients of employment insurance benefits will emphasize current labour needs.

- *Want to start your own business?* A variety of government programs exist to assist Canadians to become self-employed. For example, entrepreneurs who demonstrate that their business has market and sales potential and long-term viability, and who have expertise in the field, may be eligible for loans and consulting advice through the Business Development Bank of Canada. In Ontario, funding is available for research infrastructure, for international research, and for green technology, while students may receive a grant of up to $3,000 to start a summer business.

These examples of government spending make up only a tiny sample of the variety of ways that the public sector works to improve the quality of life for Canadians.

Governments have many major recurring expenditure items (see Table 8.3), none greater than the programs that are collectively referred to as the *social safety net*. Over time, especially since the hardships of the Great Depression, governments have invested more into the expansion of the welfare state, and these systems vary greatly from jurisdiction to jurisdiction, given each province's and territory's authority over the policy area. There is no definitive list of government-funded programs that fit within the social safety net category, but we can broadly distinguish between *entitlements* and *insurance programs*.

↻ For a discussion of the social safety net, see The Politics of Fiscal Federalism, beginning on page 103 of Chapter 3.

a) Entitlement Programs

Entitlement programs represent part of the social contract between Canadians and their government. Citizens can be reasonably confident that these supports will always be available as resources allow, though the specific eligibility criteria and scope of services may be subject to change. As the welfare state has expanded, the federal government has created policies that entitle eligible citizens to receive financial assistance. This is often in conjunction with provincial governments; alternatively a federal program may supplement autonomous provincial policies. The most notable ones focus on supporting citizens prior to their normal working years, and after they exit the workforce.

A major federal government policy, initiated in 1944, is the family allowance, commonly referred to as the baby bonus. The financial needs of families with young

baby bonus A government policy that awards money to parents of young children.

TABLE 8.3 | Federal Government Expenditures

Expenditure	Percentage (%) of Total Program Expenses
Direct program expenses: $122.1 billion	
Operating expenses	32.1
Transfer payments	14.6
Capital amortization	2.0
Major transfers to persons: $70.4 billion	
Elderly benefits	16.0
Employment Insurance benefits	7.0
Children's benefits	5.1
Major transfers to other governments: $58.5 billion	
Canada Health Transfer (CHT)	11.4
Canada Social Transfer (CST)	4.7
Other health and social transfers	0.1
Fiscal arrangements	7.1
Gas Tax Fund	0.8
Other major transfers	0.5
Other transfers*	–1.3*
Total program expenses: $251 billion	100%

*Reflects recovery of a tax point transfer from Quebec under the terms of the CHT and CST.
Note: Rounded figures using 2012-13 data. Percentages calculated by authors.
Source: Government of Canada, Budget Plan (2013): Table 4.2.6. www.budget.gc.ca/2013/doc/plan/chap4-2-eng. html#a0-Chapter-4.2:-Fiscal-Planning-Framework.

BRIEFING NOTES
Entitlement Programs and the Federal Spending Power

Previous federally sponsored programs like the Universal Child Care Benefit and the Millennium Scholarship initiative are prime examples of the use of the federal spending power, through which Ottawa spends in areas of provincial jurisdiction. As described in Chapters 2 and 3, these sorts of pan-Canadian programs are welcomed by provincial governments that favour government intervention, national standards, and additional revenues; they are opposed by provincial governments that prefer to maintain constitutional authority over social programs.

children became acute as soldiers returned from war and the baby boom began. Initially a universal program, the family allowance provided monthly payments of $5 to $8 to parents for every child in their care who was up to 16 years of age. Renamed the Universal Child Care Benefit, prior to the 2015 election, it paid each family $160 per month for every child under 6 years of age, and $60 per month for every child between 6 and 17 years of age. This monthly payment was in addition to a federal tax credit for two-parent families, worth up to $2,000. To assist low-income families and those with children with disabilities, the federal government also maintained the Canada Child Tax Benefit, which paid eligible families over $175 a month for each child under 18 years of age. This suite of family-based programs was the topic of significant debate in the 2015 federal election campaign, and subject to change by Justin Trudeau's government, who pledged to move away from universal benefits to ones targeted at lower-income families. Some provincial governments have separate baby bonus and assistance programs provided in addition to the family allowance.

We also take for granted that most Canadian children attend publicly funded schooling from kindergarten to grade 12, with private schools and home schooling available as alternatives. Provincial governments fund and maintain these school systems, with financial support from the federal government through the Canada Social Transfer (CST). However, Canadian governments have not made it a priority to fully subsidize post-secondary education. Most of the costs of public college and university programming are paid for by provincial governments; nevertheless, tuition fees, textbooks, living costs, and other expenses are the responsibility of students. The expense of a post-secondary education is such that it could prevent students from lower income households from enrolling. To address this policy problem, in 1964 the government of Canada introduced the Canada Student Loans program. The program provides loans to eligible students that begin incurring interest six months after graduation. Most provinces and territories supplement Canada Student Loans with their own student loan and grant programs. These funds are intended to be supplemented with other funding, including non-repayable grants and savings accumulated in a Registered Education Savings Plan. The idea is to subsidize the costs of studying at a public post-secondary school for those who demonstrate financial need, while

Canada Student Loans A federal program that helps qualifying students access post-secondary education by awarding them interest-free repayable loans while they study full-time.

Bernard Weil/GetStock.com

Most estimates now peg the average Canadian student's loan debt at over $25,000 by the time they complete or abandon their post-secondary education. What are the societal impacts of saddling graduates with this much debt, if they are unable to secure well-paying jobs? What other public policy tools, beyond student loan programs, would be effective in achieving the desired outcomes?

simultaneously placing responsibility on students, who will gain a competitive edge in the job market, to fund their own education.

Graduates of post-secondary programs will likely gain higher earnings than they would without a college or university degree. But people participating in the workforce will experience different results. Those who are independent and not working may qualify for social assistance to provide them with a minimum level of income. Partially funded through the Canada Social Transfer, this government program is a provincial responsibility, and so it varies in nature across the country. Those deemed eligible for social assistance may receive basic benefits for food, clothing, personal care, household maintenance, and utilities, as well as funding for rent or a mortgage.[10] If circumstances warrant, recipients may qualify for municipal tax payments, eye exams, prescription glasses, a prescription drug card, medical supplies, medical equipment, medical transportation, private childcare if it is related to employment or training, and/or funeral expenses. This policy is not without its critics, particularly on the political right. Those on the left have led the charge to combat the social stigma of government handouts through an evolution in language that has seen social assistance go from being called "the dole" and "welfare" to "income support" or "income assistance." While social assistance ensures that everyone has a minimum income and quality of life, it is seen as particularly inequitable to those struggling to get by on minimum-wage jobs, known as "the working poor."

Upon exiting the workforce, most Canadians will see their income levels decline. The financial pressures on senior citizens who have fixed incomes can be acute,

social assistance Financial support provided by government to citizens with no other recourse to income.

especially for those who did not contribute to a pension plan or amass personal savings, who do not own their own home, and who have medical expenses. People employed outside the public sector, contract workers, homemakers, widowers, renters, and those with health problems are particularly vulnerable. Moreover, as people live longer, their finances need to stretch further. For these reasons women tend to be in greater need than men.

In 1927, the federal government consulted with provinces in creating a pension plan for retired Canadians, which awarded funds to applicants if they could demonstrate financial need. This was replaced in 1952 with the Old Age Security (OAS) pension, which was the country's first universal pension program for Canadians 65 years and older.[11] As of 2015, recipients of the OAS pension may obtain approximately $550 a month, and recipients who have a low income also receive a Guaranteed Income Supplement (GIS) as a top-up. However, seniors who earn over $100,000 annually have the OAS amount fully clawed back by the government.

The OAS and GIS are designed to ensure that all seniors have a basic minimum income regardless of the extent to which they participated in the workforce. Those who do work have a greater ability to save for retirement, but many would not do so unless obligated by law. In 1966, the Canada Pension Plan (CPP) was created as a mandatory retirement savings program. Workers are required to pay into the CPP fund, up to an annual limit, and their contributions are supplemented with CPP contributions that are made by their employer; workers who reside in Quebec pay into the Quebec Pension Plan (QPP) instead. When they turn 65, contributors are eligible to begin receiving monthly CPP payments as are their widows and widowers, if applicable; alternatively, they may opt for early retirement at the age of 60, or earlier if they become disabled, but in this case they will receive lower payments.

Many Canadians, buoyed by the advertising of the financial services industry, have dreams of retiring to a life spent living in exotic tropical locations with abundant golf courses and vineyards to visit. As retirement approaches, many may begin to realize that the CPP, which pays out approximately $600 to $1,000 a month depending on circumstances, is unlikely to cover much beyond their normal living expenses. This is why the federal government introduced the Registered Retirement Savings Plan (RRSP) and Tax-Free Savings Account (TFSA) programs mentioned in the Inside Canadian Politics box on page 323, to encourage Canadians to save for their own retirements. It is also why the Ontario government is leading the charge to create a provincial retirement pension on top of the CPP.

There are growing concerns that the CPP and other pension plans are underfunded. Payments made by current employees are invested and are used to finance the pension cheques of current retirees. But as the baby boomers exit the workforce, there will be a large number of retirees drawing on pension funds with a smaller pool of workers contributing. Canadians are living longer, and so retirees are drawing more funds from their pension than was budgeted. Moreover, as a defined benefit program, the CPP guarantees a set payout regardless of how much workers contributed or how successful the government's investments have been. This raises further questions about the CPP's sustainability at current contribution and payout rates. Similar challenges confront other public- and private-sector pension plans. The solution proposed so far by the federal government has been to provide alternative savings options and

Canada Pension Plan
A mandatory federal retirement program funded by workers and employers.

INSIDE CANADIAN POLITICS
How Does the Government Encourage Canadians to Save for Future Expenses?

Governments use their tax codes to provide incentives for Canadians to save for the future. As a matter of policy, government needs people to save for their future expenses in order to maintain a solid social and economic foundation for society. Governments mandate these savings through worker and employer contributions to the Canada Pension Plan (CPP), but the program may not provide sufficient income to all retirees. Indeed, as discussed below, a tense debate is underway about enriching the CPP and related entitlement programs to ensure the stability of Canada's retirement system.

In the meantime, the federal government incentivizes citizens to voluntarily save for retirement by offering them the option to *defer* taxes until the money they save can accumulate enough interest to cover them. For instance, the federal government's Registered Retirement Savings Plan (RRSP) allows Canadians to defer taxes on a proportion of their saved income, and receive a tax rebate for any taxes they paid on the income at the time of investment. Canadians do not pay taxes on these funds until they withdraw them from their account, at which point they have likely earned a significant amount of interest on their investment. Similarly, Canadians can save for a child's post-secondary education through a Registered Education Savings Plan and/or for a disabled dependant's needs through a Registered Disability Savings Plan. The federal government has also established a Tax-Free Savings Account (TFSA) system, which allows Canadians to save up to $5,500 a year without being taxed on any income earned on the investment. This is not a deferred tax program, but rather allows Canadians to accumulate tax-free interest on their savings.

VOX POP
To what extent do governments need to provide rules and incentives for Canadians to save for their future? What other public policy tools could be used to ensure the next generation of retirees is in a solid financial position when they stop working?

encourage people to take responsibility to save for their own retirement, although in the 2015 election campaign the Trudeau Liberals pledged to consider potential enhancements to CPP during the 2015 election campaign. Some provincial governments have proposed a more aggressive approach, either by increasing CPP premiums for current workers or creating province-specific pension plans. As pensions are an area of joint federal–provincial responsibility, and as the Canadian population continues to age, retirement income is likely to be one of the most controversial areas of intergovernmental negotiations in the decades to come.

b) Insurance Programs

Publicly funded insurance programs are available to Canadians when an urgent need arises. As with any insurance program, a large number of people pay into it, but at any given time only a minority use it. Moreover, the full cost of the insured service is not necessarily covered, and there may be a deductible that has to be paid by the user.

medicare A publicly
funded health care service
administered by each
province with the financial
support of the federal
government.

↻ The Canada Health
Transfer is explained on
pages 110–12 of Chapter 3,
on federalism.

When Canada was formed, public health services were offered by charities; today, medicare is the crown jewel in the country's social safety net. Since 1966, Canada's interconnected provincial healthcare insurance programs have existed as an area of provincial jurisdiction under broad national standards. Each jurisdiction has a public health insurance program that provides universal access to medical care regardless of a citizen's financial means. The Canada Health Act, 1984, identifies the conditions that provinces and territories must follow when delivering basic services if they wish to qualify for funds available through the Canada Health Transfer. As previously mentioned, there are five main principles that provincial health services must adhere to. They must be:

1. universal (i.e. everyone qualifies),
2. comprehensive (i.e. must cover all insured services),
3. accessible (i.e. must not impose financial barriers to essential services),
4. portable (i.e. citizens receive service in other provinces), and
5. publicly administered (i.e. not for profit).

Canada's healthcare system is both a source of pride to Canadians and a source of concern. In public opinion surveys it is regularly cited as a point of differentiation from the United States (particularly prior to "Obamacare") and part of the Canadian identity. Yet there are constant complaints about timely access to family physicians; long wait times to see specialists; frustrations about costs and procedures that are not covered; and studies that show that public healthcare is of lower quality than private healthcare. Furthermore, the system is under increasing strain as the average age of the population increases, and as concerns persist over the federal government's obligation to provide health services to Aboriginal Canadians. Political insiders now snidely remark that because of the growing expenses, we will one day see the provincial minister of health, not the minister of finance, deliver the provincial budget.

Debates abound: To what extent should the federal government be involved in an area of provincial jurisdiction? What can be done about wait times? How far should residents of rural communities be expected to travel to access care? Should a two-tier

BRIEFING NOTES

Healthcare and Socialized Medicine in Canada

As the debate over so-called "Obamacare" raged south of the border from 2008 to 2013, Republican conservatives were fond of referring to Canada's medicare system as "socialized medicine." Republicans used the term pejoratively, even though few Canadians identify themselves as socialist and few socialists would label Canada's universal system as achieving full equality of result. Republicans also inaccurately equated the Obama administration's model with the Canadian one. While the latter employs a single-payer model with provincial and territorial governments paying healthcare providers for Canadians' health services, the Obama administration's Affordable Care Act requires individual Americans to purchase health insurance from corporations that, in turn, pay providers for their customers' services.

public/private system be allowed, where those Canadians who can afford more timely or sophisticated care should be allowed to pay out-of-pocket? Should a *pharmacare* program be established to subsidize the costs of medication? Should hospital parking fees be included in the Canada Health Act? No matter what the policy options are, the fact remains that spending demands are increasing, which reduces the range of policy solutions that policymakers have at their disposal.

The other major federal public insurance program is employment insurance (EI), which provides temporary income to workers who have been laid off. The Unemployment Insurance Act (1941), which was renamed the Employment Insurance Act in 1996 to reduce negative connotations, requires that workers pay EI premiums through payroll deductions (i.e. money deducted from their paycheques). Approximately 2 per cent of Canadians' earnings fund a national insurance program, which is administered by the federal government. Workers who have paid the premiums and who have worked the minimum number of insurable hours may be eligible to receive EI benefits if they are let go by their employer (but not if they were fired for cause) or if they choose to take parental leave. The program also provides benefits to individuals who leave work owing to sickness or to care for a sick family member. After a brief unpaid waiting period, normally claimants may receive about half of their insurable earnings, subject to a maximum amount, for up to just less

employment insurance
A mandatory government insurance program, funded by employees and employers, that provides temporary income to workers who lose their jobs.

Dale Brazao/GetStock.com

Social policy in Canada exists primarily—but not exclusively—in the provincial/territorial realm. For instance, Canada maintains a so-called "patchwork" of provincial and territorial childcare systems, with each government operating a unique set of programs and standards. These range from a heavily subsidized and regulated system in Quebec to a predominantly private and non-profit system in Alberta. Despite periodic promises by party leaders, the federal government's role has remained limited to funding provinces through the Canada Social Transfer, and subsidizing Canadian parents through various tax credits and benefit programs. What are the advantages of this decentralized form of policymaking? Why don't more politicians question why government subsidizes the childcare costs incurred by those working parents who can afford to pay?

than a year. They may also access resources to help them find work through regional EI offices, and they may qualify to participate in a funded job training program. Once their EI benefits are used up, citizens may apply for other government programs, such as social assistance.

The employment insurance program is a source of just as much controversy as pensions and publicly funded healthcare. Defenders point out that it supports seasonal economies in rural areas, such as agriculture, fishing, and tourism, which have recurring layoffs. The program can encourage employers to distribute finite work hours among available employees; for instance, instead of one person being employed year-round, the availability of EI provides an alternative of four people working for 13 weeks. In this way, defenders argue, EI creates an efficient economy that optimizes the availability of labour and supports rural communities. Others aren't so convinced. They believe that the EI program creates a false economy, and maintain that it is a disincentive for repeat users to work year-round or to relocate to find work. They remark that provincial governments, which are responsible for social assistance spending, are incentivized to fund so-called "make work projects," whereby workers do menial tasks for the sole purpose of working enough hours to qualify for EI. Defenders and critics alike do share one concern: that the EI fund is too large, and is running a significant surplus. Whether this signifies that premiums are too high or that benefits are too difficult for workers to access is a matter of debate.

The biggest source of policy disagreement around employment insurance policy is its regional inequities. The 2008 economic crisis brought this to the fore. Ontario labourers and others who had never filed a claim lost well-paying jobs only to learn exactly how difficult it was to access an insurance program they had paid into for their entire working lives. This is because over 50 regional categories treat laid-off workers differently depending on where they live in Canada. Some premiers began lobbying for change, but could not agree on reforms. Ontario wanted a single national standard; western Canada wanted the categories reduced to just three regions (urban, rural, remote); Quebec was wary of the additional costs of change; and the Atlantic premiers were most satisfied with the system as it existed. For its part, the federal Conservative government sought to place more onus on repeat claimants to travel for available work, thereby creating a two-tier system of new applicants and repeat users—reforms that Justin Trudeau's Liberals have pledged to reverse.

Two other public insurance programs are worth mentioning. Federal, provincial, and municipal governments all have some form of disaster financial assistance programs. These are intended to assist people in greatest need in the event of a calamity causing damage that will not be covered by a private-sector insurance program, such as flooding. The other noteworthy program is public motor vehicle insurance, which is offered by Crown corporations in British Columbia, Manitoba, Quebec, and Saskatchewan. The governments of these provinces have determined that a no-fault insurance program is in the public interest in the expectation that it will result in lower rates. It is a rare example of the government operating in a sector of the economy that is traditionally serviced by the private sector, as it is in other jurisdictions. In provinces where motor vehicle insurance is offered only by the private sector, there is periodically public pressure, particularly from the NDP, to switch to a publicly owned insurance provider.

Toward Good Government

Patronage and the Merit Principle

Competent public administration, capable policy analysis, and vibrant pluralism generally characterize the high standards of Canadian governments. Despite the operating mantra of "good government" it is inevitable that allegations of outdated practices and frustrations with policy blunders will arise.

Those who hold senior positions within government and within agencies, boards, and commissions (ABCs) perform important roles in public administration, but they are sometimes criticized as beneficiaries of a system that is rife with patronage. More formally known as *clientelism*, patronage is a cultural practice that reflects an expectation among the supporters of a political party, its leader, and/or its candidate(s) that they will receive something in return for their loyal service. The prime minister and the premiers of large provinces literally have thousands of positions to fill, while in smaller provinces such posts number in the hundreds. Appointments to ABCs receive limited scrutiny, and they tend to be made as rewards for supporters of the government party. In some jurisdictions, the appointment process is secretive, while in others citizens are eligible to apply for positions; in all cases, the choice of whom to appoint is an executive power. Furthermore, the operations of ABCs do not receive nearly the same level of opposition or media attention as does the business of a government department. Some partisans receive appointments irrespective of their apparent qualifications, and the practice may create a culture of entitlement within the government party. So why does the practice exist? Patronage positions are necessary when the primary criterion for the job is the executive's trust that the appointee will advance the government's agenda. The availability of such positions motivates people to participate in politics and encourages party loyalty. Patronage was the bastion of the first party system (see Chapter 9), but increasingly the practice has drawn public criticism and rebuke. As a result, there has been a gradual move toward opening up such government positions for public competition.

Patronage runs counter to the merit principle. This holds that government jobs and contracts should be publicized and open to competition, and awarded to the most competent applicants. Under the merit principle, all citizens should be eligible to apply for government positions, formal criteria should be consistently applied to evaluate candidates, and the most qualified person should be offered the job. Equally, there are standardized rules for disciplining employees and terminating their employment. This means that the government cannot discriminate against applicants and employees on the basis of socio-demographic characteristics or their political activities outside work hours; nevertheless, even with the existence of the merit principle, some demographic cohorts are disproportionately represented in the public service and some bureaucrats do face pressure to hide or curtail their spare-time political activities. In the federal government, the Public Service Commission is responsible for the professionalism of staffing, and ensures that non-senior positions are free from political influence. The commissioner of official languages is responsible for ensuring all federal institutions abide by the terms of the Official Languages Act, effectively promoting the use of English and French in the federal bureaucracy and as part of its hiring practices. There

> **patronage** The awarding of government jobs, contracts, and/or other financial benefits to friends of the government party.

> **merit principle** The notion that the most qualified candidate should be awarded a position, contract, or other financial benefit.

↻ See Diversity in the Civil Service, beginning on page 509 of Chapter 13, for an explanation of employment equity programs.

are also provincial and territorial equivalents that exist to enforce the merit principle at those levels. Job vacancies are advertised, applications are screened by a committee, candidates are interviewed and tested, and the committee decides who should be offered the position. As well, employment equity programs exist to improve the representation of underrepresented groups in the public service.

Financial Mismanagement and Unethical Behaviour

Public interest in political appointments pales against the media attention and legislative debate associated with a political scandal. A notorious example occurred when the federal minister of fisheries overruled food inspectors in 1985 and allowed cans of possibly spoiled tuna to be sold to consumers. The minister did so out of worries that the packaging plant in St Andrews, New Brunswick, would be shut down, causing 400 employees from the small community to be laid off. However, when the media and opposition learned of his decision, controversy erupted; within a week, the minister resigned on the grounds of individual ministerial responsibility. Eventually, the plant workers found themselves out of work when the manufacturer, StarKist, closed the plant saw amid rapid declines in its market share. As a policy response to the so-called "tainted tuna" scandal, the government passed rules to remove a minister's power to overrule inspectors, and greater attention was given to the importance of quality control measures. If there is a silver lining to bad policy, it is that its detection and the ensuing debate lead to new policies that are designed to prevent a repeat situation. Even then, there are no guarantees. In 2000, seven people died and thousands became sick when the water supply in Walkerton, Ontario, became contaminated with *E. coli* bacteria that went undetected because of some falsified reports by two brothers working in the Walkerton Public Utilities Commission. In 2008, 22 people died after a listeriosis outbreak was traced to cold cuts processed in Toronto, and partial blame was placed on government policies that allowed the industry to self-regulate.

It is said that the difference between ethical breaches in British and Canadian government is that an offending British politician can't keep his hands to himself, while an offending Canadian politician can't keep his hands out of the till.[12] Indeed, in Canada sex scandals are sporadic compared with British and American politics, in part because the Canadian media and political elite tend to treat politicians' personal lives as off limits, unless there is a clear implication for public policy. At the federal level, the most significant sex scandal occurred during the Cold War, when cabinet ministers and other high-ranking government officials cavorted with Gerda Munsinger, who was allegedly a Soviet spy. Another case involved the solicitor general's forging the signature of his lover's husband on an abortion document in the late 1970s. Further indiscretions have included the minister of defence visiting a strip club in 1985 during a working visit to West Germany, and the minister of foreign affairs leaving cabinet documents at his ex-girlfriend's house in 2008. In all of these cases the minister was demoted to the backbenches by the prime minister.

By far the greater challenge in Canadian politics has concerned the dispensing of public goods. **Pork barrel politics** involves the cabinet's authorizing government spending in electoral districts where there is support for the governing party or where local projects may translate into votes and donations. "Pork" commonly refers to

pork barrel politics The partisan allocation of government spending to select constituencies, especially those districts held by the governing party.

public funds being used for government programs or initiatives, such as public infrastructure projects or grants for businesses promising to create local jobs. For example, the Harper government's Economic Action Plan was widely panned as a pork barrel program, with Conservative ridings in Ontario routinely receiving more funds than ridings held by other parties.[13] Pork barrel politics is widely practised by governments across Canada and is a public policy outcome that results from the activities of elected officials who want to "bring home the bacon" for their constituents. It is broader than patronage because even those who support a different political party, leader, and/or candidate(s) may benefit from the government spending. To some, pork barrel politics and patronage are unscrupulous; to others, they are forms of smart politicking that operates within the law.

What is beyond the pale is anything that breaks or circumvents the spirit of the law. There are too many scandals to list, but we can distinguish among isolated acts by individuals, behaviour by multiple public officials that in part can be attributed to the nature of the system itself, and mass collusion between political actors seeking to defraud the government for their own personal gain and/or their political party. The following are examples of isolated acts by individuals from different political parties:

- In 2002, it was revealed that the Liberal minister of defence had violated conflict of interest rules by awarding a $36,500 contract to prepare a 14-page report to a former girlfriend and that the topic that was outside of the contractor's area of expertise. The minister resigned from cabinet but three years later was appointed to the Senate.
- In 1995, the RCMP alleged that former PC prime minister Brian Mulroney had received kickbacks from an international lobbyist working for aircraft manufacturer Airbus. While Mulroney was in power, Airbus won a multimillion-dollar government contract to supply airplanes to Air Canada, which at the time was a Crown corporation. Mulroney sued the government for defamation and won. However, a decade later, the media reported that Mulroney indeed accepted money from the lobbyist. In 2007, Prime Minister Harper announced the creation of the "Commission of Inquiry into Certain Allegations Respecting Business and Financial Dealings Between Karlheinz Schreiber and the Right Honourable Brian Mulroney," which became known as the Oliphant Commission. Mulroney testified that he received $225,000, and the Commission concluded that there was no evidence of work being performed for these payments.

The following examples highlight systemic behaviour by multiple individuals:

- In 2015, the New Democratic Party was publicly rebuked and ordered to repay $2.75 million for using House of Commons funds to pay the salaries of political party staff working in Montreal, Quebec City, and Toronto.
- From 2006 to 2015, auditors questioned the legality of the expense claims of members of the Newfoundland and Labrador legislature, then the Nova Scotia legislature, and then the Senate. The Senate scandal, which was not confined to any one party, led to the resignation of one senator, the suspension of three others by their peers, and the firing of the former chief of staff to Prime Minister Harper for writing a $90,000 personal cheque to cover the expenses of one of the senators.

UP FOR DEBATE

Is political patronage still necessary in today's Canada? The debate supplement at the end of this chapter gives some of the arguments on both sides, and offers questions and resources to guide a discussion around this pressing topic.

Examples of mass collusion include:

- In the wake of the 1995 Quebec referendum, the Liberal Party launched a program to raise the profile of the federal government among Quebecers, leading to what became known as the sponsorship scandal (see the Inside Canadian Politics box on page 454 of Chapter 11).
- In 2006, the federal Conservative Party ran afoul of Elections Canada for circumventing party spending limits in an episode since known as the "in and out" scandal (see pages 393–4 in Chapter 10).

INSIDE CANADIAN POLITICS

Was the Pacific Scandal the Biggest Political Scandal in Canadian History?

The most common scandals in Canadian politics have implicated government parties in kickback schemes, where someone within government is given a secret payment for helping a firm to secure a government contract. The Pacific Scandal, though it occurred close to 150 years ago, remains for many the most egregious political scandal in Canadian history, although parallels may be drawn to more recent episodes.

In the 1870s, two business consortiums were bidding for a lucrative government contract to build the Canadian Pacific Railway. During the 1872 general election, a representative of one of the groups donated at least $350,000 (roughly $6.6 million in today's dollars) to the Conservative Party, and when the Conservatives were returned to power, that consortium was awarded the railway contract. When some Liberals broke into a government office, they discovered a telegram from Prime Minister John A. Macdonald pleading for the funds. In the resulting kerfuffle, some Conservative MPs crossed the floor, the government fell on a non-confidence motion, and the governor general asked the Liberals to form the government. It is the only time in Canadian federal politics that power has switched hands without a general election. The Macdonald Conservatives lost the ensuing election; nevertheless, afterwards they went on to win four consecutive majority governments.

Similar episodes in federal politics include the 1931 Beauharnois Scandal, where it was revealed that the Liberal government had received kickbacks for awarding a contract for a power dam, and the sponsorship scandal of the early 2000s, discussed at length in Chapter 11. In both cases the prime minister attempted to weather the political storm, with information about the Beauharnois matter coming to light *after* a change of government, and the government falling on a non-confidence vote *after* a commission of inquiry delivered its first report. By comparison, in the Pacific Scandal, not only did the prime minister resign, but the governor general turned to the official opposition party to form the government.

THE LESSON

While governments may be held accountable by their legislatures and the Crown, and may be ousted for unethical behaviour, the electorate can be just as quick to forgive parties and politicians for their misdeeds.

VOX POP

What are the most effective public policy tools when it comes to reducing the frequency or severity of scandals involving the public purse?

THEY SAID IT

Political Elites Caught with Their Hand in the Till

I must have another ten thousand. Will be the last time of asking. Do not fail me. Answer today.

> —private telegram from Conservative prime minister John A. Macdonald to railway businessman Hugh Allan, seeking campaign funds in what would become the Pacific Scandal

Individual members of the Liberal party may have done what they should not have done. . . . The party is not disgraced but it is in the valley of humiliation.

> —House of Commons speech by Liberal prime minister William Lyon Mackenzie King, reflecting on the Beauharnois Scandal

I made a serious error of judgment in receiving a payment in cash for this assignment even though it was decidedly not illegal to do so. That mistake in judgment was mine alone. I apologize and I accept full responsibility for it.

> —commission of inquiry testimony from former PC prime minister Brian Mulroney, reflecting on the Airbus affair

I am sorry that we weren't more vigilant; that I wasn't more vigilant. Public money was misdirected and misused. That's unacceptable.

> – televised address by Liberal prime minister Paul Martin, reflecting on the sponsorship scandal

I do want to speak to the PM before everything is considered final. . . . We are good to go from the PM. . . .

> —emails from Conservative prime minister Stephen Harper's chief of staff, allegedly negotiating a private payment to a Conservative senator to offset the repayment of improper expense claims

These episodes provide a glimpse at what is evidently a systemic problem. In all cases, stronger accountability practices and increased transparency would have reduced the possibility of misusing public funds.

There are many ways that the government attempts to limit the possibility of financial mismanagement and unethical conduct. Government personnel, including members of cabinet, are subject to the rule of law, including the Criminal Code of Canada. The Financial Administration Act states that the federal government must take "appropriate measures to promote fairness, openness and transparency in the bidding process for contracts" (section 40.1). Strict campaign finance laws limit the amount of money Canadians can donate to federal political parties, and prevent unions and corporations from contributing. Most federal government contracts are put out for public tender and follow a rigorous evaluation process. Public opinion research reports must be submitted to Library and Archives Canada within six months. Government departments and agencies prepare annual reports. Lobbyists are required to register with most governments, and basic information about their activities is made public. These are just some of the many internal government policies that have been crafted in response to past problems. As well, legislatures employ a number of officers, including conflict of interest and ethics commissioners.

↻ See Chapter 10 for a full account of Canada's campaign finance laws.

↻ See page 228 of Chapter 6 for a discussion of offices of the legislature.

At the federal level, some of these policies were introduced as part of the Accountability Act, which was the most sweeping reform legislation in recent memory. It was introduced by the Harper government in 2006 in response to the sponsorship scandal and the report of the Gomery Commission. The Act's changes included; increased scope of investigation for the auditor general; whistleblower protection to allow public servants who spot wrongdoing to speak out; and stricter rules for lobbyists,

Accountability Act
Sweeping 2006 federal legislation whose rules were designed to reduce the possibility of unethical conduct in government.

in particular requiring that five years lapse between the time government insiders may leave their positions and begin a lobbying career. Nevertheless, there are those who call for the government to go further. For instance, the Liberal Party under Justin Trudeau has promoted a so-called "open Parliament plan" that would require parliamentarians to proactively disclose their travel and hospitality expenses and make meetings of the House of Commons' secretive Board of Internal Economy open to the public. The Trudeau Liberals have also pledged to make government information more accessible, and embrace "open data" initiatives.

↻ See Lobbyists, beginning on page 478 of Chapter 12, for a discussion of lobbying rules in Canada.

Concluding Thoughts

Political actors in Canada sort out ways to resolve public policy problems through a combination of intergovernmental relations, media posturing, and politicking. Many Canadians found out after the stock market correction of 2008 and resulting global economic recession that the social safety net is full of holes. Employment insurance favours residents in some areas of the country over others. There are arguments that businesses and workers should have to pay more into the Canada Pension Plan because payouts to retirees are insufficient. The affordability of post-secondary education is a concern due to rising tuition fees, housing expenses, and student debt. Complaints about healthcare include growing wait times, medication expenses, and homecare costs, and the system is struggling to keep up with increasing demand as baby boomers age. The lack of a national childcare program compromises the ability of some parents, especially women, to participate in the workforce. Public-service unions are criticized for defending the remuneration of civil servants, some of whom earn more than private-sector workers in comparable positions. Amid all of this, there are ongoing frustrations about finding ways to meaningfully assist the working poor, the unemployed, and the homeless. Addressing these priorities is expensive, and yet many working Canadians feel overtaxed as it is, and want less of their money spent on programs they feel they do not benefit from. Inspired by populist politicians promising to deliver the same services at a lower cost by rooting out inefficiencies in the system, they are demanding tax cuts and more focused and efficient spending of government resources on core public services. As ever, public policy is buffeted by competing ideologies, and policymakers remain challenged to strike a balance between the most effective and most popular blend of taxing and spending.

For More Information

Want a deeper perspective into how public policy and public administration operate at the provincial level of government? See Michael M. Atkinson and colleagues' *Governance and Public Policy in Canada: A View From the Provinces* (University of Toronto Press, 2013). As well, for an appreciation of the institutionalized role of patronage, have a look at Jeffrey MacLeod's 2006 account of failed attempts at reform in Nova Scotia, "Clientelism and John Savage" (*Canadian Journal of Political Science* 39, no. 3: pp. 553–70).

Problems understanding the principal–agent problem? If you are mathematically inclined, then consult Sanford J. Grossman and Oliver D. Hart's 1983 article "An Analysis of the Principal–Agent Problem" (*Econometrica* 51, no 1: pp. 7–45).

Interested in learning about the difficulties of reconciling partisan and political interests with those of the public service? A broad theoretical approach can be found in "Civil Servants, Managerialism and Democracy," by Morton R. Davies (*International Review of Administrative Sciences* 64 (1998): pp. 119–29). For a Canadian take, see Reg Whitaker's chapter "Politics versus Administration: Politicians and Bureaucrats" in the book *Canadian Politics in the 21st Century*, edited by Michael Whittington and Glen Williams (Thomson Nelson, 2007).

Wondering how public administration is evolving in Canada? Learn about the concept of new public management in Allan Tupper's chapter "New Public Management and Canadian Politics," in *Reinventing Canada: Politics of the 21st Century*, edited by Janine Brodie and Linda Trimble (Pearson, 2003). See also Peter Aucoin's "New Public Management and New Public Governance: Finding the Balance," in *Professionalism and Public Service: Essays in Honour of Kenneth Kernaghan*, edited by David Siegel and Ken Rasmussen (University of Toronto Press, 2003).

How does public opinion influence public policy? Stuart Soroka and Christopher Wlezien investigate in "Opinion Representation and Policy Feedback: Canada in Comparative Perspective" (*Canadian Journal of Political Science* 37, no. 3 [2004]: pp. 531–59). For a different type of perspective, see Manoj Hastak, Michael B. Mazis, and Louis A. Morris, "The Role of Consumer Surveys in Public Policy Decision Making" (*Journal of Public Policy & Marketing* 20, no. 2 [2001]: pp. 170–85).

To what extent does public policy matter to voters on Election Day? Éric Bélanger and Bonnie M. Meguid explain that the policy positions of Canadian political parties matter only to those voters who think that a given issue is important. See "Issue Salience, Issue Ownership, and Issue-Based Vote Choice," in *Electoral Studies* 27, no. 3 (2008): pp. 477–91.

Doing some topical research about public policy in Canada? Visit the website of Policy Options magazine: www.irpp.org.

Want to explore "pracademia"—the intersection of worlds of public-service practitioners and public administration academics? The Institute of Public Administration Canada (http://ipac.ca) provides a venue for pracademics to interact and discuss matters of public policy. They also publish a leading journal on the subject, *Canadian Public Administration*.

Deeper Inside Canadian Politics

1. Some advocacy groups that advance the cause of political minorities receive government funding. However, they are some of the government's biggest critics. Do you agree or disagree that some interest groups should be given public funding? How should governments decide which ones to fund?

2. Patronage tends to be decried by the public, attacked by the political commentators and the opposition, and derided by editorial cartoonists. Yet no matter what political party is in power, it persists. Under what circumstances do you feel that patronage is acceptable and even necessary?

3. Budget deficits and public debt are common because politicians tend to be praised for making spending promises and criticized for spending cutbacks. And for a politician to propose a tax increase today is fraught with risk. In this way, politicians are incentivized to "buy votes with voters' own money," as the saying goes. To what extent is this a public policy problem?

UP FOR DEBATE

Is political patronage still necessary in today's Canada?

THE CLAIM: YES, IT IS!

Patronage is a tool used to bind political coalitions, and for this reason it remains necessary for political executives to govern effectively.

Yes: Argument Summary

Clientelism—also known as patronage—has a longstanding place in democracies worldwide, including in Canada. Its persistence reflects the reality that often the most important criterion for a job in politics is a willingness to be loyal to the political executive. Alternatives such as using committees to decide on appointments, of opening positions up to the electorate, or of turning matters over to the Public Service Commission are romantic notions that ignore the mechanics of running government. It may be maligned, but patronage is popular among the political class, and it is deeply entrenched in Canadian politics.

Yes: Top 5 Considerations

1. Patronage is often confused with pork barrel politics. While there is some overlap, the former usually refers to favouritism in government appointments, and the latter to the allocation of government funds to community projects. Extensive regulations exist to inhibit the presence of patronage in the awarding of government contracts, notably the public tendering process.

2. The appointment of friends of the party in power assures the government party that its agenda will be implemented rather than stonewalled. The mandarins who adhere to the merit principle may not reflect the values of the broader public as expressed in a recent election or measured in opinion polls. Patronage ensures the smooth, accountable operation of the state, which is legitimately governed by people popularly elected by the citizenry.

3. Patronage glues political parties together and helps ensure that public officials are all on the same page. The aspirations of parliamentarians and partisans to hold an appointed public position is a key component of party discipline that has proven necessary for political parties' success and the stability of government.

4. Politics involves the brokering of competing demands. Patronage is a deal-making tool that can be leveraged to encourage opinion leaders to unite communities of competing interests and to promote their interests among party elites.

5. The political executive's appointment power can be used as a tool of affirmative action to counterbalance the inequalities that result from democratically elected positions. Patronage has allowed some of the highest public positions, including governors general, lieutenant governors, ministers, senators, judges and others, to be filled by qualified candidates from groups that have traditionally been overlooked by electors, including women, non-whites, non-anglophones, and people with disabilities. In this way, patronage is not nearly as illiberal as its critics suggest.

Yes: Other Considerations

- Patronage is one of the few perks available to reward those who volunteer their time in politics. In some areas of the country it is part of the local political culture, and those attempting reforms have learned that it is exceedingly difficult to do so.

- All opposition parties criticize patronage, and yet once in government, all parties practise it. Likewise, Canadians who oppose patronage may view things differently if they are the ones who benefit from the spoils.

- Political appointees who make poor decisions

can be quickly replaced; however, the civil service has so many protections that the dismissal of incompetent bureaucrats may not be feasible. Furthermore, job security may create the very conditions that lead to underperformance.

THE COUNTERCLAIM: NO, IT ISN'T!

Patronage is outdated, unethical, and outrageous.

No: Argument Summary

The blatant use of the executive power to practise patronage and reward supporters is out of step with modern notions of democratic government. It is understandable that cabinet and members of the Prime Minister's Office or Premier's Office need to be appointed; however, the process of selecting candidates to become senators, judges, and chairs of government agencies and board positions is increasingly questioned. There is little reason why the process used by the political executive to fill public positions should not be open to more public scrutiny and participation.

No: Top 5 Considerations

1. Patronage in Canada is a holdover from the immediate post-Confederation era, when the government party was expected to fill the civil service with friends. It may encourage corruption and is at odds with the values of a modern liberal democracy. For example, the leadership of a political party may promise a lucrative appointment to prevent whistleblowers or wrongdoers from going public.

2. The modern civil service strictly adheres to the merit principle and employment equity. Patronage is incompatible with the bureaucracy because it undermines the bureaucracy's apolitical values of evidence-based decision-making, its standards of professionalism, and its concern for demographic representation. It introduces fears of dismissal, the promotion of party interests over the public interest, constant suspicion,

turmoil when there is a change of government, and the exploitation of the civil service to prop up the government party in election campaigns.[14]

3. The growth of government and the important role that it plays in Canadians' lives increases the importance of appointing only the most highly skilled, trained, and experienced candidates to senior positions in the public service.

4. The clandestine nature of many patronage appointments is a telling indicator that political elites know that their decisions prioritize the interests of their party over those of the general public. Government announcements made late on a Friday and appointing celebrities to the Senate are two standard tricks to manage decisions that would otherwise attract negative publicity.

5. Each new head of government introduces experiments with reforms to operate a more ethical government. As prime minister, Stephen Harper periodically refused to appoint any senators and required that the suitability of his first nominee to the Supreme Court be scrutinized by an all-party parliamentary committee. However, over time these reforms complicated the ability to govern, and Harper eventually appointed partisans just as his predecessors did.

No: Other Considerations

- The ability to distribute the spoils of office exclusively among supporters may be legal, but by today's standards it is unethical.

- Prominent Canadian journalist Jeffrey Simpson once wrote, "patronage is the pornography of politics, enticing to some, repulsive to others, justified as inevitable, condemned as immoral, a practice seldom considered a fit subject for polite discussion."[15]

- When PC Party leader Brian Mulroney delivered his "you had a choice, sir" knockout punch in the leaders' debate of the 1984 election, he was referring to the authority of the prime minister to put a stop to the practice of patronage politics.

- Extensive rules may exist to prevent government contracts being awarded on the basis of partisanship, but the sponsorship scandal occurred nonetheless.

Discussion Questions

- How realistic is it to expect members of the political executive to work with senior government officials who were hired through the non-partisan merit system?
- Why do you think opposition parties criticize patronage, but once in power, they do the same thing?
- How much weight do you place on the argument that when a political party forms the government, it needs to hire its own friends as a counterbalance to all of the friends that were hired by the outgoing administration?
- Do you know anyone who has benefited from political patronage? In your opinion, should that position have been opened up to public competition, or not? Explain.
- The first minister's appointment power has arguably hastened the number of political minorities holding top government positions. Does this change your opinion about patronage? Why or why not?
- To what extent would an independent, advisory panel assuage critics' concerns with the prime minister's power to select senators for appointment?

Where to Learn More about Patronage in Canadian Politics

Matthew Flinders and Felicity Matthews, "Think Again: Patronage, Governance and the Smarter State," *Policy & Politics* 38, no. 4 (2010): pp. 639–56.

Alan Gordon, "Patronage, Etiquette, and the Science of Connection: Edmund Bristol and Political Management, 1911–1921," *Canadian Historical Review* 80, no. 1 (1999): pp. 1–33.

Jeffrey MacLeod, "Clientelism and John Savage," *Canadian Journal of Political Science* 39, no. 3 (2006): pp. 553–70.

Public Service Commission of Canada, "Public Service Impartiality: Taking Stock" (Ottawa: 2008). Available at www.psc-cfp.gc.ca/plcy-pltq/rprt/impart/impart-eng .pdf.

Steffen W. Schmidt, Laura Guasti, Carl H. Landé, and James C. Scott, eds, *Friends, Followers and Factions: A Reader in Political Patronage* (University of California Press, 1977).

Jeffrey Simpson, *Spoils of Power: The Politics of Patronage* (Toronto: HarperCollins, 1988).

David E. Smith, "Patronage in Britain and Canada: An Historical Perspective," *Journal of Canadian Studies* 22, no. 2 (1987): 34–54.

PART II
Politics and Politicking

9 POLITICAL PARTIES

Inside this Chapter

- What is a political party?
- What types of political parties exist in Canada?
- Which political ideologies underpin party politics in Canada?
- What do party leaders do, and how are they selected?
- What are a party's parliamentary and extra-parliamentary wings?
- What is partisanship and party discipline?

Inside Political Parties

Political parties and their leaders are by far the most visible actors in Canadian democracy. As you've read, their reach extends into every corner of the political system, not only organizing the executive and legislative branches but also, quite controversially, playing a role in the structure of the judiciary. Canadians are most familiar with their role in elections, however, with visions of party colours and banners symbolizing what it means to campaign for office.

Despite their prominent place in Canadian democracy—or perhaps *because of* their visibility—political parties have attracted a number of unflattering labels, many of which are undeserved. Indeed, a number of misconceptions surround political party politics in Canada, so as you read through this chapter, bear the following truths in mind.

 Canadian democracy does not depend on the existence of political parties. While parties have done a great deal to institutionalize their role in Canadian democracy, recent and historical reform movements demonstrate that they may be dispensable. Indeed, the early days of Confederation and present-day politics in Northwest Territories and Nunavut suggest alternatives to partisanship, or at least strong party discipline. And the periodic, but often pivotal, role played by independents raises real questions about the utility of political parties in the twenty-first century.

 Parties do not exist solely to campaign for office. Political parties are never more visible than when their candidates are campaigning for election, yet that is not the principal function of parties. Quite to the contrary, political parties play a role in all corners of government, not to mention civil society. This is part of the reason they have become so deeply embedded in Canadian political culture.

Parties are not the shapeless, outdated, elite-driven organizations they are sometimes made out to be. Like all stereotypes, this misperception carries enough truth to be persuasive. Yet Canada's political parties are by no means bereft of principle or grassroots support. If they were, and if they failed to evolve with the times, they would certainly not have survived the century-and-a-half since Confederation.

Peering inside Canada's political parties means peeling back the many layers that make up their organizations, and tracing their development through several unique party system eras.

Overview

Mainstream political parties, particularly the governing party federally or in a province or territory, receive considerable media and public attention. However, a lot goes on behind the scenes that the media tend to ignore, and there are more political parties than most people realize. To understand political parties in Canada we need to dissect their organizational apparatus and enumerate the variety of activities that they are involved with. Normally, we expect that members of a political party will

What the 2015 Election Means for Political Parties

Visit the *Inside Canadian Politics* flipboard to learn about the latest developments in the area of Canadian political parties.

Go to http://flip.it/gblag.

work together because they hope to win an election and form the government, but in fact parties have many other reasons for engaging in the public sphere. It is only with an appreciation of what is involved with political parties that we can truly begin to understand how politics works in Canada.

UP FOR DEBATE

Should Canada's political parties do more to recruit members of underrepresented groups as candidates?

Keep this question in mind as you read through the chapter. Consult the end-of-chapter debate supplement for more material to help you engage in an informed discussion of the topic.

Political Parties in Canada

The Nature and Role of Political Parties

Political parties have historically been the mechanisms through which most organized political activity occurs in Canada. A **political party** is a formal organization of politically minded citizens who unite under a common label and contest elections. Political parties bring together competing perspectives and unite like-minded people who seek to shape government decisions. They are thus political clubs that seek to influence and change public policy.

political party A political entity that runs candidates in elections in an attempt to shape government policy and laws.

Political parties are arguably the most dominant political actors in the Canadian political system. They emerged in the nineteenth century out of a need to organize policy debate and representation in the legislature. Since that time, they have grown beyond the confines of the legislature to help organize elections. Furthermore, their diversity has grown as a reflection of the vibrancy of pluralism, the public sphere, and political opinions.

Not surprisingly, political parties attract considerable media and public attention. They are also the subject of extensive study by political scientists. There are many ways of thinking about political parties and evaluating their behaviours, some of which are presented in this chapter. But what do political parties actually do? Among their many roles:

- *Aggregating interests:* Political parties operate as vessels that collect the many points of view on countless issues, use varied mechanisms for identifying a position on any given issue, and advocate the best way forward.
- *Articulating interests:* Political parties promote different ways of looking at issues and encourage public discussion about government.
- *Selecting a leader:* Political parties are the organizations through which people who want to lead the government are identified and selected.
- *Choosing candidates:* Political parties coordinate the process of recruiting people who are willing to stand for election and become representatives in the legislative assembly.

- *Running election campaigns:* Political parties field candidates who will run under the party banner, often providing candidates with communications resources and a common policy platform with which they can connect with voters.
- *Promoting a government agenda:* Political parties help the voting public identify the slate of candidates and policies they want to control the government.
- *Coordinating a legislative agenda:* Political parties organize legislative affairs, ensuring that there is political cohesion rather than instability, and that politics operates more smoothly than it would otherwise.

As you can see, a good deal of what political parties do involves identifying and connecting with potential voters. In today's digital world, this involves sophisticated methods of data gathering and management, as illustrated in the Opportunities Available box on page 342.

Types of Political Parties

In Canada, political parties barely existed in 1867, when John A. Macdonald led the elites who congregated within the Liberal–Conservative Party into elections against a loosely organized Liberal Party. Elite parties such as these were closed cadres of the upper class. They were foremost concerned with organizing votes within the legislature and, secondarily, with appealing to those male citizens who were eligible to vote.

> **elite party** A small political party run by people with ascribed social status.

Laura Politis

Volunteering on an election campaign is an excellent way for young people to gain first-hand experience in politics. What are the advantages and disadvantages of becoming involved in partisan politics? What are other avenues for young people to influence the political system?

Opportunities Available

Knowledge of Canadian Politics and Government Preferred!

Provincial Data Director

BC New Democratic Party (BC NDP)

The BC New Democratic Party (BC NDP) seeks a highly experienced and motivated individual for the full-time position of Data Director to lead its data services department. The BC NDP data services department provides comprehensive data systems design and maintenance, data management and analytics for BC NDP communications, fundraising, and field operations. We seek an experienced individual with a combination of technical and political skills and the leadership to manage these services. The position will report to the Provincial Director.

Responsibilities

- Manage and coordinate all data needs of BC NDP staff and partners.
- Lead the development, implementation and integration of fundraising, field and communications tools.
- Work with consultants and other BC NDP staff responsible for the acquisition, enhancement, and management of data files.
- Work with vendors to acquire data sources that can enhance targeted outreach and to acquire tools to contact targets and manage systems that will track work.
- Manage file access for BC NDP organizations and constituency associations. This includes administration, training, and targeting.
- Create accountability systems that will aid the provincial leadership team in decision-making.
- Lead the development and implementation of an effective analytics reporting system to assist managers in the assessment of departmental performance.
- Advise departmental leads on data best practices.
- Make recommendations and provide strategic support regarding ways to make data and database operations more efficient and effective.
- Ensure organizational compliance with all applicable privacy and information security laws.

Qualifications

- Candidates should have an understanding of common direct voter contact programs, online fundraising and volunteer engagement tools, and at least one cycle of experience in the use of data to drive effective decision-making.
- Candidates should have a diplomatic, professional approach to problem solving while working independently or on a team, as well as the ability to manage several tasks/projects concurrently and prioritize work effectively.
- Strong data and programming skills are required; familiarity with other online electoral/advocacy tools and constituent relationship management tools is a plus.
- Strong database and spreadsheet skills are required, as is willingness and aptitude to learn new technical skills.
- Experience working with statistical models, and using results to aid in planning.
- Candidates must have a demonstrated capacity to describe technology and data systems and outputs in simple language.
- Must be a self-starter willing to work long irregular 'campaign-style' hours and to travel as needed. The ideal candidate will have a demonstrated history of persistence and resourcefulness in solving technical and data problems.
- Ability to communicate effectively, works well under pressure, is detail oriented, and meets deadlines.
- Experience managing staff centrally and remotely.

Compensation

The position is a unionized position with generous salary and benefits and is compensated according to the terms of the CUPE 3787 agreement.

Location

Vancouver, BC.

Source: John Horgan, NDP: https://www.bcndp.ca/jobs/6271

The caucus tended to make most decisions, including who the leader should be. Those who ran the party controlled the distribution of resources and privileges; they performed little campaigning; and they placed a high priority on their personal contacts.

When the franchise was extended to women and property qualifications to vote were lifted, political parties needed to reach across class divisions and empower their members. This gave rise to the mass parties that emerged in Canada's second party system, beginning after World War I. A variety of forces helped to decentralize the major parties' power structure, and extended a role for grassroots party members in leadership selection, policy design, and electioneering. The emphasis turned from organizing elites to reforming society, and the party leadership became more accountable to the party membership as the size of the political party grew. Compared to an elite party, a mass party's membership cares less about the personality of the party's leader than the ideas that the leader espouses. Such a party may therefore have close ties with quasi-political organizations, such as labour unions, advocacy groups, or business groups.

For the most part, pure elite and mass parties have been phased out of Canadian politics, and remain historical "ideal types." In 1966, American political scientist Otto Kirchheimer identified a classification that remains applicable to the most successful Canadian political parties today.[1] The primary objective of what he labelled a catch-all party is to find ways to win in order to improve society, which means appealing to voters with varying viewpoints and adapting to the preferences of the majority. Compared to mass parties, the catch-all, or big tent, party places greater emphasis on the charisma of the party leader, and the professional communication of broad messages supplants grassroots activism. The importance of individual party members is therefore diminished, and made even less significant by the catch-all party's priority on raising funds from sources outside its membership, including government subsidies. This means that a catch-all party is not normally left-wing or right-wing, though an ideological party can shift to the centre without abandoning its core ideological principles. For instance, at times the Conservative Party of Canada behaves as a catch-all party, because it downplays some of its conservative principles to appeal to voters outside its traditional base. This may mean, for example, choosing to run budget deficits in the face of an economic downturn, or opting not to appeal court decisions that result in more liberal social policies, like same-sex marriage.

mass party A grassroots political party characterized by its efforts to sign up members.

catch-all party A competitive political party that prioritizes the design of effective public policy and election strategies.

BRIEFING NOTES
Labelling Political Parties

Outsiders can find it challenging to apply consistent labels to political parties, and insiders are sometimes offended by the categories in which political scientists place their organizations. In this sense, it is often best to consider party types—elite, mass, catch-all, brokerage, market-oriented, and so on— as markers of party *behaviour* at any given time, as opposed to permanent classifications. These are subject to change and, to a large extent, the perspective of the individual applying the label.

THEY SAID IT

Canadian Political Scientists on Brokerage Party Politics

[Brokerage parties] canvass and delineate the varied interests of the electorate, seeking to broker a coalition of supporters.

—Harold Clarke et al. (1996)[5]

Marked by compromissory leadership, an aversion to ideology, and an absence of consistency in policies and programs, brokerage parties in Canada

have crowded around the centre of the political spectrum, seeking support from essentially the same voters.

—John Courtney (1988)[6]

[Brokerage parties are] essentially similar organizations opportunistically appealing to a variety of interests; ideology distinguishes neither the party activists nor the positions adopted by the parties. . . . They are in essence *Tweedledum and Tweedledee*. Elections involve competition among the "Ins" and the "Outs."

—Janine Brodie and Jane Jenson (1996)[7]

VOX POP

Brokerage politics depends on finding middle ground among voting groups with very different—sometimes competing—regional interests. Is this a productive way of generating policies that will be widely popular or a tactic that risks watering down the party's principles?

brokerage party The Canadian term for a catch-all party that brokers competing regional demands.

In Canada, the term brokerage party is often used as a synonym for a catch-all party. Brokerage and catch-all parties are similar in that they aim to listen to citizens, identify policies that will appeal to competing viewpoints, and attract people who feel that the party embodies the public's values. A brokerage party differs, though, in that it explicitly attempts to reconcile the wide variety of regional interests found in Canadian society. In this way, brokerage parties have been described as Canada's "shock absorbers," confining regional conflict within party organizations rather than promoting open disputes between parties.[2] The Liberal Party of Canada is an excellent example of a brokerage party because of its history of brokering competing demands from different areas of the country, particularly Quebec and the rest of Canada. Brokerage parties are less common at the provincial level; with more homogeneous populations, provincial parties are able to appeal to a narrower set of interests while still maintaining the level of popular support necessary to win seats and form governments. This said, in many provinces, parties do need to appeal to at least two or three different regions to win enough seats to form government.[3] In Manitoba, for instance, parties need to cobble together support from at least half of the province's four main regions: the remote north, the rural south, North Winnipeg, and South Winnipeg.[4]

In recent years, other categories of political parties have been posited to reflect changing dynamics of party politics. The list includes but is not limited to the *cartel party*, the *electoral–professional party*, and the *horizontal party*. In fact, owing to technological changes, the brokerage party is arguably becoming obsolete. Provinces compete in a global economy, news media no longer operate in a regional vacuum, opinion surveys have become affordable, and statistical modelling enables the targeting of voters in ways that reduce the importance of regional dimensions. Modern

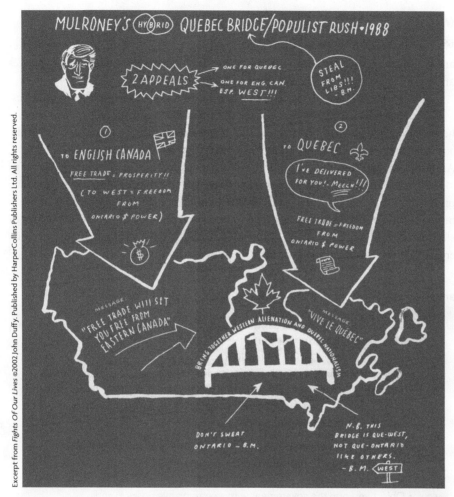

In *Fights of Our Lives*, John Duffy, public affairs consultant and veteran Liberal Party insider, provides a series of "playbooks" for party success over the ages. This one, from the 1988 federal election campaign, embraces the brokerage party ideal by mapping out a strategy to reconcile the competing interests of French and English Canada. What sort of brokerage strategies were used in the most recent federal election? What about in the most recent provincial election in your jurisdiction?

political parties have become professionalized: they know that in order to be competitive, they must work with political consultants—including media, marketing, opinion research, and social media experts—to identify and win over floating and undecided voters. The consequences include an obsession with message control, an emphasis on images over substance, the practice of permanent campaigning, and prioritizing the interests of the party centre over the grassroots. The integration of advanced research and communication techniques means that electors are targeted based on their shared interests that transcend provincial or regional boundaries. This has contributed to a shift in the regional fault lines of politics, where it matters less what province an elector lives in than whether the elector lives in a city, a suburb, or a rural area. The days of brokering provincial interests appear to have evolved into a landscape of so-called "retail politics," where ground-level salesmanship is used to peddle policies and promote brands of leadership at an individual level.

↻ See pages 157–58 of Chapter 4, on regionalism, for a discussion of code politics and how political parties continue to exploit regional differences for political gain, despite the growth of retail politics.

Major and Minor Parties

We can distinguish between two types of political parties in Canada. *Major parties* are professional organizations with a significant daily presence, while *minor parties* are those that are largely dormant until an election campaign is pending.

A major party is a political party that has significant public support and resources. Major parties typically feature leaders who see themselves as competing to become the head of government, or leader of the official opposition at the very least. In other terms, a major party may considered simply any party that has members in the legislature. According to one prominent definition, major parties are those with either "governing" or "blackmail" potential; that is, they are perceived to be strong enough to win elections or, if not, to exert such a threat as to be able to influence the policy positions of those in power.[8] Major parties in Canada tend to have a long history of being competitive in elections, to field candidates in all available electoral districts, and/or to have their leaders participate in mid-campaign leaders' debates (see Table 9.1).

major party A political party that has many supporters and a large organizational infrastructure.

TABLE 9.1 | Political Parties Whose Candidates Were Elected in Recent Federal Elections

Party Name and Logo	Characteristics
Bloc Québécois*	• Type: Mass party that leans to the left • Political ideology: Quebec nationalism • Objective: Advance Quebec's interests; advocate unique status within Canada; establish the conditions for a successful referendum on sovereignty-association • Policies include: Support for Quebec art and culture; pressure on Ottawa to allow Quebec to keep more tax revenues
Conservative Party of Canada	• Type: Right-wing catch-all party • Political ideology: Conservatism; economic libertarianism; electoral–professional and brokerage politics • Objective: Form the government with a conservative policy agenda • Policies include: Tougher sentences for dangerous offenders; lower taxes
 Green Party of Canada*	• Type: Left-wing mass party • Political ideology: Environmentalism • Objective: Advance an agenda of environmental and left-wing social policies • Policies include: Reduction of automobile emissions; increased taxes on polluters
 Liberal Party of Canada	• Type: Catch-all party that leans to the left • Political ideology: Electoral–professional and brokerage politics • Objective: Form the government with a policy agenda that appeals to the median voter • Policies include: Stronger national programs; increased foreign aid
 New Democratic Party	• Type: Left-wing catch-all party • Political ideology: Democratic socialism and brokerage politics • Objective: Form the government with an agenda that appeals to unions and the working class • Policies include: National childcare program; higher taxes on corporations

*Although these parties were represented in the House of Commons after the 2015 federal general election, they did not elect enough members to achieve official party status and were arguably minor parties.

Source: Adapted from Elections Canada (www.elections.ca), Apathy Is Boring (www.apathyisboring.com).

Conversely, a **minor party** is typically little more than a fringe organization that operates with little public support on a shoestring budget and that has elected few, if any, legislators. Its volunteers are frequently asked to run as candidates in ridings that they do not live in, and with almost no prospects of winning. Minor parties rely on inexpensive modes of communication such as the Internet. Their leaders are typically unknown to most citizens, and if they do manage to attract media attention, it is owing to public curiosity or a sense of fair play. Nevertheless, they are participants in the Canadian party system, and reflect the ideal that competing political viewpoints are welcome in a democracy.

Not long ago, a minor political party contesting the federal election was required to field a minimum of 50 candidates in order for its party name to be listed on the ballot. This rule, which was in effect from 1993 through 2000, effectively excluded tiny and

minor party A small political party with much less support or infrastructure than a major party.

Most minor parties face an uphill battle when it comes to contesting elections. With few notable exceptions, most recently the Reform Party, minor parties are unable to win seats. Why would a party exist, and why would people join it, if it had little chance of winning?

TABLE 9.2 | Minor Political Parties in Recent Canadian Federal Elections

Party Name and Logo	Characteristics
Animal Alliance Environment Voters Party of Canada	• Characteristics • Type: Left-wing mass party • Political ideology: Environmentalism • Objective: Advance an agenda of environmental policies that favour animal rights • Policies include: Ban cosmetic testing on animals; improve treatment of farm animals
 Canadian Action Party	• Type: Left-wing mass party • Political ideology: Economic nationalism • Objective: Advance an agenda of protectionist economic policies • Policies include: Promote local agriculture; increase federal government financial transfers so provinces will reduce tuition fees
Christian Heritage Party	• Type of party: Right-wing mass party • Political ideology: Christianity • Objective: Advance an agenda of policies that reflect Christian values • Policies include: Public education programs to reduce unhealthy lifestyles; promotion of adoption over abortion
Communist Party of Canada	• Type: Left-wing mass party • Political ideology: Socialism • Objective: Advance an agenda of socialist economic policies • Policies include: Government-funded childcare; significant increase to the minimum wage
Libertarian Party of Canada	• Type: Right-wing mass party • Political ideology: Libertarianism • Objective: Advance an agenda of libertarianism • Policies include: Reduce government subsidies, reduce taxes
Marijuana Party	• Type: Left-wing mass party • Political ideology: Libertarianism • Objective: Advance an agenda of decriminalizing marijuana • Policies include: Legalizing marijuana
Marxist–Leninist Party of Canada	• Type: Left-wing mass party • Political ideology: Communism • Objective: Advance an agenda of communist economic policies • Policies include: Nationalizing banks; withdrawal from free trade agreements
Online Party of Canada	• Type: Brokerage party • Political ideology: Populism • Objective: Advance an agenda developed through contributors' online votes • Policies include: Direct democracy using the Internet; unspecified Senate reform
Pirate Party of Canada	• Type: Mass party • Political ideology: Libertarianism • Objective: Advance an agenda of the free copying of electronic data • Policies include: Decriminalize private file-sharing; increase privacy protections

TABLE 9.2 | continued

Party Name and Logo	Characteristics
 Progressive Canadian Party*	• Type: Right-leaning mass party • Political ideology: Fiscal conservatism, democratic socialism • Objective: Advance a red tory policy agenda • Policies include: Support for small business; environmental protections
Rhinoceros Party	• Type: Mass party • Political ideology: Anarchism • Objective: Promote anti-partyism through unusual policies • Policies include: Abolishing the House of Commons but preserving the Senate; decriminalizing all drugs
United Party of Canada	• Type: Left-leaning mass party • Political ideology: Fiscal conservatism, democratic socialism, environmentalism • Objective: Advance a policy agenda that will bring Canadians together • Policies include: Promotion of renewable energy; universal access to post-secondary education
Western Block Party	• Type: Right-wing mass party • Political ideology: Western nationalism • Objective: Separation of Western provinces from Canada • Policies include: Direct democracy; lower taxes

*Not affiliated with the former Progressive Conservative Party of Canada, which became the Conservative Party in 2003, or with Progressive Conservative parties at the provincial level.

Source: Adapted from Elections Canada (www.elections.ca), Apathy Is Boring (www.apathyisboring.com).

poorly financed political organizations. It was designed to prevent the participation of nuisance or fringe parties that were disruptive to mainstream parties and those that used satire to mock the political system, such as the Rhinoceros Party (see Table 9.5). But the rule also contravened the democratic principle of free and fair elections. One deregistered minor party, the Communist Party of Canada, took the matter to court. In a 2003 judgement, the Supreme Court of Canada struck down the 50-candidate rule, declaring that it contravened provisions in the Charter of Rights and Freedoms that protect the democratic rights of citizens. In particular, the Court upheld the primacy of section 3 of the Charter, which stipulates that "Every citizen of Canada has the right to vote in an election of members of the House of Commons or of a legislative assembly and to be qualified for membership therein." This ruling meant that the 50-candidate rule provisions in the Canada Elections Act could no longer be enforced.[9] Since the 2004 federal election there has been no candidate minimum to register a political party. The number of minor political parties has increased as a result (see Table 9.2).

Party Ideologies

Regardless of their reputation as amorphous, "big tent" organizations, and their traditional focus on appealing to voters along regional lines, major political parties in Canada are by no means devoid of ideology. In fact, it is difficult to describe or

ideology A set of ideas that form a belief system underpinning a particular political or economic theory.

↻ Socialism, liberalism, conservatism, and other terms related to ideology are discussed in detail in Chapter 1 and summarized in Figure 1.3; see especially pages 11–16.

left-wing Characterized by a political tendency that promotes higher taxes and a bigger role for government while promoting proactive measures to secure social equality.

right-wing Characterized by a political tendency that promotes lower taxes and a smaller role for government, while supporting traditional social hierarchies and those resulting from competition.

A **traditional social democrat** advocates a branch of socialism that remains committed to replacing capitalism with a more co-operative economic system. A **third-way social democrat** advocates a branch of socialism that accepts capitalism and aims to harness it to achieve equality of result.

A **welfare liberal** seeks to achieve equality of opportunity in social terms. A **business liberal** seeks to achieve equality of opportunity in economic terms.

explain Canadian party politics without reference to terms like *left*, *right*, and *centre*, or *socialism*, *liberalism*, and *conservatism*.

Generally speaking, left-wing parties advocate increasing taxes on the incomes of the wealthy and big business, so that these revenues may be used to create and strengthen social programs. This fits with their progressive view of society, whereby those who are disadvantaged are provided with supports to achieve equality. Examples of left-wing parties include the NDP, the Bloc Québécois, and the Green Party of Canada.

By comparison, right-wing parties advocate the merits of reducing taxes as a means of stimulating economic growth in the private sector. By reducing the size of government they can keep taxes low but at a cost of reduced government services. This fits with their objective of building a society that is more self-reliant and less dependent on the state. Examples of right-wing parties include the Conservative Party of Canada and the former Reform Party of Canada.

Nestled somewhere in between the left and the right is the Liberal Party of Canada, which historically has defended national unity by accommodating regional and social cleavages, and has been motivated to adopt policies that it believes will give it the best chance of winning elections and forming government. Other federal parties, like the Bloc Québécois and Greens, often defy categorization on the traditional left–right spectrum. This is because their core values—be they Quebec nationalism or environmentalism—place them on different ideological planes compared to the New Democrats, Liberals, and Conservatives. This said, most BQ and Green policies may be placed on the left side of the spectrum (e.g. support for a woman's right to choose to have an abortion), while others like tax relief may place them on the right.

Canadian political parties are best considered amalgams of the various ideological groups, as depicted in Figure 9.1. In general, though it is not always the case, traditional and third-way social democrats tend to support the New Democratic Party, just as welfare and business liberals tend to support the Liberal Party. Historically, the Progressive Conservative Party was home to both red and blue tories, with Social Credit, Reform, and the Canadian Alliance more closely representing the interests of neo-liberals and neo-conservatives. Since the merger of Canadian Alliance with the Progressive Conservatives in 2003, when they became known as simply the Conservative Party of Canada, the old and new right have effectively united, with the latter emerging predominant.

Canadian Political Parties

Canada's Federal Party Systems

Given that party politics in any jurisdiction evolves over time, political scientists have a tendency to identify eras of stable party competition. Each of these periods tends to end with a fracturing of the party system, when electors express mass disenchantment at the ballot box, ushering in a period of renewal.

In Canada there are thought to have been at least three party systems at the federal level, each occurring during a different era of Canadian politics. Building on research conducted by political scientist R. Kenneth Carty (1988), whose later work

BRIEFING NOTES

Big and Small "l" Ideologies

It is important to distinguish partisan labels like "big-C" Conservatives and "big-L" Liberals from adherents of particular ideologies like "small-c" conservatives and "small-l" liberals. While many, if not most, small-c conservatives vote Conservative, not all of them do. By the same token, not all big-L Liberals ascribe to liberal values.

It is also important not to confuse American definitions of these terms with Canadian ones. A liberal in the United States might well be considered a socialist in Canada, and yet a conservative in Canada might actually get along better with the American liberal than with an American conservative. This is because politics south of the border is further to the right of the political spectrum than it is in Canada. For this reason, it is usually the case that Conservative prime ministers in Canada are more left-wing than American presidents, regardless of whether a president is a Democrat or a Republican.

with William Cross and Lisa Young (2000) described the evolution of Canadian party systems through the turn of the twenty-first century,[10] we can identify these three eras as follows:

1. from Confederation to World War I
2. from the inter-war period through to the late 1950s
3. from the 1960s through the early 1990s.

A fourth party system era has since taken shape, following an interval marked most noticeably by the fracturing of the Progressive Conservative Party in 1993 and the re-emergence of a united Conservative Party of Canada in 2004.

Each of these long periods of relative stability has been defined by a unique mix of political parties and a unique set of rules (both formal and informal) governing competition among them. Transition periods between them have varied in length, lasting anywhere from one to several election cycles and typically featuring minority governments, a proliferation of minor parties, and experimentation with new institutions and models of party behaviour.

To illustrate how party labels and the fortunes of political parties change over time, we need only look at the results of each formative election that marked the beginning or end of each federal party system (see Table 9.3). The first party system (*1867 to 1917*) was characterized by power rotating between the Conservative and Liberal parties, which were the only two major parties of the period. Some historians note that the first nationwide party election did not occur until 1898, although nascent party organizations did exist before that time. The dominant mode of campaigning involved these elite parties appealing to local notables whose financial resources and sway over their constituency's voters were crucial to a party's victory. Many party elites also owned or controlled local newspapers, which served as organs for the party-in-favour. Party leaders were usually proven politicians, chosen by and among the parliamentary caucus.

A **red tory** supports a form of "old right" conservatism that promotes the preservation of the social fabric and government institutions. A **blue tory** supports a form of "old right" conservatism that promotes economic nationalism and smaller government.

A **neoliberal** advocates a form of "new right" conservatism that favours less government intervention in the economy. A **neoconservative** advocates a form of "new right" conservatism that promotes the protection of traditional values, as well as community safety and national security.

party system A particular constellation of political parties guided by a unique framework of behaviour.

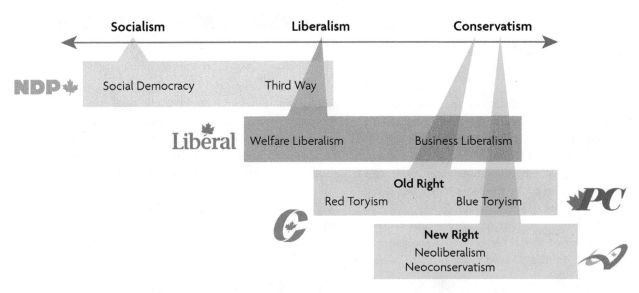

FIGURE 9.1 | Historically Where Canada's Major Federal Parties Sit on the Political Spectrum

Think ideology doesn't matter? This American niche dating site expanded to Canada in 2013 to help conservative singles find their ideal ideological mate. Is ideological compatibility a deal-breaker for you in assessing a potential life partner?

BRIEFING NOTES

Party System Eras

Just as the way ideological labels are applied to different party organizations can be controversial, so, too, can the start and end points of Canada's party system eras be a source of dispute. The following discussion suggests that there have been at least three party system eras, separated by transition periods of varying lengths:

- *1867 to 1917* – first party system era
- *1921 to 1957* – second party system era
- *1962 to 1993* – third party system era
- *2011 onward* – fourth party system era

That a fourth party system began with the 2011 general election is open to debate; more election results will be needed for political scientists to arrive at a consensus.

Insiders and outsiders may take issue with the precise cut-off points of these eras in general, and the identification of the newest party system in particular. It is important to note that these are offered as frames of reference to better understand the evolution of Canadian party politics, not as hard-and-fast timelines.

The second party system (*1921 to 1957*) saw several mass parties gain traction at the expense of elite parties. These new organizations, including the Progressives and their successors Social Credit and the Co-operative Commonwealth Federation, brought innovation to Canadian party politics. For instance, their success put

TABLE 9.3 | Results of Pivotal Canadian Federal Elections

Party	Number of Seats Won (% vote)				
	1867	*1921*	*1962*	*1993*	*2011*
Bloc Québécois	—	—	—	54 (13.5%)	4 (6.1)
Conservative*	101 (50.0)	50 (30.5)	116 (37.3)	2 (16.0)	166 (39.6)
Green	—	—	—	0 (0.2)	1 (3.9)
Labour	—	3 (2.7)	—	—	—
Liberal	80 (49.0)	116 (40.7)	99 (37.4)	177 (41.3)	34 (18.9)
NDP	—	—	19 (13.4)	9 (6.9)	103 (30.6)
Progressive	—	58 (21.1)	—	—	—
Reform Alliance	—	—	—	52 (18.7)	—
Social Credit	—	—	30 (11.7)	—	—
United Farmers	—	3 (0.8)	—	—	—
Other/independent	0 (1.0)	5 (5.1)	1 (0.2)	1 (3.6)	0 (1.0)
Total Seats	181	235	265	295	308

*Includes variants of party name

Note: Party affiliations were not formally recorded by Elections Canada until 1963.

Source: Data reproduced with permission from the Parliament of Canada. Parliament of Canada (2013). "Electoral results by party." http://www.parl.gc.ca/Parlinfo

CP Picture Archive/Fred Chartrand

Although the Liberal Party under Jean Chrétien (*left*) claimed a majority victory in the 1993 election, it relied heavily on near-sweeps of Ontario and Atlantic Canada. In defeat, rival parties gained strength in different regions of the country. Lucien Bouchard (*centre*) guided the Bloc Québécois to Official Opposition status with wins in 54 ridings—all in Quebec. The Reform Party of Preston Manning (*right*) garnered most of its 52 seats in Saskatchewan, Alberta, and BC, while the NDP, under Audrey McLaughlin (*second from the right*), likewise claimed all 9 of its seats west of Ontario. The Progressive Conservatives, behind Prime Minister Kim Campbell (*second from the left*), won just 2 seats (in Quebec and New Brunswick), a historic low for the party. What factors do you think contributed most to the collapse of Canada's system of regional brokerage?

pressure on the two mainstream parties to change their leadership selection processes from caucus conventions to more open conventions. Notwithstanding the regional focus of these mass parties, the overwhelming tenor of the second party system was one of brokerage, with the Liberals and Progressive Conservatives building bridges across regional divides to form majority governments.

This brokerage became easier during the third party system (*1962 to 1993*), with the advent of national media and broadcast television. While the independent press and radio had allowed new parties, like Social Credit, to build regional followings in the second party system, the Liberals, PCs, and New Democrats used nationwide TV to build pan-Canadian agendas and support. In this way, technology helped the NDP become entrenched as the third major federal party, although it never attained official opposition status in this era. This made Canada a "two-plus" party system with two major parties and a third major competitor.

This period of stability was interrupted by the largest earthquake in Canadian electoral history: the 1993 election. Its reverberations lasted the better part of the next decade, resulting in significant regional instability that led to a long period of multipartyism, with as many as five major parties competing for votes in various regions of the country. In many ways, the 1993–2003 interlude mirrored the sort of regional tensions that marked earlier transitions. Just as the Progressives emerged in the 1920s and Social Credit had become emboldened in the 1950s, so, too, did the Bloc Québécois and the Reform Party gather strength in the late 1980s and early 1990s.

As we'll see in greater detail later in this chapter, the nature of this instability changed in the early twenty-first century, as regional tensions during a period of Liberal majority government began to wane, only to be replaced by divisive partisanship and gamesmanship during three successive minority governments in 2004, 2006, and 2008. A lull descended in 2011, when electors awarded a majority government to the Conservative Party; the NDP became the official opposition for the first time; the Liberal Party earned the fewest number of seats in its history; the Bloc Québécois was reduced to four seats; and the Greens elected their first member of Parliament. One or more electoral cycles will be required to establish the validity of this fourth party system. The Liberal Party's victory in 2015, for instance, challenged the notion that Conservative governments, NDP strength, and a thoroughly divided left were hallmarks of the latest era of party competition. Nevertheless, we can see that, like earlier eras, the latest system of party competition has some unique features.

Canada's Provincial Party Systems

Political parties operate in all 10 provinces and in Yukon (see Table 9.4). In most provinces, but not all of them, the most competitive parties are those that are affiliated with a federal counterpart. The nuances of provincial politics are such that it can be difficult for many people to recognize the extent to which a party has national ties. Just because two parties share the same label does not mean that they are like-minded or collaborative. Equally, just because two parties have different names does not necessarily mean they oppose each other, although it certainly increases the possibility.

As at the federal level, each province features its own set of party systems. So, too, does Yukon—the only territory with partisan representation as opposed to consensus government. The premiers and governing parties for these various systems can be

↻ Consensus government is discussed in Chapter 6, in the section on territorial legislatures: see pages 247–48.

TABLE 9.4 | Registered Political Parties in Recent Canadian Provincial/Territorial Elections

Province/Territory	NDP	LIB	PC	GRN	Other(s)
British Columbia	✔	✔		✔	Conservative Party
Alberta	✔	✔	✔		Wildrose Party, Alberta Party
Saskatchewan	✔	✔		✔	Saskatchewan Party
Manitoba	✔	✔	✔	✔	
Ontario	✔	✔	✔	✔	
Quebec		✔			Parti Québécois, Coalition Avenir Québec, Option Nationale, Québec Solidaire
New Brunswick	✔	✔	✔	✔	People's Alliance of New Brunswick
Newfoundland and Labrador	✔	✔	✔		
Nova Scotia	✔	✔	✔		
Prince Edward Island	✔	✔	✔	✔	
Yukon	✔	✔			Yukon Party
Northwest Territories					No political parties
Nunavut					No political parties

Note: Includes only political parties that obtained at least 1 per cent of the total vote in the 2011–15 election cycle.

found in the appendix at the back of this book. In general, provincial party systems have come in the following main varieties:

- *one-party dominant systems*, featuring long periods of rule by one party organization (as historically with the Progressive Conservatives and Social Credit in Alberta)
- *two-party brokerage systems*, featuring close but largely non-ideological competition between Canada's two longest-running parties, the Liberals and PCs (as in New Brunswick and PEI)
- *polarized two-party systems*, featuring close and pitched competition between two ideologically polarized parties (as with the NDP and Liberals in BC, the Sask Party and NDP in Saskatchewan, and the Liberals and Parti Québécois in Quebec)
- *two-and-a-half party systems*, featuring two major competitors and a weaker but still relevant third party (as in Manitoba, where the NDP and PCs lead the Liberals, and Nova Scotia and Newfoundland and Labrador, where the NDP serves as the province's third party, after the Liberals and PCs)
- *three-party systems*, where competition is tight among three relatively well-balanced parties (as in Ontario, where the Liberals, PCs, and New Democrats are relatively evenly matched, and Yukon, where the Yukon Party, Liberals, and New Democrats divide the vote).

Jurisdictions move in and out of these categories as competitive dynamics change. For decades, Ontario featured a one-party dominant system governed by the PCs' "big blue machine," and Nova Scotia has only recently transitioned away from a traditional two-party system with the rise of the NDP to power. Yet, these transformations are often very slow and may be influenced by a party's relationship with its federal counterpart.

Political scientist Rand Dyck (1992) described the linkages between federal and provincial parties in the following way.[11] Integrated parties are characterized by the teamwork, ideological similarities, and sharing of resources between federal and provincial units. The NDP is a classic case of an integrated party, as are the Liberal parties in the Atlantic provinces. In each case, the federal party organization is fully integrated with the provincial parties because they share fundraising apparatuses, lists of supporters, party workers, and policy objectives. For example, the NDP's top strategists who worked on the 2011 federal campaign were dispatched to British Columbia to run the party's provincial campaign in 2013. In general, Atlantic Canada has tended to feature the most integrated political parties; ties between federal and provincial organizations are much weaker in the rest of Canada.

Unlike integrated parties, confederal parties share the same or a similar label but do not see eye to eye. Their leaders and parliamentarians may privately or publicly criticize each other, they may have different ideologies, and each side may see the other as getting in the way of an agenda. The federal Liberal Party and the BC Liberal Party are a good example of party units that have different ideologies and few formal ties, as the BC Liberals tend to have closer connections with the federal Conservatives. Likewise, the provincial Quebec Liberal Party brings together federalists from all three major parties at the federal level.

As well, a number of provincial Progressive Conservative parties have had strained, if not icy, relations with the federal Conservative Party, whose constitution

integrated parties Federal and provincial political parties whose behaviours and organization are interconnected.

confederal parties Federal and provincial parties that operate autonomously from each other, even though they may have similar names.

states that it shall not establish provincial parties. An excellent example occurred in Newfoundland and Labrador during the 2008 federal election. As a result of a dispute between PC premier Danny Williams and Conservative prime minister Stephen Harper, the former urged Canadians to vote "anything but Conservative." Williams's so-called "ABC campaign" reached beyond Newfoundland and Labrador to the point where the Newfoundland PC Party bought advertising space on a billboard along Toronto's Gardiner Expressway advising Ontarians not to vote Conservative. The campaign succeeded to the extent that the federal Conservatives won no seats in Newfoundland during the 2008 election; however, it appears to have had no impact elsewhere in the country.

Lastly, there are many truncated parties, which do not have namesakes at both levels. Organizations like the Yukon Party, Saskatchewan Party, and Alberta's Wildrose Party do not run candidates at the federal level. These parties tend to ally themselves with the federal Conservatives, however. Historically, the Reform Party of Canada refused to run candidates at the provincial level; many Social Credit and PC voters in the Western provinces chose to support Reform at the federal level. The Bloc Québécois and Parti Québécois are another example of sister organizations that share resources but not the same name.

> **truncated party** A federal or provincial political party that does not have a similarly named party at the other level of government.

Provincial elections, like federal elections, can feature a number of minor political parties that seek to advance an agenda but are not in contention to win any seats, let alone form the government. The number of political parties may be related to how difficult it is to register a party, the diversity of public opinions, and the ability to organize and fundraise. Thus the variety of political actors in one province is not necessarily indicative of party competition elsewhere. For instance, in Canada's westernmost province, minor parties that earned less than 1 per cent of the vote in the 2013 provincial election were the Advocational Party, BC Vision, the BC Excalibur Party, BC First, the BC Marijuana Party, the BC Social Credit Party, the British Columbia Party, the Christian Heritage Party of BC, the Communist Party of BC, the Helping Hand Party, the Platinum Party, Unparty: The Consensus-Building Party, the Work Less Party, and Your Political Party (YPP). Conversely, in Canada's easternmost province, only the three major parties and a handful of independents contested the 2011 Newfoundland and Labrador election.

Political parties have a much smaller presence at the territorial and municipal levels of government in Canada. Of the three territories, only Yukon has parties; in Northwest Territories and Nunavut, candidates run as independents, and later participate in consensus government. During election campaigns, in some large cities and small towns there are electoral alliances of like-minded candidates who pool resources to campaign under a local banner. In most municipalities, candidates officially run as independents, though some may have an affiliation with a federal or provincial party that they may or may not communicate to electors.

The Evolution of Major Parties

Understanding the evolution of Canadian party politics can be challenging without reference to some sort of family tree (see Figure 9.2), whose components we discuss next.

At the federal level, the only constant in Canadian party politics has been the Liberal Party of Canada. Nicknamed "the Grits"—a moniker that dates back to a

> **Liberal Party** A brokerage party that has governed Canada at the federal level longer than any other major party.

pre-Confederation movement for democratic reform—the party began by promoting business liberalism and has evolved to promote welfare liberalism. Its key strength has been its ability to act as a broker of the English–French divide, a role that has seen it currying the favour of Quebec, to the great frustration of western Canada. The party's pro-Quebec image, along with its reluctance to move more forcefully to implement free trade, prompted many Western and rural Liberals to form a splinter party in the period between the two world wars. The Progressives ran successfully under a variety of banners, forming provincial governments (under the banner "United Farmers") in Ontario, Manitoba, and Alberta, and winning enough seats to become the official opposition in Ottawa in 1921. However, on principle, the Progressives handed the third-place Conservatives the official opposition title and function, seeing them as arcane relics of traditional party politics. Most Progressives returned to the Liberal fold by 1925, having convinced the party's establishment of the need to balance rural and Western interests with those of central Canada and the cities. The Liberals went on to become a powerhouse from that point through 2006, controlling the federal government for long periods of uninterrupted rule, including 1935–57, 1963–79, and 1993–2006.

natural governing party
A single party whose long-term dominance has become institutionalized.

This hegemony has caused many observers to call the Liberals Canada's natural governing party. The party's success has been based on an appeal to the median voter that balances left-wing policies of communitarianism with appeals to right-wing

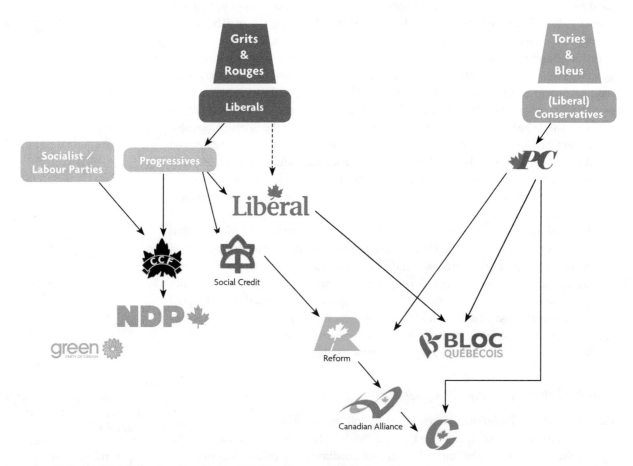

FIGURE 9.2 | The Canadian Federal Political Party "Family Tree"

individualists. Notably, the Liberals have been successful at cultivating support from the business community while maintaining a progressive public image on social issues.[12] From 1896 to 2006, every Liberal leader had become prime minister, and the party had never placed worse than second in a general election. In the ensuing decade, the party experienced more difficulty. Leaders Stéphane Dion and Michael Ignatieff led the Liberals to poor showings in the 2008 and 2011 general elections, respectively, and soon after resigned. Liberal partisans hoped that new leader Justin Trudeau could reclaim some of the success experienced by his father, Pierre Elliott Trudeau, who led the party from 1968 to 1984 and was prime minister for almost the entire time. Those hopes were well-placed, when the younger Trudeau led his party to a surprise majority victory in 2015.

Throughout the twentieth century, the Conservative Party of Canada, together with its predecessors, acted as the main alternative to the Liberal Party. Its ideology began as traditionalist tory conservatism and loyalty to Britain, particularly the monarchy. The party's principles have since evolved to attract fiscal, religious, and social conservatives. This clustering of different points of view and political agendas has meant that the Conservative Party has often served as a mechanism to bring together people who are frustrated with Liberal governance, particularly residents of Western and rural Canada. Some of the Conservative Party's leaders have won the most lopsided election victories in Canadian history, with John A. Macdonald winning five majority governments in the late nineteenth century, John Diefenbaker winning the biggest federal landslide ever in 1958, and Brian Mulroney capturing the largest number of seats in Canadian history in 1984. Yet the party has seen these periods of success offset by precipitous failures, most notoriously in 1993, when it went from being the government to winning just two seats. In the midst of constitutional negotiations over the Meech Lake and Charlottetown Accords, many Progressive Conservatives left the party to found the Reform Party (1987) or else joined with disgruntled Liberal Party members to form the Bloc Québécois (1991). This was the most significant instance of the party's being unable to maintain its coalition of ideological factions, and over time it has changed its name a number of times in an effort to

Conservative Party A centre–right major party that has periodically formed the government of Canada.

↻ The creation of the Bloc Québécois is discussed later in this chapter on pages 365–6.

BRIEFING NOTES

Names as Political Brands

The wide variety of names used to label political parties in Canada can be bewildering. The confusion is heightened when some of the names appear to be oxymorons, like "Liberal–Conservative" and "Progressive Conservative." Others—like the Saskatchewan Party, Canadian Alliance, Parti Québécois, Western Canada Concept, and Confederation of Regions—avoid ideological references altogether. Such naming conventions, in evidence throughout Canadian history, are part of a strategy taken up by party leaders and their advisers to build bridges between ideological camps. For this reason, it is best to consider these names as *brands* and not as *ideological labels*.

The Canadian Press/Fred Chartrand

Ontario Liberal premier Kathleen Wynne, on stage with federal Liberal leader Justin Trudeau prior to the 2015 election. Four provinces and one territory have had Liberal heads of government who were women. Yet the Liberals are the only major federal party that has never had a woman leader at the national level. Does this surprise you? What might explain this?

broaden its appeal (see Table 9.5). The latest incarnation was formed in 2003, when the Canadian Alliance Party (previously known as the Reform Party) and the Progressive Conservative Party merged to become the Conservative Party of Canada. The new party's first leadership contest was held in 2004 and was won by Stephen Harper. Under Harper, the Conservative Party went on to win a minority of seats in the 2006 and 2008 elections, and formed a majority government after the 2011 election. The Conservatives' defeat in 2015, and Stephen Harper's subsequent resignation as leader, leaves many questions in terms of the party's future.

TABLE 9.5 | Name Changes of Major Political Parties in Canada

Political Party	Formerly Known as . . .
Conservative Party of Canada (since 2003)	• Liberal–Conservative Party* (1867–73, 1920–30) • Conservative Party (1873–1920, 1930–42) • Progressive Conservative Party (1942–2003)**
Liberal Party of Canada	• Liberal-Reform Party (1867–78)
New Democratic Party of Canada (since 1961)	• Co-operative Commonwealth Federation (1932–61)

*Variations of this terminology were used at different times. The party also presented itself as the Unionist Party in the 1917 federal election and headed the so-called Union government.

**In 2003 the PC Party merged with the Canadian Alliance Party to form the Conservative Party of Canada. The Canadian Alliance was created in 2000 as a rebranded version of its predecessor, the Reform Party of Canada.

There are a few nuances about the Conservative Party that are worth noting. First, in a tradition dating back to seventeenth-century Britain, partisans and the party are commonly referred to as "Tories." Second, the federal Conservative Party is not officially affiliated with provincial Progressive Conservative parties. The federal Conservative Party changed its name to the Progressive Conservative (PC) Party in 1942, when Manitoba premier John Bracken became leader and appealed (largely in vain) to those who supported the Progressive Party of the era. Provincial parties followed suit, and to this day in all but three provinces (BC, Saskatchewan, and Quebec), they are known as the provincial PC Party. Third, ideological splits and coalitions have often occurred on different approaches to conservatism. The neoliberal ideology espoused by Prime Minister Harper, and before him the Reform and Canadian Alliance parties, is free-market individualism. Neoliberals like Harper believe in lower taxes, smaller government, and libertarianism, while blue tories in the party recognize the important role of the state in the economy. Neoconservatives often clash with neoliberals over the role of the state in enforcing moral standards, and with red tories over the importance of protecting traditional family values. Meanwhile, red tories may have supported the now defunct federal Progressive Conservative Party and currently identify with a provincial PC Party, or even the NDP, more than with the federal Conservatives. As political scientist Gad Horowitz once explained, "At the simplest level, [a red tory] is a Conservative who prefers the CCF–NDP to the Liberals, or a socialist who prefers the Conservatives to the Liberals, without really knowing why."[13]

Unlike the Conservative and Liberal parties, the New Democratic Party of Canada (NDP) does not trace its roots back to Confederation. Rather, its origins are in the post–World War I social gospel movement led by labour activists such as J.S. Woodsworth. Their mobilization of people concerned about the inequities of capitalism and the effects of the Great Depression led to the creation in 1932 of the Co-operative Commonwealth Federation (CCF). Despite the fact the party formed the provincial government in Saskatchewan in 1945, the CCF's supporters grew frustrated with underwhelming election results, including winning just eight seats in the 1958 federal election. In 1961 the party formally united with organized labour and rebranded itself as the NDP.

Over time the NDP has gradually moved away from an outright rejection of capitalism toward espousing a third-way, communitarian approach. This includes higher taxes on big business and the wealthy, stronger social programs, strict environmental protections, and a reduced role in military conflict. However, despite this shift toward the centre, the party has tended to fare poorly in Canada's winner-take-all electoral system, and in most elections it would have won many more seats under a system of proportional representation, where the number of seats won corresponds to the percentage of popular votes. At the same time, the left-wing radicalism espoused by some of the party's most hardline supporters has inhibited gains among many voters. Notwithstanding its breakthrough in the 2011 federal election, the NDP's victories have been achieved mostly by influencing public policy when the Liberal Party has formed the government, notably when Liberal minority governments turned to the NDP for support in the 1960s. The party's electoral success has been confined to provincial elections, where its affiliated units have formed the government in six provinces (BC, Alberta, Saskatchewan, Manitoba, Ontario, and Nova Scotia).

New Democratic Party
A left-wing major party that has historically been more successful at the provincial level of government than at the federal level.

↺ The components of Canada's social safety net are discussed at length in Chapter 8, on public policy and administration: see especially pages 317–26.

INSIDE CANADIAN POLITICS
How Did the CCF Evolve into Today's NDP?

Today's NDP is very different from its origins. The seeds of the party were sown by frustrated workers and the unemployed after World War I. Socialist uprisings in Europe, notably in Russia, played a role in inspiring the Winnipeg General Strike of 1919. The implications of Canada's being without a strong social safety net became clear in the early 1930s, during the Great Depression. Rising unemployment rates showed no signs of abatement, a drought devastated farms, and families were in need of food. Capitalism seemed to favour the rich at the expense of the poor.

In 1932, prominent members of fledgling left-wing protest parties including the United Farmers, the Progressive Party, and the Labour Party joined forces. The Co-operative Commonwealth Federation (CCF) was formed, and at its 1933 convention, members adopted the so-called Regina Manifesto. This policy document called for the CCF to replace the free-market forces of capitalism with government management of the economy through democratic socialism, a system that depended on nationalizing several sectors of the economy.

A mass party, the CCF was unable to wrest control of the government from its rival catch-all parties, despite its success in some provincial elections (notably in Saskatchewan, under Tommy Douglas). During the Cold War, critics decried the CCF's sympathies for communism, and in 1956 the party attempted to move toward the political centre by passing the Winnipeg Declaration. The new policy plank allowed the CCF to continue to embrace its socialist principles while now promoting the Keynesian economic approach of government spending to stimulate economic growth. In the late 1950s, the party continued to move away from the far left. The CCF formed an alliance with the Canadian Labour Congress, and for three years supporters from both camps worked to create a new party. At a party convention in 1961, the CCF was dissolved and the New Democratic Party (NDP) was born.

The new party espoused more tempered leftist policies and marked an evolution from the CCF's origins as a protest party. The preamble of the NDP's constitution pledged a belief in "the application of democratic socialist principles to government." This included championing the needs of individuals including the poor, supporting a sustainable environment, and seeking peace. But the constitution also declared the NDP's positions against "the making of profit" and for "the principle of social ownership" and "economic and social planning." Although the party's popular support broadened, it remained disadvantaged by the single-member plurality (SMP) electoral system, and at times was marginalized by the Liberal Party's claiming credit for adopting NDP policies such as medicare. According

Federal Protest Parties

protest party A party that galvanizes elector frustrations with the major political parties.

Since the early twentieth century there has been a revolving door of protest parties that have been outlets for voters to express their frustrations. Many began as inconsequential fringe parties but, unlike organizations such as the Rhinoceros Party of Canada, some protest parties have eventually attracted sufficient support in an election to influence the outcome. The electoral system plays a significant role in rewarding protest parties: those organizations that have a national focus tend not to elect many MPs, whereas those parties whose support is concentrated in a region can disrupt the party system.

Green Party A left-wing protest party that promotes environmentalism.

In recent years, the Green Party of Canada has played a significant role in elections and party politics. Its core philosophy of environmentalism also draws in

to public opinion polls in 1987, the NDP was, for the first time, Canadians' preferred choice to form a government. Yet once again it placed third in the ensuing election. By 1993, the NDP was reduced to nine seats in Parliament and would spend a decade in fourth place in the House of Commons.

The NDP's evolution toward a catch-all party accelerated when Jack Layton became its leader in 2003. In four elections from 2004 to 2011, the party positioned Layton as prime ministerial, and emphasized populist policies that would appeal to mainstream Canadians, such as lower credit card fees. The SMP system (also known as "first past the post") worked to their advantage in 2011, when a surge of Quebec support helped the party win 59 seats in that province alone and, for the first time, the NDP formed the official opposition.

The party embraced many of the third-way policies and marketing techniques that had earlier propelled UK's New Labour and Tony Blair to victory. However, while Blair formally divorced Labour from socialism in the mid-1990s, the NDP's constitution still espoused socialist principles throughout Layton's tenure. At the party's 2013 convention, under new leader Thomas Mulcair, NDP delegates voted 960 to 188 for a change in wording and philosophy. The preamble was amended to promote the progressive principles of "greater equality, justice, and opportunity" in a "more just, equal, and sustainable Canada." The NDP's new economic policy declared that "governments have the power to address the limitations of the market in addressing the common good." In explaining the party's move toward the centre, Mulcair said: "That's the way to connect and reach out beyond our traditional base. A lot of Canadians share our vision and our goals in the NDP. We've just got to make sure that by modernizing, by using the language that resonates with a wider public in Canada, that we'll be able to do what we have to do, which is to defeat [the Conservative government led by] Stephen Harper."[14]

THE LESSON

Major political parties at the federal level in Canada are often challenged to balance their adherence to ideological principles, on one hand, and the need to engage in catch-all strategies in order to gain power, on the other. Tony Blair put it bluntly: "Power without principle is barren, but principle without power is futile."

elements of fiscal conservatism, social progressivism, and democratic idealism. From its founding in 1983 through the early 2000s, it was a fringe organization that earned less than 1 per cent of the vote. Two major political changes catapulted the Greens from the fringe to national attention. First, the Canada Elections Act was amended in 2003 to provide political parties with state funding, using a formula that awarded money for each vote received. This per-vote subsidy incentivized the Green Party to get votes in every available electoral district across the country, and in 2004 it became only the fourth Canadian party ever to field a full slate of candidates. Second, the environmental movement in Western societies saw a surge in support, epitomized by the popular and critical acclaim, including an Academy Award, for the documentary film *An Inconvenient Truth* (2006), in which former American vice-president Al Gore set out his concerns about global warning. Support for the Green Party surged.

By 2008, concerns about climate change were so great that Canada's national broadcast networks bent to popular demand to include Green Party leader Elizabeth May in the leaders' debates; previously, only political parties with a seat in Parliament had been invited. The party is regularly cited as the preference of 5 to 8 per cent of respondents in public opinion polls, but has had difficulty translating this popular support into seats. This is due largely to the fact that the party's support is spread thinly across the entire country, rather than being geographically concentrated. The Greens perform best in British Columbia, and in 2011 and 2015, May won a seat in the BC riding of Saanich–Gulf Islands to became her party's first elected member of Parliament. In 2013, the Green caucus doubled in size when a New Democrat MP left the NDP caucus and crossed the floor. The phasing out of the per-vote subsidy by 2015 will put more revenue pressure on all of the parties, but especially the Greens.

↻ The election challenges facing the Greens are discussed in the context of PR electoral systems in Chapter 10, on elections: see pages 401–2.

The flaring up of regional grievances has had the most significant implications for Canadian party politics, however. In western Canada, a number of protest parties rose to prominence between World War I and World War II, and their appeal sometimes extended east of Manitoba. For instance, the Progressive Party (1914–30) was a vehicle for farmers who were upset about tariffs and rising train freight rates. They had alliances with the United Farmers parties that had organized in provinces across Canada, particularly in Alberta, Manitoba, and Ontario. In those provinces, Progressives placed increased pressure on the governing Liberals to implement democratic reforms, notably the extension of the franchise to women. The Progressives established a regional alternative to the two-party system dominated by the Liberal and Conservative

The Canadian Press/Justin Tang

Demonstrators attend a rally on Parliament Hill. The Marijuana Party is a federal protest party that has been running candidates on a single issue—the decriminalization of recreational marijuana use—since 2000. In 2015, the issue was taken up as part of the Liberal Party's platform, and became a legislative priority for the new Liberal government. Are protest parties like the Green Party and the Marijuana Party only relevant until their causes go mainstream? Do they still serve a role, even if their policies are adopted by major parties?

parties, and placed second in the 1921 election. That same year, Canada's first woman MP, Agnes Macphail, was elected as a member of the upstart party. But it had no formal leader, and, as noted earlier this chapter, supporters gradually gravitated back to the Liberal Party or on to other movements. On the left, the Progressives gave rise to the CCF, while those on the right launched Social Credit (1935–93). The "Socreds" were a band of conservatives and populists whose original goal of radical financial reform gradually gave way to more mainstream forms of neoconservatism and neoliberalism. Forming the provincial government in Alberta from 1935 to 1971, the Socred movement faded elsewhere on the Prairies in the 1950s but still found support as the "Ralliement des créditistes" in Quebec into the 1960s, and was successful in some BC provincial elections until the early 1990s, when it disbanded.

More recently, the aforementioned Reform Party (1987–2000) emerged as a Western-based conservative protest party whose leader, Preston Manning, promoted an agenda captured in the slogan "the West wants in." He had worked alongside his father, Alberta premier Ernest Manning, in building Social Credit support throughout the 1960s. Reform's familiar ideology of demanding smaller and more responsible government appealed to neoliberals, neoconservatives, and disgruntled Westerners alike. To many people's surprise, 52 Reform MPs were elected in the 1993 election, and the party went on to form the official opposition in 1997. Preston Manning led a rebranding of the party into the Canadian Alliance (2000–3), but was unsuccessful in his ensuing leadership bid. The Canadian Alliance was formed in an attempt to attract remaining supporters of the federal Progressive Conservative Party as well as "blue Liberals" (Liberal partisans who are partial to fiscal conservatism), all so that the party could achieve a breakthrough in Ontario and usurp the Liberal Party's grip on government. Although the Alliance formed the official opposition after the 2000 general election, this was a disappointment to partisans. Stephen Harper, an original Reform MP who had not sought re-election in 1997, returned to party politics by seeking and winning the leadership of the Alliance. As leader, he pushed an agenda to merge the Alliance with the PC Party, which resulted in the creation of the Conservative Party of Canada in 2003.

Regional protest parties have also found success in Quebec. Unlike other protest parties operating at the federal level, these organizations have fielded candidates exclusively in that province and have had no aspirations of forming the government. The earliest was the Ligue Nationaliste Canadienne (1900–12), a fledgling organization created by disgruntled Liberal MP Henri Bourassa, who sought to bring together Quebecers who were frustrated with British imperialism. The Bloc Populaire Canadien (1942–47) emerged in response to anger about the possibility of conscription in World War II and similarly attracted Quebec nationalists. But by far the most successful Quebec protest party has been the Bloc Québécois. It was formed by nationalists who were frustrated by the defeat of the Meech Lake Accord in 1990. The Bloc attracted disgruntled Liberals and Progressive Conservatives, in particular federal PC minister Lucien Bouchard, who became the party's leader. The BQ promoted sovereignty–association and shocked Canadians by forming the official opposition after the 1993 election. In the aftermath of the failed 1995 Quebec referendum, the Bloc began championing Quebec's concerns generally, particularly with respect to social democracy, but also on issues such as demanding tougher laws against biker gangs, stoking public anger about the sponsorship scandal, and advocating the need

↻ Western alienation is discussed in the concept of sectionalism in Chapter 4, on regionalism: see pages 136–37.

Bloc Québécois A left-leaning protest party that promotes Quebec nationalism.

to fix the fiscal imbalance. But its raison d'être began to wane with the popularity of the sovereignist movement. By 2011, the party was devoid of new policy ideas, setting the stage for many Quebecers to turn to the NDP instead. While more than doubling its seat total in 2015, the Bloc once again failed to achieve official party status in the House of Commons, leaving the immediate future of the party in doubt.

Party Candidates and Independents

In order to represent a party in an election, a person must first be nominated, and this may involve contesting a nomination campaign. In *Candidates and Constituency Campaigns in Canadian Elections*,[16] political scientist Anthony Sayers classified Canadian parties' election candidates into four groups:

- *Star candidates* are the handful of high-profile people whose involvement is actively promoted by the party centre and who may be asked to speak publicly on behalf of the party. In Canada, unlike the United States, it is rare for a star candidate to be a pop culture celebrity. Normally the star candidates in Canadian politics are people who have held senior positions in business, advocacy groups, or not-for-profit organizations.
- *Party insiders* are people who have worked their way up through the party over the years and are extremely well connected internally, especially with the party leader.

THEY SAID IT

Stephen Harper on the Bloc Québécois and Sovereignty

In an effort to blunt their attacks on the status quo, major parties take every opportunity to brand protest parties as extremist. The Conservative Party of Canada, for instance, is fond of referring to the NDP and Bloc Québécois as "socialists" and "separatists," respectively. Consider the following statement by Prime Minister Stephen Harper:

> In spite of the popularity of the Bloc and other sovereigntist parties, support for sovereignty itself has fallen dramatically since our government came to office.

When the election comes I can be sure that the one subject [leader of the Bloc Québécois] Mr Duceppe isn't going to talk about during the election is sovereignty. You know he goes to Washington and he talks about sovereignty, he goes to Europe and he talks about sovereignty, but he never talks about sovereignty to Quebeckers any more. That's a sign of how the mission of that party has faded.[15]

—Prime Minister Stephen Harper (2011)

VOX POP

Why do you suppose the Prime Minister would draw attention to the sovereignty issue, when—in his own words—it had declined in importance?

- *Local notables* are people who are well known in the electoral district in which they hope to run, and whose candidacy tends to be more formidable than media coverage suggests. A local notable may be a mayor or a city councillor, or the leader of a community interest group.
- *Stopgap candidates* are more common than major political parties are willing to admit. Stopgaps are people whose candidacy goes uncontested, who run in a riding where there is no active electoral district association, and who operate a campaign on a shoestring budget. A stopgap is little more than a name on the ballot for the party because the prospects of winning are very weak; the candidate likely risks not even qualifying for the minimum vote threshold (currently 10 per cent of the vote) to qualify for a partial return of election expenses from Elections Canada. Stopgaps are often students, party volunteers, and idealists who want to help the party and who engage their families and friends for support. Although their electoral prospects are dim, once in a while they are elected amidst a sweeping electoral tide that favours one party's candidates above all others'.

In each election there are candidates who run as independents. These people are not formally affiliated with a political party. Sometimes they simply wish to put their names forward in the election process; other times they are former partisans, even MPs, who have severed their relationship with a party. The election of

UP FOR DEBATE

Should Canada's political parties do more to recruit members of underrepresented groups as candidates? The debate supplement at the end of this chapter gives some of the arguments on both sides, and offers questions and resources to guide a discussion around this pressing topic.

independent A candidate or parliamentarian who is not officially affiliated with a political party.

In 2011, Ruth Ellen Brosseau was working at a Carleton University pub when she became a stopgap candidate for the NDP in Berthier–Maskinongé, Quebec. As someone who did not even live near the riding, she was an example of a parachute candidate who was dropped in as a name on the ballot. Despite her francophone-sounding surname, she barely spoke French. She vacationed in Las Vegas during the campaign and did not visit the riding even once. Nevertheless, Brosseau was elected amidst the "Orange Wave" that propelled numerous New Democrat stopgaps to victory in Quebec. A similar wave brought many rookie New Democrats into the government caucus following the 2015 Alberta election. What do you think it takes for a stopgap candidate like Brosseau to be elected? What do they need to do to get re-elected as Brosseau was in the 2015 election?

INSIDE CANADIAN POLITICS

Do Independent Candidates Face Discrimination?

Independents face many barriers to election in Canada. A major party label, when listed on the ballot next to a name, can offer voters a very powerful cue. More than this, however, the electoral laws and rules of campaigning often discriminate against independent candidates. As but one example, at the federal level, only political parties are allowed to raise funds between election periods. This prevents independents from collecting donations or issuing tax receipts to their contributors outside of the formal election campaign. Edmonton-based independent MP Brent Rathgeber (who was elected as a Conservative before leaving the party in between elections) raised this objection during parliamentary debates surrounding a series of amendments to the Canada Elections Act, but his calls for equal treatment of partisan and non-partisan candidates went unheeded by the government and official opposition.

VOX POP

Why do you think independent candidates are prohibited from receiving donations between election periods?

independents in general elections or by-elections is exceedingly rare in Canada. A member of Parliament who has been kicked out of a party for taking a stand on an issue of concern to constituents may have a chance at re-election, as may a popular party insider who has failed to secure the party nomination because the party centre approved a different candidate. But there are no guarantees. For instance, Louise Thibault was elected as a Bloc MP in 2004 and 2006, but resigned from the party to sit as an independent in 2007 and was defeated by the new Bloc candidate in the 2008 general election. As a consequence, parliamentarians who leave their party do so knowing that their chances of re-election are low, unless they cross the floor to a popular alternative.

Structure of Political Parties

To further understand political parties, we must unpack their many parts. There are three basic types of people who are affiliated with a political party. There are those who are formally involved with the internal machinery of the party (the *extra-parliamentary wing*), those who represent the party in a legislature (the *parliamentary wing*), and those who have a psychological attachment to the party whether or not they have any formal role (*partisans*).

The Extra-parliamentary Wing

Political parties have common organizational structures. The most formalized parties have their own constitution to establish basic matters such as the party's name, its principles, and its objectives. A party constitution outlines eligibility criteria for joining the party, guidelines for maintaining a senior party council or board of directors, and requirements for controlling the party's finances. It informs the coordination of election readiness by stipulating rules for party conventions, where members vote on policies and select a leader; rules for running electoral district associations; and rules for representing the party as an election candidate. There may also be information about committees and commissions, as well as details about any official affiliation with other political organizations (including unions or professional associations). Guidelines about the method for changing the constitution are identified, so that the party may evolve to reflect party members' priorities. The components of party constitutions are therefore integral to how a political party takes shape.

The federal Conservative, Liberal, and New Democratic party constitutions share many commonalities, and yet each has distinctive elements. Each identifies the party principles, namely the shared values, ideologies, and purposes of the party. For the Conservative Party, this includes "A belief in a balance between fiscal accountability, progressive social policy and individual rights and responsibilities"; for the Liberal Party, the principles of "individual freedom, responsibility and human dignity in the framework of a just society, and political freedom in the framework of meaningful participation by all persons"; and for the NDP, the building of "sustainable prosperity and a society that shares its benefits more fairly."

Party members are those people who have formally applied to belong to a party, have likely paid a membership fee, and are expected to help advance the party's objectives. All residents of Canada above a specified age may apply for membership as long as they do not simultaneously belong to another party. Party members are eligible to formally participate in party activities, normally in the riding where they live. For example, the Conservative Party constitution states that individual members may attend local party meetings, may seek election to the board of directors of their electoral district association, may stand for election to be a delegate at a national party convention, and may vote in such internal party contests. In addition to individual membership, the NDP provides affiliated membership to "trade unions, farm groups, co-operatives, women's organizations and other groups" that share the party's values. That party designates formal roles and titles for members of organized labour within its organizational hierarchy, including a vice-president position and two positions on the party executive. It also reserves up to thirty positions for representatives of national labour organizations on the party's national council.

The internal organizational structures of federal political parties vary somewhat but in general resemble the model shown in Figure 9.3. Provincial and territorial parties are supported by similar frameworks, albeit on a smaller scale, with fewer layers and internal bodies. Each party's extra-parliamentary wing is coloured in yellow, and consists largely of party members and their delegates, most of whom are volunteers. Political parties attempt to maintain a presence in each electoral district through a local branch of the party. An electoral district association (EDA), commonly referred to as a *riding association* or a *constituency association*, is a formal arm of the party that engages grassroots members in the electoral district where they live. EDAs are regional arms of each party that provide members with an opportunity to participate in public affairs, policy development, and election readiness. Members are eligible to attend meetings to discuss strategic matters and to select EDA executives, convention delegates, and the party's local election candidate. They are an organizational mechanism

party convention An official gathering of party delegates to decide on matters of policy and/or leadership.

party member A person who formally belongs to a political party, having joined by purchasing a membership.

electoral district association The local organization of a political party operating within the boundaries of an election riding.

through which parties communicate with party activists, initiate local fundraising events, identify potential candidates, and stay in touch with local concerns.[17] In some cases, a party may also operate provincial associations as a means of coordinating local activity. In areas of the country where the party is popular, there tend to be vibrant district associations with intense competition for executive positions and the opportunity to represent the party in an election. The reverse is also true: in places where the party is unpopular, there may not even be an electoral district association, which inevitably results in the recruitment of a stopgap candidate at election time.

Each federal political party has some sort of organizational hierarchy to integrate members and EDAs while performing a central management function. Membership in national bodies normally comprises party members from across Canada; people who hold public office at the federal or provincial level of government are typically ineligible for a high-ranking position within the extra-parliamentary wing by virtue of their position. The hierarchy ranges from people who are responsible for the party's day-to-day management to the participants in special interest branches of the party, such as its youth wing. The latter may include commissions—which the NDP

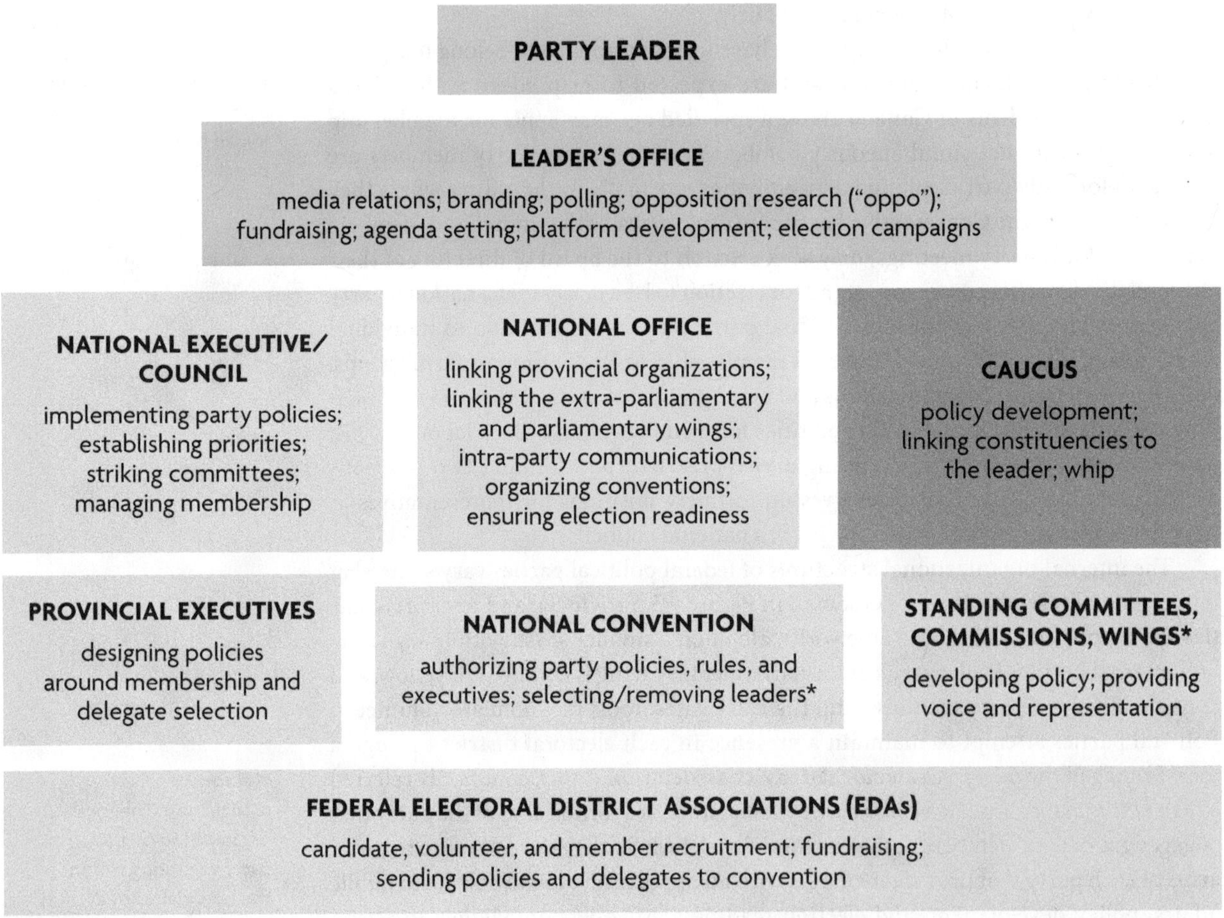

PARTY LEADER

LEADER'S OFFICE
media relations; branding; polling; opposition research ("oppo"); fundraising; agenda setting; platform development; election campaigns

NATIONAL EXECUTIVE/ COUNCIL
implementing party policies; establishing priorities; striking committees; managing membership

NATIONAL OFFICE
linking provincial organizations; linking the extra-parliamentary and parliamentary wings; intra-party communications; organizing conventions; ensuring election readiness

CAUCUS
policy development; linking constituencies to the leader; whip

PROVINCIAL EXECUTIVES
designing policies around membership and delegate selection

NATIONAL CONVENTION
authorizing party policies, rules, and executives; selecting/removing leaders*

STANDING COMMITTEES, COMMISSIONS, WINGS*
developing policy; providing voice and representation

FEDERAL ELECTORAL DISTRICT ASSOCIATIONS (EDAs)
candidate, volunteer, and member recruitment; fundraising; sending policies and delegates to convention

FIGURE 9.3 | Typical Structure of Federal Political Parties

* Not all parties have this component/role.

constitution defines as "a formal organization, internal to the party, which regroups members on a basis of identity, or around a specific political issue"[18]—in order to provide a forum for those members who have a shared interest. The Liberal and New Democrat constitutions expressly identify and formalize the role of youth in their parties. By comparison, the Conservative Party constitution merely remarks that the formalization of youth forums and post-secondary campus organizations will be addressed by the party's national council through bylaws.

The organizational structure to coordinate internal party affairs can be extensive. To illustrate, the Liberal Party designates a number of executive officers, namely the national party president, two vice-presidents, a policy chair, and a membership secretary. Those executive members belong to a national board of directors that includes the party leader, the past president, the president of each provincial or territorial association, one member of the Liberal Party caucus, and the chair of each of the party's special interest commissions. Those commissions include one each for Aboriginal people, women, youth, and seniors, which themselves may operate local clubs. The members of the national board of directors, the president of every party EDA, and the chairs of the provincial or territorial special interest commissions also belong to the party's council of presidents. That body is tasked with an annual review of the party's strategic, organizational, and fundraising plans. Those plans are formulated by the party's standing committees, namely its national management committee, its national revenue committee, its national election readiness committee, and its national policy and platform committee. As well, each party employs staff in its national office. They provide an array of organizational supports, such as media monitoring, event planning, liaising with EDAs, fundraising drives, and ensuring election readiness.

Political parties periodically hold formal gatherings that bring together current and past high-ranking party officials with delegates sent from each EDA. A party convention is a forum to amend the party's constitution, receive information from the party executive including the leader, shape party policy, and elect members of the party's national executive. Resolutions are introduced, debated, and voted upon. A convention is therefore akin to a party's internal legislative assembly and acts as the supreme decision-making body over party affairs, subject to Canadian law. Party conventions are normally held every two years, unless circumstances warrant a special meeting (such as the selection of a new party leader). Conventions keep the party executive accountable to the membership, balance the interests of the leadership with those of the grassroots, generate publicity and public interest, and generally stimulate team-building.

Party Leaders

The party leader is the chief public official for the party. He or she is the public face of the party who acts as its primary spokesperson. The leader embodies the party's principles, leads it in the legislature and during an election campaign, and is ultimately responsible for making decisions. Among the powers of a federal party leader is the authority to inform Elections Canada of the registration or deregistration of the party or its electoral district associations; to accept or overrule local nominations for a candidate to represent the party in a general election or by-election; and to act as a

party leader The head of a political party's legislative wing.

signatory on other official documents, such as the formal appointment of a registered agent of the party. The Liberal Party constitution enumerates the responsibilities and powers of its leader as follows:

(a) speak for the party concerning any political issue
(b) be guided by the party policies and the party platform
(c) report to every meeting of the council of presidents
(d) report to the party at every convention
(e) in consultation with the national president, appoint the national campaign co–chairs
(f) appoint the national policy vice-chair
(g) appoint four additional members of the national policy and platform committee
(h) take part in the development of the party policies and party platform . . .
(i) designate the caucus accountability officer to report to the council of presidents and each biennial convention of the party on the implementation of the party policies by the caucus.[19]

↺ The role of the PMO is discussed throughout Chapter 5, on the executive: see especially pages 178–79.

Given all of these responsibilities, leaders are often supported by a sizeable staff, located in the leader's office. The prime minister's office (PMO) and premiers' offices often serve this purpose for parties in power.

What does not appear in any party constitution is just how supreme the authority of the party leader is in practice in Canada. In order to secure the position, a leader must have significant support within the party across the country, and once installed, he or she appoints supporters to key positions. In other parliamentary democracies there are mechanisms to remove an unpopular leader, even if that person is head of the government. For instance, in Australia the leadership review vote is conducted within caucus, rather than as an extra-parliamentary exercise.[20] Seeking to emulate that power for parliamentarians, a Conservative MP introduced a private member's bill in the House of Commons. The Reform Act passed in 2015 and will, as in Australia, allow the caucus to decide if a leadership review vote is warranted.

leadership review A vote held at a party convention on whether a leadership contest should be held.

Leadership reviews seek the formal endorsement of party delegates that the current leader should continue in the role. A leadership review may be held at a party

THEY SAID IT

Comedian Rick Mercer on Party Leadership Conventions

As much as I love an election, I love a leadership convention even more. From a showbiz perspective politics doesn't get much better than this. In an election the parties turn on each other; in a leadership convention a party turns on itself. This leads to a whole new level of carnage and destruction . . . just too much fun.[21]

—Rick Mercer, 2008

INSIDE CANADIAN POLITICS
Are All Leaders Vulnerable to Review?

Seemingly perplexing situations occur as a result of leadership reviews. Normally party leaders seek to secure a strong endorsement from delegates in order to demonstrate their popularity within and control over the party. At the 1983 federal Progressive Conservative Party convention, leader Joe Clark received 66.9 per cent support in a leadership review vote, yet he shocked everyone by proclaiming that he had chosen to resign. Somewhat unusually, Clark announced that he would be a contestant in the ensuing leadership race to reclaim his vacated position, which he hoped would return him with a strong mandate to lead. Instead, Brian Mulroney was crowned Tory leader, and went on to lead the party to victory in the 1984 and 1988 general elections. In 1992, a public opinion poll indicated that Mulroney's public support sat at just 11 per cent, but there was no revolt in the Progressive Conservative Party or significant internal movement to replace him; he resigned on his own terms a year later.

Conversely, popular and successful leaders may also meet their demise at the hands of party members. In 2006, Alberta premier Ralph Klein resigned after receiving barely half of all votes in a leadership review following his fourth consecutive, massive election victory just two years earlier. Prime Minister Jean Chrétien led the Liberal Party to three consecutive majority governments from 1993 to 2000, and subsequent polls continued to indicate that he was the most popular of the federal party leaders at the time. However, the prime minister was less popular than his finance minister, Paul Martin, who lost to Chrétien in a party leadership convention in 1990. In public, Chrétien and Martin were all smiles and appeared as a formidable team; in private, they feuded, to the point that staffers became go-betweens because the two men would not talk to one another directly. So-called "Martinites" had been slowly assuming control of caucus, EDAs, and the party executive apparatus, while simultaneously engaging in fundraising and cultivating a positive public image of their leadership aspirant. In 2002, Chrétien kicked Martin out of cabinet, prompting the latter to begin orchestrating a leadership review vote at the next party convention. Later that year, Chrétien announced that he would be stepping down, which set the stage for Martin to win the party's leadership convention in 2003 with 94 per cent of delegate votes.

THE LESSON

The threat of an internal putsch illustrates why it is that a leader's first priority must be to keep party members, and chief rivals, happy. Not even the most successful leaders in general election campaigns are immune to such internal threats.

convention, usually at the first convention after an unsuccessful general election campaign. The leadership review provides a mechanism for an opponent to assume control of the internal party apparatus in order to apply pressure from within, but it also acts as a mechanism to potentially convince party members of the supremacy of the leader. Technically, the leader requires only a majority of votes to continue, but in practice the threshold is much higher. Ever since the Joe Clark episode, chronicled in the Inside Canadian Politics box above, party leaders are expected to resign if they receive less than a two-thirds endorsement from party delegates, even if the party constitution does not stipulate such a requirement.

leadership contest An election within a political party to select a leader.

A **leadership contest** occurs when a party leader vacates the position and a new leader needs to be selected; in between, the party may appoint an interim leader, who normally does not seek the leadership. If there is more than one applicant, then a leadership race ensues, culminating in a party vote. Leadership hopefuls tour the country (or province), participate in debates, sign up members, and attract media attention. The stakes are especially high if contestants are vying to replace a sitting head of government. This sometimes results in a situation where party members, not the general public, choose the next prime minister or premier. Examples of prime ministers who ascended to the job in this manner include Pierre Trudeau, John Turner, Kim Campbell, and Paul Martin. Recent provincial and territorial premiers who were designated to the position

INSIDE CANADIAN POLITICS
Selecting Canadian Party Leaders

Canadian political parties have used a myriad of voting systems to select their leaders. In general, these sets of rules have become more inclusive over time, allowing a greater number and diversity of individuals to participate. At present, five different models are used:

- *Caucus choice*. In the nineteenth and early twentieth centuries, party leaders were selected by and from among the organization's elected representatives. Today, most parties reserve caucus-only choice for the selection of interim leaders, who serve as the party's head following the resignation of a leader and until the official selection of a replacement.
- *Delegate conventions*. Initially held behind closed doors, in so-called smoke-filled rooms filled with party elites, conventions have evolved into televised events involving party faithful numbering in the hundreds. Depending on the party, these delegates include party notables (legislators, extra-parliamentary executives), leaders of affiliated organizations (such as unions), representatives of the party's special wings (youth, women's, Aboriginal) if any, and envoys elected by the various electoral district associations. Collectively, these delegates—and not the grassroots party members, themselves—vote to choose the leader. The remaining forms of leadership selection allow party members a more direct role in leadership selection.

- *One-member, one-vote*. First adopted by the Parti Québécois in 1985, the OMOV universal balloting process has emerged as one of the most common leadership selection processes among Canadian parties. As its name suggests, each party member receives one vote when it comes to selecting the leader. Different parties have different rules for determining how a winner is eventually chosen, with most using multiple rounds of voting or rank-ordered ballots in contests featuring more than one contender. Many parties are also experimenting with telephone and online voting to increase access to the voting process.
- *Weighted constituencies*. Under this system, each electoral district is assigned an equal number of points, which are then distributed to leadership candidates based on their share of the popular vote in that constituency. For instance, when Stephen Harper ran for the leadership of the Conservative Party of Canada in 2004, each of the 308 constituencies was allotted 100 points. When Harper captured 51 per cent of the votes in the Nova Scotia district of Sackville–Eastern Shore, he was allotted 51 points (compared with Tony Clement's 10 and Belinda Stronach's 39). When points were tallied across all 308 constituencies, Harper emerged victorious with 17,298 of a total 30,808 points.
- *Hybrid*. While the weighted constituency model combines the simplicity of the one-member, one-vote model with the importance of achieving

include Alison Redford and Jim Prentice (Alberta), Christy Clark (British Columbia), Greg Selinger (Manitoba), Kathleen Wynne (Ontario), Darrell Pasloski (Yukon), Wade MacLaughlin (PEI), and Paul Davis (Newfoundland and Labrador). Most, but not all, of these leaders went on to form governments in the subsequent general election.

The method of selecting a leader has changed over the years and reflects evolutions in mass communication discussed above. In the newspaper era and the age of elite parties, the leader was selected by the party's parliamentarians; in the radio and television era, as mass parties took shape, leaders were selected at special conventions by party delegates from electoral districts; with advances in telecommunications and transportation, parties gradually expanded the leadership selectorate to include all

geographic representation, the hybrid model balances the advantages of OMOV with the participation of underrepresented groups. In hybrid systems, all party members cast a ballot for the leadership candidate of their choice. These votes are then weighted according to a specific set of rules. For instance, when the federal NDP selected Jack Layton in 2003, the votes of all party members were weighted at 75 per cent of the total, with the remaining 25 per cent of votes being reserved for unions.

Jurisdiction	Delegate Convention	One-member one-vote	Weighted constituencies	Hybrid
Canada	Liberal	NDP, BQ	Conservative	
British Columbia		NDP	Liberal	
Alberta		Liberal, PC, Wildrose		NDP
Saskatchewan		NDP, Sask Party		
Manitoba	NDP	Liberal, PC		
Ontario	Liberal	PC		NDP
Quebec*	Liberal	PQ, Option nationale		
New Brunswick		NDP, PC	Liberal	
Nova Scotia	PC, NDP	Liberal		
Prince Edward Island		NDP, Liberal, PC		
Newfoundland and Labrador	PC	Liberal, NDP		
Yukon	Liberal	Yukon Party, NDP		

Source: Wesley and Loewen 2012, with updates by authors

Model employed by each party's most recent contested leadership election is listed.

*Québec solidaire has no official "leader," but rather two co-spokespeople. Coalition Avenir Québec has yet to adopt a formal constitution; its first leader, François Legault, was its founder.

VOX POP

What are the major advantages and drawbacks associated with each of these leadership selection methods? And what are the factors that would lead a party to choose one over the others?

BRIEFING NOTES

Dark Horse Candidates in Nomination Races

Parties have different sets of rules when it comes to the selection of their leaders. Some voting systems are highly adversarial, pitting front-runners in a heated and divisive struggle for the leadership of the party. This type of competition can allow so-called "dark horse" candidates to emerge victorious, as supporters of the leading contenders refuse to shift their support to the closest rival and prefer to endorse a least-hated alternative. This dynamic played out at opposite ends of the country, in two different parties, on the same weekend in December 2006. After four rounds of balloting, the Liberal Party of Canada chose Stéphane Dion as

its eleventh leader, after a bitterly contested campaign between front-runners Bob Rae and Michael Ignatieff. At the same time, the Alberta PCs chose Ed Stelmach as the province's thirteenth premier. Stelmach's low-profile campaign was overshadowed by the heated rivalry between red tory Jim Dinning and new right conservative Ted Morton. In the end, neither Stelmach nor Dion lasted long as leaders, campaigning in just one general election each. This is not to say that a dark horse candidate cannot go on to enjoy a longer career as party leader, as evidenced by former Ontario premier Dalton McGuinty, who was a longshot to win his party's nomination in 1996.

party members; and in the Internet era, leaders are starting to be selected by anyone recruited by leadership contestants, whether they are party members or not. This is enabled by new technologies that include televoting and online voting, sometimes with limited scrutiny of the voter's eligibility. Some parties continue to use traditional delegate conventions, occasionally providing special votes for particular groups like youth and labour. Others employ voting systems that allow party members to vote directly for the leader, sometimes weighting these votes according to the size of each member's constituency. Moreover, the rules for leadership contests have evolved, and contestants to lead a federal party are subject to the financial limits specified in section 435 of the Canada Elections Act.

The Parliamentary Wing

party caucus All members of a political party who hold a seat in the legislature.

The parliamentary wing of a party consists of its caucus (those members of the party who hold a seat in the legislature) and the people who work directly for those public officials. Party caucuses at the federal level may include both MPs and senators; at the provincial level, the party caucus comprises all of that party's members of the provincial legislative assembly. The caucus meets regularly *in camera*, or in private: these meetings are not open to extra-parliamentary members of the party, nor are they open to the media or the general public. In camera caucus meetings provide an opportunity for members of the legislature to receive information from the party leadership and a forum for them to voice their concerns behind closed doors. At times, caucus discussions can be heated affairs, but once the meeting is over, any dissent is not disclosed, so that the party may present a unified front to the public. As discussed below, strict discipline means members risk being expelled from the party should they break ranks or speak about what happens during caucus meetings.

The number of people belonging to a party caucus varies considerably and reflects the party's performance in the most recent general election. A federal political party that has a majority government and that has been appointing senators for many years will have a caucus of more than two hundred parliamentarians. Conversely, at the start of the 42nd Parliament, the Bloc Québécois caucus had only ten MPs, and the Green Party just one. Since neither party was represented in the Senate, that was the extent of their respective caucuses. The limited human resources of smaller parties are compounded when they have fewer than 12 MPs, which is the threshold for a party in the House of Commons to be granted official party status. This parliamentary designation brings with it extra financial resources and eligibility to participate in Question Period. With the exception of Quebec, which requires a dozen MNAs for a party to acquire official status, the threshold is lower for provincial legislatures, ranging from eight seats in Ontario to the conventional practice of at least one seat in PEI and in Newfoundland and Labrador. Official party status in the legislature should not be confused with whether a party has registered with an election agency, or the corresponding eligibility to include the party label on an election ballot next to a candidate's name.

As discussed in great detail in Chapters 5 and 6, parties sit on either the government or opposition benches, with prominent parliamentarians being assigned ministerial or shadow ministerial roles.

Partisans

Not all people involved in party politics are card-carrying members, elected delegates, or members of a legislative assembly. People who identify with a political party are known as partisans. Some of the most ardent partisans are members and become deeply involved with the extra-parliamentary and/or parliamentary wings of a party. These partisans choose to spend their time working to advance a political cause. Other partisans may give money to a party, volunteer in an election campaign to persuade others to vote for the party's candidate, or otherwise support the party. In short, they are loyal to the party and have a psychological attachment to it.

It is important to distinguish between a person's partisan identification and her or his voting behaviour. Not all Liberal partisans vote for Liberal candidates, for example, just as not all Liberal voters feel a strong attachment to the party. There is mixed evidence about whether the strength of partisanship in Canada has been waning. In the past, the connection that people had with a political party was more likely to be related to their dependency on patronage and "pork barrel" politics. Today, partisanship remains a prominent force, even though laws prohibit leaders from offering their supporters tangible rewards like government jobs or contracts. Indeed, even when party identification was in flux in the early 2000s, at least a third of Canadians continued to support the same party consistently from election to election, and even those who voted for a different party still identified with their original party.[22]

This said, the inducements of career advancement and bringing home the goods for constituents are still used to ensure that party supporters voice their frustrations in private and never in public. Even though Canadian electors are increasingly open to party switching, the one aspect of partisanship that appears to be solidifying is party discipline. Party discipline refers to the internal party conformity that is expected and

---

official party status The minimum number of elected members a party needs to question the government in the legislature and qualify for other resources and privileges.

↻ The government's cabinet and the opposition's shadow cabinets are discussed on pages 181–90 of Chapter 5, on the executive. The roles of different actors in Parliament are discussed on pages 222–26 of Chapter 6, on the legislature.

partisan Someone who identifies with, and is a staunch supporter of, a political party.

↻ Party discipline is defined and discussed at length in Chapter 6, on the legislature: see especially pages 217 and 226–8.

INSIDE CANADIAN POLITICS

What Happened with Floor Crossers and Independents in the 38th Parliament?

Floor crossing is an episodic event. Two cases stand out in recent memory because of the unusual circumstances and intense public interest. In 2004, business mogul Belinda Stronach decided to enter politics by contesting the leadership of the Conservative Party of Canada, and was runner-up to Stephen Harper. Soon afterward she ran as the Conservative candidate in the Ontario electoral district of Newmarket–Aurora and was elected with 42 per cent of the vote. In 2005, just as it appeared that the Liberal government headed by Prime Minister Paul Martin could fall on a budget vote, Stronach crossed the floor to the Liberals. Unusually, she was instantly made a cabinet minister, which drew controversy about the ethics of the Liberals leveraging public resources for their own political gain. Stronach was re-elected in the 2006 and 2008 general elections as a Liberal MP, after which she chose not to seek re-election.

The Conservatives were outraged by Stronach's floor crossing, and yet one of Stephen Harper's first acts as prime minister was to leverage the perks of office as Martin had done before him. During the 2006 federal election, Liberal cabinet minister David Emerson warned people not to vote Conservative and publicly admonished Harper. Emerson was re-elected in the riding of Vancouver Kingsway with 43 per cent of the vote, well ahead of the Conservative candidate, who placed third with 18 per cent. Emerson was due to lose his post as a minister when the Conservatives formed the government. Surprisingly, when Harper unveiled his first ministry, Emerson was included as a Conservative minister. For days, protesters picketed in front of Emerson's constituency office, demanding that he resign. The media coverage was so negative and lasting that Emerson did not seek re-election.

In the same 2005 budget vote that sparked Stronach's floor-crossing, independent MP Chuck Cadman also played a leading role. First elected to the House of Commons under the Reform and Canadian Alliance banners in 1997 and 2000, respectively, Cadman lost his local Conservative Party nomination race in the lead-up to the 2004 federal election. Cadman decided to run as an independent in that election, and won, becoming the only person not affiliated with a political party to win a seat in that campaign. Undergoing chemotherapy to treat his end-stage skin cancer, Cadman nevertheless made a dramatic trip to Ottawa to cast a decisive vote in support of the minority Liberal government's 2005 budget. Unbound by the constraints of party discipline, Cadman could have voted against the budget, causing the government to fall and triggering an election. His actions demonstrate the powerful, albeit rare, influence independent MPs can wield in hung parliaments.

VOX POP

Should floor crossers be required to resign their seats and seek re-election before serving in another party's caucus? How about parliamentarians who are expelled or who resign from caucus to serve as independents?

enforced by the party leadership. Partisans exert control on each other to ensure that they do not deviate from the directives issued by the party centre, namely the members of the leader's inner circle. This stands in contrast with the members of various colonial, provincial, and federal assemblies of the nineteenth century who became known as "loose fish" and "shaky fellows" because their voting behaviour was unpredictable.

Nevertheless, partisans sometimes decide to switch parties. When a legislator does so, it is known as crossing the floor. The expression describes the action of a member of a legislature who leaves the party seated on one side of the chamber to join those on the other side, often having her or his chair literally moved across the aisle in the process. The decision to cross the floor is a personal one, and thus the motivations are not fully understood. The reasons tend to be philosophical differences with party leadership, frustration with the political system, and/or an opportunity for career advancement. Those who switch parties may do so to improve their own clout, as when an opposition MP or MLA joins the government side in the hope of accessing the perks of office, or when a government backbencher leaves after accepting that upward mobility is impossible within that party. There is a lot of media attention when someone crosses the floor because it is a controversial action and is treated as a win or a loss for the corresponding parties. Although some constituents welcome such a decision, others criticize it as unethical and call for the member to resign so that a by-election can be held. A floor crosser may not necessarily be re-elected in a future general election because many of the partisans who previously voted for their party's candidate will choose to vote once again for the same party. Those who are truly disaffected may choose to sit as an independent rather than join an opposing party. In that case, they face even greater constraints in terms of resources and prospects for re-election.

When someone crosses the floor or resigns from the party caucus, there is inevitably discussion about whether that elected official should be required to resign from office and represent his or her new party in a by-election. Federal laws preclude that possibility: once someone is elected, he or she is unlikely to be forced to vacate the seat until the next general election. British Columbia is the only jurisdiction in Canada to have recall legislation that allows people to petition to force a by-election.

crossing the floor A situation in which a member of the legislature leaves one political party to join another.

↻ See the ICP box on page 216 of Chapter 5 for a description of floor-crossing at the provincial level, in Alberta.

Concluding Thoughts

Political parties play a dominant role in Canadian political society. They are the lifeblood of political debate, elections, and legislative activity. At any given time there are a variety of major and minor political parties with diverse ideologies, objectives, and proposed public policies seeking the public's attention. In Canada, the strength of party discipline is such that independent thoughts are normally expressed behind closed doors, at a convention, in caucus, or at constituency association meetings. This raises questions about the quality of democratic discourse and concerns about the limited ability of non-partisans to influence government policy. Moreover, partisanship contributes to polarizing debate and to excessive power concentrated in the party leader's inner circle, especially within the prime minister's office or a premier's office. Canadian democracy is conceivable without political parties; indeed, it functions without them in two of the three territories and in many of Canada's largest cities. Yet, while many critics would like this sort of non-partisan politics to spread to other quarters, parties have become so entrenched in the electoral process that it is difficult to imagine Canadian politics without them.

For More Information

Want an insider's perspective on campaigning within Canada's three major federal parties? Read insights from party strategists like Tom Flanagan (*Harper's Team: Behind the Scenes in the Conservative Rise to Power*, McGill–Queen's University Press, 2007), Warren Kinsella (*Fight the Right: A Manual for Surviving the Coming Conservative Apocalypse*, Random House, 2012), and Brad Lavigne (*Building the Orange Wave: The Inside Story behind the Historic Rise of Jack Layton and the NDP*, Douglas & McIntyre, 2013).

Want to understand the inner workings of Canadian political parties? Look no further than *Rebuilding Canadian Party Politics*, an informative work by R. Kenneth Carty, William Cross, and Lisa Young (UBC Press, 2000).

How has the way that political parties recruit members, mobilize support, fundraise, and communicate changed in Canada over time? Find out in Dan Azoulay's article "The Evolution of Party Organization in Canada since 1900," *The Journal of Commonwealth & Comparative Politics* 33, no. 2 (1995): pp. 185–208.

To what extent are political parties similar to franchises such as McDonald's? One of Canada's preeminent scholars on party politics, R. Kenneth Carty, explores the matter in "The Politics of Tecumseh Corners: Canadian Political Parties as Franchise Organizations," *Canadian Journal of Political Science* 35, no. 4 (2002): pp. 723–45.

Why does the electoral system reward regional protest parties and punish pan-Canadian parties? Find out in Alan C. Cairns's seminal article on the matter, "The Electoral System and the Party System in Canada, 1921–1965," *Canadian Journal of Political Science* 1, no. 1 (1968): pp. 55–80.

Has Canada entered a fifth party system? Is the era of brokerage politics over? How has state funding of political parties contributed to the growth of the Green Party of Canada? These and other questions are examined in *Parties, Elections, and the Future of Canadian Politics*, a collection edited by Amanda Bittner and Royce Koop (UBC Press, 2013).

Despite its setback in 2015, is it possible that the Conservative Party of Canada can supplant the Liberal Party as Canada's natural governing party? Scholars weigh in. See Michael D. Behiels's "Stephen Harper's Rise to Power: Will His 'New' Conservative Party Become Canada's 'Natural Governing Party' of the Twenty-First Century?," *American Review of Canadian Studies* 40, no. 1 (2010): pp. 118–45. Take a look also at Faron Ellis and Peter Woolstencroft's "The Conservative Campaign: Becoming the New Natural Governing Party?," in *The Canadian Federal Election of 2011*, ed. Jon Pammett and Christopher Dornan, (Dundurn Press, 2011).

Are minor, fringe, and protest parties better able to compete with major parties in the Internet age? Tamara Small thinks not. Find out why in "Equal Access, Unequal Success: Major and Minor Canadian Parties on the Net," *Party Politics* 14, no. 1 (2008): pp. 51–70.

It may surprise you, but there is no evidence that party leaders are growing in importance in Canadians' voting decisions—apparently, our attachment first and foremost to parties remains the strongest predictor of voting behaviour. Not convinced? Take a look at Elisabeth Gidengil and André Blais's chapter "Are Party Leaders Becoming More Important to Vote Choice in Canada?" in *Political Leadership and Representation in Canada*, edited by Hans J. Michelmann, Donald C. Story, and Jeffrey S. Steeves (University of Toronto Press, 2007).

How are party leaders selected across Canada? Jared Wesley and Brett Loewen provide a summary in chart form on page 257 of their article "'Getting Better All the Time'?: Leadership Selection and the Manitoba NDP," *Canadian Political Science Review* 6, no. 2-3 (2012): pp. 255–66.

How does local campaigning vary between high-profile candidates, local notables, party insiders, and stopgaps? Anthony Sayers explains in *Parties, Candidates and Constituency Campaigns in Canadian Elections* (UBC Press, 1999).

Do women have a more difficult time becoming party leaders because of the way they are treated by the media? Linda Trimble finds that they may, in fact, have some advantages. For more, see "Gender, Political Leadership and Media Visibility: *Globe and Mail* Coverage of Conservative Party of Canada Leadership Contests," *Canadian Journal of Political Science* 40, no. 4 (2007): pp. 969–93.

Looking to understand what different political parties are all about? Visit the websites of federal and provincial political parties, which are easily located using your favourite search engine.

Interested to see how well your views match with the policy programs of political parties in Canada (and beyond)? Take the quiz at http://votecompass.com/.

Interested in learning more about the history of Canada's "fringe" parties? See the CBC's historical coverage of Libertarians, Marxist–Leninists, Rhinos, and others, archived in its video library under the title *Outside Looking In: Small Parties in Federal Politics*: http://www.cbc.ca/archives/topic/outside-looking-in-small-parties-in-federal-politics.

Can't get enough of party politics? Tune into to weekly and Sunday-only politics shows on CBC and CTV, or get your daily fix on CPAC. Monitor *The Hill Times* weekly newsmagazine. Subscribe to a political party listserv, "like" a politician or political journalist on Facebook, and follow your favourites on Twitter.

Deeper Inside Canadian Politics

1. In addressing what he views as major misconceptions, Joseph Wearing (1996) lists what he considers to be five "myths" about Canadian party politics:

   - that the history of Canadian parties begins in 1867
   - that the Conservative and Liberal parties are virtually indistinguishable brokerage, pro-business parties
   - that third parties have been constantly stifled by the two older parties, which have stolen all their progressive policies anyway
   - that the two older parties have kept alive antiquated conflicts between religious groups, regions, and French and English in order to prevent the emergence of a "modern" party system based on class divisions
   - that the resulting party system makes Canada an anomaly among modern nations. . . . [23]

   Prepare your own evaluation of any two of these "myths." Are they as misleading as Wearing argues, or is there more truth to some of them than he allows?

2. Throughout much of Canada, democracy is defined by party politics. This places a number of obstacles in the way of independents seeking office. Identify three main barriers confronting independents, and ways in which each of these may be overcome.

3. On page 376, you read about how the rules surrounding the 2006 leadership contests in the Liberal Party of Canada and PC Party of Alberta resulted in victory for two dark horse candidates. Research the precise rules surrounding these two contests, or more recent ones where a dark horse candidate won. What would the outcomes have looked like under different voting systems?

UP FOR DEBATE

Should party leaders take positive actions to increase the presence of women and other underrepresented Canadians in legislatures?

THE CLAIM: YES, THEY SHOULD!

The best way to ensure that the views of women, visible minorities, Aboriginal people, and other traditionally marginalized groups are reflected in government decision-making is for political parties to take steps to ensure that more of them are nominated and elected.

Yes: Argument Summary

A healthy democracy must be pluralistic—that is, it must include representatives with an array of socio-demographic characteristics to reflect the views of society as a whole. A legislature that is consistently composed primarily of older white men, many of them drawn from the wealthiest socioeconomic class, cannot adequately speak for the people whose interests it is designed to represent. Canadian political parties (less so the NDP) are responsible for the noticeable lack of women, Aboriginal people, members of visible minority communities, persons with disabilities, and other traditionally marginalized Canadians in our legislatures. The vast majority of our legislators carry party banners during election campaigns, meaning that inclusive legislatures require inclusive slates of candidates. Canadian party leaders hold a veto over who carries their party's banner in election campaigns, and they should use this power to ensure their election slates are more representative of the Canadian population. Occasionally, this may mean rejecting a party nominee who was democratically selected by local party members and installing someone else. These and other support measures are needed to increase their representation in the legislature and in the political executive, including extensive candidate searches, target or quota-setting, mentorship, and financial assistance.

Yes: Top 5 Considerations

1. Section 3 of the Charter of Rights and Freedoms states that every Canadian citizen has a right to be a member of a legislative assembly, while section 15 states that every Canadian is legally equal and cannot be discriminated against on the basis of "race, national or ethnic origin, colour, religion, sex, age or mental or physical disability." Sometimes positive actions are required to overcome this sort of discrimination and achieve the democratic ideal of diversity enshrined in the Charter.

2. Parties are the gatekeepers to Canadian democracy. Unless parties take active steps to ensure people from traditionally disadvantaged groups have a fair chance of being nominated to become candidates, there is little chance that any will be elected to the legislature. Research demonstrates that many people from underrepresented groups have just as much chance of being selected by voters in a general election as those from mainstream political communities. The key is ensuring they are nominated in the first place, and that responsibility lies with parties.

3. Party leaders have not shied away from ensuring party insiders, star candidates, and local notables win nomination battles. Using this prerogative to ensure greater demographic diversity would be a far more noble cause.

4. Democracies around the world are taking steps to implement quotas and support systems to ensure

that people from underrepresented groups, like women, are sufficiently represented. The 1995 Beijing Platform for Action, which was signed by all members of the United Nations' World Conference on Women, established that a minimum of 30 per cent of senior government positions should be filled by women. Canada has failed to achieve these targets, largely because parties are failing to run enough female candidates.

5. Political parties have the means to nurture the engagement of traditionally marginalized people through mentorship, special training opportunities, and recognition of special accommodation. Parties can make a difference by providing resources like fundraising assistance and childcare support for candidates, as well as ethnic outreach.

Yes: Other Considerations

• Getting candidates from traditionally underrepresented groups onto the ballot is more difficult than most people realize. It's true that there are plenty of women, Aboriginal people, allophones, LGBTT activists, and youth who are involved in the political process in some manner, but helping these people to step forward as candidates for office requires more than mentorship: they require help to overcome institutional barriers to their candidacy, and political parties can provide this help through quotas that level the playing field.

• Beyond reform of internal party rules, legislative change is an option that party-dominated legislatures have been unwilling to debate. For instance, governing parties could pass legislation that designates a number of seats in the legislature for traditionally underrepresented groups, or opposition parties could propose to create dual-member constituencies to ensure each district is represented by one woman and one man.

• As Prime Minister Justin Trudeau said in response to a reporter who questioned why gender parity was a priority when selecting members of his cabinet, "It's 2015."

THE COUNTERCLAIM: NO, THEY SHOULDN'T!

A strong democracy must encourage unfettered political competition for seats in the legislative assembly.

No: Argument Summary

Free and fair elections are the embodiment of democracy. This involves the freedom to put one's name forward to seek election, the freedom of party members at the grassroots to select their preferred candidate, and the freedom of voters to choose who best represents them—as individuals or as communities. The special treatment of people from underrepresented groups may be well-meaning, but it is anti-democratic. It is largely a symbolic effort that does little to meaningfully empower women, Aboriginal people, ethnic minorities, and other politically underrepresented groups. Well-intentioned party elites with the power to intervene in the nomination process should not meddle in the democratic process, but rather must give the general public the opportunity to render their own judgement on which candidates should be elected.

No: Top 5 Considerations

1. In a free and fair election process, people must be able to compete in open nominations to represent the political party of their choice, rather than have that opportunity closed off by party elites. Anything else is an unhealthy practice for a political party hoping to attract a critical mass of supporters.

2. A party's success during a general election campaign does not result from nominating weaker candidates over stronger candidates solely on the basis of gender, ethnicity, or social characteristics. Research demonstrates that Canadians place little value on the local candidate when casting a ballot, meaning that there is little electoral incentive for party leaders to diversify their slates and little reason to expect Canadians would notice if they did.

3. Candidate quotas are problematic. They can become divisive for the party when the leadership's preferred candidate is imposed against the wishes of the grassroots who have followed proper democratic process to identify their own choice. This can result in a new form of democratic dissatisfaction, and backlash against the same sense of inclusiveness quotas are designed to promote.

4. In order to meet artificial quotas, party elites are more likely to endorse people from traditionally marginalized groups in uncontested nominations in weak seats. As a result, these candidates often end up as cannon fodder during elections, further perpetuating the perception of discrimination and underrepresentation.

5. If inclusiveness were truly a top-of-mind concern for Canadians, they would vote with their feet, punishing or rewarding parties based on the candidates they nominate, or supporting efforts to reform the electoral system. As it stands, parties with the most homogeneous campaign slates tend to win more seats than those with a greater demographic balance. And Canadians have repeatedly rejected electoral reform options that would create incentives for parties to run a more diverse field of candidates.

No: Other Considerations

- The progressive nature of a candidate and/or seats quota system is controversial. Those who seek to advance "elect more women" or "elect more minorities" agendas may attract narrow-minded righteous ideologues whose politics are an affront to those who have a more open-minded view of democracy and are satisfied with the status quo.
- There is a tenuous linkage between affirmative action, on one hand, and inclusive legislatures, on the other. It is possible to support employment equity policies that introduce counter-discrimination hiring practices within the public service, and still be vehemently opposed to special status for traditionally-marginalized people who run for election to a legislative assembly.

Discussion Questions

- What are the advantages and disadvantages of giving a party leader final say over whether or not a candidate can represent the party in an election campaign?
- Why do you think that women might have a more difficult time getting elected than men? What about Aboriginal people as compared with non-Aboriginal people? Candidates with visible disabilities versus candidates without? Poor versus wealthy? Young versus old?
- To what extent do you think a candidate's sexual orientation affects his or her ability to be elected?
- Would you support the government's putting aside a pool of money for members of political minority groups to use in a bid to win their party's nomination? Why or why not?

- Given its progressive social values, it may not be surprising that the New Democratic Party was the first major Canadian party to have a woman leader (Audrey McLaughlin, 1989–95)—and yet, this happened only in 1989. Why do you think it took so long for this to happen?
- Given that conservativism tends to cater to traditional, "white male" values, why is it that the Conservatives were the first to appoint a woman to cabinet (Ellen Fairclough, in 1957); the first to elect a black member of Parliament (Lincoln Alexander, in 1968) and to appoint him to cabinet (in 1979); and the only party to be led by a woman prime minister (Kim Campbell, in 1993)?

Where to Learn More about Canadian Political Parties' Recruitment of Traditionally Underrepresented Groups

Karen Bird, "The Political Representation of Visible Minorities in Electoral Democracies: A Comparison of France, Denmark, and Canada," *Nationalism and Ethnic Politics* 11, no. 4 (2005): pp. 425–65.

Jerome H. Black, "Entering the Political Elite in Canada: The Case of Minority Women as Parliamentary Candidates and MPs," *Canadian Review of Sociology* 37, no. 2 (2000): pp. 143-66.

Miki Caul, "Political Parties and the Adoption of Candidate Gender Quotas: A Cross-National Analysis," *Journal of Politics* 63, no. 4 (2001): pp. 1214–29.

William Cross and Lisa Young, "Candidate Recruitment in Canada: The Role of Political Parties," in *Parties, Elections, and the Future of Canadian Politics*, ed. Amanda Bittner and Royce Koop (Vancouver: UBC Press, 2013): pp. 24–45.

Lynda Erickson and R.K. Carty, "Parties and Candidate Selection in the 1988 Canadian General Election," *Canadian Journal of Political Science* 24, no. 2 (1991): pp. 331–49.

Royce Koop and Amanda Bittner, "Parachuted into Parliament: Candidate Nomination, Appointed Candidates, and Legislative Roles in Canada," *Journal of Elections, Public Opinion and Parties* 21, no. 4 (2011): pp. 431-52.

Mona Lena Krook and Pippa Norris, "Beyond Quotas: Strategies to Promote Gender Equality in Elected Office," *Political Studies* 62, no. 1 (2014): pp. 2-20.

R.E. Matland and D.T. Studlar, "The Contagion of Women Candidates in Single-Member District and Proportional Representation Electoral Systems: Canada and Norway," *The Journal of Politics* 58, no. 3 (1996): pp. 707–33.

Anthony M. Sayers, *Parties, Candidates, and Constituency Campaigns in Canadian Elections* (Vancouver: UBC Press, 1999).

Melanee Thomas and Marc André Bodet, "Sacrificial Lambs, Women Candidates, and District Competitiveness in Canada," *Electoral Studies* 32, no. 1 (2013): pp. 153–66.

Manon Tremblay and Réjean Pelletier, "More Women Constituency Party Presidents: A Strategy for Increasing the Number of Women Candidates in Canada?," *Party Politics* 7 (2001): pp. 157–90.

10 DEMOCRACY AND ELECTIONS

Inside this Chapter

- What are the key principles and values underpinning democracy in Canada?
- What are the rules and regulations governing Canadian democracy?
- How do these ideals and rules "play out" during election campaigns?

Inside Democracy and Elections

Canadian democracy is built on the premise of free and fair elections. Indeed, Canada is recognized around the world as a model for election administration, with our politicians and public officials serving as advisers and observers in democracies across the globe. But precisely how do Canadians keep their elections so "free" and "fair"? What sorts of rules are in place to ensure that all eligible Canadians have the opportunity to cast ballots and run for office? Are the rules stringent enough to prevent democratic fraud, yet loose enough to permit free speech and open competition? Just how fair are these rules, considering that they are drafted by the winners of past elections? And, all told, do Canadians really have a direct voice in their political affairs? The answers to these and other questions reveal some important maxims about the way elections are run in this country:

What the 2015 Election Means for Democracy and Elections

Visit the *Inside Canadian Politics* flipboard to learn about the latest developments in the area of Canadian elections.

Go to
http://flip.it/gblag.

 Canadians lack real tools of direct democracy. Referendums and plebiscites aren't all that common in Canada, although when they occur they tend to be viewed as defining moments that shape political outcomes. In reality, no referendum is binding on a Canadian government, as ultimate sovereignty rests with the Crown and not the people. This means that all public policy outcomes are always contingent upon government support.

 Canadians do not elect their prime ministers and premiers. It may seem like a technicality, but Canadians elect a local representative. Their ballots do not contain a list of people who are competing to become the head of government. It is the monarch's representative who appoints a head of government, based on that person's ability to command support in the legislature. Media coverage of elections and party advertising focuses so much on party leaders that it's easy to overlook the importance of local representation.

Meaningful electoral reform is possible. While recent efforts to transition away from the first-past-the-post system toward more proportional forms of representation have failed, provinces have experimented with alternative voting systems in the past. In addition, many jurisdictions have initiated other changes to their systems of elections, including improving the accessibility of the voting act itself.

In this chapter we will explore these and other inconvenient truths as we peer at the underbelly of Canadian democracy and elections.

Overview

Many Canadians appear to take for granted the opportunity to elect the public officials who steer government decisions. Barely more than half of all eligible voters turn out at the polls in an average Canadian election, and as years pass, fewer voters report having a strong sense of obligation to do so. Studies suggest that the civic duty to vote is in decline, especially among Canadian youth. At the same time, research confirms that Canadians are less knowledgeable than ever about politics and elections in this country. Findings like these reveal a real need to revisit the foundations of Canadian democracy to gain a better appreciation for, and understanding of, how our system works.

This chapter discusses the core dimensions and customs of Canadian democracy, and the important role that elections play in sustaining it. In tracing the evolution of Canadian democracy, the chapter exposes the diversity of systems that exist in various parts of the country.

Democracy in Canada

Canada, as presented in Chapter 1, is a liberal democracy, characterized by equality, rights, and freedoms preserved through free and fair elections and the rule of law. It hews to the most basic tenets of democracy, which hold that there must be regular, non-violent elections; that the winner of elections assumes control of the government; that the people are represented by elected officials in a general assembly; that two or more political parties contest the elections; and that power alternates over time.[1] As a liberal democracy, Canada should produce a government that is organized to reflect society's interests, and that raises and spends money in a manner that is approved by a majority of the public's elected representatives.

As we have seen, however, Canadian democracy is more complicated than this: it features a distinct blend of representative, federal, parliamentary, electoral, and partisan elements that distinguish it from other liberal democracies. General elections are held at least every five years, and several high-profile referendums allowed the country's electors to vote on specific issues; some provinces have even employed the tools of direct democracy like recall and initiatives. But despite these cases of direct democracy, Canada is first and foremost a *representative democracy*, where citizens elect politicians to make decisions on their behalf. Furthermore, as discussed in Chapter 2, Canadians live in a *federation*, whereby they elect representatives to serve in two sovereign orders of government, at the federal and at the provincial/territorial level. In this regard, Canada resembles the United States and differs from unitary states like the United Kingdom. At the same time, the Canadian system is built on Britain's Westminster parliamentary traditions: instead of having an elected head of state and a strict separation of powers between the legislative and executive branches, as found in presidential systems and republics like the United States, Canadian democracy features a *constitutional monarchy* grounded in the principle of responsible government. Save for, and in stark contrast to, the consensus-based systems that persist in Northwest Territories and Nunavut, the Canadian political system is also unmistakably party-oriented. In short, Canadian democracy is complex, and it is unique.

Suffrage

Many Canadians take democracy for granted, without stopping to think of the many societies throughout the world that still do not have free and fair elections—free from coercive influences and fair in terms of their impartiality. They also do not consider that Canadians had to struggle to get the right to vote, known as suffrage.

At Confederation, if you were a 21-year-old man of British descent who owned property or was the head of a household, then you were eligible to vote; otherwise, you

suffrage The right to vote in an election.

had little voice in the political system. The constitution initially authorized provincial governments to decide who should have the *franchise*, or the right to vote.[2] This recognized the local nature of the way elections were administered, but eligibility questions soon emerged. Should voters have to own land, or a house? Should immigrants be allowed to vote? What about workers who had arrived from other provinces? In Nova Scotia, if you collected social assistance, you were ineligible. So, too, were those who worked for the post office in Quebec, and Aboriginal people living in Ontario, Manitoba, or British Columbia. By the early 1900s, political pressure succeeded in broadening eligibility, but only among men.

Things began to change for women during World War I. Suffragettes such as Nellie McClung petitioned for the right to vote, gave public lectures, met with politicians, and staged a play in Winnipeg to raise public awareness that the situation was both unfair and ridiculous. In 1916, Manitoba became the first province to allow women to vote, followed later that year by Saskatchewan and Alberta. The next year the laws were changed in Ontario and BC, and for the first time a woman, Louise McKinney in Alberta, was elected to a Canadian legislature.

These suffragette movements would influence federal politics, but only enough for the governing party to change the election laws to its advantage. Prime Minister Robert Borden's Conservative government, which supported allocating more resources for the war effort, passed the Military Voters Act and the Wartime Elections Act in advance of the 1917 Canadian election. These pieces of legislation gave the vote to any current or former woman belonging to the Canadian armed forces, including Canada's military nurses. But the government's two acts went much further than this

Greg Perry

Why do you think so many Canadians take their voting rights for granted? At what point does voter apathy pose a threat to Canadian democracy?

to ensure that people sympathetic to Canada's commitment to its World War I allies would be casting a ballot. They stipulated that any woman directly related to someone serving in the Canadian forces, even if that person had died, was now eligible: wives, sisters, mothers, grandmothers. Moreover, these laws took away the right to vote from thousands of Canadians, such as Mennonites, because they spoke German, and immigrants born in an enemy country. In other words, while some women were now allowed to vote in federal elections, other women and members of other marginalized groups were not.

At this point, the move toward universal suffrage gathered momentum. Legislatures across the country changed laws to allow women to both vote and be candidates for elected office on the same basis as men. The one exception was Quebec, where women were struggling for equality in other areas, such as the right to own property; they turned their attention to suffrage only in the 1930s, finally gaining the right to vote at the outset of World War II (see Table 10.1)

Even though the franchise was being broadened, the rules still favoured citizens of British origin. Certain Canadians still did not have the right to vote, or had that right taken away. Aboriginal people were eligible only if they agreed to relinquish their status as a registered Indian. There was limited pressure on the government for this to change, in part because some Aboriginal people felt that voting in Canadian elections would only legitimize their assimilation. Racism figured prominently once again

TABLE 10.1 | "Democratic Firsts" for Canadian Women

Jurisdiction	Gained Right to Vote	Gained Right to be a Candidate	First Candidate to Win Office	First to Join Cabinet	First to Head a Government	First 50/50 Cabinet
Canada	1918*	1919	1921	1957	1993 (Kim Campbell, Progressive Conservative)	2015
BC	1917	1917	1918	1921	1991 (Rita Johnston, Social Credit)	—
AB	1916	1916	1917	1921	2011 (Alison Redford, Progressive Conservative)	2015
SK	1916	1916	1921	1982	—	—
MB	1916	1916	1920	1966	—	—
ON	1917	1919	1943	1972	2013 (Kathleen Wynne, Liberal)	—
QC	1940	1940	1961	1962	2012 (Pauline Marois, Parti Québécois)	2007
NB	1919	1934	1935	1970	—	—
PE	1922	1922	1970	1982	1993 (Catherine Callbeck, Liberal)	—
NS	1918	1918	1960	1985	—	—
NL	1925	1925	1930 (1975 as a province of Canada)	1979	2010 (Kathy Dunderdale, Progressive Conservative)	—

*Many Aboriginal women and men did not gain the right to vote until 1960.

Source: Elections Canada, *A History of the Vote in Canada*, 2nd edn (Ottawa: Office of the Chief Electoral Officer of Canada, 2007): p. 64, Table 2.4. Also Linda Trimble, Jane Arscott, and Manon Tremblay, eds, *Stalled: The Representation of Women in Canadian Governments* (Vancouver: UBC Press, 2013).

in World War II, when the intensity of war carried over to Canadian voting rules. The biggest culprit was British Columbia, which revoked the vote from Aboriginal people and Asian Canadians, notably those of Chinese, Japanese, and Indian descent. After Japan bombed Pearl Harbour in 1941, Parliament opted to disenfranchise many Japanese Canadians living elsewhere in Canada. It was 1948 when those laws were repealed, but it was not until 1960 that all Aboriginal people living in Canada were given the franchise in federal elections. Since then, in the late 1980s, the right to vote was given to federally appointed judges, and in the early 1990s it was extended to many prisoners and to Canadians with significant mental disabilities. However, prisoners serving a sentence of two years or more continued to forfeit their right to vote until the Supreme Court of Canada ruled that prohibition to be unconstitutional. Since the *Sauvé* decision (2002), all adult Canadian citizens are eligible to vote in federal elections, save for the two highest-ranking officials at Elections Canada, namely the chief electoral officer and deputy chief electoral officer.

Election Laws

Establishing who is eligible to vote is just one of many aspects of elections regulated by laws. The rule of law helps ensure that elections are fair and democratic. Think of politics as a high-stakes game: there are written rules that govern the behaviour of the players, and there are unwritten ethical boundaries that are open to interpretation. Referees are tasked with organizing the competition and ensuring that the rules are followed. Some key terms from the "rulebook" are explained in Table 10.2.

TABLE 10.2 | Key Terms and Officials in Election Administration

Term	Summary	Function
advance polls	Polling stations that are open roughly a week before Election Day to allow people who will be unavailable on Election Day to vote in advance.	To ensure that everyone has the opportunity to vote, including political staffers, who will be busiest on Election Day.
chief electoral officer	Responsible to the legislature, the independent person who bears responsibility for overseeing the entire election.	To issue election writs, appoint returning officers, ensure that election workers are trained, officially recognize political parties, etc.
list of electors	A central database of the name, sex, date of birth, and address of every Canadian who is eligible to vote.	To allow election workers and election candidates to communicate directly with electors and check if they have voted.
polling stations	Accessible rooms in local buildings where booths are set up for people to vote.	To organize voters into clusters, minimizing the likelihood of long lineups and wait times on Election Day.
returning officer	A person in every electoral district who oversees the administration of the election in that area and who is supported by a team of workers, including the deputy returning officer and poll clerks.	To ensure that someone is locally responsible for overseeing the election of a candidate.
scrutineer	Also known as a "candidate's representative," this individual observes the counting of the ballots.	To ensure all of his or her candidate's votes are counted.
special ballot	A ballot that is submitted by mail rather than cast at a polling booth.	To allow people to vote who cannot do so in person, such as people travelling or temporarily living away, members of the Canadian Forces, and people in jail.

INSIDE CANADIAN POLITICS
Should the Voting Age be Lowered to 16?

In 1970 the voting age in federal elections was lowered from 21 to 18 years. Should it be lowered even further?

Some argue that the voting age should be lowered from 18 to 16 years. After all, in many provinces, 16-year-olds can obtain a driver's licence, they can join the Canadian Forces, and they can be tried as an adult in court. Here are some of the major arguments on both sides of the debate:

Sun Media

School boards in some provinces hold mock votes to coincide with provincial and federal elections, so that students—such as the ones shown here, at St Kateri Catholic School in Grande Prairie—can see how their results compare with those of the broader electorate. At what age do you think citizens should be allowed to vote in provincial and federal elections?

For lowering the voting age to 16

- It would get young people involved in elections.
- The number of Canadian voters would increase.
- Politicians would pay more attention to young people's concerns.
- Getting young people involved would increase their likelihood of voting when they become adults.
- The importance of civic education in schools would increase.

Against lowering the voting age to 16

- The overall election turnout percentage would likely decrease because so many 16- and 17-year-olds wouldn't vote.
- Young people would be the least informed and most impressionable voters.
- The international standard for voting eligibility tends to be 18.
- More legal rights apply to adults 18 years and older, who have more at stake in an election.
- Many young people oppose the idea because they feel uninformed.

Something to look for when studying political reform is what advocates and decision-makers would stand to gain. When looking at voting age, three themes are common.

First, some politicians use the issue to appeal to young voters, who tend to be some of the most energetic volunteers. Also, a student in high school today might be old enough to vote by the next election. Standing as a proponent of lowering the voting age could enhance a politician's popularity among members of this young demographic.

Second, the politicians who advocate lowering the voting age tend to belong to an opposition party. The issue of voting age gives them an opportunity to criticize and embarrass the government.

Third, compared with older voters, young people are more likely to support progressive policies that are left of centre on the political spectrum, and they have historically been more likely to support radical change. For this reason, political parties such as the NDP, the Greens, and the Parti Québécois tend to be supporters of lowering the voting age, whereas the Conservative Party, because it tends to attract older voters, would be more hesitant.

VOX POP
What effect could lowering the voting age have on election outcomes?

At the federal level, detailed election rules are passed by Parliament, and the resulting legislation is known as the Canada Elections Act. The Act designates the chief electoral officer, who reports to Parliament rather than to the prime minister, as the head of Elections Canada, the non-partisan organization that administers federal elections. Examples of the types of duties that a chief elections officer for a municipal election is tasked with are presented in the Employment Opportunities box on page 396. The duties for chief electoral officers at the federal and provincial levels are considerably broader.

Each of the 338 electoral districts has a returning officer who is appointed to oversee the election in that area. To increase public awareness of election rules, Elections Canada routinely coordinates information campaigns, including drawing upon the list of electors to mail voting reminder cards so that citizens are informed about when and where they can vote. Temporary staff are hired to work at polling stations on Election Day to verify voters' eligibility to vote in the riding, to pass out paper ballots, and to count the votes for each candidate when the polls close. Electors such as those who are travelling or temporarily living out of the country can apply to vote by special ballot so that they can receive a package to submit their vote by mail.

Canada's election rules govern the behaviour of candidates and their supporters, and evolve over time (see Table 10.3). Among the many offences under the Canada Elections Act are voting more than once, preventing candidates from accessing a public area to communicate with electors, and, on the part of an employer, not giving staff time to vote. Similar rules exist across the country at the provincial and territorial levels, which is not to suggest that there are not variations.

Just how serious an offence is it to break an election law? It can be quite serious, as the case of former Conservative Party staffer Michael Sona illustrates. In 2014, Sona was found guilty of election fraud and sentenced to nine months in prison plus a year on probation for his involvement in arranging a "robocall"—an automated phone call—designed to direct voters in Guelph, Ontario, to a nonexistent polling station on the day of the 2011 federal election. In 2015, former Conservative Party MP Dean Del Mastro was sentenced to a month in jail and banned from seeking elected office for five years, after he was found guilty of exceeding campaign spending limits and trying to cover it up. Such charges are exceedingly rare, however. Typically, enforcement of election law is very difficult, and the sanctions for anyone found guilty tend to be minimal, such as a fine rather than jail time. One of the likely reasons for the rarity of cases like Sona's and Del Mastro's is the significant risk that opponents will publicize any transgressions. In this sense, rule-breaking is limited less by fear of formal enforcement than by fear of public humiliation, the likelihood of sanctions imposed by the offender's political party, and the reduced chances of getting re-elected. For example, during the 2011 federal election, a Liberal campaign worker in Toronto was spotted taking Green Party brochures out of residents' mailboxes and replacing them with brochures for the Liberal MP seeking re-election.[4] A Green Party volunteer took photos of the offence and posted them online. The news media pounced on the story, and in short order the Liberal candidate (who was not re-elected) was pressured to fire the worker, although no formal charges or sanctions were pursued.

But when rules are interpreted differently, the matter can head to court. For instance, Elections Canada alleged that in 2006, the federal Conservatives broke the spirit of some financing laws through some shifty accounting that came to be known as the "in and out" scandal. In 2008, it was front-page news when the RCMP raided the national headquarters of the governing Conservative Party to collect evidence related to the allegations. Ultimately, in late 2011, the Conservative Party pleaded guilty to exceeding the limit on advertising spending in 2006; the party was fined $52,000 and repaid over $230,000 received in government election subsidies. The Conservatives dropped plans to appeal the case to the Supreme Court after the Crown withdrew charges against four Conservative members, including two senators.[5] Justice may have been served under the law, but by then the party had won three consecutive elections and avoided facing the issue as a significant topic of discussion during a campaign.

The most common role for the courts in settling election controversies is a judicial recount. If the margin of victory is very small (0.1 per cent or less, at the federal level), the law dictates there must be another count of the ballots. This process is overseen by a judge, who makes rulings on any questionable ballots. For instance, voters are instructed to mark a ballot with an "X" to identify their choice. Some voters, as a form of protest, intentionally ignore this instruction and instead write a message of complaint, resulting in a spoiled ballot. But many voters, ignorant of the rules, use a checkmark instead of an X, or they circle the name of their preferred candidate. Should a vote count if an elector draws a happy face next to a candidate's name? What if an elector crosses off all but one candidate's name? In a close race, these are the sorts of interpretations that can decide the outcome, and a judge is the final authority.

Electoral System

single-member plurality (SMP) An electoral system whereby the winner of a district needs just one vote more than the number amassed by the runner-up.

The rules of Canada's single-member plurality (SMP) electoral system, also known as *first past the post*, are quite simple. Areas of the country are divided into electoral districts, also known as *ridings* at the federal level or *constituencies* at the provincial level. In each district, a variety of candidates appear on the ballot, including designated representatives of different political parties, and sometimes independents who are not party representatives. After the votes have been counted, the candidate with the most votes wins, even if the margin of victory is just one vote and regardless of whether most voters marked their ballot for other candidates. The party that wins the most districts almost always forms the government because it will control the legislature. In this sense, each federal election consists of hundreds of simultaneous individual elections, all fought under the same rules, but each featuring its own unique campaign dynamics. The same SMP system governs elections in every province and territory, although some jurisdictions have experimented with other electoral systems in the past and have contemplated reforms more recently.

Like the US and the UK, Canada is one of the few countries to use a single-member plurality electoral system. By contrast, two-thirds of the world's voters cast their ballots in some form of proportional representation (explained below) or mixed system, as did the residents of several Canadian provinces in the early twentieth century. In short, while there are many other federations, parliamentary democracies, and nations with SMP electoral systems, no other country has quite the same mixture of these elements as Canada does (see Figure 10.2 on page 399).

SMP may be ubiquitous across Canada, but it is by no means the only electoral system possible. As you read this, discussions are likely occurring about how to reform the electoral system, given that the Justin Trudeau Liberals pledged to introduce a new system by 2017. Canada's use of SMP places it in rare company. Across the democratic world there are over a dozen different types of electoral systems, of which Table 10.4 provides a small sampling. These different electoral systems are distinguished by three main factors: their electoral formula, their ballot structure, and their district size.

BRIEFING NOTES

What Is the Fair Elections Act?

In 2014, the Fair Elections Act changed the rules for federal elections in Canada. It was passed by the House of Commons and the Senate after the government integrated amendments to some of the more controversial aspects of the bill (Bill C-23). Those MPs who turned out for the vote on Bill C-23 cast their ballots along party lines: Conservatives favoured the bill, while NDP, Liberal, Bloc Québécois, and Green MPs voted against it. Some of the new rules are as follows:[3]

1. *Stricter vouching.* Voters who arrive at the polling station without proof that they live in the electoral district are permitted to vote, provided (a) they sign an oath of residency, and (b) that person's residency is vouched for by another valid voter, who must also sign an oath. Previously, a voter information card and/or vocal vouching were permitted (The Trudeau Liberals have vowed to repeal this provision.).

2. *Reduced Elections Canada communications.* The elections agency is no longer permitted to engage in advocacy to encourage voter turnout. Instead, the focus of its election communications is to provide Canadians with information about when, where, and how to vote.

3. *Change in the chief electoral officer's tenure.* The person holding this title retains the position for up to 10 years. Previously the post could be held until the age of 75.

4. *Reassignment of the commissioner of Canadian elections.* New offences exist, such as impersonating a candidate or an election official. Tasked with policing election rules, the commissioner is no longer an Elections Canada official but a member of the office of the director of prosecutions.

5. *Party access to voting data.* Political parties will be provided with official information about which Canadians voted and which did not. In the past, parties had to compile this information themselves by assigning scrutineers to sit at polling stations.

6. *Nomination of polling station employees.* Political parties' electoral district associations (EDAs) and the parties themselves may nominate polling station workers (specifically, deputy returning officers and poll clerks). Previously, only a party's local candidates could do so.

7. *Higher donation limits.* The amount that Canadians can donate to a campaign increased to $1,500 as of 2015, with an increase of $25 annually after that. Candidates can also give more to their own campaigns than they could previously.

8. *Stricter rules for robocalls.* Anyone who deploys a recorded telephone message during an election campaign is now required to maintain details of the recording and when the call was made. The information must be kept for three years. More restrictions and tougher penalties were also introduced.

9. *Restrictions on third-party advertising.* Elections Canada refers to interest groups and other organizations that engage in political communication but which do not field candidates as "third parties." The Fair Elections Act broadened the limits on third-party spending to encompass pre-campaign advertising.

Opportunities Available

Knowledge of Canadian Politics and Government Preferred!

Chief Elections Officer

Department of Legislative Services, City of New Westminster, British Columbia

The City of New Westminster requires a Chief Elections Officer with specialized knowledge and considerable experience in the administration of elections. Reporting to the Director of Legislative Services, duties will include coordinating the planning and implementation of all operations leading up to the General Local Election and ensuring that legislative and legal requirements are applied and followed. Other duties will include hiring, training and supervising the work of a large number of election staff; and liaising with a wide variety of internal and external contacts, including elected officials, regarding election matters. The Chief Elections Officer will coordinate the preparation and maintenance of a variety of complex material related to election administration while exercising considerable independence of judgment and action, within the parameters of legislated and corporate procedures.

Requirements

- Thorough knowledge of applicable sections of the Municipal Act and other relevant Provincial statutes, as well as City bylaw provisions and other rules, policies and procedures governing the work performed; thorough knowledge of the requirements pertaining to the use by the City of the Provincial Voters' List.

- Ability to interpret, explain and apply election law, procedures and policies.
- Ability to select and train election staff, and to plan, assign, supervise and review the work.
- Ability to develop and implement a complex operational plan. Ability to develop and implement programs such as staff training and public awareness.
- Strong ability to work independently and exercise judgement.
- Ability to function effectively under pressure and to meet inflexible deadlines.
- Considerable knowledge of the geography and demographics of the City of New Westminster.
- Technical ability to ensure production of ballots in accordance with vote counting equipment standards.
- Technical ability to order, have produced, and test election memory chips, and ensure placement in appropriate voting place machines.
- Technical ability to train election staff to generate election night reports, separate memory chip packs from the vote counting equipment for transport and accumulation, and accumulate accurate results in an appropriate format.
- Strong oral and written communication abilities.

Source: Civic Info BC, "Find careers" (2014), www.civicinfo.bc.ca/161.asp?jobpostingid=22208#.UxLAwfldWSo.

The *electoral formula* is the way that votes are translated into seats. Some systems declare the winner based on whether the candidate captured a plurality (or the most) of the votes cast, while others demand that the victor receive support from a majority (at least half) of electors. Still others assign seats proportionally, basing a party's representation in the legislature on its total share of the popular vote across the country, not on the number of geographic districts it wins; other systems involve some mixture of these formulas. As its name suggests, Canada's single-member plurality system belongs to the first of these main types. The others—majority, proportional, and mixed—exist elsewhere and at times have appeared at the provincial level throughout Canadian history.

TABLE 10.3 | Examples of Rationale for Current Federal Election Rules

Old Rules	Problem	Current Rule
Electors stood up and publicly announced who they were voting for.	Electors could be threatened about how to vote.	Electors are given a secret ballot so that nobody can see how they have voted.
No limits existed on fundraising or spending.	Candidates with wealthy supporters had a big advantage.	Limitations on fundraising and spending evens the playing field.
Electors were enumerated through door-to-door canvassing.	Collection of information by this means was labour-intensive.	Data for the list of electors is continuously updated through government records.
Election finance matters were secretive.	Candidates could feel pressured to return favours to donors.	Fundraising and spending details must be reported and publicly released after the election.
Businesses and unions could donate money and labour.	Organizations might seek favours from elected officials.	At the federal level, only citizens are allowed to donate to parties and candidates.
Political parties qualified for government funding, based on the number of votes received.	Parties could become dependent on the state, with little incentive to fundraise from supporters.	Per-vote funding subsidies have been eliminated.

Source: Adapted from Elections Canada, *A History of the Vote in Canada* (Ottawa: Minister of Public Works and Government Services Canada, 1997).

The second main element of an electoral system concerns the way in which the vote choice itself is framed. Distinguishing between *ballot structures* involves a pair of considerations. First, are voters expected to cast only one ballot at one point in time, or are there multiple rounds of voting involved in each election? Is there a single Election Day, or do voters gradually narrow the field of candidates over a longer period of time? Second, does the voting process require voters to select only their top choice of candidates (a *categorical ballot*), or does it require them to rank the candidates in order of preference (a *preferential ballot*)? Under SMP, in federal contests, Canadians cast a single ballot by placing a single mark next to their favoured candidate. Again, this has not always been the case in provincial elections and the SMP system is certainly not common outside North America.

District size is the third and final element of an electoral system. Size here refers to the number of elected representatives awarded for a single district, not to the size of the district's geographic area or population. The concept of having more than one representative may seem foreign to many Canadians. Most have grown accustomed to having a single member of Parliament (MP) at the federal level and—depending on where you live in Canada—a single member of the House of Assembly (MHA), member of the Legislative Assembly (MLA), member of the provincial Parliament (MPP), or member of the National Assembly (MNA) at the provincial level. Hence, the use of the term *single-member* plurality system. Many Canadians are unaware that in the past, voters often sent several representatives to the same legislative body.

↺ See Figure 6.1 for a breakdown of provincial legislatures across Canada.

Each electoral system is based on a different set of values and objectives. Some systems may perform well in terms of representing different geographic regions, for instance, while others may be better at representing different demographic groups (women, Aboriginal people, newcomers, and so on). In parliamentary systems, some may be likely to produce majority governments, whereby the governing party controls the legislature, while others may be designed to produce hung parliaments, which force

INSIDE CANADIAN POLITICS

Should Canadians Be Able to Vote Online?

If we can manage our bank accounts online and renew our driver's licences over the Internet, then surely the technology exists for us to be able to vote online—doesn't it? This is becoming a burning question as voter turnout declines and as mobile technology becomes a bigger part of Canadians' lives. Online voting would be more convenient and could increase election participation among youth, people who are confined to their homes, people with special needs, people who have to commute a long way to vote, and people who are too busy to line up at a polling station. It would also reduce the possibility of human errors and the need for judicial recounts. Governments around the world are studying online voting and it is being tested in some elections where the stakes are lower, such as municipal and students' union elections. Indeed, section 18 of the Canada Elections Act states that the chief electoral officer may carry out studies on electronic voting, but that adopting such a process would need Parliament's approval.

The biggest concern with online voting is the possibility of election fraud. The only way that an online system would be adopted is if the highest form of secure technology had the full confidence of elected officials, election administrators, and the public. There are also significant set-up and maintenance costs to keep up with the latest technology. The system would need to be tested, electors would need to be informed about how to use it, and regular polling stations would still need to be staffed because not everyone would choose or be able to go online. There is also a lack of evidence that an abundance of non-voters would suddenly become online voters; many refrain from participating in elections for reasons other than the inconvenience, meaning that online voting would simply make it easier for routine voters to cast a ballot. Lastly, public confidence in online voting technology in Canada remains hampered by the controversies surrounding several recent experiments by political parties who used online voting to select their leaders.

This said, electronic voting continues to gain momentum in some corners of the county, including Halifax, which held its first e-vote in 2008. For now, though, it seems that most Canadians will have to make do with lining up for a paper ballot and using a pencil to mark it with an "x" in most elections.

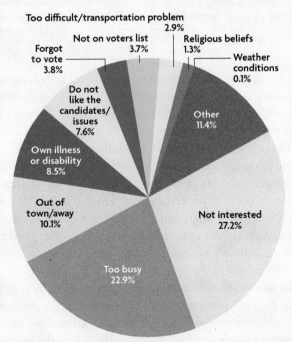

FIGURE 10.1 | Canadians' Reasons for Not Voting in a Federal Election

Source: Data from Statistics Canada, "Reasons for Not Voting in the May 2, 2011 Federal Election," *The Daily* (5 July 2011).

VOX POP

The chart above illustrates the results of Statistics Canada research on why people did not vote in federal elections. Given these reasons, what impact do you think online voting would have on voter turnout?

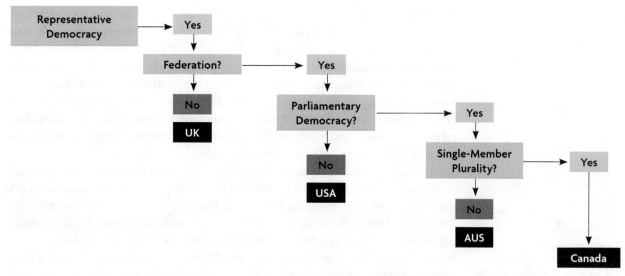

FIGURE 10.2 | Democracy in Canada Compared with Australia, Great Britain, and the United States

competing parties to co-operate. Some may be more accessible and more easily administered, while others may be more difficult to understand and expensive to operate.

By contrast, single-member plurality systems like Canada's tend to be easily understood by voters, generate decisive results, and produce a direct link between representatives and their constituents. Marking an "X" on a ballot is easy to understand, as is the notion that the candidate receiving the most votes—and the party winning the most seats—is the victor. This sort of first-past-the-post system also often produces clear-cut winners, by virtue of translating pluralities in the popular vote into majorities in the legislature. And, by providing voters with a clear sense of who represents them in the legislature (just one member of Parliament), constituents have no difficulty attributing blame or credit come Election Day.

There are obvious tradeoffs involved, however. While decisive, SMP systems often produce disproportional results in terms of how votes are translated into seats for political parties. Canadian federal elections consist of not one but several hundred races,

TABLE 10.4 | Electoral Systems Used Internationally

Electoral System	Examples	Electoral Formula	District Size
Alternative Vote (AV)	Papua New Guinea	majority	single-member
Block Vote	Kuwait, Lebanon, Syria	plurality	multi-member
List Proportional Representation	Spain, Israel, Finland	proportional	multi-member
Mixed-Member Proportional (MMP)	Germany, New Zealand, Venezuela	plurality & proportional	single-member & multi-member
Single-Member Plurality (SMP)	**Canada**, United States, United Kingdom	**plurality**	**single-member**
Single Non-transferable Vote (SNTV)	Afghanistan, Jordan, Indonesia	plurality	multi-member
Single Transferable Vote (STV)	Australia, Ireland, Malta	proportional	multi-member
Two-Round Plurality	France	plurality	single-member

and the percentage of seats won by a party can be quite different from the percentage of the total vote obtained. A party that goes on to form the government may have won a majority of these contests (and thus at least half of the seats in the legislature), but none of these individual victories needs to be based on a majority of the votes cast in each riding. In contests where three parties have candidates, for instance, it is possible for a candidate to win with just 34 per cent of the votes cast, even though 66 per cent of voters chose someone else. If a party wins enough of these close, multi-candidate races, it may win enough seats to form government without necessarily winning a majority of all of the votes cast across the country.

Indeed, in Canadian politics, winning a federal election has seldom required collecting a majority of support among all voters. Since the emergence of Canada's multiparty system following the First World War, only three Canadian governments have won a majority of the popular vote. We call these *earned majorities*. The remaining elections resulted in either *manufactured majorities* (15 times, including the 2015 federal election), or minority governments (13 times) (see Figure 10.3). Such a high number of hung parliaments, where no one party obtains a majority of seats, even questions the ability of Canada's SMP system to produce the decisive results that its proponents tout.

Nonetheless, first-past-the-post systems are known for producing disproportional, even counterintuitive, results. Consider the outcomes of the following provincial elections, all of which were waged under SMP rules. Frank McKenna's Liberal Party won the 1987 New Brunswick election by a substantial margin in terms of the popular vote, winning 60 per cent of all ballots cast compared to just 29 per cent for the Progressive Conservatives and 11 per cent for the New Democrats. In a purely proportional system, the Liberals would have been entitled to a healthy legislative majority, with 60 per cent of the seats. However, under the first-past-the-post formula, McKenna became the second premier in Canadian history to lead a party that won 100 per cent of the seats in the legislature; previously, the PEI Liberals won all of the Island's 30 seats in 1935. Without an opposition, McKenna's government chose

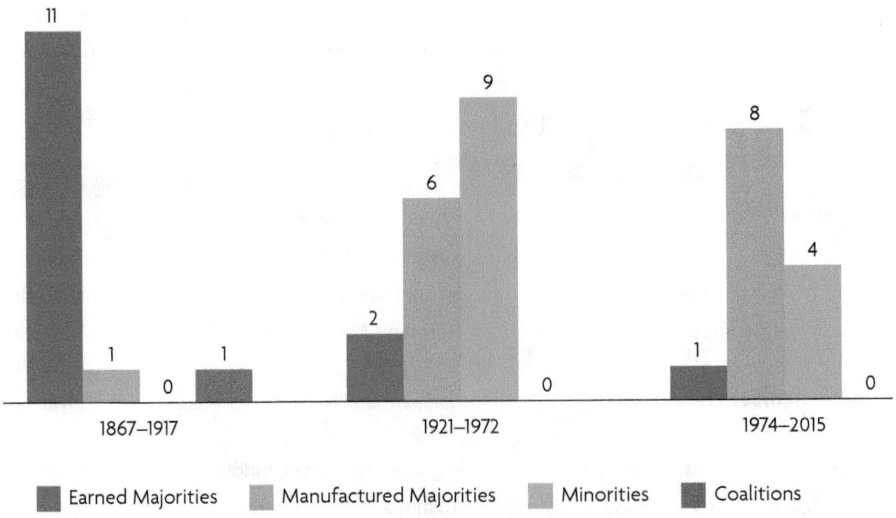

↺ Earned and manufactured majorities are defined and explained in the discussion of majority governments in Chapter 6, on the legislature.

FIGURE 10.3 | Federal Government Compositions since 1867

to answer questions from journalists and opponents from the press gallery during Question Period, to maintain the veneer of responsible government.

In other instances, SMP rules have contributed to "wrong" winners and losers. This occurs when a party wins the greatest share of the popular vote and yet it nevertheless fails to win the greatest share of seats in the legislature. For example, in 1999 the Saskatchewan Party won the highest share of vote with 39.6 per cent and elected 25 candidates. However, the Saskatchewan NDP stayed on as the government because it won 29 seats, even though it earned 0.88 per cent fewer votes than its chief rival; meanwhile the Saskatchewan Liberal Party won just 4 seats, even though 20.2 per cent of electors voted for its candidates. Wrong government outcomes are made possible by the fact that first-past-the-post rules discriminate against parties who build *deep* bases of support in a small number of ridings and parties whose support is spread too *thinly* across all constituencies. A total of 11 Canadian elections have produced wrong winners and losers, as depicted in Table 10.5.

Others argue that the first-past-the-post system prevents Canadians from feeling that their votes really matter in the outcome of the election. Because votes are tabulated on a riding-by-riding basis, citizens who live in uncompetitive districts may feel uncompelled to cast a ballot, as the chance that their single vote may tip the balance is so small. This is known as the **voter's paradox**: because the costs of voting (investing time to become informed, going to the polling station, etc.) outweigh the potential benefits (the low probability of casting the deciding ballot), the act of voting may be considered illogical. SMP and other electoral systems that confine the voter's choice to a specific local race may exacerbate the voter's paradox. A citizen who lives in a constituency with a **safe seat**, where the result is predictable before any votes are cast, may feel less inclined to participate in the election; conversely, Canadians who live in districts with closer races—the so-called **swing districts** that political parties pay the most attention to—are more likely to feel that voting matters. In Canada, there are more safe seats than swing districts, leading many Canadians to feel that their votes are wasted on candidates that seemed destined to win or lose by a considerable margin. By ensuring that the popular vote more closely matches the number of a party's seats in the legislature, proportional representation (PR) electoral systems are designed to limit the number of so-called "wasted votes" and orphaned voters.

PR systems are designed so that the number of party representatives who are elected is proportionate to the party's share of the vote. One outcome, if Canada were

voter's paradox The situation facing a voter whose single ballot is unlikely to influence the outcome of the election, making the costs of voting greater than the potential benefits.

safe seat An electoral district in which the incumbent party is highly likely to be re-elected.

swing district A riding or constituency where the election outcome is uncertain.

TABLE 10.5 | "Wrong" Winners and Losers in Canadian Elections since 1945

Jurisdiction	Election Years
Federal	1957, 1979
British Columbia	1996
Saskatchewan	1986, 1999
Ontario	1985
Quebec	1966, 1998
New Brunswick	1974, 2006
Nova Scotia	1970
Newfoundland and Labrador	1989

INSIDE CANADIAN POLITICS
How Did One Vote Change Canadian History?

In his book *Just One Vote* (University of Manitoba Press, 2009), Ian Stewart tells how a series of one-vote elections changed the course of Canadian history.

The story began in 1986, when Jim Walding won a local NDP party nomination battle in Manitoba by a single ballot. Sitting as an MLA in 1988, Walding voted against his own New Democratic Party in a legislative vote, marking the first time that a sitting

majority government was defeated by a member of its own caucus. The NDP loss triggered an election, which brought the Manitoba Progressive Conservatives to power with a minority government. With its legislature divided, the provincial government was unable to pass the Meech Lake Accord, which killed a nationwide effort to amend the Canadian constitution.

THE LESSON

If that single NDP party member hadn't supported Walding in his 1986 nomination race, the entire course of Canadian history might have turned out quite differently.

to adopt the PR system, could be that smaller parties like the Greens, whose support is spread across the country, would have a greater chance to elect a larger number of representatives. Its proponents argue that PR guarantees that every vote counts as equally as possible toward the eventual outcome, and that for this reason it encourages more citizens to participate in elections. Switching to a PR system is often advocated by people who find faults in the results of an SMP system. Such claims often overlook that all electoral systems have their own strengths and weaknesses.

A benefit of the SMP system is that it reflects geographic diversity, in that each member of the legislature represents a territorially defined district. Unfortunately this geographic representation often comes at the expense of other types of communities. Consider the experience of two traditionally marginalized groups in Canada: francophones and women. The former group is geographically concentrated, both within the province of Quebec and in several other ridings elsewhere in Canada. This clustering allows members of the group considerable political clout, in that should they have a set of collective interests and objectives, they may band together as a voting block to elect and influence a series of elected representatives to sit on their behalf in the legislature. To a lesser extent, the same may be true of members of other smaller socio-cultural communities who live in close proximity to one another (e.g. Filipinos in north Winnipeg, Italians in south Toronto, and African Canadians in Preston, Nova Scotia).

This experience contrasts with that of groups that are not defined by territory, such as Canadian women. Without a substantial majority in any single riding, women do not have the same sort of collective power in Canada's geographically defined system of representation. Other electoral systems, particularly those based on proportional representation, tend to better reflect these groups as they combine votes across a larger geographical area and provide incentives for parties to appeal to non-territorial

INSIDE CANADIAN POLITICS
What Happened When British Columbia Tried to Reform its Electoral System?

The most recent push for electoral reform in British Columbia began when the opposition Liberal Party pledged to establish Canada's first Citizens' Assembly on Electoral Reform. The BC Liberals were a "wrong loser" in the 1996 provincial election, having won more total votes than the incumbent New Democratic Party while failing to win more seats.

Upon reaching office in 2001, the Liberals followed through on their promise and established a panel of British Columbians from across the province to study and make recommendations about the future of the first-past-the-post system. Four years later, the Citizens' Assembly on Electoral Reform recommended that the province move to a single transferable vote system in future elections. The option was put to a vote in

a referendum held in conjunction with the 2005 BC election. Over 57 per cent of British Columbians voted in favour of the switch, including a majority of voters in all but two of the province's 79 districts. This was not enough to displace the first-past-the-post system, however, as the referendum rules required that at least *60 per cent* of voters (and a simple majority in at least 60 per cent of districts) support the change.

Falling just shy of this threshold, reformers convinced the government to convene a second referendum, which took place alongside the 2009 BC election. The second result cast serious doubt over the future of electoral reform in the province, as only 39 per cent of British Columbia voters voted in favour of adopting the proposed new system.

VOX POP
Given all this, what are the prospects for electoral reform in British Columbia?

communities, including labourers, non-heterosexuals, and ideologues. In this sense, opponents of SMP often cite its lack of inclusiveness.

Given these and other significant drawbacks, it should come as little surprise that Canadians periodically consider alternatives to the first-past-the-post system. While short-lived or abortive, these historical experiments at the provincial level are worth considering. Most took place in western Canada in the first part of the twentieth century. At different points, elections in British Columbia (1951–3), Alberta (1924–55), and Manitoba (1920–55) were conducted using a combination of AV in rural areas and STV in cities. In each case, the provincial government introduced the new systems out of a populist commitment to democratic reform, and in each case, it ended the experiment out of concern that its own grip on power was loosening under the new rules. Elsewhere, Saskatchewan employed a block vote system in its various urban centres (1921–64), and Prince Edward Islanders used a dual-member system to send one councillor and one assemblyman to the provincial assembly under familiar first-past-the-post rules (1893–1996). Since then, electoral reform movements have risen and subsided across the Canadian provinces.

Electoral reformers suffered similar setbacks elsewhere in Canada during the period between the two BC referendums discussed in the Inside Canadian Politics box at the top of this page. Maritime governments struck a pair of commissions to investigate the matter. The Commission on Prince Edward Island's Electoral Future

mixed-member
proportional (MMP)
system An electoral system
that combines geographic
and partisan representation
by providing extra seats to
parties whose share of seats
is lower than their share of
the popular vote.

urged Islanders to adopt a mixed-member proportional (MMP) system, a recommendation Island voters rejected by a healthy margin in the subsequent 2005 plebiscite (64 per cent to 36 per cent, with only one-third of eligible Islanders turning out to vote. In 2015, the PEI government announced that a referendum would be held on choosing between SMP, proportional representation, and preferential ballot. Assembled in 2004, the New Brunswick Commission on Legislative Democracy also recommended a move to MMP. Premier Bernard Lord pledged to hold a referendum on the reform in 2008, but his government fell two years before the vote could be held. Skeptical of the new model and its prospects for passing a referendum, subsequent New Brunswick governments have elected not to proceed.

Reform met with similar results in central Canada. In Ontario, a citizens' assembly recommended a move toward MMP, which voters promptly rejected in a 2007 referendum (by a 63–37 percent margin). "Wrong losers" in 1998, the Quebec Liberals also promised changes to their province's electoral system. Detailed study by committees, a commission, and the province's chief electoral officer suggested the benefits of a mixed-member formula. The Quebec government has resisted implementing these recommendations, however, owing to a lack of consensus around the specifics of the new system and a healthy dose of reluctance as a result of reform failures in other Canadian provinces.

Thus, while Canadians across the country have either adopted or considered changes to their electoral system, these flirtations with reform have been fleeting.

VOX POP

After taking the time to research some of the seven alternatives to SMP listed in Table 10.4, do you believe that political leaders should be actively pursuing electoral form at the federal and provincial/territorial level? Which alternative makes the most sense to you?

Apportionment

↻ Intra-state political
institutions are discussed
at length on pages 115–16
of Chapter 3, on federalism
in Canada.

Sorting out how to distribute seats in the House of Commons is one of the most politically charged and complex processes in all of Canadian politics. Deciding how many MPs are allocated to each province is an understandably sensitive matter, given the importance of regional representation in the intra-state federal institutions like Parliament. While some attention must be paid to representing historical communities of interest and the terms of previous constitutional settlements, consideration must also be given to the changing demographics of Canadian society.

Two key elements are used to calculate the size and shape of federal ridings:

- *electoral formulas*, as discussed, establish how many House of Commons seats each province is entitled to
- *electoral boundary rules* establish the means by which constituency maps are drawn.

Taken together, these laws and regulations set guidelines for—and limitations on—electoral commissioners as they strive to ensure all Canadians receive effective representation in their elected assemblies.

These opportunities and challenges were evident in a recent round of reforms to the structure of the Canadian House of Commons. As part of its 2012 democratic reform package, the Harper government introduced a new formula for distributing seats in the House of Commons. These reforms aimed to address the perception that Canadians in the provinces with the fastest-growing populations (Alberta, BC, and Ontario) had become increasingly underrepresented over time. The number of electors per MP in these provinces was substantially higher than in other parts of the country, and solving this growing discrepancy required one of two solutions: remove seats from slower-growing provinces (notably those in the Atlantic region) and reassign them to the high-growth ones, or add more seats to the House of Commons to accommodate the population shifts. Given the political outcry the former solution would have caused, the Conservative government opted for the latter course of action and adjusted the electoral formula accordingly.

The number of seats in the House of Commons increases over time as Canada's total population increases. The new formula boosted the total number of MPs from 308 to 338. Of these additional 30 seats, Ontario received 15, Alberta and British Columbia received 6 each. Even though its population was not increasing, Quebec received 3 more MPs. The addition of seats to Quebec was a late revision to the government's plans, and came in response to political pressure from the Official Opposition and the Government of Quebec to protect the province's proportionate and historic share of seats in the House of Commons. Quebec is home to approximately 24 per cent of the Canadian population, and has traditionally been accorded one-quarter of the seats in the House of Commons.

The new electoral formula is grounded in a standard of 111,166 people per riding in 2011. This quotient is indexed to the average provincial population growth starting in 2021, which will allow the formula to account for future shifts in population among the provinces. The new formula also adds a representation rule to prevent any provinces from losing any seats as a result of future seat redistributions. In all, the new four-step process is used to determine how many seats each province receives under the new formula:

1. *Step 1* – Determine the initial provincial seat allocation. This is done by dividing the provincial population by the electoral quotient (set at 111,166).
2. *Step 2* – Apply the minimum seat guarantees. This is done by considering the number of additional seats each province receives as a result of two constitutional provisions: the Senate floor rule (which specifies that no province shall receive fewer MPs than it has senators) and the grandfather floor rule (which states that no province shall have fewer seats than it did in 1985).
3. *Step 3* – Apply the new representational rule, which states that no province that is currently overrepresented should emerge underrepresented as a result of the new formula.
4. *Step 4* – Add the territorial seats: one each for Yukon, Northwest Territories, and Nunavut.

Taken together, these steps will produce the allocation of seats shown in Figure 10.4 following the next redistribution, which was completed prior to the 2015 federal election.

Redistribution (or *redistricting*) is the legal process by which electoral boundaries are redrawn. The task is usually completed once per decade. In several jurisdictions,

redistribution The formal process used to periodically adjust electoral boundaries.

the process coincides with the decennial census that produces an official count of
the number of citizens, which allows consideration of population shifts within and
among the Canadian provinces. As a provincial population changes both internally
and in relation to its neighbours, it becomes necessary to revise the electoral boundaries to ensure effective and relatively equal representation for all Canadian voters. At
the same time, provisions are put in place to protect communities of interest, whose
representation may require special modifications to the standard one-person, one-
vote ideal.

In Canada, redistribution is conducted using a series of independent boundaries
commissions, at both the federal and the provincial/territorial levels. The precise
makeup of these commissions differs depending upon the order of government and
the jurisdiction involved. Some commissions are made up of government or cabinet
appointees (as in British Columbia), while others are made up of ex-officio members
whose place on the commission comes by virtue of their holding a position in another
organization (as in Manitoba). The terms and mandates granted to each commission also vary, with some being allotted the ability to add seats to the legislature and
others not; some being held to a strict number of electors per district, and others
being permitted considerable variance between constituencies; some commissions
being required to hold public consultations, and others performing their duties with
little public influence.

This independent process is designed to prevent gerrymandering—the highly
partisan practice of drawing boundaries to favour one political party over its opponents. The term was coined by a *Boston Gazette* reporter in reference to Governor
Elbridge Gerry's redrawing of the Massachusetts state senate map, such that the
shape of certain districts in the Boston area came to resemble the shape of a salaman-
der. Despite the reasonably transparent work of boundaries commissions, there are
inevitably claims of gerrymandering in Canada when redistricting occurs. Pundits

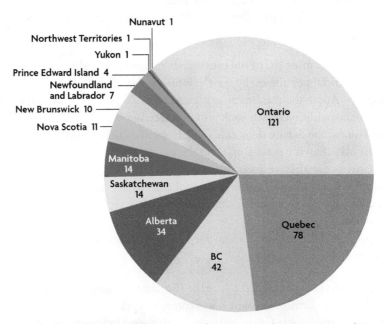

FIGURE 10.4 | Share of Seats in the House of Commons, by Province and Territory

identify boundary changes that appear to lump known supporters of opposition parties together in an alleged attempt by the governing party to create wasted votes in SMP elections.

To provide guidance in the drawing of electoral boundaries, governments typically establish a series of permitted deviances by which commissions may stray when creating districts. These deviances are calculated by dividing the entire population by the total number of districts; they then take this quotient (or average district size), and allow the commissioners to vary by a certain percentage (up or down) when creating each new constituency. Saskatchewan has Canada's strictest deviance formula, allowing its commissioners only 5 per cent leeway from the provincial norm. This means that the most populous constituency cannot have more than 5 per cent more people than the average district, and the least populous district cannot have more than 5 per cent fewer people than the average district.

All Canadian jurisdictions allow for some exceptions to these deviances. Most exceptions involve northern and remote communities, to preserve a certain number of seats in the legislature for these traditionally marginalized groups. Manitoba,

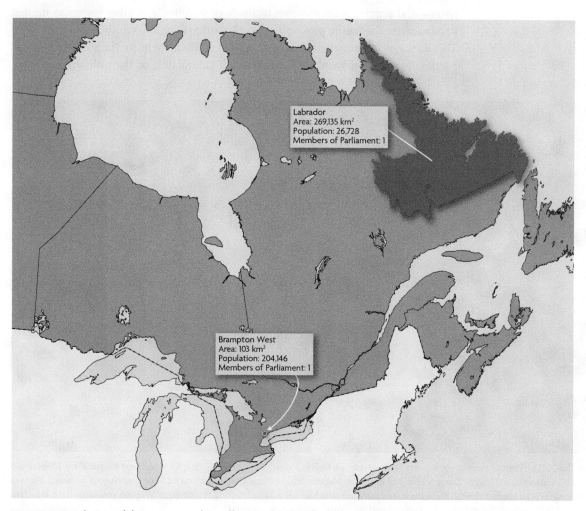

Labrador
Area: 269,135 km²
Population: 26,728
Members of Parliament: 1

Brampton West
Area: 103 km²
Population: 204,146
Members of Parliament: 1

FIGURE 10.5 | Canada's Largest and Smallest Federal Ridings, by Population

for instance, establishes two variance formulas: one for the south (10 per cent) and one for the north (25 per cent). Similar northern allowances are in place in Alberta and Saskatchewan. Other exceptions involve ethnic or cultural communities. Nova Scotia's legislation allowed its electoral commission the latitude to create a predominantly African-Canadian district in the form of the Preston constituency. Rooted in the area for several generations, African Canadians make up about two-thirds of this majority-minority district, a fact that contributed, in part, to the election of the province's first black MLA, Yvonne Atwell, in 1998.

Campaign Finance

Campaigning is one of the most resource-intensive activities in Canadian politics. It is an expensive and intense undertaking for parties, candidates, organizers, journalists, political scientists, election authorities, and other actors. It costs an immense amount of time and money to plan, conduct, deliver, police, and follow an election campaign. The direct costs of the election—including paying and training poll officials, printing ballots, renting space for offices and polling sites, mounting voter education campaigns, and acquiring information technology, supplies, and other resources needed to administer the voting process itself—amount to over $200 million per campaign. This does not include the approximately $65 million spent by the various political parties, $45 million spent by the individual candidates, or the millions of dollars

Ian Dalsin

Ahead of the 2015 provincial election in Alberta, 24-year-old Ian Dalsin vowed, on Facebook, that he would eat his hat if his 20-year-old friend and NDP candidate Thomas Dang won a seat in the legislature. Shown here, Dalsin lost the bet but was true to his word. He was hardly the only one to scoff at the NDP's chances in a province that had seen 44 years of PC dominance. Why do you suppose it is so rare for 20-year-olds to get elected in federal, provincial and territorial elections in Canada?

spent by electoral district associations (political parties' local riding organizations) on activities including advertising, voter mobilization, staff salaries, rent, publicity, polling, and litigation. All told, each Canadian federal election costs well over $350 million in direct administration and campaign costs alone. That amounts to over $10 per Canadian for every election, and this figure does not include the millions spent by media organizations and researchers, the untold number of unpaid hours contributed by volunteers, or the increased government spending stemming from the various platform pledges of the victorious party.

While high, these numbers pale in comparison to those involved in American elections. Parties, candidates, and interest groups alone spent billions of dollars in the various contests in 2012. At over $20 per American, these figures do not include the costs of actually *administering* (let alone reporting on or researching) the election.

Why the great disparity between Canada and the United States? Part of the explanation lies in the different values that underpin each democracy. If Canada's political culture leans more toward *equality*, America's tilts more toward *freedom*. This has real implications for the way money is regulated in each political system. In Canada, campaign finance laws promote equality and justice among parties and candidates, placing stricter limits on how much each citizen can contribute to political parties and candidates, and how much these actors can spend on elections; Canada's laws often involve some level of public funding to help even the playing field among parties. In the United States, limits on contributions and spending are viewed as limits on Americans' freedom of (political) expression. As a result, Canadian elections do not feature as much fundraising activity or lavish spending as is the case south of the border.

When it comes to politics and elections, money carries with it several negative connotations. Some link money to concerns with bribery and corruption. The Pacific Scandal and the sponsorship scandal illustrate what can happen when public funds are used for partisan purposes. In both instances, the government of the day provided its party's corporate financiers with kickbacks in return for their campaign contributions, and in both cases, the electorate's response was resolute. John A. Macdonald's Tory government, in 1874, and Paul Martin's Liberal government, in 2004 and 2006, were punished in general elections. Beyond buying influence, critics fear money in politics further perpetuates Canada's *vertical mosaic*—a term coined by sociologist John Porter in his 1965 book of the same name. The metaphor draws on the notion that Canada can be considered a cultural mosaic, with different ethno-cultural communities preserving their distinct character rather than feeling pressure to assimilate. Porter's *vertical* mosaic captures the idea that the ethno-cultural tiles are arranged hierarchically, with English-speaking white, Anglo-Saxon, protestant (WASP) men at the top, dominating Canadian society, leaving those from non-WASP backgrounds generally excluded from political and corporate power.

Political party and campaign finance regulations are legal rules that are designed to mitigate the negative influence of money in politics. Ultimately, the stringency of a state's system of political finance rules depends on which of the following two values are most important to lawmakers: ensuring political actors have the resources necessary to contest elections and engage the public in a meaningful democratic exercise, or ensuring that well-heeled special interests do not have an inordinate amount of influence on politics and elections.

campaign finance regulations Laws that govern political fundraising and/or spending.

Political finance regimes consist of three sets of rules, governing *revenue* (or contributions to political parties), *expenditures* (the amount and type of spending parties can conduct), and *disclosure* (the nature of public reporting required for donations and spending). Limits are usually placed on both revenue and expenditures, to prevent the most affluent citizens and most well-off parties from dominating the political competition.

Party Revenues

Canadian political parties generate revenue from a wide range of sources, from membership dues and contributions from individual supporters, to a variety of government subsidies. At the federal level, political contributions to political parties (including candidates, electoral district associations, and leadership contestants) are restricted in terms of both source and amount. Only individual Canadians can donate to federal parties, meaning that corporations, unions, and other so-called third parties are not permitted to contribute funds. Similar restrictions exist in some, but not all, provinces. Likewise, at the federal level and in some other jurisdictions, individuals are restricted in the amount of money they can donate. As of 2015, this amounted to $1,500 in any calendar year to a registered federal political party's national organization, $1,500 to a candidate or constituency association, and $1,500 to a contestant in a party leadership contest. These limits also pertain to in-kind contributions, such that non-monetary donations of services or goods (e.g. volunteering to set up a candidate's website, or loaning the party a campaign bus) must be counted against one's donation limit, based on the commercial value. Candidates and leadership contestants are also limited in the amount of money they can contribute to their own campaigns, up to $1,000 for the nomination and up to $1,500 for the general election. These contribution rules were put in place to limit the role of powerful corporate and organizational interests in elections, and to prevent affluent Canadians from attaining undue influence over the political process. Similar models are also in place provincially in Quebec, Manitoba, Nova Scotia, and Alberta.

Political parties also receive a variety of government subsidies, which have traditionally come in three main forms. The first consists of election spending rebates, whereby parties and candidates are reimbursed for a certain proportion of their election expenses. Political parties are reimbursed for 50 per cent of their election spending as long as they meet a minimum support threshold. Candidates a refund of 60 per cent of their expenses if they receive 10 per cent of the vote.

Tax credits are the second form of government subsidy, although these funds are often forgotten when it comes to calculating the amount of state sponsorship. When individual Canadians donate to political parties, they can deduct the amount from their taxable income. These tax credits do not flow directly to the political parties per se, but they represent forgone revenue that the government would have otherwise collected (and spent on other priorities). In this sense, tax credits do constitute a subsidy to political parties—and one that is far more generous than the subsidies given to registered charities or other organizations. For federal-level contributions up to $400, for instance, Canadians are able to deduct 75 per cent of the amount from their tax payable. This rebate decreases proportionally, as the contributions increase.

political contributions Donations to a political candidate, group, or cause.

third parties The Elections Canada term for interest groups.

government subsidy Public funds used to support an individual, group, or cause.

A third government subsidy consists of annual direct public funding, also known as a *per-vote subsidy*, which rewards parties for each vote received in the previous general election. Provided a party receives a minimum level of support (usually between 2 and 5 per cent of the vote), it would be entitled to a certain dollar amount per ballot cast in its favour (usually between 2 and 5 dollars). At the federal level, these annual funds were introduced as a way of offsetting bans on big donations and of levelling the playing field for smaller parties. However, in 2011, the Harper government announced that it would phase out the per-vote subsidy at the federal level, and in April 2015, the last of these quarterly allowances were sent out, marking an end to the program. Per-vote subsidies are still paid out by some provincial governments, such as those of Quebec and Manitoba, but the elimination of this subsidy at the federal level increases the onus on political parties to fundraise.

VOX POP

Which of the three subsidies most benefits larger parties, and which are most valuable to smaller parties? Why should political parties receive subsidies at all?

Party Spending Limits

Parties and candidates are not only restricted in terms of the funds that they raise, but also in terms of the funds that they are allowed to spend. At the federal level, spending limits are legal restrictions on expenditures, which are calculated based on the number of ridings a party contests and the number of voters in those ridings. National party organizations fielding a full slate of 338 candidates were permitted to spend just under $55 million each on the 2015 election (or $2.15 per eligible Canadian voter). Likewise, candidates' spending is limited based on the number of voters in their constituencies, with a sliding scale allowing for greater per capita spending in smaller, more sparsely populated districts.

> **spending limits** Legal restrictions on how much money can be spent in a campaign.

Many observers perceive certain loopholes in these spending limits. The "in and out" affair, which occurred during the 2006 federal election campaign, serves as one example. As explained earlier in the chapter, the Conservative Party of Canada shifted $1.3 million between its national organization and local constituency associations in an effort to spend more money on advertising in swing ridings; having exceeded national party spending limits, party organizers were forced to repay over $230,000. Previously the Bloc Québécois was involved in an in-and-out scheme in the 2000 election.

> ↺ The "in and out" affair is explained in greater detail earlier in this chapter, on page 394.

Disclosure

The final component of Canada's campaign finance regime consists of the rules governing disclosure. National party organizations, local district associations, candidates, and leadership contestants are all required to report publicly on their various fundraising and spending activities. This is to ensure that the public is aware of precisely who is donating to whom in a given campaign. Candidates must file their audited electoral campaign returns within four months, and national party organizations within six months of Election Day. Among other details, these returns must include

> **disclosure** Revealing otherwise private information, such as campaign expenses.

the names and addresses of all donors who contributed over $200, and the amount and type of expenditures incurred. Penalties for non-compliance range from the denial of election rebates to jail terms and fines.

While these rules do bar corporations, unions, and interest groups from donating directly to political parties, the laws do not prevent third parties—that is, registered individuals and organizations who spend money on advocacy during the campaign without seeking office—from participating in elections altogether. They are allowed to advertise during campaigns. According to section 319 of the Canada Elections Act, a political advertisement is any message

> transmitted "by any means during an election period," which is "intended to *influence* how an elector might vote, by *promoting or opposing* a registered party or the election of a candidate, including a message that takes a *position on an issue* with which a registered party or candidate is associated." [Emphasis added.]

This definition differs from what is in place in the United States, where advertisements are unregulated so long as they do not explicitly contain the so-called "magic words" *vote for* or *vote against*. Third parties that wish to spend over $500 in advertising must register with Elections Canada, identify themselves as the ads' sponsors, spend no more than $150,000 in any one election (including all markets), and spend no more than $3,000 in any one district. Again, these regulations were put in place to

In Canada and the United States, political actors question the constitutionality of campaign finance laws. The American Supreme Court has ruled that "money is speech," meaning that to restrict an individual's right—or even a *corporation's* right—to spend money during a campaign is tantamount to infringing on their freedom of speech. Why do you suppose courts in the United States reached such a different view of democracy than courts in Canada, which have ruled that restrictions on campaign financing actually enhance the democratic system?

prevent well-heeled interest groups from dominating the discussion during election campaigns. While challenged as limiting Canadians' freedom of expression, these rules were upheld in the Supreme Court's *Harper* decision in 2004. That failed constitutional challenge was initiated by Stephen Harper while he was the president of a conservative lobby group.

Campaigning

National Campaigns

Election campaigns are high-profile events that tend to occur roughly every two to four years and follow a common pattern. An official election campaign begins when the legislature is dissolved by the governor general or, at the provincial level, by the lieutenant governor. This can be prompted by one of three things: a request by the head of the governing party (a prime minister or premier), a defeat of the governing party on a major vote in the legislature, or the end of the five-year period since the last election took place, five years being the maximum term allowed under the Canadian constitution. Legislation requiring fixed-date elections, whereby elections are held on a designated day every four years (unless the legislature is dissolved before then), have become common, but the constitution's five-year rule is the upper limit. When the legislature is dissolved so that new members can be elected, a writ of election for every electoral district is issued by the chief electoral officer, which officially sets in motion the nomination of candidates, the hiring of election workers, and the setting up of polling stations. Election Day usually occurs on a Monday or Tuesday.

> **writ of election** A legal document dissolving a legislature and marking the official start of an election campaign.

The Four Stages of an Election Campaign

Canadian elections tend to follow four unofficial stages:

1. the pre-writ period
2. the phony war
3. the leaders' debate
4. the post-debate period.

The *pre-writ period* encompasses the days, weeks, or even months leading up to the start of the official election campaign. The governing party prioritizes good news, so the government's budget may be full of new spending initiatives and tax cuts, the details of which are announced many times to achieve the best possible news coverage. The parties may seek to spend on advertising and other promotional activities during this period because election laws regulating such behaviour apply only during the official campaign period. It has become increasingly common for political parties, as soon as an election is over, to behave as though the next Election Day is just around the corner, and they wage a permanent campaign of ongoing electioneering during the inter-election period.

The official campaign period begins when the writ is issued; at the federal level, official campaigns last for a minimum of 36 days, during which the rules of the Canada Elections Act apply. People who follow elections refer to period leading up to

> **permanent campaign** The practice of electioneering outside of an election period, especially by leveraging government resources.

the first debate as the *phony war*, because this is when electors are just starting to pay attention and the stakes are not as high.[6] It is a time when most campaign organizations are getting set up, when candidates are being nominated, and when there is still time to recover from a mistake. The national media designate reporters to follow the major party leaders around the country. The leader's tour begins on the first day and features party leaders making campaign stops while surrounded by an entourage of party workers. The presence of journalists travelling with the leader gives party strategists the opportunity to arrange low-risk visual events that will generate positive news coverage, such as a visit to a local candidate's headquarters for a rally, a speech to supporters in a friendly riding, or a photo op at a local landmark, such as a restaurant or a market. The leaders are accompanied by a team of personnel who manage every detail of the appearance and handle media inquiries. The leader, party staffers, and the reporters travel across the country together on a chartered airplane or buses.

During the phony war period, party strategists finalize the details of their election platforms, the manifestos that itemize the party's policy proposals, spending commitments, and general pledges if elected. Each party sets up an information command centre known informally as the "war room," where a team of strategists issue news releases, monitor opponents' communications, issue rapid response counterattacks, and handle special requests. Armed with opinion research data, the parties use political marketing strategies and communications tactics in an attempt to inform and persuade targeted segments of the electorate.

Traditionally, the midpoint of the campaign is the *leaders' debates*, which are organized by major media organizations and which mark the start of the period where

leader's tour A visit of various electoral districts by the party leader and an entourage of staffers and journalists.

election platform A list of political pledges announced before or during an election campaign.

↻ A similar incident from the 1974 federal election is discussed in Chapter 11 on page 449.

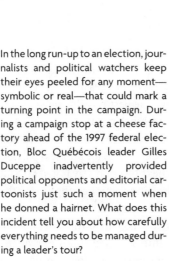

In the long run-up to an election, journalists and political watchers keep their eyes peeled for any moment—symbolic or real—that could mark a turning point in the campaign. During a campaign stop at a cheese factory ahead of the 1997 federal election, Bloc Québécois leader Gilles Duceppe inadvertently provided political opponents and editorial cartoonists just such a moment when he donned a hairnet. What does this incident tell you about how carefully everything needs to be managed during a leader's tour?

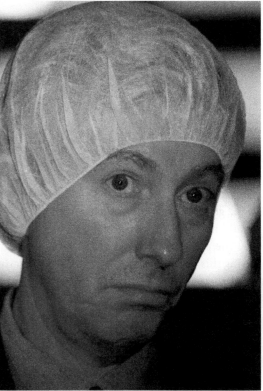

The Canadian Press/Paul Chiasson

THEY SAID IT

Famous Lines from Canadian Leaders' Debates

You had an option, sir. You could have said, "I'm not going to do it, this is wrong for Canada, and I am not going to ask Canadians to pay the price." You had an option, sir, to say "no," and you chose to say "yes" to the old attitudes and the old stories of the Liberal Party. That, sir, if I may say respectfully, that is not good enough for Canadians.

—Progressive Conservative leader Brian Mulroney chastising Liberal PM John Turner in 1984 for appointing Liberals to government jobs. Mulroney's party went on to win 211 of 282 seats.

I have news for you: I intend to make this country work. Because if there's one commitment I've made to my children, it is that I'm going to pass on to them the country I've received from my parents.

—PC leader Jean Charest arguing with Bloc Québécois leader Gilles Duceppe in 1997. Charest's party experienced a short-lived bump in opinion polls.

No 2-tier healthcare.

—Handwritten sign held up by Canadian Alliance leader Stockwell Day in the 2000 leaders' debate. The party, like its predecessor, the Reform Party, was routinely accused by opponents of having a secret agenda to privatize the Canadian healthcare system.

You say you've got a plan. Where is it? Where's your platform? Under the sweater?

—NDP leader Jack Layton to Conservative PM Stephen Harper in 2008, in a mocking reference to Harper's image management. Harper had been panned for wearing a blue sweater vest in advertising designed to make him appear more likeable.

Why do you have the worst attendance record in the House of Commons of any member of Parliament? If you want to be Prime Minister, you'd better learn to be a member of Parliament first. You know, most Canadians, if they don't show up for work, they don't get a promotion. You missed 70 per cent of the votes.

—NDP leader Jack Layton criticizing Liberal leader Michael Ignatieff in 2011 for his House of Commons absenteeism. Layton's party went on to form the official opposition, while the Liberals dropped to historic lows.

I'll give you a number: nine.

—Liberal leader Justin Trudeau in response to a 2015 debate question from NDP leader Tom Mulcair about what constitutes a clear majority in a sovereignty referendum. Trudeau was referring to the nine Supreme Court Justices who ruled 50%+1 is insufficient.

VOX POP

When it comes to leaders' debates, are strategists and the media too concerned with the knockout blow? How might a change in format produce a better debate of policy issues?

many electors begin paying attention. These forums are the only planned meetings of the major party leaders to deliberate each other's policies. The debates are designed to allow the leaders to make their pitches directly to viewers while attempting to get the better of their opponents before an audience of citizen viewers, journalists, and opinion makers. At the federal level, televised debates in English and in French have traditionally been held on back-to-back nights, organized by a consortium of broadcasters. In 2015, five independently-staged debates took place, with all the major leaders only attending one organized by the consortium of broadcasters—its French-language debate. In each election, the organizers tinker with the format, determining whether, for example, the leaders should be standing at lecterns or sitting around a table. Journalists and sometimes carefully screened electors pitch questions that one or all leaders are expected to answer. The leader of the governing party and/or of the party that is ahead in opinion polls tends to go on the defensive, while the opposition leaders seek to discredit that party.

The 1984 leaders' debate has become the standard for all other debates in Canada. In the debate's most memorable exchange, Progressive Conservative leader Brian Mulroney delivered a stinging criticism of Liberal Prime Minister John Turner over a slew of party supporters who had been appointed to government jobs. Mulroney went on to lead his party to the biggest landslide in Canadian federal election history, and that decisive episode has come to be known as the *knockout punch*. Indeed, the question that everyone asks after a leader's debate is, who won? Not only are the debates portrayed as the most important event of the campaign, but political scientists have found that a leader's performance can have a tremendous impact—favourable or unfavourable—on the image of the entire party.[7]

In the *post-debate period*, the stakes are high, as Canadians finalize their voting intentions. The parties intensify their campaigning, sharpen their messages, attack their opponents, and increase their advertising. The controversial tactic of running critical advertising spots, or attack ads, intensifies during this period. At the same time, campaign organizers take additional measures to insulate their candidates from the sort of devastating mistake, or campaign gaffe, that could destabilize their messaging and their chances of winning. Local candidates are increasingly urged not to participate in all-candidate debates because the audience is stacked with committed partisans and there is a risk of bad media coverage that could undermine the

CBC Licensing

In 2012, Elections Canada announced it would no longer prohibit news outlets from releasing any election night results until the last polls in BC and Yukon had closed, finding the ban nearly impossible to enforce in the era of social media. Why did the ban make sense? Do you think it should be illegal for individual Canadians to post election results in their region before polls have closed in the rest of the country? How would this be enforced?

campaign not just locally but nationally. Party leaders stay focused on delivering scripted speeches, and may limit or even refuse reporters' questions.

In the final days of the campaign, the party leaders visit a handful of swing districts where they are trying to shore up support, before completing their tour in their own riding or constituency. On Election Day, the news media cover the leaders as they go to vote and report on the traffic through local polling stations. A media blackout prohibits political advertising and the communication of previously unreleased opinion poll data. Party workers known as *scrutineers* observe the voting process throughout the day and during the vote count. That evening, after the last of the polls has closed, journalists begin reporting the vote results as the ballots in each poll are counted. Using statistical analysis of voting patterns, the media can project the outcome based on early results and declare a victor before the final results are tallied. These projections are typically reliable, although there have been occasions where networks have had to reverse their announcements. Leaders and candidates give victory or concession speeches, and pundits begin to assess the reasons why parties and candidates won or lost. The most organized of campaigns will engage in a post-campaign evaluation, in which organizers and strategists they take stock of what worked and what didn't so that they can learn for the next campaign.

↻ Negative advertising—and whether it is good or bad for Canadian politics—is a theme that runs throughout Chapter 12, on communication.

Voter Turnout in Canadian Elections

Regardless of the election outcome, there is also the matter of how many people voted. Voter turnout, which is the proportion of registered electors who voted, is seen as an indicator of the vibrancy of democracy. The trend in Canada (see Figure 10.6) and other Western nations is a decline in elector participation. Lower turnout is predicted to continue because fewer young people are voting, and it is presumed they are less likely than the youth of previous generations to take up voting later in life. Non-voters give a variety of reasons for staying home. "Too busy" and "not interested" top the list, followed by, among others,

voter turnout The proportion of eligible electors who cast ballots in an election.

- was away
- was ill
- did not like the choices
- forgot
- was not on the voters list
- found voting too difficult
- prevented by religious beliefs
- prevented by weather conditions.[8]

↻ See the ICP box on page 398 of this chapter for a visual summary of these findings.

At the core is that many voters feel like voting doesn't make a difference and the contest is not competitive. By comparison, people who vote tend to have a heightened civic duty, which is a sense of obligation to participate in the polity, and are more interested in politics (see Figure 10.7).[9]

How serious a concern is lower turnout? It suggests that Canadians are not engaged in elections, are ill-informed about public policy, and are taking democracy for granted. Or it may signify that people are reasonably content with the status quo and make a conscious decision that voting is not worth the effort. One explanation is the *voter's paradox*, discussed earlier. Economists and rational-choice theorists have

FIGURE 10.6 | Turnout in Canadian Federal Elections, 1945–2015

Note: 2015 turnout is a preliminary figure from Elections Canada and does not include people who registered on election day.

long argued that it is illogical to vote. They argue that because the chances that a single vote will decide the outcome of the election are so minuscule, it is incomprehensible that any elector would bother spending any time or effort paying attention to election campaigns, making a decision, and driving to the polls. One economist has calculated that the expected benefit from voting must be over 8 billion times the cost of voting.[10] Clearly, people vote for reasons other than to personally influence the outcome, such as the positive feelings they get from being part of a group and exercising their democratic right to participate in such an important civic event.

Turnout fluctuates between elections, and varies widely across Canada at both the federal and provincial/territorial levels (see Table 10.6). Among the reasons for turnout variation are the density of population, the amount of time that has passed since a previous campaign, and the time of year that the election is held.[11] One constant is that residents of Prince Edward Island tend to be more likely to vote than other Canadians, regardless of the nature of the election. Complicating matters, it can be difficult to compare data over time given that the franchise has been extended, and not all Canadians appear on the government's list of electors. Nevertheless, the level of turnout raises questions about the legitimacy of democratic government in Canada, especially if we consider the frequency of manufactured majorities. As it stands, a majority government tends to be formed on the basis of securing approximately 40 per cent of the votes cast, which produces wins in more than half of the contested seats. As we have discussed, this in itself is problematic. But when only two-thirds of electors cast a ballot, this means that only about a quarter of eligible electors have actually voted for the political party that forms a majority government—a calculation that assumes that everybody is accounted for on the official list of electors. Delving deeper, we may find that different socio-demographic clusters of electors have disproportionately voted for or against the governing party, and that the socio-demographic composition of elected officials does not align with that of the electorate. We also

Most likely to vote

Least likely to vote

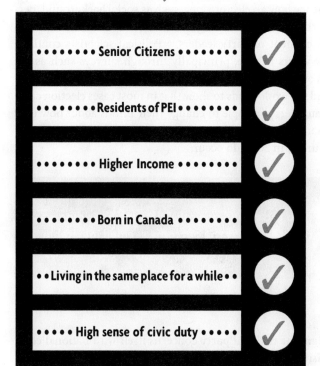

FIGURE 10.7 | Canadians Most and Least Likely to Vote

know that political parties reach out to some voters more than others, especially older citizens over young voters. All of this suggests that the political executive is bound to be out of touch with the needs and wants of the general public and certain cohorts.

TABLE 10.6 | Federal and Provincial Election Turnout by Province, 1993–2013

Province	Average Federal Election Turnout (%)	Average Provincial Election Turnout (%)	Higher Federal or Provincial Participation? (%)
British Columbia	63.4	62.4	federal: +1.0
Alberta	59.0	51.2**	federal: +7.8
Saskatchewan	63.3	68.8	provincial: +5.5
Manitoba	61.2	60.8	federal: +0.4
Ontario	62.8	55.7	federal: +7.1
Quebec	66.2	72.3	provincial: +6.1
New Brunswick	67.4	71.2	provincial: +3.8
Nova Scotia	63.6	66.2	provincial: +2.6
Prince Edward Island	72.1*	82.5*	provincial: +10.4
Newfoundland and Labrador	53.4**	69.7	provincial: +16.3

*Highest in Canada.   **Lowest in Canada.

Source: Adapted from Lori Thorlakson, "Explaining the Federal-Provincial Turnout Gap in the Canadian Provinces, *Canadian Political Science Review* 9, no. 1 (2015): Table 1, p. 170.

For all of this effort, do national campaigns matter? Studies show that many non-campaign factors influence how an elector votes, such as social background, personal beliefs and values, party identification/allegiance, views on economic matters, opinions on issues, and assessment of party leaders.[12] Political scientists continue to attempt to measure how voters behave, principally through surveys such as the Canadian Election Study, Vote Compass, and the Comparative Provincial Elections Project, and research around the world tends to show that in most cases election campaigns do not cause large numbers of people to change their minds about how they intend to vote. Nevertheless unexpected results, such as the NDP Orange Wave in 2011 or the Trudeau Liberals' triumph in 2015, do occur.

VOX POP

If an election were being held today, and one candidate in your riding was so heavily favoured over the others that the outcome seemed inevitable, would you vote? Why or why not? What would have to change to make you more or less likely to vote?

Local Campaigns

During an election campaign, the national party concerns itself with national communications such as advertising, media coverage of the leader's tour, and press releases. These are collectively known as the "air war," in reference to a desire to control the media airwaves. At the same time, candidates are competing to earn the right to represent an electoral district, such as Winnipeg North or Dartmouth–Cole Harbour. This is where the "ground war" occurs. Candidates and local campaign workers interact directly with electors by knocking on doors, phoning electors, distributing brochures, and putting up lawn signs. Much of their focus is on identifying potential supporters so that on Election Day, they can contact favourable voters and encourage them to get out to the polls, a process known as *getting out the vote*, or GOTV.

GOTV Efforts to mobilize supporters to vote, such as telephone reminders.

party nomination An internal contest to decide who should represent a party locally in an upcoming election.

For most candidates, the process of seeking election involves a lot of work.[14] Two formal stages must be completed to become an election candidate. The first is to win the party nomination. If more than one person is interested, there is a nomination contest, which is a mini-election among local party members, who vote on which candidate should represent the party in the upcoming election. The internal contest is run by the party. Contested nomination races indicate a popular belief that the party's candidate may be elected, whereas uncontested nominations are a sign either that one candidate, such as an elected official seeking re-election, has the nomination locked up or that the party's eventual nominee stands little chance of winning the general election. The second stage is signing the nomination papers for the election authorities, including securing the signatures of some local electors to demonstrate that they endorse the candidate. This is accompanied by a deposit that gets returned if post-election paperwork is completed. Of course candidates who intend to run as independents do not need to seek a party nomination.

A candidate for election is required to appoint an official agent to authorize the campaign's election spending, which is later audited. Many people erroneously think that local candidates are supported by a huge team of paid consultants and workers.

INSIDE CANADIAN POLITICS
What Was the "Orange Wave"?

Jack Layton led the federal New Democratic Party in the 2004, 2006, and 2008 federal election campaigns. Opinion surveys consistently indicated that Canadians liked Layton but not enough that they would vote NDP. In each election his party's seat count improved, but nevertheless the NDP placed fourth behind the Conservatives, the Liberals, and the Bloc Québécois.

At the outset of the 2011 campaign, the NDP seemed destined for another fourth-place finish. The characteristically robust Layton just had hip surgery and needed a cane; in public he seemed physically frail and perhaps not up to the rigours of a drawn-out campaign. But something happened that surprised everyone, including Layton. Around the time of the leaders' debates, Quebecers began to turn away from the Bloc Québécois. As opinion polls showed that the "Orange Wave" of increasing NDP support was real, it began to spill over into other parts of Canada, and the momentum seemed to energize Layton. The media began to scrutinize the party's platform and profiled various NDP candidates, some of whom were university students, party volunteers, and other stopgap candidates parachuted into Quebec ridings with little

hope—initially, at least—of winning. Nevertheless, on Election Day, the party made history, winning a majority of seats in Quebec and the second-most seats overall. Layton became the NDP's first-ever leader of the official opposition. Meanwhile, the Liberal Party placed third for the first time in its history, and the Bloc was reduced to a rump of four MPs.

The NDP's achievement was bittersweet, as three months later, Layton passed away from cancer, triggering a search for a new party leader and a new member of Parliament for the riding of Toronto–Danforth. In an open letter to Canadians, Layton declared: "[L]ove is better than anger. Hope is better than fear. Optimism is better than despair. So let us be loving, hopeful and optimistic. And we'll change the world."[13] His words may have inspired a new generation of NDP supporters, including those that supported the "Orange Crush" in the 2015 Alberta provincial election. However, despite periodically leading in public opinion polls, and a reasonably error-free campaign, in 2015 the "Orange Wave" became the "Orange Crash." Tom Mulcair led his party to its second-best performance in terms of seats (44 MPs), but nevertheless it is once again relegated to being the third party in the House.

THE LESSON
Campaigns can have a profound impact on improving a party's standing in the legislature.

That may be true in the case of celebrity candidates, but typically the campaigns of lower-profile candidates in Canada are managed by a small core of volunteers, many of whom may be the candidate's personal friends and family; sometimes the candidate her- or himself doubles as the campaign manager. The trend, however, is to pay campaign workers, especially on Election Day, when fewer people are available or interested in committing to volunteering with a campaign.

Political parties engage in a seats triage to identify which electoral districts they will retain with minimal effort, which ones they are unlikely to win, and which seats will be close races.[15] They focus their resources on the close races, where a visit by the party leader and prominent candidates, some extra advertising, and additional workers may tip the scales. This typically leaves candidates in safe seats, incumbents

seats triage The identification of swing ridings where campaign resources should be concentrated.

incumbent An elected official who currently represents an electoral district.

seeking re-election, and candidates in unwinnable races to their own devices. But how much does this matter? Research suggests that the effects of the local ground war are minimal, usually accounting for less than 10 per cent of the vote, and that they matter only in extremely close races.[16]

By-elections

Sometimes a special election, known as a by-election, is needed to fill a vacancy in an electoral district before the next general election occurs. Vacancies occur when an elected official resigns or dies while in office. Resignations occur for a myriad of reasons: for example, a sitting politician may accept an appointment to the Senate or an ambassadorship; may decide to run as a candidate in a municipal or provincial election campaign; or may be forced to step down over a scandal. Sometimes a politician will resign a safe seat to give an incoming party leader who is not currently a member of the legislature an opportunity to get elected. At other times the person simply retires owing to ill health. Within a number of months, the prime minister, through the governor general, announces that a federal by-election will be held for electors in that district to vote for a new representative.

Since the question of which party will form the government isn't at stake, local issues and candidates matter more. Even so, by-elections are usually seen as a test in which local voters have the chance to send a message about their satisfaction with the governing party. For this reason, and because voter turnout tends to be lower than in a general election, the winner of a by-election will not necessarily be re-elected in the following general election when national media coverage intensifies.

Direct Democracy in Canada

Canada may be first and foremost a representative democracy, but over the course of Canadian history, there have been moments when citizens have been called upon to provide first-hand input into the policy-making process. Typically this is done through either a plebiscite or a referendum. The federal government has held two major national plebiscites in Canadian history, concerning the prohibition of alcohol (1898) and the desirability of military conscription (1942), and one national referendum on the Charlottetown Accord (1992).

Referendums are exceedingly rare in Canada because they tend to be on divisive policy issues and risk disrupting the social order. All three federal referendums were relatively close, and each revealed a unique set of regional cleavages within the Canadian electorate. The prohibition plebiscite passed by a margin of 2 per cent (51–49), with substantial majorities in English Canada (particularly the Prairies and the Maritimes) voting in favour. The conscription plebiscite produced similar regional results, albeit with a larger proportion (65 per cent) of Canadians voting in support of establishing a military draft. Quebec voters sided overwhelmingly *against* each proposal, making the province the only one to vote "no" to both prohibition (81.2 per cent) and conscription (72 per cent). Historians cite numerous explanations for these outcomes, most of them having to do with Quebec's unique political culture and relationship with the federal government and rest of Canada. For reasons explained in Chapter 2, the referendum on the Charlottetown Accord failed nationally (55 per cent

BRIEFING NOTES
Referendums and Plebiscites

For most intents and purposes, the terms *referendum* and *plebiscite* are synonymous in Canada. Strictly speaking, however, a plebiscite is a *non-binding* instrument to ascertain the public's opinion on an issue of public policy, while a referendum is a *binding* public vote on a concrete

variety of policy alternatives. The word *referendum* is used much more commonly, and many people use it to refer to any type of direct vote by citizens on a policy, without observing the nuances of binding and non-binding votes. For this reason, we treat the terms as interchangeable.

to 45 per cent), achieving majority support only in PEI (74 per cent), Newfoundland (63), New Brunswick (62), Northwest Territories (61), and Ontario (50). Once again Quebec opposed the referendum issue. In all three referendum cases the proposed policy did not proceed, though in World War II the government wavered for two years before eventually establishing conscription. This latter point reveals the contingent nature of direct democracy in Canada: unlike the situation in the United States, where referendums may be binding and lead directly to new legislation, in Canada the choices made by the electorate still require the support of the government of the day in order to be implemented.

The Canadian provinces and territories have served as political laboratories for experiments with direct democracy. In terms of province-wide referendums and plebiscites, provincial governments were most active in the early twentieth century, particularly on the issue of liquor (see Table 10.7). All told, four provinces held a total of twelve separate votes on prohibition, temperance, and the sale of spirits, with plebiscites in Alberta (1915, 1923, 1957), Ontario (1924), Quebec (1919), and PEI (1878, 1893, 1901, 1923, 1929, 1940, 1948). Aside from these decisions, provincial and territorial governments have convened referendums on a wide range of topics, from taxes, gambling, and shopping, to potatoes and automobiles. Perhaps most significantly, governments have sought direct public input on weighty democratic and constitutional issues, including abortion, religious schooling, electoral systems, borders, and whether to join or leave Confederation. It should be noted that the James Bay Cree also held a referendum surrounding the 1995 Quebec sovereignty vote, with 96 per cent of the people voting to stay in Canada rather than join a sovereign Quebec. Moreover, every province except Nova Scotia, Ontario, and Manitoba have legislated requirements to hold a plebiscite prior to tabling any amendment to the Constitution of Canada in their respective legislatures (although Manitoba has a requirement to hold public consultations before doing so).

In addition to direct votes on issues of public policy, several provinces have experimented with the introduction of recall legislation—a formal process that allows the electorate to petition the government for the removal of a member of the legislature between elections. In jurisdictions where such legislation exists, a petition signed by a significant proportion (usually 40 per cent) of registered voters in the member's constituency is enough to have the elected official cease to hold office. That individual

↻ Canada's regional cleavages are discussed in Chapter 4, on regionalism. See especially pages 140–50, on regionalism in Quebec.

↻ The debate surrounding conscription is discussed in Chapter 14, on Canada's place in the world.

recall Legislated process by which electors of a given district may petition for a by-election.

may, however, run in the by-election that is triggered by the successful recall. In this way, recall legislation is intended to ensure that members of the legislature remain accountable, responsive delegates of their constituents.

Although recall legislation is common in the United States, it has not taken hold in Canada. Alberta's experience lasted only two years, at which point Premier William Aberhart repealed his own Recall Act (1935) amid a threat posed by his own constituents to use the law against him. As it stands, British Columbia is the only province to have enacted and employed recall legislation. Since its introduction in 1996, the province's chief electoral officer has processed two dozen recall petitions. While none

TABLE 10.7 | Referendums and Plebiscites in the Canadian Provinces and Territories

Province	Issue	Result
British Columbia	Initiative and recall plebiscite (1991)	supported introduction of legislation allowing initiatives and recall
	Treaty referendum (2002)	supported certain principles in treaty negotiations with First Nations
	Referendum on electoral reform (2005 and 2009)	rejected single transferable vote electoral system
	Harmonized Sales Tax (HST) referendum (2011)	approved repeal of HST
Alberta	Electrification plebiscite (1948)	approved continued private distribution of electricity
	Daylight Saving Time plebiscites (1967, 1971)	rejected, then approved, the adoption of Daylight Saving Time
Saskatchewan	Abortion plebiscite (1991)	rejected public funding of abortions
	Constitutional amendment plebiscite (1991)	approved mandatory referendums on constitutional amendments
	Balanced budget plebiscite (1991)	approved enacting balanced budget legislation
Manitoba	No provincial plebiscites or referendums	
Ontario	Referendum on electoral reform (2007)	rejected mixed-member proportional system
Quebec	Referendum on sovereignty-association (1980)	rejected sovereignty-association
	Referendum on Quebec sovereignty (1995)	rejected sovereignty
New Brunswick	Video lottery terminal referendum (2001)	approved retaining video lottery terminals
Nova Scotia	Sunday shopping plebiscite (2004)	rejected establishing Sunday shopping
Prince Edward Island	Automobile plebiscite (1913)	government suppressed results
	Potato plebiscite (1954)	approved of Potato Marketing Board
	Fixed-link crossing plebiscite (1988)	approved creation of bridge to NB
	Video lottery terminal referendum (1997)	approved removal of all video lottery terminals
	Plebiscite on electoral reform (2005)	rejected mixed-member proportional electoral reform
Newfoundland and Labrador	Referendums on Confederation (1948)	approved entering Confederation
	Schools referendums (1995, 1997)	rejected, then approved disbanding religious schools
Yukon	No territorial plebiscites or referendums	
Northwest Territories / Nunavut	Northwest Territories division plebiscite (1982)	approved dividing Northwest Territories
	Nunavut Creation Referendum (1992)	endorsed the Nunavut Land Claims Agreement
	Northwest Territories boundary plebiscite (1992)	approved the NWT–Nunavut boundary
	Nunavut capital plebiscite (1995)	approved Iqaluit as capital of Nunavut

Note: Excludes municipal plebiscites and referendums.

was officially successful in removing a member of the Legislative Assembly, in that the petitions either did not receive enough signatures or else failed procedurally, one process did contribute to an MLA's resignation. Often, the threat of recall is enough to persuade a government to reconsider its course of action on a particular issue, as was arguably the case with members of the BC Liberal government when they relented to pressure to hold a referendum on the Harmonized Sales Tax (HST) in 2011.

Concluding Thoughts

Elections are complex, fundamental events in Canadian democracy. So much time and effort goes into ensuring they are contested vigorously, reported objectively, studied rigorously, and conducted fairly that it is somewhat surprising—even disappointing—that so many Canadians decide not to participate. Studies indicate that, for as many as 6 in 10 non-voters, Canada's political system is *too* complicated for them to engage in any meaningful way. Books like the one you're reading, and courses like the one you're probably taking, are designed to help inform would-be voters of how the various facets of Canadian democracy function. Ultimately, however, it is up to citizens to learn what they need to in order to become effective members of the traditional political community—should they wish to do so.

↻ See the ICP box What Happens When Direct Democracy Meets Tax Policy, in Chapter 8 for a consideration of British Columbia's HST referendum.

↻ For an answer to the question, Why Isn't Direct Democracy More Common in Canada?, see the ICP box in Chapter 2.

For More Information

How is the Canadian system of government designed for Canadians' views to be represented? Peter Aucoin, Jennifer Smith, and Geoff Dinsdale tackle this question in *Responsible Government: Clarifying Essentials, Dispelling Myths and Exploring Change* (Canadian Centre for Management Development, 2004). Available at www.csps-efpc.gc.ca/pbp/pub/pdfs/P120_e.pdf.

How do Canadians define "representation"? Cameron Anderson and Elizabeth Goodyear-Grant shed light on the topic in "Conceptions of Political Representation in Canada: An Explanation of Public Opinion," *Canadian Journal of Political Science* 38, no. 4 (2005): pp. 1029–58.

Does Canada need more referendums? Richard Johnston, André Blais, Elisabeth Gidengil, and Neil Nevitte take a critical look at the topic in *The Challenge of Direct Democracy: The 1992 Canadian Referendum* (McGill–Queen's University Press, 1996).

How does Canada's electoral system compare with those found in other mature democracies? Henry Milner and his colleagues help contextualize Canada's electoral reform movement in *Steps Toward Making Every Vote Count* (University of Toronto Press, 2004).

Why do you suppose efforts and experiments with electoral reform have been so short-lived in Canada? Dennis Pilon explores the topic in his book *The Politics of Voting: Reforming Canada's Electoral System* (Emond Montgomery, 2007).

To what extent is the SMP electoral system's exaggeration of support for the winning party a problem? Peter Russell examines Canada's parliamentary system of government in *Two Cheers for Minority Government: The Evolution of Canadian Parliamentary Democracy* (Emond Montgomery, 2008).

Does gerrymandering exist in Canada? Exactly how are electoral boundaries designed? Find out in John C. Courtney's *Commissioned Ridings: Designing Canada's Electoral Districts* (McGill–Queen's University Press, 2001).

Do election rules in Canada seem strict? Should taxpayers subsidize political parties? Editors Lisa Young and Harold Jansen are among a variety of authors who examine political finance rules in their book *Money, Politics, and Democracy: Canada's Party Finance Reforms* (UBC Press, 2011).

Want to learn more about the history of federal, provincial, and territorial campaigns in Canada? Visit the CBC Archives to view hundreds of video and radio clips dating back to the early twentieth century: www.cbc.ca/archives/categories/politics/elections/elections.html, or search: CBC archives elections.

Need all of the latest information on upcoming Canadian elections? For polls, seat projections, newsfeeds, historical results, and more, visit the Election Almanac: www.electionalmanac.com.

Want to compare the laws, rules, and regulations that govern the various federal, provincial, and territorial elections? Elections Canada maintains an up-to-date *Compendium of Election Administration in Canada*. Search: Elections Canada compendium.

Itching to see the latest (and historical) Canadian political advertisements? Visit the CanuckPolitics YouTube channel by searching: YouTube Canuck Politics ads.

Interested in becoming an "Everyday Political Citizen"? Visit the Samara website to learn more about improving citizen engagement through research and education: www.samara.com.

Deeper Inside Canadian Politics

1. The provincial electoral district of Preston was created in Nova Scotia in 1993, with African Canadians making up nearly two-thirds of its residents. Is this sort of "majority minority" district the most effective means of representing the province's rural African-Canadian community in the Nova Scotia Legislature?

2. Critics have often accused parties (and governments) of rigging the rules surrounding elections to ensure their own success. Is there empirical evidence of this in Canadian history?

3. Should new rules be established to regulate negative campaign advertising in Canada?

4. Imagine a friend of yours announced the intention not to vote in an upcoming election. "It's not worth the hassle—what difference would it make anyway?" What arguments would you use to change your friend's mind?

UP FOR DEBATE

Do election campaigns matter in Canada?

THE CLAIM: YES, THEY DO!

Election campaigns are vital to Canadian democracy

Yes: Argument Summary

Cynics are misinformed about the fundamental purpose of election campaigns. These contests are not designed to present diametrically opposed viewpoints on major public policy issues. Regular pitched battles of that sort would not only destabilize Canadian democracy, but would mask that—on most major issues—Canadians are in fundamental agreement. When parties present citizens with similar positions (in favour of public healthcare or opposed to military intervention, for instance), they are behaving rationally and responsibly by reflecting the interests of mainstream Canadians. Instead of placing voters in the position of having to decide which party or candidate is on the correct side of the issues, campaigns ask voters to choose who would be best at handling the issues in the years ahead, and whose priorities align best with their own. And voters often use the opportunity presented by a campaign to change their minds about who they want to govern.

Yes: Top 5 Considerations

1. Election campaigns are contests between competing agendas and competencies. Most election platforms present voters with a list of the top five or six issues a party wants to address, and the campaign is spent trying to convince voters that the party's leadership is the one best suited to managing those issues. In this sense, election campaigns do present voters with meaningful democratic choices.
2. Even though there is broad agreement over most fundamental (so-called "valence") issues, Canadian politics is not devoid of heated ideological debates or detailed policy discussions. In brokerage systems like Canada's, these battles are fought *within* political parties, in advance of election campaigns. Citizens' input is collected, and consensus is generated at local constituency meetings, at leadership and policy conventions, and within caucus, producing the sort of practical, widely accepted positions we see in campaign platforms. Were it not for this level of pre-election brokerage, Canadian elections would be fractious, divisive affairs, quite possibly threatening national unity on a quadrennial basis.
3. Research challenges the notion that the Canadian electorate is as aligned (or partisan) as popular conception would suggest. Canadians do not identify as strongly or consistently with particular political parties the way voters in other countries do. As "free agents," Canadian voters are often open to persuasion during election campaigns.
4. Electors often do change their minds in the lead-up to Election Day. For instance, public opinion polls in advance of recent provincial elections in Alberta (2012) and British Columbia (2013), and the 2004 federal election, predicted massive victories for opposition parties. Indeed, polls released *in the midst* of those campaigns suggested the governing parties were headed for defeat. Yet the incumbents' campaigns convinced voters otherwise, not only preserving their hold on power but increasing voter turnout in the process.
5. Despite the fact that political parties are constantly campaigning, writ periods are often the only opportunity otherwise occupied Canadians have to assess their representatives. Many Canadians may tune into politics only in the final weeks or days of the campaign. But when they do, experience shows they do make meaningful (and surprising) decisions.

Yes: Other Considerations

- Election campaigns are integral to free and fair elections—a core premise of Canadian democracy. Without them, we would live in an autocratic system of government.
- The fact that there is widespread agreement on major policy issues is not an indicator of the failure of Canadian democracy. It's a sign that political parties are fulfilling their duty to broker varied interests to prevent them from tearing the country apart.
- Attacks on personal (versus professional) character aside, so-called "negative campaigns" draw important contrasts between the abilities of various leaders to govern in citizens' best interests.
- Democracy doesn't simply "happen" during campaigns. As focused as we may be on voter turnout, it is also important to ask why more Canadians do not take an interest or get involved in politics between elections.
- Not all campaigns are devoid of policy debates. Some, like the 1988 federal "free trade election" or the 1960 Saskatchewan "medicare election," are akin to referendums on important issues.

THE COUNTERCLAIM: NO, THEY DON'T!

Election campaigns don't matter as much as some people think, and in some ways may actually be harmful to the quality of Canadian democracy.

No: Argument Summary

Electioneering and even voting don't matter quite as much as politicians and campaign workers suggest. Many Canadians already know exactly how they are going to vote, regardless of what happens during an election campaign. Among the remainder, many are tuned out from politics completely, while many others become turned off by the negativity of campaign mudslinging. Increasing numbers of citizens appear to be figuring out that it is irrational to invest the time and effort in following a campaign when a single vote is so unlikely to change the outcome of the election. Moreover, the reality is that where electioneering was once confined to a relatively short period leading up to an election, the state of play today features a permanent campaign of relentless politicking. As a result, even without much of a formal campaign, Canadians have all the information they need to make an informed vote on Election Day.

No: Top 5 Considerations

1. Canadians don't pay much attention to political campaigns. The first half of an official campaign is commonly referred to as the "phony war" because there is such low interest.
2. Canadian campaigns do not feature the great debates one would expect from a fully functioning democratic system. Parties rarely present contrasting positions on major issues. Those voters who *do* pay attention to campaigns are exposed to relentless negativity and horse-race coverage. So focused are they on identifying and mobilizing supporters that politicians rarely make any effort to engage citizens in a genuine dialogue during campaigns.
3. "An election is no time to discuss serious issues" is a quote attributed to Prime Minister Kim Campbell. Party leaders rarely go into great detail about what they plan to do after an election, and local candidates are often muzzled when it comes to their own views on public policy. As a result, election campaigns hardly confer any sense of a democratic mandate for the winning party.
4. Roughly two-fifths of the Canadian electorate is made up of partisans. These voters will support the same political party regardless of election campaign dynamics.
5. Political parties are increasingly practising the "permanent campaign," which makes the official campaign period leading up to the election virtually indistinguishable from the rest of the time between elections.

No: Other Considerations

- Leaders' debates, for all of the media attention they're given, rarely make a difference to the final result.
- For all of the work by individual candidates and

their volunteers, local campaigning is thought to affect no more than 10 per cent of the vote.

- The media are guided by opinion polls that lead to "horse-race" coverage that ignores the parties and candidates that are likely to lose. For many parties and candidates, especially those considered "minor," this makes an election a frustrating and unfair experience.
- Political parties elected to form the government rarely introduce radical changes. The adage "Liberal, Tory, same old story" exemplifies the public's frustration with opposition parties adopting the policies of the party that they replaced in government.
- Parties often campaign on vaguely defined policies designed to appeal widely to the electorate (particularly "hard-working middle-class families"); a party's real legislative agenda becomes apparent only once it takes office.
- While campaigns were once the only real way for voters to get to know their local candidates, the Internet has become the simplest way for interested electors to familiarize themselves with local representatives and the issues at play in their riding.

Discussion Questions

- Could you imagine a system with longer terms, fewer federal elections, and more opportunities for direct democracy, giving Canadians the opportunity to vote on key issues? What would be the advantages and disadvantages of such a system?
- Since voter turnout is on the decline, could an opinion poll based on a scientifically defined representative sample of eligible voters ever become a substitute for an election, plebiscite, or referendum as we know them today?

- Research has demonstrated that while most Canadians object to the use of negative advertising, negative ads are undeniably persuasive and effective in shaping voter opinions. Why does this contradiction exist? What's the solution?
- Have you ever worked in an election campaign? If so, how did you get involved? If not, what would it take to engage you? A compelling candidate? An issue you feel strongly about? The excitement of playing a role in a heated political contest?

Where to Learn More about Election Campaigns in Canada

André Blais and Martin M. Boyer, "Assessing the Impact of Televised Debates: The Case of the 1988 Canadian Election," *British Journal of Political Science* 26 (1996): pp. 143–64.

André Blais, Elisabeth Gidengil, Richard Nadeau, and Neil Nevitte, "Measuring Party Identification: Canada, Britain, and the United States," *Political Behavior* 23 (2001): pp. 5–22.

R. Kenneth Carty and Munroe Eagles, *Politics Is Local: National Politics at the Grassroots* (Don Mills, ON: Oxford University Press, 2005).

Harold D. Clarke, Lawrence LeDuc, Jane Jenson, and Jon Pammett, *Absent Mandate: Interpreting Change in Canadian Elections*, 2nd edn (Toronto: Gage, 1991).

Anthony Downs, *An Economic Theory of Democracy* (New York: Harper & Row, 1957).

Tom Flanagan, "Political Communication and the 'Permanent Campaign'," in *How Canadians Communicate IV: Media and Politics*, ed. David Taras and Christopher Waddell (Edmonton: Athabasca University Press, 2012), pp. 129–48.

Elisabeth Gidengil, Neil Nevitte, André Blais, Joanna Everitt, and Patrick Fournier, *Dominance and Decline: Making Sense of Recent Canadian Elections* (Toronto: University of Toronto Press, 2012).

Jane Green, "When Voters and Parties Agree: Valence Issues and Party Competition," *Political Studies* 35 (2008): pp. 629–55.

Richard Johnston, André Blais, Henry E. Brady, and Jean Crête, *Letting the People Decide: Dynamics of a Canadian Election* (Montreal and Kingston: McGill–Queen's University Press, 1992).

Heather MacIvor, ed., *Election* (Toronto: Emond Montgomery, 2010).

William H. Riker, "Political Theory and the Art of Heresthetics," in *Political Science: The State of the Discipline*, ed. A.W. Finifter (Washington, DC: American Political Science Association, 1983).

Jared J. Wesley, "In Search of Brokerage and Responsibility: Party Politics in Manitoba," *Canadian Journal of Political Science* 42 (2009): pp. 211–36.

11 POLITICAL COMMUNICATION

Inside this Chapter

- What are the characteristics of Canada's political media?
- What is e-government?
- What are the major theories and practices of political communication?
- What is political marketing?

Inside Political Communication

To *really* understand Canadian politics, you need to appreciate the ways that political information is communicated. This is more than recognizing the different types of media that link political elites with voters; this means understanding the inner dynamics of the communications game. Much of the information about politics and government that Canadians are exposed to is shaped by various political actors with their own agendas; it is up to citizens to maintain a healthy skepticism. The era of e-politics offers citizens the opportunity to access more political information than ever before. However, the speeding up of news cycles and sharing of information has both positive and negative implications for Canadian democracy.

The significant amount of change in the realm of political communication over recent decades has introduced questions about the roles of old and new media in covering Canadian politics. In spite of the changing communication landscape, the following maxims apply.

- 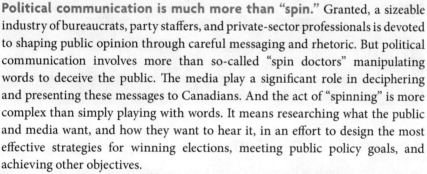 **The emergence of the Internet as a dominant communication platform does not mean the end for traditional political media.** Citizen journalists have risen in prominence over the last decade. Yet they rely heavily on the members of the parliamentary press gallery for their content and to expand their reach. For their part, traditional media sources have also evolved, shifting toward online delivery methods.

- **Political communication is much more than "spin."** Granted, a sizeable industry of bureaucrats, party staffers, and private-sector professionals is devoted to shaping public opinion through careful messaging and rhetoric. But political communication involves more than so-called "spin doctors" manipulating words to deceive the public. The media play a significant role in deciphering and presenting these messages to Canadians. And the act of "spinning" is more complex than simply playing with words. It means researching what the public and media want, and how they want to hear it, in an effort to design the most effective strategies for winning elections, meeting public policy goals, and achieving other objectives.

- **Even in an era of 24-hour news cycles and public demand for transparency, politicians are not bound to answer journalists' questions.** An arsenal of new online investigative techniques helps the media perform an essential role in Canadian democracy. But Canadian political elites are not obliged to talk with journalists. The only requirement is that the government be held to account in the legislature. If cabinet ministers manage to avoid providing answers during Question Period, then why should we expect them to behave any differently before the press? Make no mistake: most politicians, whether in the legislature or in the media scrum outside, are fond of communicating with the public, but their messages are seldom direct replies to questions posed by opponents and hostile reporters.

Overview

At its heart, political competition pits one set of ideas against others, with opponents vying to convince the public that their particular interpretation of reality is most accurate. Governments will portray themselves as able stewards in times of prosperity, and capable defenders in times of turmoil and change. Their opponents will attempt to downplay such positive interpretations of political reality, or blame the government for any downturn in fortunes. In short, all political communication consists of a

What the 2015 Election means for Political Communication

Visit the *Inside Canadian Politics* flipboard to learn about the latest developments affecting political communication in Canada.

Go to
http://flip.it/gblag.

selection of information that is presented in a certain manner. The trick for audiences is to understand what the main facts are. This can be difficult when information is projected in a slanted manner and when some information is not publicly disclosed.

Political communication comprises the modes, as well as the strategies and tactics, of disseminating information. In this chapter we differentiate between the *mainstream media*, which provide Canadians with most of their political news, and *Internet*, *online*, or *digital* media, which have quickly become a vital source of political information. We introduce key theoretical concepts that shape political information, such as horse-race coverage and information subsidies. We explain that government elites are participating in a permanent campaign that treats every day like there is an election going on, and we distinguish between the types of political advertising. Finally, we introduce relatively recent trends in political communication in Canada, such as political marketing and branding. We conclude by observing the importance of public opinion research in politics and governance, which in Canada is used foremost to inform communication decisions.

UP FOR DEBATE

Is negative political advertising good or bad for Canadian democracy?

Keep this question in mind as you read through the chapter. Consult the end-of-chapter debate supplement for more material to help you engage in an informed discussion of the topic.

The Politics of Spin

In politics nothing is as it seems.[1] People form inaccurate impressions of public actors and government. Why is this? In part, it is that public opinion is based on political ideologies and partisanship. But more than this, it is that people often lack the information to figure out what is real. Political information is delivered to the consumer with biases, with turns of phrase used to present a story at a favourable angle, and with key details often hidden from public scrutiny. Political leaders project images of strength even when they are weak, and the media choose to emphasize certain aspects while ignoring others. Government supporters lavish praise on the party in power, while opponents and pundits hurl criticism. But the general public also bear responsibility, for they may lack the interest to probe more deeply into an issue.

The politics of illusion are everywhere. When senator Mike Duffy was facing allegations that he filed improper expense claims and accepted a $90,000 cheque from Prime Minister Harper's chief of staff to repay the money to Parliament, he defended himself in a passionate speech to the Senate. Duffy claimed that the prime minister said to him, "It's not about what you did. It's about the perception of what you did that's been created in the media."[2] The statement, regardless of whether it can accurately be attributed to Harper, suggests that political elites operate in a world where perception is reality. Duffy, who had a successful career as a political journalist, was well aware of how difficult it is to counter what the public *perceives* to be true. This is a downside of Canada's mediated democracy, where citizens depend on the media to act as an intermediary between them and their political leaders, rather than having (or being able) to obtain information themselves. At one extreme are citizens who place far too much trust in the media and believe everything that they hear; at the other, those who distrust all political information and are partial to conspiracy theories. In between is a society where political actors, journalists, and citizens alike struggle to assess what is fact, what is spin, and, most difficult of all, what is omitted from the public narrative. This is especially challenging when political communication draws heavily on emotion.

Before delving into the theories and strategies of political communication, we present a case that highlights the importance of communication in politics: the coalition crisis of 2008. The crisis occurred during a tumultuous period in Canadian politics, one that nearly brought down the government mere months after a general election. The pivotal episode involved an intense power struggle featuring all of the major parties, but in the version of events given to the public, it was all about defending the interests of Canadians. In the story that follows, be mindful of the different communication techniques and frames used by the political actors involved. It is a lesson in how the competition for power in Canada is as much over votes and seats as it is for control over reality and the hearts and minds of Canadians.

The story begins in September 2008, when Prime Minister Harper requested that Governor General Michaëlle Jean dissolve Parliament. The request was granted despite the passage, only the year before and by Harper's own administration, of fixed-date election legislation. The fixed-date election law was designed to prevent a prime minister from calling a snap election before the expiry of Parliament's four-year lifespan, and yet this is exactly what Harper was seeking to do. Publicly, the prime minister positioned the early election as necessary because Parliament had become dysfunctional; in reality, the opposition parties were probably correct that he wanted to go to the polls before global economic troubles worsened.[3]

In the mid-October 2008 election, voters returned the Conservative government with 19 seats more than the party won in 2006, but it was not enough to form a majority government. With 143 of 308 seats, the Conservatives would have to rely on support from at least one of the Liberals (77 MPs), the BQ (49 MPs), or the NDP (37 MPs) to survive votes of confidence. The legislature was so divided that Parliament's two independent MPs had the potential to hold the balance of power on some votes. After leading his party to its worst result in modern memory, Stéphane Dion announced his resignation as Liberal leader, effective May 2009. Nevertheless, behind the scenes, NDP strategists were contemplating how to reach out to the Liberals to form a coalition government.

In mid-November, at the onset of an economic recession, MPs returned to Ottawa for the opening of the 40th Parliament, with all party leaders pledging a new climate of civility in the House of Commons. But on 26 November, NDP leader Jack Layton grew concerned when CTV reported that the Harper government was about to announce that the per-vote funding subsidy provided to political parties would be wound down.[4] This would cripple the finances of the opposition parties, who relied upon these state subsidies. They would have to lay off party staff, many of whom

mediated democracy
A democratic society that relies on the media to provide citizens with information about politics and government.

↻ The coalition crisis is discussed in the ICP box on page 220 of Chapter 6, on the legislature. The discussion of hung parliaments that begins on page 217 includes an explanation of coalition government.

worked tirelessly on the recent election campaign. They would have less money for public outreach and travel. They would likely have to reduce their communication and research budgets. Their election readiness and competitiveness relative to that of the Conservatives, who were flush with cash from donations received from individual supporters, would be seriously undermined.

When finance minister Jim Flaherty delivered his fiscal update to the House of Commons the next day, it contained other "poison pills" that were designed to divide the opposition caucuses and force them into taking positions contrary to their well-known stances. In particular, there was no new government spending to stimulate economic growth (a Liberal demand), but there was a pledge to restrain the ability of civil servants to strike (an NDP no-go). As the measure was a confidence vote, the Conservative government would fall without the support of some non-Conservative MPs.

The opposition parties reacted with outrage about the fiscal update, taking care not to emphasize their anxieties about the elimination of government funding for political parties. They signalled that they would form a coalition government should the Conservative government be defeated and should Governor General Jean decide to transfer the reins of power, rather than dissolving Parliament for the third time in three years. They maintained that together they were the ones who had a majority of seats (163 to the Conservatives' 143) and argued that a majority of Canadians had voted for them (54 per cent, compared with 37.7 per cent who voted Conservative). That they united in an unprecedented manner so quickly underscores the perceived urgency of their financial predicament and the ferocity of prior backroom planning. The Conservatives had not campaigned on the most controversial components of the fiscal update, including the party financing issue, but nor had the opposition parties publicly discussed their willingness to enter into a coalition.

Prime Minister Harper scheduled a rare press conference to denounce the opposition leaders' plans. He labelled it an undemocratic plot by "socialists and separatists" and privately urged party members to increase their financial contributions to his party. Later that day, the Liberal Party tabled a motion of non-confidence in the House of Commons, prompting the government to delay a vote on its fiscal update motion for one week. All the while, former Liberal prime minister Jean Chrétien and former NDP leader Ed Broadbent were privately negotiating the terms of a coalition deal.

On 29 November, the Conservative government announced that it would remove the party financing element from the fiscal update. The NDP held a conference call to discuss the development but mistakenly sent the dial-in information to Conservative MP John Duncan, instead of NDP MP Linda Duncan. The call was recorded and leaked to the media the next day. Layton was heard bragging about his role in orchestrating the coalition plan prior to the 2008 election. This revelation played into the Conservatives' message that the coalition scheme was a longstanding plot to undermine the will of the Canadian electorate. Nevertheless, finance minister Flaherty announced that the government had also backed down on its right-to-strike provisions.

By this point, the public agenda had been set: the opposition parties were preparing to form a coalition government. On 1 December, Dion, Layton, and Bloc Québécois leader Gilles Duceppe held a joint news conference to sign an agreement stating their intentions to govern. Their accord was expressed as putting Canadians' interests first during the economic crisis. Liberal MPs would hold 18 of 24 cabinet positions, plus the prime ministership, and the NDP would hold six spots. The Bloc Québécois would not hold any cabinet seats, but Bloc MPs would vote with the coalition government on confidence matters. "We are ready to form a new government that will address the best interests of the people instead of plunging Canadians into another election," said Dion, who under the coalition accord would become prime minister while a search for a new Liberal leader could be initiated.[5] The opposition parties trumpeted their commitment to stimulus spending on public infrastructure, housing, and key industries, as well as worker supports such as skills training and easier access to employment insurance. The coalition government would also pursue cap-and-trade environmental policy (an NDP demand) and corporate tax cuts (a Liberal priority). The accord and the parties' communications made no mention of preserving the per-vote subsidy that the Conservatives had vowed to eliminate in their November fiscal update.

The next day, it became known that the prime minister was planning to ask the governor general to prorogue Parliament, ostensibly to provide a cooling-off period, but also to forestall the inevitable vote of non-confidence. All political parties commenced an aggressive communications campaign, using advertising, public relations, and social media to support their positions. Communications spin and wedge politics were evident: opponents of the coalition decried the illegitimacy of "the separatist coalition"; supporters of "the majority coalition" accused the PM of attempting to dodge a confidence vote with an undemocratic move to prorogue Parliament.[6] Rallies were organized across Canada. Green Party leader Elizabeth May announced her support for the coalition; Conservatives alleged her allegiance was purchased with the promise of a Senate seat. The leader of the provincial Parti Québécois, Pauline Marois, used the turmoil as proof that Canadian democracy was dysfunctional and as grounds for Quebec separation. Prime Minister Harper read her remarks aloud in the House of Commons, receiving applause from the Bloc Québécois and silence from its coalition partners. He also claimed that the opposition leaders had refused to display a Canadian flag at their signing ceremony, despite photographs and video that prove otherwise. The media reported that later the Conservative caucus was heard singing O Canada, which fed a growing image in English Canada that patriots were defending the government from a separatist takeover. Public opinion polls found that a majority of Quebecers and supporters of the three opposition parties were in favour of the coalition, but that a majority of Canadians outside of Quebec were opposed, as were almost all Conservative supporters.[7]

The parties' communications rolled along. At 7 p.m. on 3 December, Prime Minister Harper delivered a rare, pre-recorded, prime time televised address, once again deploring the notion of a coalition government as undemocratic. The four-and-a-half minute message appeared on all major television and radio networks. Layton and Duceppe deferred to Dion to deliver the coalition's address. The Liberal leader's taped address arrived 30 minutes late at the networks, at which point many had returned to regularly scheduled programming; those viewers who did see it would have been unimpressed by the production quality, if not the content. A book positioned immediately behind Dion titled Hot Air was visible as the would-be government leader was speaking. Scathing reviews observed that the video appeared to have been filmed on a camera phone and judged that it lacked the strength and substance required of a prime minister-in-waiting.[8] Dion's chief of staff publicly apologized for the debacle that editorials in *The Globe and Mail* branded "amateur hour." The next day, a number of prominent Liberals publicly called for Dion to immediately step down as leader. The communication stumble effectively marked the end of the coalition project.

On 4 December, the prime minister met with the governor general to make his formal request that she prorogue Parliament. She assented, thereby ending the first session of the 40th Parliament. Within days, Dion announced his resignation as Liberal leader. In the New Year, the second session opened with the government's throne speech, which introduced a budget that contained stimulus spending provisions and left untouched the per-vote subsidies. The Liberals, now led by Michael Ignatieff, supported the budget, thus assuring the continuity of the government.

The importance of communication in this episode is underappreciated. The coalition case is upheld in political science as evidence that Canada's adherence to Westminster parliamentary traditions helps to maintain order in times of high tension, preventing constitutional crises and ensuring the continuity of power. It also prompts conversation about Canada's electoral system and its aversion to coalition government, despite its long history of practice in Europe.[9] What is less well understood is the effort that the parties placed on appealing to the hearts and minds of Canadians. Message spin was used by the opposition to seek power on the initial pretence that they were motivated by defending the interests of ordinary Canadians, rather than their own self-preservation; by comparison, nationalistic communication was used by the governing Conservatives to frame the debate as one between

Hundreds of Canadians across the country took to the streets on the weekend of 6–7 December 2008 to express their views on the coalition crisis. Some sided with the opposition parties, supporting their efforts to forge a coalition government, while others turned out in support of the governing Conservatives, decrying the coalition as an affront to democracy. Considering the resolution of the crisis, which side do you think won? What were the keys to victory?

Canadian patriots and Quebec separatists, and delegitimize the democratic credibility of a coalition government. Political elites across the country weighed in with their opinions, and engaged Canadians expressed their views online, on talk radio, in letters to the editor, and in public rallies. All told, a variety of political communication strategies and tactics were employed, which attracted the attention of even those Canadians who otherwise do not pay attention to politics, and prompted an emotional response across the country.

The Media Landscape in Canada

Traditional Media

As the example of the coalition crisis shows, there are many ways that political actors send and receive information. Outside of personal communication, the most important channel is the mainstream news media, in particular newspaper, radio, and television outlets. Together, these media form a large network that enables information to be transmitted among political actors, individual media outlets, and the general public. The news media act as a broker between political elites and the people they represent: politicians often allow news coverage to guide their decision-making, while for the attentive public, the news informs their knowledge of political happenings.

Journalists keep politicians in check: they filter political information and follow election campaigns. The mainstream media are normally divided into print media (mostly newspapers) and broadcast media (radio and television). The media are in a constant state of evolution as a result of technological change. When Canada was formed in 1867, then-recent innovations allowed large printing presses to mass-produce millions of pages in a single day, and small local presses could produce handbills. The party press consisted of partisan newspapers that gained income from printing government advertisements and official notices. These newspapers were operated by publishers who were sympathetic to a political party, and their readership was made up foremost of elites.[10] The editorial content, sometimes authored by the printer, routinely savaged political opponents.

party press Early newspapers that relied on government advertising and that were blatantly partisan.

As literacy rates improved, there was growing demand for mass distribution of newspapers. The so-called "penny press" earned revenues through low-cost subscriptions and business advertising. This increased the expectation for non-partisan news, and by the early twentieth century, the party press was fading away. This is not to suggest that ideological slants did not persist. For instance, since its founding, the *Toronto Star* has been a proponent of the welfare state, and today its left-wing bias is well known. Likewise, Postmedia sources, including the *National Post*, are known to espouse conservative views, particularly in their editorial content.

Newspapers adjusted to the onset of radio in the 1920s by becoming the authoritative source for news details. By comparison, radio was able to deliver news quickly, in a manner that could resonate with audiences. As politicians realized that their own voices could be transmitted into citizens' living rooms without being filtered through journalists, they gravitated toward the medium. Radio was particularly important in the early twentieth-century populist and progressive movements in the Canadian prairies, helping Social Credit and Co-operative Commonwealth Federation leaders like Bill Aberhart, Ernest Manning, and Tommy Douglas attain and retain office.

But it was the emergence of television in the 1950s that fundamentally changed politics across the country. Video resonates on an emotional level with viewers, and moving images enable the transmission of contextual information. An often cited example is the 1960 US presidential debate, in which radio listeners felt that the more knowledgeable Richard Nixon was the better debater, but those watching on TV were transfixed by a dapper John F. Kennedy.[11] While the analogy is far from perfect, historians suggest that Pierre Elliott Trudeau's public image gave him a similar advantage over Progressive Conservative leaders like Robert Stanfield. Television has broad reach and connects with undecided voters; however, it is expensive and non-participatory. Although some efforts are made to get viewers to join online conversations by hosting polls, posting hashtags, or setting up feedback lines, television programming tends to treat electors as passive participants who have no ability to shape what is covered.

Today, the mainstream media serve diverse needs and are in a constant state of flux ushered through technological change. The *Toronto Star* and *The Globe and Mail* have the highest print circulations in Canada, but the latter's role as Canada's national newspaper is evolving, given that print editions are no longer available in some areas of the country. Subscription-based national and city newspapers are having to compete with streamlined dailies distributed for free to commuters (like *Metro*), free community newspapers that serve specialized markets, and news services that cater to specific ethnic communities. Politics is also covered in newsmagazines such as *Maclean's*, whose content has shifted from summaries of weekly events to long-form investigative pieces and analysis of topical debates. Radio now tends to be used to communicate political information through short news clips and call-in programs. Charles Adler hosts the most popular Canadian syndicated daily political talk radio program; the only national program, CBC Radio's *Cross Country Checkup*, fields calls every Sunday, while regional stations across the country operate their own call-in programs. Traditional television programming is under stress as the multichannel universe expands, as consumers grow accustomed to obtaining content on demand, and as people discontinue cable service in favour of online media streaming. Fewer and fewer Canadians are getting their news from the same national news broadcasts in the same way they did a generation ago.

A media organization that is acutely aware of the need to evolve in response to changing consumer behaviour is Canada's national public broadcaster. The Canadian Broadcasting Corporation (CBC) and its French division, Société Radio-Canada (SRC), are maintained by the federal government to differentiate Canadian broadcasting from private-sector broadcasters and insulate Canadian listeners from the cultural influences of American media. The CBC was created based on a recommendation of the 1929 Royal Commission on Radio Broadcasting (which also led to the formation of the Canadian Radio-television and Telecommunications Commission, or CRTC, the body that administers the Broadcasting Act). Canada's first national broadcaster was the Canadian Radio Broadcasting Corporation (CRBC), established by the federal government of R.B. Bennett in 1932. It gave way to the CBC in 1936. Since that time, the CBC has long had a major presence in Canadian broadcasting, and the creation of its 24-hour news channel in 1989 both fed and intensified the demand for political information.

According to CBC News journalistic standards and practices, its news division operates at arm's length from the government in its duty to produce factual journalism that reflects a variety of opinions and perspectives from across Canada. CBC staff

Canadian Broadcasting Corporation A Crown corporation that is Canada's national public broadcaster.

↻ Chapter 14, on Canada in the world, features much on Canadians' efforts to distinguish themselves from Americans. See especially the section Canadian Identity Today, beginning on page 547.

Opportunities Available

Knowledge of Canadian Politics and Government Preferred!

Reporter–Editor

CBC/Radio-Canada

As a Reporter/Editor, your primary objective is to perform reporting and editorial assignments related to the gathering, writing and presentation of program material for all three of our media platforms: Radio, Television and the Web. You will develop and maintain contact with a variety of sources as well as work in close co-operation with your program unit. You will have demonstrated success in your role by gathering and reporting information from various sources, conducting an analysis of facts and information gathered, drawing conclusions or raising issues requiring further investigation, and contributing ideas, written scripts, and program content. You will also, as required, critically edit material written by others, present information and/or analysis on air in a variety of formats, and perform other production or administrative tasks associated with the smooth functioning of the newsroom, program unit or station. Your work will be governed by CBC's journalistic and broadcasting policy and protocols.

Qualifications

- A university degree or equivalent along with three years of directly related experience
- Ability to work in a cross-cultural environment
- Ability to work quickly, under pressure, to meet deadlines
- A demonstrated interest in the social, political and cultural life of Northern Canada
- Excellent writing, reporting, technical and on-air presentation skills
- Clearly demonstrated reliability
- A mature, enthusiastic and positive attitude and an excellent ability to contribute to a team environment
- Initiative, flexibility, creativity and curiosity
- Willingness and ability to learn new tasks and try tasks outside of your normal range of work
- Established and credible presence on Social Media
- Demonstrated ability to use social media and other resources to build contacts and sources
- Ability to travel within Northern Canada on assignment

Notes

- Please include in your application an online link to your demo.
- Candidates may be subject to skills and knowledge testing.
- CBC/Radio-Canada is committed to reflecting our country's diversity.

Source: CBC Licensing/CBC, "Current Openings" (2014), https://cbc.taleo.net/careersection/2/jobdetail.ftl.

uphold some of the highest standards of journalism in Canada and are expected to be mindful that a single minor error can undermine an entire news report. However, these standards and focus on Canadian programming come at a cost: while its budget continues to decline, the CBC still receives over $1 billion annually from the federal government to finance its programming. This is supplemented by advertising revenues on the television network and CBC website. CBC Radio, which also has local affiliates like CBC Television, is commercial-free. An example of the type of career opportunities that exist within the CBC is presented in the box on page 439.

The CBC offers weekday political news programs; so do the main competitors of its English division, CTV and Global. Indeed, the public broadcaster is no longer the primary source of information or entertainment for Canadians; CTV News long ago eclipsed CBC News as the most popular news program. Moreover, whereas CTV and Global own the rights to top American programs such as *The Big Bang Theory*, which command high advertising revenues during prime time, the CBC must fund its own programming, such as *Murdoch Mysteries*, which has a Canadian focus but earns lower ratings. A mechanism to counter this disadvantage is the CRTC's requirement that all radio and television broadcasters—public and private—must, as a condition of their broadcast licence, feature a significant amount of Canadian content (often referred to as CanCon). The challenge for all broadcasters, especially the CBC, is to produce original Canadian content that attracts enough viewers to justify the considerable costs. With intensifying competition from digital media, the business models of traditional media are in a state of flux. Canadians can increasingly obtain content on demand, meaning that fewer people are attached to watching programming at scheduled times. An exception is live events such as breaking news or sports. The CBC experienced a major loss of advertising revenue when Rogers outbid the public broadcaster for the rights to broadcast NHL hockey games. Stations like CBC Newsworld and W Network are under pressure as cable providers move to a so-called "pick and pay" model that gives cable subscribers greater choice about which extra channels to pay for. Meanwhile, increasing numbers of Canadians are choosing to cut the cable cord altogether. Media executives must figure out how to generate popular CanCon in this changing media environment.

A further source of concern for the CRTC is media conglomeration. The mergers and acquisitions of media companies is a worldwide trend that creates efficiencies because the same content can be shown on multiple platforms. For example, Montreal-based Québecor operates two major French-language newspapers, the Sun Media newspaper chain, the TVA network and TVA publishing, Vidéotron cable and Internet services, Canoe websites, and the Archambault music retailer. Other media giants include Bell Media, Postmedia, Rogers Communications, and Shaw Media. The associated disappearance of small media operations reduces the variety of local and ideological perspectives available to Canadians. As online offerings become the staple of media consumption, the CRTC's position is that "Canadian television must deliver compelling and diverse programming in an age of digital technology marked by an abundance of channels and on-demand content available on many platforms (cable, satellite, the Internet, mobile devices)."[12] Given the global reach of the Internet, it is difficult to imagine how the CRTC can police media content as it has in the past.

Another institution of the mainstream media that has evolved is the press gallery. Each legislature has a press gallery comprising accredited journalists who are

CanCon Laws requiring that media outlets operating in Canada provide a minimum level of Canadian-produced programming.

press gallery Political journalists who monitor government business and who personally observe proceedings in the legislature.

©Friends of CBC Broadcasting. Reused with Permission.

Many of those who support the CBC believe that, as a public broadcaster, the so-called "Mother Corp" is more likely to investigate matters in the public interest than is a private-sector broadcaster that derives its revenues from commercial advertising. Critics of the CBC argue that the broadcaster reaches only a narrow segment of the body of taxpayers who keep it on the air. What do you think is the value of having a national public broadcaster? How well does the CBC deliver that value, particularly when it comes to coverage of Canadian politics?

assigned to cover government and legislative proceedings. The chamber of each legislature reserves seating and office areas for the press gallery so that they can be assured of space to report on parliamentary business. They are granted special access to some areas of the legislature in order to allow them to interact with public officials. As such, they perform an institutional function as the so-called fourth estate, which is a reference to journalists theoretically being included among the other three branches of government (executive, legislative, and judicial). The fourth estate consists of professional journalists and media outlets in the print (magazine, newspaper) and broadcast (television, radio) sectors, and increasingly some online-only media. Their role is considered so important to good government that they are determined to obtain any political information that they deem to be in the public interest.

In recent years, the press gallery's dominant role as the purveyors of political journalism has been under stress. The erosion of the newspaper industry, the conglomeration of media outlets, the rise of citizen journalists, and the availability of information online have created a perfect storm to reduce their clout. This has been exacerbated by government officials who perceive media elites as problems rather than partners in the dissemination of political messages. Stephen Harper's refusal

fourth estate An informal term for the media, implying that a free press is so vital to democracy that it is on par with the three branches of government (executive, legislature, judiciary).

to meet with members of the Canadian parliamentary press gallery on their terms stands out (see the Inside Canadian Politics box below), particularly in comparison with the early approach of his successor, Justin Trudeau. By comparison, the Ottawa press gallery's interactions with opposition parties are cordial, as is the case between most politicians and members of press galleries elsewhere in the country.

Digital Media

Of course, Canada's traditional media are under tremendous pressure from the growing popularity of Internet-based digital media. Given how ubiquitous information communication technologies (ICTs) have become in Canadians' lives, it is easy to overlook how quickly politics and society have changed in the digital age. Email gained popularity in the early 1990s as a means to share information with many people simultaneously. In the 1993 Canadian federal election, political party headquarters were experimenting with email, and they made do with a limited number of dedicated phone lines for fax machines. That year, the United Nations and the White House launched basic websites, which consisted of static information and hyperlinks, with very little interactivity. The era of Web 1.0 allowed political actors, governments, and the media to post static information online to a worldwide

INSIDE CANADIAN POLITICS
How Should the Prime Minister Deal with the Press Gallery?

Political leaders and the press have a love–hate relationship. They both need each other, but their position is enhanced by controlling the other.

This tension came to the fore soon after Stephen Harper became prime minister. The Canadian parliamentary press gallery had become accustomed to questioning leaders at will and to asking ministers questions as they exited cabinet meetings. In an effort to control the agenda, Harper's communications staff informed the press gallery that the prime minister's office—not the journalists themselves—would now decide who could ask questions at news conferences. Furthermore, the times and locations of cabinet meetings would no longer be public knowledge.

Ottawa-based journalists were apoplectic. Many gallery members refused to attend Harper's news conferences and decried his demands as worthy of a dictatorship government. But those who acquiesced, including many local media outlets across the country, benefited from exclusive access to the prime minister. This persisted during the 2011 and 2015 election campaigns, during which Harper was accused of staying in a bubble because journalists were required to stand a distance away from him. This approach stood in stark contrast with that of Liberal leader, Justin Trudeau, whose promises of a more transparent government matched his more open style in engaging the mainstream media. Upon taking office, Prime Minister Trudeau reinstated press conferences in the National Press Theatre and promised a new era of openness with the gallery.

VOX POP
How do you feel about a prime minister shunning the press gallery? Do politicians have an obligation to engage with the media on the media's terms?

Sean Kilpatrick/The Canadian Press

The Sun News Network ceased broadcasting in February 2015, less than four years after it arrived on the scene to provide balance in a broadcasting environment perceived by some to be dominated by a left-wing media bias. Poor ratings led to the demise of the network, which had drawn comparisons with the American network Fox News for its provocative right-of-centre views on Canadian politics and social issues. To what extent is there a prevailing bias in Canadian news reporting? How desirable and feasible is it to offer a balance of perspectives?

audience. This began to erode the mainstream media's control over political information because the Web introduced a cost-efficient means of global communication that anyone with computer skills could initiate. Even so, in the 2000 Canadian election, many candidates in Canada still did not have a website, nor did many Members of Parliament.[14]

The emergence of Web 2.0 in the early 2000s allowed interactivity and content collaboration between users. This gave rise to blogs with feedback forums, news sites with comments pages, file sharing, and social networking. The 2004 federal election saw the popularity of blogs, the emergence of attack websites, and the widespread use of Blackberries by campaign operatives and journalists. By the 2006 campaign, daily photographs from the campaign trial were uploaded to political websites, and

BRIEFING NOTES

Web 1.0 and Web 2.0

Insiders often use buzzwords to describe the quickly evolving nature of the Internet. Web 1.0 is best considered a read-only version of the Internet, allowing one-way communication between the author(s) and their audience. By contrast, Web 2.0 has allowed political actors to communicate with their followers on a two-way basis (through social media, enhanced email, forums, and so on).

podcasts were created. In the 2008 campaign, websites were professionally produced and hosted short videos. YouTube, Facebook, and Twitter existed, but at that point were not regularly used in Canadian politics.[15] Today, email communication, websites, and social media are major components of everyday politicking. Mainstream media are also big users of ICTs, but they are struggling to compete with free information available on political websites such as *The Huffington Post*, *iPolitics*, and *rabble.ca*. The rise of these outlets, and the emergence of citizen reporters, has produced a new genre of political watchdog.

ICTs have changed the practice of politics and political communication, though perhaps not quite as much as technophiles would have us believe, and not necessarily for the better. Web 1.0 and 2.0 allow more efficient, faster, and more engaging ways of doing many things that have always been practised. Political candidates and parliamentarians have always been able to interact with electors, but now that they can do so electronically, they are expected to respond to issues faster than ever. Journalists can break news as soon as it happens, but must do so more frequently. Newspapers in particular have had difficulty adapting to the volume of information and compressed timelines.

Arguably it is the non-elites who have benefited most from the rise of ICTs. Small political parties, interest groups, and grassroots movements now have a low-cost mechanism to stay in touch with their membership and to push their agenda. Citizens interested in politics have a forum for spontaneous and flexible debate. They can locate detailed information on matters ranging from parliamentarians' voting records to the minutiae of a policy announcement. They can attract mainstream media attention by complaining online; easily mobilize supporters of a cause to an event; send, receive, and discuss breaking information; and quickly upload photos and video for viewing by a mass audience. Local and government information that otherwise might not attract public attention comes to the fore; conversely, rumours, falsehoods, negativity, and hate speech can flourish, too. In the past, a citizen who was unhappy with government would make time to author a letter and would wait weeks to receive a well-researched reply; now, the moment something happens, an angry message can be sent out on a smartphone by a person expecting an immediate response and solution. This tyranny of the urgent is having implications for public policy and governance. More than ever before, we live in a world where speed, emotion, visuals, and personal stories may take precedence over thoughtful, evidence-based decisions. Moreover, citizen journalists, bloggers, and other online contributors, many of them partisan, are typically not professionally trained or regulated, and they have no formal role in the institutions of the state, such as the parliamentary press gallery. Canadians may have access to more political information than ever, but they must be sterner judges of the sources, content, and tone of the messages communicated to them.

We now find ourselves in the age of e-democracy. It is a concept that promises to use ICTs to democratize political decision-making and stem the tide of declining public engagement in politics.[16] E-democracy enhances the potential for existing political activities by using the Internet to engage citizens in policy discussion and the sharing of information. It connects citizens with candidates, elected officials, journalists, and interest group leaders. It is a means of providing ready access to political platforms, of discussing political ideas, and of building social capital. But for all of its potential, in practice, e-democracy is proving to provide less social cohesion than optimists had

↻ See Social Media Politics in Alberta, on page 488 of Chapter 12, for an example of a recent, successful social media campaign in Canadian politics.

e-democracy The use of information communication technologies to get citizens involved in politics.

hoped. Arguably, it also introduced unprecedented acrimony to political discourse, as parties, candidates, and interest groups use the technology to narrowcast their often divisive messages to specific segments of the population, a trend we will consider later in this chapter. In this way, ICTs can bring together like-minded citizens who reinforce each other's views and denigrate opponents. E-democracy also changed methods of journalism, as the practice of cultivating inside sources has been displaced by the practice of monitoring social media feeds of political insiders.

ICTs have also transformed how government services are delivered. E-government involves the use of websites, email, videoconferencing, and social media to supplement the use of call centres and electronic kiosks. It has expanded the ability of government to be available around the clock and has re-shaped the way that government bodies interact with each other. Citizens with access to a computer or mobile device can readily obtain accurate information from government bodies in any jurisdiction. They can pay taxes and fees, obtain forms, and submit applications. The Government of Canada's main website (www.canada.ca) and its Service Canada site (www.servicecanada.gc.ca) are prominent examples. Among the top government website searches are information about the Canada Pension Plan, employment insurance, the GST/HST credit, jobs, old age security, tax documents, records of employment, social insurance numbers, and birth certificates.[17]

As political communication scholar Andrew Chadwick explains, there are four categories of e-government that are widely recognized by political scientists.[18] The form of e-government that we have been considering thus far, which involves the online availability of government information, services, announcements, and job competitions, is known as *government-to-citizens*, or G2C. Another public form of e-government is *government-to-business* (G2B), in which ICTs are used to provide support services to businesses, to attract investment, and to inform business operators about regulations, permits, and licensing and zoning matters. But ICTs have also changed the operations *within* government. Because the public service is so large and is spread across a large area (spanning multiple time zones in the case of the federal government), the government uses ICTs internally to communicate with its employees. G2E (*government-to-employee*) includes making information available about internal job competitions, human resources policies, and special initiatives, often through a password-protected intranet. Finally, *government-to-government* (G2G) involves interactions among public servants in different jurisdictions, such as between bureaucrats in federal, provincial, and territorial departments of health. G2G uses SharePoint sites and videoconferences to allow governments to consult with each other, to gather information about laws and best practices, and to share data.

An important safeguard against government secrecy and corruption is freedom of information legislation (also known as *access to information*), which has taken on a new meaning in the e-government era. Access to information requires, by law, that the government make its internal documents available to the public upon request. It improves government transparency by allowing citizens to obtain data that would otherwise be unavailable. To curtail nuisance inquiries, a nominal application charge (e.g. a $5 fee) must accompany each request, and further charges may be required if the request exceeds an internal research time limit. Applications are routinely filed by opposition parties, journalists, and public advocates seeking to understand government decisions and to exploit discrepancies with a minister's explanation of the

e-government The interactive use of information communication technologies to deliver public programs and services.

freedom of information A legal requirement that governments release information upon request, subject to certain restrictions.

matter. To ensure impartiality, the identity of the applicant is not widely disclosed within the public service, unless permission to do so is explicitly granted.

As the expectations of government transparency increase, so does the volume of access to information requests. Many government bodies are proactively posting information online through e-government initiatives. In 2011, for example, the federal government launched its Open Data pilot project, which has made over 270,000 datasets publicly available online at http://open.canada.ca/en. It also posts online its responses to all completed access to information requests so that others may benefit from the disclosed data. Nevertheless, governments are criticized for not being sufficiently transparent, and for obstructing requests. Some internal files cannot be publicly disclosed; for instance, the Department of Defence could not release secret information about the Canadian military without sparking public safety concerns, and many provincial governments are relieved of their duties to release information that may be detrimental to their ability to conduct intergovernmental relations. Moreover, the political executive needs to be free to deliberate a full range of policy options without fear of public sanction. Consequently, cabinet documents, briefing notes, and anything else that is prepared for ministers is often ruled off-limits. So, too, are many materials prepared for negotiations with other governments. This can be a problem, because documents that arguably should be publicly available are heavily redacted, and requests can take months longer to complete than the legislation allows.

Despite the broadening of freedom of information laws and the advent of e-government, there has recently been a palpable sense that the Canadian government has become even more secretive. In 2011, the federal Conservatives fell on a motion of non-confidence after they had been found in contempt of Parliament for refusing to release information requested by the opposition parties about the military mission in Afghanistan. In 2012, an international report ranked Canada fifty-first out of 89 nations on its commitment to upholding access to information principles.[19] Furthermore, critics of the Open Data pilot project (such as Democracy Watch, an Ottawa-based advocacy group) say that the government is bombarding people with quantitative data which do little to assist them with understanding the rationale for policy decisions.

The Open Data project illustrates the mixed success that e-government has in this country. While the project has made an abundance of information available, public servants may overlook that not everyone can readily access and navigate the Internet: while close to 8 in 10 Canadians have daily Internet access, e-government leaves others behind, such as those with certain disabilities. The reduction of personnel and the outsourcing of technical expertise can result in service disruptions. With ICTs, governments have become more accountable than ever before, but transparency has not occurred at the pace demanded by critics. ICTs offer the potential to permit citizens to have greater interactivity with political elites and public servants, but there has been some reluctance in Canada to seek out feedback on public policy, with the exception of some pilot projects. As well, ICTs can be used by political elites to bypass the mainstream media and communicate directly with citizens, thereby diminishing the mediation role of the fourth estate.

hacktivism Politically motivated damage inflicted on government information communication technologies.

The most significant downside of e-democracy and e-government is that ICTs pose a security risk. Hacktivism is a disruptive form of online political activism that exploits weaknesses in e-government. In essence, it is electronic civil disobedience.

Hacktivism ranges from political agitators defacing website content to political enemies engaging in electronic surveillance. International hactivist organizations, such as Anonymous and WikiLeaks, destabilize social order as they promote a philosophy that government should be completely open and transparent. The presence of hacktivists means that it is essential for government records and financial data to be actively protected from unauthorized access. However, the need to guard against a security breach extends well beyond ICTs: the 2013 loss by Human Resources and Skills Development Canada of an external hard drive containing personal information for 500,000 Canadians who had received student loans comes to mind. Conversely, local political actors also engage in hacktivism, although their motivation is not to destabilize government but rather to inflict political harm on their opponents. This has included the launch of a denial of service attack on the NDP voting system during the party's 2012 federal leadership convention, and a Liberal staffer accessing a fake Twitter account from a House of Commons computer to tweet details about the minister of public safety's divorce. Periodically, there are media reports of government computers being used to change the content of a minister's Wikipedia entry, and party staffers may use fake names to post comments to online feedback forums. Hacktivism can also be a source of political comedy: the scrolling electronic signs on Toronto's GO Transit trains were once reprogrammed by a hacker so that every three seconds commuters saw the message "Stephen Harper Eats Babies." The realities of e-democracy reinforce our understanding that democracy involves the conflict of political ideas rather than idealized notions of decisions arrived at by public consensus.

Political Communication Frameworks and Tactics

Communication is an essential if not primary activity of anyone involved in politics and government. Political parties, candidates, elected officials, interest groups, social movements, lobbyists, journalists, and voters all seek to inform and influence each other. In a democratic society like Canada's, where rights and freedoms are constitutionally protected, the free-flowing exchange of perspectives, ideas, and data is essential to a vibrant public sphere. German philosopher Jürgen Habermas, in his seminal work *The Structural Transformation of the Public Sphere* (1962), articulated the need for reasoned public debate among the middle class, not just the political elite. He believed that good government was more likely if a society was made up of well-read citizens who freely conversed about politics in coffee houses and other social settings. The general public must be informed and engaged in public affairs, Habermas reasoned, in order to constrain the power of government elites. However, not all political dialogue can occur face to face in small venues, and the quality and quantity of public debate is shaped by media technology. The influence of technology on communication is so profound that in the 1960s Canadian scholar Marshall McLuhan argued that "the medium is the message," meaning that the same information is subject to change across different mediums.[20]

public sphere The venue for group and public discussion about social problems and government.

To get in front of an issue and advance a political cause in the public sphere, you need to do more than talk around the water cooler or in line at Tim Hortons, however. Political actors push ideas, public problems, and policy solutions in a bid to

↻ Agenda setting is discussed in the context of the policy cycle in Chapter 8, on public policy: see page 295.

↻ The Senate scandal is discussed in Chapter 6, in the ICP box on pages 210–11.

↻ Reasons for the decline in voter turnout are discussed in Chapter 10, on elections: see the section Voter Turnout in Canadian Elections, beginning on page 417.

horse-race coverage
Media attention focused on who is leading in public opinion.

attract news media coverage and penetrate the public consciousness. This is known as *agenda setting*. Topics that rise to the top of the public agenda apply pressure on political elites for prompt action; those that fall off the public agenda or never make it are more likely to be ignored. For instance, if we are to believe media coverage, the Senate scandal that dominated the news in 2013 was apparently the only matter of national political interest during much of that period. The official opposition led Question Period each day with questions about the PMO's involvement, and this cued the media to report on it. But every day that the scandal was in the news was another day that less sensational issues, including important matters of public policy, were bumped off the public agenda.

The growth of media has meant that there is an ever increasing demand for content. We expect the fourth estate to scrutinize government, to filter political information, and to follow election campaigns. The reality of modern journalism is that specialist reporters are being replaced by multitaskers who are familiar with many topics but are intimately familiar with few. Moreover, there is increasing competition between media outlets to attract audiences, causing them to place more emphasis on sensationalist tactics. The detailed analysis of politics and public policy is cast off to specialist publications and programming, such as *The Hill Times* and the Cable Public Affairs Channel (CPAC). In mainstream media, political news is projected in a manner that emphasizes competing points of view, builds stories with dramatic arcs, and focuses on the personalities of political actors. The old adages in journalism that "if it bleeds, it leads" and that journalists should "comfort the afflicted and afflict the comfortable" certainly apply to political media. The negative tone of political reporting, combined with the intensity of partisan attacks and negative political advertising, has turned many people off politics altogether. The corresponding withdrawal from public affairs by many citizens has been dubbed a "spiral of cynicism" by American scholars Joseph Cappella and Kathleen Hall Jamieson.[21] This is believed to be a contributing factor to low voter turnout in elections.

One cause of the spiral of cynicism is the emphasis the media place on reporting about political mudslinging and the results of public opinion surveys. Many journalists tend to approach the entirety of an election campaign as a sporting contest. They focus on which political party or leader is ahead in the polls, and speculate on the reasons for the lead and whether it is likely to grow, shrink, or hold. This competition frame is fuelled by political parties who engage in negative treatment of their opponents. Horse-race coverage results when the media make it a priority to report on who is winning, as indicated by the latest polls, while giving scant attention to contestants who are forecast to lose or the issues at the heart of the campaign. The mediated horse race tends to feature most prominently during election campaigns when the stakes are highest. Every announcement and gaffe is interpreted as having implications for the party's standings in the polls. As the campaign winds down, the media increase their focus on the horse race between the parties and leaders most likely to form government, while the coverage of uncompetitive parties and independent candidates, perceived as less important, diminishes. Opinion polls also guide editorial decisions about which issues to prioritize, and what to ignore.

The winners-and-losers narrative of the political horse race matters because media coverage informs public opinion and political power. The biased perspective (intended or not) that the media and political actors present about a subject is known as a *frame*. Framing is the manner in which a person, organization, or issue is publicly communicated. When framing is practised by skilled political communicators, it simplifies complex matters in a purposeful manner that fits the sender's position (this sort of political framing is also known as "spin"). When framing is used unintentionally by non-political actors, it reflects the communicator's ideological bias.[22]

A notable case of media framing occurred during the 1974 federal election campaign. Progressive Conservative Party leader Robert Stanfield had a staid public image compared with that of the more dashing Pierre Elliott Trudeau, leader of the Liberal Party and prime minister of Canada. One of Stanfield's handlers began tossing a football around with Stanfield on a North Bay airport tarmac. A Canadian Press photographer was present and took a roll of photos. The next day, the photo that appeared in newspapers across Canada, including on the front page of *The Globe and Mail*, depicted a distraught Stanfield at the one moment that he fumbled a catch. That iconic photo continues to be held up as the framing bias exhibited by the media and the reason why political handlers attempt to inoculate politicians from unscripted media opportunities.

The treatment of politics as a horse race has extended beyond the official campaign period and into governance. This results in a game frame, where everything that political actors do is reduced to a conversation about who wins and who loses. Unlike horse-race politics, which is informed by statistically reliable opinion survey data, the game frame may be informed by anything that indicates the public mood, such as media straw polls, call-ins to talk radio, letters to the editor, social media conversation, and public protests. The media extend their horse-race thinking by applying this strategic lens in interpreting political events. So, rather than emphasizing the substance of public policy, media coverage might concentrate on declaring a victor. Consider, for instance, the mini-crisis that erupted over recognizing Quebec as a nation. Thanks largely to the media's presentation of the episode, it is widely

> **framing** The shaping of information so that communication recipients will interpret it in a manner that is advantageous to the sender.

> **game frame** A strategic filter applied by the media on political decisions and events with a view to declaring winners and losers.

> ↺ The Quebec nation motion is explained on page 148 of Chapter 4, on regionalism.

The Canadian Press/Doug Ball

Robert Stanfield drops the ball in this now infamous photo (*second from the right*) that made *The Globe and Mail*'s front page during the 1974 election campaign. Other photos taken by the same photographer showed Stanfield catching the ball. Why would a newspaper editor have chosen to use this one? What effect would you expect it to have on Stanfield's campaign? Would a photo of Pierre Trudeau dropping a football have been treated the same way, or have the same impact? What is the lesson for today's politicians, given that citizens have cameras on their smartphones?

BRIEFING NOTES

The War Metaphor

The game frame posits that every move by political actors is communicated through a prism of who is winning and who is losing. Given this focus, it is unsurprising that the game frame is often extended to incorporate the use of war metaphors. Media often identify certain competitive ridings as "battleground constituencies," for example. They may refer to door-to-door campaigning and nationwide advertising campaigns as the "ground war" and "air war," respectively. After leaders' debates, the media ask which leader "scored a knockout punch." Politicians and political operatives often join in the metaphor, as well, referring to their campaign headquarters as "bunkers" or "war rooms." In fact, the very word "campaign," is borrowed from military terminology, where it was originally used to describe a set of operations conducted over open land. The use of sports and war metaphors apply a masculine lens to politicking in Canada, which can have a detrimental effect on the inclusiveness of the public sphere.

remembered for the way Stephen Harper emerged victorious from a difficult situation. Media critics and political scholars are concerned that the game frame is no longer restricted to major events but rather pervades political journalism, no matter how trivial or significant the issue under examination is. Which is not to say that academics are immune to using the game frame themselves—after all, there are publications that offer a ranking of first ministers in an attempt to identify the best PM (Mackenzie King, in one study[23]) or premier (Alberta's Peter Lougheed, in another[24]).

It is not only journalists who advance this tone of discussion but also the political pundits who provide *infotainment*, that is, information delivered in an entertaining manner. The news media has always been a forum to blend opinion with facts in an effort to explain events and educate audiences in an engaging manner. They often make use of political pundits who draw on their own experiences with party politics and government to offer colour commentary. It is common for members of the press gallery to share their behind-the-scenes observations and impressions. Political insiders such as former or current politicians and party workers regularly discuss public affairs with a partisan slant. Pollsters welcome the opportunity to share their insights in part because they can leverage their public profile to generate research contracts. Political scientists likewise provide detached commentary that is grounded in scholarship and broader perspective. Collectively their analysis of political affairs frames each political event as a contest.

The media's need to deliver fresh and interesting content while operating under tighter financial constraints leads to them accepting what are known as information subsidies. The communication activities of governments and political actors are largely designed with an objective of accommodating the media's needs. If content can be created and delivered to media outlets free of charge, then there is a greater likelihood that the media will reproduce that content. Information subsidies include news releases with prepared quotes and ready-made bullet points, content issued through social media such as tweets, and packaged text, still images, audio, and video distributed by other means. In particular, they include news conferences and other staged

information subsidy Free packaged content provided to the media in a manner that is designed to meet their needs.

photo ops designed especially for the media and known as *pseudo-events* because they are a blurred reality. Given the time pressures and dwindling resources facing twenty-first–century journalists, the temptation to simply relay these pre-packaged messages can often be overwhelming.

Consider the following two examples of pseudo-events as a form of information subsidy. Each year, the Canadian Taxpayers Federation organizes a mock annual awards ceremony. Members of the media are invited to a staged event where representatives in formal wear announce the winners of spray-painted golden pigs (representing government largesse) to the public official, bureaucrat, or body of government deemed to have exhibited the most egregious spending, taxation, regulation, or accountability practices.[25] A more sporadic event that appeared to be impromptu, but which was in fact planned and staged for communication purposes, occurred in October 2009. In an effort to soften his image, Prime Minister Harper appeared unannounced on stage at the National Arts Centre performance of cellist Yo-Yo Ma. Harper shocked attendees when he proceeded to play the piano and sing a Beatles song. The appearance led the news for days, was a most-viewed YouTube video during the period, and was featured on government webpages. It also prompted encore performances by the prime minister in subsequent years, including the singing of

The Canadian Press/Fred Chartrand

Interest groups often struggle to draw media and public attention to their causes. The Canadian Taxpayers Federation hosts an annual mock awards gala highlighting what it views as the worst instances of government waste at all levels. The event is co-hosted by mascot "Porky the Waste Hater" and has often attracted media focus. Where is the line between sensationalism and political advocacy? What distinguishes a successful media campaign from an unsuccessful stunt?

Guns 'N' Roses' *Sweet Child O' Mine* at the 2014 Conservative Party Christmas party, which was leaked to the media. These are but a few of the many pseudo-events that compete daily with the publicity tactics of other interest groups, political parties, and governments for public attention.

Inevitably, the content of information subsidies and other political information is filtered and reduced by the news media. This is so that the media can present complex information in a digestible manner to diverse audiences who have varied background awareness and fickle tastes. As well, journalists themselves may be unfamiliar with the subject matter, and are faced with the need to become instant experts on a given topic each day. This presents a challenge for public officials who are dealing with complicated issues but must communicate in a simple manner. There is also considerable danger that information may be framed differently than they intended, which can jeopardize their agenda. The most skilled political communicators are able to design information subsidies that are brief and clear enough that the media will use them unaltered, ensuring that the message gets across as intended.

Political Advertising and Permanent Campaigning

permanent campaign
The practice of electioneering outside of an election period, especially by leveraging government resources.

All of these communications practices are components of what is commonly known as the permanent campaign. Activities that were once restricted to the official campaign period are increasingly practised and honed between elections. This is especially true for the governing party, which attempts to leverage the perks of office to its partisan advantage. Timeworn tactics include delivering good-news budgets in election years, re-announcing government spending initiatives, and using the free mailing privileges accorded to members of the legislature. This is in addition to countless micromanagement practices, such as requiring that government media products refer to the first minister's name (e.g. "the Harper government" instead of "the Government of Canada") and styling news conference podium signs with party messaging. Examples involving ICTs include the use of party colours on non-partisan government websites, the creation of government websites that promote core party messages, and the leveraging of government ICTs by the office of the prime minister or premier.

Government Advertising

By far the most controversial aspect of permanent campaigning is government advertising. According to Public Works and Government Services Canada, government advertising is used to "communicate with Canadians about policies, programs, services and initiatives, public rights and responsibilities, and risks to public health, safety and the environment."[26] But as Jonathan Rose explains in *Making Pictures in Our Heads: Government Advertising in* Canada,[27] this definition misses a crucial point: that government advertising, while explaining public policy, does so in a way that props up the governing party. Indeed, government advertising has a sordid history of being used for quasi-partisan purposes. There are checks in place to reduce the possibility of partisanship in the content of government-funded advertising. The most restrictive regime exists in Manitoba, where government officials are barred from publicly releasing almost all information about government programs and services during an election or by-election campaign. This includes the use of social media, and only permits the government and bureaucracy to release information when required by law or when involving a public health concern or emergency. At the federal level, the planning process, from strategic conception to post-campaign evaluation, is designed to involve many organizations that are required to give their approval (see Figure 11.1). But since cabinet is responsible for the overall strategic direction of the government, and since senior political staffers are involved in both the initiation and approval of advertising programs, government advertising often appears to do little more than support a partisan agenda. This leads to concerns that government advertising is a questionable use of public resources. For instance, the Harper Conservative government was widely criticized for spending tens of millions of dollars annually to advertise its policy initiatives, such as the Economic Action Plan, tax relief measures for families, and the commemoration of the War of 1812.

Some jurisdictions in Canada have passed legislation to reduce the possibility of partisan government advertising. Ontario's Government Advertising Act (2004) states that the province's government advertising "must not be partisan" and requires that an Advertising Review Board oversee all advertising that involves public funds. In Manitoba, government advertising, including most forms of government announcements, must undergo additional scrutiny by top civil servants before being released in the so-called "red zone" leading up to an election.

Notwithstanding these rules, government communications, especially advertising, are routinely on the edge of being political propaganda. Propaganda is an escalation of framing, for it involves the intentional use of biased communications

> propaganda One-sided persuasive communication that communicates falsehoods by virtue of its selective exclusion of truths.

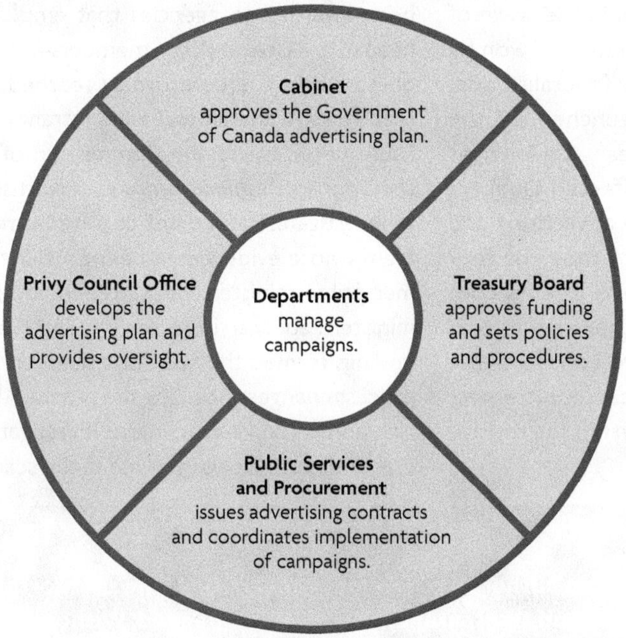

FIGURE 11.1 | Roles and Responsibilities of Federal Organizations in Government Advertising

Source: Reproduced from Public Works and Government Services Canada, "How It Works" (2014), www.tpsgc-pwgsc .gc.ca/pub-adv/roles-eng.html.

as part of a power struggle, and typically employs images intended to provoke an emotional response.[28] There are different types of propaganda ranging from provocative messages about public policies to psychological brainwashing. The mildest form of propaganda projects the sponsor in a positive light through choice of words; for instance, animal welfare groups and foreign governments refer to the seal "hunt" and the "slaughter of baby seals," while the industry and domestic governments refer to the "taking" of seals during a "humane harvest."[29] A similar war of words occurs over

INSIDE CANADIAN POLITICS
How Did Government Advertising Lead to a Political Scandal?

Many governments have been accused of using their taxpayer-funded advertising budget to enhance their public standing on the pretext of educating the citizenry about new programs and policies. Critics argue that such partisan advertising constitutes a misuse of public funds. But in the late 1990s and early 2000s, the federal Liberal Party found itself embroiled in a scandal about an advertising campaign that was not only promoting the government of the day but also lining the pockets of party supporters and the Liberal Party itself.

The sponsorship scandal began in the wake of the 1995 Quebec sovereignty referendum, won by the narrowest of margins by the federalist side. The sponsorship program was launched by the governing Liberal Party under Jean Chrétien as part of its effort to win back disaffected Quebecers. The original intent was to use advertising and other communication strategies to raise the federal government's profile by highlighting its contributions to Quebec industries. The program was meant to be subtle, as there were concerns that an aggressive campaign would cause bitterness among Quebecers still recovering from the divisive referendum vote.

The sponsorship program attracted the attention of the media after *The Globe and Mail* filed access-to-information requests to obtain contracts awarded by the Chrétien government. The paper learned—and in 2002 reported—that over $500,000 had been spent on a report that could not be located. This news prompted journalists, the opposition, and the auditor general to probe for more information, and led to considerable upheaval within the government. The auditor general's 2004 report found that close to $100 million in advertising contracts had been awarded to agencies that employed or were headed by Liberal Party members—often for little or no work. The controversy reached such a state that in 2004, the Liberal administration, now led by Paul Martin, called the Commission of Inquiry into the Sponsorship Program and Advertising Activities to investigate. Retired Justice John Gomery headed a team whose evidence-gathering included calling former prime minister Jean Chrétien and sitting prime minister Paul Martin to testify. The Gomery report findings formed the basis of a number of policy and process changes, including the federal Accountability Act, and it sparked a criminal investigation into several of the principals involved in the scandal.

THE LESSON

The cabinet has the legal authority to authorize government advertising. The sponsorship scandal shows why accountability measures and transparency processes are needed. Without limitations, governing political parties may be tempted to exploit government resources for their own advantage, and if given the chance, some officials may engage in illegal behaviour.

INSIDE CANADIAN POLITICS
Are PMO Videos an Act of Transparency or of Propaganda?

In 2014, the prime minister's office launched "Stephen Harper: 24/7," a weekly newsmagazine summarizing behind-the-scenes daily activities of the prime minister. Each short video was an edited collection of documentary footage compiled over the previous week by PMO videographers with exclusive access to the prime minister. The short productions featured flattering images, an uncritical narrator, and patriotic music. While the videos were unquestionably one-sided, they did provide information about the prime minister's busy itinerary that the mainstream media was not in the habit of reporting—at least, not in a cohesive manner: attending public events, meeting with cabinet ministers, announcing spending commitments, touring the country, shaking hands

with senior citizens, attending a hockey game with his son, and so on. The news media raised concerns that this was reminiscent of North Korean propaganda depicting supreme leader Kim Jong-un; in reality, the inspiration was more likely Barack Obama's "West Wing Week" videos. But, as *The Huffington Post* pointed out, the first of the PMO videos made no mention of climate change activists getting past Harper's security to disrupt his speech that week, of protesters clamouring outside one of the depicted events, or of controversy waging at the time over the destruction of Department of Fisheries and Oceans records.[31] At the time of writing, it is unclear whether prime minister Justin Trudeau will continue the practice of producing weekly videos.

VOX POP

What value do Canadians receive for public funds being used to finance the weekly production of video documentaries about the prime minister? What are the advantages and disadvantages of the media drawing upon this type of information subsidy?

how to refer to Alberta's petroleum reserves: whether you use the word "tar sands" or "oil sands" is a clue to which side of the issue you're on.[30] At the extreme, propagandist regimes operate a totalitarian state, whereby the messages of party elites are omnipresent and free speech is a crime. George Orwell's *1984* fictionalized this extreme; however, the atrocities of Nazi Germany, the cult of personality cultivated by North Korean autocrats, and the monitoring of online communication in China are all too real. In this context, the propaganda campaigns of which Canadian governments are sometimes accused are easily dismissed as routine politicking. Nevertheless, their actions do warrant scrutiny (see, for instance, the discussion of the PMO's "24/7" videos above).

In addition to government advertising, the public is exposed to advertising funded by political parties. In the past, this sort of advertising was largely confined to the official election campaign, but like so many other electioneering practices, party-sponsored advertising is now to be found during the inter-election period. Political advertising is more common when major parties select a new leader, because there is an immediate struggle to define that person's public image; when an election is approaching, in order to avoid campaign spending restrictions; and during minority government, when the possibility of a snap election looms.

Kinds of Political Advertising

There are generally considered to be four types of political ads. *Positive advertising* promotes uplifting messages. This type of advertising is of the "feel good" variety and may use inspirational messages or humour. Typically it is somewhat ineffective because it fails to resonate on an emotional level and is not memorable.

A more direct approach is *comparative advertising*. This contrasts the strengths of a party or candidate against the weaknesses of an opponent (named or implied). For instance, it may begin with negative information communicated in sinister tones but then transition to positive information using an uplifting tone. Comparative ads are used to favourably differentiate the message sponsor and are reasonably effective because they present a problem (the opponent) and a solution (the sponsor).

To many people's dismay, advertising that does nothing more than exploit the weaknesses of an opponent is arguably the most effective form of political advertising. Negative political advertising denigrates an opponent—typically a leader or candidate—and his or her politics. This campaign approach may be widely criticized, but audiences, including journalists, are thought to ultimately prioritize negative information over positive information, in spite of the outrage they generate. Negative ads are thought to contribute to critical media coverage, which in turn results in a despondent electorate that dislikes and distrusts politics and government.[32] They have become an essential tactic because research has shown that as much as people dislike them, viewers' and listeners' initial frustration with the sponsor is likely to be

negative political advertising Paid communication that criticizes an opponent's policy or record, and which may verge on attacking the person.

During the 1993 federal election campaign, the Progressive Conservatives ran negative advertisements highlighting what they saw as Liberal leader Jean Chrétien's lack of leadership qualities. One of these ads featured images like this one, which critics felt drew attention to Chrétien's slight facial deformity caused by Bell's palsy. What sorts of personal characteristics are off-limits when it comes to attack ads?

overwhelmed by their ability to recall the negative message communicated with the target of the ad.[33] Another reason that negative advertising is so effective is that the news media engage in an adwatch and treat the latest controversial ads as news, which increases their reach at no cost to the sponsor. It's worth noting, too, that negative advertising often is not designed to win over new voters as much as it is meant to mobilize a party's base of committed supporters, to make them more likely to vote or to encourage them to increase their donations to the party.

The fourth type of political advertising takes negative advertising a step further. *Attack advertising* belittles someone's personal life or physical characteristics rather than the person's politics. Attack ads are widely considered to be beyond the pale and risk backfiring. In Canada, people often refer to the backlash against the so-called "Chrétien face ads" in the 1993 federal campaign as the limits of public tolerance. Since then, political parties have exercised caution about criticizing opponents' looks or personal lives, which is not to say that it does not happen. This brings us back to the importance of framing, because it helps to explain why political advertising often attempts to exploit the weaknesses of individual politicians rather than philosophical ideas, party brands, or public policy.

UP FOR DEBATE

Is negative political advertising bad for Canadian democracy? The debate supplement at the end of this chapter gives some of the arguments on both sides, and offers questions and resources to guide a discussion around this pressing topic.

INSIDE CANADIAN POLITICS

Why Are the 1993 Chrétien "Face Ads" Still Relevant Today?

The 1993 Canadian federal election was a watershed moment for negative advertising in Canadian politics. The positive bounce that an unpopular Progressive Conservative government had received with the appointment of Kim Campbell as prime minister began to erode during the election campaign. PC Party strategists tested advertising in focus groups to assess how voters would react to TV spots that attacked Liberal leader Jean Chrétien. The ads used unflattering photographs of Chrétien that appeared to highlight his partial facial paralysis caused by Bell's palsy, while voiceovers made statements such as, "Is this a prime minister?" and "I would be very embarrassed if he became Prime Minister of Canada."

When the advertisements ran on television, the PCs' internal polling found that they succeeded in weakening public impressions of Chrétien.

However, there was significant political fallout. The Liberal Party coordinated a cross-country phone-in campaign among its supporters, urging them to express outrage that these ads had crossed the line, and anger for making fun of someone's disability. So acute was the public backlash—including within the PC Party—that Campbell immediately pulled the ads against the advice of her strategists. On Election Day, the Liberals formed a majority government, and the PCs were reduced to only two seats.

The case is a notorious example of the implications of using negative advertising to attack an opponent's physical characteristics rather than to deride their politics. Today, "going neg" is often seen as a necessary evil, but Canadian practitioners are mindful not to repeat the PCs' mistakes of "going personal."

VOX POP

Do you think that Prime Minister Campbell was right to pull her party's attack ads and overrule the advice of some of her party's top strategists?

Political Marketing

The competitive nature of political advertising is evidence of the lengths that political parties will go to to promote their point of view and attract voter support. In *Shopping for Votes: How Politicians Choose Us and We Choose Them*, veteran political journalist Susan Delacourt describes the evolution of Canadian political parties' use of sales and marketing techniques.[34] She chronicles the history of Canadian consumerism and democracy and examines how, over time, business marketing practices have entered the realm of Canadian politics. These practices are founded on the principle that political parties must research the marketplace of political consumers and shape their products and communications to meet voters' needs and wants. In practice, however, political elites have used research intelligence to inform ways to promote what matters to themselves in a manner that is most likely to generate public support.

In Canada and elsewhere, a new variation of the catch-all party is gaining acceptance among political scientists: the market-oriented party. This emergence of this type of party, as posited by political marketing scholar Jennifer Lees-Marshment, reflects the growing tendency by British political parties to embrace marketing principles.[35] In her model, the elite parties of yesteryear were concerned with their own priorities rather than with public opinion, and mass parties used opinion research foremost to figure out how to sell themselves to electors. Conversely, an idealized notion of the market-oriented party is one that uses research to estimate what the demands of the electorate are so that it can make internal changes to respond to those preferences. It is a version of the catch-all party that has become professionalized by engaging consultants with specialized skillsets and an ability to make use of the latest marketing and communication technology. Idealistically, a market-oriented party is highly democratic; however, in practice it does not exist, at least in Canada. This is because, as mentioned, Canadian parties are prone to prioritizing the preferences of political elites. They may focus exclusively on the needs of the narrowest segment of the electorate necessary to achieve their goals and often slide into the realm of propaganda. As suggested in Chapter 9, it is perhaps most helpful to consider political parties as exhibiting behaviours of brokerage or market-orientated organizations, rather than trying to pigeon-hole them as belonging to a particular class of party.

A related, emerging area of research considers political parties as *brands*. A brand is a synthesis of all communication impressions that are absorbed by a consumer, who may develop an emotional attachment as a result. It extends beyond symbols, such as a logo or slogan, to encompass core messages, media coverage, and personal interactions that collectively inform a mental image of the brand. The evoked image of the brand in an elector's mind becomes an information shortcut for her or him to pass judgement. Most scholarship about political brands has surrounded the rebranding of Britain's Labour Party under the leadership of Tony Blair.[36] His communications team recast the party as "New Labour" and were relentless in their practice of media management to control the image of the party, the leader, and the Labour government.

Branding appears to be more applicable to Canadian politics than is the broader conceptualization of political marketing. The limited scholarship about political branding in Canada has tended to focus on the practice of branding the country in international tourism.[37] However, some emerging work has looked at party branding on the right by the Conservatives[38] and on the left by the NDP.[39] An undertone is that the need to control the message contributes to party discipline.

---

market-oriented party A political party that uses research data to design policies that satisfy voters.

↻ See Types of Political Parties, beginning on page 341 of Chapter 9, for an explanation of catch-all and brokerage parties.

↻ Party discipline is defined and discussed at length in Chapter 6, on the legislature: see especially pages 217 and 226–8.

Any public representative of a political party in Canada is expected to promote a consistent and authorized message. This guideline applies not only to members of the caucus but also to public spokespeople and local constituency officials and volunteers. The importance of "message discipline" has increased with the reach of the media; gone are the days when partisans could say one thing in one region of the country, while their fellow partisans said something different, even contradictory, in another. In Canada today, whatever is said by a representative of a political party must align with what other representatives say. This encompasses remarks made at public events, to the news media, via social media, on websites, in newsletters, through email, and by any other form of communication. In short, sameness is expected, regardless of one's personal opinions.

It can be frustrating for elected officials to publicly support a party decision or policy that they vehemently oppose in private. They were elected to represent their constituents in a democratic country where free speech is protected both in the constitution and to an even greater degree within the legislature. But party leaders exert considerable power, while the people's representatives complain of feeling reduced to little more than trained seals. Studies, pundits, political scientists, and even some elected officials routinely suggest that MPs should have more freedom. So why do party members accept party and message discipline? Not everyone does, but those who do have many reasons. They may recognize that politics is not about getting one's own way all the time and that they must choose which issues to exert their political capital on. A political party that operates as a cohesive whole presents itself in the media as capable of governing and pushing forward its agenda; this contrasts with the alternative of instability resulting from party infighting and bending to pressure from lobbyists and special interests. For the government party, there is a heightened need to enforce party discipline because at all times the party must maintain the confidence of the legislature. There can be significant peer pressure to comply; going along with the party means that you remain part of the in-group, but operating as a free agent invites the risk of being socially and professionally ostracized. In short, the benefits of going along with party discipline often outweigh the disadvantages to those involved. A result is that the message discipline expected of political parties turns MPs into brand ambassadors.

↻ For a review of the convention of party discipline, see Chapter 6, on the legislature. See especially the section The Partisan Composition of Legislatures and the end-of-chapter debate supplement.

Public Opinion Research

Political marketing and political branding theories hold that political parties use public opinion research both to inform their political communication and also to select which policies to prioritize. The thinking is that in order to win, a party must jettison unpopular policies and emphasize those that will most likely resonate with targeted segments of the population. Narrowcasting is used to maximize the efficiency of communicating with the slivers of the electorate who are likely to respond to a micro-policy. Opinion research is gathered to identify targeted groups of citizens and to understand their media consumption habits. Media planning data such as detailed audience ratings statistics, combined with internal party database information about supporters, are scrutinized to identify the most cost-effective advertising opportunities to reach the identified cohorts. Whereas political parties once campaigned largely on a constituency basis in the first party system, a regional basis in the second, and a pan-Canadian basis in the third, parties now target their appeals to specific groups of individuals, often through specialty publications or television channels, email

narrowcasting A form of campaigning in which parties choose communications that will target narrowly-defined groups of voters.

↺ See Canada's Federal Party Systems, beginning on page 350 of Chapter 9, for a review of the first, second, and third party systems in Canada.

lists, and social media. In his books *Harper's Team* and *Winning Power: Canadian Campaigning in the 21st Century*, Tom Flanagan explains how political parties compile information about supporters and use it for direct voter contact.[40] This involves compiling databases of supporters and sending them information by email. Direct voter contact is a cost-effective way to bypass the filter of the mass media and control the message that is received by target audiences. The Conservatives, under Flanagan's direction, were initially masters at this, but the other parties have caught on and now regularly issue direct appeals. Typically this is used as a fundraising mechanism rather than as an information tool.

Political communication is thus supplemented or shaped by quantitative and qualitative public opinion research. The government is a major consumer of data about Canadians' views on various topics. In particular, departments use *focus groups* to test policy ideas and communication concepts, and *opinion surveys* to inform their decisions (see Table 11.1). As with advertising, the potential exists for partisan use of government-funded opinion research and the awarding of contracts to party supporters. To curtail this possibility, departments planning to invest in public opinion research must observe standardized procedures, including subjecting the project to a competitive bidding process, and must consider the input of specialists within the public service. As well, commissioned research reports must be made publicly available online within a determined period, according to the internal policies of some governments, including those of Canada, Alberta, and Saskatchewan.

Within the government, public opinion research is used

- to inform changes to communication activities;
- to devise ways to improve the delivery of programs and services; and
- to monitor issues that matter to Canadians.

The media, as we have seen, tend to use polling data for horse-race coverage and to identify whether government and political parties are behaving in a manner that is in line with the general public's preferences. Political parties are motivated by the opportunity to implement a political agenda and control the public purse. They use opinion data as a form of strategic intelligence that can guide them to victory and avoid mistakes.

Research intelligence is the basis for a sophisticated selection of media choices. For instance, the federal Conservative Party has identified fans of hockey and curling, particularly men, as potential supporters. Rather than advertising on programming that is watched by many citizens, such as the evening news, they choose to concentrate their advertising budget on programs watched by hockey and curling fans. We might think that this would be specialty sports networks, but in fact media statistics indicate that animated comedy programs such as *The Simpsons* would be more likely to reach their intended audience.[41] This is reinforced by other forms of narrowcasting such as direct mail, email blasts, online advertising, social media, and strategically selected photo ops. While narrowcasting creates opportunities for political parties, it is a concern because it means that these parties are communicating with only some members of the audience and are purposely excluding likely opponents. Consequently, today's civil society is dividing into factions of people who self-select which media to be exposed to, and who likely receive communication mostly from the political party that they already support. This is reinforced by the fact that many

TABLE 11.1 | Quantitative and Qualitative Public Opinion Research Tools

	Quantitative Research	Qualitative Research
Most common tool	Opinion surveys: the administration of a questionnaire to a representative sample of a population	Focus groups: the moderation of discussions with small meetings of 8–12 recruited people
Purpose	To obtain a statistically reliable snapshot of opinions	To obtain a deep understanding of attitudes from select cohorts
How data are used	To engage in a statistical analysis of a dataset and apply conclusions to the larger population	To consider the feelings, language, and ideas expressed by participants to inform generalizations
Limitations	Difficult to obtain a deep understanding of public attitudes; caller ID and mobile phones are resulting in lower response rates; online surveys may produce questionable results	Requires considerable advance planning; produces highly subjective data; is expensive; takes longer than surveys to administer; involves travel
Examples of research reports for federal government departments	• Client satisfaction survey (Canadian Transportation Agency) • Public opinion on the environment (Environment Canada) • Survey assessing Canada's Economic Action Plan's jobs and growth campaign (Finance Canada)	• Television ad "disaster check" focus groups (Public Safety Canada) • Focus group research on views of government spending (Treasury Board of Canada Secretariat) • Focus testing of radio and print creatives for the national anti-drug strategy (Health Canada)

Source: Adapted from Canada, "Public Opinion Research Reports" (2014), www.porr-rrop.gc.ca/index-e.html.

interest groups employ these same marketing techniques when targeting their audiences. These are among the reasons why the idealized notion of political marketing that enhances democracy does not exist in Canadian politics.

Pollsters

Another technique practised by parties, well-funded interest groups, and some think tanks is to hire a research company to compile public opinion data. This information is useful both in terms of understanding where Canadians stand on issues of importance to the advocacy group, as well as measuring the party's or organization's success in influencing public opinion. The presidents and vice-presidents of polling firms have become ubiquitous in Canadian public affairs. These **pollsters** are regularly in the news disclosing the results of their firm's latest opinion survey and privately may offer counsel to the leaders of political parties and interest groups. Technological change, including computer-assisted telephone interviewing, reduced long-distance toll charges, and advances in online surveys, means that polls have become affordable and commonplace. In addition to compiling *quantitative* (i.e. numerical) data, pollsters offer deeper insights obtained through *qualitative* research methods such as focus groups, which are used to test advertising and policy ideas (see Table 11.1). Examples of major public opinion research firms in Canada include EKOS, Ipsos, Léger, Nanos Research, Abacus Data, and Pollara Strategic Insights, who are publicly represented by pollsters such as Frank Graves, Darrell Bricker, Christian Bourque, Nik Nanos, David Coletto, Bruce Anderson, and Michael Marzolini. Their training and use of social science research methods allow pollsters to speak with a detached credibility that distinguishes them from most political commentators.

pollster A senior employee of a research company who oversees the administration of public-opinion surveys.

INSIDE CANADIAN POLITICS
Political Communication and Campaign Strategy

Canada's most successful political strategists take all of this wisdom into account when engaging in election campaigns (or the permanent campaign in general). Broadly speaking, political parties, interest groups, and other actors use one of two types of strategies: *confrontation* or *articulation*.

According to the confrontation approach, parties and organizations compete by taking opposing positions on questions of policy or ideology. Campaigns feature debate and dialogue so that, when one party speaks to an issue, its opponent engages directly by taking an opposing side on that issue. This results in a great debate over issues of public policy, such as whether to engage in war, whether to raise taxes, or whether to privatize certain public services. These sorts of debates are exceedingly rare in Canadian politics, as there are very few issues on which Canadians are deeply divided. Knowing that the majority of Canadians stand on one side or another on most issues, there is little incentive for parties to engage in direct confrontation.

Parties taking the articulation approach talk past each other: instead of assuming divergent policy positions, the parties engage each other by selectively emphasizing different issues and manipulating the political agenda to their advantage. For instance, parties often conduct market research to determine which issues their party owns, which is to say the issues on which voters trust them most to handle. The party then attempts to prime the media and the public by placing those issues at the top of the campaign agenda, while remaining strategically ambiguous about issues that their opponents own. Right-wing parties typically own issues like taxation and debt relief, while left-wing parties own issues like education and healthcare.

Alternatively, parties may attempt to elevate so-called *wedge issues* to the forefront of public debate. Wedge issues are those that divide their opponents internally, creating dissension among their ranks and possibly demobilizing or converting their followers. If an environmentalist party knows that an opponent's followers are deeply divided over whether to establish a carbon tax, for example, it may launch a communication campaign to raise public awareness over the issue in an attempt to drive a wedge into its opponent's base.

Lastly, parties may engage in what is known as "dog whistle politics," highlighting issues that are of particular interest to a small group of core supporters but that fail to resonate (or even register) with the general public. Parties will often use coded language when raising these issues, so as not to draw attention (much like a dog whistle catches the ears only of dogs and not humans). Consider, for example, the use of terms like "individual responsibility" by right-wing parties, or "working families" by left-wing parties. These terms mean a lot to each party's respective base, and carry with them strong ideological connotations. Yet their significance may escape the attention of most Canadians. As a result of using these articulation strategies, parties develop competing policy packages featuring distinct sets of priorities for the future, rather than specific, contrasting policy prescriptions.

Most political scientists today recognize that parties compete both through direct confrontation and through articulation (or selective emphasis). Depending on the organization involved, and varying from time to time, parties may take opposing positions on the same issues or engage in competitive agenda-setting.

VOX POP

Thinking back to the 2015 federal election, did you see more evidence of direct confrontation or of articulation? Why do you suppose the parties involved chose the communication strategies they did? Which topics might have been considered "wedge issues" or examples of "dog whistle" politics?

Concluding Thoughts

Political communication is fast-changing, and yet the basic theoretical principles remain constant. No matter what medium or innovative technology is used by political elites to provide information to their audiences, central concepts such as framing, permanent campaigning, and branding will apply. As journalists and political actors seek to outwit each other in the media game, and as new information emerges in the age of e-politics, the rest of us remain confronted with the age-old challenge of discerning what is true, what is spin, and what is hidden from public view.

For More Information

Intrigued by the media's coverage of the coalition crisis, and the role of television in political communication? Lydia Miljan examines the use of frames in English television news coverage of the crisis in her 2011 article "Television Frames of the 2008 Liberal and New Democrat Accord" (*Canadian Journal of Communication* 36: pp. 559–78). Peter Russell and Lorne Sossin invited leading political scientists and constitutional experts to explore Canada's *Parliamentary Democracy in Crisis* (University of Toronto Press, 2009). As well, a chronology of events as seen through the eye of political journalists is available in the *Maclean's* article "Inside a Crisis That Shook the Nation," by John Geddes and Aaron Wherry (11 December 2008, available online).

Want to learn more about the public sphere and how the concept remains relevant today? Grab a coffee and go to a public space to read editors Christian J. Emden and David Midgley's 2012 collection *Beyond Habermas: Democracy, Knowledge, and the Public Sphere* (New York: Berghahn Books).

Concerned about the sponsorship scandal? The most authoritative source is the Commission of Inquiry into the Sponsorship Program and Advertising Activities, which produced two final reports, collectively known as the Gomery Report. John Wanna raised questions about the failures of ministerial responsibility during the scandal in his 2006 article "Insisting on Traditional Ministerial Responsibility and the Constitutional Independence of the Public Service: The Gomery Inquiry and the Sponsorship Scandal" (*Australian Journal of Political Science*, 65: pp. 15–21). Kirsten Kozolanka provided a critical account of government communications and its politicization in "The Sponsorship Scandal as Communication: The Rise of Politicized and Strategic Communications in the Federal Government" (*Canadian Journal of Communication* 31 (2006): pp. 343–66).

Interested in negative political advertising in Canadian politics? Given that negative advertising has pervaded Canadian politics, it is surprising that so little research has been conducted on the topic. Ken Whyte's 1994 story in *Saturday Night*, "The Face That Sank a Thousand Tories: How a Conservative, 'Personal Attack' Ad on Chrétien Caused the Loudest Backfire in Canadian Political History" (109: pp. 14–18) provides a good overview of the debacle concerning the Chrétien "face ads." However, all of the attention given to those TV spots overlooks the harshness of the "Mr Sage" radio ads that attacked Prime Minister Mackenzie King a half-century earlier. For more on that, see Ian Ward's article "The Early Use of Radio for Political Communication in Australia and Canada" (*Australian Journal of Politics & History* 45 (1999): pp. 311–30).

Curious about the concept of political marketing? A variety of Canadian perspectives and case studies can be found in *Political Marketing in Canada*, edited by Alex Marland, Thierry Giasson, and Jennifer

Lees-Marshment (UBC Press, 2012). Daniel Paré and Flavia Berger have written about the use of political marketing by the Conservative Party in "Political Marketing Canadian Style? The Conservative Party and the 2006 Federal Election" (*Canadian Journal of Communication* 33 (2008): pp. 39–63), and David McGrane has examined its practice by the New Democratic Party in his chapter in *The Canadian Federal Election of 2011*, edited by Jon H. Pammett and Christopher Dornan (Toronto: Dundurn, 2008).

Want to monitor or participate in minute-by-minute conversations about Canadian politics? Twitter is an ideal venue for following topical discussions. Visit PoliTwitter.ca's list of top hashtags: http://politwitter.ca/page/canadian-politics-hash-tags.

Interested in the state of e-government in Canada today? Check out the Government of Canada's main Web portal: www.canada.ca.

Curious about the extent of Open Data in the federal government? Visit open.canada.ca/en to see what sort of information is on offer.

Want to view the latest direct messages from the the Prime Minister of Canada? The Prime Minister's missives are available at pm.gc.ca.

Deeper Inside Canadian Politics

1. Much has been made of Web 2.0 and the ensuing rise of citizen journalists in Canadian politics. Which do you think is more effective at holding governments accountable in Canada: the mainstream media or digital media? Why?

2. In other countries, interest groups have emerged in an attempt to provide objectivity to the public sphere. For example, factcheck.org employs researchers to verify political statements made by American political players. Is there a role for such services in Canadian politics? Why or why not?

3. Compare the content and communication methods found in the Canadian prime minister's weekly online messages with those of the American president. What are the major similarities, and what explains the major differences?

UP FOR DEBATE

Is negative political advertising bad for Canadian democracy?

THE CLAIM: YES, IT IS!
Negative political advertising hurts democracy.

Yes: Argument Summary

Negative communication is damaging democracy worldwide. When negativity is used in political advertising, particularly in videos, it employs psychological techniques to generate an emotional response among audiences. Consequently, viewers become agitated, even outraged, about the message, the message sponsor, and the political realm as a whole. Over time, turnout in elections has been declining, and the negative advertising that turns people off politics is widely thought to be a contributing factor. The bad things that politicians say about each other undermine any attempts to improve citizen engagement and increase election turnout. Moreover, this contributes to a negative tone about politics in media coverage, and it results in a so-called spiral of cynicism. Political activism that uses negative communication goes against the spirit of democracy.

Yes: Top 5 Considerations

1. The use of horror themes (e.g. black backgrounds, grainy slow motion, black and white images, menacing music, unflattering photos, shocking headlines, judgemental narration) are designed to upset electors, causing them to become distressed about and suspicious of politicians, political parties, and politics.
2. People who get angry at negative ads are likely to express their frustration with the political process by not voting.
3. Negative ads make politics appear evil and childish; they do little to inspire intelligent debate on the issues.
4. Negative advertising distorts truths and promotes a frame about a leader or candidate that is unfair. It borders on the kind of attack advertising that denigrates the personal characteristics of politicians but that has nothing to do with their political competencies.
5. Negative advertising is increasingly being used by interest groups, whose use of unregulated information communication technologies to distribute negative video is also more common.

Yes: Other Considerations

- It is inevitable that negative advertising will descend into attack politics. Negative advertising lowers the quality of democratic discourse to name-calling and image framing rather than elevating democracy into a sophisticated debate about public policy.
- Small jurisdictions such as Prince Edward Island and Newfoundland and Labrador are less likely to feature negative advertising than are larger jurisdictions. This speaks to an understanding in small communities that being harshly critical about politicians has harmful effects on a politician's family and on that person directly.

THE COUNTERCLAIM: NO, IT ISN'T!
Negative political advertising results in better government.

No: Argument Summary

Negative advertising is a legitimate tool of political activism and is unjustly criticized. Democratic romanticists somehow think that politics should be about peaceful discussion in an honourable manner. In reality, political actors seek out media coverage to set and control the public agenda; they attempt to frame issues and the image of opponents; and they campaign for the hearts and minds of electors. Negative advertising draws public attention to perceived (and often real) weaknesses of opponents and therefore performs a service for electors. A combination of positive, comparative, and negative communication is an excellent way to inform people about their political choices.

No: Top 5 Considerations

1. Negative advertising holds governments accountable for their decisions and political parties for their policy positions. Even the threat of negative advertising may keep them from acting rashly.
2. The media and voters pay attention to negative advertising. Negative ads are the best way to grab the public's attention about issues of concern.
3. There is a difference between negative and attack advertising. If used properly, negative advertising promotes truthfulness in political discourse by using facts to dispel myths, information to confront media slants, and data to counter partisan falsehoods.
4. Political advertising may increase voter turnout by activating non-voters and motivating partisans to get involved. It increases perceptions that more is on the line and gives partisans a reason to mobilize supporters to the polls.
5. Political parties that "go neg" are more likely to be supported by electors than those parties that insist on being positive and not responding to attacks. The failure of the frontrunner NDP to deploy negative messages in the 2013 British Columbia election campaign is thought to have contributed to the Liberals' re-election.

No: Other Considerations

- There are no laws against negative advertising; in fact, it is the epitome of free speech, which is protected in the Charter of Rights and Freedoms.
- The media treat negative advertising as news and offer important context by explaining the ads to viewers. This holds the sponsors of negative advertising accountable.
- Negative information can, to some electors, be useful information that helps inform their vote decision. What one elector may dismiss, another elector may perceive to be important.

Discussion Questions

- How can lawmakers possibly regulate negative advertising that appears online?
- How can we limit negative political advertising without infringing the constitutional protection of free speech?
- Why do you think so much attention is paid to the negative aspects of politics instead of the positive side?

- Think about some recent political advertising that you have seen or heard. Was it primarily positive or negative? Do you think it was effective? Why or why not?
- To what extent do you agree with the claim that negative advertising holds politicians accountable and is therefore an important component of a democratic system of government?

Where to Learn More about Negative Political Advertising

Stephen Ansolabehere and Shanto Iyengar, *Going Negative: How Political Advertisements Shrink and Polarize the Electorate* (New Haven, CT: Free Press, 1995).

Ted Brader, *Campaigning for Hearts and Minds: How Emotional Appeals in Political Ads Work* (Chicago: University of Chicago Press, 2006).

Geoffrey Haddock and Mark P. Zanna, "Impact of Negative Advertising on Evaluations of Political Candidates: The 1993 Canadian Federal Election," *Basic and Applied Social Psychology* 19, no. 2 (1997): pp. 205–23.

Victor Kamber, *Poison Politics: Are Negative Campaigns Destroying Democracy?* (New York: Plenum Press, 1997).

David Mark, *Going Dirty: The Art of Negative Campaigning* (Lanham, MD: Rowman and Littlefield, 2006).

Bruce Pinkleton, "The Effects of Negative Comparative Political Advertising on Candidate Evaluations and Advertising Evaluations: An Exploration," *Journal of Advertising* 26, no. 1 (1997): pp. 19–29.

Jonathan Rose, "Are Negative Ads Positive? Political Advertising and the Permanent Campaign," in *How Canadians Communicate IV: Media and Politics*, ed. David Taras and Christopher Waddell (Edmonton: Athabasca University Press, 2012).

12 POLITICAL ACTIVISM

Inside this Chapter

- What are interest groups, and different types of interest groups?
- What are social movements?
- What is lobbying?

Inside Political Activism

Legislatures, courtrooms, and party headquarters are not the be-all and end-all of Canadian democracy. And it is fortunate that they are not. These traditional venues are often exclusionary, with participants (intentionally or unintentionally) establishing rules and internal cultures that insulate them from challenges by traditionally

What the 2015 Election means for Political Activism

Visit the Inside Canadian Politics flipboard to learn about the latest developments affecting political activism in Canada.

 Go to
http://flip.it/gblag.

marginalized groups and minority opinions. Special interest groups pursue other avenues to influence the political process. Because these political activists operate outside the traditional arena of Canadian democracy, they have often been the subject of certain misconceptions relating to their role and importance in the political process. Bear in mind the following maxims as you read through the chapter.

 Special interest groups have limited influence on Canadian politics. Interest groups are sometimes portrayed as powerful, well-financed organizations that hold undue sway over politicians and political decision-making. In fact, most interest groups and social movements face enormous resource challenges and institutional barriers in engaging governments and achieving their policy objectives.

 Lobbying in Canada is not the clandestine, corrupt, and anti-democratic practice it is often made out to be. The media and the entertainment industry have cultivated an image of lobbyists as shady figures using secret meetings, bribes, and other discreditable means to coerce elected officials. However, in reality, lobbying has always been an indispensable means of connecting societal interests to government, and the practice is becoming increasingly regulated and professionalized over time.

 Protests and public demonstrations are not the only—or even the most common—forms of political activism. Activists engage in a variety of ways with various parts of the Canadian political system, from elections and social media campaigns to backroom negotiations and courtroom confrontations.

Overview

Citizens seek to influence public policy in many ways other than through the more traditional channels of elections (representation) and the courts (litigation). In this chapter, we explore different components of political activism. This includes the pressure exerted by interest groups, the societal demands of social movements, and the influence of lobbyists on setting the political agenda.

UP FOR DEBATE

Should election spending by interest groups be regulated?

Keep this question in mind as you read through the chapter. Consult the end-of-chapter debate supplement for more material to help you engage in an informed discussion of the topic.

Political Activism

↻ The topic of pluralism is taken up on page 294 of Chapter 8, on public policy.

In a pluralist democracy, public policy is influenced by competing ideologies, interests, and pressures. Different political worldviews, discussed in Chapter 1, help to frame the competition among political parties, described in Chapters 9 and 10, on parties and elections respectively. Another way of influencing public policy and monitoring government behaviour is to mobilize supporters of a principle or a belief to pressure elected officials. This is the trade of interest groups, the organized political associations that promote an agenda without fielding election candidates or aspiring to govern. Interest groups in Canada normally use communication tactics in an effort to compel the political executive to respond to their demands in a manner that is advantageous to their membership. Consequently, they are in a constant struggle to attract media attention and generate public sympathy for their cause. So effective are they at using the media that Canadian interest groups have been described as "necessary links in the processes of communication that bind government and people."[1]

Interest groups are alternatively called *advocacy* or *pressure groups*, or *special interests*. Elections Canada refers to them as *third parties*, in the sense that they are actors outside the formal world of political parties and politicians. Their role in a pluralist democracy is an important one, for they attract attention to issues that political parties, the media, and the voting public may otherwise ignore. On the other hand, their political influence can at times undermine democratic principles if they become actively involved in secretive decision-making processes among political elites. Critics of the invisible role that interest groups have in political decision-making argue for greater regulation, but the courts have rejected many of these arguments in favour of sections of the Charter of Rights and Freedoms upholding the principles of free speech and freedom of association. Table 12.1 presents a selection of interest groups, their goals, and their tactics.

Interest groups perform a wide range of functions in Canadian democracy. As catalysts and activists, they help promote or highlight public policy issues that might otherwise go unnoticed. They provide a critical link between citizens and government, communicating challenges, research, and solutions from the grassroots of society to those in positions to do something with them. This communication is a two-way street, with many interest groups helping to support, explain, or legitimize government actions to their members or the general public. Select interest groups may actually serve on behalf of the government, monitoring compliance with state legislation or regulations, or even formally delivering programs and services on behalf of government.

Interest groups are thus a vital link between elected officials and the general public. They have a more direct and substantive connection with many Canadians than do political parties. Whereas there are three to five major federal political parties, there are, by comparison, over 20,000 interest groups in Canada. They can be as small, representing the interests of a handful of people or organizations, or they can be as large as a formal institution that represents an entire industry and/or millions of citizens. Their politicking includes lobbying, fundraising, litigation, and the release of research reports. Mostly, however, they specialize in political communication such as advertising, public relations, direct marketing, social media, public meetings, and protests. The emergence of social media has revolutionized the way special interests link leadership executives with the grassroots. An example of the type of career opportunities that exist in this sector is presented in the Opportunities Available box on page 472.

Interest groups become especially active during an election campaign, when they increase their efforts to exert the influence of their membership on political parties, the media, the general public, and, ultimately, the government. They send letters to party leaders and to candidates seeking to establish positions on issues of importance to the group's membership. They mobilize their supporters by recommending how to vote and, in some cases, may make a determined effort to defeat certain candidates.

interest group A political organization that seeks to influence public policy without competing for election.

TABLE 12.1 | Canadian Interest Groups and Their Tactics

Interest Group	Objective	Examples of Pressure Tactics
CANADA WITHOUT POVERTY / CANADA SANS PAUVRETÉ Canada Without Poverty	Eliminate poverty in Canada	• policy education and development • promotion of human rights • deliver presentations and respond to media • conduct workshops and online courses
Canadian Association of Petroleum Producers	Ensure the economic sustainability of the Canadian oil and gas industry	• commission opinion polls • coordinate industry awards • deliver presentations • respond to government regulations
cfs fcéé Canadian Federation of Students	Promote post-secondary students' viewpoints	• analyze government policies • mail information to politicians • run Travel CUTS travel agency catering to students
Canadian Taxpayers FEDERATION Canadian Taxpayers Federation	Promote lower taxes, monitor wasteful spending, keep politicians accountable	• conduct media interviews • speak at events • launch petitions and organize supporters to contact politicians • publish *The Taxpayer* magazine
CARP CARP (previously known as Canadian Association of Retired Persons)	Promote retirement security, equitable access to health care and freedom from age discrimination for older Canadians	• inform government of position on legislation and policies • poll members on policy issues and government proposals • conduct media interviews, debates, and discussions
Egale Canada Human Rights Trust Egale Canada Human Rights Trust (previously known as Equality for Gays and Lesbians Everywhere)	Promote human rights for lesbians, gays, bisexuals, transgendered Canadians	• participate in court cases • stage annual equity fundraising gala • organize safe schools campaign
LIFECANADA VieCanada LifeCanada	Facilitate communication among educational pro-life groups across Canada	• provide pro-life educational resources • promote the activities of educational pro-life groups, including conferences, marches, national polling, and advertising campaigns
madd* Saving Lives, Supporting Victims Mothers Against Drunk Driving	Stop impaired driving and support victims of this violent crime	• provides victim services • delivers youth programs across country • educates general public through awareness campaigns • promotes legislative best practices in impaired driving
Physicians *for a* Smoke-Free Canada Physicians for a Smoke-Free Canada	Reduce illnesses caused by tobacco smoking and second-hand smoke	• research tobacco industry • work with departments of health • meet with groups in developing countries
PSAC AFPC Public Service Alliance of Canada	Representing federal public servants as a labour union	• negotiate labour issues • coordinate protests and strikes • testify at parliamentary committees

INSIDE CANADIAN POLITICS
Farmer Politics

In the early twentieth century, farmers constituted one of the most influential groups in Canadian politics, particularly in Ontario and western Canada. Because agriculture was such a dominant industry and because Canadian legislatures were so heavily weighted toward rural representation, farmers' support was integral to federal parties wishing to form majority governments in Ottawa. When the Conservatives and Liberals balked at farmers' demands for free trade with the United States, for lower freight rates to transport grain and farm implements, and for greater control by the Western provinces over their natural resources, they found themselves abandoned by the farmers, who formed their own political party. The newly minted Progressives won enough seats in the 1921 federal election to place second, although they rejected the title "official opposition" out of principle. They did so because they wished to distinguish themselves from old-line parties like the Liberals and Conservatives, and felt that individual members should represent their constituents rather than simply toe the party line in Parliament. Only after the Liberal Party made a concerted effort to address the farmers' grievances did the Progressives disband. Several went on to form new parties, however, including Social Credit and the Co-operative Commonwealth Federation.

Farmer support was also absolutely essential to any would-be premier seeking power at the provincial level. Farmers in different provinces exerted their political clout in different ways. In Alberta, Manitoba, and Ontario in particular, they formed their own parties under the "United Farmer" banner. In each province, United Farmers formed the government at one point, and remained affiliated with the federal Progressives. In Saskatchewan, however, the farmers decided to remain an interest group—the Saskatchewan Grain Growers' Association—rather than form their own party. In an effort to retain power, the Liberal Party of Saskatchewan actively courted the Association, naming several of its members to their executive committees and inviting them into cabinet. Arguably, the farmers in the Association retained as much power as their counterparts in Alberta, Manitoba, and Ontario, despite opting to remain outside the traditional realm of party politics.

THE LESSON

Organized interests have options when it comes to mobilizing politically. They may choose to become interest groups and ally themselves with existing parties, or form their own political parties to challenge old-line actors for control over the government.

While third parties can include established, high-profile organizations such as the Canadian Labour Congress, the International Fund for Animal Welfare, and the National Citizens Coalition, some of the special interest groups that get involved in federal elections are much narrower, such as the Vancouver Fire Fighters' Union Local 18 or the group Save Our Prison Farms. As well, some people register their own names as third parties, as do organizations that purport to promote democratic reforms. This occurs because third parties are required by law to register with Elections Canada if they spend $500 or more on advertising, and their total spending is limited to about $3,000 per electoral district. These limits are intended to strike a balance between the constitutional protection of free speech and the considerable influence—and deep pockets—of some groups compared with others.

Money is an important determinant of an interest group's success, but it is by no means the only factor. Indeed, success itself is defined in many ways among interest groups. For some, it entails raising public consciousness about an issue or set of concerns; for others, it involves directly influencing the development of public policy; for still others, it may involve a more partisan objective of shaming or ultimately defeating the party in power. To achieve any of these objectives, however, interest groups require a core set of tools and attributes, some of which are under their control and some of which rely upon outside forces. Among the internal factors, successful interest groups often have sizeable memberships or followerships, allowing them to speak credibly when telling policymakers that they have the backing of a substantial portion of the electorate. CARP (formerly known as the Canadian Association of Retired Persons) boasts over 300,000 members, for instance, while Greenpeace Canada reports nearly 90,000 financial supporters, which the group counts as anyone who has donated to

Opportunities Available

Knowledge of Canadian Politics and Government Preferred!

Advocacy Officer

National Association of Federal Retirees

The Advocacy Officer is responsible to the Manager, Advocacy and Communications, for monitoring and researching relevant policy (particularly as they relate to pensions, healthcare, seniors and veterans) and producing advocacy materials and events in support of the Association's Strategic Advocacy plan. The incumbent will build relationships with stakeholders, identify opportunities to shape policies, and support the advocacy work of the National Association of Federal Retirees' branches. The successful applicant will have the following key attributes:

- A university degree in political science, communications or related field, or an equivalent professional qualification;
- At least 5 years' experience in communications, policy-based work, or advocacy-related communication;
- Experience in writing, editing and proofreading advocacy materials and conducting research for public dissemination;
- Experience conducting policy analysis;
- Excellent editing, writing and proofreading skills in both official languages (English and French);
- Experience with relevant information technology, including website content management;
- Strong interpersonal communications skills; and
- The ability to manage multiple assignments independently, with a high level of organization and attention to detail.

Source: Canadian Public Relations Society, "National Association of Federal Retirees" (2014), http://cprs.ca/careers/job_listing.aspx?jbno=4555. brian-masse-constituency-assistant-casework-permanent-part-time-30-hoursweek.

their organization in the past 18 months. These followers are most effective when they are held together by a common set of beliefs and goals, thus requiring interest group leaders (much like party leaders) to define the organization's core values and objectives and to nurture the relationships among followers and between the membership and the leadership. This has become an increasingly challenging task in an era of declining social capital, when membership in community organizations and interest groups has become less common and when the benefits derived from joining such groups are less obvious. Last century, joining membership-based organizations like Rotary, Kinettes, or Lions clubs or being an active participant in a union or professional organization meant deriving some form of solidary benefit from merely taking part. In today's era of social media and virtual communities, the incentive for this form of communal experience is diminishing. In this sense, there is an important distinction between those interest groups made up largely of so-called "chequebook" members (people who do little more than donate money to the cause) and those with a more active and cohesive membership. It is worth noting that measuring this cohesiveness requires more than simply counting an organization's number of Twitter followers or Facebook likes. Lastly, interest groups require what have been called *tangible* and *intangible* resources.[2] The former involve money, access to funds, office space, staff, a functional and effective Web presence, and other types of hard assets. Intangible resources are of a softer variety and include experience and expertise in fields like public administration and

The Nova Scotia Teachers Union pulled this ad in October 2013 after Elections Nova Scotia deemed it to be political advertising. In order to comply with the province's Election Act, the union was required to register as a third party or else suspend its political advertising. What about this ad makes it political? Why would a union need to engage in political advertising?

marketing; a strong brand, track record, and reputation; and a broad network enhanced by deep relationships with key decision-makers. Tangible and intangible resources are mutually reinforcing, in that it takes hard assets to acquire soft ones, and soft assets—when used effectively—can help to generate hard ones.

An interest group's prospects for success also rely on a host of external factors beyond its direct control. The party in power can often determine the group's access to policymakers and even funding, with interest groups enjoying more influence when a like-minded government is in office. Women's groups, for instance, have been more influential at the federal level when the Liberal Party has been in power; PC and Conservative governments have reduced funding to these groups and allowed them more limited access to the decision-making process. The salience and popularity of the group's cause is also an obvious but significant factor, as is the presence of supportive allies or unsupportive opponents. Unions, on one hand, and taxpayers' organizations, on the other, are excellent examples of how interest groups on each side of the political spectrum often band together and oppose their political foes. Altogether, these external elements are why many interest groups spend so much of their efforts on supporting or defeating governments, raising public awareness and sympathy for their causes, and developing deeper networks with other organizations.

Taken together, these internal and external factors are all necessary keys to most interest groups' success. Taken separately, none of them is sufficient to prevent the organization's failure. It takes more than simply a solid website and social media campaign or a sizeable bank account and a supportive government to reach one's goals.

Interest Groups

Many interest groups are considered institutionalized, which is to say that they are so well organized that they have become entrenched within the state political system. Institutionalized interest groups are headed by political elites who have advanced the same core arguments for years. These groups play the Ottawa game by applying political pressure through standard tactics such as news conferences, lobbying, and coordinated letter-writing campaigns. They typically feature a well-defined organizational structure and a stable membership, so continuity is assured even if there is employee or member turnover, and their objectives tend to encompass a variety of connected issues and concerns. Examples of institutionalized interest groups include the Canadian Labour Congress, Equal Voice, Greenpeace Canada, and the Retail Council of Canada.

institutionalized interest groups Pressure groups that have become entrenched political organizations.

The success of an institutionalized interest group hinges on its inclusion of people who are very familiar with how government works and who the key players are. This group might include former government officials and high-ranking members of political parties. The institutionalized interest group focuses on the implications of specific legislation or financial decisions and negotiates concessions from government officials. The values and credibility of the organization are paramount, such that the group's leaders will prioritize winnable policy gains and accept defeat on unmovable issues.[3] Institutionalized interest groups are so entrenched in the political system that they are treated as credible opinion leaders even while pushing their own values. While they may have begun as outsiders, they have become part of Ottawa politics.

Institutionalized interest groups are in this way different from upstart interest groups that champion grassroots issues. Issue-oriented interest groups are outsiders who tend to lack internal cohesion and are often unorganized. They are the opposite of institutionalized in that they tend to have few resources, experience personnel turnover, and often have little insider experience in the processes of government or political elites. They have a difficult time accomplishing their objectives, which tend to be just one or two issues of concern, limiting the breadth of their appeal. Some such organizations have a short lifespan, such as Canadians Rising Up for Democracy, the Elizabeth Will Group, and the group Immigration Practitioners and Academics for a Just Immigration Policy, all of which were registered third parties in the 2011 election, but none of which were registered for the 2015 election campaign. Others linger for years, such as the Save Our Prison Farms organization. The ability to communicate information via the Web and social media has been a boon to these groups. In Canadian politics today, they can organize, raise funds, and apply public pressure in ways that were previously unimaginable.

> **issue-oriented interest groups** Loosely-organized political organizations that focus on a core issue.

The types of political issues that institutionalized and issue-oriented interest groups champion are diverse. There is no definitive way to classify groups on the basis of their political concerns. One attempt has identified a dozen typologies, including single-issue, trade association, labour union, intergovernmental, professional association, civil rights, religious, agricultural, public interest, corporation, think tank, and charity.[4] Another has clustered the concerns of local interest groups into the categories of business, labour–agricultural, moral–ethical, social service, noneconomic interests, and environmental and consumer.[5] For simplicity's sake we can distinguish between the groups that act to advance the interests of their membership and the groups that are motivated to advance the broader public interest.[6] *Self-interested groups* include organizations representing businesses and labour unions such as the Canadian Bankers Association, the Canadian Labour Congress, and Canadian Manufacturers & Exporters. These operations tend to represent a large membership, are reasonably well financed, and are often motivated by the pursuit of economic benefits. For instance, the role of the Canadian Pharmacists Association, according to its website, is to emphasize "innovation, advocacy, education, information and collaboration" in the pharmacy field and to "influence decision makers on a wide range of issues" of concern to pharmacists.[7]

The corporations and trade associations that finance these private interests tend to give institutionalized interests a financial and organizational advantage over *public interest groups*. Public interest groups promote policies that they feel will benefit broader society or a political minority group. Examples of public interest groups include the Canadian Jewish Congress, the Council of Canadians with Disabilities, and the National Action Committee on the Status of Women. Some have considered National Aboriginal Organizations (NAOs) to be public interest groups. Although many NAO leaders would eschew the label, as it suggests they are non-governmental actors (see Chapter 13), these organizations do engage in activities similar to those of advocacy groups. For instance, the role of the Assembly of First Nations is to

> advocate on behalf of First Nations as directed by Chiefs-in-Assembly. This includes facilitation and coordination of national and regional discussions and dialogue, advocacy efforts and campaigns, legal and policy analysis,

↻ National Aboriginal Organizations are discussed beginning on page 527 of Chapter 13, on diversity and representation.

communicating with governments, including facilitating relationship building between First Nations and the Crown as well as public and private sectors and general public.[8]

Such equality-seeking groups emphasize improved circumstances for particular individuals; by comparison, quality-of-life groups focus on change for the betterment of Canada as a whole. Examples include Greenpeace and Amnesty International, which have Canadian chapters that promote environmental and social justice throughout the world. In this vein, charities and post-secondary institutions might be considered public interest groups as well, and it may surprise some citizens to learn that such organizations engage in the lobbying of public officials.

Some interest groups receive financial grants and contributions from the federal government to sustain their activities. This recognizes that some public interest groups play an important role in a pluralist society but lack the financial certainty of the larger groups with whom they compete. Take, for example, the Council of Canadians with Disabilities. As a constituency, persons with disabilities have acute needs; generally do not tend to seek election or become parliamentarians; are dispersed across the country; tend to belong to a lower socioeconomic cohort; and may experience more difficulty with engaging in political activism than other groups. In recognition of these unique circumstances, the federal government has deemed that it is in the public interest to provide financial support to the Council and, at times, to

National Firearms Association

Categorizing interest groups may be more difficult than it appears. Consider this information piece from Canada's National Firearms Association. How would you characterize the NFA as a special interest group: institutionalized or issue-oriented? Self-interested or public interest?

its provincial member groups. This has included core operational funding, grants for research projects, and monies for special initiatives, among other things.[9]

In this respect, governments and government agencies may have a significant impact on an interest group's access to funds. Gaining and retaining designation as a registered charity, for example, can have a real impact on an organization's ability to raise funds, as Dying with Dignity found when the Canada Revenue Agency revoked its status in 2015. Reductions in the amount, and restrictions on the use, of government grant monies can also affect an interest group's bottom line. The Conservative government under Prime Minister Harper placed such limits on the ability of Status of Women Canada to fund advocacy and lobbying activities of women's groups, for instance, unspoken reasons for which included the groups' close working relationship with opposition parties and the Conservative party's aversion to state sponsorship of special interests.

Think Tanks

Whereas interest groups generate funding through donations and membership drives, think tanks obtain income by selling consulting services, receiving financial gifts, and/or receiving grants through their affiliation with government or a university. Think tanks conduct research on public policy issues in order to stimulate public discussion about their ideas and proposed solutions. They seek to advance an agenda that is based on an analysis of objective information such as economic data, census data, or labour force data. As advocacy organizations, they seek media coverage of their research-based policy proposals, and their employees offer expert commentary in a manner that is projected as objective and non-partisan, even though their ideological slants are normally well known. Take, for example, the Manning Centre for Building Democracy, whose mantra is "building Canada's conservative movement," or the left-wing Broadbent Institute, whose slogan is "We fuel progress."

Canadian think tanks focusing on economic policy and whose board members are foremost from the private sector include the Atlantic Institute for Market Studies, the C.D. Howe Institute, and the Fraser Institute. Conversely, think tanks that study social policy and promote social justice include the Canadian Centre for Policy Alternatives, the Council of Canadians, the David Suzuki Foundation, the Pembina Institute, and the Broadbent Institute. Those organizations' board members are more likely to be affiliated with labour unions, community activism, and the public sector. Other think tanks, such as the Canada West Foundation, the Frontier Centre, and the Mowat Centre, promote regionalist perspectives, attracting people from both the right and left of the political spectrum. So, too, do think tanks devoted to public policy, in general, like the Institute for Intergovernmental Relations and the Institute for Research on Public Policy. There are a plethora of other research institutes embedded in universities, as well, typically associated with faculty in political science and economics.

In many ways, think tanks in Canada fulfill a role played by political parties in European democracies, where public policy research and development is contained within the formal party apparatus. In fact, sometimes Canadian think tanks are commissioned (or cajoled) to perform policy studies on behalf of governments.

This type of policy work is illustrated by the Conference Board of Canada, which bills itself as "the foremost independent, evidence-based, not-for-profit applied

think tank An organization that performs research as a means of public advocacy.

THEY SAID IT

Think Tanks Promoting Preferred Policy Options

NEW STUDY: Canada–U.S. relations remain marked by trade barriers, disputes.

—The Fraser Institute (@FraserInstitute)

REFORM OR ABOLISH THE SENATE? Check out the Manning Foundation's new site and vote for YOUR favourite option!

—Manning Centre (@manningcentre)

Canada's top CEOs make 171 times more than average worker & 194 times more than average woman worker.

—The Canadian Centre for Policy Alternatives (@ccpa)

Tell the feds to listen to the people and reject the #Enbridge #NorthernGateway pipeline.

—The Council of Canadians (@CouncilofCDNs)

research organization in Canada."[10] The organization disseminates evidence-based research about economic trends, organizational performance, and public policy issues, all in support of an agenda to achieve a more competitive economy for Canada. It employs experts in "conducting, publishing, and disseminating research; forecasting and economic analysis; helping people network; running conferences; developing individual leadership skills; and building organizational capacity." The Conference Board's activities are similar to those of an interest group, including issuing news releases, responding to media requests, coordinating a member database, hosting conferences, publishing reports, holding webinars, and testifying to legislative committees. Yet it is often commissioned by governments to produce independent reports (such as the Council of the Federation's studies into the vertical fiscal imbalance). Like any interest group or think tank, it seeks to inform decision-makers and to influence public policy. For example, recommendations presented in the Conference Board's 2013 report *The Future of the Postal Service in Canada* contributed to Canada Post's initial decision to phase out door-to-door mail delivery in urban areas and to nearly double the price of postage stamps. Aside from the emphasis on research, a key difference between many think tanks and interest groups is the remark on the Conference Board's website that they "do not lobby for specific interests." This requires some explanation of the work of lobbyists.

Lobbyists

lobbying Personal communication with public office-holders initiated by advocacy groups as part of an effort to influence decisions.

Some strategies of political activism, such as letter-writing campaigns and protests, go only so far in pressuring public officials to take action; behind-the-scenes support is needed. Consequently, a core activity carried out by most institutionalized interest groups is the lobbying of political elites. Lobbying involves communicating directly with public office-holders, normally through in-person meetings, in order to advance policy objectives. This can include conversations about proposed or existing legislation, regulations, policies and programs, or efforts to secure grants and other financial benefits. The term originated from the practice of waiting in the lobby of the legislature to intercept legislators and political staff in order to curry favours.

Nowadays lobbying is a profession: a lobbyist is a professional who is paid to provide strategic advice to clients and to provide access to decision-makers in government. Lobbyists draw upon their personal connections with the political elite to act as intermediaries and advance their clients' policy objectives. They tend to be industry experts, political party insiders, and/or former senior political or government staffers.

Lobbyists may be employed exclusively by a corporation, they may work for an interest group, or they may be independent hired guns whose consulting services are available for a fee. The latter tend to be the employees of government relations and public affairs firms, such as Earnscliffe Strategy Group, Summa Strategies, Hill+Knowlton Strategies, and Crestview Strategy. Some have also suggested that governments lobby each other, although practitioners of intergovernmental relations would view their profession otherwise. Several provincial, territorial, and Aboriginal governments have established offices in Ottawa to build closer relationships with key federal decision-makers. This often involves lobbying-like behaviour.

Lobbying is a legitimate activity with a poor public image. It is an essential means of ensuring that political elites are aware of the range of implications of public policy in a pluralistic society. However, by nature it is clandestine, and the absence of transparency gives pause about whether its practice enhances or harms democratic discourse. Lobbying raises concerns that undue influence is for sale, and that those who stand to benefit from changed public policy engage in surreptitious behaviour. At its best, lobbying ensures that politicians and bureaucrats make informed decisions

> **lobbyist** A person or firm hired to communicate directly with public office-holders in order to advance a client's public policy agenda.

Occupy Austin

The Occupy movement was among the most successful social movements in recent memory in terms of raising public consciousness—albeit around a loosely defined set of public policy concerns. Initiated by the Canadian anti-consumerist group Adbusters and peaking in 2011–12, the movement was purposefully nebulous, lacking any institutional structure or leadership because most of its adherents were railing against the entire notion of organized interests. One of the lasting impacts of Occupy remains the salience of the term "the 99%," which has come to symbolize the power disparity and income inequality between the world's richest 1 per cent and the rest of the population. Why do you think Occupy was more successful than many established political parties and interest groups when it came to raising the profile of income inequality?

that take into account stakeholder perspectives; at worst, high-stakes politicking can lead to unethical activities such as bribery or graft, with lobbyists offering financial kickbacks to public officials in return for government contracts, and elected officials peddling their influence.

The Government Relations Institute of Canada, an interest group for government relations and public affairs professionals, has a code of professional conduct. At all times, members of the Institute are expected to comply with laws regarding lobbying, campaign finance, political activities, and business–government relations. In addition, they must not knowingly circulate falsehoods or misleading information, and must avoid conflicts of interest and other forms of professional impropriety.[11] Likewise, the federal Commissioner of Lobbying of Canada, who is an agent of Parliament, administers a code of conduct that is based on concepts identified in the Lobbying Act. The core principles of that act, which have been carried over into some provinces' legislation, are to uphold the importance of access to public officials and the transparency of lobbying activities. To encourage transparency, information about which lobbyists are working for whom and which government bodies they are lobbying must be publicly disclosed (see Figure 12.1 and Figure 12.2). Moreover, the Accountability Act bans people who have held senior positions in the federal government or public office from lobbying for a period of five years after leaving their government post. In practice, this means that the media and critics can monitor the behaviour of governments and lobbyists, and that aspiring lobbyists with inside connections must wait at least one electoral cycle before they can leverage their contacts.

↺ The implications of the Accountability Act are considered on page 331 of Chapter 8, on public policy.

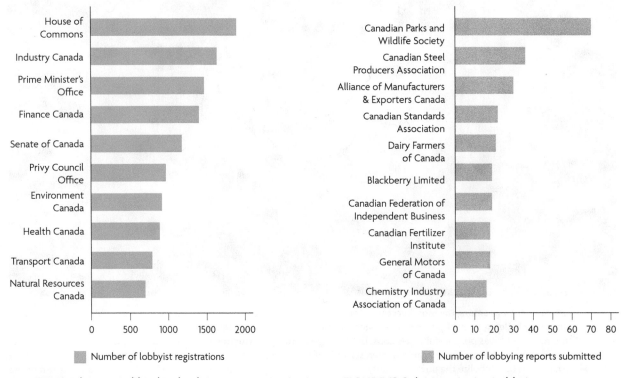

Number of lobbyist registrations

Number of lobbying reports submitted

FIGURE 12.1 | Most-Lobbied Federal Government Institutions   **FIGURE 12.2 | Most Active Lobbyists**

Note: Figures 12.1 and 12.2 based on 2013 data.

Social Movements

As any of the aforementioned pollsters would tell you, healthcare and the economy regularly resonate as the top public policy priorities to Canadians. Periodically, the perceived importance of these issues is displaced by major events, such as a terrorist attack, which stokes fears about public safety, or a series of unpredictable weather events, which raises concerns about climate change. Society's sudden interest in an issue can cause citizen groups to stand up and urge government action. When these groups call on the public, and not just governments, to rethink their values and adopt a new outlook on an issue, the phenomenon becomes a social movement.

A social movement is a shared mindset among people seeking to change the public's views about an issue, and to alter their behaviour. Whereas an interest group is a formal organization that uses political communication to pressure political elites, and a think tank uses research to prompt public debate about policy options, a social movement exerts broad social pressure for policy change. People who are at the forefront of a social movement are not necessarily members of a political party or interest group; rather, they are collectively an informal group of people who share a common concern, often on a topical issue. The concerns and goals of social activists—even of those within the same movement—may be wide-ranging, drawing on such varied ideologies as feminism, environmentalism, anti-capitalism, libertarianism, neo-conservatism, and Aboriginal rights, to name only a few. For this reason,

> **social movement** A collection of members of the general public who share a public policy concern and urge government action and changes to social values and behaviour.

> ↻ The history of voting rights in Canada is discussed in Chapter 10, on elections: see the section titled "Suffrage," on pages 388–91.

> ↻ Affirmative action policies are explained in the section "Toward Reducing Canada's Democratic Deficit," in Chapter 13, on diversity and representation.

The Canadian Press/Fred Chartrand

In 2015, the House of Commons unanimously passed a motion to remove the sales tax on feminine hygiene products. Similar motions raised in the federal and provincial legislatures had failed to carry, but the latest attempt, brought forward by NDP MP Irene Mathyssen, was buoyed by an online petition that gathered over 72,000 signatures in just five months. What combination of factors do you think contributed to the success of this particular initiative and its support by all political parties? In other words, why were activists successful in 2015 when similar efforts had failed previously?

it can be difficult for policymakers to immediately solve the policy problem at the heart of a social movement because the activists' concerns are so wide-ranging and lacking in specificity. Moreover, although the proponents may attract public sympathy, their demands may not be palatable to broader society. Consequently, successful

THEY SAID IT

The Idle No More Movement

Idle No More calls on all people to join in a peaceful revolution, to honour Indigenous sovereignty, and to protect the land and water.

INM has and will continue to help build sovereignty and resurgence of nationhood.

INM will continue to pressure government and industry to protect the environment.

INM will continue to build allies in order to reframe the nation-to-nation relationship; this will be done by including grassroots perspectives, issues, and concerns.

—Idle No More vision statement, 2014[12]

The Canadian Press/Geoff Robins

Compare the Idle No More vision statement with the description of the Assembly of First Nations presented on pages 475–6 earlier in the chapter. How do the two statements differ? In what ways do they reflect the differences between a social activist organization and a social movement?

social movements are those that contribute to a different way of thinking among political elites; over time, they can influence an array of policy decisions, such as the extension of voting rights to women and the practice of affirmative action within the public service.

Social movements are seen as an expression of the rejection of traditional politics and institutions.[13] They are a mechanism for frustrated citizens to express their political views and to participate in the political process in an unconventional manner. This gives rise to the idea that they are a form of "new politics" that is untarnished compared with the corruption and inequalities of "old politics" practised by the political establishment, comprising traditional political elites in major political parties, institutionalized interest groups and the mainstream media, and even academics. Their activism is motivated by a shared ideology and notions of democratic idealism rather than necessarily personal gain. While members of social movements likely recognize the importance of voting, they believe that change is more likely if society itself is transformed. As such, they are an important component of the political process, and complement the efforts of established political interests.

A well-known challenge for many interest groups and social movements is that people who do nothing to help can nevertheless benefit from the efforts of those working tirelessly to effect change. The conundrum of free riders who do not join in political activism campaigns and who benefit regardless is known as the collective action problem. In *The Logic of Collective Action: Public Goods and the Theory of*

collective action problem
The notion that people whose interests are promoted by a group will benefit from its efforts whether or not they actively participate.

Patrick LaMontagne

Social media has become an effective tool for drawing attention to social causes ranging from the return of kidnapped African schoolchildren to the protection of animal rights. Critics of "slacktivism" argue that retweeting hashtags, signing online petitions, and sharing or liking videos are ego-driven gestures that appeal to our sense of altruism but diminish rates of more productive engagement, like attending a political rally, donating to a food bank, or volunteering at a homeless shelter. Defenders argue that one young person with a smartphone can do more to raise civic engagement than a thousand people at a protest. What do you think: does social media promote or diminish political activism?

Groups (1965), American economist Mancur Olson theorized that people gain the most when a small group to which they belong achieves a favourable policy outcome; in larger groups, which have higher expenses and broader objectives, there is a more diffuse commitment to the movement's core principles. To address this quandary, and to encourage people to participate in a large group or movement, it is essential that formal membership offer special incentives. This is why interest groups promote members-only rates on consumer products (e.g. insurance, groceries, travel) and exclusive subscriptions to industry journals, magazines, or newsletters.

In the case of social movements, the notion of offering special incentives is impractical, given that there is normally no formal organization that coordinates membership benefits. However, visible participation in a social movement can offer participants an improved social status. For instance, people who display a sticker or badge with a political message, coffee drinkers who attach their reusable cups to the outside of their backpacks, men who grow moustaches as part of the "Movember" fundraiser for prostate cancer, and people who "like" a Facebook page devoted to a particular movement may be incentivized by the public attention they receive from communicating a cause. The latter has given way to accusations of slacktivism, with critics noting that people who join movements through social media seldom engage directly or meaningfully in promoting the change it advocates.

slacktivism Actions taken by individuals to appear part of a social movement, but which have no direct impact on the fulfilment of its objectives.

Activism: Then and Now

The Manitoba Schools Question

Political elites are confronted with making difficult decisions that inevitably favour some interests and ideologies over others. The pressure that the political executive face can be so significant that they may avoid addressing the issue in public, let alone attempt to resolve the debate. The decision not to make a decision on a pressing cause is criticized, and upsets those pushing for favourable treatment, but when a delay happens, it is because the cabinet has estimated that the alternatives are worse.

The intensity of competing political interests is well illustrated by the Manitoba schools question, which remains among Canada's most significant policy crises. It is an example of how political pressure is applied on politicians between elections. It shows how a localized policy dispute can become a national issue that can fracture a political party and divide the country.

Manitoba schools question A formative dispute over the funding of education that exposed religious, language, and intergovernmental tensions in Canada.

At the crux of the Manitoba schools dispute was section 93 of the British North America Act, 1867. Section 93 confers authority on provinces to make laws concerning education. However, it also stipulates that the rights of denominational schools must be upheld, and that Protestant or Roman Catholic minorities can appeal to the federal cabinet if they feel that their rights have been affected by the province.

In 1870, the federal government's Manitoba Act created the province of Manitoba and included a clause to protect existing religious schooling. But as more and more English-speaking Protestants settled in Manitoba, the growing English-speaking majority applied pressure on the provincial government to cease funding French schools for Roman Catholics. Bowing to public pressure, the Manitoba legislature passed the Public Schools Act (1890), ending the government's funding of religious schools and leaving French-language Catholic schools to raise funds in order to continue to operate. Rather than interfere, Prime Minister John A. Macdonald was satisfied to let the matter wind its way through the courts. This upset his party's Quebec MPs, who felt the protections outlined in section 93 were an important part of Quebec's constitutional bargain.

When Macdonald died while holding office in 1891, the governor general appointed Senator John Abbott to be prime minister. Prime Minister Abbott was in office when Britain's top court, the Judicial Committee of the Privy Council (JCPC), ruled that the Public Schools Act was legal. Consequently, Manitoba's French Catholic minorities proceeded to appeal to the federal cabinet to have the provincial law overturned. But Abbott resigned, and justice minister John Thompson was appointed prime minister. Thompson likewise stalled for time by asking the courts to review the matter to verify that cabinet did indeed need to make a decision. Thompson died in office, too, leading the governor general to appoint Senator Mackenzie Bowell as prime minister. When the JCPC ruled in 1895 that the federal cabinet did indeed have the duty to intervene, Bowell proposed that Manitoba should create and fund a Catholic school board. Internal party rancour led four ministers (three of them francophone) to resign in a bid to pressure Bowell to implement federal remedial legislation that would repeal the provincial government's law. Three of these ministers returned, but then seven ministers—all Protestants—resigned in an effort to get Bowell to resign. The government was in crisis.

The governor general resolved the situation by appointing member of Parliament Charles Tupper prime minister and reappointing six of the ministers. Tupper prepared remedial legislation to repeal the province's Public Schools Act; however, the Conservatives had been in power for nearly five years, the constitutional limit. The Liberal party, led by Wilfrid Laurier, prolonged debate in the House of Commons until an election had to be called, and the remedial bill died on the order paper. During the 1896 election campaign, Laurier did not commit to a proposed solution, promising only "sunny ways and sunny days" to negotiate an amicable way forward. When Laurier assumed office as prime minister, he brokered a compromise that would require the province to fund French Catholic education, but only if there were a minimum of 10 students per funded school.

The debate over religious education funding has periodically reappeared and continues to be a divisive issue. In 1905 it was a source of heated debate when Alberta and Saskatchewan were created. In the 1990s, it was the subject of two contentious provincial referendums in Newfoundland, which concluded with voters supporting the government's creation of a single school system instead of funding religious-only school systems. During the 2007 provincial election campaign in Ontario, which has a publicly funded Catholic school system, a central issue was a proposal by the Tories to extend public funding to Jewish and Muslim schools. Electors rejected the idea by re-electing a Liberal government. In each of these cases, powerful interest group organizations exerted pressure on political parties in a bid to secure a favourable government decision.

The case of the Manitoba schools question is a historic example illustrating that political executives are often called upon to make difficult decisions that have the potential to divide Canadians, and even their own caucuses. It demonstrates that pressure is applied by organized interests on political parties, in particular the cabinet, to act on the demands made by those groups. Sometimes policy disputes can attract significant media attention and become so controversial that competing interests cannot be satisfied. This is especially true when deep and cross-cutting cleavages are involved, as was the case in this instance concerning the English Protestant / French Catholic divide. In such circumstances, politicians may avoid making a decision by sending the matter to a committee, commissioning a study, or even referring

INSIDE CANADIAN POLITICS
When Does Political Activism Go Too Far?

A key difference between political parties and political activists is that political parties are institutions, and as such, they attract more attention. Conversely, advocacy groups face a constant dilemma to figure out ways to get their demands on the public agenda. To spur political action, they need to generate public awareness of an issue and build buy-in for how government policy should be changed. They need to mobilize the public and media to generate pressure on politicians and on ministers. Otherwise, the political executive is likely to pursue a different agenda, and may make decisions that create new concerns for special interests.

Without news coverage, it is considerably more difficult to get on the public agenda and effect change. Many advocacy groups employ a standard mix of public relations activities, such as communicating via social media, issuing media advisories, publicizing a website, and perhaps organizing a protest. However, unless they initiate something unusual, their efforts are unlikely to be deemed newsworthy. Consequently, advocacy groups often resort to publicity stunts to attract media attention. But if publicity stunts are commonplace, they are no longer newsworthy. As a result, some groups pursue radical tactics. At times these are unsanctioned and committed by fanatical fringes of the organization or movement.

Consider the following examples of political activism. Some were organized by opposition political parties and/or by interest groups; others were an outcome of global social movements; still others were spontaneous acts by individuals. Not all of these actions were necessarily sanctioned by the leaders of an interest group or movement. In your opinion, which ones go too far?

- At the national archives in Ottawa in 1983, a man asked to see a copy of the Canadian constitution. He then poured red paint over it. He wanted to protest the Canadian government's granting the US permission to test cruise missiles over Canadian airspace.
- In 2015, student groups in Quebec voted to boycott post-secondary classes to protest planned spending cuts by the provincial government. When some students attended class at l'Université du Québec à Montréal (UQAM), masked intruders turned off the lights in classrooms, shut off computers, and chastised the students for not respecting the boycott.[4]
- Periodically, farmers draw attention to their demand for government aid by driving their slow-moving tractors in convoy along highways and city streets on their way to Ottawa.
- The town of Oka, Quebec, sought to expand a golf course onto land that was traditionally used by Mohawk people. Previously the courts had rejected the Kanesatake Mohawks' claim over the land. In response to the town's plans, some Mohawks erected a barricade to prevent access to the area. The arrival on the scene of the Sûreté du Québec sparked an exchange of gunfire, and a police officer was killed. The Mohawks crushed police cars, which became part of the barricade. An end to the Oka Crisis was negotiated after a

the matter to the courts. Eventually, the matter may become an issue to which even an election may not bring finality, as the persistence of linguistic tensions in Manitoba demonstrate. But what it does not show is that interest groups are far more numerous and organized today. Moreover, their efforts and tactics are sometimes clandestine and are not always in the public interest.

standoff that captured Canadians' attention during the summer of 1990. The town of Oka backed off its land development plans, and Canadian governments began examining their relations with Aboriginal people. Nobody was charged in the death of SQ corporal Marcel Lemay.

- Amidst the 2010 G8/G20 Toronto summit meetings, peaceful anti-capitalism protests turned violent when some people employed so-called "black bloc" tactics. Their identity concealed with black clothing, they vandalized buildings and burned a police car, as the riot police sought to restore order.

- During the Occupy movement that began in New York's Zuccotti Park in 2011 before spreading to other North American cities, people set up tents to camp out in public places, and refused to leave when police and municipal officials attempted to disband the protesters. Advocates argued that this was peaceful protest to raise awareness of economic disparities between the world's richest and poorest citizens. Critics warned of health and safety issues associated with allowing people to camp for such an extended period in public spaces.

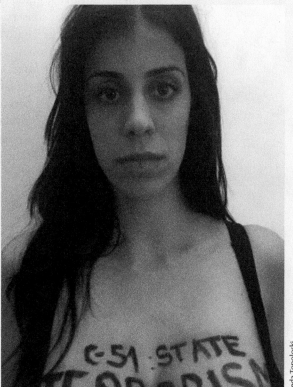

Neda Topaloski

In 2015, Neda Topaloski's topless protest against the federal government's anti-terrorism legislation in the public gallery of the House of Commons earned her an RCMP ticket for public indecency and a one-year ban from the Parliament Hill precinct. A member of Femen—a European movement that uses nudity to protest various causes—Topaloski defended this form of protest in an interview with *Maclean's* in which she said: "Women's bodies are used all the time to sell a million things. . . . [W]e decided to use that, but speak for ourselves and take back our bodies and identities and make them subjects, not objects."[5]

VOX POP

What role do avant-garde activists like Femen play in Canadian democracy today? Where is the line between productive public advocacy and sensationalism?

Social Media Politics in Alberta

Political scientists are challenged when it comes to measuring the impact of social media campaigns on politics. Unpacking how voters, politicians, bureaucrats, and others make political decisions is immensely difficult. This said, there have been a number of recent high-profile incidents in Alberta that suggest the power of Facebook, Twitter, and YouTube is growing—and with it, the influence of grassroots social movements.

Consider first the 2012 Alberta provincial election, a heated two-way race between the governing Progressive Conservatives (PCs) and the upstart Wildrose Party. Wildrose entered the campaign with a sizeable lead in public opinion polls, but that advantage gradually shrank owing to several high-profile incidents involving the party's social conservative wing. Seizing on what many viewed as homophobic and racist remarks from Wildrose candidates, a group of young Albertans produced a two-and-a-half minute YouTube video entitled "I Never Thought I'd Vote PC." In it, the group of left-leaning twenty-somethings listed the many reasons they would vote strategically for the Progressive Conservatives to prevent the Wildrose Party from assuming control of government. The video went viral, and while proof of strategic voting, let alone the impact of the video itself, is far from conclusive, many observers credit it for helping to influence the many Albertans who had not yet decided whether or how to vote. The PCs ended up winning the election, with surveys suggesting that a high proportion of progressive voters supported the governing party. According to the video's creator, Aviva Zimmerman:

> We are a group of young Albertans (ages 22 to 27) who are concerned of what our province will look like under a Wildrose government.
>
> We got this project together in 48 hours, so we were not prepared for the media storm this created. We were hoping to create a video that would speak to our peers—young and liberal Albertans who were not going to vote because they could not stomach the thought of voting PC.
>
> We did not mean to offend anyone. This was a tongue-in-cheek satire. . . . We must stress, we are not affiliated with any party—not funded by or organized by—any party. We are simply young people who have a strong opinion.[6]

Two years later, left-leaning Albertans made a similar use of Twitter to influence the government's policy on gay–straight alliances (GSAs). Rejecting a Liberal backbencher's bill that would have required any public or private school to support students seeking to establish a GSA, the government introduced its own bill attempting to balance the rights of the students with the religious freedoms of parents and school boards. The left-leaning reaction on Facebook and Twitter—using the hashtags #ableg and #Bill10—was so swift and one-sided that it prompted the government to retract its bill within days and ultimately reintroduce and pass legislation that mirrored the Liberals' original bill. Thus, a combination of partisan, interest group, academic, student, and other grassroots pressure on social media resulted in a sudden and major shift in government policy.

What is perhaps most remarkable about these incidents is that they both occurred in what most experts label as Canada's most conservative province. This demonstrates the potential for grassroots social movements—with or without the support of established parties and interest groups—to influence the traditional political process.

Concluding Thoughts

The common objective of interest groups and social movements is to bring about change. They place different emphasis on the primary targets of that change, however. While most interest groups ultimately intend to pressure government decision-makers, social movements tend to focus on members of society as a whole. Consequently, their tactics differ, because one is focused on getting the attention of political elites while the other is concerned with building awareness among the wider population. Inevitably, the leaders of Canada's most prominent interest groups are themselves part of the establishment and political elite, which is in sharp contrast with the grassroots appeal of a social movement.

Political activism is at the intersection between having a government that is accountable to the people and a government that can carry out its business without fear of public repercussions. Increasing opportunities to get involved in politics are, paradoxically, occurring at the same time that more people appear to be tuning out. Nevertheless, the control of political elites is gradually declining, as ordinary Canadians are able to generate and disseminate political information as never before. In the past, voters were largely passive participants who were fed whatever policies and issues political actors and media elites offered on the menu. Now, anyone with a smartphone can blog their thoughts, tweet their observations, or create a video that might go viral. The nature of Web 2.0 is evolving so rapidly with advancements in computing hardware, software, and bandwidth that political communicators are constantly trying to get out in front of the newest trend.

For More Information

Want to learn about some of the pressure tactics used by interest groups and social movements? Consider Karin Braunsberger and Brian Buckler's 2009 analysis of the boycott of Canadian seafood that has been used to pressure the federal government to ban the seal hunt: "Consumers on a Mission to Force a Change in Public Policy: A Qualitative Study of the Ongoing Canadian Seafood Boycott," *Business and Society Review* 114: pp. 457–89.

Why do governments and political parties focus on the policy needs of particular target populations rather than society as a whole? Explore in Anne Schneider and Helen Ingram's "Social Construction of Target Populations: Implications for Politics and Policy," *American Political Science Review* 87 (1993): pp. 334–47.

How does the government engage the public? Find out some ways that government could become more citizen-oriented in Katherine A. Graham and Susan D. Phillips's 1997 study "Citizen Engagement: Beyond the Customer Revolution" (*Canadian Public Administration* 40: pp. 255–73); see also Keith Culver and Paul Howe's "Calling All Citizens: The Challenges of Public Consultation" (*Canadian Public Administration* 47 (2004): pp. 52–75).

What do disengaged Canadians have to say about politics? Samara is an interest group that seeks to improve the quality of democracy in Canada, in part by conducting research. One of their reports discusses the political powerlessness felt by ordinary Canadians. For more, see the following, by Heather Bastedo and colleagues: "The Real Outsiders: Politically Disengaged Views on Politics and Democracy" (2011), available at www.samaracanada.com.

Deeper Inside Canadian Politics

1. Interest groups often have limited resources and options when it comes to strategy. Public persuasion, litigation, and lobbying each carry with them their own risks, benefits, and costs. Imagine you are advising one of the following groups. Which strategy would you offer as your recommendation, and why?

    a) A pro-life group seeing to re-criminalize abortion.

    b) A neighbourhood association seeking to block the building of a new stadium in your community.

    c) A trade union opposed to the expansion of the Agreement on Internal Trade.

2. The Idle No More and Occupy movements captured nationwide attention at around the same time. Yet neither has demonstrated the staying power or success of earlier social movements, like those surrounding the environment or women's rights. Why do you suppose this is?

UP FOR DEBATE

Should limits on election spending by interest groups be eliminated?

THE CLAIM: YES, THEY SHOULD!
Spending limits represent a constraint on free speech and are undemocratic.

Yes: Argument Summary

In a democratic society, freedom of speech must be sacrosanct in political debates. Those in power should not be permitted to control or limit the messages expressed by special interest groups during an election campaign; to do so is anti-democratic. Current limits on the amount of advertising third parties can buy in the run-up to voting day are clearly a mechanism to muzzle groups that could otherwise help determine the outcome of the election. Should the country's political elites be the ones to decide what information or viewpoints Canadians are exposed to? If Canadians do not like the ideas they hear, they will choose to ignore such communication, and may even take action against the source. As the US Supreme Court has reasoned, a constitutional freedom does not truly exist if limits are then placed on that freedom. Deep-pocketed political interests should be allowed to spend money on political communication as they see fit.

Yes: Top 5 Considerations

1. Having access to money is essential for communicating with citizens. Therefore, limiting third-party election spending is akin to limiting political communication. For democracy to function, it is imperative that the political elites who are in power do not limit the ability of others to hold them accountable, which includes the ability to provide information to Canadians during an election campaign.

2. In Canadian federal politics as well as in several provinces, corporations and labour unions are not allowed to donate money to political parties or candidates. That they are also limited in their election spending is excessive.

3. In the United States, the Supreme Court ruled in 2010 that interest group spending could not be restricted, because this would violate the First Amendment's constitutional provision that "Congress shall make no law...abridging the freedom of speech". In Canada, the Charter of Rights and Freedoms stipulates that Canadians must have "freedom of thought, belief, opinion and expression" (Section 2b).

4. The Supreme Court of Canada ruled that third-party election spending limits are in the public interest, but it has also ruled that legislation restricting the participation of small political parties is unconstitutional. This demonstrates an ideological slant that supports free speech for small voices but that denies free speech for other political voices regardless of size and how much popular support they enjoy.

5. There is nothing to prevent wealthy organized interests from circumventing regulations by funding—instead of a single interest group—multiple interest groups united in a common policy objective. The challenges involved in closing these loopholes make attempts at regulation fruitless.

Yes: Other Considerations

- Restricting spending by third-party election participants does a disservice to democracy if that money would have been used to provide positive information and add to constructive debate.

- Because the constitution does not distinguish between the freedom of speech for individuals and the freedom of speech for interest groups or other political organizations, we should infer that the freedom applies to all equally. This freedom should apply irrespective of financial capacity.

THE COUNTERCLAIM: NO, THEY SHOULD NOT!

Spending limits on special interests are essential in a functioning pluralistic and democratic society.

No: Argument Summary

Interest groups perform an important function in Canadian politics. However, wealthy organizations have a greater capacity to pressure political elites and potentially influence government decisions. It is imperative that spending by interest groups be regulated, especially during election campaigns.

No: Top 5 Considerations

1. In 2004, the Supreme Court of Canada ruled that restricting spending by interest groups is justified under the Charter of Rights and Freedoms' provision that freedom of speech may be subject to "reasonable limits prescribed by law as can be demonstrably justified in a free and democratic society" (section 1). In this ruling, the court emphatically denied a petition brought by the National Citizens Coalition, a conservative interest group that was advocating the removal of such spending limits (and whose president at the time was Stephen Harper).

2. Allowing unlimited spending by special interests risks harming the very foundations of democracy by allowing people and groups with greater resources to have greater influence over the political process and government decision-making. Breaking up this concentration of funds creates the level playing field that is essential to a healthy democracy.[17]

3. History shows that concentrated money is often spent on the sort of negative advertising that turns people off the political process. Negative advertising campaigns sponsored by well-funded advocacy groups have played a formative role in a number of recent provincial election campaigns. This has been cited as a serious concern by chief election officers and has led to some provincial legislatures, attempt to introduce stricter regulations.

4. Spending limits and regulations reduce the possibility of corruption. Under the Canada Elections Act, after a general election the names of donors and a group's spending activities must be reported to Elections Canada. The information is then made available for public scrutiny.

5. There is little indication that interest groups are unable to operate in Canada within the existing regulations. Over 50 registered interest groups spent money during the 2015 federal election campaign. This ranged from deep-pocketed institutionalized groups like the Canadian Union of Public Employees to tiny protests like Voters Against Harper that communicated only through the Internet.[8]

No: Other Considerations

- Most industrialized democratic nations impose some sort of limits on the influence of big money in political campaigns. Equalizing the communication playing field for all political interests through regulation has been deemed to be the greater good over unregulated free speech.

- In the United States, the formidable influence of political action committees (PACs) and so-called "super PACs" that bundle money is a major public concern. Incidents have included the notorious Swift Boat Veterans for Truth group, which during the 2004 presidential campaign ran negative ads with claims that were so far-fetched that it spawned the term "swiftboating" to refer to political falsehoods.

- Without regulation, the perception of influence of big money in Canadian politics could reduce citizens' confidence in their democratic system of government.

Discussion Questions

- To what extent should the government limit how much interest groups can spend during election campaigns?
- Should interest groups be treated differently than political parties when it comes to restricting their election activities? Why or why not?
- Why do you think that supreme courts in Canada and the USA have arrived at different interpretations concerning the constitutional protection of free speech?
- Libertarians like the National Citizens Coalition have been especially critical of spending limits. Why do you think this is?
- In your opinion, should the government provide subsidies to poorly funded interest groups to help them communicate during election campaigns?

Where to Learn More about Interest Groups in Canada

Robert G. Boatright, *Interest Groups and Campaign Finance Reform in the United States and Canada* (Ann Arbor, MI: University of Michigan Press, 2011).

F.L. Morton and Avril Allen, "Feminists and the Courts: Measuring Success in Interest Group Litigation in Canada," *Canadian Journal of Political Science* 34 (2001): pp. 55–84.

Jacquetta Newman and A. Brian Tanguay, "Crashing the Party: The Politics of Interest Groups and Social Movements," in *Citizen Politics: Research and Theory in Canadian Political Behaviour*, ed. Joanna Everitt and Brenda O'Neill (Don Mills, ON: Oxford University Press, 2002).

Iain Ramsay, "Interest Groups and the Politics of Consumer Bankruptcy Reform in Canada," *University of Toronto Law Journal* 53 (2003): pp. 379–423.

Leslie F. Seidle, ed., *Interest Groups and Elections in Canada*, vol. 2 of the Research Studies of the Royal Commission on Electoral Reform and Party Financing (Toronto: Dundurn, 1991).

Hugh G. Thorburn, "Interest Groups and Policy Making in Canada," in *Party Politics in Canada*, ed. Hugh G. Thorburn and Alan Whitehorn (Scarborough, ON: Prentice-Hall, 2000).

13 DIVERSITY AND REPRESENTATION

Inside this Chapter

- How is diversity defined and represented in Canadian democracy?
- What steps are being taken to reduce Canada's democratic deficit?
- How (well) is diversity represented in the civil service, in civil society, and through the courts?
- What lessons do the experiences of Aboriginal people impart about representation in Canada?

Inside Diversity and Representation

Canada prides itself on being a pluralistic country, and Canadian citizens pride themselves on being among the world's most tolerant and most accepting of diversity. But what precisely does it mean to "accept diversity," and exactly how is this diversity *represented* in Canadian democracy? Outsiders may be surprised at the barriers that continue to prevent certain Canadians from engaging more meaningfully in Canadian democracy. And they may be offended by those who find little cause for alarm in the relatively low proportion of women, Aboriginal people, visible minorities, young people, and members of other traditionally marginalized groups in various parts of the political system. Exposing oneself to deeper debates about diversity and representation reveals some unsettling misconceptions. As you read through this chapter, keep in mind the following aspects of representation in Canada.

What the 2015 Election means for Diversity and Representation

Visit the *Inside Canadian Politics* flipboard to learn about the latest developments affecting diversity and representation in Canada.

Go to
http://flip.it/gblag.

 Canada's self-image as a "mosaic" can undermine efforts to advance multicultural equality. Canadians have embraced the metaphor that celebrates the country's diversity by depicting Canada as a mosaic of differently coloured tiles that together produce a rich and complex picture of multicultural harmony. In reality, the mosaic identity makes it easier to ignore some of the persistent ethnocultural inequalities in Canadian society, not to mention other forms of discrimination based on social identities other than race.

 Some of Canada's traditionally marginalized groups have overcome barriers to political representation. It is true that politics in Canada continues to be largely a white man's game. But there are success stories that buck this trend—of women, for instance, reaching positions of power, and of certain institutions that feature an overrepresentation of certain traditionally marginalized groups. The challenge is to learn and apply lessons from these areas of success, while not letting this anecdotal evidence cloud our view of the barriers that remain.

 Aboriginal Canadians are not much better "represented" in Canadian politics today than they were decades ago. New avenues of representation have opened up for Aboriginal people living in Canada, but self-government remains elusive, and paternalistic and colonial treatment remains the norm.

UP FOR DEBATE
Are affirmative action programs needed in the Canadian public service?

Keep this question in mind as you read through the chapter. Consult the end-of-chapter debate supplement for more material to help you engage in an informed discussion of the topic.

Overview

As much as regionalism (Chapter 4) is a defining characteristic, non-territorial diversity is a true touchstone of Canadian political culture. The concept is so engrained in the country's political psyche that it can be difficult to remember a time when near-universal respect for individual and group rights was contested in this country. This is not to say that every Canadian is accepting of her fellow citizens. Nor is it to say that all Canadians receive equal voice or treatment in Canadian politics. What it does suggest is that certain cultural norms have developed that frown upon most forms of intolerance and discrimination in Canadian society and democracy. Traced back to the writings of John Murray Gibbon, the salience of what he called the *Canadian Mosaic* (1938) is the product of generations of socialization. It has real political implications for the way citizens and politicians approach diversity, how Canadians are treated under the law, and how people view the representativeness of Canada's political institutions.

Representing the Canadian Mosaic

To appreciate the depth of diversity and multicultural values in Canada, try the following exercise. Assemble a small group of Canadians—family members, classmates, neighbours—and ask them to fill in the blanks of the following sentence aloud:

> When it comes to multiculturalism, Canada is a _____ while the United States is a _____.

mosaic A metaphor used to depict Canada's multicultural character, which features and encourages many distinct yet interdependent ethnocultural communities.

melting pot A metaphor used to depict the multicultural character of the United States, which subsumes ethnocultural communities under the broader "American" identity.

In unison, most will respond that Canada is a mosaic, a country whose ethnocultural makeup resembles a tapestry with patches of many different shapes, colours, and sizes. Canadians of all backgrounds are encouraged to promote their cultural heritage and traditions, and maintain ties to their ancestral homelands. By contrast, the US is typically viewed as a melting pot, a term most Americans embrace as a symbol of the country's willingness to subsume all cultures within a common "American" culture. Indeed, the motto inscribed on the US seal—*E pluribus unum*, or "Out of many, one"— is often taken as an expression of this ideal, though it was originally used to characterize the US as a federation of unified states. While these symbols—mosaic and melting pot—are most often associated with the two countries' treatment of racial, ethnic, religious, and linguistic diversity, a broader interpretation of diversity incorporates factors like gender, sexual orientation, Aboriginal status, age, and ability, among others.

↻ For more on what it means to say that Canada is a representative democracy, see page 41 in Chapter 2, on the constitution.

Like diversity, the concept of representation lies at the heart of any discussion of Canadian democracy. To say that Canada is a "representative democracy" carries with it the notion that Canadians are being *represented*, which is to say that someone else is granted the authority to speak on their behalf. But how, and by whom?

Hanna Pitkin's seminal research on the topic suggests there are four main types of representation, all of which bear on Canadian democracy. Citizens may feel a sense of symbolic representation when they feel a strong attachment to a particular political actor or entity. This symbolism means that they may identify with a specific person or institution to the extent that it appears to embody or personify their own place in politics and government. Whereas Pitkin reserves this type of connection for religious communities (e.g., Christians may feel symbolically represented by Jesus), it is not uncommon for some Canadians to feel a somewhat similar symbolic attachment to the Queen, or to inanimate objects like the flag or the healthcare system.

symbolic representation A political attachment to someone or something that is seen to epitomize what it means to be a part of one's political community.

descriptive representation A political attachment to someone viewed as sharing one's background or social profile.

More often than not, however, we tend to think of representative democracy in one of three other ways. Descriptive representation exists to the extent that Canadians feel that certain of their elected officials stand for people like them. Also

THEY SAID IT

Multiculturalism in Canada

When it comes to multiculturalism, Canada is unique. Its population is truly an ethnic, linguistic and cultural mosaic. Is Canada making the most of this diversity?

—Radio Canada International (@RCInet)

Tory senator's stunning argument: multiculturalism is a fraud committed for political gain.

—New Canadian Media (@NewCdnMedia)

Multiculturalism in its controversial glory: Is Canada a "country without a core culture"?

—National Post (@nationalpost)

Census 2011 release on languages: is multiculturalism stifling bilingualism?

—CTV Montreal (@CTVMontreal)

VOX POP

Multiculturalism is not just a social ideal but official government policy, protected in the Charter of Rights and Freedoms and enshrined in the Canadian Multiculturalism Act, 1988. There are critics of this approach, however. What are the benefits of enshrining multiculturalism in law? What are the downsides to making multiculturalism a national policy?

known as "mirror representation," this sentiment is common among citizens who value the presence of certain personal attributes among those they send to the legislature, be it based on gender, language, ethnicity, race, region, or other characteristics. Women who prefer to vote for female candidates, or men who refuse to do so, prize descriptive representation over other forms, for example.

Other Canadians may seek more formalistic representation from their elected officials. This broadminded way of thinking is most closely associated with the notion that members of the legislature serve as trustees of the public good. Once elected, politicians sit in the legislature as stewards of government, making collective decisions based on the needs of the entire population, rather than (simply) their own specific constituency. A voter who supports an MLA for her ability to craft provincial policy rather than her ability to deliver specific services or programs to the community has a formalistic view of representation.

This contrasts with substantive representation, whereby elected officials serve as delegates of their own constituents. People who feel substantively represented do not perceive that their interests are subsumed by those of the broader community. Rather, they sense that their politicians are working directly for *them*, and expect their locally elected representative to prioritize *their* interests over broader ones.

formalistic representation
A political attachment to someone by virtue of that person's status as a legitimately elected official.

substantive representation
A political attachment to someone in a position to defend or promote one's own interests.

In essence, the level of satisfaction that you feel about Canadian democracy depends upon how well you feel the system is performing in terms of representing you in any of these four ways. Some Canadians value descriptive representation over a more formalistic form, while others prize a more substantive connection with their representatives. Some citizens see these various forms of representation as being linked, so that descriptive representation is a prerequisite to substantive representation, for instance. Others look for different forms of representation from different types of representatives, viewing MPs differently than MLAs, for example.

Given these various definitions, it is not surprising that Canadians have long debated the quality of Canadian democracy when it comes to incorporating the country's various forms of diversity. Critics suggest that Canada suffers from a democratic deficit, meaning that its political institutions fail to live up to the democratic standards and expectations of its citizens.[1] John Porter was among the first academics

democratic deficit The gap between peoples' expectations for the performance of democratic institutions and the perceived performance of those institutions.

Jim Young

Canadians are represented not only by elected officials. Prime ministers often select senators on the basis of their ability to represent the country's diversity in Parliament. Consider the tenure of Anne Cools, the first black Canadian to serve in the Senate. An Ontarian, Cools was born in Barbados in 1943, studied at McGill University in Montreal, and was a social worker prior to her appointment, focusing particularly on curbing domestic and family violence. She ran unsuccessfully as a Liberal candidate in the 1979 and 1980 federal elections, contesting the Toronto-area district, Rosedale. In 1984, Pierre Trudeau appointed Cools to represent Ontario in the Senate, where she served as a Liberal for 20 years. She crossed the floor to the Conservatives in 2004, abandoning the Liberals over issues including same-sex marriage. Just three years later, she was removed from the Conservative caucus for voting against the 2007 federal budget. As of 2015, she is Canada's longest-serving senator and sits as an Independent. According to her own biography, she is married and a member of the Anglican Church of Canada. Which Canadians does Cools represent in the Senate, and under which forms of representation?

THEY SAID IT

Democratic Representation in Canada

Democracy demands that elected members be able to realize fully the role for which they have been chosen.

—Liberal prime minister Pierre Trudeau

I was criticized for being too much concerned with the average Canadians. I can't help that; I am one of them!

—Progressive Conservative prime minister John Diefenbaker

Government, in the last analysis, is organized opinion. Where there is little or no public opinion, there is likely to be bad government, which sooner or later becomes autocratic government.

—Liberal prime minister Mackenzie King

A successful politician must not only be able to read the mood of the public; he must have the skill to get the public on his side. The public is moved by mood more than logic, by instinct more than reason, and that is something that every politician must make use of or guard against.

—Liberal prime minister Jean Chrétien

to study the issue from a social scientific perspective. His 1965 book *The Vertical Mosaic: An Analysis of Social Class and Power in Canada* peeled back the curtain on the Canadian business and political elite. The study revealed that, far from being an egalitarian system in which all cultures had equal opportunity and equal representation in the Canadian power structure, the country's fabled cultural mosaic was structured hierarchically (i.e. vertically), so that certain cultures were dominant—namely, white, English-speaking men of British ancestry.

While the Quiet Revolution in Quebec, advancements in women's equality, the success of ameliorative programs, and reductions in discrimination have modified this picture somewhat, there remain real gaps in Canada's political institutions in terms of descriptive representation. Statistics tend to support the contention that women, visible minorities, and Aboriginal people are underrepresented in Canadian legislatures, based on their respective proportions of the population. It is important to note that, in Canada, the term *visible minority* does not include Aboriginal people, who make up a separate category. In twenty-first–century Canada, women typically make up only 25 per cent of members of Parliament, despite the fact they represent over half of the population. Visible-minority groups tend to make up 20 per cent of the population, yet occupy only 10 per cent of seats in the House of Commons, while Aboriginal people, who comprise 4 per cent of Canadians, typically occupy only 2 per cent of the seats. Similar patterns are found in municipal and provincial legislatures.[4] Statistics portray a similar situation for minority language communities as well. Francophones

visible minorities Non-Aboriginal Canadians who are non-white in colour or non-Caucasian in ethnicity.

Aboriginal people First Nations, Métis, or Inuit living in Canada.

in predominantly anglophone regions remain largely underrepresented, although the reverse is also true. Allophones—those whose first language is neither French nor English—are underrepresented throughout much of Canada. In recent years the

INSIDE CANADIAN POLITICS
What Proportion of Canadians Have Multiple Ethnic Identities?

Typical discussions about minority political participation in Canada continue to reveal two harsh realities: first, that minority groups tend to be underrepresented in the country's political institutions; and second, that there has been slow, uneven, protracted growth in the number of minority officials in Canadian legislatures. While accurate in a broad sense—in that the political opportunity structure continues to discriminate against members of many ethnic minority groups—these observations require refinement in light of recent trends in multiple identification.

More Canadians than ever are reporting multiple ethnic identities. According to 2011 census data, over 4 in 10 Canadians (42.1 per cent) report having ancestors from more than one ethnic group, up 6 percentage points since the 1996 level of 35.8 per cent. At the same time, attitudes toward the multicultural "mosaic" have grown more positive over time. As Warren Kalbach argues, "Assuming that most of those with multiple origins including either of or both French and English, or even Canadian, origins, have experienced some degree of assimilation by the bicultural dominant population, a significantly different picture of Canada's cultural mosaic emerges. *Rather than withering away, the British and French bicultural base can be seen to have been augmented through the intermarrying of members of minority ethnic origins with members of the two culturally dominant groups.*"[2] The fact that these demographic changes at the mass level have reached the elite level is to be expected.

Some analysts argue that the longer an ethnic group is established in Canada, the more likely its members are to assimilate into the majority society, or to engage in *exogamous marriage* (marrying outside of one's ethnic group). In this vein, Warren Kalbach may offer insight into why Canadians of eastern European backgrounds have achieved this status while Aboriginal groups, visible minorities, and others have not: "There is considerable evidence that the more different one's culture is perceived to be from that of either of Canada's founding [cultural] groups, the stronger one's ethnic identity and 'ethnic connectedness' to one's ethnic community in Canada, the longer it may take to become sufficiently integrated and assimilated to become a fully participating member of Canadian society on a basis of equality."[3] This argument holds that there is a hierarchy of acceptance in Canadian society, such that minority groups that are perceived to be most similar to the majority group tend to face fewer obstacles to societal participation.

To be certain, elements of the formal political opportunity structure—including the electoral system, the structure of political parties, campaign finance regimes, voter preferences, and others—continue to pose formidable obstacles to the representation of ethnic minorities in our legislatures. Yet there may be other factors preventing their political participation, including barriers to minority integration, in general.

VOX POP
How do people with multiple ethnic identities fit into the conventional view of representation and diversity in Canada? Are there any special measures that should, or could, be taken to ensure the representation of Canadians with multiple ethnic identities?

proportion of allophones as a share of the Canadian population has risen considerably, while the proportion of francophones has been declining (see Figure 13.1).

For these reasons, most political scientists recognize the predominance of white, anglophone, Protestant men, whose control over the Canadian state has remained virtually unassailable since the eighteenth century. "To talk of political participation of ethnic groups without coming to terms with this central fact of 'Anglo-dominance',"   argue Dahlie and Fernando, "is akin to narrating the Red Riding Hood story with no reference to the wolf!"[5]

Toward Reducing Canada's Democratic Deficit

Barriers to Political Participation

Not everyone is convinced that Canada suffers from a democratic deficit. Not all provinces and territories experience the same representational gaps, for example. Some, like Quebec, perform better when it comes to representing women; others, like Manitoba, perform better at representing visible minorities. And not all minority groups remain excluded from office; in fact, some have achieved substantial *overrepresentation* in city halls, provincial assemblies, and Parliament. This trend is especially evident in urban and western Canada, where there has been a gradual, but noticeable, increase in the number of politicians of non-British origin.[6] Nevertheless, representational gaps persist.

Meanwhile, proponents of formalistic representation argue that legislators and judges ought not to be selected on the basis of their demographic characteristics. Their merit—in particular, their ability to deliberate and make decisions on behalf of the entire polity—is of utmost importance regardless of their background. Others feel that affirmative action policies—designed to ensure Canada's political institutions

affirmative action
A policy or policies consisting of proactive measures to guarantee the descriptive representation of traditionally underrepresented groups.

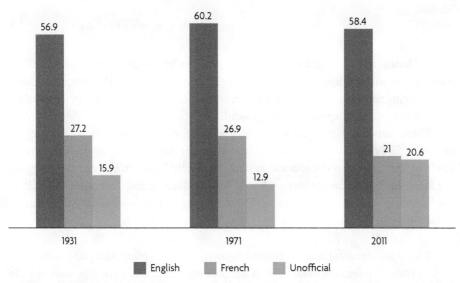

FIGURE 13.1 | Share of Official and Unofficial Languages in Canada (1931, 1971, 2011)

Sources: Historical Statistics of Canada, "Table A185-237 Mother tongues of the population, census years, 1931 to 1976," www5.statcan.gc.ca/access_acces/archive.action?l=eng&loc=A185_237-eng.csv; Census 2011, "Linguistic Characteristics of Canadians," www12.statcan.gc.ca/census-recensement/2011/as-sa/98-314-x/98-314-x2011001-eng.cfm.

Tony Caldwell/Ottawa Sun/SunMedia

How many people in this photo do you think would identify themselves as a "visible minority"? This is the sort of challenge confronting political scientists who study diversity, many of whom are forced to use photos and short biographies of politicians as a basis for assigning them visible-minority status. The term *visible minority* is used in federal legislation and in Statistics Canada's census, but is recognizing all "non-white" Canadians as a demographic group separate from "white" Canadians an outdated approach to measuring equality of representation? Considering the "white" category includes a host of ethnic minority groups, including Ukrainians and Scandinavians, where do you draw the line on what is visible? And who should determine whether someone fits in a particular cultural category: a researcher, a policy analyst, or the person being labelled?

are well balanced in terms of race, ethnicity, and gender—impose artificial quotas. To these critics, such policies favour descriptive representation over all other definitions, and discriminate against so-called whitestream Canadians—those of Caucasian, often British, English-speaking background.

whitestream Canadians
Caucasians who have formed the traditional mainstream of Canadian society; previously known as WASPs, or white Anglo-Saxon Protestants.

These important normative disputes aside, few observers would dispute the empirical fact that certain groups of Canadians participate at lower rates in various levels of the Canadian democratic system. In its 2013 report *In from the Margins*, the Standing Senate Committee on Social Affairs, Science and Technology identified the following groups as either vulnerable or facing significant barriers to inclusion in Canada:

- *Recent immigrants* typically are less fluent in Canada's official languages, encounter difficulty finding work in their fields of expertise, and earn less income than their non-immigrant peers (see Chapter 13 in the Senate committee report).
- *Visible minorities* are projected to make up 25 per cent of Canada's population by 2031. Lower rates of employment and income contribute to higher rates of

poverty among visible minority Canadians, and persistent racism and other forms of intolerance continue to cause discrimination against their full inclusion in Canadian society and their underrepresentation in various political institutions (including Parliament and the civil service).

- *Religious minorities*—those Canadians who identify as neither Protestant nor Catholic—have grown substantially over the past two decades. Hindus, Buddhists, and Sikhs, in particular, have been the targets of discrimination. Religious intolerance was identified as the cause of nearly 400 reported hate crimes in 2010 alone.
- *Sexual minorities*—lesbian, gay, bisexual, transsexual, transgender, two-spirit, intersex, and queer Canadians—are a diverse group unto themselves. Collectively, and unlike other traditionally disadvantaged groups, LGBTT individuals have suffered from "invisibility," in that their identities may remain largely hidden from view and unrecognized in formal policies and programs that promote social inclusion. Sexual minorities are more likely than heterosexuals to experience physical and sexual abuse, harassment, and discrimination.
- *Urban Aboriginal people* face lower standards of living than their non-Aboriginal counterparts, reflected in poorer levels of health, education, and income. Gang and criminal activity is also more prevalent among urban Aboriginal people. While the committee's report was confined to Canadians in urban areas, Aboriginal people in rural and remote communities encounter many of the same barriers.
- *Individuals with disabilities* comprise one in every seven Canadians, yet discrimination persists. On average, people with disabilities have income levels 20 per cent below the Canadian average.
- *Youths and seniors* also face challenges in terms of employment and connections to the workforce.

In making its recommendations to address the barriers facing these groups, the Senate committee focused primarily on income mobility as a path to greater equality and inclusion. For the most part, however, political scientists are in consensus that real barriers remain when it comes to the descriptive (if not substantive) representation of the same traditionally marginalized groups in Canadian politics. The question is why, and the answer is multifaceted, particularly considering the fact that different groups face unique obstacles.

Factors underpinning the underrepresentation of traditionally marginalized groups can be divided into two general categories: those that affect the "supply" of willing and able officials, and those affecting the "demand" for them among Canadians and the existing political class.[7]

Factors affecting the so-called "supply" side are driven by the deeper societal biases that foster not just barriers to political representation but social exclusion more generally. Members of traditionally marginalized groups are less likely to consider themselves suitable for public office, given a lack of role models in those positions and longstanding societal assumptions of their subordinate role in politics. A lack of resources also impedes the supply of capable candidates for office. Members of traditionally marginalized groups are often less affluent and less well-connected to existing political networks, two factors that limit their ability to raise the funds and elite or grassroots-level support necessary to compete for office.

Conversely, on the "demand" side of the equation, these individuals also face a host of systemic barriers to political representation. Traditional political cultures often favour older white men. This discrimination can be embodied in political institutions as well, creating an entire system that is unwelcoming to members of traditionally marginalized groups. Some voters and party members may find Muslim candidates undesirable from a descriptive standpoint, for instance. Such perceptions may convince elites not to recruit or support a person of Islamic faith as their party's candidate on the ballot. Similar gender biases are also built into many Canadian political institutions, including legislative schedules that discriminate against parents (more typically mothers) seeking to balance a career in politics with family responsibilities.

In sum, these supply-side and demand-side obstacles *turn away* many individuals who would otherwise be fit and willing to pursue enhanced political representation, while also *turning off* many people from wanting to participate in the first place.

Efforts at Reform

When it comes to assessing the representativeness of Canadian democracy, most scholars and students begin by examining legislatures (Chapter 6). To understand why so few traditionally underrepresented Canadians sit in the House of Commons or provincial and territorial assemblies, consider the process involved in gaining a seat. First, the individual must decide whether he or she *wants* to seek office; for a whole host of reasons, the individual often does not. With lower-than-average incomes, many members of immigrant, visible-minority, and Aboriginal communities lack the resources necessary to build a political career while seeking or maintaining outside employment. For others, including many women, sexual minorities, and people with disabilities, the political life is quite simply unattractive. They may view Canadian politics as exclusionary and discriminatory and not wish to put themselves (or their friends and families) through the intense, often prejudiced rigours of modern campaigns. Others, particularly some Aboriginal people, may question the legitimacy of the Canadian political system entirely. These same barriers also discourage or prevent traditionally marginalized groups from gaining non-elected positions within the civil service, the judiciary, and other parts of government. These socioeconomic and psychological barriers are real, and in many ways, they are the most difficult challenges to address as they are deeply embedded in Canadian society. Eliminating these challenges would essentially involve ending discrimination and poverty, which afflicts marginalized communities disproportionately. These are significant challenges, in and of themselves.

In terms of more immediate steps, some suggest that marginalized Canadians require more role models in positions of power. Seeing "someone like me" in elected office can send a powerful, positive message to would-be candidates, counteracting the many negative messages they encounter during their formative years. Women, visible-minority members, and people with disabilities serve as powerful role models when they gain office. The case of gay and lesbian politicians is different, because while they may be vocal champions of the rights of LGBTT Canadians, they may choose to keep their sexuality private, which makes them spokespersons but not role models. This led comedian Rick Mercer, in 2011, to call on Canadian politicians to

THEY SAID IT

Pierre Trudeau on the Homosexual Movement in Canada

There's no place for the state in the bedrooms of the nation. What's done in private between adults doesn't concern the Criminal Code.

—Liberal justice minister Pierre Trudeau, 1967

VOX POP

Pierre Trudeau made this famous comment while defending his government's decision to decriminalize sexual activity between people of the same sex. Since then it has served as a rallying cry for champions of sexual freedom. Yet it took over three decades to achieve marriage equality, and much remains to be done to protect the rights of transgender Canadians. What sorts of barriers remain when it comes to the political equality of LGBTT Canadians, and why do they persist?

go beyond simply saying "it gets better" in response to LGBTT youth being bullied: he called on them to "come out" publicly as both political champions and role models for the LGBTT community.[8] The challenge, then, is twofold: first, to empower members of traditionally marginalized groups to attain positions of power, and second, to encourage them to serve actively as role models for future generations.

An individual from a traditionally marginalized group is likely to face systemic obstacles to gaining a seat in the legislature even if he or she has made the decision to seek office. The most imposing of these barriers are institutional, with discrimination built into Canada's electoral laws and broader political system. There has been some progress in narrowing the resource advantage traditionally enjoyed by older white men. Canadian women, for instance, are better educated and earn higher salaries than ever before, and continue to close the conventional occupational status gap between men and women. At the same time, in provinces like Quebec, Manitoba, Nova Scotia, and Alberta, and at the federal level, campaign finance laws have been reformed to "level the playing field" in terms of the resources necessary to mount effective political campaigns. These laws have placed limits on the amount of money each candidate can spend, and the amount that each candidate can donate to his or her own campaign. At the same time, these laws have restricted the ability of well-heeled citizens to finance candidates and parties, barred unions and corporations from donating to campaigns, and limited the ability of third-party interest groups to campaign during elections. Together, these reforms have gone some way toward limiting the material advantages enjoyed by Canada's traditional political elite. The results are mixed. While changes to campaign finance laws in Quebec and Manitoba coincided with an increase in the number of women in their legislatures, it is difficult to draw a direct causal link, particularly when similar gains have failed to materialize at the federal level. Campaign finance reform is not a panacea for inequities in political representation.

↻ For more information on campaign finance laws, see the section Campaign Finance beginning on page 408 of Chapter 10, on elections.

↻ Canada's single-member plurality system, its advantages, and its disadvantages are discussed in Chapter 10, on elections: see Electoral System, beginning on page 394.

candidate quotas Hard-and-fast requirements established by some political parties to improve the proportion of candidates from traditionally underrepresented groups.

parachute candidate A candidate selected by the party leadership without necessarily consulting or seeking the approval of local constituency members beforehand.

Canada's electoral institutions remain some of the most imposing and talked-about barriers to equal representation. Most reformers focus here first, aiming to change the "rules of the game" rather than addressing the underlying reasons why so few people are able or choose to "play the game" in the first place. Of these institutions, Canada's single-member plurality (SMP) electoral system is the primary target. Critics argue that SMP systems like Canada's foster an intense form of competition—one that favours traditionally dominant candidates, including men, older Canadians, and members of whitestream society. Moreover, unlike systems that elect multiple members per district (as in Norway), single-member plurality systems like Canada's do not encourage parties to balance their campaign slates with an equal number of men and women. By contrast, some forms of proportional representation (PR) provide incentives for political parties to nominate candidates from a variety of socio-demographic backgrounds. This is especially true in list-PR systems, where parties are required to publicize their full slate of candidates, thus allowing citizens to assess their representativeness and commitment to diversity.

Given these barriers, some reformers have sought incremental changes to Canada's electoral system. As discussed in Chapter 9, the Liberals and New Democrats have long-established internal structures that ensure the representation of women and traditionally disadvantaged groups within the party apparatus. The most successful of these structures have come into play at the party nomination stage. For example, most provincial and federal political parties require that local constituency associations conduct an active search for nominees from traditionally marginalized groups as a condition of signing their chosen candidate's nomination papers (thus certifying him or her to run under the party's banner during an election). This policy is in addition to programs for training or financing candidates from traditionally marginalized groups. The policy does not guarantee that a candidate from a marginalized group will win the nomination, let alone the broader election. It only ensures that the candidate's name will appear on the party-level ballot.

Some parties have taken these reforms one step further, by imposing goals ranging from soft targets to hard quotas on the number of women or visible minorities in their overall slate of candidates. In 1985, the federal NDP set an ambitious goal of making 50 per cent of their candidates women. Eight years later, the Liberal Party followed suit by setting a 25 per cent target. In 2015, 43% of NDP candidates were women, as were 31% Liberal candidates, and 19% of Conservatives.[9] The Conservative Party maintains no such targets, revealing an ideological divide among Canada's major parties when it comes to representation of traditionally marginalized groups. Right-leaning parties are less likely to see the need or value in providing supports to help members of traditionally disadvantaged groups overcome historical discrimination, favouring free and open competition for office among individuals subject to the same set of rules.

One of the major concerns cited by Conservatives at both the federal and provincial levels has to do with the party leadership overriding the choice of local party members. To meet self-imposed country- or province-wide quotas, parties are often forced to recruit parachute candidates to run in certain constituencies. This may mean appointing a nominee that local party members do not favour, or even one who does not live in the district, as a means of balancing the party's overall campaign slate.

Effectiveness of Reforms

The results of these incremental reforms are mixed. While research shows that traditionally marginalized candidates, particularly women, are just as likely to win a seat as their traditionally dominant counterparts—provided they first win the party nomination—parties nonetheless have a difficult time recruiting nominees from these groups. Since 2009, women have constituted around one-third of all legislators in British Columbia and Quebec—the highest proportions in Canada. Gender balance has been more difficult to achieve elsewhere, with women making up closer to 20 per cent of legislators in Atlantic Canada, and men making up three of every four MLAs and MPs in Ontario and the Prairies. Over the same period, federal parties have also failed to achieve gender parity in terms of their campaign slates. The New Democrats, Bloc Québécois, and Greens have come closest, with approximately one in three of their candidates being women. The Liberals and Conservatives have traditionally lagged in this measure. Moreover, when parties do attempt to take proactive steps to guarantee women's representation, they are often accused of parachuting traditionally marginalized candidates into unwinnable races, leaving traditionally dominant candidates to contest the more competitive districts.

The success of women and members of traditionally underrepresented groups in district-level elections goes a long way to determining their success in executive positions. Unless they are elected as members of a legislature, they are highly unlikely to be selected to serve in cabinet or as a party leader. This is borne out by statistics on the gender and ethnic balances across Canada, as first ministers are often challenged to find enough suitable MPs or MLAs to build a diverse cabinet. Many have used the rule of thumb that the same proportion of women will be selected to serve in cabinet as serve in the government caucus. This said, for a brief period in 2007, the Quebec government became the first in North America to feature a cabinet with complete gender parity. Alberta replicated the feat following the 2015 provincial election, as did Justin Trudeau in his first cabinet.

The challenges of representation at the district level are accentuated when it comes to the party leadership. Historically, federal party leaders have been whitestream men, and very few members of visible minority communities have served as leaders of Canada's major political parties at the provincial level.

The gender balance has been just as slow to materialize among party leaders, both federally and provincially. Prior to 2008, Rita Johnson (BC premier 1991–2), Kim Campbell (Canadian prime minister 1993), and Catherine Callbeck (PEI premier 1993–6) stood out as Canada's first and only female first ministers. Their short-lived tenures, combined with the fact that only Callbeck led her party to victory in a general election, diminished the weight of these milestones. Since 2008, there has been dramatic growth in the number—and prominence—of women in leadership positions, at least at the provincial and territorial level. The premiers' table approached gender parity in 2013, when six of thirteen premiers were women, including those representing the four largest provinces. Collectively, they represented nearly two-thirds of all Canadians. Canada's first openly gay first minister, Kathleen Wynne of Ontario, became premier after being selected by her party to replace sitting premier Dalton McGuinty; she later led her party to victory in the 2014 provincial election.

The challenges of assembling cabinet are discussed in Chapter 5, on the executive: see page 183, on balancing geographic representation and socio-demographic considerations.

THEY SAID IT

Marie Deschamps on the Importance of Having Bilingual Judges

On retiring from the Supreme Court in 2012, Marie Deschamps offered the following reflections on whether bilingualism should be a requirement for Supreme Court justice appointees:

> I think it makes the life of the judge much easier when the judge is bilingual. The end result, I don't think it makes a difference. For the judge to be able to convey their own ideas in the language that everyone will understand, it's better to be bilingual. . . . [That said,] sometimes it's difficult. There are some parts of the country where it's more difficult to have bilingual judges. They might be a qualified candidate and they can learn on the job when they come. In the end, I think it's important that everyone become bilingual.

—Former Supreme Court justice Marie Deschamps, in an interview with the CBC[10]

VOX POP

Why is it important to maintain linguistic representation on the Supreme Court? How important are these reasons compared with the need to maintain relative gender parity or ethnic diversity?

Of note, months later, Wade MacLauchlan of Prince Edward Island became Canada's first openly gay man to serve as a provincial premier.

Somewhat ironically, *unelected* democratic institutions often better reflect Canada's socio-demographic diversity. Take, for example, the Supreme Court of Canada. With the requirement that at least three justices must be from Quebec, to offer expertise in adjudicating cases involving the province's civil code, the Supreme Court is almost assured of linguistic balance between English and French. Moreover, there is ongoing debate as to whether bilingualism should be made a formal requirement for selection of *all* justices to the Supreme Court. In 2000, Beverley McLachlin became the first woman to serve as chief justice, and by virtue of holding that position is also a deputy of the governor general of Canada. From 2005 to 2012, four of the nine Supreme Court justices were women. The court has been much slower to reach representativeness in ethnic or socio-economic terms—largely a historical by-product of a homogeneous legal profession. As law schools, like universities in general, become more diverse, so, too, should the courts become more inclusive over time.

While much maligned for being undemocratic, Canada's appointed Senate demonstrates the paradoxical place of appointed bodies in modern democracies. Because they are unelected—and thus not directly accountable to Canadians like their delegates to Parliament—many feel senators represent Canadians in more descriptive and formalistic (if not substantive) ways. In fact, for decades, the Senate has been more inclusive than the House of Commons when it comes to the socio-demographic backgrounds of its members. While women typically comprise barely one in four MPs, for

The Canadian Press/Jeff McIntosh

Naheed Nenshi's election as Calgary's mayor in 2010 was remarkable for many reasons. Not only had he defied early polls to become the first Muslim to win a big-city mayoral race in North America; at 38, he also represented a new generation of progressive leadership in a province known for its conservative political culture. Nenshi's performance and popularity made him Canada's first recipient of the "World Mayor" prize, issued by the City Mayors Foundation in 2014. Would Nenshi have enjoyed as much success had he decided to enter provincial or federal politics instead? Is the nature and structure of municipal politics more or less inclusive when it comes to representing diversity?

example, over one-third of all senators are women. Prime ministers have also been known to select senators to represent minority communities of interest, including francophones outside Quebec. This is one of the reasons why advocacy groups acting on behalf of traditionally marginalized groups continue to support an appointed Senate over an elected one.

The contemporary debate over Senate elections raises the fundamental conundrum of modern democratic reform. Should we make our institutions more accountable by opening more positions up to direct election? Americans elect a far greater range of officials than Canadians do: they elect not only senators but also judges and even dogcatchers, for example. Or should we retain the ability of elected leaders to appoint representatives, thus helping prospective candidates avoid the obstacles that often prevent members of traditionally disadvantaged groups from competing effectively in elections? In the end, one's position on these questions depends on one's perspective on representation, in general.

Diversity in the Civil Service

Diversity is also reflected in the Canadian bureaucracy, although in different ways and to varying degrees across the country. The federal public service applies the principle of employment equity to its hiring practices, as a means of ensuring that the

employment equity A federal government policy requiring civil service managers to proactively consider employing women, people with disabilities, Aboriginal people, and visible minorities.

bureaucracy reflects the diversity of the Canadian public it serves. Justice Rosalie Abella, head of the 1983–4 Royal Commission on Equality in Employment, coined the term to differentiate the Canadian approach from the American concept of "affirmative action" discussed above, which faced backlash for its focus on preferential hiring. Rather than establishing hard quotas, as affirmative action does, employment equity policies involve setting goals and targets for government managers, encouraging them to establish training and recruitment programs aimed at four target groups and to treat all applicants equally when hiring. This "equality of opportunity and treatment" approach is distinct from the "equality of result" expected from most affirmative action programs.

Employment equity is a federal government policy designed to improve the representation of traditionally underrepresented groups in the civil service and federally regulated industries. Co-administered by the Treasury Board Secretariat and Public Service Commission (PSC)—an independent agency reporting to Parliament—employment equity seeks to eliminate barriers and provide equitable access to federal government jobs for qualified members of four traditionally underrepresented groups identified under the Employment Equity Act:

- women;
- Aboriginal people;
- persons with disabilities; and
- members of visible-minority communities.

In previous decades, francophones were also considered a priority group under the employment equity framework. In pursuing employment equity, the PSC bases its hiring on the principles of non-discrimination and merit, which hold that every Canadian should have equal opportunity to compete for public-sector employment, and that the sole criterion for selection should be fitness for the job. This policy of employment equity should not be confused with the concept of pay equity, which seeks to end gender-based discrimination standing in the way of "equal pay for work of equal value" (as enshrined in section 11 of the Canadian Human Rights Act).

pay equity A policy designed to eliminate gender-based discrimination in terms of how federally regulated employees are paid.

Similar employment equity policies exist in other Canadian jurisdictions, but few (if any) have had as much success as the federal government's in terms of improving the representativeness of the bureaucracy. As seen in Table 13.1 and Table 13.2, the proportion of women, Aboriginal people, people with disabilities, and members of visible minorities in the federal public service has increased dramatically over the past three decades. In fact, employment equity policies have been so successful that of the four target groups, only people with disabilities remain underrepresented, and an argument could be made that members of the other three minority groups are now *overrepresented* compared to their proportion of the general population. This said, just as there remains a lack of traditionally disadvantaged people in leadership positions in most parties and private-sector organizations, so, too, do bureaucracies remain challenged to attain diversity among their highest ranks. This means that, while a majority of civil servants may be women, this proportion decreases the further up the management chain you measure.

Not everyone supports the concept of employment equity. Critics feel that the policy amounts to reverse discrimination, excluding otherwise qualified individuals

TABLE 13.1 | Proportion of Men and Women in the Federal Public Service, 1983–2012 (%)

	1983	1993	2003	2012
Men	58.2	52.9	46.7	44.9
Women	41.8	47.1	53.3	55.1

Source: Demographic Snapshot of the Federal Public Service, 2012, http://www.tbs-sct.gc.ca/res/stats/demo12-eng.asp, Office of the Chief Human Resources Officer, Treasury Board of Canada Secretariat, 2015

TABLE 13.2 | Representation of Employment Equity–Designated Groups in the Federal Public Service, 2006–7 and 2011–12

Employment Equity–Designated Group	2006–7	2011-12
Women	54.5	55.3
Aboriginal people	3.9	4.5
People with disabilities	5.5	5.7
Members of a visible-minority group	9.8	13.3

Source: Demographic Snapshot of the Federal Public Service, 2012, http://www.tbs-sct.gc.ca/res/stats/demo12-eng.asp, Office of the Chief Human Resources Officer, Treasury Board of Canada Secretariat, 2015

from jobs in favour of members of traditionally marginalized groups. This issue came to a head in 2010, when Sara Landriault reported that she had been excluded from applying for a position as an administrative assistant with the federal government. After answering that she was neither Aboriginal nor a member of a visible minority in the online application form, Landriault said she was informed she did not meet the criteria for the job and was prevented from applying. The incident sparked a review of the federal government's employment equity policy, with Treasury Board president Stockwell Day stating: "While we support diversity in the public service, we want to ensure that no Canadian is barred from opportunities in the public service based on race or ethnicity." Federal immigration minister Jason Kenney added: "We are in favour of appropriate diversity in the public service and reasonable efforts to achieve it, but we don't think any Canadians should be excluded from applying within their government. It's okay to encourage people from different backgrounds to apply, but in our judgement it goes too far to tell people that if they are not of a particular race or ethnicity they cannot apply [for a job] that is actually funded by their tax dollars."[10]

Diversity in Civil Society

Debates over the representativeness and inclusiveness of Canada's political system are not confined to the realm of elected or appointed officials. The issues reach much more deeply into civil society, challenging policymakers to identify and address both political and social inequalities. Interest groups have been at the forefront of these efforts to address inequality by putting pressure on elected officials and by engaging the media and the public in discussion of the issues.

In recent decades, these discussions have centred on the need for reasonable accommodation of diversity in Canadian laws and institutions. The concept of

civil society The community of citizens in Canada, outside the realm of government.

reasonable accommodation Adjustments to policies that allow for the inclusion of traditionally disadvantaged groups without causing undue hardship to others.

↻ Interest groups are discussed throughout Chapter 12, on activism.

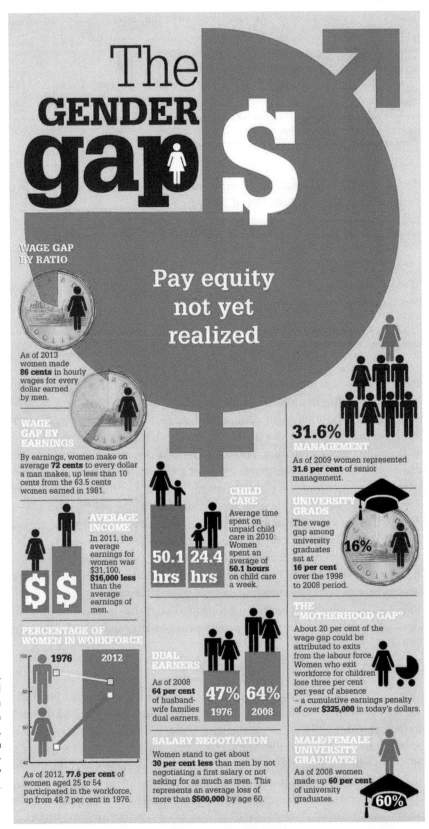

FIGURE 13.2 | The Gender Gap in Canada

Women are not only underrepresented in traditional political institutions in Canada. They remain disadvantaged in the corporate world and broader society, as well. What are some of the common reasons behind the lack of gender equality in Canada's public and private sectors?

THEY SAID IT

Competing Points of View on Employment Equity

We can continue to achieve greater diversity in the public sector without prohibiting people from applying for jobs on the grounds of their race or ethnicity. It's a very simple principle and I think it's something the vast majority of Canadians would appreciate. Excluding Canadian citizens from applying for employment in their government is profoundly illiberal. What we're articulating here is an essentially liberal value of equality of opportunity and equality under the law.

—Jason Kenney, Conservative MP and then-minister of citizenship and immigration[12]

We shouldn't apologize for doing that. Sometimes the pendulum has to swing the other way before it finds balance in the middle.

—Pat Martin, NDP MP

If [the Conservatives] do what they're trying to do then there won't be any protections for aboriginals and visible minorities.

—Marcel Proux, Liberal MP

reasonable accommodation means that governments must make appropriate adjustments to policies (i.e. accommodations) so that people from traditionally disadvantaged or marginalized groups are able to exercise their rights and freedoms on an equal basis with those from mainstream society. It also ensures that these adjustments do not place a disproportionate burden on the state and civil society (i.e. that they be reasonable). Thus, reasonable accommodation requires governments to balance being inclusive and equitable with being practical and not placing undue hardship on the state or its citizens.

Ultimately, most questions of reasonable accommodation boil down to whether the rights and freedoms enjoyed by members of a minority community outweigh those of the broader community, or whether the practices or beliefs of one community should be imposed on or integrated into the other. Section 15 of the Charter of Rights and Freedoms provides the legal foundation for those seeking reasonable accommodation in Canada, as do provincial human rights codes. Consider the following questions:

- Should Canadians whose religion requires the wearing of certain types of clothing have to conform to the uniform codes imposed by the Canadian military or RCMP? Should they be able to wear religious articles while playing organized sports, or should sport associations have the ability to ban their use?
- Should Aboriginal people in Canada have the right to access unique, culturally sensitive programs and services, like education, health and justice systems?
- Should Canadians whose beliefs prohibit the taking of photographs or unveiling of the face be required to produce photo ID to drive, vote, or secure a passport?

- Should Canadian children whose religion involves carrying a weapon (like the Sikh ceremonial kirpan) be allowed to carry these weapons to school?
- Should small-budget community organizations be required to install wheelchair ramps on aging buildings?
- Should religious schools be allowed to prevent gay, lesbian, bisexual, or transgendered teachers from working in their classrooms? Should they be forced to allow student-led gay–straight alliance groups?
- Should governments be required to offer government services in all languages required by their citizens?

While these sorts of questions have prompted debates across Canada, the volume of discussions has been highest in the province of Quebec. Given that its francophone majority constitutes a continent-wide minority, and given the province's long history of controversial policies designed to protect the dominant language and culture, it is not surprising that Quebec has become the epicentre for debates over reasonable accommodation.

In 2007, Quebec Premier Jean Charest struck a Commission on Accommodation Practices Related to Cultural Differences (also known as the Bouchard–Taylor Commission) to investigate the relationship between the province's white, francophone, predominantly secular majority and its various minority cultural communities. The commission held public consultations throughout the province, hearing from over 3000 Quebecers and receiving over 900 written submissions. In their final report, released in 2008, the commissioners reached the conclusion that the Government of Quebec must take steps to establish Quebec as a formally secular state, and actively address discrimination in society. Among their 37 recommendations were the following:

secular state A religiously neutral governing regime.

- remove the crucifix located above the speaker's chair in the National Assembly
- abandon prayers at government meetings and state functions
- prohibit judges, Crown prosecutors, police officers, prison guards, and the speaker of the National Assembly from wearing religious signs in the course of their duties (but not prevent other civil servants from doing so)
- permit students to wear religious symbols in class, but not allow them to be exempt from compulsory courses (e.g. sexual education) on the basis of religion
- encourage paid leave for religious holidays, in both the public and private sector
- increase funding to organizations supporting immigrant women
- pass legislation to enshrine, and launch an aggressive campaign to promote, interculturalism in Quebec as a means of ending all forms of discrimination, including those based on gender, race, religion, sexual orientation, physical ability, and other social factors.

The Commission did not make any formal recommendations on the need for linguistic accommodation, deeming the state of the French language beyond its scope.

In part because of its minority government position, and in part because such questions divided his own government caucus, Premier Charest chose not to follow up on many of the commission's recommendations. However, the issue re-emerged as a central campaign theme in the 2010 provincial election, which brought the Parti

Québécois (PQ) to power under another minority government. As part of its campaign platform, the PQ promised to introduce a Charter of Quebec Values as a means of defining the secular nature of the Quebec state and society.

The government introduced its charter in fall 2013, sparking heated debates not only in Quebec but across Canada. Initially titled the "Charter affirming the values of State secularism and religious neutrality and the equality between women and men, and providing a framework for accommodation requests," the legislation (Bill 60) aimed to establish the neutrality of the Quebec state. It prohibited all civil servants from wearing "conspicuous" religious symbols, and required all citizens to leave their faces uncovered when providing or receiving a government service. Critics charged that the PQ was attempting to undermine minority rights while cultivating a siege mentality in Quebec amid complaints from Ottawa and the rest of Canada over its failure to respect the Canadian Charter of Rights and Freedoms. Proponents viewed the Charter of Quebec Values as the embodiment of the Report of the Bouchard–Taylor Commission and a firm definition of secularism (*laïcité*), as distinct from multiculturalism, in modern Quebec society. The controversial bill never became law because the Parti Québécois minority government was defeated by the Quebec Liberals in the following general election.

In 2015, the provincial Liberals presented their own "neutrality" legislation, Bill 62 (or An Act to Foster Adherence to State Religious Neutrality and, in Particular, to Provide a Framework for Religious Accommodation Requests in Certain Bodies). While it fell short of an outright ban on all religious symbols and does allow for accommodations under certain circumstances, the law nonetheless prevents civil servants from wearing face-covering garments while at work and members of the public requesting services from doing the same.

THEY SAID IT

The (Proposed) Charter of Quebec Values

In England, they get into fights and throw bombs at one another because of multiculturalism and people get lost in that type of a society.

—Premier Pauline Marois[13]

The prospect of physicians, nurses and other health-care workers having to leave their institutions to ensure these basic freedoms is unthinkable and devastating.

—Dr Michael Malus, Chief of Family Medicine at the Jewish General Hospital[14]

The only contact most Quebecers have with the Islamic world are violent images repeated ad infinitum: wars, riots, bombs, the World Trade Center attack, and the Boston Marathon; it's also the image of female subordination to the male and the violence inflicted if women refuse to submit. The reflex is clear: We don't want that here!

—Jacques Parizeau, former premier of Quebec[15]

Zunera Ishaq, a Sunni Muslim, took the oath of Canadian citizenship in October 2015 after winning a series of court battles affirming her right to do so while wearing her niqab. The government had fought to uphold the ban on the face-covering niqab, with Conservative prime minister Stephen Harper arguing: "I believe, and I think most Canadians believe, that it is offensive that someone would hide their identity at the very moment where they are committing to join the Canadian family." The divisive issue came to the forefront during the 2015 federal election campaign, with some branding the niqab a symbol of Muslim oppression of women and others holding it up as an important religious right. How would you set the limits of reasonable accommodation in a case such as this?

These sorts of controversies and tensions are not unique to Quebec. Similar, smaller-scale debates have occurred across Canada over the course of the past century. Moreover, while ethnic and religious rights tend to dominate these discussions, reasonable accommodation also involves addressing the needs of other minority groups (including Aboriginal people, LGBTT people, allophones, people with disabilities, and others). And the requirements of reasonable accommodation apply more broadly than just to governments. Employers are also required to provide such protections for employees (see *O'Malley and Ontario Human Rights Commission v. Simpsons-Sears*). In many ways, then, conversations about reasonable accommodation tend to overlap with those concerning the need for employment equity and affirmative action in Canada.

Diversity and the Courts

Advocates of inclusion have advanced their cause by many means, including entering politics to reform the electoral process and legislatures from within, and educating the public on the depth of Canada's democratic deficit so that citizens will put pressure on their elected officials to initiate reforms. Beyond these traditional channels, diversity activists have sought redress and progress through the courts, appealing to judges whose role is to remain independent of the historical and majoritarian influences found elsewhere in the Canadian political system. At times, this has made the courts the greatest protectors of traditionally disadvantaged groups in Canada. Consider the role of the judiciary in promoting:

↻ The rule of judicial impartiality is one of three core principles of Canada's justice system: see page 258 in Chapter 7.

- the political equality of women (the 1929 *Persons* case established that women were equally entitled to serve in the Senate and, by extension, other political offices);
- abortion rights (the 1988 *R v. Morgentaler* decision ruled that criminal sanctions placed on abortions violated women's rights);
- the inherent rights of Aboriginal people (the 1990 *R v. Sparrow* case established that Aboriginal rights predated the Charter, and could not be infringed);
- the rights of sexual minorities (the 1995 *Egan v. Canada* case read gay, lesbian, bisexual, and transgender rights into the Charter of Rights and Freedoms); and
- the rights of sex-trade workers (the 2013 *Bedford v. Canada* case deemed that anti-prostitution laws were unconstitutional on the basis that they exposed prostitutes to harmful situations by causing them to practise their trade in secret).

In many, but not all, of these instances, the courts acted in advance of political will and even public opinion. They struck down laws that were discriminatory and contrary to the Bill of Rights or Charter of Rights and Freedoms, the latter of which prohibits discrimination based on race, national or ethnic origin, skin colour, religion, gender, age, disability, or sexual orientation. They re-interpreted others to match the principles of fairness and equality. In other instances, the courts acted not in response to an individual citizen or advocacy group's request, but—on the urging of governments—on their own initiative.

↻ For more information on the rights protected under Canada's constitution, see The Charter of Rights and Freedoms on page 68 of Chapter 2.

The Charter of Rights and Freedoms is not the only piece of legislation protecting minority rights in Canada. As discussed in Chapter 2, the federal Bill of Rights continues to play a role. So, too, do various federal, provincial, and territorial human rights codes, which are adjudicated by a series of human rights commissions and tribunals across Canada. Like the formal court system, these quasi-judicial bodies play a key role in protecting and promoting diversity in Canadian political life.

human rights commissions and tribunals Quasi-judicial panels that investigate and/or adjudicate citizens' complaints about discrimination prohibited by human rights laws.

At the federal level, the Canadian Human Rights Act prohibits any federal government department or agency, or any federally regulated employer, from discriminating on the basis of race, national or ethnic origin, skin colour, religion, age, sex, marital or family status, sexual orientation, disability, or pardoned conviction. The Canadian Human Rights Commission handles complaints of discrimination against the federal government in terms of its employment practices and delivery of services to Canadians, including those under the Canadian Human Rights Act and the Employment Equity Act. If a complaint cannot be resolved, the commission may choose to investigate further, referring some cases to the Canadian Human Rights Tribunal. Much like a court of law, the tribunal holds hearings into those cases, and may order certain remedies, including compensation or fines, if the discrimination complaint is found to have merit. The decisions of the tribunal may be reviewed by the Federal Court, with a range of further appeals reaching all the way to the Supreme Court of Canada. Similar

Canadian Human Rights Commission Body empowered to adjudicate discrimination complaints against federally regulated bodies.

↻ See the ICP box on page 229 of Chapter 6 for an explanation of how free votes were allowed on the matter of same-sex marriage.

INSIDE CANADIAN POLITICS

How Did the Courts Resolve the Marriage Equality Debate?

Canada was deeply divided over the issue of same-sex marriage in October 2004. While courts had legally recognized it in half of the provinces and one territory, public opinion polls and academic surveys showed that support for the concept of allowing two men or two women to marry had remained below 50 per cent throughout the previous decade. It came as no surprise, then, that the federal government's own caucus was divided over the issue.

In June 2003, Prime Minister Jean Chrétien announced his government's intention to introduce legislation legalizing same-sex marriage. It was a bold announcement, considering that just four years earlier, the House of Commons had overwhelmingly passed a resolution affirming the definition of marriage as "the union of one man and one woman to the exclusion of all others." Many Liberals had voted in favour of this traditional definition. Chrétien's government had taken steps to recognize other legal rights of same-sex couples, such as extending common-law benefits to gays and lesbians for things like pensions. However, it had stopped short of including marriage among those rights.

Crucially, Chrétien decided to refer his Civil Marriage Act to the Supreme Court of Canada *before* introducing it to Parliament, asking the Court three questions:

1. Could the federal government change the definition without the permission of the provinces?

2. Would same-sex marriage violate the Charter of Rights and Freedoms?

3. Would the Charter protect religious officials from being compelled to perform same-sex marriages?

This decision was reinforced by his successor, Prime Minister Paul Martin, who added a fourth question, asking the Court directly whether the traditional definition of marriage was consistent with the Charter.

This *Reference Re: Same-Sex Marriage* effectively lifted the issue out of Parliament's hands and placed it in those of Canada's highest court. In reaching its decision on whether the traditional definition of marriage infringed upon the equality rights found in section 15 of the Charter of Rights and Freedoms, the Supreme Court was able to rely on previous decisions handed down by provincial courts. Among them, the Ontario

human rights laws and codes, commissions, and tribunals exist throughout the provinces and territories, although specific grounds for discrimination, remedies available, and particular processes differ from jurisdiction to jurisdiction.

The most controversial cases appearing before these bodies have surrounded the issue of hate speech. These cases have often pitted protections found in various human rights codes against provisions found in the Charter of Rights and Freedoms. The Charter both promotes multiculturalism and preserves Canadians' freedom of religion and expression, while the Criminal Code of Canada prohibits the spreading of "hate propaganda." The latter forbids "any writing, sign or visible representation that promotes genocide" or "incites hatred against any identifiable group." Tribunals and courts have been challenged to define specifically what constitutes "hatred." They have sought to establish whether limitations on freedom of expression are justifiable and, if so, under what circumstances.

Alberta has been home to two such controversial cases. One involved a high school teacher, James Keegstra, who was charged under the Criminal Code in 1984 for instructing his students that the Holocaust had been fabricated to generate sympathy

hate speech Messages that promote harm or aggravated contempt of an identifiable group of people.

Court of Appeal's opinion in *Halpern v. Canada* proved most persuasive. In that ruling, judges had found that the traditional definition of marriage offended the dignity of people in same-sex relationships. It had also rejected the claim that the traditional definition could be defended on the basis of the necessity of procreation: the Ontario court had found that many heterosexual marriages do not rear children, that many homosexual couples do, and that neither type of couple would be likely to stop procreating were the definition of marriage to change.

The Supreme Court ruled in favour of same-sex marriage proponents, finding that the federal government did have the authority to change the definition of marriage, that same-sex marriage did not violate the Charter, and that it did not infringe upon the freedom of religion by compelling anyone to perform such marriages. The Supreme Court chose not to answer the prime minister's fourth question, concerning the constitutionality of the traditional definition of marriage. The justices argued that the issue had already been decided by lower courts, and that the federal government had not challenged those rulings.

Armed with this opinion, Prime Minister Martin introduced the Civil Marriage Act to Parliament in February 2005, and it received Royal Assent in July of that year. This made Canada the fourth country in the world (behind the Netherlands, Belgium, and Spain) to provide legal support for same-sex marriage on a nationwide basis.

Almost immediately, public opinion in Canada shifted to support the concept of same-sex marriage, climbing on a national basis the way it had climbed regionally in response to earlier lower court rulings. The reason, in part, speaks to the weight Canadians place in the legitimacy conferred by the courts.

VOX POP

What is the proper role of the courts when it comes to policymaking on deeply divisive issues like same-sex marriage? What other policy tools were available to the federal government, and how effective would they have been at achieving the government's objectives?

for Jews. The case went all the way to the Supreme Court of Canada, which ruled that, while Keegstra's right to freedom of expression had been violated, this violation was justified in order to prevent hatred against an identifiable group. A second case involved cartoons that caused an international furor when they first appeared in 2005 in the Danish newspaper *Jyllands-Posten*. The cartoons depicted the prophet Muhammad, an act that is considered blasphemous among devout Muslims. The editors of the Danish newspaper defended their decision to publish the cartoons on the grounds they wanted to spark a debate about Islam and censorship. Months later, Calgary-based *Western Standard* re-published the cartoons, prompting Muslim groups to file a pair of complaints with the Alberta Human Rights and Citizenship Commission. One of these complaints was eventually withdrawn, while the commission dismissed the other.

The role of the courts and tribunals in promoting diversity has raised the ire of critics. Some take issue with the judiciary's choice to favour group rights over individual ones, or positive entitlements over negative liberties. Others take a broader view, challenging the supremacy of appointed judges over elected legislatures, and arguing that judges have become unaccountable, unelected lawmakers. Proponents of

INSIDE CANADIAN POLITICS

What are Canada's International Commitments to Human Rights?

Canada is a party to 8 of 10 core UN human rights commitments, including the so-called International Bill of Rights, which encompasses the Universal Declaration of Human Rights (1948), the International Covenant on Civil and Political Rights (1976), and the International Covenant on Economic, Social and Cultural Rights (1976). Canada is also party to the following:

- the International Convention on the Elimination of All Forms of Racial Discrimination (1969)
- the Convention on the Elimination of All Forms of Discrimination against Women (1981)

- the Convention Against Torture and other Cruel, Inhuman or Degrading Treatment or Punishment (1987)
- the Convention on the Rights of the Child (1990)
- the Convention on the Rights of Persons with Disabilities (2008).

Canada is not a party to two other UN human rights conventions, those concerning migrant workers and the secret abduction or imprisonment of persons whose whereabouts remain hidden from the public.

VOX POP

Why do you suppose Canada has refused to become party to the International Convention on the Protection of the Rights of All Migrant Workers and Members of Their Families? How about the International Convention for the Protection of All Persons from Enforced Disappearance?

---

the judiciary's role look to the courts as an important, more impartial access point to government. They view judges as independent, expert arbiters in disputes over minority rights, providing a crucial check against the tyranny of the majority.

Beyond these domestic laws, Canada is also a signatory to several United Nations declarations and conventions, including the Universal Declaration of Human Rights, the Declaration on the Rights of Disabled Persons, and the Convention on the Elimination of Discrimination against Women. Canada also supports other UN conventions, including the Declaration on the Rights of Indigenous Peoples, though it may not officially sign, fully adopt, or implement them. While not directly enforceable by international law, these declarations hold their signatories to account through a combination of investigation and moral suasion. Upon request, the federal government has invited UN rapporteurs to tour the country; meet with government officials, civil society groups, and ordinary Canadians; and study and report on the state of human rights in Canada. UN agencies often make these requests after being approached by aggrieved interest groups and communities based in Canada. Previous UN reports have criticized Canada's treatment of First Nations peoples, its lack of progress in meeting the needs of persons with disabilities, and its continued use of religiously segregated schools. Often in collaboration with the provinces and territories, the federal government is obligated to respond publicly to these reports, detailing how it intends to address any shortcomings or explaining why it chooses not to do so. Ultimately, this form of public transparency, not any formal sanctions, ensures Canada meets its international human rights obligations.

UN declarations and conventions Commitments made by many UN members to uphold and advance common causes in their respective countries.

Aboriginal Representation in Canada

This brings us to one of the most critical and controversial aspects of representation in Canada: that of Aboriginal people. Our approach to the topic differs somewhat from what is found in other textbooks, in that we do not argue that indigenous politics exists in an academic or political vacuum, separate from broader discussions about democratic diversity. In our view, the subject of Aboriginal representation highlights both the shortcomings and the successes of Canadian democracy in general. This is why we place it at the culmination of this chapter, as the representation of Aboriginal people is as much about First Nations, Métis, and Inuit as it is about Canada as a whole. It has as much to teach us about the historic subjugation and contemporary oppression of Aboriginal people as it has to teach us about the evolution and future of Canadian sovereignty, Canadian democracy, and its representative institutions.

To begin, consider the fact that many Aboriginal people are "represented" by more "representatives" than most other Canadians. Like other Canadians, some Aboriginal people may feel represented by town or city councillors, MLAs, and MPs, not to mention their mayors, premiers, and prime minister. In addition, many Aboriginal people also feel represented by their local band council and chief; their tribal councils and treaty negotiators; or their regional or National Aboriginal Organization leaders. Some Aboriginal people reject some of these representatives as being illegitimate, and the quantity of these representatives should not be conflated with increased access to or influence in policymaking. Understanding these complex relationships helps us to better understand the democratic perspectives not just of Aboriginal people but of Canadians as a whole.

BRIEFING NOTES

The Language of Aboriginal Representation

A wide variety of terms have been used to describe Aboriginal people in Canada, some imposed by governments, developed by academics, and adopted by Aboriginal people themselves. The Constitution Act, 1982, recognizes Indians, Métis, and Inuit as Aboriginal peoples living in Canada. According to mainstream standards developed by the Canadian political science community, *Aboriginal* should be used as an adjective only, and the expression *Aboriginal Canadians* should be avoided in favour of *Aboriginal people in Canada*, since not all Aboriginal people embrace Canadian citizenship. *People* is used when referring to a group of individuals or the entire Aboriginal community; *peoples* is used only when referring to distinct groups (as in the Gitxsan, Nisga'a, and other Aboriginal peoples). *Indigenous* is an increasingly common synonym for *Aboriginal* and is used the same way to refer to Indigenous people living in Canada.

Although it is embedded in some federal legislation, the word *Indian* has gradually given way to *First Nations*, just as *Eskimo* has been superseded by *Inuit*. Where possible, it is advisable to use the self-defined name of the community being discussed instead of more general terms (e.g. a Mi'kmaq woman, instead of a First Nations woman or an Aboriginal woman).

Definitions and Designations

Constitutionally, Aboriginal people comprise four distinct groups: status Indians, non-status Indians, Métis, and Inuit. According to the 2011 National Household Survey, approximately 1.4 million Canadians identify themselves as belonging to one of these groups, and their population sizes vary considerably across Canada (see Figure 13.3).

Nearly half (49.8 per cent) of Aboriginal people in Canada are considered status Indians. The term derives from the Indian Act and applies to all First Nations individuals who are registered with the federal government, making them eligible for federal programs, services, and benefits. Prior to reforms in 1985, it was possible to lose one's status under the Indian Act for a variety of reasons, ranging from attending university or pursuing certain occupations to marrying a non-status man or opting to vote in federal elections. These regressive policies were reversed through Bill C-31, although it is still possible to lose status through several generations of marriage and procreation among non-status individuals.

All Aboriginal people who are not registered under the Indian Act and do not have an official "status card" are considered "non-status." This includes the 15.3 per cent of First Nations people who are not defined by the federal government as falling under the Indian Act (making them non-status Indians) as well as all Métis and Inuit, who lack status under the Indian Act.

Many, but not all, status Indians are also members of a band. In this sense, a band is a group of status Indians for whom reserve land has been assigned, or who have been so designated by the Crown.[16] Some bands are distributed over several reserves,

> **status Indian** A First Nations person registered and entitled to certain rights under the Indian Act.

> **non-status Indian** A First Nations person who is not registered under the Indian Act.

> **band** A group of status Indians defined by the federal government.

> **reserve** A tract of land owned by the federal government and set aside for First Nations peoples.

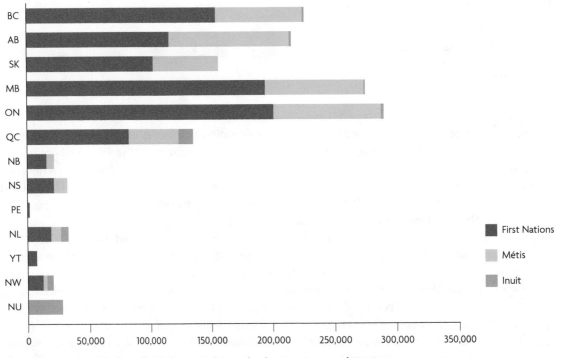

FIGURE 13.3 | Self-Identified Aboriginal Peoples by Province and Territory

Source: Data from Statistics Canada, 2011 National Household Survey

but some have no reserve land whatsoever. Moreover, only about half of all status Indians live on reserve; the remainder live in towns and cities, often retaining their membership in the band. Complicating matters, not all people living on reserves are status Indians; many non-status Indians, Métis, and non-Aboriginal people do so, although they are not members of the band.

Many bands were defined by the federal government with little or no regard for the history or cultural ancestry of the communities affected. As a result, some bands consist of multiple First Nations, and several bands may join together to form a more culturally succinct political group, operating under a single tribal council. Through the band system, the federal government also imposed British-style values and institutions without regard for traditional modes of governance. Liberal democratic forms of representation replaced centuries-old communitarian, hereditary, matriarchal, elder-centric, or consensus-based systems, to which some Aboriginal communities are only now returning.

As the governing body for all band members (whether on- or off-reserve), a band council is chaired by a chief and elected by band members. Chiefs and band councils are responsible for reporting to the federal government on the expenditure of certain funds, and serve as the primary liaison between band members and the federal Ministry of Aboriginal Affairs and Northern Development. To administer some programs and services (including healthcare, policing, and children's services), band councils will often form corporations and enter into formal agreements with federal, provincial, and territorial governments.

Comprising 30 per cent of Canada's Aboriginal population, Métis include those who self-identify as being of mixed First Nations and European ancestry, and who maintain some historical connection to and acceptance by a Métis community. There remains considerable cultural and legal debate over the constitutional status of Métis peoples in Canada, with conflicting views on whether they qualify for certain treaty rights or other forms of nationhood.

> **band council** Governing body elected by members of a band.

↻ See page 280 of Chapter 7 for a discussion of how the federal and provincial governments have worked with some First Nations bands to establish independent Aboriginal police forces in Alberta.

> **Métis** Aboriginal people with mixed First Nations and European ancestry.

BRIEFING NOTES
Identity, Status, and Membership

Self-identification is only one part of how Aboriginal people are categorized in Canada. Through a paternalistic set of policies and labels, the federal government continues to define Aboriginal people according to their eligibility for various government programs and services.

In this sense, is important not to confuse the term "status" (a legal definition) with "membership" in a particular First Nation, Métis nation or settlement, Inuit community, or other Aboriginal group. Membership in these groups is often defined internally, while status is defined by the federal government.

It is also important not to confuse status under the Indian Act with treaty entitlements. While many Aboriginal people may carry both status and treaty cards—which grant them distinct sets of benefits and rights—the two are not synonymous. Not all Aboriginal people with treaty rights are status Indians; some non-status First Nations and Métis people claim treaty rights. And not all status Indians have treaty rights; large tracts of land in Canada are not covered by treaties, yet their First Nations inhabitants are still eligible to register for status under the Indian Act.

The **Inuit** are Indigenous people whose ancestral homeland lies in the northern-most lands of North America, mostly between Labrador and Northwest Territories, in close proximity to the Arctic Ocean. With just under 60,000 Inuit in Canada, the group makes up 4.2 per cent of all Aboriginal people, but forms a majority of the population of Nunavut.

Demographics and Representation

Regardless of these complex definitions, the portrait of Aboriginal life in Canada is stark: there remain sizeable gaps in socioeconomic well-being between Aboriginal and non-Aboriginal people in Canada. Many but not all Aboriginal communities tend to feature

- lower-than-average incomes and higher unemployment;
- lower graduation rates and education levels;
- lower standards of living, including housing, community services, and public utilities;
- higher rates of crime and incarceration; and
- poorer health outcomes, whether measured in terms of life expectancy, chronic disease, substance abuse, mental illness, suicide, or other terms.

At the same time, Aboriginal people make up some of the youngest and fast-est-growing communities in Canada (see Figure 13.4).

Despite the upward trend in Aboriginal population and the very serious issues facing First Nations, Métis, and Inuit in Canada, Aboriginal people remain under-represented in Canadian legislatures and appointed offices. Moreover, the participation rates of Aboriginal people in federal, provincial, and territorial elections are substan-tially lower than voter turnout rates among the non-Aboriginal population, lagging behind the national average by as much as 20 percentage points in some instances.

There are two schools of thought on these trends. One, based on research con-ducted by political scientists like Patrick Fournier and Peter John Loewen,[17] sug-gests that Aboriginal people tend to share the same socioeconomic characteristics of non-voters in the non-Aboriginal population. Aboriginal communities simply pos-sess these features to a much broader and deeper extent. Considering that Aboriginal people in Canada are generally younger, have lower levels of education and income, have fewer political resources (including political knowledge and information), and have a weaker sense of civic duty than the general population, it should come as little surprise that they tend to vote in lower numbers than non-Aboriginal Canadians. From this perspective, closing the so-called "turnout gap" requires narrowing the soci-oeconomic gap that exists between Aboriginal and non-Aboriginal people in Canada.

A second school of thought, espoused by scholars like Kiera L. Ladner and Michael McCrossan,[18] holds that a unique combination of historical, socio-cultural, institutional, and attitudinal barriers stand in the way of Aboriginal engagement in Canadian elections. By virtue of centuries of discrimination and colonialism, many Aboriginal people lack confidence in the institutions of the Canadian state, and fail to see elections as producing legitimate, democratically representative results for themselves and their communities. Over a century's worth of policies and legislation

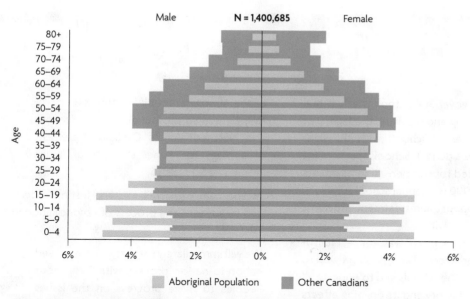

FIGURE 13.4 | Aboriginal and Non-Aboriginal Age Pyramids

Source: Statistics Canada, 1996, 2001 and 2006 Censuses of Population, and 2011 National Household Survey, AANDC tabulations.

have helped to institutionalize Canada's racism against Aboriginal people, beginning with the Indian Act, 1876, which defined First Nations people as wards of the federal government, imposed a regressive reserve system and paternalistic form of band governance, and stripped away most remnants of self-government. In the mid-twentieth century, cross-culture foster placement and adoption programs removed Aboriginal children from their families and placed them in non-Aboriginal homes. Forced relocation programs moved entire communities like the Innu of Davis Inlet to make way for economic development or to facilitate what governments viewed as more productive ways of life for the displaced residents.

Perhaps no institution is more emblematic of Canada's paternalistic approach to Aboriginal people than the residential schools system, which attempted to assimilate Aboriginal children by forcibly removing them from their communities and placing them into state and religious boarding schools. Many children were permanently separated from their families, and some experts, including those on the Truth and Reconciliation Commission, have characterized the residential schools system as an instrument of cultural genocide, with Aboriginal customs and languages being forbidden in the classroom as a means of extinguishing them entirely. In addition, widespread physical, psychological, and sexual abuse occurred at these schools, setting generations of Aboriginal people on a cycle of family violence and patterned substance use on a scale not experienced by any other group in Canada.

The cumulative effects of these institutions has been devastating for Aboriginal people and their communities, helping to explain but by no means justify the enduring gap between their living standards and those of Canada's non-Aboriginal population. It also helps to explain the deep sense of mistrust felt toward the Canadian state, and the corresponding reluctance among many Aboriginal people to participate in the conventional institutions of Canadian democracy.

residential schools system
A program of state- and church-run schools designed to assimilate Aboriginal children into whitestream Canadian society.

INSIDE CANADIAN POLITICS

How Is the Federal Government Approaching Reconciliation?

In 2007, the federal government took the first real step toward recognizing and resolving the legacy of Canada's Indian residential schools with the signing of the Indian Residential Schools Settlement Agreement. It provided for compensation payments to the estimated 110,000 residential school survivors, and also included support and treatment programs and commemorative activities.

Just as important to many was the establishment of the Truth and Reconciliation Commission to explore the impact of the schools and to educate all Canadians about this history and its ongoing effects on all parts of society. The commission's interim report was released in June 2015.

In June 2008, with leaders of all National Aboriginal Organizations and dozens of residential school survivors in attendance in the House of Commons, Prime Minister Stephen Harper offered an apology for the Government of Canada's role in the program. Part of his remarks are included here:

> To the approximately 80,000 living former students, and all family members and communities, the Government of Canada now recognizes that it was wrong to forcibly remove children from their homes, and we apologize for having done this. We now recognize that it was wrong to separate children from rich and vibrant cultures and traditions, that it created a void in many lives and communities, and we apologize for having done this. . . . The burden of this experience has been on your shoulders for far too long. The burden is properly ours as a Government and as a country. . . . The Government of Canada sincerely apologizes and asks the forgiveness of the Aboriginal peoples of this country for failing them so profoundly. . . . (Indigenous and Northern Affairs Canada, "Statement of apology to former students of Indian Residential Schools")

On the campaign trail in 2015, Justin Trudeau pledged to advance the process of reconciliation in several areas:

> We will immediately re-engage in a renewed nation-to-nation process with Indigenous Peoples to make progress on the issues most important to First Nations, the Métis Nation, and Inuit communities—issues like housing, infrastructure, health and mental health care, community safety and policing, child welfare, and education. . . .
>
> We will immediately launch a national public inquiry into missing and murdered Indigenous women and girls in Canada, to seek recommendations on concrete actions that governments, law enforcement, and others can take to solve these crimes and prevent future ones. . . .
>
> To support the work of reconciliation, and continue the necessary process of truth telling and healing, we will work alongside provinces and territories, and with First Nations, the Métis Nation, and Inuit, to enact the recommendations of the Truth and Reconciliation Commission, starting with the implementation of the United Nations *Declaration on the Rights of Indigenous Peoples*. (Liberal Party of Canada, 2015, "Real Change: A New Plan for a Strong Middle Class," pp. 46–8.)

VOX POP

Do you think the federal government's actions to date represent an appropriate and proportional response to address the legacy of residential schools? Why or why not?

The White Paper and National Aboriginal Organizations

The residential schools era is one of the saddest chapters in this history of Aboriginal people's relationships with Canadian governments, and the road to reconciliation was by no means direct. In 1969, the federal government released its *White Paper on Indian Policy*, a somewhat ironically titled document that proposed to dismantle the Indian Act and assimilate Aboriginal people into whitestream Canadian society. Prime Minister Pierre Trudeau and his minister of Indian affairs, Jean Chrétien, based the policy prescription on the principle of equality, arguing that converting reserve land to private property, settling outstanding land claims and extinguishing treaties, and devolving responsibility over "Indian affairs" to the provinces would result in fairer treatment of Aboriginal people.

Aboriginal groups were quick to condemn the government's proposals. During the consultations prior to the white paper's release, many Aboriginal groups asked the government to amend (not abolish) the Indian Act: they wanted to see Aboriginal rights enhanced, not extinguished; Aboriginal representation in federal decision-making increased, not submerged; and federal fiduciary responsibility for Indian affairs increased, not merely handed off to the provinces. Facing vocal opposition across the country, the federal government abandoned the white paper soon after it was released.

Marta Iwanek/GetStock.com

In June 2015, the Truth and Reconciliation Commission released its summary report, including a list of 94 calls to action. Consult the report, which is widely available online. Which of the recommendations do you feel are the most difficult to implement? Are there other ways to promote reconciliation among Aboriginal and non-Aboriginal people in Canada?

National Aboriginal Organizations (NAOs) Five bodies formally recognized as representing the interests of different Aboriginal groups across Canada.

The white paper left a lasting mark on Aboriginal politics in Canada, however, as it hastened the birth of the first National Aboriginal Organizations (NAOs). Prior to the 1960s, Aboriginal political groups were almost entirely regional, based around individual tribes or bands, or confined to specific provinces. The 1969 white paper convinced many Aboriginal leaders of the importance of forming pan-Canadian organizations to lobby, litigate, and engage in public persuasion.

Aboriginal communities across Canada have gradually developed a greater number of increasingly specialized and sophisticated institutions to represent their interests on the national (and international) stage (see Figure 13.5). The evolution of NAOs has coincided with various waves of constitutional negotiations.

The first truly pan-Canadian organization, the National Indian Advisory Council, was a creation of the federal government. Established in 1961 to represent status and non-status Indians and Métis in their dealings with Ottawa, NIAC broke apart amid diverging interests among its members. First Nations groups founded two new organizations: the National Indian Brotherhood, representing status Indians, and the Native Council of Canada, representing non-status Indians and Métis. The Brotherhood has since become the Assembly of First Nations, while the groups represented by the Native Council have developed a pair of separate organizations: the Congress of Aboriginal Peoples and the Métis National Council. Meanwhile, Aboriginal women banded together to form the Native Women's Association of Canada, and Inuit Canadians founded the Inuit Tapirisat of Canada (later re-christened the Inuit Tapiriit Kanatami). A series of regional and provincial Aboriginal organizations have also developed, sometimes affiliated with the NAOs, sometimes at

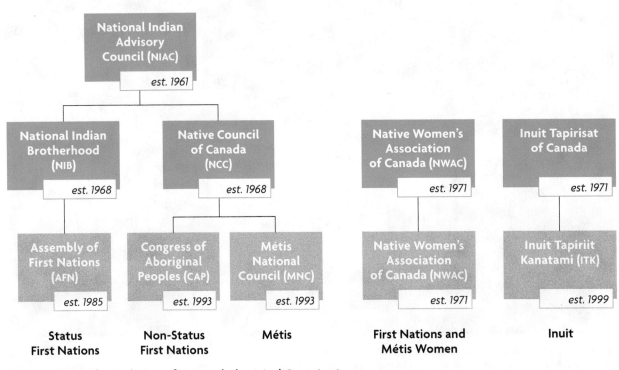

FIGURE 13.5 | The Evolution of National Aboriginal Organizations

odds with them. An example of the type of career opportunities that exist within such organizations is presented in the Opportunities Available box below.

As these NAOs formed, federal, provincial, and territorial governments took notice, and this level of pan-Canadian unity helped force Aboriginal rights closer and closer to the forefront of megaconstitutional negotiations in the 1970s and 1980s. When first ministers drafted the terms of patriation, they were pushed by groups like the National Indian Brotherhood to enshrine the Royal Proclamation and treaty rights in the new Constitution Act, and promise future rounds of direct constitutional negotiations with Aboriginal leaders. During the Charlottetown round of constitutional negotiations in the early 1990s, first ministers promised to recognize and take steps to fulfill the inherent right to Aboriginal self-government and to "safeguard and develop their languages, cultures, economies, identities, institutions, and traditions, and to develop, maintain and strengthen their relationship with their lands, waters and environment, so as to determine and control their development as peoples according to their own values and priorities and to ensure the integrity of their societies." While the Charlottetown Accord ultimately failed, the inclusion of

Opportunities Available

Knowledge of Canadian Politics and Government Preferred!
Justice Project Coordinator

Violence Prevention and Safety, Native Women's Association of Canada

The Native Women's Association of Canada is seeking a project coordinator to plan and organize a dialogue session for input into the development of the draft Justice Framework to address Violence Against Aboriginal Women and Girls. The successful candidate will work under the supervision of the Director of the Violence Prevention and Safety Department.

Major Duties

- Identify and invite dialogue session participants
- Secure a venue for the event
- Identify and invite a facilitator that is knowledgeable in the subject area
- Attend to all logistics regarding the travel and accommodation of the dialogue session participants
- Organize the recording of the dialogue session and the development of the post-dialogue teleconference or Webinar
- Track the progress and quality of work being performed

- Develop status, draft and final report
- Other related duties, as required

Essential Knowledge, Skills and Competencies

- Knowledge of issues affecting Aboriginal women
- Knowledge of the Canadian justice system in relation to Aboriginal women
- Superior oral and written communication skills
- Effective time management skills
- Strong sense of tact, diplomacy, maturity and professionalism
- Highly motivated, positive attitude and the ability to work independently
- Possess analytical skills and decisiveness
- Ability to work as part of a team, demonstrating flexibility and efficiency
- Political and cultural sensitivity is required
- Must have knowledge of Aboriginal diversity
- Advanced computer and IT skills

Source: Native Women's Association of Canada (2014), www.nwac.ca/current-opportunities.

↺ The reasons for the failure of the Charlottetown Accord are discussed on pages 64–5 of Chapter 2, on the constitution.

Aboriginal rights provisions was due, in no small part, to the success of NAO leaders and Aboriginal community organizers in elevating such issues to the top of the political agenda.

Today, the five officially recognized National Aboriginal Organizations—the AFN, the Congress of Aboriginal Peoples, the Métis National Council, the Native Women's Association of Canada, and the Inuit Tapiriit Kanatami—are invited to annual meetings with the premiers in advance of each summer gathering of the Council of the Federation. In 2009, premiers directed all provincial and territorial ministers of Aboriginal relations to work together with NAO leaders to examine ways of working together to improve the lives of First Nations, Inuit, and Métis peoples across Canada. Together, these ministers and leaders formed the Aboriginal Affairs Working Group, which meets at least once a year to discuss progress in priority areas, including improving educational, economic, and housing outcomes in Aboriginal communities, and ending violence against Aboriginal women and girls. The federal minister of Aboriginal affairs and northern development is invited to each working group meeting, and has attended twice since 2009; this may change with the Trudeau Liberals. On occasion, the federal minister meets with NAO leaders on a bilateral or multilateral basis; the prime minister has also done so, but less frequently.

National Aboriginal Organizations may be the most convenient means for federal, provincial, and territorial (FPT) governments to engage with Aboriginal people on a pan-Canadian basis (although most FPT governments prefer to deal with local Aboriginal communities as opposed to NAOs). The NAO model falls well short of what many feel is the most appropriate model for Aboriginal representation in Canada: a nation-to-nation approach.

Toward Aboriginal Self-Government?

In the midst of the Charlottetown round of constitutional negotiations, the federal government launched a Royal Commission on Aboriginal Peoples (RCAP), whose 1996 report—*People to People, Nation to Nation*, released two decades before the Truth and Reconciliation Commission completed its investigation into residential schools—sought to restore justice and sow the seeds of reconciliation between Aboriginal and non-Aboriginal people in Canada. After five years, over one hundred public hearings, and dozens of academic studies, the Royal Commission reached a simple conclusion: "The main policy direction, pursued for more than 150 years, first by colonial then by Canadian governments, has been wrong." Whether intentional or guided by ignorance, assimilationist policies that had aimed to modernize Aboriginal communities and forge equality between Aboriginal and non-Aboriginal Canadians had done far more damage than good.

To remedy the situation, RCAP outlined the premises for Aboriginal self-government in Canada, as follows:

Royal Commission on Aboriginal Peoples (RCAP) An investigation launched to study the relationship between Aboriginal and non-Aboriginal people in Canada.

- For many Aboriginal peoples, the right to be self-governing is derived from the Creator, who gave each nation responsibility for caring for the land and each other;
- Aboriginal self-government is protected through international law, which states that all peoples have the right to "self-determination," including the freedom to choose their own forms of government;

- Aboriginal self-government was recognized by the first European settlers, and was never ceded by Aboriginal people (through conquest, treaty, or otherwise); and
- Aboriginal self-government is enshrined in the Canadian constitution, which acknowledges that it predated Confederation and was a key element of the bargain that allowed non-Aboriginal people to found this country.

The way forward, argued the commissioners, required a re-assessment of the status and role of Aboriginal people in Canada. This renewed relationship would have to be built on four principles:

- *recognition*, which involved mutual acknowledgment by Aboriginal and non-Aboriginal people of each other's unique laws and institutions;
- *respect*, which would require regard for the unique rights and status of Aboriginal people in Canada;
- *reciprocity*, necessitating the encouragement of both Aboriginal and non-Aboriginal people to share benefits from their relationship; and
- *responsibility*, with each partner being accountable for their actions and commitments.

The commissioners recommended these principles be enshrined through new and renewed treaties.

According to RCAP, these values could be reflected within three models of self-government. In *Nation Government*, individual Aboriginal peoples would choose how to exercise their own sovereignty within their respective boundaries, particularly in areas of cultural, social, and economic development. In *Public Government*, Aboriginal people would form the majority in a territory shared with non-Aboriginal people and, by virtue of being selected by all people through democratic structures, govern on behalf of all residents regardless of their heritage. Finally, in *Community of Interest Government*, Aboriginal people in urban areas would form the minority of the population yet exercise control over education, social services, and economic development through devolution arrangements with provincial governments.

Other RCAP recommendations included the following:

- formal government recognition of past injustices, the inherent right to self-government, and a separate constitutional order of government for Aboriginal people
- the creation of dual (Canadian and First Nation) citizenship
- the consolidation of over 600 Indian bands into 60 to 80 nations
- increased funding for Aboriginal governments
- the creation of a Lands and Treaties Tribunal to formalize and streamline the resolution of outstanding land claims
- the creation of a "House of First Peoples" to advise Parliament and, eventually, pass legislation respecting Aboriginal people in Canada.

The RCAP report generated much debate among Canadians, politicians, and academics, particularly surrounding the notion of Aboriginal self-government. Three general approaches have emerged. One, embodied by the RCAP report, proposes a nation-to-nation paradigm in which Aboriginal people constitute autonomous

treaty federalism A system of governance recognizing the equal-order relationship between First Nations and the Crown.

third order of government A constitutionally recognized status for First Nations people, on par with the federal and provincial orders.

government units, albeit highly interdependent with those of the Canadian state. Treaty federalism is among the most widely accepted models under this approach. Articulated by scholars like James Youngblood Henderson, James Tully, and Kiera Ladner,[19] treaty federalism adds a layer of representation to the traditional concept of Canadian federalism. It acknowledges that sovereignty in Canada is not simply divided between the federal and provincial orders of government; it is also invested in Aboriginal people through the inherent right to self-government.

This has given rise to the notion that Aboriginal people constitute a third order of government in Canada. Contrary to the traditional interpretation of the Canadian constitution, Aboriginal affairs would no longer be an area of federal jurisdiction, and the federal government would not hold sovereign authority over Aboriginal people. Just as provincial powers are not delegated to provincial governments by the federal order, neither would Aboriginal rights and authority be delegated by provincial or federal governments. Under the treaty federalism model, treaties have helped to define the relationship between the federal, provincial, and Aboriginal orders, and must be respected, expanded, and extended to new territories in order to fully realize Aboriginal self-government in Canada. In this sense, the federal government's responsibility for "Indian affairs" is confined to implementing existing treaties and negotiating future ones.

The RCAP report contained a series of recommendations that would have built a new constitutional order along these lines. This included the recognition of a separate Aboriginal order of government, parallel to the federal and provincial orders, with sovereignty over the governance and welfare of Aboriginal people, and the creation of a separate "House of First Peoples." Other suggestions have included establishing Aboriginal-specific electoral districts and court systems, and guaranteed seats in Parliament or at the first ministers' table. These sorts of institutional reforms would help to integrate Aboriginal people into the various branches of government as a separate and equal order.

RCAP's harshest critics sit at the opposite pole of perspectives on the future of Aboriginal self-government. Many opponents of the parallelism approach argue against establishing separate institutions or systems of rights for Aboriginal people, viewing such provisions as placing group rights over the individual rights shared equally among all Canadians. One of the most critically acclaimed proponents of this viewpoint is Tom Flanagan, whose *First Nations? Second Thoughts* remains only one of two books to have won both the Donner and Donald Smiley prizes for best work in public policy and political science. In it, Flanagan challenges the notion that Aboriginal people have an inherent right to self-government, and suggests that fostering further separation between Aboriginal and non-Aboriginal modes of governance would only exacerbate the socioeconomic gaps that exist between the two communities. Flanagan suggests that colonization and the disappearance of Aboriginal customs and ways of governance is an inevitable part of Canada's evolution, and that efforts to impede or roll back this process are both futile and counterproductive. Rather than stand in its way, Flanagan advocates embracing this evolution, extending notions like property rights to Aboriginal communities as a means of facilitating their advancement.

Flanagan's critics have labelled his work "assimilationist," with many arguing his proposals go even further than those advanced in the Trudeau government's 1969 white paper. For his part, Flanagan does not eschew the label, saying:

In order to become self-supporting and get beyond the social pathologies that are ruining their communities, [A]boriginal people need to acquire the skills and attitudes that bring success in a liberal society, political democracy, and market economy. Call it assimilation, call it integration, call it adaptation, call it whatever you want: it has to happen.[20]

A third approach has emerged as a mid-point between the parallelism of treaty federalism and the integration-minded model advanced by scholars like Flanagan. This citizens plus model was popularized by political scientist Alan Cairns in his 2000 book of the same name. According to Cairns and his supporters, Aboriginal people retain all of the rights accorded to all Canadians (including those contained in the Charter of Rights and Freedoms) *plus* a set of rights unique to Aboriginal people (including those embodied in the Royal Proclamation of 1763, treaties, and government legislation). According to this view, Aboriginal self-government should be considered within the confines of the Canadian state and citizenship, without the formal establishment of independent, sovereign nation-states, and without subsuming it under the current constitutional order. Cairns's approach emphasizes the commonalities and shared interests between the Aboriginal and non-Aboriginal communities in Canada, and acknowledges that—like many non-Aboriginal people—Aboriginal people often hold multiple identities. These differences and similarities should be recognized, while forging a common, pan-Canadian set of interests and political community.

Debates between these three worldviews have been fought not just in the public and political spheres but also in the courts. In the *Calder* (1973) and *Guerin* (1984) decisions, for example, the Supreme Court ruled that Aboriginal title to land could pre-date white settlement. In the *Sparrow* (1990), *Van der Peet* (1996), and *Marshall* (1999, 2007) cases, the court held that Aboriginal hunting and fishing rights are "evolving" and constitutionally protected against provincial regulation. Through the *Delgamuukw* (1997) and *Haida Nation* (2004) cases, the court established that the Crown has the duty to consult Aboriginal groups prior to developing lands to which they could stake claims. And in *Tsilhqot'in Nation* (2014), the Supreme Court of Canada ruled that, while underlying control over the land rests with the Crown, Aboriginal peoples with valid title claims must be consulted and accommodated before any decisions are made with regard to the use and management of the land, including its natural resources.

Indeed, as not all lands in what is now Canada were formally ceded to the British or Canadian Crown, Aboriginal people continue to stake land claims. In light of this fact, the British Columbia and federal governments continue to negotiate land claims settlements in the province, the most comprehensive of which was the Nisga'a Treaty. The 1999 final agreement marked the first of its kind in one hundred years in BC, and provided for a form of self-government for the 5500 Nisga'a peoples living in the Nass River Valley of BC. The newly formed Nisga'a government has legislative authority over some land and resources management issues, taxation, citizenship, language, and culture. These laws exist in parallel with federal and provincial laws, and are subject to the Canadian constitution, including the Charter of Rights and Freedoms. The Nisga'a government may also make laws in areas like health and social services, environmental protection, and transportation, although federal or provincial laws continue to hold primacy. In addition to recognizing these powers, the treaty and related agreements

citizens plus The notion that Aboriginal people (ought to) hold a special set of rights in addition to those conferred by Canadian citizenship.

land claims Statements of Aboriginals' entitlement to territory within Canada.

Nisga'a Treaty Land claims agreement struck between the Nisga'a Tribal Council, the Government of Canada, and the Government of BC.

THEY SAID IT

Excerpts from "A Message Regarding the Rights of the Crees"

In response to the prospect of a "yes" vote in the 1995 Quebec referendum, the James Bay Cree released the following statement about their own constitutional position.

We are Eeyouch. We are a people. We have our own land, Eeyou Astchee. We are an organized society of Aboriginal people forming part of the community of the world's indigenous peoples. We are the original inhabitants of our territory, and have occupied our land and governed ourselves for the past 9,000 years.

At least four times—in 1670, 1870, 1898, and 1912—Eeyou Astchee, our traditional lands and waters, have changed status, purportedly, transferred between kings as gifts, or deeded between colonial companies and governments, all without our knowledge, and certainly without our consent. It has always been assumed that we the James Bay Crees, the actual owners and occupants, simply passed with the land, without voice, without the right to determine or even know what was being done with us.

Now in 1995, although we live in a modern and democratic state, protected by the Canadian Constitution with its Charter of Rights and Freedoms, our people and our territory may once again be transferred from sovereign to sovereign, this time from Canada to what may become the newly independent state of Quebec. And although there is now a United Nations, with a Universal Declaration of Human Rights and a vast array of international human rights instruments that should protect us, a process has been set in motion that would forcibly remove the Crees from Canada, and incorporate us and our lands in this new state. . . .

The myth persists in Quebec and elsewhere in Canada, that this country consists of two founding nations or peoples. This fiction constitutes a practical denial of our presence, our rights and status, and our role in the history, economy, and well-being of this country.

Now, as Canada debates its own possible dis-integration, many would prefer once again to conduct this debate without facing the troubling and far-reaching questions regarding our rights as an Aboriginal people. Many Aboriginal peoples would also prefer to stay in the background and allow the "non-natives" to fight this out among themselves.

For the Crees this is no longer possible. It is our people and our own land that is being threatened, and the Crees must be heard or we may become the victims of our own silence, passed along with the land. . . .

[We] have been making extensive preparations to defend ourselves. We know our rights, and we can reply strongly to every one of the many false arguments that have been made by those who consider it in their own interest to deny our rights.

This debate will continue in Canada—the need to recognize and respect the rights of the Crees and other Aboriginal peoples in order to advance the well-being of all of its citizens, to strengthen its democracy, its respect for human rights, and its future as a country that includes Aboriginal peoples in its own vision of itself.

That has not yet happened. Perhaps the unity debate, and the examination of Cree rights and status that it brings into focus, will help to bring this about. That is certainly one of our goals, and perhaps the most important reason to read this study.

In any case, this is certain: The Crees will be here. We are not going anywhere. Nothing will be done with us, now or in the future, without our informed consent.

—Grand Chief Matthew Coon Come

transferred nearly $250 million to the Nisga'a, provided ongoing (but gradually tapering) federal and provincial transfers for the delivery of health, education, and social services by the Nisga'a government, and recognized over 2000 square kilometers of land as Nisga'a territory. In these ways, the Nisga'a treaty came closest to establishing what RCAP had labeled the "Nation Government" model of self-government.

At the same time, the federal government was also negotiating the 1993 Nunavut Land Claims Agreement, which culminated in the creation of a new, Inuit-majority northern territory in 1999. Nunavut's territory was carved out of the eastern portion of Northwest Territories, and is the largest subnational unit in North America, with also the lowest number of inhabitants. The Nunavut territorial government retained the same constitutional status as the governments of Northwest Territories and Yukon, with jurisdiction over land use management, economic and resource development, and property taxation remaining subject to federal oversight. As in the Northwest Territories, Nunavut's legislative assembly operates a form of consensus government,

Nunavut Land Claims Agreement An agreement between the Inuit (Tunngavik Federation of Nunavut) and the Government of Canada, resulting in the creation of the Territory of Nunavut.

Lee Narraway

Not unlike Newfoundland and Labrador's entry into Confederation, the creation of Nunavut in 1999 took decades—and a substantial amount of direct democracy—to achieve. In an initial territory-wide plebiscite in 1982, 56 per cent of Northwest Territories voters agreed that the territory should be divided. In a second plebiscite, held 10 years later, the proposed border between NWT and Nunavut was endorsed by 54 per cent of voters. A third vote, in November 1992, saw the Nunavut Land Claims Agreement and the establishment of the new territory endorsed by 85 per cent of NWT residents who voted. Are plebiscites a necessary mechanism to establish new provinces and territories in Canada? Should all Canadians be consulted on the matter? What other processes could be put in place to ensure minority and majority interests—both within the territory and in the rest of Canada—are balanced?

with no political parties. In these ways, Nunavut approaches what RCAP referred to as the "public government" model of Aboriginal self-government.

The debates between Ladner, Flanagan, Cairns, and their followers are unlikely to subside in the foreseeable future, and neither are the representational challenges underlying them. As mentioned, Canada's Aboriginal population is substantially younger and is growing far more quickly than the non-Aboriginal population, particularly in the West. Between 1971 and 2011, Canada's population, on the whole, grew by just over 50 per cent; the Aboriginal population grew nearly ten times as quickly over that period (487 per cent), and high birth rates continue to place Aboriginal people among the fastest-growing demographic groups in Canada. Considering these trends, in the years to come, Canadians of all ethnic and cultural backgrounds will continue to face questions about the appropriate, fair, and just representation of Aboriginal people in Canada.

Concluding Thoughts

As a project in liberal democracy, Canada has always been a case study in the accommodation of difference. In Chapter 2, we discussed how Confederation aimed to achieve unity through diversity. Centuries prior to 1867, Canada was forged through the bridging of ethnic, cultural, and linguistic divides. These divisions have multiplied since, creating a complex set of overlapping cleavages.

We began this chapter by pointing out the widespread consensus surrounding Canada's mosaic, and how deeply ingrained multiculturalism has become in its political ethos and national identity. We closed by highlighting how contested the components of that mosaic really are, and how much work remains to incorporate diversity into Canada's democratic institutions. While the country has come a long way in terms of recognizing the value of acceptance, accommodation, and reconciliation, significant barriers remain to the full participation of traditionally marginalized groups in Canadian society. The most viable way to reduce the democratic deficit will remain one of the most contested topics in Canadian politics in decades to come.

For More Information

How inclusive are each of the major institutions of Canadian democracy? Led by William Cross, the Canadian Democratic Audit team compiled a series of 10 volumes on the subject, covering everything from political parties and legislatures to the courts and interest groups. Read *Auditing Canadian Democracy* (UBC Press, 2010) for a full synopsis of their findings.

How inclusive are Canada's city governments? In *Electing a Diverse Canada*, editors Caroline

Andrew, John Biles, Myer Siemiatycki, Erin Tolley, and their contributors examine the *Representation of Immigrants, Minorities, and Women* in nine of Canada's largest cities (UBC Press, 2008).

What explains the lack of women in positions of political power? Linda Trimble, Jane Arscott, and Manon Tremblay have assembled a comprehensive volume on the matter, entitled *Stalled: The Representation of Women in Canadian Governments* (UBC Press, 2013).

Are there other perspectives on Aboriginal self-government in Canada? For a rejoinder to Tom Flanagan's *First Nations: Second Thoughts* (McGill–Queen's University Press, 2000) and Alan Cairns's *Citizens Plus* (UBC Press, 2000), see Annis May Timpson's edited volume *First Nations, First Thoughts: The Impact of Indigenous Thought in Canada* (UBC Press, 2009).

Interested in the gender balance of Canada's legislatures today? Equal Voice Canada (www.equalvoice.ca) maintains a running tally of the number of women in Parliament and provincial assemblies.

How did Canadian public opinion evolve so quickly on the issue of LGBTT rights? J. Scott Matthews explores "The Political Foundations of Support for Same-Sex Marriage in Canada," *Canadian Journal of Political Science* 38, no. 4 (2005): pp. 841–66.

Want to learn more about the history of LGBTT rights in Canada? Established by researchers at the University of Lethbridge, Mapleleafweb, a political education website, offers a concise history: http://mapleleafweb.com/features/same-sex-marriage-canada, or search: Maple Leaf Web same sex marriage.

Want to read the highlights of the 1996 Royal Commission on Aboriginal Peoples Report? Go to: www.aadnc-aandc.gc.ca/eng/1100100014597/1100100014637, or search: 1996 RCAP report.

Confused about how the Indian Act operates? Mapleleafweb has assembled an excellent primer. Search: Maple Leaf Web Indian Act.

Want to hear the latest results of the Truth and Reconciliation Commission? Visit the TRC website: www.trc.ca.

Want to learn more about integration, diversity, and immigrant integration in Canada? Visit the Metropolis Project website: http://canada.metropolis.net/.

Looking for a debate on the merits of race-based affirmative action in other countries? *The Economist* hosted one. Search: Economist affirmative action debate.

Deeper Inside Canadian Politics

1. People from traditionally marginalized groups face many common challenges to their fair representation in Canadian democracy. They also face many barriers unique to their own respective groups. Consider the obstacles encountered by Aboriginal women in Canada. Outline five key challenges they face by virtue both of being members of an Indigenous community and of being women, comparing these to those faced by both Aboriginal men and Caucasian women.

2. Are provincial and territorial governments more inclusive than the federal government when it comes to representing diversity? Why or why not?

3. In Chapter 4 we discussed the evolution of Quebec nationalism and the challenges facing its proponents. Compare and contrast these experiences with those of Canada's Aboriginal people. Which group is more likely to achieve sovereignty (or self-government), and why?

UP FOR DEBATE

Are affirmative action programs needed in the Canadian public service?

THE CLAIM: YES, THEY ARE!

Affirmative action is needed to ensure that the government workforce reflects the diversity of Canada's population.

Yes: Argument Summary

A democratic society should be governed by people who reflect the diversity of the broader citizenry. Historically, the Canadian public service has been made up predominantly of white men of western European heritage, particularly in senior management roles. The American practice of affirmative action, which involves quota-based hiring, can do far more to correct this bias than the training and recruitment practices in place under the program of employment equity currently favoured by the federal government.

Yes: Top 5 Considerations

1. The use of affirmative action policies to address discrimination against disadvantaged groups is protected by the constitution. Section 15 of the Charter of Rights and Freedoms specifies equality rights and explicitly allows "any law, program or activity that has as its object the amelioration of conditions of disadvantaged individuals or groups including those that are disadvantaged because of race, national or ethnic origin, colour, religion, sex, age or mental or physical disability." The argument that such policies in fact discriminate against better qualified candidates is invalid.
2. The hiring and fast-tracking of certain Canadians into management positions is the most viable way of "righting a wrong" and adjusting for the underrepresentation of certain groups within the public service.
3. Affirmative action programs contribute to pay equity and promotes human resource practices that are sensitive to different groups. For example, they can lead to employment policies that are responsive to employees' childcare obligations or the rights of employees in same-sex partnerships to family benefits.
4. Recent immigrants experience particular challenges entering the Canadian workforce. They may have difficulty having their employment and education credentials recognized, they may not be fluent in either of Canada's official languages, and they may not be sufficiently familiar with local cultural nuances that lead to a job offer. Private-sector employers are often especially reluctant to hire recent immigrants. The government can help them find work in the public sector through affirmative action policies.
5. The importance of affirmative action programs in the public service is magnified by the absence of such quotas in most areas of the legislative and executive branches of government.

Yes: Other Considerations

- For multiculturalism to thrive in Canada, the government must itself be a cultural mosaic.
- Hiring quotas can help public service employers fill positions with specialized needs that only recent immigrants or ethnic minorities can provide. For example, Citizenship and Immigration Canada has a special need for employees who are fluent in various langauages and familiar with different ethno-cultural practices, while Aboriginal Affairs and Northern

Development Canada places an added importance on ensuring that its employees are familiar with Aboriginal culture.

- With Canada's birth rate sitting below replacement level, young, skilled immigrants are needed more than ever to fill a variety of jobs vacated by an aging workforce. Skilled immigrants may be more likely to come to Canada and contribute meaningfully to society if it has affirmative action policies in place.

THE COUNTERCLAIM: NO, THEY AREN'T!

Affirmative action is undemocratic because it favours certain candidates over others on the basis of gender, ethnic background, and other social characteristics.

No: Argument Summary

Affirmative action is built on a very specific and limiting view of Canadian democracy—one that favours descriptive over substantive representation, group over individual rights, minority over majority interests, equality of result over equality of opportunity, and government intervention over free-market competition. At its most successful, Canadian democracy involves a greater balance between these conflicting values.

No: Top 5 Considerations

1. One of the greatest challenges associated with designing affirmative action policies surrounds the fairness in defining which groups should be eligible for unequal treatment. These decisions inevitably sow deeper divisions in Canadian society, and amount to government-directed social engineering.
2. Affirmative action programs aim to treat the symptoms of discrimination, not its root causes. Enforcing certain types of hiring does not in itself improve the attitudes of employers and other workers toward members of minority groups. By holding descriptive representation as both its means and its end goal, affirmative action fails to address the underlying causes of discrimination in the broader Canadian political culture.
3. To follow this metaphor, the cure (i.e. hiring quotas) may be worse than the disease (i.e. discrimination), as they serve only to perpetuate the politics of difference. As John Roberts, chief justice of the US Supreme Court, has stated, "the best way to stop discrimination on the basis of race is to stop discriminating on the basis of race."[21]
4. Once established, affirmative action programs and policies are very difficult to wind down or abolish, regardless of their lack of effectiveness. Several political parties in Canada have had quota systems in place for over two decades, and yet gender parity in their caucuses remains elusive.
5. Recent statistics suggest that the groups that affirmative action programs are designed to help are already well represented in the workforce.

No: Other Considerations

- In prioritizing merit over group identity, Canada's system of employment equity attempts to avoid the negative consequences of pure affirmative action.
- The beneficiaries and non-beneficiaries of employment equity programs can both experience a negative self-image in response to such programming.[22]
- Affirmative action programs that establish hiring quotas do not necessarily consider the types or quality of occupations that are consequently filled by members of minority groups.
- To qualify for special treatment in hiring, people must register their special status. This can be a source of concern for people belonging to non-visible minority groups, such as persons with disabilities.

Discussion Questions

- Do you think there is a fundamental difference between affirmative action programs and employment equity programs? What are the strengths and weaknesses of each approach?
- Once hiring in the public service meets or exceeds its affirmative action targets, would it nevertheless be perceived as politically incorrect to cancel the programs?
- Many new Canadians do not speak English or French as a first language. What is the best way to ensure that they are not at a significant disadvantage in government hiring? How can the government ensure that those employees who are not fluent in either official language can perform their duties?
- Is the democratic spirit upheld or infringed when members of a particular demographic group are purposely hired over equally qualified candidates?
- In your opinion, should political parties be required to follow some variation of the employment equity programs that are used in government?

Where to Learn More about Affirmative Action and Employment Equity in Canadian Government

John Grundy and Miriam Smith, "Evidence and Equity: Struggles over Federal Employment Equity Policy in Canada, 1984–95," *Canadian Public Administration* 54, no. 3 (2011): pp. 335–57.

Rana Haq and Eddy S.W. Ng, "Employment Equity and Workplace Diversity in Canada," *International Handbook on Diversity Management at Work: Country Perspectives on Diversity and Equal Treatment*, ed. Alain Klarsfeld (Cheltenham, UK: Edward Elgar, 2010).

Ivona Hideg and D. Lance Ferris, "Support for Employment Equity Policies: A Self-enhancement Approach," *Organizational Behavior and Human Decision Processes* 123, no. 1 (2014): pp. 49–64.

Harish C. Jain, Frank Horwitz, and Christa L. Wilkin, "Employment Equity in Canada and South Africa: A Comparative Review," *International Journal of Human Resource Management* 23, no. 1 (2012): pp. 1–17.

Harish C. Jain, et al., "Effectiveness of Canada's Employment Equity Legislation for Women (1997–2004): Implications for Policy Makers," *Industrial Relations* 65, no. 2 (2010): pp. 304–29.

Eddy S.W. Ng and Ronald J. Burke, "A Comparison of the Legislated Employment Equity Program, Federal Contractors Program, and *Financial Post* 500 Firms," *Canadian Journal of Administrative Sciences* 27, no. 3 (2010): pp. 224–35.

14 CANADA'S PLACE IN THE WORLD

Inside this Chapter

- How have Canada's ties to Britain and the United States changed over time?
- How has Canada's international political status evolved?
- What have Canada's military priorities been?
- What types of multinational organizations does Canada belong to?
- How does Canada participate in improving the global community?

Inside Canada's Place in the World

The twentieth century was supposed to be the century of Canada—at least, according to Prime Minister Wilfrid Laurier. With its vast territory, abundant natural resources, and burgeoning population growth through immigration, the future looked bright

What the 2015 Election means for Canada's Place in the World

Visit the *Inside Canadian Politics* flipboard to learn about the latest developments affecting Canada's place in the world.

Go to
http://flip.it/gblag.

for the young dominion. Laurier's optimism about Canada's future was drastically overstated, however, at least in terms of his designs on world domination. Gradually, Canada did manage to throw off some shackles of its colonial past, taking control first of its own economy, then its military, then its symbols, and finally its constitution. But this process took over 100 years to complete, and many still consider Canadian sovereignty to be a work in progress. Indeed, some outsiders view Canada's evolution as moving from the grip of Britannia into the orbit of Americana. In the process, Canadian global leadership has never really materialized, as it continues to work in the shadows of greater countries.

This outsider's view fits well with Canadians' modest self-image. Yet it drastically oversimplifies Canada's role on the international stage. As you read through this chapter, bear in mind the following maxims about Canada's place in the world.

 Canada is still in its adolescence. Canada may have been born 150 years ago, but it has taken the better part of the period since 1867 for the country to achieve maturity as a fully sovereign nation. In many ways, Canada is still far younger than other advanced industrial countries.

 Canada charts its own course on foreign policy. Many people believe that Canadian foreign policy is effectively American foreign policy. However, while its economic and military dependency on the United States is beyond dispute, Canada's relationship with its American neighbour is far more nuanced than some observers suggest.

 Canada has more clout than you might think. Some students believe that Canada shies away from bold action on the international stage. Its interventions may be few and far between, but Canada's status as a middle power has allowed it to exert significant influence on issues like global trade and human rights, from time to time.

Peering inside Canada's place in the world means gaining an accurate sense of the country's role and position within the international community, as well as its own mission and identity.

Overview

Canada may be one of the largest landmasses in the world, and it may rank among the globe's most advanced industrial societies, but its politics are defined far more by domestic factors than by global ones. The country has rarely harboured ambitions grander than supporting its own citizens, offering cautious support for its allies, and making modest foreign aid contributions. Canada has operated in the shadows of two international giants, with British imperialism ceding to American continentalism in the mid-twentieth century, and historically its leaders have been preoccupied with managing internal political tensions. Indeed, Canadians have tended to support politicians who champion local matters, governments that are inward-looking, and prime ministers who can hold their own on the international stage without necessarily "punching above their weight." Yet despite these modest expectations, Canadians have served admirably as members of the international community, participating in the most significant military conflicts of our times, lending talent to important acts of international diplomacy, and embracing, if not leading, efforts at globalization.

From Colony to Dominion to Country

Understanding Canada's status as a constitutional monarchy—not an independent republic—is crucial to understanding its role in the international community. Its formal connection to the United Kingdom has far-reaching implications for its behaviour as a global citizen. Whatever aspirations Canadians may have to divest themselves of British rule, they have collectively determined that they are not in a hurry to do so.

Until 1931, when the Statute of Westminster was passed, all British laws were in force in Canada, as well as in Australia, Newfoundland (a British colony at the time), New Zealand, and South Africa. Even then, the Canadian constitution, known rightly as the British North America Act, 1867, remained a British statute. It was only with the passage of the Constitution Act in 1982 that Canada secured the ability to change its constitution without requiring the approval of the British Parliament.

Moreover, Canada did not exercise military independence until the Second World War; prior to that, Britain spoke for Canada in international forums, and Canadians initially served under British military units. True Canadian citizenship did not exist until the Canadian Citizenship Act came into force in 1947, prior to which "Canadians" were considered a subset of British subjects. It took until 1949 for the Supreme Court of Canada to become the country's highest court, displacing the British-based Judicial Committee of the Privy Council; in the same year, Newfoundland joined Confederation following two referendums on the issue.

The Birth of a "New Nationalism"

The subsequent decades marked a turning point in Canada's history. During the 1960s in particular, several major trends, personalities, and forces converged to produce a unique setting for political debate about Canada's place in the world. Canada was nearing its centennial and, like any major birthday, the moment provided ample opportunity for reflection on the past and projection toward the future. Monuments were erected and historical celebrations were held to commemorate Confederation, while Expo '67, the world fair held in Montreal, promised to give Canada and other members of the global community a glimpse at tomorrow. Coming together to celebrate these events was a Canadian population that had undergone a dramatic transition of its own. Demographically, the country in 1960 was made up of more poly-generation Canadians than ever before, thanks largely to the post-war baby boom. On the whole, the increase in native-born Canadians meant relatively weaker kinship ties with Britain and the rest of Europe. At the same time, overall immigration levels remained relatively high after the war, with the percentage of non–English- and non–French-speaking Canadians soaring to new heights. This prompted some observers to proclaim the new immigrants, who came largely from central and eastern Europe, a third official segment of the Canadian population after the English and French (and to the notable exclusion of Canada's Aboriginal peoples). As Canada looked toward its second century, its cultural makeup was no longer dominated by its British and French constituents.

↻ Canada's status as a constitutional monarchy is explained in Chapter 2, on the constitution; see especially page 43.

Statute of Westminster A British law that permitted its Dominions to opt out of future legislation passed by the British Parliament.

↻ The Constitution Act is discussed throughout Chapter 2; see especially The BNA Act and Legislation since 1867, beginning on page 50.

Canada's political culture and institutions took longer to evolve. The two world wars had ended only decades prior to the 1960s, and their impact left lasting scars. After fighting with and in defence of the British empire, a large group of veterans and their families, perhaps more than any other segment of the population, retained strong emotional ties with the mother country. As the epigraph on one Normandy grave site attested, many veterans saw themselves as "the sons of William the Conqueror come back to claim his land." These sentiments ran contrary to post-war political and economic trends, as Britain began to lose its influence on the world stage. American isolationism in the interwar period had delayed the onset of symptoms, but by the 1960s, it became apparent that

INSIDE CANADIAN POLITICS
How Did Canadians Choose their Flag?

For many of today's young Canadians, it is difficult to picture a union jack or red ensign flying on Parliament Hill, or to imagine a time when the maple leaf did not represent Canada on flagstaffs around the world. Yet the adoption of the Canadian flag in 1965 symbolized the evolution of both the Canadian state and its people. To many at the time, the new maple leaf flag became the embodiment of Canada's new place within the Commonwealth of Nations, within North America, and within the world as a whole. At the same time, the flag announced the birth of a new cultural dynamic within her own borders—a tribute to the changing nature of relations among the "founding" and "new" races.

In 1867, as a British dominion, Canada's national flag was the Union Jack. This turned out to be unsuitable in war because of the need to distinguish military units and the nationalist stirrings among Canadian soldiers. To fill the gap, a modified version of the Union Jack, known as the Red Ensign, became Canada's unofficial flag.

During the 1963 federal election campaign, Liberal leader Lester B. Pearson promised to create an official flag, and upon becoming prime minister he unveiled his preferred design. The so-called "Pearson pennant" featured three red maple leaves on a white backdrop with vertical blue bars on each of the left and right sides. The maple leaf was a political symbol that had been used for years in songs and in the uniforms of Canadian sports teams. But the idea was dismissed as an affront to Canada's British heritage by the Conservative Party, while war veterans preferred the Red Ensign. Some thought combining the ensign with another cultural symbol, like the fleur-de-lis, would help provide balance.

A national debate ensued. Conversations in public places, in classrooms, and around the dinner table contributed to the evolution of a more modern and independent Canada. An all-party parliamentary committee reviewed approximately 6000 design submissions. It settled on the red-and-white maple leaf design that we know today—the same motif that appeared in a 1903 Quebec political cartoon.[1]

In the beginning, the flag debate was divided largely along regional lines, as reinforced by political parties' support bases. Progressive Conservative leader and former prime minister John Diefenbaker led the fight against the so-called "Pearson pennant." The Canadian flag, Diefenbaker argued, should reflect the contributions of the county's two founding peoples—the French and the English—by incorporating the fleur-de-lis and the union jack. As a symbol, the Conservatives turned to the red ensign, Canada's national flag since its sanction by Mackenzie King in 1945. Through modifications that would place the fleur-de-lis in a more prominent position and would add a single green maple leaf, the Tories proposed the ensign as a means of commemorating Canada's three stages of government: from French, to British, to Canadian administration.

On the other side of the aisle, members of Parliament from Quebec advocated a new, "distinctive" Canadian flag with no emblems to tie it to foreign

British hegemony had declined considerably in the wake of the two world wars. Part of a larger anti-colonialist movement that saw several former colonies gain their independence, Canada was beginning to distance itself from its traditional colonial identity.

In this context, a "new nationalism" was born in Canada, centred around three main goals:

- the adoption of a national anthem
- the development of a distinctive national flag
- the patriation of the constitution.

↺ Political cultures are defined and described beginning on page 127 of Chapter 4, on regionalism.

nations. The Liberal Party, whose caucus relied heavily on the contentment of its large French-speaking contingent, came out in strong support of this position. A new flag, they contended, ought to be introduced to symbolize the future of the Canadian nation and the unity of its peoples. Prime Minister Lester Pearson remarked that the proposed maple leaf flag would be "something around which all Canadians, new and old, native born and naturalized, of all racial stocks, can rally, and which will be the focus of their loyalty to Canada." Along these lines, the design ought to be "mutually acceptable" to all Canadians, and contain a central symbol which would "divide us the least."

After a rancorous discussion in the House of Commons, and amid minority government conditions, the Flag Act, 1965, was passed, and the maple leaf became Canada's national emblem. Thus, on the eve of the centennial of Confederation, and amid a hung parliament, Canada had adopted a new national symbol that helped sever symbolic ties to its British heritage.

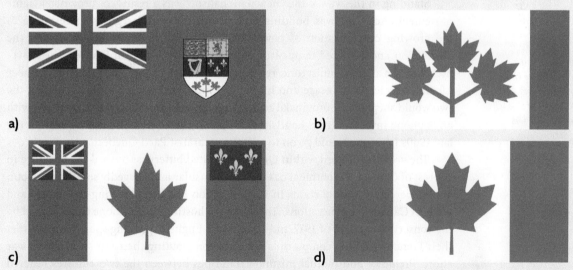

FIGURE 14.1 | (a) The Red Ensign **(b)** The Pearson Pennant **(c)** The Diefenbaker Proposal **(d)** The Canadian Flag

VOX POP

Given this, do you agree that a single-symbol flag was the best choice, or would a dual-symbol flag have been more appropriate? How do you think the new flag has influenced Canada's sense of nationalism?

BRIEFING NOTES

Nationalism and Patriotism in Canada

It may be more accurate to call the 1960s an era of new Canadian *patriotism* or *national identity*, as opposed to a new nationalism. As discussed in Chapter 4, political scientists reserve the term *nationalism* to refer to ethnically homogeneous communities with common ties to a shared homeland and a design, if not grip, on self-government.

This scarcely described the cultural shift underway in post-war Canada, considering that its driving force was multicultural. That said, the shorthand term "new nationalism" does fit well with the public vernacular and helps situate Canada in a global movement toward self-determination that was underway at the time. See Nationalism in Canada on page 139.

↺ See The Path to Patriation, beginning on page 57 of Chapter 2.

The anthem question had been settled rather easily, though not formally, with the selection of the French-Canadian song *O Canada*, which had been Canada's unofficial anthem since the dawn of World War II. The flag question was far more divisive, pitting former Progressive Conservative prime minister John Diefenbaker, with his binational vision of a flag pairing the French fleur-de-lis with the British Union Jack, against Liberal and Créditiste opponents, who championed a single-symbol pennant based on the now iconic maple leaf. The latter camp won out in 1965, as discussed in the Inside Canadian Politics box on pages 544–5. The road to patriation was even longer: it would take another two decades to achieve consensus on the amending formula necessary to bring the constitution home to Canada.

↺ See Regionalism in Quebec, beginning on page 140 of Chapter 4, for a discussion of the Quiet Revolution and Quebec nationalism.

Standing in the way of the "new nationalism" was a resurgent provincial rights movement. Activism was building among provinces and regions in response to the growing centralization of government authority that had begun during the Depression and gathered momentum during World War II. In Quebec, the movement took on an isolationist tone, resulting in the birth of the Quiet Revolution under Liberal Premier Jean Lesage and his cabinet minister René Lévesque. Together, the two would shepherd in provincial reforms designed to annul Quebec's marriage with anglophone investors from English Canada and the United States. However, in the late 1960s Lévesque would go on to lead the separatist Parti Québécois.

The growing discord within Quebec reignited bitterness toward the province in the rest of Canada. Resentment of Quebec, its insular and allegedly selfish behaviour, and its perceived special status in Confederation had been brewing in Ontario and western Canada for generations. The flames of hostility were, at one time, fanned by the conscription crises of 1917 and 1942, when English-speaking Canadians felt that their French-speaking compatriots were not contributing their fair share to the war effort. Prejudice and mutual misunderstandings between the two cultures festered in the early post-war period, only to erupt throughout the second half of the twentieth century. Holding these regional factions together within the bosom of a single state—the age-old dilemma facing Lord Durham and his successors—was becoming increasingly difficult by the 1960s. Yet it was a task that many hoped was achievable under the mandate of "new nationalism."

Federally, the political party system appeared to provide little help in this endeavour. The period between 1957 and 1963 was one of the most turbulent party transitions in history. Following the "Diefenbaker interlude," in which the Conservatives earned three consecutive governments and began building closer military ties with the United States, the Liberals returned to power in 1963 with a tenuous minority government. Prime Minister Lester B. Pearson's Liberals would be forced to rely on the support of the system's third parties—the New Democrats, Social Crediters, and Créditistes— in their efforts to push through "new nationalist" reforms. Internally, Quebec was overrepresented in the Liberal caucus, holding 46 of the party's 128 seats. The Tories, meanwhile, had seen their support base dwindle to a constituency confined to rural Ontario and the West. This captivity of the Conservative Party would last until the Mulroney era, forcing the Conservatives to adopt its supporters' anglo-Canadian agenda for much of the 1960s and 1970s.

Thus, with Canada on the verge of its centennial, the country was very mindful of the implications of its new position in the world, its role in the Commonwealth, and its relationship with the United States. Though hampered somewhat by rumblings in the federal and political party systems, a "new nationalism" boldly emerged to promote the country's modern persona.

Canadian Identity Today

Despite the "new nationalism" of the 1960s and the patriation of the constitution two decades later, Canada retains many significant ties to Britain. To this day, the Canadian head of state is the British monarch, whose primary representative is the governor general. The Queen retains a prominent, if symbolic, place on Canadian stamps and currency. At investiture, many elected officials, public servants, and all new citizens are still required to pledge their allegiance to the British monarch.

By virtue of Canada's historical connection to Britain, it is one of the 54 members of the Commonwealth of Nations, a group that also includes Australia, Bangladesh, India, Nigeria, Pakistan, South Africa, and, of course, the United Kingdom. Created in 1949, the Commonwealth brings together nation-states that have a constitutional relationship with Britain, although Mozambique and Rwanda are members with no such connection.

Commonwealth An association of nation-states with ties to the United Kingdom.

The relationship between Britain and Canada has deep partisan, ethnic, and ideological undertones. Conservatives are traditionally attached to the mother country, whereas Liberals have tended to advance Canadian independence and English–French dualism. Conservative prime ministers have exhibited their loyalty by brokering a British-style constitution (Macdonald), pledging support to Britain during wartime (Borden), becoming a British Lord after leaving office (Bennett), and proclaiming allegiance to the Union Jack (Diefenbaker). Conversely, Liberal prime ministers have refused a British knighthood (Mackenzie) and have steadfastly avoided engagement in British military conflict (Laurier, King, Pearson); they have also presided over the creation of Canadian citizenship (King), the Canadian flag (Pearson), the Order of Canada (Pearson), official bilingualism (Pierre Trudeau), and the patriation of the constitution (Pierre Trudeau). This political divide continued under Stephen Harper, whose Conservative government made a point of reinvigorating Canada's connection to the monarchy. The Military Command once again became known as the Royal Canadian Navy and the Air Command as the Royal Canadian Air Force. Canadian embassies and consulates around the world, as well as the Foreign Affairs building in

Ottawa, were ordered to display portraits of Canada's head of state, the Queen. New citizens were given new guidebooks espousing the importance of the monarchy. Such incremental changes were widely seen as an attempt to counter decades of Liberal policies that gradually detached Canada from Britain. The game continued after the Liberals won the 2015 federal election. One of the first acts of the new Trudeau government was to remove the portrait of the Queen from the foyer of the Foreign Affairs headquarters, which had been put there by the Conservatives.

At the same time as the ties between Britain and Canada were loosening, Canada's relationship with the United States grew stronger. This so-called "Americanization" was taking place in North America and western Europe. The Cold War was pulling many states, including Canada, into the American political and military orbit, while, at the same time, the United States moved in to fill the economic vacuum left by Britain's exit from the seat of power. Economically, Great Britain ceased to be a major financial centre after the devastation of World War II, and American investment in Britain's former allies and colonies reached even higher levels under the Marshall Plan and private-sector initiatives.

By the 1960s, it was apparent that the most remarkable American investments had occurred in Quebec, where English-speaking US interests had assumed vital control of the economy thanks to the accommodative policies of early twentieth-century Quebec premiers like Louis-Alexandre Taschereau and Maurice Duplessis. Yet the backlash against such widespread Americanization was not confined to Quebec. Canadians everywhere expressed a fear of being absorbed into the mainstream American culture and a desire to preserve Canada's unique position in North America.

Described in greater detail below, Canada and the United States developed a closer, but at times tense, military and economic partnership. While the two countries would have notable fallings-out over military issues—including Canada's refusal to arm nuclear missiles in the North and to join the US in its armed conflicts in Vietnam and Iraq—and trade disputes over issues like automotive manufacturing, beef, and softwood lumber, the overall relationship between Canada and the United States remains the strongest among any two countries in the world.

Perhaps just as importantly, Canada during the post-war period moved closer to the United States in cultural terms, prompting some to applaud and others to decry the Americanization of Canadian culture. The advent of broadcast television in the 1960s brought an influx of American stations, with American news and entertainment programming that overwhelmed the burgeoning "new nationalism" being developed around the Centennial. The federal government responded by implementing stringent new Canadian content (or "CanCon") laws, mandating Canadian broadcasters to carry a certain proportion of Canadian-made shows and regulating them through the Canadian Radio-television and Telecommunications Commission (CRTC). They also bolstered the mandate and role of state-owned media, namely the CBC and Radio-Canada; established federal funding agencies, including the National Film Board, Telefilm Canada, and the Canadian Television Fund, to support Canadian artists and producers; and placed foreign ownership restrictions on Canadian media providers, including newspapers and magazines. Over time, the arrival of the Internet and global telecommunications has made such protectionist measures difficult to maintain, if not obsolete. American culture continues to pervade much of the Western and non-Western worlds, including Canada.

↻ See page 438 of Chapter 11, on political communication, for a discussion of the role of the CRTC.

The Americanization of Canadian popular culture has not necessarily corresponded with the Americanization of Canadian political culture. In general, Canadian politics remains defined by its more "deferential" character that is rooted in its British foundations, while lacking the more populist aspect that characterizes politics in the United States. For instance, Canadians place more trust in government authority than Americans do, which is one reason why the former are more willing to support gun control laws than the latter. Canadians also pride themselves in maintaining a multinational, multicultural society. Their "mosaic" ideal of a Canada that allows immigrant groups to preserve their ethnic identity stands in contrast to the American "melting pot," where immigrants are expected to assimilate into the broader American culture. Canadians view themselves, and are often viewed by others, as more collectivist and egalitarian than their American counterparts. This is evidenced, in some ways, by the more universal character of Canada's healthcare system and the country's approach to marriage equality. The Canadian political character is thus arguably an American–European hybrid, because Canada's economic values are similar to the United States, but its moral values tend to be more in line with Europe's (see Table 14.1).

A connected concept is patriotism, which is an expression of loyalty to one's community. Patriotism is normally characterized by a passionate national identity. It activates political emotions such as pride, allegiance, and a sense of belonging to a group. Canadian patriotism is a work in progress when compared with the self-assurance of the American political identity. The United States was formed after a violent revolt against the British, the Declaration of Independence, and a subsequent civil war. Its identity has been forged by economic innovation, international military action, cultural exportation, and overt patriotism. By comparison, Canada has never aspired to be more than a middle power, and operates in the global shadow of its southern neighbour. It was formed nearly a century after the American Revolution that saw residents loyal to Britain flee northward through legislation passed by the British Parliament. The motivation behind the push to grow the Dominion of Canada in the West was the anticipated westward expansionism of the United States. As Sir John A. Macdonald put it at the time, "I would be quite willing, personally, to leave [the West] a wilderness for the next half century, but I fear that if Englishmen do not go there, the Yankees will."[3] It was not until Canadians were called upon to participate in a series of global wars that the Canadian national identity began to crystallize. At issue was growing opposition to the authority of the British, who expected Canadians to dutifully engage in British conflicts. A Canadian consciousness grew as Canadians

↻ See Representing the Canadian Mosaic, beginning on page 496 of the previous chapter, for an explanation of how the mosaic and melting pot ideals differ.

patriotism An emotional connection with a homeland, normally one's country.

middle power Canada's status as an intermediary, rather than a leader, in international affairs.

↻ See Origins of Regionalism in Chapter 4, beginning on page 152, for an explanation of how the American Revolution sparked migration to the Maritimes and Ontario.

TABLE 14.1 | Summary of Political Culture Differences, Canada and the United States

Canada	United States
• elitist, deferential	• populist, skeptical
• multicultural "mosaic"	• uni-national "melting pot"
• collectivist, egalitarian	• individualist, libertarian
• capitalism, larger government, higher taxes	• free-market capitalism, smaller government, lower taxes
• episodic modest patriotism	• unrelenting bold patriotism

Shown here in a Stephen Harper media conference, the logo for Canada's 150th anniversary was unveiled in 2015. According to Ariana Cuvin, the 19-year-old University of Waterloo student who designed the logo: "The base of the leaf is made up of four diamonds . . . with 9 more expanding outwards from them, meant to represent the 4 provinces that formed Canada after Confederation in 1867, eventually growing to the 13 provinces and territories. The repeated shape is meant to create a sense of unity, and the 13 shapes forming the leaf represents our togetherness as a country. . . . The multi-coloured iteration gives a feeling of diversity while the red one shows pride and unity."[2] Cuvin's design is very similar to Canada's centennial logo (*at left*), created by 24-year-old graphic designer Stuart Ash in 1964, which uses 11 equal-sized triangles to represent the 10 provinces and the north. What does the similarity between the two logos suggest about Canadian identity and political culture? Do you feel the Canada 150 logo "reflects Canada as a diverse nation with a rich past and promising future," as the Government of Canada suggested? Why or why not?

served abroad, participated in rancorous debates at home over conscription, and collectively marked military victories and defeats. Since that time, Canadian patriotism has been expressed episodically, seldom in politics and more often on the socio-cultural stage, as at the Olympics.

Defence, Terrorism, and Diplomacy

Historically, Canada's approach to foreign policy has been defined

- by its position as a so-called middle power sharing a continent with the world's leading superpower;

THEY SAID IT

Pop Culture Converges with Political Culture

Popular culture often embodies a national identity. Roots clothing and Tim Hortons restaurants are examples of iconic Canadian consumer brands that have used patriotism and nationalism to sell their products. Equally, artists and athletes routinely embody a national identity, whether they are singing about their homeland or competing on the international stage. Sometimes the crossover between commerce, pop culture, and politics can be blurry. Take, for instance, the Molson Canadian "I Am Canadian" television advertising campaign from the early 2000s. One of the ads in that campaign, titled "The Rant," tapped into a sense of Canadian patriotism with undertones of anti-Americanism. Against a backdrop displaying a Canadian flag and other images of Canadiana, the commercial begins with the Canadian everyman taking the microphone on stage. His speech starts quietly, as though the speaker lacks self-assurance, but it soon gains momentum and becomes a confident declaration of Canadian identity:

> I'm not a lumberjack, or a fur trader, and I don't live in an igloo or eat blubber, or own a dog sled. And I don't know Jimmy, Sally, or Suzy from Canada, although I'm certain they're really, really nice. I have a prime minister, not a president. I speak English and French, not American, and I pronounce it "about," not "a boot." I can proudly sew my country's flag on my backpack. I believe in peacekeeping, not policing; diversity, not assimilation; and that the beaver is a truly proud and noble animal. A tuque is a hat, a chesterfield is a couch, and it is pronounced *zed*, not *zee—zed!* Canada is the second largest landmass, the first nation of hockey, and the best part of North America! My name is Joe, and I am Canadian! Thank you.

There are similar tones of national identity in the poem "We Are More" by Shane Koyczan, a spoken word artist from western Canada, who himself is the image of a Canadian everyman. "We Are More" was commissioned by the Canadian Tourism Commission. Koyczan voiced his work to the world at the opening ceremonies of the Vancouver 2010 Winter Olympic Games. Go to YouTube to find Koyczan's reading of the poem; search: Koyzcan we are more.

VOX POP

Nationalism and patriotism evoke pride, but they are worrisome because they tend to involve the politics of selective memory and invented traditions. What aspects of Canada are conveniently overlooked or overstated in "I am Canadian" and "We are More"?

- by its tendency toward "soft power" (or diplomacy) and peace-building, instead of "hard power" (military force) and intervention;
- by its penchant for multilateralism and the use of international alliances over unilateralism and "going it alone"; and
- by its preference for preserving human security of individuals abroad, versus the need to intervene to preserve its own state security.

We examine each of these tendencies in the following sections.

Defence

Canada's military has evolved with the maturation of Canada itself. The past worries of American expansionism above the forty-ninth parallel have been replaced by a sense of security that comes from sharing the longest unprotected border in the world with the globe's mightiest military force. A major factor driving Ontario, Quebec, New Brunswick, and Nova Scotia toward Confederation in 1867 was the threat of America's territorial ambitions, known as "manifest destiny." The young dominion relied on British military protection, and as new provinces joined the union—Manitoba in 1870, British Columbia in 1871, PEI in 1873, Alberta and Saskatchewan in 1905—it became clear that Canada needed its own military. However, there were concerns, especially in French Canada, that Canadian troops would be used for the advancement of British interests. These concerns crystallized during the South African Boer War (1899–1902). That far-away military conflict had nothing to do with Canadian security, and yet all members of the British Empire, including the Dominion of Canada, were required to participate.

In the early twentieth century, Canadian political leaders attempted to resolve the need for a homegrown military that would not be subservient to Britain. Liberal prime minister Wilfrid Laurier accepted that Canada would fulfill its obligation to support Britain in the Boer War, but in doing so he determined that Canada would offer only volunteers, and that their participation would be conditional on being funded by the British government. Later, in 1910, his administration created the Royal Canadian Navy, though this was not a popular decision, particularly in Quebec. Liberal prime minister William Lyon Mackenzie King likewise pushed back against the automatic deployment of Canadians whenever Britain became embroiled in an international dispute. When Britain threatened war over a dispute involving the Turkish seaport of Chanak in 1922, the call came for Canadians to engage in the conflict. King, however, delayed sending troops by first consulting Parliament. The matter was still being debated when the Chanak crisis passed and the point was made: Canada would no longer automatically be involved in British military conflicts.

The need for a well-resourced Canadian military was most acute during the world wars. In World War I, the administration of Conservative prime minister Robert Borden was faced with pressing demands for an army, military equipment, and war funds, not to mention the rationing of limited supplies. In World War II, Prime Minister King likewise faced the urgency of limited soldiers and resources. As both wars dragged on and the casualties mounted, it became clear that Canada was expected to provide troops beyond those who had already volunteered. Heated political discussions over conscription were inevitable and risked fracturing Canada's tender political union. The notion of forcing able-bodied citizens to participate in military conflict is a highly contentious and divisive issue. When war broke out in 1914, Prime Minister Borden pledged that "there will not be compulsion or conscription," but by 1916 he had privately resigned himself to the inevitability of a military draft. He understood that such a controversial policy would provoke a rift between English and French Canada.

The gravity of World War I led Borden to propose the need for conscription. As he anticipated, the topic was a heated issue, especially in Quebec, where many were opposed to fighting under the command of the British Empire. In 1917, his government

⟳ See the ICP box Why Was Federalism the Preferred Model for Canada? on page 85 of Chapter 3, for an explanation of the American belief in manifest destiny.

conscription A compulsory war draft by the government to recruit soldiers.

THEY SAID IT

Prime Minister Borden on the Possibility of Conscription in World War I

We have more than two-and-a-half millions of French Canadians . . . and I realize that the feeling between them and the English-speaking people is intensely bitter at present. The vision of the French Canadian is very limited. He is not well informed and he is in a condition of extreme exasperation by reason of fancied wrongs supposed to be inflicted upon the compatriots in other provinces, especially Ontario. It may be necessary to resort to compulsion. I hope not, but if the necessity arises, I shall not hesitate to act accordingly.

—Private letter authored by Prime Minister Borden (1916)[4]

passed the Conscription Act and the Military Service Act, requiring most able-bodied men aged 20–45 to enroll in military service. Canada's most divisive general election ensued later that year, with pro-conscription English Canadians supporting Borden's (renamed) Union Government Party, and anti-conscription French Canadians supporting Laurier's Liberal Party. To put the ethnic polarization in perspective, consider that of the 153 seats won by the Unionists, just 3 were in Quebec (in primarily anglophone areas). Meanwhile, of the Liberals' 85 seats, there were 62 in Quebec and just 2 in western Canada. The next year, anti-conscription protest marches and rioting in Quebec resulted in the deaths of four civilians. Fortunately, World War I ended before conscription was fully implemented.

Conscription re-emerged in World War II under Prime Minister King, who was among the few anglophones who publicly expressed opposition to it in World War I. King's style of politics was strategically ambivalent. His position is captured in a pledge he made to the House of Commons in 1942: "Not necessarily conscription, but conscription if necessary." This famous statement continues to be cited as an illustration of the *brokerage* approach to Canadian politics—the need to deal with

For an explanation of brokerage parties, see Types of Political Parties, beginning on page 341 of Chapter 9.

BRIEFING NOTES

The Legacy of the World Wars

Students and others sometimes question whether it is important to learn about military conflicts that, in many cases, took place over a century ago. Simply put, it is, for these conflicts divided Canadian society so deeply that they forever altered the political party system; for instance, the legacy of debates around conscription explains why the Conservatives do not have a formal provincial political party in Quebec. Changes to political strategy resulted, because approaches to conscription evolved into what became known as "brokerage" party politics. As well, concern grew about Canadian human rights, because internment experiences helped shape a new generation of human rights codes that persist to this day. The world wars also marked the birth of a new form of Canadian identity, and the transition from Canada's status as a former British colony to a full-fledged member of the international community.

THEY SAID IT

Poet F.R. Scott on Prime Minister King's Style of Politics

How shall we speak of Canada,

Mackenzie King dead?
The Mother's boy in the lonely room
With his dog, his medium and his ruins?

He blunted us.

We had no shape

Because he never took sides,
And no sides
Because he never allowed them to take shape.

He skillfully avoided what was wrong

Without saying what was right,
And never let his on the one hand
Know what his on the other hand was doing.

The height of his ambition

Was to pile a Parliamentary Committee on a
    Royal Commission,
To have "conscription if necessary
But not necessarily conscription,"
To let Parliament decide—
Later.

Postpone, postpone, abstain.

Only one thread was certain:

After World War I
Business as usual,
After World War II
Orderly decontrol.
Always he led us back to where we were before.

He seemed to be in the centre

Because we had no centre,
No vision
To pierce the smoke-screen of his politics.

Truly he will be remembered

Wherever men honour ingenuity,
Ambiguity, inactivity, and political longevity.

Let us raise up a temple

To the cult of mediocrity,
Do nothing by halves
Which can be done by quarters.

—F.R. Scott, "W.L.M.K." (1957)[5]

contentious political issues, usually running along regional fault lines, by appearing to satisfy opposing sides in a debate without capitulating to either. Aware of the political strife associated with conscription, and the fragile nature of Canadian unity, the prime minister urged Canadians to have their say at the ballot box in a national plebiscite. Although 63 per cent of voters expressed support for conscription in the 1942 non-binding referendum, this masked the major regional divide and ethnic cleavage: while 83 per cent of anglophones had voted in favour, 76 per cent of francophones voted against the compulsory draft. As he had done in the Chanak crisis, King succeeded in delaying a decision, and once again the war ended before conscription recruits were compelled to be sent into battle.

The scope of devastation wrought by the world wars is indescribable. Tens of millions of people were killed and injured. Among them, over 65,000 Canadians died in World War I battles, and more than 45,000 were killed during World War II. Over 1.5 million Canadian men and women served in the Canadian Forces over the course of the two wars, almost 200,000 of whom were wounded in battle. It is a gross understatement to say that the human costs and political repercussions of the wars are far too extensive to discuss here. Suffice it to say that as a small reward for its sacrifices, Canada was granted greater say in British war planning and its own place at international conferences. Moreover, the wars prompted a crystallization of the Canadian identity, as a self-visualization that is indelibly linked to Britain and yet is fundamentally distinct. World War I soldier patches marked one of the first uses of the maple leaf as a national symbol, for instance.

As Canada's independence from Britain has matured, it has independently joined international organizations where it can assert its interests and form alliances with others. After World War II, global politics split into factions as the Cold War settled in. International relations were characterized by the dominance of two superpowers and competing ideologies, with Western nations aligning with the liberal democracy of the United States, and Eastern nations formalizing alliances with the communist Soviet Union. In 1949, the North Atlantic Treaty Organization (NATO) was formed to unite the defence of 12 Western nations, including Canada. To this day, NATO persists

North Atlantic Treaty Organization (NATO) International military alliance of Western nations.

War Archive/GetStock.com

Canadian governor general Alexander Cambridge (*front right*) hosts World War II Allied leaders Canadian prime minister Mackenzie King (*back left*), US president Franklin Roosevelt (*front left*), and British PM Winston Churchill (*back right*) at the Citadelle of Quebec, 1943. As Scott's poem on page 554 makes clear, King's style was to avoid controversial decisions. In 1942, he held a plebiscite on conscription while other Allied countries sent troops. When Canada hosted two wartime conferences, here in 1943 and again in 1944, King was not invited to the table with Churchill and Roosevelt. To what extent do you think this was a result of his indecisive approach to conscription?

to defend and advance the security objectives of its members through political and military means. Its political objectives are the promotion of democratic values, consensus decision-making, and collaboration on defence issues. Its crisis management activities range from protecting people from natural disasters to initiating military strikes against hostile regimes. NATO is foremost an instrument of mutual security and collective deterrence. Article 5 of the North Atlantic Treaty states that:

> The Parties agree that an armed attack against one or more of them in Europe or North America shall be considered an attack against them all. Consequently they agree that, if such an armed attack occurs, each of them, in exercise of the right of individual or collective self-defence recognised by Article 51 of the Charter of the United Nations, will assist the Party or Parties so attacked by taking forthwith, individually and in concert with the other Parties, such action as it deems necessary, including the use of armed force, to restore and maintain the security of the North Atlantic area.[6]

A Cold War counterfoil to NATO was the Warsaw Pact, an agreement that united seven Eastern Bloc countries including Czechoslovakia, East Germany, and Poland in a military alliance with the Soviet Union in 1955. When the so-called "Iron Curtain" fell in 1991, and as armament reduction pacts were signed, communism and the Soviet bloc no longer challenged the supremacy of the United States or its ideology,

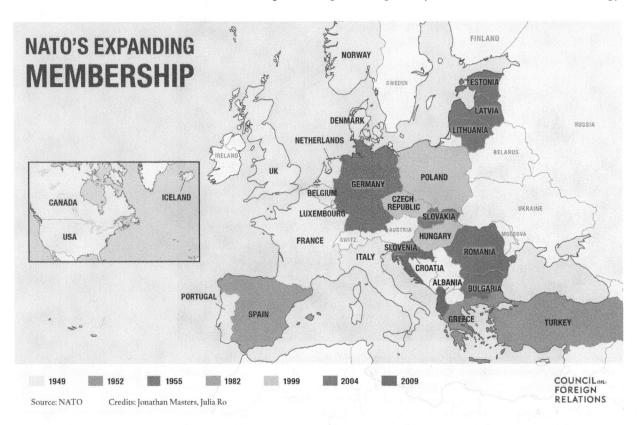

FIGURE 14.2 | Membership in the North Atlantic Treaty Organization

Source: Council on Foreign Relations

and the importance of NATO appeared to be waning. However, the September 11, 2001 terrorist attacks in the United States, as well as other episodes such as the November 2015 Paris attacks, demonstrated the need for protection against security threats from stateless combatants. A number of nation-states have joined NATO since that event, including many former members of the Warsaw Pact. Currently, NATO membership stands at 28 states (see Figure 14.2).

NATO military operations have included bombing in Bosnia and Herzegovina (1995), Kosovo (1999), and Libya (2011), and the deployment of troops to Afghanistan after September 11. Canadian soldiers were engaged in NATO combat operations in the Afghanistan War between 2006 and 2011. All told, 158 Canadians gave their lives in service of their country, and over 2000 were injured. As with Canada's past military conflicts, support for the Afghanistan mission was highest in western Canada, and opposition was most pronounced in Quebec. As well, Conservative partisans and men tended to favour the mission; women, young people, and supporters of the NDP, Green Party, and Bloc Québécois tended to be opposed.[7] This time concerns about British imperialism were replaced by opposition to American interventionism.

Membership in NATO has afforded Canada the security of alliances with some of the world's most formidable military forces. Canada has further leveraged the deterrence strategy through a separate alliance with the United States. In 1958 the two countries signed the **North American Air Defense Command** (NORAD) to create a joint air defence system. NORAD's monitoring of air (and, since 2006, of water) activity warns of a possible attack on North America by aircraft, missile, space, or waterways. As with NATO, its objectives shifted after the Cold War, and once again after 9/11. NORAD has intensified its air patrols and has provided air defence for potential terrorism targets such as G8 summits, the Vancouver Winter Olympic Games, and the NFL's Super Bowl. The bi-national organization also coordinates a security response to emerging situations: for instance, in 2009 a Thunder Bay flight school student stole a small airplane and flew into US airspace, prompting a sortie interception by two F-16 fighter aircrafts. On a lighter note, many Canadians hear about NORAD every Christmas Eve, when it issues news bulletins about its tracking of Santa Claus's progress through airspace around the world. The organization's Canadian region headquarters is the 1 Canadian Air Division in Winnipeg.

> **North American Air Defense (NORAD)** A Canada–US air defence agreement.

As the mention of Santa news bulletins suggests, not all military personnel are directly engaged in armed combat. Canadian forces personnel are often deployed to assist Canadians in times of domestic natural disasters, like floods and wildfires. Later in this chapter we will examine Canada's distinguished record in international peacekeeping, which involves diffusing dangerous situations. Those on the front lines are supported by other members of the Canadian Armed Forces, including engineers, healthcare specialists, technicians, sensor and radar operators, administrators, and emergency responders. An example of the type of non-combat career opportunities that exist within the Forces is presented in the Opportunities Available box on page 558.

Terrorism

Among the nearly 3000 people who were killed in terrorist attacks on 11 September 2001 were 24 Canadians who died when the World Trade Center buildings collapsed. Those catastrophic acts of coordinated terrorism had far-reaching implications

Opportunities Available

Knowledge of Canadian Politics and Government Preferred!
Public Affairs Officer Canadian Forces

What They Do

Public Affairs Officers provide sound communications advice at the tactical, operational, and strategic levels, and act as key advisors to military commanders during domestic and international operations.

Public Affairs Officers are advisers on all aspects of external and internal communications. They are skilled in developing, executing, and evaluating communications approaches designed to inform the public of the Forces roles, activities, and work.

The primary responsibilities of a Public Affairs Officer are to:

- Analyze and evaluate attitudes in the national and international media
- Contribute to policy development
- Gather and provide information internally & externally
- Communicate with journalists, special interest groups, and individuals regarding Defence

Working Environment

Public Affairs Officers work in a modern office setting. They may work in a wide variety of environments such as major bases and various headquarters across

Canada and abroad. They may also be required to deploy anywhere in the world to support Forces operations during times of conflict, peace support operations, or humanitarian missions.

Career Development

Public Affairs Officers are initially placed in positions that expose them to a variety of tasks and situations. With this experience, they may be deployed on international operations and exposed to different types of media. As they gain knowledge and experience, senior Public Affairs Officers have opportunities to develop plans and policies that influence the way public affairs are conducted, including national-level public affairs issues.

Public Affairs Officers who demonstrate the required ability, dedication, and potential are selected for opportunities for career progression, promotion, and advanced training.

Related Civilian Occupations

- Public Relations Specialist
- Media Relations Manager
- Marketing Strategist
- Journalist
- Special Events Coordinator

Source: Abridged from http://www.forces.ca/en/job/publicaffairsofficer-63. Accessed October 21, 2015.

worldwide. American airspace was shut down, and airplanes from around the world—some of which might have been carrying other terrorists—were diverted to Canadian airports. Under Canada's Aeronautics Act, only the minister of transport has the authority to issue emergency orders related to Canadian airspace. Minister David Collenette communicated instructions via cellphone from a speeding van as he travelled from Montreal to Ottawa. He allowed Canadian-bound airplanes to proceed to their destinations, ordered flights with sufficient fuel to return to their points of departure, and allowed remaining flights to land in Canada. He determined that, in an effort to minimize potential casualties, redirected flights should attempt to land at airports in less populated regions of the country. This set in motion what became known as Operation Yellow Ribbon, as 17 airports across Canada accepted over 30,000 displaced passengers on more than 200 diverted aircraft, led by 40 planes that landed in Halifax, NS, 38 that landed in Gander, NL, and 34 that landed in Vancouver,

THEY SAID IT

Transport Minister David Collenette Reflecting on Canada's 9/11 Response

Looking back at the Canadian response [10 years ago, on 11 September 2001], I continue to be amazed at how the behemoth that is government acted so nimbly. Experts, notwithstanding their rank, gave orders to top brass and were obeyed. In a culture that invented the "paper trail," we adopted a paperless model. Nothing was written down. All briefings were oral. We relied on personal relationships to get things done. Everyone shared knowledge. No one held back. The informal relationships and comradeship developed and nurtured over the years carried the day.

—former minister of transport David Collenette[8]

BC. Gander's population of less than 10,000 nearly doubled with the unexpected arrival of 6700 guests needing food, accommodation, and basic necessities. Local residents donated bedding; the Canadian Forces provided cots; temporary beds were set up in churches, schools, and community centres; and volunteers, including the Salvation Army, coordinated meals. After five days, the last of the diverted flights left Canadian soil.

Soon after the immediate crisis had passed, Parliament approved a series of sweeping policy changes, beginning with the Anti-terrorism Act (2001). The act's full title identified its purpose, namely to "amend the *Criminal Code*, the *Official Secrets Act*, the *Canada Evidence Act*, the *Proceeds of Crime (Money Laundering) Act* and other *Acts*, and to enact measures respecting the registration of charities, in order to combat terrorism." Among the government organizations created after 9/11 were the Canada Border Services Agency, which oversees the movement of goods and people into and out of Canada, and the Canadian Air Transport Security Authority, which is responsible for screening air passengers and baggage. A number of government bodies were granted more authority to share information with police: the Canada Revenue Agency, responsible for collecting taxes, now provides data about charities that may have connections with terrorist organizations, and border services share data about travellers and goods arriving in Canada. While many of the increased security measures operate behind the scenes, anyone travelling at a Canadian airport, marine port, or train station has been affected by new, more rigorous passenger screening. Given the sweeping nature of the Anti-terrorism Act, its provisions are subject to regular review.

Canada has been affected by several acts of domestic and international terrorism. One of the most recent of these occurred in October 2014, when an armed attacker shot and killed a soldier standing guard at the National War Memorial in Ottawa before entering the Centre Block at Parliament Hill, where he himself was fatally shot. The incident occurred two days after a man used his car to attack two soldiers in Saint-Jean-sur-Richelieu, Quebec, killing one, in what the prime minister called a terrorist act inspired by the extremist group ISIL (the Islamic State of Iraq and the Levant). Close to 30 years before these events, Canada experienced its worst act of mass murder when bombs hidden in luggage were checked in for two flights at Vancouver International Airport. One bomb detonated at a Tokyo airport, killing two baggage handlers; the other exploded on board Air India Flight 182, downing the Boeing 747 jumbo jet into the Atlantic Ocean and killing 329 people, of whom 280 were Canadian citizens. The bomb-maker, one of multiple suspects belonging to a Sikh separatist group residing in British Columbia, was the only person convicted; two alleged co-conspirators were found not guilty due to lack of evidence after a lengthy trial in the early 2000s. Twenty-five years after the tragedy, the Commission of Inquiry into the Investigation of the Bombing of Air India Flight 182 identified errors by Canadian security organizations, including the failure of agents to recognize the sound of a test bomb being detonated while spying on suspects. In the words of the Commission, "Government agencies were in possession of significant pieces of information that, taken together, would have led a competent analyst to conclude that Flight 182 was at high risk of being bombed by known Sikh terrorists."[9] Within days of the report's release, Prime Minister Harper issued a public apology on behalf of the Government of Canada.

The most episodic case of homegrown terrorism involved bombings carried out by a Marxist–nationalist terrorist organization known as the Front de libération du Québec (FLQ). The FLQ advocated the use of violent tactics against wealthy anglophones and English businesses in Quebec to advance the separatist cause. Over 200 violent crimes were attributed to the organization in the 1960s, including bank robberies and the detonation of bombs set in Canada Post mailboxes and within the Montreal stock exchange, leading to five deaths. Their campaign of fear culminated in the October Crisis of 1970. On 5 October 1970, a cell of the FLQ kidnapped a British diplomat. A ransom demand was issued for gold, the release of political prisoners, access to an airplane, and the publication of an FLQ manifesto. Five days later, another

October Crisis A period of escalating FLQ terrorism in October 1970, which prompted the federal government to invoke the War Measures Act and suspend civil liberties.

THEY SAID IT

Excerpt from Stephen Harper's Apology for the Air India Bombing

The destruction of Air India Flight 182 on June 23, 1985, was and remains the single worst act of terrorism in Canadian history. . . . This was not an act of foreign violence. This atrocity was conceived in Canada, executed in Canada, by Canadian citizens, and its victims were themselves mostly citizens of Canada. . . . It is not enough to say that the system failed. . . . [T]o make matters worse, the families of the victims were for years after treated with scant respect or consideration by agencies of the Government of Canada. These are things for which honour and duty require that the Government of Canada—the government that called this inquiry—now apologize. I stand before you, therefore, to offer on behalf of the Government of Canada, and all Canadians, an apology for the institutional failings of 25 years ago and the treatment of the victims' families thereafter.

—Prime Minister Stephen Harper[10]

FLQ cell kidnapped Quebec's minister of labour, Pierre Laporte. The Canadian military was dispatched to patrol Ottawa and streets in Quebec.

On 16 October, after considering intelligence that the FLQ possessed enough dynamite to destroy buildings, the federal cabinet authorized use of its emergency power and invoked the War Measures Act. This suspended civil liberties and personal freedoms in order to mobilize state resources against insurrection. The police were empowered with the ability to arrest citizens and detain them without charge. This overruled the legal principle of *habeas corpus*, which pertains to a citizen's right to have a judge evaluate whether the government's case is arbitrary.

Minister Laporte's body was found in a car trunk the day after Trudeau invoked the emergency power. Over the next two months the police arrested several FLQ members, although others evaded capture and conviction for many years. When the crisis subsided after the British diplomat's release in December 1970, there had been nearly 500 arrests of people whom the police suspected of promoting left-wing extremism. At the time, the scope of the emergency power was identified within the War Measures Act; today, many of the federal government's emergency powers are identified in the Emergencies Act (1988). The Emergencies Act outlines the types of emergencies that exist and what government powers may be invoked in extraordinary circumstances. It stipulates the need for a parliamentary debate and the need to report to Parliament.

There have been other sporadic acts of terrorism carried out on Canadian soil. In 1984, a man used a submachine gun to kill three employees at the Quebec legislature, in a failed attempt to attack Parti Québécois MNAs. In 1989, a gunman shot and killed 14 women at the École Polytechnique in Montreal. The anti-feminist entered

emergency power The ability of the federal government to exercise extraordinary authority in a time of crisis.

↺ For more on emergency powers, see the discussion of emergency federalism on page 99 of Chapter 3.

↺ See Principles of Canadian Justice, beginning on page 256 of Chapter 7, for an explanation of *habeas corpus*.

THEY SAID IT

Excerpt from Pierre Trudeau's National Address about the FLQ

I am speaking to you at a moment of grave crisis, when violent and fanatical men are attempting to destroy the unity and the freedom of Canada. . . . If a democratic society is to continue to exist, it must be able to root out the cancer of an armed, revolutionary movement that is bent on destroying the very basis of our freedom. For that reason the Government, following an analysis of the facts, including requests of the Government of Quebec and the City of Montreal for urgent action, decided to proclaim the War Measures Act. It did so at 4:00 a.m. this morning, in order to permit the full weight of Government to be brought quickly to bear on all those persons advocating or practising violence as a means of achieving political ends. The War Measures Act gives sweeping powers to the Government. It also suspends the operation of the Canadian Bill of Rights [the precursor to the Charter of Rights and Freedoms]. I can assure you that the Government is most reluctant to seek such powers, and did so only when it became crystal clear that the situation could not be controlled unless some extraordinary assistance was made available on an urgent basis. . . . To bow to the pressures of these kidnappers . . . would be not only an abdication of responsibility, it would lead to an increase in terrorist activities in Quebec. It would be as well an invitation to terrorism and kidnapping across the country.

—Prime Minister Pierre Trudeau, 16 October 1970[11]

a classroom, separated the men and women, and shot the women before targeting women in other areas of the building and then killing himself. The "Montreal massacre" is marked each year on 6 December, which since 1991 has been designated a

Bringing military personnel onto the streets of Ottawa, the October Crisis produced scenes that may appear foreign to Canadians today. How did the Pierre Trudeau government's approach differ from the Harper government's approach toward the October 2014 attacks on Parliament Hill? Under what circumstances would governments consider, or be justified in, invoking emergency powers and suspending Canadians' rights and freedoms today?

National Day of Remembrance and Action on Violence Against Women. Other potentially tragic incidents have had safer outcomes. In 1989, a man who was angry about the Lebanese Civil War hijacked a Montreal bus and ordered it driven to Parliament Hill, where it became stuck in mud, and, after a standoff with police, the hostages were released. In 1999, two members of al-Qaeda hid explosives in the trunk of a car, and one of them drove it onto a ferry in Victoria, BC, which was headed for the state of Washington. American customs agents found the explosives and thwarted a plot to bomb the Los Angeles International Airport at the turn of the millennium. In 2006, approximately 400 police officers raided homes in Toronto and Mississauga, Ontario, to make arrests and collect evidence concerning terrorist plots developed by al-Qaeda sympathizers. Members of the so-called "Toronto 18" (18 people were arrested) had been monitored for months as they made plans to bomb the Toronto Stock Exchange and other public and government buildings. A number were charged under the Anti-terrorism Act for plotting what a judge later called an act of terrorism that "would have resulted in the most horrific crime Canada has ever seen."[12]

At the centre of the counter-terrorism efforts that thwarted the Toronto 18 was the Canadian Security Intelligence Service (CSIS). CSIS agents are engaged in espionage, counter-intelligence, and counter-terrorism to manage the risk of domestic and foreign security threats. The spy agency's routine duties include administering security checks on incoming new Canadians and assessing clearance for senior government jobs. Its agents undertake such extraordinary tasks as entering private buildings, engaging in eavesdropping, and reviewing government data on suspects. CSIS can seek further special powers with the authorization of the relevant minister or warrants from a judge.

After the September 11 terrorist attacks, CSIS commanded more resources. Its current budget of half-a-billion-plus dollars is threefold what it received annually in the late 1990s. Part of the agency's budget allocation is used to pay informants: in the case of the Toronto 18, for example, CSIS agents paid informants millions of dollars to obtain intelligence that helped put an end to the plot.

CSIS reports to a federal minister and cabinet. Unlike most other government agencies, its activities are not eligible to be scrutinized by Parliament. The three civilians who make up the independent Security Intelligence Review Committee (SIRC) monitor CSIS on the public's behalf. The SIRC members meet about nine times a year to consider complaints about CSIS and to review situations where CSIS has denied security clearance to Canadians. The civilians' recommendations to cabinet are secret, but the committee does file an annual report with Parliament about reviews and complaints that the SIRC has investigated; we know, for example, that in recent years the SIRC has examined how the spy agency used new warrant powers and have considered allegations of racial profiling. The prime minister, after consulting with leaders of the opposition parties, recommends to the governor general who should be appointed to the SIRC. That Canadians appear to trust that the SIRC acts in the public interest—or that they remain blissfully unaware of its existence—is the epitome of the country's political culture of "peace, order, and good government."

Operating through the Department of National Defence is a spy agency even more secretive than CSIS—so secretive, in fact, that it existed for over three decades without the public's knowledge. The Communications Security Establishment Canada (CSEC) engages in high-level monitoring and sharing of international intelligence.

Canadian Security Intelligence Service (CSIS) Canada's spy agency.

↻ The doctrine of peace, order, and good government, or POGG, is discussed throughout Chapters 2 and 3; see especially the section Centralization and Decentralization, beginning on page 91 of Chapter 3.

Communications Security Establishment Canada (CSEC) Canada's electronic communications spy agency.

THEY SAID IT

CSIS and the Presence of Foreign Spies in Canadian Political Institutions

In 2010, the head of CSIS warned that spies within two unnamed provincial cabinets were providing information to an unnamed foreign government (he implied the culprit was China, though these allegations have never been publicly substantiated). In 2015, the *Globe and Mail* investigated the ties to China of a minister in the Ontario government.

> We're in fact a bit worried in a couple of provinces that we have an indication that there's some political figures who have developed quite an attachment to foreign countries. The individual becomes in a position to make decisions that affect the country or the province or a municipality. All of a sudden, decisions aren't taken on the basis of the public good but on the basis of another country's preoccupations. . . . There are several municipal politicians in British Columbia and in at least two provinces there are ministers of the Crown who we think are under at least the general influence of a foreign government.
>
> —CSIS director Richard Fadden, 2010[13]

> For me, it is how I am able to bridge Canada and China. I can be in a position to promote both jurisdictions for the benefit of the people. I think that's important. . . . I have nothing to hide. [CSIS] can carry out their perception but I have nothing, nothing, for them to investigate. They can take my phone, they can take my government phone, they can take my house phone, but they will not get anything because I am not what they perhaps may be suspecting.
>
> —Michael Chan, Ontario minister of citizenship, immigration, and international trade, 2015[14]

↺ Hacktivism is defined on page 446 of Chapter 11, on political communication.

Whereas CSIS (pronounced *SEE-sis*) prioritizes human sleuthing, CSEC (pronounced *SEE-sik* or *SEE-sek*) is concerned with foreign security threats that are communicated via radio, telephone, email, text, and other electronic means. It also tests the vulnerabilities of government computer systems (to guard against hacktivism). In the late 1990s, with its Cold War *raison d'être* of monitoring communists rendered defunct, CSEC saw its yearly budget decline to $100 million. Since the 9/11 terrorist attacks and with the growth of digital media, the profile and importance of this covert organization have increased. Today, the CSEC budget is approximately five times what it was at the end of the 1990s, and its workforce has increased from 900 to over 2100 people. Among the many clients of its intelligence services are CSIS, the RCMP, the Privy Council Office, the Departments of National Defence and Foreign Affairs, and the federal Treasury Board Secretariat.[15] It also shares intelligence with counterpart agencies in the US, the UK, Australia, and New Zealand, in a partnership known as "the Five Eyes." This covert arrangement has drawn the ire of the Security Intelligence Review Committee, which has warned that information gathered by a Canadian agency could end up being used against Canadians when they travel abroad.[16]

Unique among Five Eyes partners, CSEC is not subject to significant oversight. Since 1996 only a retired judge has been authorized to scrutinize its activities and submit a report to Parliament. As it is, concerns have been raised that CSEC allegedly co-operated with its American counterpart, the National Security Agency, which spied on world leaders at the G20 summit in Toronto in 2010. There have also been questions raised about CSEC's monitoring of Brazil's energy sector, ostensibly to the advantage of Canadian industry.[17] Some public scrutiny did occur in 2014, when the head of CSEC was questioned by the Canadian Senate's security and defence committee. CBC News reported that the agency had been collecting data from public Wi-Fi at Canadian airports to track the movements of Canadian travellers as they connected at different airports. The basis of the report was a top-secret file released by American whistleblower Edward Snowden. In response to questioning, the head of CSEC revealed that the organization had, indeed, been analyzing the Wi-Fi data, even though its mandate precludes the authority from monitoring the private communication of Canadian citizens. He explained that no actual conversations were monitored, and that the object of the surveillance was only the hidden metadata attached to electronic communication, which yields such details as date, time, contact information, geographic locations, and volume of transmitted information.[18]

VOX POP

The 2014 attacks on Parliament Hill sparked debate over what distinguishes "terrorism" from more mainstream criminal acts. How would you define "terrorism," and what sort of litmus test should public policymakers apply before using such terminology?

Diplomacy

Canada maintains an official presence in other countries. Canadian ambassadors are recognized by the host nation as state diplomats, as are the foreign representatives of some provincial governments. Together, they operate out of a government office known as an embassy or out of smaller offices known as consulates. Ambassadors perform a variety of ceremonial and bureaucratic roles: for example, they maintain formal relations between the two countries, such as by representing Canada at official events; they promote local awareness of Canada, such as by sponsoring Canada Day festivities; and they act as service points for Canadian citizens travelling abroad, by providing assistance with passport and other issues. Periodically, governments formally express dissatisfaction with policies in a host nation by recalling their ambassador. For instance, in 2012 Canada ended diplomatic relations with Iran by closing its embassy in Tehran, because Iran was allegedly providing military support to the Syrian government amidst a civil war. Conversely, Britain and the United States recalled their ambassadors in Syria, but Canada maintained that its ambassador would stay to deliver stern messages to senior Syrian officials. From time to time, Canadian ambassadors have played an intermediary role, characteristic of their position as a middle power. The Academy Award–winning movie *Argo* depicted just such an incident, when the Canadian ambassador to Iran, Ken Taylor, and his officials aided in the exfiltration of six American embassy staff following the siege of the American embassy.

United Nations (UN)
The world's primary international political body.

The foremost political forum for international diplomacy is the United Nations (UN). Canada was one of the original signatories of the League of Nations, an intergovernmental organization formed after World War I with an objective of achieving world peace through disarmament and other policies. It was the precursor to the UN, which was formed in 1945 at the conclusion of World War II. The Charter of the United Nations and Statute of the International Court of Justice was signed by 51 member nations (including Canada), and took effect after it was endorsed by the world's five great powers as the UN Security Council's permanent members (China, France, Russia, United Kingdom, United States). That document identifies the four purposes and principles of the UN, namely:

INSIDE CANADIAN POLITICS

Should the Government of Canada Monitor Canadians' Internet Use?

Whenever Canadians use the Internet on a personal computer, and every time their mobile phones connect with a cellphone tower, they are transmitting data. The degree to which these processes fall short of privacy may not occur to them. Search engines like Google use search and email data to customize the advertising that visitors see; whenever people visit a website, a "cookie" tracking device is installed on their computer; and photos and video uploaded to social networking sites become property of the site. Because people are exposed to information that suits them, this allows businesses to advertise more efficiently, which allows media companies like Google and Facebook to be profitable without charging users a fee for their services. This makes some people suspicious and, in an age of identity theft, even fearful. But even the nonchalant among us should have concerns. For instance, online travel companies have shown higher prices to people shopping online from Macintosh computers, because algorithms have indicated that they have more discretionary income than people using generic brands of computers.[19]

Of greater potential concern is how the government monitors our online behaviour. In order to carry out surveillance, it is essential that the methods used by government agents not become public knowledge. This raises philosophical questions. On the one hand, most people would want the authorities to catch those involved with a cybercrime, such as distributing child pornography, cyberbullying, promoting hate speech, and conspiring to commit acts of terrorism or anti-government fraud. On the other hand, how can security intelligence officers and the police distinguish between law-abiding citizens and online criminals? What type of information should be shared with foreign governments? Is it appropriate for public servants in government departments to actively monitor the social media communications of critics and activists? How do we keep government monitoring accountable?

Canada's privacy laws were not designed to address such fundamental questions. In a democratic system, there is a need for public oversight of such clandestine activities by the state. This is a challenge with respect to matters that cannot, by their nature, be publicly disclosed due to the potential harm to the very citizens the state is trying to protect.

VOX POP

To what extent should the Canadian government police online behaviour? When is it appropriate for information to be exchanged with foreign governments?

- to maintain international peace and security;
- to promote equal rights and self-determination;
- to pursue international co-operation on socioeconomic issues with an objective of upholding human rights; and
- to attempt to unify nations to achieve these objectives.

Collectively, the United Nations' work ranges "from sustainable development, environment and refugees protection, disaster relief, counter terrorism, disarmament and non-proliferation, to promoting democracy, human rights, gender equality and the advancement of women, governance, economic and social development and international health, clearing landmines, expanding food production, and more" in a bid to create "a safer world for this and future generations."[20]

At the United Nations headquarters in New York, representatives from 193 member nations attend meetings of the General Assembly and may participate in a variety of councils, committees, specialized agencies, funds, and programs. Of these, the UN Security Council is perhaps the most influential body in the world. It comprises the five aforementioned permanent members, who have veto power, and ten rotating members elected by members of the General Assembly for two-year terms. The Security Council has the power to issue binding resolutions on matters that include initiating peacekeeping missions, authorizing diplomatic and economic sanctions, and approving the use of international military force. It has authorized a number of peacekeeping operations—recent notable examples include the United Nations Mission of Support in East Timor (2003–5) and the United Nations Stabilization Mission in Haiti (2004–present)—and military interventions, such as during the Korean War (1950–3) and the First Gulf War (1990–1).

Canada was elected as a non-permanent member once per decade during the twentieth century but has not held a seat on the prestigious body since 2000. It was a source of consternation to some in 2010 when Canada experienced its first failed bid (Germany and Portugal were elected). For critics, this affirmed Canada's diminished international status, and was a consequence of the Conservative government's international policies. To others, Canada was a victim of the mysteries of closed-door

BRIEFING NOTES

Ambassadors and High Commissioners

The highest-ranking Canadian diplomats serving in Commonwealth nations are referred to as *high commissioners* rather than *ambassadors*. On occasion, Prime Minister Harper selected former provincial premiers for such diplomatic posts. In choosing former Manitoba premier Gary Doer (a New Democrat) as Canada's ambassador to the United States and former BC premier Gordon Campbell (a Liberal) as Canada's high commissioner to the United Kingdom, the prime minister appeared to prize executive, diplomatic, intergovernmental, and international experience over party patronage.

bargaining for votes, and the outcome should be contextualized with the fact that over 60 countries have never been a member of the Security Council.

Those who were upset with the snub were mindful that it has been a source of Canadian pride that Canada played a significant role in establishing the UN's peace-keeping role. In 1956, Lester B. Pearson was Canada's minister of external affairs when the Suez Canal crisis erupted. Egypt had proclaimed its desire to control the important shipping link and was invaded by Britain, France, and Israel. Canada's position as a middle power allowed Pearson to take a lead role in achieving a diplomatic solution through the United Nations. He proposed at the General Assembly that an international peacekeeping force should be created. Military resources provided by countries from around the world, including Canada, coalesced to form the United Nations Emergency Force and contributed to diffusing the crisis. The next year, Pearson was awarded the Nobel Peace Prize for his efforts; he would go on to become prime minister in 1963.

Recognized by their blue berets, UN peacekeepers today include military and police personnel from 122 countries and provide on-the-ground support to foster peace and security. This includes attempting to stabilize conflicts, supporting the fortification of stable law enforcement, and assisting with the repatriation of refugees. Canadian peacekeeping missions have tended to avoid frontline conflict and have prioritized the distribution of humanitarian aid, providing emergency shelter, clearing landmines, and supervising elections.

A result of Pearson's proposal was that Canada gradually assumed a middle power image associated with international peacekeeping that persisted into the twenty-first century. Canadians chaired working groups and helped fund the involvement of non-governmental organizations in a negotiation process that led to the creation of the International Criminal Court in 2002, the world's first permanent international court to consider charges of genocide, crimes against humanity, and crimes of war. Prime Minister Jean Chrétien's decision in 2003 that Canada would not join the American-led "coalition of the willing" to invade Iraq—a mission that was not sanctioned by the UN—was consistent with this image and with many of his Liberal predecessors' approach to military conflict. Canada's role as a middle power explains, in part, why the government's decision to send Canadian troops to participate in combat roles in the NATO-led conflict in Afghanistan was initially kept quiet in 2002. Liberals in particular have taken pride in a cautious international presence. To some, this is a testament to

THEY SAID IT

Comedian Rick Mercer on Canada as a Middle Power

Canada's defence policy is very simple: we don't really need one because America's defence policy is also very simple. Basically, if you mess with America, they will kill you. Because we're attached to America, nobody messes with us.

—Rick Mercer[21]

Canada's self-reliance and its respect for self-determination; to others, it is an approach that is emblematic of a country whose citizens like to think that they are global leaders, but who in practice tend to be unwilling to support dynamic initiatives and instead allow more powerful allies to engage in global conflicts in their shared interests.

One aspect of Canada's status as a middle power is that its interests abroad have been overridden by domestic concerns. Government spending on the military and on humanitarian aid has tended to take a back seat to spending on domestic infrastructure and the welfare state. Spending on the military was so constrained by the Liberal government in the 1990s that it became an embarrassing topic in some Canadian circles during that period; but even after the subsequent Conservative government significantly increased military budget allocations, Canada remained focused on other domestic priorities (see Figure 14.3). Conversely, the Conservatives' support for combat operations in Afghanistan and changes to the country's international aid priorities are thought by some to have damaged Canada's international image. The return to office of the Liberals in 2015 means a return to more foreign aid and less funding for combat operations. Whether under the direction of a Conservative or a Liberal prime minister, the federal government's policy decisions have historically tended to cautiously support allies in major international disputes; to derive a sense of security that is afforded by international alliances; and above all, to recognize that Canadians prioritize domestic policy matters. This is by no means unique to Canada: as American Speaker of the House of Representatives Tip O'Neill observed, all politics is local.

This is not to suggest that Canada's limited clout in international affairs is a reflection of closed-mindedness, isolationism, or ethnic nationalism. Rather, Canadian interest in internationalism is foremost expressed through its domestic policies, in particular a willingness to embrace international cultures. Emigration to Canada is turning its cities into global villages. About a fifth of Canadians are immigrants (see Figure 14.4); whereas most of them used to arrive from Europe, today there is a mixture of arrivals from Africa, Europe, the southern American hemisphere, and especially Asia (see Figure 14.5). As discussed in Chapter 13, the priorities of anglophones and

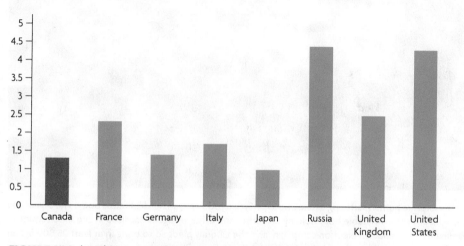

FIGURE 14.3 | Military Spending as a Percentage of GDP in G8 Countries

Source: 2012 data, Stockholm International Peace Research Institute (SIPRI) Military Expenditure Database.

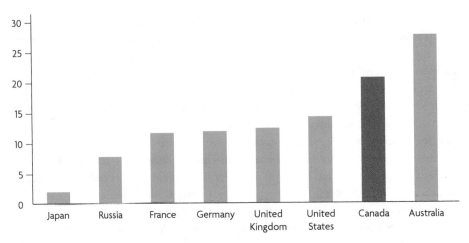

FIGURE 14.4 | Immigrants as a Percentage of Total Population in G8 Countries

Source: United Nations, "Trends in International Migrant Stock: The 2013 Revision."

AP/DHA

Rarely does a single image so poignantly capture human suffering as the photo of Syrian toddler Alan Kurdi's lifeless body. The 3-year-old washed up on a beach in September 2015 after the inflatable boat holding his father and other refugees capsized in the Mediterranean Sea. The refugee crisis suddenly dominated the Canadian election campaign, and the Liberals pledged to bring in at least 25,000 Syrian refugees. Why do you suppose it took a heart-wrenching photograph for Canadian media, politicians and voters to pay attention to a crisis that had been going on for months?

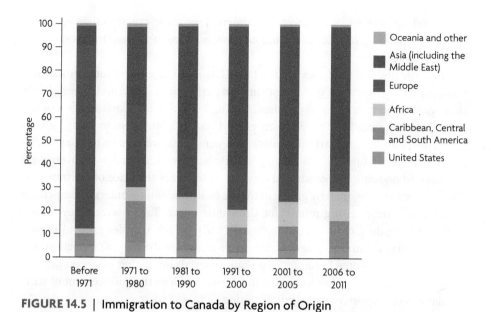

FIGURE 14.5 | Immigration to Canada by Region of Origin

Source: Statistics Canada, "Immigration and Ethno-diversity in Canada," *National Household Survey* (2011).

francophones have dominated Canadian politics, but this has been shifting with the increasing population of allophones. Canada is increasingly a "cultural mosaic" of different ethnic perspectives as people from around the world become Canadian citizens.

Globalization and International Trade

Canada is an exporter nation, and always has been. The United States and Canada are each other's largest trading partners, and their economic relationship is the world's most lucrative, worth over $616 billion in two-way trade per year. Trade with the United States makes up almost two-thirds of Canada's gross domestic product (GDP), prompting many to raise alarm over Canada's dependence on the US economy and concerns over the need to diversify its trade with other countries (especially China, India, and the European Union). This said, since the mid-1980s, Canada has maintained a trade surplus with the US, meaning that it exports more to the United States (largely in the form of energy and natural resources) than it imports in return (largely in manufactured goods). By contrast, Canada maintains a trade deficit with all of its remaining partners.

Trade Agreements

As a trading nation, Canada has always had an interest in global markets. In the age of globalization, advanced industrialized nations like Canada have been abandoning their protectionist economic policies in favour of trade liberalization. Free trade, also known as *reciprocity*, is a bi-national or multi-national policy whereby businesses can freely buy and sell goods and services in each other's jurisdiction. It provides domestic exporters with access to external markets and, owing to competition, the price of

free trade The elimination of financial and regulatory barriers to allow unfettered market access.

goods and services edges lower for consumers. Free trade can stimulate economic growth by encouraging sales and promote efficiency through a need to invest in productivity measures.

Historically, the very idea of free trade has met fierce opposition in Canada, invoking strong overtones of nationalism and anti-Americanism and forming deep cleavages in the political party system. Dating back to Confederation, businesses have argued the need for government protections to allow them to compete with their American counterparts. Historically, federal governments in both countries used tariffs to nurture the growth of domestic businesses. A tariff is a government levy applied on imported goods and services. This makes the price of the imported item more expensive, thereby giving domestic businesses and workers a competitive edge locally, while raising money for the public purse. Tariffs were a key feature of the Macdonald Conservatives' National Policy, which was designed to protect local industry, labour, and agriculture from outsiders. In the 1878 election, the Conservatives promoted lower duties on raw materials but higher duties on finished goods. This was in addition to non-tariff barriers, such as the enforcement of strict regulations on importers and legal protections afforded to domestic companies. All of these measures angered farmers, whose livelihoods depend on open markets. Resentment was particularly strong in Ontario and western Canada, giving rise to the populist movement and Western alienation and leading to the formation of the Progressive Party.

As the importance of exports grew, particularly after World War II, Canadian businesses also developed a greater desire to negotiate the elimination of tariffs so that they could obtain access to the marketplace in America, which was replacing Britain as Canada's biggest trading partner. As well, free trade advocates argued that eliminating tariffs could benefit consumers by bringing them a greater range of products at lower prices overall, and that domestic businesses must prepare to compete with multinational corporations as free trade spread to other parts of the world. However, opponents have maintained that eliminating tariff protections puts Canadian jobs at risk and could lead to fewer Canadian-owned companies. Their warnings include the threats that Canada's trading partners would ignore a free trade pact to protect their own businesses, that the Canadian economy would become Americanized, and that Canadian culture would disappear.

In the 1988 federal election, Prime Minister Brian Mulroney, his Progressive Conservative Party, and big business interests promoted a free trade agreement with the United States, while the Liberals, the NDP, and labour unions registered passionate opposition. This contrasted with the 1878 campaign, when the Liberals had been the proponents of free trade, and the Conservatives and business were protectionists. The emotional contest culminated in the Mulroney PCs winning a majority of seats on 43 per cent of the popular vote. The following year, the Canada–US Free Trade Agreement took effect, and in 1992, Mexico joined when the three countries signed the North American Free Trade Agreement (NAFTA). Decades later, we can see that Canadian businesses have benefited from access to the American market, and that trade between Canada and Mexico now far exceeds trade between Canada and Britain (see Figure 14.6 and Figure 14.7). Conversely, trade with China has increased substantially in the absence of a free trade deal, and amidst the hesitation of some Canadians to engage with that country because of its poor human rights record.

---

tariff A form of tax applied to imported goods and services.

↻ See The Evolution of Major Parties, beginning on page 357 of Chapter 9, for more on how the Liberal Party's position on free trade caused divisions within the party.

↻ Western alienation is explained in Chapter 4, beginning on page 136.

North American Free Trade Agreement A free trade agreement between Canada, Mexico, and the United States.

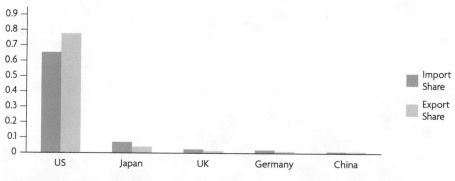

FIGURE 14.6 | Canada's Top Five Merchandise Trade Partners in 1992

Source: Industry Canada North American Industry Classification System (NAICS) Trade Statistics.

As critics feared, some NAFTA trade disputes have harmed Canadian exporters. In the early 2000s, the George W. Bush administration introduced protectionist politics to support US softwood lumber and cattle industries. President Barack Obama has mused about leaving NAFTA, and after the 2008 recession, the US government introduced "buy American" provisions in its stimulus spending initiatives, shutting out Canadian businesses as suppliers for lucrative American public-sector contracts. But overall the advocates of free trade have thus far proven to be correct. Prime Minister Harper signed new free trade deals with Central and South American countries (see Figure 14.8), and Canada has worked on huge international pacts with the European Union known as the Comprehensive and Economic Trade Agreement (CETA) and with countries across the globe on the Trans-Pacific Partnership (TPP). Despite some outrage by the NDP and some industry groups, the agreements barely made a ripple in the 2015 election campaign. The deals will likely be presented to Parliament for debate in the future. For many Canadians, free trade is now believed to be an economic benefit to Canadian businesses and workers alike.

Related to issues surrounding free trade are debates over the appropriate level of foreign direct investment in Canadian industries. As an exporting nation, and with higher demand for capital than domestic sources can provide, the Canadian economy relies heavily on investment from companies (and often governments) from other countries. Well over three-quarters of foreign direct investment flows into Canada from the United States, although an increasing proportion is being derived from

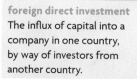

foreign direct investment
The influx of capital into a company in one country, by way of investors from another country.

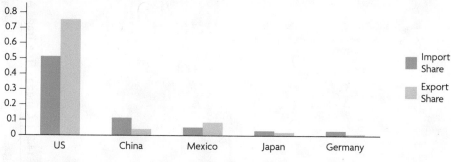

FIGURE 14.7 | Canada's Top Five Merchandise Trade Partners in 2012

Source: Industry Canada North American Industry Classification System (NAICS) Trade Statistics.

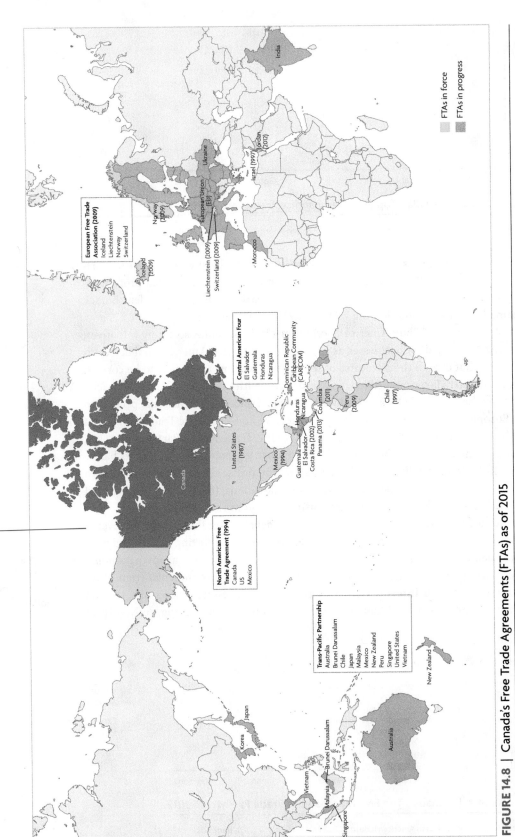

FIGURE 14.8 | Canada's Free Trade Agreements (FTAs) as of 2015

North American Free Trade Agreement (1994)
Canada
US
Mexico

Central American Four
El Salvador
Guatemala
Honduras
Nicaragua

European Free Trade Association (2009)
Iceland
Liechtenstein
Norway
Switzerland

Trans-Pacific Partnership
Australia
Brunei Darussalam
Chile
Japan
Malaysia
Mexico
New Zealand
Peru
Singapore
United States
Vietnam

FTAs in force
FTAs in progress

Source: Data from Foreign Affairs, Trade and Development Canada, "Canada's Free Trade Agreements" (2014), www.international.gc.ca/trade-agreements-accords-commerciaux/agr-acc/fta-ale.aspx?lang=eng.

other sources, including Chinese investors and state-owned enterprises. This influx of foreign capital, which is now most prevalent in the energy sector, poses serious questions and challenges for the federal government.

This is why the federal government regulates foreign spending in Canada, determining whether high-level investments are in the best public interest of Canadians. On one hand, foreign direct investment is necessary to stimulate economic growth, create jobs, and spur innovation. On the other hand, it can create a culture of dependency on foreign sources of capital, expose the Canadian economy to foreign influence or control, and result in the outflow of profits to investors outside the country. Critics feel the rules surrounding this "national interest" determination are unnecessarily opaque, with provincial governments and foreign investors seeking clarity to allow for a more predictable investment environment.

Canadian politicians also periodically embark on self-initiated trade missions. A trade mission is a networking opportunity for businesspeople who hope to strike deals and for politicians who hope to sign bilateral relations agreements. The head of government leads a group of government officials and members of the business community to prearranged meetings with foreign counterparts. There is much media fanfare as the participants are celebrated for promoting international awareness of economic opportunities and for stimulating economic growth. This includes the so-called "Team Canada" missions led by Prime Minister Chrétien from 1998 to 2002, during which he was accompanied by the minister of international trade as well as a number of premiers. Provinces initiate their own trade missions as well, including annual junkets organized through the Council of the Federation. Larger provinces also seek to advance their policy interests by setting up official offices in foreign cities, often national capitals. As of 2014, Alberta had international offices in 10 locations; British Columbia had trade and investment representatives in 6 global cities; and Quebec had a network of delegations, bureaus, and trade branches in 26 locations.

International Economic Forums and Organizations

Canada participates in a number of international forums and organizations where the foremost objective is to advance economic interests. Increases in global economic trade have been facilitated by the World Trade Organization (WTO), which seeks to minimize regulatory burdens between nation states. Its mantra of "open trade for the benefit of all" epitomizes a philosophy that tariffs and government subsidies inhibit global economic growth. The WTO's core activities include helping to negotiate reduced barriers to international economic trade and creating mechanisms for settling trade disputes. Founded in 1995, and with 149 members, the WTO comprises the majority of the world's nation-states, including Canada. Its predecessor, the General Agreement on Tariffs and Trade (GATT), was formed in 1947 and facilitated rounds of trade negotiations that set the framework for a global economy characterized by reduced tariffs.

Canada is also a member of the Group of Eight (G8)—currently known as Group of Seven (G7)—which brings together the leaders of some of the world's most advanced economies in an annual summit. It originated in 1975 as a meeting of the leaders of France, Germany, Italy, Japan, the United Kingdom, and the United States to deal with the oil crisis. The next year, Canada joined the group (making it the G7),

World Trade Organization (WTO) An international organization whose members voluntarily follow agreed economic policies.

G8/G7 Annual meeting of the leaders of eight of the world's most industrialized economies.

INSIDE CANADIAN POLITICS

What are Provinces Doing to Promote Trade Within Canada?

Free trade between Canada and foreign entities may be booming, but non-tariff barriers persist to limit economic trade *within* Canada. The scope of inter-provincial protectionism is too extensive to describe in detail here, but the list of barriers includes dis-criminatory registration requirements for non-local businesses; local content and purchasing provisions; residency requirements for worker qualifications; different standards for food products; discrimina-tory practices in the sale of alcoholic beverages; and barriers to the processing of natural resources.

In 1995, the government of Canada, all 10 prov-inces, the Northwest Territories, and Yukon signed the Agreement on Internal Trade (AIT) in an effort to address these issues. At the same time, these gov-ernments formed the Committee on Internal Trade, which is made up of federal, provincial, and territo-rial ministers who seek to negotiate the reduction of interprovincial trade barriers. As the president and chief executive officer of the Canadian Chamber of Commerce put it:

It's ironic that the provinces were able to find common ground with our agreement with Europe, and yet they have a difficult time sitting in the same room to discuss trade amongst themselves. At the same time that we're undertaking the most ambitious international trade agenda in Canadian his-tory, we remain divided internally. It's sober-ing to think of a future where it is easier for Ontario to trade with Europe or India, than for Alberta to trade with Quebec.[22]

The stubborn interprovincial trade protections that linger in Canada prove that domestic politics can sometimes be pricklier than international rela-tions. It has also convinced some regions to cre-ate their own freer trade zones, with BC, Alberta, and Saskatchewan now forming the New West Partnership, Ontario and Quebec collaborating on economic and climate issues, and Atlantic Provinces pursuing greater harmonization of their economies.

VOX POP

Why do you suppose Canada's internal trade barriers between its provinces and territories are, in many ways, more insurmountable than its trade barriers with other countries?

Agreement on Internal Trade (AIT) Federal-provincial-territorial agreement to lower internal trade barriers within Canada.

and in 1998 Russia was added to become the eighth member. Russia has since been suspended from the group due to the West's dispute over Russia's recent foray into Ukraine. Traditionally some leaders of African countries are also invited to attend some sessions. The G8 annual summits attract global media attention because some of the world's most powerful heads of government promote their economic and for-eign policy agendas, while also discussing topical world issues. The idea for a parallel Group of Twenty (G20) was advanced by Paul Martin while he was Canada's finance minister in the Chrétien government. Martin saw a need for an annual forum to bring together finance ministers and central bank governors from the world's major econ-omies to discuss financial markets, financial stability, and economic co-operation. The first meeting of the G20 was held in 1999, and the first summit of G20 leaders was held in 2008. When the global economic crisis of 2008 occurred, the G20 convened in Washington, DC, to identify the causes of the problem, to discuss possible policy responses, and to establish ways to reform financial markets.

The G8 and G20 summits have become an opportunity for interest groups and social movements to coordinate protests in an attempt to attract world attention to their concerns. When Canada hosted the G8 and G20 summits in Ontario in 2010, there was considerable criticism of the federal government's spending on security, infrastructure, and media events. Opposition parties raised concerns about Conservative pork-barrelling to improve ridings held by Conservative MPs, and questioned the installation of a $57,000 temporary "fake lake" exhibit to generate media interest while also promoting tourism in the Ontario cottage country region of Muskoka. But the real controversy was associated with peaceful protests that turned violent. Four police cars were burned, storefront and bank windows were smashed, and masked protesters threw projectiles at police. Over 400 people were arrested and, for the first time in Toronto's history, the police deployed tear gas. Canada is scheduled to host the G8 again in 2018.

Another international organization that Canada belongs to is the Asia–Pacific Economic Cooperation (APEC) forum. APEC brings together 21 Pacific Rim countries—among them Australia, China, Indonesia, Japan, Mexico, Russia, Thailand, and the United States—to discuss economic matters. The association was formed in 1989 to promote economic integration throughout the region, and uses the tagline "advancing free trade for Asia–Pacific prosperity." As with the WTO, it advocates economic growth through the reduction of trade barriers, encouraging private-sector business investment, simplifying rules, and reducing administrative burdens. APEC holds an annual summit to encourage dialogue between international leaders. In 1997, Vancouver hosted the APEC forum, which was marred by public demonstrations. Media coverage showed the RCMP pepper-spraying protesters; when asked to comment on the affair, Prime Minister Chrétien quipped, "For me, pepper, I put it on my plate." The RCMP Complaints Commission initiated a public inquiry and concluded in 2001 that poor planning by police leadership was to blame for the excessive use of force.

↻ See Chapter 12 for a comprehensive introduction to political activism.

↻ Pork barrel politics is explained in the section Financial Mismanagement and Unethical Behaviour, beginning on 328 of Chapter 8.

APEC A multinational economic organization of Pacific Rim countries.

International Development

In addition to furthering its own security and economic interests through interactions with other nations, Canada is involved in a number of international organizations that promote democracy, human rights, the rule of law, and the socioeconomic development of emerging economies.

As mentioned earlier, Canada is a member of the Commonwealth of Nations, whose organizational values are to promote democracy, human rights, and the rule of law. Every two years it holds a meeting of heads of government, where recent priorities have been discussions aimed at the strengthening of "development and democracy ... good governance, human rights, gender equality, and a more equitable sharing of the benefits of globalization."[23] From time to time, Canada assumes a leadership role in the Commonwealth. For three decades beginning in the early 1960s, successive Canadian prime ministers applied international pressure, particularly through the Commonwealth, to end apartheid in South Africa. More recently, former prime minister Stephen Harper attempted to assert this moral suasion when he refused to attend the 2013 Commonwealth Summit in Sri Lanka, in protest of the host country's violations of the human rights of its Tamil minority.

Canada also participates in the Organisation internationale de la Francophonie (the OIF, or simply La Francophonie), a network of countries where the French language and/or culture flourishes. In this way the organization resembles the Commonwealth of Nations in bringing together countries or regions with ties to a homeland. For example, the Commonwealth Games are held every four years, as are the Francophonie Games; both feature a variety of Olympic sports, as well as non-Olympic sports (such as lawn bowls in the case of the Commonwealth) and cultural events (such as poetry, song, and traditional dance in the case of the Francophonie).

La Francophonie's activities are centred on more than just the French language, culture, and education: it also seeks to promote peace, democracy, human rights,

La Francophonie
Association of nation-states and regions with French language and cultural connections.

The Commonwealth is often criticized for failing to achieve consensus on the need to advance economic, social, and humanitarian causes. What sorts of barriers lie in the way of progress in these areas? How might they be overcome?

sustainable development, digital technologies, and sport. The organization holds biennial summits where members' heads of state and/or heads of governments convene to discuss topical issues and to celebrate their shared culture. When Quebec City hosted the leaders' summit in 2008, the French president addressed the Quebec legislature, signed an agreement to recognize the qualifications of professionals trained in either France or Quebec, and met privately with Prime Minister Harper to discuss free trade with Europe. In addition, ministerial conferences are held on a focused policy matter, such as Internet access or human security.

The Francophonie is the only multilateral government organization where Canada has consented to provinces (in this case Quebec and New Brunswick) holding full membership alongside countries such as Belgium, France, Switzerland, and a number of former Belgian and French colonies in Africa. Traditionally, the Canadian cabinet includes a minister responsible for La Francophonie, who also meets annually with provincial and territorial minsters responsible for francophone affairs.

Canada's primary foreign investment body operates through the Department of Foreign Affairs. From 1968 until 2013, the Canadian International Development Agency (CIDA) was the country's leading international investment arm and was responsible for administering foreign aid programs. In the 2013 federal budget, the Conservative government announced that CIDA would be absorbed within the Department of Foreign Affairs, and the two bodies would operate as the Department of Foreign Affairs, Trade and Development (DFATD). A key policy mandate of the current body is to improve the efficiency, focus, and accountability of international aid programs that assist people living in poverty. Funding programs must meet certain criteria, including an established need for aid, a likelihood of benefiting from Canadian support, and overall objectives consistent with Canadian foreign policy. Funds are prioritized for local food sustainability (e.g. agriculture), children and youth (e.g. education), and economic growth (e.g. local business development). Overall values promoted by DFATD are environmental sustainability, gender equity, and democratic governance, although the ministry has been criticized for focusing too heavily on the economic implications of its foreign aid.[24] This tone is likely to see an abrupt shift under the Justin Trudeau Liberals.

The amount of foreign aid a country gives is typically measured as a proportion of its gross national income, or GNI. Figure 14.9 shows Canada's level of international

BRIEFING NOTES

Quebec's Role on the International Stage

In addition to its formal role in the Francophonie, Quebec also enjoys a seat as part of Canada's permanent delegation to the United Nations Education, Science, and Culture Organization (UNESCO). The agreement with the federal government, signed in 2006, allows Quebec to select a representative to speak directly on its behalf in forums convened by UNESCO bodies. Together, these two guarantees help distinguish Quebec from other Canadian provinces, some of whom do maintain international offices across the world (chiefly to promote trade and investment).

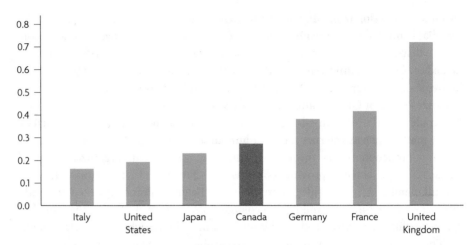

FIGURE 14.9 | Official Development Assistance (ODA) as a Percentage of Gross National Income (GNI) in G7 Countries

Source: Based on data from OECD (2012), "Development aid: Net official development assistance (ODA)", Development: Key Tables from OECD, No. 1. DOI: http://dx.doi.org/10.1787/aid-oda-table-2012-1-en

development assistance compared with that of other G7 countries. As we can see, Canada falls in the middle of the pack. The United Kingdom, Germany, and France commit more than Canada does, whereas the United States, Japan, and Italy offer proportionately less. Each country has its own reasons for its commitments; for instance, the United States might argue that in dollar terms it offers more than any other country, and that this is in addition to its considerable investments in global security.

In Canada, as elsewhere, the pressure to allocate limited resources to other countries must be weighed against domestic pressures to allocate those resources at home. To take one single example, the Federation of Canadian Municipalities has pushed for federal funding for affordable housing, arguing that millions of low-income households need money for new construction or infrastructure maintenance.[25] Why does that matter? Because it is a reminder that Canadian politicians are incentivized to respond to domestic interests, media pressure, and party members' priorities. If we believe that most elected officials want to be re-elected, then it is natural that they will consider that public opinion polls routinely show that Canadians prioritize healthcare, job creation, taxation, the environment, accountability, and other policy matters *within* Canada. Moreover, government budgets tend to operate in a deficit situation, and it is difficult for finance ministers to defend foreign spending at a cost of cuts to domestic spending initiatives. The exception is when an international humanitarian crisis rockets to the top of the public agenda, which in turn results in public expectations that government will help. In such situations the government of Canada commits special financial support to the affected nation and may deploy human resources expertise such as the Canadian Forces' Disaster Assistance Response Team (DART). In recent years, the federal government has pledged that for a specified period it will match Canadians' personal donations to charitable organizations such as the Red Cross that are best suited to dispatch appropriate aid.

One of the ways that DFATD promotes its objectives is by working through international agencies. For instance, the Organization of American States (OAS; not to be confused with the same acronym for Old Age Security), founded in 1948 but

UP FOR DEBATE

Should Canada give more money for foreign aid? The debate supplement at the end of this chapter gives some of the arguments on both sides, and offers questions and resources to guide a discussion around this pressing topic.

with roots dating back to 1890, is a regional political association of all independent states in the Americas. The OAS brings together 35 nations in North, Central, and South America to advance democracy, development, human rights, and security in the hemispheres. Given that its original objective was to restrict European influence on the Americas, and to expand the influence of the United States, Canada did not become a permanent observer in the OAS until 1972, and opted not to join until 1990. Canada has since become one of the organization's largest financial contributors, and provides supports such as election observation, legal assistance, and humanitarian aid. DFATD is an active participant in initiatives of the OAS, including "the promotion of human rights, socioeconomic development and poverty alleviation, energy conservation, gender equality, corporate social responsibility, as well as financial assistance for rapid response to political and humanitarian crises."[26]

In recent years Canada has been promoting its sovereignty over Arctic lands. Canada is a founding member of the Arctic Council, which promotes co-operation and interaction among Arctic states. The organization is a means of advancing

The Canadian Press/Jeff McIntosh

Canada's Arctic is patrolled by the Canadian Rangers, a sub-component of the Armed Forces Reserve, who carry out national security and public safety missions in remote and sparsely settled regions. Establishing a military presence in the North has become an important priority, as Canada competes with seven other countries (Russia, Sweden, Norway, Iceland, Denmark, Finland, and the US) for the right to the land at the top of the world—and the prized reserves of subsea oil beneath. What considerations should be applied when deciding which countries have sovereignty over Arctic lands, ice, and waterways? What role should Canada's military play in promoting its claims to sovereignty in the Arctic?

the interests of Canada's Arctic Indigenous peoples along with those of Denmark, Finland, Iceland, Norway, Russia, Sweden, and the United States. Organizations such as the Inuit Circumpolar Council are formally engaged as permanent participants. The council's objectives include improving the lives of Arctic residents, preparing for environmental emergencies, addressing pollution in the Arctic, and conserving Arctic flora and fauna.

This chapter has touched on only some of the many aspects that make up Canada's international presence. In addition to the multinational organizations that have been mentioned, Canada participates in a number of other initiatives, such as the Organisation for Economic Co-operation and Development (OECD), the World Bank, and the United Nations Educational, Scientific and Cultural Organization (UNESCO). Canada has been a signatory to countless international agreements, such as the 1997 Kyoto Accord on climate change, from which it subsequently withdrew in 2011. It was the proponent of an international agreement to ban landmines, signed by over 160 nation-states, which became known as the Ottawa Treaty (1997).

Concluding Thoughts

When thinking about Canada's place in the world it is easy to overlook what a young country it is. Nation-states around the globe have centuries of history, identity formation, and infrastructure. By comparison, the great-grandparents of Canadian baby boomers were alive when the Dominion was formed, and many baby boomers were themselves involved in the 1960s national debate about creating a Canadian flag. In Canada's early years, politicians prioritized expansionism, population growth, economic development, public infrastructure, and military protectionism. Even though the world wars of the twentieth century forced Canada to look outward, its political focus remained decidedly inward. After World War II, government policies emphasized social programming, while identity formation was shaped under the stress of national unity conflicts. In recent years, Canada has morphed from being opposed to free trade to welcoming it; national unity concerns have (tentatively) given way to pocketbook issues that transcend provincialism; and an image of peacekeeping has been re-imagined by soldiers engaged in battle. Canada's place in the world, as with its own social fabric, is in a constant state of evolution.

Woven throughout Canada's role in international affairs are such underlying values as increasing concern about human rights. Close observers of Canadian politics can detect differences in approach between Conservative and Liberal governments. The ethnic electoral fault lines associated with twentieth-century divisions over conscription persist among Canada's major political parties today, with the Liberal Party experiencing more success east of Manitoba, and Conservatives seen as a more attractive proposition west of Ontario. Quebec was opposed to Canadian participation in the war in Afghanistan, just as it has historically been opposed to military conflicts dating back to the Boer War. However, other divisions have eroded: whereas free trade was a polarizing issue in several federal elections, the negotiation of a trade deal with the European Union has been embraced across the political spectrum. Canada's place in the world is evidently at once predicable and ever changing.

For More Information

How has Canadian foreign aid been spent?
Contributors to *Struggling for Effectiveness: CIDA and Canadian Foreign Aid*, edited by Stephen Brown (McGill–Queen's University Press, 2012), explore such matters as the scope of Canadian donations to developing nations, the federal government's food security policies, and the challenges associated with reforming foreign aid practices.

Should Canada's role as a middle power prioritize peacekeeping over military-building? Definitely peacekeeping, according to Robert W. Murray and John McCoy. Read their article "From Middle Power to Peacebuilder: The Use of Canadian Forces in Modern Canadian Foreign Policy," *American Review of Canadian Studies* 40, no. 2 (2010): pp. 171–88.

What is the modern role for NORAD? Consider the arguments of David S. McDonough in his 2012 article "Canada, NORAD, and the Evolution of Strategic Defence," *International Journal* 67, no. 3: pp. 755–69.

After the FLQ crisis, why did Quebec separatists shun violence and choose democratic means to pursue their political goals? Lee Dutter investigates in "Why Dogs Don't Bark (or Bomb) in the Night. Explaining the Non-development of Political Violence or Terrorism: The Case of Quebec Separatism," *Studies in Conflict & Terrorism* 35, no. 1 (2012): pp. 59–75.

How does a free trade deal get negotiated? Michael Hart details the negotiations that culminated in the Canada–US Free Trade Agreement in *Decision at Midnight: Inside the Canada–US Free-Trade Negotiations* (UBC Press, 1994).

What role do provinces and territories play in international trade negotiations? In December 2013, the *International Journal: Canada's Journal of Global Policy Analysis* published a special edition on this topic.

Learn about the compelling story of how Canadian minister of transport David Collenette's day unfolded on 9/11. His recollections a decade later were recorded by *Maclean's* magazine (Search: Macleans up in the air 911).

Consider what can be done about extremism and terrorism in Canada. Perspectives on terrorist groups in Canada, terrorist financing, and how 9/11 changed Canada can be found in *Terror in the Peaceable Kingdom: Understanding and Addressing Violent Extremism in Canada*, edited by Daveed Gartenstein-Ross and Linda Frum (Washington, DC: Foundation for Defence of Democracies, 2012), (Search: defend democracy peaceable kingdom).

Gain an appreciation for the government's response to the Air India disaster. See the summary of the commission of inquiry into the disaster, by searching "Air India report".

Expand your awareness of multinational organizations and international forums. Plenty of information about the United Nations (www.un.org/en), the World Trade Organization (www.wto.org), the Commonwealth (thecommonwealth.org), and La Francophonie (www.francophonie.org) is available online.

Interested in why it took a photo of a dead toddler to draw attention to the Syrian refugee crisis? PhD student Sean Fleming argues that it humanized a collective and distant issue, in "The Syrian refugee crisis and the salience of international issues," *Canadian Election Analysis 2015: Communication, Strategy and Democracy* (UBC Press): 90-91.

UP FOR DEBATE

Should Canada give more money for foreign aid?

THE CLAIM: YES, IT SHOULD!

Canada should increase its foreign aid to help combat poverty in developing nations.

Yes: Argument Summary

The scope of global need for foreign aid is incomprehensible, with malnourishment, disease, sexual violence, inadequate environmental standards, and a lack of basic education being some of the many chronic problems that are most acute in developing countries. The United Nations target for foreign aid is 0.7 per cent of an industrialized nation's gross domestic product; Canada commits roughly half of this objective. Western nations can minimize human suffering if they choose to prioritize humanitarian aid over domestic politics. There is moral and altruistic need for the federal government to build on its peacekeeping image by taking a leadership role in the international community in allocating more funds to combat global poverty. For as Bono of U2 once said, "the world needs more Canada."

Yes: Top 5 Considerations

1. Reducing global poverty has been, and should be, the primary purpose of Canadian foreign aid. There is a moral imperative for the Government of Canada, whose citizens enjoy some of the best living standards in the free world, to help those in greater need living in impoverished societies. Relying on corporations and citizens to donate to their preferred causes is not enough.

2. Canada's position as a middle power means that it can leverage the political value of funds that would have otherwise been committed to its military. Through foreign aid, Canada can reward foreign governments that prioritize improving the quality of life of its citizens, form alliances with like-minded leaders, and redirect support from regimes with poor human rights records. This can inspire other developing nations to follow suit and reduces the conditions that lead to stateless combatants targeting Canada.

3. It is imperative that countries like Canada commit their resources in order to advance the objectives of multinational organizations like the United Nations (UN) and the Organisation for Economic Co-operation and Development (OECD). Improving human rights, promoting democracy, advancing the equality of girls and women, encouraging sustainable economic development, and distributing medicine to those in need are noble values. Without concrete, government-sponsored action, those in need are left only with unfulfilled promises.

4. So-called "economic diplomacy," whereby industrialized nations prioritize trade and economic investment in emerging economies, is a capitalist approach to solving a problem that requires a communitarian mindset. Trade liberalization may serve the interests of businesses in large economies while exploiting smaller ones, thereby worsening the plight of the poor rather than allegedly helping them.

5. Countless organizations in Canada, including the Canadian offices of global advocacy groups such as Amnesty International and Doctors Without Borders, seek to fill the foreign aid policy vacuum. Political parties should listen to these perspectives and show leadership by advancing an international development agenda.

Yes: Other Considerations

- By engaging Canadian businesses in public aid programs as opposed to using public funds, the government legitimizes attempts by profit-motivated commercial interests to present themselves as corporate citizens. This may increase the influence of the private sector over public policy, divest the government of its own responsibilities, and harm Canada's international image.

No: Argument Summary

On behalf of all Canadians, the federal government spends over $5 billion annually on foreign aid programs benefiting more than 100 countries, and many Canadians choose to make individual donations. Idealists who romanticize Canada's international role and believe that its foreign aid budgets should be increased have little appreciation for the complexity of the task. In reality, to meet the interests of transparency and public accountability while remaining viable, any foreign aid dedicated to eradicating global poverty and related foreign development initiatives must also generate some benefits to Canada.

No: Top 5 Considerations

1. The top priority for politicians and governments in Canada is to improve the quality of life of Canadian citizens. It is naive to think that political elites can maintain power if they are criticized for diverting public funds toward citizens in other countries. As long as Canadians pressure their government to spend more locally, or to cut their taxes, then their elected representatives will be incentivized to respond in kind.

2. The amount of foreign aid distributed by the federal government doesn't tell the whole story.

Canadian citizens, corporations, religious organizations, and other groups have the option of giving their own money to charities that dispense foreign aid. Charitable donations are subsidized through tax deductible status, and in the event of an episodic crisis (e.g. a natural disaster) the federal government tends to match the donations of Canadian citizens and corporations.

3. The public often thinks that political leaders are the ones who make foreign aid decisions. In truth, the complexity of international relations and offering assistance to developing nations means that it is largely, and necessarily, a bureaucratic process led by international aid organizations. Achieving transparency, value, and accountability for Canadian taxpayer dollars spent on foreign aid is challenging in this context.

4. This said, money given to developing nations needs to be spent in an efficient manner to optimize its impact. Public policy operations within Canada are subject to transparency and regular program evaluation to ensure that money is being spent appropriately. The same standard of care is needed for foreign aid programs.

5. News media coverage of foreign aid polices can be moralistic, simplistic, and judgemental without comprehending the complexity of the policy problems. This introduces all sorts of biases into decisions about where to allocate limited assistance. For instance, the government may respond to pressure to direct aid to geographic areas that the media pays attention to, but the media has difficulty generating coverage of remote locations where help may be needed most.

No: Other Considerations

- Public opinion surveys routinely indicate that foreign aid is not a top priority of Canadians. Accordingly, it tends to be a minor element of political parties' campaign platforms and is an afterthought in Canadian election news coverage.

Discussion Questions

- How can the Canadian government ensure that money given to foreign organizations is used in an appropriate manner?
- Why do you think Canadian politicians spend so little time advocating for foreign aid?
- What are the strengths and weaknesses of a policy where the Canadian government offers to match what Canadian corporations and individuals donate?
- Should Canadian provinces, territories, and municipalities get involved in foreign aid programs?
- Is it right that the government attaches criteria to foreign aid, such as requiring that Canadian businesses benefit from any spending?

Where to Learn More about Canada and Foreign Aid

David R. Black and Rebecca Tiessen, "The Canadian International Development Agency: New Policies, Old Problems," *Canadian Journal of Development Studies* 28, no. 2 (2007): pp. 191–212.

Stephen Brown, ed., *Struggling for Effectiveness: CIDA and Canadian Foreign Aid* (Kingston and Montreal: McGill–Queens University Press, 2012).

John Cameron, "CIDA in the Americas: New Directions and Warning Signs for Canadian Development Policy," *Canadian Journal of Development Studies* 28, no. 2 (2007): pp. 229–49.

Hans Morgenthau, "A Political Theory of Foreign Aid," *American Political Science Review* 56, no. 2 (1962): pp. 301–9.

David R. Morrison, *Aid and Ebb Tide: A History of CIDA and Canadian Development Assistance* (Waterloo, ON: Wilfrid Laurier University Press, 1998).

Douglas A. Van Belle, Jean-Sébastien Rioux, and David M. Potter, *Media, Bureaucracies and Foreign Aid: A Comparative Analysis of the United States, the United Kingdom, Canada, France and Japan* (New York: Palgrave Macmillan, 2004).

FIRST MINISTERS OF CANADA

Prime Ministers since 1867 and Premiers since 1945

Canada

YEARS	PRIME MINISTER	PARTY*
1867–73, 1878–91	John A. Macdonald	Conservative
1873–8	Alexander Mackenzie	Liberal
1891–2	John Abbott	Conservative
1892–4	John Thompson	Conservative
1894–6	Mackenzie Bowell	Conservative
1896	Charles Tupper	Conservative
1896–1911	Wilfrid Laurier	Liberal
1911–20	Robert Borden	Conservative
1920–1, 1926	Arthur Meighen	Conservative
1921–6, 1926–30, 1935–48	Mackenzie King	Liberal
1930–5	Richard Bennett	Conservative
1948–57	Louis St Laurent	Liberal
1957–63	John Diefenbaker	Conservative
1963–8	Lester Pearson	Liberal
1968–79, 1980–4	Pierre Trudeau	Liberal
1979	Joe Clark	Conservative
1984	John Turner	Liberal
1984–93	Brian Mulroney	Conservative
1993	Kim Campbell	Conservative
1993–2003	Jean Chrétien	Liberal
2003–6	Paul Martin, Jr	Liberal
2006–15	Stephen Harper	Conservative
2015–	Justin Trudeau	Liberal

*The federal Conservative party has experienced name changes over time; see Chapter 9.

Provinces

British Columbia

YEARS	PREMIER	PARTY
1941–7	John Hart	Liberal–Conservative coalition
1947–52	Byron (Boss) Johnson	Liberal–Conservative coalition
1952–72	W.A.C. Bennett	Social Credit
1972–5	Dave Barrett	New Democratic Party
1975–86	Bill Bennett	Social Credit
1986–91	Bill Vander Zalm	Social Credit
1991	Rita Johnston	Social Credit
1991–6	Mike Harcourt	New Democratic Party
1996–9	Glen Clark	New Democratic Party
1999–2000	Dan Miller	New Democratic Party
2000–1	Ujjal Dosanjh	New Democratic Party
2001–11	Gordon Campbell	Liberal
2011–	Christy Clark	Liberal

Alberta

YEARS	PREMIER	PARTY
1943–68	Ernest Manning	Social Credit
1968–71	Harry Strom	Social Credit
1971–85	Peter Lougheed	Progressive Conservative
1985–92	Don Getty	Progressive Conservative
1992–2006	Ralph Klein	Progressive Conservative
2006–11	Ed Stelmach	Progressive Conservative
2011–14	Alison Redford	Progressive Conservative
2014	Dave Hancock	Progressive Conservative
2014–15	Jim Prentice	Progressive Conservative
2015–	Rachel Notley	New Democratic Party

Saskatchewan

YEARS	PREMIER	PARTY
1944–61	Tommy Douglas	Co-operative Commonwealth Federation
1961–4	Woodrow Lloyd	CCF/New Democratic Party
1964–71	Ross Thatcher	Liberal
1971–82	Allan Blakeney	New Democratic Party
1982–91	Grant Devine	Progressive Conservative
1991–2001	Roy Romanow	New Democratic Party
2001–7	Lorne Calvert	New Democratic Party
2007–	Brad Wall	Saskatchewan Party

Manitoba

YEARS	PREMIER	PARTY
1943–8	Stuart Garson	Liberal–Progressive coalition
1948–58	Douglas Campbell	Liberal–Progressive coalition / Liberal–Progressive majority
1958–67	Duff Roblin	Progressive Conservative
1967–9	Walter Weir	Progressive Conservative
1969–77	Edward Schreyer	New Democratic Party
1977–81	Sterling Lyon	Progressive Conservative
1981–8	Howard Pawley	New Democratic Party
1988–99	Gary Filmon	Progressive Conservative
1999–2009	Gary Doer	New Democratic Party
2009–	Greg Selinger	New Democratic Party

Ontario

YEARS	PREMIER	PARTY
1943–8	George Drew	Progressive Conservative
1948–9	Thomas L. Kennedy	Progressive Conservative
1949–61	Leslie Frost	Progressive Conservative
1961–71	John Robarts	Progressive Conservative
1971–85	Bill Davis	Progressive Conservative
1985	Frank Miller	Progressive Conservative
1985–90	David Peterson	Liberal
1990–5	Bob Rae	New Democratic Party
1995–2002	Mike Harris	Progressive Conservative
2002–3	Ernie Eves	Progressive Conservative
2003–13	Dalton McGuinty	Liberal
2013–	Kathleen Wynne	Liberal

Quebec

YEARS	PREMIER	PARTY
1944–59	Maurice Duplessis	Union Nationale
1959–60	Paul Sauvé	Union Nationale
1960	Antonio Barrette	Union Nationale
1960–6	Jean Lesage	Liberal
1966–8	Daniel Johnson, Sr	Union Nationale
1968–70	Jean-Jacques Bertrand	Union Nationale
1970–6	Robert Bourassa	Liberal
1976–85	René Lévesque	Parti Québécois
1985	Pierre-Marc Johnson	Parti Québécois

1985–94	Robert Bourassa	Liberal
1994	Daniel Johnson, Jr	Liberal
1994–6	Jacques Parizeau	Parti Québécois
1996–2001	Lucien Bouchard	Parti Québécois
2001–3	Bernard Landry	Parti Québécois
2003–12	Jean Charest	Liberal
2012–14	Pauline Marois	Parti Québécois
2014–	Philippe Couillard	Liberal

New Brunswick

YEARS	PREMIER	PARTY
1940–52	John B. McNair	Liberal
1952–60	Hugh John Flemming	Progressive Conservative
1960–70	Louis Robichaud	Liberal
1970–87	Richard Hatfield	Progressive Conservative
1987–97	Frank McKenna	Liberal
1997–8	Ray Frenette	Liberal
1998–9	Camille Thériault	Liberal
1999–2006	Bernard Lord	Progressive Conservative
2006–10	Shawn Graham	Liberal
2010–14	David Alward	Progressive Conservative
2014–	Brian Gallant	Liberal

Nova Scotia

YEARS	PREMIER	PARTY
1945–54	Angus Macdonald	Liberal
1954	Harold Connolly	Liberal
1954–6	Henry Hicks	Liberal
1956–67	Robert Stanfield	Progressive Conservative
1967–70	G.I. Smith	Progressive Conservative
1970–8	Gerald Regan	Liberal
1978–90	John Buchanan	Progressive Conservative
1990–1	Roger Bacon	Progressive Conservative
1991–3	Donald Cameron	Progressive Conservative
1993–7	John Savage	Liberal
1997–9	Russell MacLellan	Liberal
1999–2006	John Hamm	Progressive Conservative
2006–9	Rodney MacDonald	Progressive Conservative
2009–13	Darrell Dexter	New Democratic Party
2013–	Stephen McNeil	Liberal

Prince Edward Island

YEARS	PREMIER	PARTY
1943–53	Walter Jones	Liberal
1953–9	Alex Matheson	Liberal
1959–66	Walter Shaw	Progressive Conservative
1966–78	Alexander Campbell	Liberal
1978–9	Bennett Campbell	Liberal
1979–81	Angus MacLean	Progressive Conservative
1981–6	James Lee	Progressive Conservative
1986–93	Joe Ghiz	Liberal
1993–6	Catherine Callbeck	Liberal
1996	Keith Milligan	Liberal
1996–2007	Pat Binns	Progressive Conservative
2007–2015	Robert Ghiz	Liberal
2015–	Wade MacLauchlan	Liberal

Newfoundland and Labrador*

YEARS	PREMIER	PARTY
1949–72	Joey Smallwood	Liberal
1972–9	Frank Moores	Progressive Conservative
1979–89	Brian Peckford	Progressive Conservative
1989	Tom Rideout	Progressive Conservative
1989–96	Clyde Wells	Liberal
1996–2000	Brian Tobin	Liberal
2000–1	Beaton Tulk	Liberal
2001–3	Roger Grimes	Liberal
2003–10	Danny Williams	Progressive Conservative
2010–14	Kathy Dunderdale	Progressive Conservative
2014	Tom Marshall	Progressive Conservative
2014–15	Paul Davis	Progressive Conservative
2015–	Dwight Ball	Liberal

*Joined Canada in 1949.

Territories

Yukon*

YEARS	PREMIER	PARTY
1978–85	Chris Pearson	Progressive Conservative
1985	Willard Phelps	Progressive Conservative
1985–92	Tony Penikett	New Democratic Party
1992–6	John Ostashek	Yukon Party
1996–2000	Piers McDonald	New Democratic Party
2000–2	Pat Duncan	Liberal
2002–11	Dennis Fentie	Yukon Party
2011–	Darrell Pasloski	Yukon Party

*Commissioners served as heads of government in Yukon until 1978.

Northwest Territories*

YEARS	PREMIER	PARTY
1980–4	George Braden	No party system
1984–5	Richard Nerysoo	No party system
1985–7	Nick Sibbeston	No party system
1987–91	Dennis Patterson	No party system
1991–5	Nellie Cournoyea	No party system
1995–8	Don Morin	No party system
1998	Goo Arlooktoo	No party system
1998–2000	Jim Antoine	No party system
2000–3	Stephen Kakfwi	No party system
2003–7	Joe Handley	No party system
2007–11	Floyd Roland	No party system
2011–	Bob McLeod	No party system

*Commissioners served as heads of government in Northwest Territories until 1980.

Nunavut*

YEARS	PREMIER	PARTY
1999–2008	Paul Okalik	No party system
2008–13	Eva Aariak	No party system
2013–	Peter Taptuna	No party system

* The territory was created in 1999 from land under the jurisdiction of Northwest Territories.

GLOSSARY

ABC An agency, board, or commission responsible for delivering a program or service, or producing goods, at arm's length from government.

Aboriginal people First Nations, Métis, and Inuit living in Canada. An increasing number of Canadian institutions, including the federal government, have begun using the term "Indigenous" instead of "Aboriginal." While recognizing the important symbolic, cultural, political, and historical differences between these terms, we have used them interchangeably throughout this textbook. *See also* **Indigenous people**.

Accountability Act A piece of sweeping legislation whose rules were designed to reduce the possibility of unethical conduct in government.

ad hoc committee A committee whose mandate is time-limited. *Also called* **working committee**.

adjournment The temporary suspension of a legislative sitting until it reconvenes.

administrative law The branch of public law involving the review of government decisions and disputes between citizens and state agencies.

administrative tribunal A quasi-judicial body empowered to decide administrative law cases, and whose decisions may be appealed to the court system.

affirmative action A policy of proactive measures to guarantee the descriptive representation of traditionally underrepresented groups.

agenda setting The use of strategies and tactics to generate public and government support for a proposed public policy.

AIT The Agreement on Internal Trade, a federal–provincial–territorial agreement to lower internal trade barriers within Canada.

allophones Canadians whose dominant language is neither French nor English.

amending formula A set of rules governing how the constitution can be changed.

APEC The Asia–Pacific Economic Cooperation forum, a multinational economic organization of Pacific Rim countries.

appointment power The authority to decide who should be hired to fill a government position.

asymmetrical federalism A system of federalism in which jurisdictional powers are distributed unequally among provinces (*see* **federalism**).

attorney general A cabinet member who is the highest-ranking elected legal officer in a jurisdiction.

auditor general The independent officer responsible for auditing and reporting to the legislature regarding a government's spending and operations.

autocracy A system of government featuring an unelected decision-maker with absolute authority.

baby bonus A government policy that awards money to parents of young children.

backbenchers Rank-and-file legislators without cabinet responsibilities or other special legislative titles or duties.

balanced budget A budget in which total government revenues equal (or sometimes exceed) total government spending.

band A First Nations group with Indian status as defined by the federal government (*see* **status Indian**).

band council The governing body of a First Nations band, elected by its members.

bicameral legislature A legislative body consisting of two chambers (or houses), e.g. the House of Commons and the Senate. *Compare* **unicameral legislature**.

bill A piece of draft legislation tabled in the legislature.

Bill of Rights, 1960 Non-constitutional legislation detailing Canadians' rights and freedoms vis-à-vis the federal government; superseded by the Charter of Rights and Freedoms in 1982.

Bloc Québécois A left-wing protest party that promotes Quebec nationalism.

blue toryism A branch of old right conservatism that promotes economic nationalism and smaller government. *Compare* **red toryism**.

boundaries commission A body that recommends changes to election boundaries.

British North America Act, 1867 Canada's first modern, written constitution.

brokerage party The Canadian term for a catch-all party that brokers competing regional demands (*see* **catch-all party**).

budget A document containing the government's projected revenue, expenditures, and economic forecasts.

budget deficit A situation in which spending exceeds revenues during a given period.

budget estimates The detailed, line-by-line statements of how each department will treat revenues and expenditures.

budget surplus A situation in which revenues exceed spending during a given period.

business liberalism   A branch of liberalism that seeks to achieve equality of opportunity in economic terms. *Compare* **welfare liberalism**.

by-election   A district-level election held between general elections.

cabinet The leaders of the political executive, consisting of the sitting prime minister, ministers, ministers of state, cabinet secretaries, and associate ministers, as appropriate.

cabinet committee A subgroup of cabinet members assigned to scrutinize a particular set of executive actions.

cabinet shuffle A change in the composition of a government's political executive between elections.

cabinet solidarity   The understanding that members of the executive remain cohesive and jointly responsible for the government's undertakings.

campaign finance regulations   Laws that govern political fundraising and/or spending.

Canada Health Act A piece of federal legislation imposing conditions on provincial governments for the expenditure of funds from health transfers.

Canada Pension Plan   A mandatory federal retirement program funded by workers and employers.

Canada Student Loans A federal program that helps qualifying students access post-secondary education by awarding them interest-free repayable loans while they study full-time.

Canadian Broadcasting Corporation (**CBC**) A Crown corporation that is Canada's national public broadcaster.

Canadian Human Rights Commission A body empowered to adjudicate discrimination complaints against federally regulated bodies.

Canadian Security Intelligence Service *See* **CSIS**.

CanCon An informal term for regulations by the Canadian Radio-television and Telecommunications Commission requiring that media outlets operating in Canada provide a minimum level of Canadian-produced programming.

candidate quotas   Hard targets established by some political parties to improve the proportion of candidates from traditionally underrepresented groups.

catch-all party A competitive political party that prioritizes the design of effective public policy and election strategies. *Compare* **brokerage party**.

caucus *See* **party caucus**.

central agencies   Coordinating bodies that steer government business across all departments.

centralized federalism   A federal system of government in which the national government has considerable power (*see* **federalism**).

Charlottetown Accord A failed accord that proposed to renew the constitution, but was defeated in a national referendum in the early 1990s.

Charter of Rights and Freedoms A portion of the Constitution Act, 1982, enshrining Canadians' core liberties and entitlements vis-à-vis their governments. *Compare* **Bill of Rights, 1960**.

Charterphiles Supporters of the enhanced role of judges in the Canadian rights regime.

Charterphobes Opponents and skeptics of the enhanced role of judges in the Canadian rights regime.

Charter-proofing Pre-emptive steps taken by a government to ensure that its proposed legislation withstands judicial review.

citizen A legally recognized inhabitant of a democratic state.

citizens plus The notion that Aboriginal people (ought to) hold a special set of rights in addition to those conferred by Canadian citizenship.

civil law   The body of rules governing disputes between or among private parties.

civil-law system A legal order based on a written code.

civil society The community of citizens in Canada, outside the realm of government.

Clarity Act A piece of federal legislation passed in 2000 that identifies the terms for the federal government to deal with a province proposing to secede.

classical federalism A federal system of government in which the federal and provincial governments operate independently of each other in their own respective areas of jurisdiction (*see* **federalism**).

cleavage   A division that separates opposing political communities.

clerk of the Privy (or **Executive**) **Council** The highest-ranking public servant in the federal or provincial/territorial bureaucracy.

coalition government   A hung parliament in which the cabinet consists of members from more than one political party (*see* **hung parliament**).

collaborative federalism   A system of federalism in which provincial governments take the lead to solve common public policy problems together (*see* **federalism**).

collective action problem   The notion that people whose interests are promoted by a group will benefit from its efforts whether or not they actively participate.

collective bargaining The formal negotiation of the terms of an employment contract between the representatives of a group of employees and their employer.

colonialism Belief in the supremacy of European settler institutions over those of Aboriginal groups, and policies and practices that support this belief.

commission of inquiry An independent body of experts created by a government to investigate a contentious area of public policy or an issue deemed to be of great public importance. *Also called* **royal commission**.

committee of the whole Another name for the body of all legislators.

common-law system A legal order based on customs, usage, and precedent.

Commonwealth (of Nations) An association of nation-states with ties to the United Kingdom.

Communications Security Establishment Canada See **CSEC**.

conditional grants Federal transfers to the provinces that may only be used for a specific purpose, and are subject to federal government restrictions or standards.

confederal parties Federal and provincial parties that operate autonomously from each other, even though they may have similar names.

Confederation The federal union of provinces and territories forming Canada, originally including Ontario, Quebec, New Brunswick, and Nova Scotia.

confidence convention The practice under which a government must relinquish power when it loses a critical legislative vote.

conscription A compulsory draft by the government to recruit soldiers for military action.

consensus government A system of governance that operates without political parties (e.g. in Northwest Territories and Nunavut).

Conservative Party A centre–right major party that has periodically formed the government of Canada.

constituency association See **electoral district association**.

constitutional convention An unwritten rule based on custom that binds political actors to adhere to the traditions of the constitutional order.

constitutional law The branch of public law dealing with the authority of the state.

constitutional monarchy A system in which the sovereignty of the Crown is maintained, but exercised by elected officials according to prescribed rules.

constitutional order The body of written and unwritten rules that govern all laws in Canada.

contempt A formal denunciation of a party's unparliamentary behaviour by the speaker of the house.

co-operative federalism A system of federalism in which the federal and provincial governments work together to solve public-policy problems (see **federalism**).

correctional system The network of community-based and institutional programs designed to detain, rehabilitate, and deter those involved in illegal activity.

Council of the Federation Organization that supports regular meetings of provincial and territorial premiers in the interest of fostering collaboration.

criminal law The body of statutory rules governing misconduct that affects not only the immediate victims but society as a whole.

critic An opposition party member assigned to scrutinize the activities of a particular minister of the Crown.

crossing the floor The process in which a member of the legislature leaves one political party to join another party.

Crown The legal concept of the monarch's supremacy over the executive, legislative, and judicial branches of government.

Crown attorney A lawyer who acts on behalf of the government when deciding how to pursue criminal cases.

Crown corporation An enterprise owned by a federal or provincial government.

CSEC The Communications Security Establishment Canada, Canada's electronic communications spy agency.

CSIS The Canadian Security Intelligence Service, Canada's spy agency.

decentralization The transfer of authority from a central government to local levels of government, typically from the federal government to provincial and territorial governments.

decentralized federalism A federal system of government in which the regional units have considerable power (see **federalism**).

declaratory power The authority of the federal government to decide that an issue falls within its jurisdiction.

democracy A system of government featuring decision-makers chosen by citizens through free and fair elections.

democratic deficit The gap between peoples' expectations for the performance of democratic institutions and the perceived performance of those institutions.

Department of Finance The central agency responsible for setting and monitoring the government's fiscal and economic policy, including overseeing the budget process.

deputy minister The highest-ranking public servant in a given government department, reporting to the department's minister.

descriptive representation A political attachment to someone viewed as sharing one's own background or social profile. (Compare **formalistic representation**, **symbolic representation**, **substantive representation**.)

devolution The act of transferring (devolving) powers from a central government to regional or local governments that remain under its constitutional purview.

dialogue model The notion that the definition of rights and freedoms is reached through the interaction of judges, legislatures, and executives.

direct democracy A system in which citizens make political decisions by voting on individual issues.

direct taxation The collection of taxes by government without using an intermediary. Compare **indirect taxation**.

disallowance The constitutional power of the federal government to veto provincial legislation and cause its termination.

disclosure The act of revealing otherwise private information, such as campaign expenses.

dissolution The process by which a Parliament or legislature is closed, resulting in a general election of new members.

distinct society A proposed designation for the province of Quebec, recognizing that it features a French-speaking majority, a unique culture, and a civil-law tradition. The designation was spelled out in the Canada Clause that would have been adopted as a preamble to the Constitution Act had the Charlottetown Accord been passed.

divided crown A monarchy whose sovereignty is split among different orders of government.

earned majority A majority government in which the governing party's share of the popular vote is at least 50 per cent. *Compare* **manufactured majority**.

e-democracy The use of information communication technologies to get citizens involved in politics.

e-government The interactive use of information communication technologies to deliver public programs and services.

election platform A list of political pledges announced before or during an election campaign.

electoral district association The local organization of a political party operating within the boundaries of an election riding. *Also called* **constituency association**.

elite party A small political party run by people with ascribed social status.

emergency federalism An arrangement in which the federal government assumes control in a national crisis (*see* **federalism**).

emergency power The ability of the federal government to exercise extraordinary authority in a time of crisis.

employment equity Federal government policy designed to improve the representation of traditionally underrepresented groups in the civil service and federally regulated industries.

employment insurance (EI) A mandatory government insurance program funded by employees and employers that provides temporary income to workers who lose their jobs.

equalization A federal transfer program designed to lessen the fiscal disparities among provinces.

executive federalism A system of federalism in which the elected leaders of federal and provincial governments make public-policy decisions (*see* **federalism**).

Fathers of Confederation The group of colonial leaders who negotiated the terms of union forming the Dominion of Canada.

federalism A constitution-based division of powers among two or more orders of government. (*See* **asymmetrical federalism, centralized federalism, classical federalism, collaborative federalism, co-operative federalism, decentralized federalism, emergency federalism, executive federalism, fiscal federalism, functional federalism, inter-state federalism, intra-state federalism, symmetrical federalism, treaty federalism.**)

federal spending power The capacity of the federal government to spend its available funds, even on areas that fall outside its constitutional jurisdiction.

federation A political system that distributes power between a central government and regional governments.

filibuster The extension of parliamentary debate, typically by opposition members, to delay the passage of a bill.

first minister diplomacy The characterization of Canadian premiers and prime ministers as the primary spokesperson of their government's interests.

first ministers The heads of government in Canada, namely the prime minister and premiers.

first ministers' meeting A formal gathering of the premiers hosted by the prime minister.

First Nations Aboriginal groups descended from a variety of historical Indigenous nations; collectively, the earliest inhabitants of North America and their descendants, other than Métis and Inuit.

first past the post *Another term for* **single-member plurality**.

fiscal federalism The manner in which revenues and responsibilities are distributed among various orders and governments (*see* **federalism**).

fiscal update A semi-annual announcement of the state of the government's economic, revenue, and spending projections.

fixed-date election law Legislation prescribing that general elections be held on a particular date, or range of dates, typically every four years.

foreign direct investment The influx of capital into a company in one country, by way of investors from another country.

formalistic representation A political attachment to someone by virtue of that person's status as a legitimately elected official. *Compare* **descriptive representation, symbolic representation, substantive representation**.

fourth estate A term for the media that implies that a free press is so vital to democracy that it is on par with the three branches of government (the executive, the legislature, and the judiciary).

framing The shaping of information so that communication recipients will interpret it in a manner that is advantageous to the sender.

La Francophonie An association of nation-states and regions with French language and cultural connections. *Also called* **Organisation internationale de la Francophonie (OIF)**.

freedom of information A legal requirement that governments release information upon request, subject to certain restrictions.

freedoms Autonomy to live and act without external restraint.

free trade The elimination of financial and regulatory barriers to allow unfettered market access.

free vote A bill or motion in the legislature on which party members, except members of cabinet, are allowed to vote however they choose without sanction.

functional federalism A system of federalism in which civil servants conduct the bulk of intergovernmental activity (*see* **federalism**).

fusion of powers An intimate connection between the authority of the executive and the authority of the legislature.

game frame A strategic filter applied by the media to political decisions and events with a view to declaring winners and losers.

Gang of Eight The eight provinces united in opposing the federal government's plans to patriate and centralize the Canadian constitution.

Gazette The official journal listing government appointments, changes to laws and regulations, and other notices.

G8/G7 Annual meeting of the leaders of eight of the world's most industrialized economies—currently known as the **Group of Seven (G7)** due to Russia's suspension from the group.

gerrymandering The purposeful manipulation of electoral districts to maximize one party's chances of winning.

goods and services tax (GST) A federal value-added tax applied to the sale of most goods and services in Canada.

GOTV Get Out The Vote, a term for efforts to mobilize supporters to vote, such as telephone reminders.

government (1) The organization of public policy and public administration. (2) The body consisting of all cabinet ministers, who remain responsible to the legislature for state decision-making.

government agency An arm's-length corporate body operating on behalf of a government.

government board A public advisory committee made up of appointed citizens.

government commission An agency of the government that provides specialized policy expertise and oversight.

government subsidy Public funds used to support an individual, group, or cause.

governor general The monarch's representative at the federal level in Canada.

Great Recession A decline in the international economy that began in 2008, triggered by the collapse of the US housing market.

green paper A government document released to explore policy options, without any commitment to the outcome.

Green Party A left-wing protest party that promotes environmentalism.

GST *See* **goods and services tax**.

habeas corpus The right not to be detained without cause or due process; the term comes from Latin and means literally "you shall have the body."

hacktivism Politically-motivated damage inflicted on government information communication technologies.

harmonized sales tax (HST) In Atlantic Canada and Ontario, a value-added consumption tax that combines both federal and provincial rates.

hate speech Messages that promote harm or aggravated contempt of an identifiable group of people.

head of government The highest-ranking official in a jurisdiction, appointed by the Crown to lead the executive.

head of state The highest-ranking figure in a sovereign state, serving as its foremost ceremonial representative.

horizontal fiscal gap Inter-provincial disparities in revenue. *Compare* **vertical fiscal gap**.

horizontal fiscal imbalance A situation in which some provinces have more than enough capacity to fund their constitutional responsibilities while others do not. *Compare* **vertical fiscal imbalance**.

horse race coverage Media attention focused on which party or leader is leading in public opinion.

house leader A member of the legislature responsible for the overall performance of his or her party in the legislative process.

House of Commons The lower house of Canadian Parliament, consisting of elected members from across the country. *Compare* **Senate**.

HST *See* **harmonized sales tax**.

human rights commissions and tribunals Quasi-judicial panels that investigate and/or adjudicate citizens' complaints about discrimination prohibited by human rights laws.

hung parliament A government in which no single party controls at least half of the seats in the legislature. *Compare* **coalition government**, **minority government**, **majority government**.

ideology A set of ideas that form a belief system underpinning a particular political or economic theory.

incarceration Court-ordered confinement in a provincial, territorial, or federal prison.

incumbent An elected official who currently represents an electoral district.

independent A candidate or parliamentarian who is not officially affiliated with a political party.

Indigenous people *Another term for* **Aboriginal people**.

indirect taxation The collection of taxes by an intermediate body on behalf of government. *Compare* **direct taxation**.

information subsidy Free packaged content provided to the media in a manner that is designed to meet their needs.

inner cabinet The members of the political executive who hold its most important portfolios, including finance, treasury board, and justice (among others).

institution A structure that defines and constrains behaviour within a political system.

institutionalized interest groups Pressure groups that have become entrenched political organizations (*see* **interest group**).

integrated parties Federal and provincial political parties whose behaviours and organization are interconnected. *Compare* **truncated party**.

interest group A political organization that seeks to influence public policy without competing for election. *Also called* **third party**.

interest rate The percentage rate of money charged by lenders to borrowers.

inter-state federalism A system of formal interactions among government officials and leaders (*see* **federalism**).

intra-state federalism A system of federalism in which regional interests are represented within the institutions of the central government (*see* **federalism**).

Inuit Aboriginal people with historic ties to the northernmost lands in Canada.

issue-oriented interest groups Loosely organized political organizations that focus on a core issue (*see* **interest group**).

Judicial Committee of the Privy Council *See* **Supreme Court of Canada**.

judicial impartiality The principle by which judges decide cases based on evidence and an objective interpretation of the law.

judicial independence The principle by which judges are free from political interference when deciding cases.

judicial review The authority of the courts to adjudicate matters of constitutional law.

jurisdiction The ultimate authority to make legal decisions, or the seat of power for such decision-making.

justice of the peace An individual appointed to provide routine, administrative judicial services.

labour union An organization of workers that represents its members' interests, especially in bargaining with their employer.

land claims Statements of Aboriginal peoples' entitlement to territory within Canada.

Laurentian myth A theory that historic perceptions of central Canadian dominance have spawned regionalist resentment in peripheral parts of the country.

leader of the official opposition Typically, the leader of the party with the second-most seats in the legislature.

leader's tour A visit to various electoral districts by the party leader and an entourage of staffers and journalists.

leadership contest An election within a political party to select a leader.

leadership review A vote held at a party convention on whether a leadership contest should be held.

leave Permission granted by a court to hear a case.

left-wing Characterized by a political tendency that promotes higher taxes and a bigger role for government while promoting proactive measures to secure social equality. *Compare* **right-wing**.

legislative committee A small group of legislators assigned to deliberate and report back to the legislature.

liberal democracy A system in which equality, rights, and freedoms are preserved through public debate and free and fair elections.

Liberal Party A brokerage party that has governed Canada at the federal level longer than any other major party (*see* **brokerage party**).

libertarian Advocating the least possible amount of state intervention in the lives of citizens.

lieutenant governor The monarch's representative in each province.

line department Units responsible for the development and delivery of policy, programs, or services under a particular portfolio.

lobbying Personal communication with public office-holders initiated by advocacy groups as part of an effort to influence government decision-making.

lobbyist A person or firm hired to communicate directly with public office-holders in order to advance a client's public-policy agenda.

lock-up The process through which invited individuals (e.g. the media) are given confidential access to budget documents before they are officially released to the public.

majority government A government in which the governing party controls at least half of the seats in the legislature. *Compare* **hung parliament**.

major party A political party that has many supporters and a large organizational infrastructure.

mandatory minimum (sentence) The shortest allowable prison term for a person convicted of certain crimes (such as firearms and gun offences) or under certain conditions (e.g. a repeat offence).

Manitoba schools question A formative dispute over the funding of education that exposed religious, language, and intergovernmental tensions in Canada.

manufactured majority A majority government in which the governing party's share of the popular vote is less than 50 percent. *Compare* **earned majority**.

Maritimes The region of Eastern Canada consisting of New Brunswick, Prince Edward Island, and Nova Scotia.

market-oriented party A political party that uses research data to design policies that satisfy voters.

mass party A grassroots political party characterized by its efforts to sign up members.

mediated democracy A democratic society that relies on the media to provide citizens with information about politics and government.

medicare A publicly funded healthcare service administered by each province with the financial support of the federal government.

Meech Lake Accord A failed constitutional accord in the late 1980s that would have recognized Quebec as a "distinct society" (*see* **distinct society**).

melting pot A metaphor used to depict the multicultural character of the United States, which assimilates or subsumes ethnocultural communities under the broader "American" identity. *Compare* **mosaic**.

member of Parliament (MP) One of the over 300 representatives elected by Canadians to serve in the House of Commons.

merit principle The notion that the most qualified candidate should be awarded a position, contract, or other financial benefit.

Métis Aboriginal people with mixed (First Nations and European) ancestry.

middle power Canada's status as an intermediary, rather than a leader, in international affairs.

ministerial responsibility The understanding that ministers remain individually responsible for the activities undertaken by staff in their respective departments.

minister of justice The member of the government responsible for the administration of the justice system within a given jurisdiction. *Compare* **solicitor general**.

minister of state A member of the legislature assigned by the first minister to provide support to cabinet by exerting leadership over a particular policy area.

minister of the Crown The political head of a government ministry responsible for directing and overseeing the activities of its departments and agencies, boards, and commissions.

minority government A hung parliament in which the cabinet consists of members from one political party (*see* **hung parliament**).

minor party A small political party with much less support or infrastructure than a major party.

mixed-member proportional (MMP) system An electoral system that combines geographic and partisan representation by providing extra seats to parties whose share of seats is lower than their share of the popular vote.

monarch The absolute head of a monarchy, whose power is typically derived by birth.

mosaic A metaphor used to depict Canada's multicultural character, which features and encourages many distinct yet interdependent ethnocultural communities. *Compare* **melting pot**.

motion A proposed parliamentary action.

multicultural Consisting of many culturally distinct groups.

NAFTA The North American Free Trade Agreement, a free trade agreement between Canada, Mexico, and the United States.

narrowcasting A form of campaigning in which parties choose communications that will target narrowly-defined groups of voters.

National Aboriginal Organizations (NAOs) Five bodies formally recognized as representing the interests of different Aboriginal communities across Canada.

nationalism A unifying ideology among people who share a common homeland, ancestry, and language or culture. *Compare* **patriotism**.

NATO *See* **North Atlantic Treaty Organization**.

natural governing party A single party whose long-term dominance has become institutionalized.

negative political advertising Paid communication that criticizes an opponent's policies or record, and which may verge on making personal attacks.

neoconservatism A branch of new right conservatism that promotes the protection of traditional values as well as community safety and national security.

neoliberalism A branch of new right conservatism that favours less government intervention in the economy.

New Democratic Party A left-wing major party that has historically been more successful at the provincial level of government than at the federal level.

Night of the Long Knives An incident in November 1981 in which the federal government and 9 of 10 provincial governments reached a deal to patriate the constitution, without the presence of Quebec government officials.

Nisga'a Treaty A land claims agreement struck between the Nisga'a Tribal Council, the Government of Canada, and the Government of BC (*see* **land claims**).

non-status Indian A person of First Nations ancestry who is not registered under the Indian Act. *Compare* **status Indian**.

NORAD The North American Air Defense Command, created through an agreement co-signed by Canada and the US.

North Atlantic Treaty Organization (NATO) An international military alliance of Western nations.

notwithstanding clause Section 33 of the Constitution Act, 1982, which permits legislatures to pass laws that breach certain rights and freedoms.

Nunavut Land Claims Agreement An agreement between the Inuit (Tunngavik Federation of Nunavut) and the Government of Canada that resulted in the creation of the Territory of Nunavut in 1999.

Oakes test A model used by the court to weigh the democratic benefits and assess the constitutionality of a law that breaches certain Charter rights.

October Crisis A period of escalating terrorism by the Front de Libération du Québec in October 1970, which prompted the federal government to invoke the War Measures Act and suspend civil liberties.

official party status The minimum number of elected members a party needs to question the government in the legislature and qualify for other resources and privileges.

omnibus legislation A bill or law that addresses a wide variety of public policy issues in a single document.

opposition days Time allotted to opposition parties to raise their own motions and legislation in the House of Commons.

parachute candidate A candidate for election in a riding who has been selected by the party leadership without necessarily consulting or seeking the approval of local constituency members beforehand.

parliamentary democracy A democratic system in which government executives must be supported by a majority of elected representatives in a legislature.

parliamentary privilege The legal immunity enjoyed by members of a legislature for things done or said in the course of their duties in the chamber.

parliamentary secretary   A member of the legislature assigned by the first minister to assist a minister in the performance of his or her duties.

parliamentary supremacy   The doctrine according to which legislatures and executives, not courts, define key elements of public policy.

partisan   Someone who identifies with, and is a staunch supporter of, a political party.

party caucus   All the members of a political party who hold a seat in the legislature.

party convention   An official gathering of party delegates to decide on matters of policy and/or leadership.

party discipline   Legislators' strict adherence to the directives of their party leadership.

party leader   The head of a political party's legislative wing.

party member   A person who formally belongs to a political party, having joined by purchasing a membership.

party nomination   An internal contest to decide who should represent a party locally in an upcoming election.

party press   Early newspapers that relied on government advertising and that were blatantly partisan.

party system   A particular constellation of political parties guided by a unique framework of behaviour.

party whip   A member of the legislature responsible for ensuring caucus members appear in the House of Commons for important votes and otherwise adhere to the principle of party discipline.

patriation   The process through which Canadian governments gained the authority to amend the country's main constitutional documents.

patriotism   An emotional connection with a homeland, normally one's country. *Compare* **nationalism**.

patronage   The awarding of government jobs, contracts, and/or other financial benefits to friends of the government party.

pay equity   A policy designed to eliminate gender-based discrimination in terms of how federally regulated employees are paid.

peace officer   A specially trained individual granted government authority to enforce laws. The term encompasses police; sheriffs; customs, corrections, parole, and conservation officers; and other officers and investigators.

per capita transfers   Funds distributed to provinces based on how many people live in their jurisdictions.

permanent campaign   The practice of electioneering outside of an election period, especially when leveraging government resources to do so.

permanent committee   *Another term for* **standing committee**.

permanent executive   Non-partisan bureaucratic officials serving at the pleasure of the Crown and its ministers.

plebiscite   A non-binding citizen vote held to inform a decision by a representative body. *Compare* **referendum**.

pluralism   The presence of diverse socioeconomic groups participating in public affairs.

POGG   The constitutional objective of peace, order, and good government. The POGG clause of the British North America Act was designed to give the federal government overwhelming authority in defining the national interest and extraordinary powers in times of national emergency.

policy   Overarching principles used to guide government decisions and actions.

policy adviser   A professional who analyzes data to assess and recommend possible courses of ongoing action.

political contributions   Donations to a political candidate, group, or cause.

political culture   A society's innate political characteristics, embodied in the structure of its institutions and the beliefs of its members.

political party   A political entity that runs candidates in elections in an attempt to shape government policy and laws.

politics   Activities involving the pursuit and exercise of collective decision-making.

pollster   A senior employee of a research company who oversees the administration of public-opinion surveys.

pork barrel politics   The allocation of government funds to select constituencies, especially those districts held by the governing party.

portfolio   An office or area of responsibility for a minister of the Crown.

power   The ability to design, control, or influence other members of a political community.

pracademic   Characterized by an approach that blends the perspectives of practitioners and academics.

premier   The head of government for a provincial or territorial government.

premier's office   Partisan staff appointed by the premier to advance the political interests of the provincial cabinet, in particular those of the first minister.

prerogative authority   Powers that are not explicitly granted to political executives and that remain vested in the Crown.

presidentialization   The concentration of executive power in the office of the prime minister or premier at the expense of broader cabinet authority.

press gallery   Political journalists who monitor government business and who personally observe proceedings in the legislature.

prime minister   The head of government at the federal level.

prime minister's office (PMO)   Partisan staff appointed by the prime minister to advance the political interests of the federal cabinet, in particular those of the first minister.

principal–agent problem   A problem arising from the fact that someone (an agent) working on behalf of a decision-maker (the principal) may not take the course of action the principal intended.

private laws Rules governing the relationships among citizens and organizations.

Privy Council The body of prominent federal politicians and officials who typically advise the governor general.

Privy Council Office (PCO) The central agency responsible for coordinating the government's overall implementation of policy.

propaganda One-sided persuasive communication that communicates falsehoods by virtue of its selective exclusion of truths.

prorogation The process by which a legislative session is closed.

protest party A party that galvanizes elector frustrations with the major political parties.

public administration The delivery and study of public policy by government.

public debt The accumulated amount borrowed by a government to finance budgets and considered owing.

public laws Rules governing individuals' relationships to the state and society.

public policy A plan or course of action chosen by a government to respond to an identified problem.

public policy cycle The common stages in public decision-making, from conception to implementation and modification.

public sphere The venue for group and public discussion about social problems and government.

Quebec nation motion A non-binding federal motion passed in 2006 that recognized the special character of the Québécois.

question period The time allotted for members of the legislature to ask questions of the government in the House of Commons.

Quiet Revolution A modernizing movement of the early 1960s in Quebec, geared toward a stronger provincial government and a greater outward expression of nationalism.

quotas *See* **candidate quotas**.

rational choice theory A theory that humans are self-interested actors whose decisions maximize their own needs and wants.

RCMP The Royal Canadian Mounted Police, a pan-Canadian police force commissioned by the federal government.

reasonable accommodation Adjustments to policies that allow for the inclusion of traditionally disadvantaged groups without causing undue hardship to others.

reasonable limits clause Section 1 of the Charter of Rights and Freedoms, which allows governments to pass laws that would otherwise contravene rights and freedoms, but which are necessary to protect other democratic norms.

recall Legislated process by which electors of a given district may petition for a by-election.

Red Chamber *Another term for* **Senate**.

redistribution (or **redistricting**) The formal process used to periodically adjust electoral boundaries.

red toryism A branch of old right conservatism that promotes the preservation of the social fabric and government institutions. *Compare* **blue toryism**.

reference cases Proceedings initiated by a government asking for the court's opinion on the constitutionality of legislation.

referendum A citizen vote whose outcome is binding on legislators. *Compare* **plebiscite**.

regionalism An allegiance or psychological connection to a territory with its own unique political characteristics.

regional minister A minister whose portfolio includes additional responsibility for government in a broad geographic area.

regulation A directive passed by the executive specifying how a piece of primary legislation is to be administered.

remand The court-ordered, temporary detention of accused offenders awaiting trial.

representative democracy A political system in which citizens elect officials to make political decisions on their behalf.

republic A system of government in which sovereignty is vested in the people, not the Crown.

reservation The constitutional power of the federal government to withhold the passage of provincial legislation, so as to cause short-term or permanent delay.

reserve A tract of land owned by the federal government and set aside for a First Nations community.

residential schools system A program of state- and church-run schools designed to assimilate Aboriginal children into whitestream Canadian society.

residual powers Any powers not specifically identified in the constitution, which default to the federal government.

responsible government A constitutional principle whereby the executive (cabinet) must be supported by a majority of elected members of the legislature.

restorative justice Drawn from Aboriginal traditions, a set of principles that emphasizes repairing relationships between criminal offenders, their victims, and the community.

riding association *See* **electoral district association**.

rights Legal claims or entitlements to have something or to act in a particular manner.

right-wing Characterized by a political tendency that promotes lower taxes and a smaller role for government while supporting traditional social hierarchies and those resulting from competition. *Compare* **left-wing**.

royal commission *See* **commission of inquiry**.

Royal Commission on Aboriginal Peoples (RCAP) An investigation launched to study the relationship between Aboriginal and non-Aboriginal people in Canada.

Royal Proclamation of 1763 The British document that set out the terms of European settlement in North America following the Seven Years' War.

rule of law The principle that no one is above the law, and that any powers granted to elected or non-elected officials must be conferred by legislation.

safe seat An electoral district in which the incumbent party is highly likely to be re-elected.

sales tax A revenue-generating tax charged by a government on the sale of applicable goods or services.

seats triage During an election campaign, the process of identifying swing districts where campaign resources should be concentrated (*see* **swing district**).

secessionism A widely held sentiment that a province or territory should leave the Canadian federation.

sectionalism An emotional connection with one's regional homeland, rather than one's country.

secular state A religiously neutral governing regime.

self-government The inherent right of a people to sovereignty (or self-determination) over their own affairs.

Senate The upper house of the Canadian Parliament, consisting of members chosen by the executive. *Also called* **Red Chamber**. *Compare* **House of Commons**.

senator One of the appointed members of the upper house of the Canadian Parliament.

7/50 amending formula A rule for passing most amendments to the constitution, requiring the consent of Parliament and the legislatures of seven provinces representing no less than 50 per cent of Canada's population.

shadow cabinet A group of opposition party members responsible for holding ministers of the Crown to account for their actions.

single-member plurality (SMP) An electoral system in which the winner of a district needs just one vote more than the number amassed by the runner-up. *Also called* **first past the post**.

slacktivism Actions taken by individuals to appear part of a social movement, but which have no direct impact on the fulfilment of its objectives.

social assistance Financial support provided by government to citizens with no other recourse to income.

social movement A collection of members of the general public who share a public policy concern and urge government action and changes to social values and behaviour.

social safety net Government-funded social welfare programs designed to assist citizens in their time of need.

solicitor general The cabinet member typically responsible for the penal and policing aspects of the justice system. *Compare* **minister of justice**.

sovereignty The power to exercise government authority over a polity within a defined geographical area.

sovereignty–association A proposed legal arrangement whereby Quebec would be politically independent but maintain economic ties with Canada.

speaker The member of the legislature responsible for presiding over its rules and general decorum.

speech from the throne A document read by the governor general or lieutenant governor, officially opening a new session of the legislature and detailing the government's plans.

spending limits Legal restrictions on how much money can be spent in a campaign.

sponsorship scandal An affair in which Liberal advertising agencies received public funds for work that was never performed.

standing committee A committee whose existence is defined by standing orders. *Also called* **permanent committee**.

standing orders The body of rules governing the conduct of the legislature.

state A structured political community with a single source of ultimate authority over its territory.

status Indian A person of First Nations ancestry who is registered with the federal government and entitled to certain rights under the Indian Act. *Compare* **non-status Indian**.

Statute of Westminster A British law that permitted its dominions to opt out of future legislation passed by the British Parliament.

stimulus Increased government spending to encourage job growth during an economic downturn.

substantive representation A political attachment to someone by virtue of their defence or promotion of one's own interests. *Compare* **descriptive representation**, **formalistic representation**, **symbolic representation**.

suffrage The right to vote in elections.

Supreme Court of Canada Canada's highest court of appeal, which displaced the **Judicial Committee of the Privy Council** (JCPC) in 1949.

swing district (or **riding**) A riding or constituency where the election outcome is uncertain.

symbolic representation A political attachment to someone or something that is seen to epitomize what it means to be a part of one's political community. *Compare* **descriptive representation**, **formalistic representation**, **substantive representation**.

symmetrical federalism A system of federalism in which provincial governments are entitled to equal powers (*see* **federalism**).

tariff A form of tax applied to imported goods and services.

taxation policy The regulations, mechanisms, and rates set by government to generate revenues from people and businesses in its jurisdiction.

tax credit A tax exemption on money spent on a specific activity, up to a specified limit.

think tank An institute or organization that performs research as a means of public advocacy.

third order of government A constitutionally recognized status for First Nations people, on par with the federal and provincial orders.

third party *Another term for* **interest group**.

third-way social democracy   A branch of socialism that accepts capitalism and aims to harness it to achieve equality of result. *Compare* **traditional social democracy**.

throne speech   *See* **speech from the throne**.

toryism   A branch of Canadian conservatism with British, communitarian roots. *See* **blue toryism**, **red toryism**.

trade union   *See* **labour union**.

traditional social democracy   A branch of socialism that remains committed to replacing capitalism with a more co-operative economic system. *Compare* **third-way social democracy**.

Treasury Board   The cabinet committee that is tasked with reviewing and authorizing government revenue and expenditure policies.

Treasury Board Secretariat (TBS)   The central agency responsible for coordinating government spending, as well as human and technical resources.

treaties   Agreements between the Crown and Aboriginal peoples establishing mutual duties and obligations.

treaty federalism   A system of governance recognizing the equal-order relationship between First Nations and the Crown (*see* **federalism**).

truncated party   A federal or provincial political party that does not have a similarly named party at the other level of government. *Compare* **integrated parties**.

two-row wampum   A ceremonial beaded belt symbolizing the parallel paths and equal-order relationship between the Crown and First Nations living in North America.

UN declarations and conventions   Commitments made by many UN members to uphold and advance rights causes in their respective countries.

unicameral legislature   A legislative body consisting of one chamber (or house). *Compare* **bicameral legislature**.

unitary system   A political system featuring a central government that chooses what powers to devolve to regional bodies.

United Nations (UN)   The world's primary international political body.

vertical fiscal gap   The revenue disparity between the federal and provincial orders of government. *Compare* **horizontal fiscal gap**.

vertical fiscal imbalance   A situation in which the federal government has an excess of revenue, and the provinces an excess of responsibilities, with respect to their constitutional obligations. *Compare* **horizontal fiscal imbalance**.

visible minorities   Non-Aboriginal Canadians who are non-white in colour or non-Caucasian in ethnicity.

voter's paradox   The situation facing a voter whose single ballot is unlikely to influence the outcome of the election, making the costs of voting greater than the potential benefits.

voter turnout   The proportion of eligible electors who cast ballots in an election.

welfare liberalism   A branch of liberalism that seeks to achieve equality of opportunity in social terms. *Compare* **business liberalism**.

welfare state   A suite of government programs, services, and financial supports designed to assist the least fortunate in society.

Western alienation   Political discontent in areas west of Ontario, normally derived from frustration with perceived political favouritism enjoyed by areas east of Manitoba.

white paper   A document outlining a government's policy commitment.

whitestream Canadians   Caucasians who have formed the traditional mainstream of Canadian society; previously-known as white Anglo-Saxon Protestants (WASPs).

World Trade Organization (WTO)   A multilateral organization whose members voluntarily follow agreed economic policies.

working committee   *See* **ad hoc committee**.

writ of election   A legal document dissolving a legislature and marking the official start of an election campaign.

NOTES

CHAPTER 1

1. Richard Simeon and David J. Elkins, eds, *Small Worlds: Provinces and Parties in Canadian Political Life* (Toronto: Methuen Publications, 1980).
2. Steve Patten, "Toryism and the Conservative Party in a Neo-liberal Era," in *Party Politics in Canada*, 8th edn, ed. Hugh G. Thorburn and Alan Whitehorn (Scarborough, ON: Prentice-Hall, 2000).
3. Jason Fekete, "No Question: Federal Leaders Often Absent for Question Period," *Ottawa Citizen* (30 Dec. 2014).
4. Kirsten Kozolanka, ed., *Publicity and the Canadian State: Critical Communications Perspectives* (Toronto: University of Toronto Press, 2014).

CHAPTER 2

1. Janet Ajzenstat and Peter Smith, *Canada's Origins: Liberal, Tory or Republican?* (Ottawa: Carleton University Press, 1995).
2. David E. Smith, *The Invisible Crown: The First Principle of Canadian Government* (Toronto: University of Toronto Press, 2013).
3. Peter Aucoin, Jennifer Smith, and Geoff Dinsdale, *Responsible Government: Clarifying Essentials, Dispelling Myths and Exploring Change* (Ottawa: Canadian Centre for Management Development, 2004).
4. Ipsos-Reid/Dominion Institute, "O Canada: Our Home and Naive Land," www.historicaCanada.ca/sites/default/files/PDF/polls/Canadaday.survey.dominioninstitute.1july08_en.pdf.
5. A month earlier, she had signed a piece of parallel legislation passed by the UK Parliament (the Canada Act 1982) officially relinquishing its control over the Canadian constitution.
6. Andrew Heard, *Canadian Constitutional Conventions: The Marriage of Law and Politics*, 2nd edn (Don Mills, ON: Oxford University Press, 2014).
7. Peter Aucoin, Mark D. Jarvis, and Lori Turnbull, *Democratizing the Constitution: Reforming Responsible Government* (Toronto: Emond Montgomery, 2011).
8. *Edwards v Canada (Attorney General)* (1929), [1930] A.C. 124.
9. National Archives (USA), "Declaration of Independence," www.archives.gov/exhibits/charters/declaration_transcript.html.
10. Christopher Moore, *1867: How the Fathers Made a Deal* (Toronto: McClelland & Stewart, 1997).
11. David Thomas, *Whistling Past the Graveyard: Constitutional Abeyances, Quebec, and the Future of Canada* (Toronto: Oxford University Press, 1997).
12. Roy Romanow, John Whyte, and Howard Leeson, *Canada . . . Notwithstanding: The Making of the Constitution 1976–1982* (Agincourt: Carswell/Methuen, 1984).

13. Keith Banting and Richard Simeon, eds, *And No One Cheered: Federalism, Democracy and the Constitution Act* (Toronto: Methuen, 1983).
14. Robert Bothwell, *Canada and Quebec: One Country, Two Histories* (Vancouver: UBC Press, 1998): p. 204.
15. Patrick Monahan, *Meech Lake: The Inside Story* (Toronto: University of Toronto Press, 1991).
16. Kenneth McRoberts and Patrick Monahan, *The Charlottetown Accord, The Referendum, and the Future of Canada* (Toronto: University of Toronto Press, 1993).
17. Richard Johnston, *The Challenge of Direct Democracy: The 1992 Canadian Referendum* (Montreal and Kingston: McGill–Queen's University Press, 1996).
18. Prime Minister of Canada, "PM declares that the Québécois form a nation within a united Canada" (22 Nov. 2006), www.pm.gc.ca/eng/news/2006/11/22/pm-declares-quebecois-form-nation-within-united-Canada.
19. David S. Law and Mila Versteeg, "The Declining Influence of the United States Constitution," *New York University Law Review* 87, no. 3 (2012): pp. 762–858.
20. Richard Sigurdson, "Left and Right-wing Charterphobia in Canada: A Critique of the Critics." *International Journal of Canadian Studies* 7–8 (1993): pp. 95–115.

CHAPTER 3

1. See, for example, Bruce E. Johansen, *Forgotten Founders: How the American Indian Helped Shape Democracy* (Boston: Harvard Common Press, 1982).
2. W.H. Riker, *Federalism: Origin, Operation, Significance* (Boston: Little, Brown, 1964): p. 5.
3. P.B. Waite, ed., *The Confederation Debates in the Province of Canada*, 2nd edn (Montreal and Kingston: McGill–Queen's University Press, 2006).
4. Peter John Boyce, *The Queen's Other Realms: The Crown and Its Legacy in Australia, Canada, and New Zealand* (Riverwood, New South Wales: Federation Press, 2008): p. 93.
5. Joe Warmington, "'I Need F-ing 10 Minutes to Make Sure He's Dead': New Rob Ford Video Surfaces," *Toronto Sun* (7 Nov. 2013).
6. Diana Mehta and Colin Perkel, "Mayor Rob Ford: 'I Really Effed up'; Admits to Buying Illegal Drugs," *Maclean's* (13 Nov. 2013).
7. Dana Flavelle, "Ford Scandal Hurting City's Global Image, Report Finds," *Toronto Star* (12 Nov. 2013).
8. Jill Mahoney, "Rob Ford Cheers on Argos on Eve of More Confrontation with City Hall," *The Globe and Mail* (17 Nov. 2013).
9. Robert Benzie, "Rob Ford Crisis: Wynne Lays out Conditions for Intervening," *Toronto Star* (14 Nov. 2013).

10. Barry L. Strayer, *Canada's Constitutional Revolution* (Edmonton: University of Alberta Press, 2013).

11. Government of British Columbia, "Requirements for British Columbia to Consider Support for Heavy Oil Pipelines: Technical Analysis" (2012), www.env.gov.bc.ca/main/docs/2012/TechnicalAnalysis-HeavyOilPipeline_120723.pdf.

12. David Cameron and Richard Simeon, "Intergovernmental Relations in Canada: The Emergence of Collaborative Federalism," *Publius: The Journal of Federalism* 32, no. 2 (2002): pp. 49–71.

13. Kathy L. Brock, "The Politics of Asymmetrical Federalism: Reconsidering the Role and Responsibilities of Ottawa," *Canadian Public Policy* 34, no. 2 (2008): pp. 143–61.

14. Government of Canada, "Prime Minister Harper Outlines His Government's Priorities and Open Federalism Approach," news release (20 April 2006), www.pm.gc.ca/eng/news/2006/04/20/prime-minister-harper-outlines-his-governments-priorities-and-open-federalism.

15. Michael Babad, "'Honorary' Third World Then: How WSJ Describes Canada Now," *The Globe and Mail* (8 Feb. 2012).

16. Budget Speech (2007), www.budget.gc.ca/2007/pdf/bkfbsfe.pdf.

17. John Richards, "Cracks in the Country's Foundation: The Importance of Repairing Equalization," *Canadian Political Science Review* 2, no. 3 (2008): pp. 68–83.

18. Adrian Morrow, "Premiers Put Canada Job Grant, CPP at Top of Agenda," *The Globe and Mail* (15 Nov. 2013).

CHAPTER 4

1. Janine Brodie, "The Political Economy of Regionalism," in *The Canadian Political Economy*, ed. Wallace Clement and Glen Williams (Montreal and Kingston: McGill–Queen's University Press, 1989): p. 139.

2. Michael D. Ornstein, H. Michael Stevenson, and A. Paul Williams, "Region, Class and Political Culture in Canada," *Canadian Journal of Political Science* 13, no. 2 (1980): pp. 227–71.

3. Allan Kornberg and Marianne C. Stewart, "National Identification and Political Support," in *Political Support in Canada: The Crisis Years*, ed. Allan Kornberg and Harold D. Clarke (Durham, NC: Duke University Press, 1983): p. 83.

4. Harold D. Clarke, Jane Jenson, Lawrence LeDuc, and Jon H. Pammett, *Political Choice in Canada* (Toronto: McGraw–Hill Ryerson, 1979): p. 404.

5. Garth Stevenson, *Unfulfilled Union: Canadian Federalism and National Unity* (Toronto: Macmillan, 1979): p. 17.

6. Brodie, "Political Economy of Regionalism," p. 141.

7. Richard Simeon, "Regionalism and Canadian political institutions," in *Canadian Federalism: Myth or Reality?*, ed. J. Meekinson (Toronto: Methuen, 1977): p. 293.

8. Ramsay Cook, *The Teeth of Time: Remembering Pierre Trudeau* (Montreal and Kingston: McGill–Queen's University Press, 2006): p. 199.

9. John Robert Colombo, *Colombo's Canadian Quotations* (Toronto: Hurtig, 1974).

10. Terence Ball and Richard Dagger, *Political Ideologies and the Democratic Ideal*, 8th edn (New York: Pearson, 2010).

11. Margaret Canovan, "Trust the People! Populism and the Two Faces of Democracy," *Political Studies* 47, no. 1 (1999): pp. 2–16.

12. Kevin Libin, "What the West Wants Next," *National Post* (28 Oct. 2011).

13. CTV News, "McGuinty Urges Voters to Put Ontario First" (8 Sept. 2008).

14. Valérie Vezina and Karlo Basta, "Nationalism in Newfoundland and Labrador," in *First Among Unequals: The Premier, Politics and Public Policy in Newfoundland and Labrador*, ed. Alex Marland and Matthew Kerby (Montreal and Kingston: McGill–Queen's University Press, 2014).

15. Antony Jay, *Lend Me Your Ears: Oxford Dictionary of Political Quotations* (New York: Oxford University Press, 2010): p. 172.

16. Quoted in George A. Rawlyk, Bruce W. Hodgins, and Richard P. Bowles, *Regionalism in Canada: Flexible Federalism or Fractured Nation?* (Scarborough, ON: Prentice-Hall, 1979): p. 2.

17. George Radwanski, *Trudeau* (Toronto: Macmillan, 1978): p. 316.

18. Philip Authier, "Péladeau skeptical of poll that shows PQ slipping, but sovereignty more popular," *Montreal Gazette* (23 Apr. 2015). http://montrealgazette.com/news/quebec/pierre-karl-peladeau-pq-slipping-in-public-opinion-but-sovereignty-option-is-up-poll.

19. Melville H. Watkins, "The Innis Tradition in Canadian Political Economy," *Canadian Journal of Political and Social Theory* 6, no. 1/2 (1982): pp. 12–34.

20. Janine Brodie, *The Political Economy of Canadian Regionalism* (Toronto: Harcourt Brace Jovanovich, 1990).

21. James Feehan and Melvin Baker, "The Churchill Falls Contract and Why Newfoundlanders Can't Get Over It," *Policy Options* (Sept. 2010): pp. 65–70.

22. Harry Eckstein, "A Culturalist Theory of Political Change," *American Political Science Review* 82, no. 3 (1998): pp. 789–804.

23. Michael McDevitt, "The Partisan Child: Developmental Provocation as a Model of Political Socialization," *International Journal of Public Opinion Research* 18, no. 1 (2005): p. 69.

24. Richard E. Dawson and Kenneth Prewitt, *Political Socialization* (Boston: Little, Brown, 1969): p. 152.

25. Harry Hiller, "Regionalism as a Social Construction," in *Regionalism and Party Politics in Canada*, ed. Keith Archer and Lisa Young (Don Mills, ON: Oxford University Press, 2000): pp. 24–40.

26. Jared Wesley, *Code Politics: Campaigns and Cultures on the Canadian Prairies* (Vancouver: UBC Press, 2011).

27. Roger Gibbins, 1998.

CHAPTER 5

1. Angus Reid Public Opinion, "Canadians Lukewarm on Monarchy, Would Pick William as Next King" (30 April 2013), www.angus-reid.com/wp-content/uploads/2013/04/2013.04.30_Monarchy_CAN.pdf.

2. Quoted in Althia Raj, "Canadian Navy, Air Force Name Change Divides NDP Caucus," *The Huffington Post* (15 Aug. 2011).

3. Quoted in Prithi Yelaja, "Royal Military Renaming Slammed as Colonial Throwback," CBC News (17 Aug. 2011), www.cbc.ca/m/news/Canada/royal-military-renaming-slammed-as-colonial-throwback-1.986039.

4. Quoted in Yelaja, "Royal Military Renaming."

5. Quoted in Yelaja, "Royal Military Renaming."

6. Susan Delacourt, *Juggernaut: Paul Martin's Campaign for Chrétien's Crown* (Toronto: McClelland & Stewart, 2013): p. 230.

7. Public remarks at Prairie Political Science Association Meetings, Banff, Alberta (15 Sept. 2013).

8. Jeffrey Simpson, *The Friendly Dictatorship* (Toronto: McClelland & Stewart, 2001); Lawrence Martin, *Harperland: The Politics of Control* (Toronto: Viking, 2010).

9. For instance, Donald J. Savoie, *Governing from the Centre: The Concentration of Power in Canadian Politics* (Toronto: University of Toronto Press, 1999).

10. In the US, members of cabinet do not hold seats in the legislature, which has more independent clout, whereas in Canada the presence of cabinet members in the legislature leads to a so-called "fusion of powers," because the people's elected representatives are meant to hold the executive to account.

11. Savoie, *Governing from the Centre*, p. 8.

12. Herman Bakvis and Steven B. Wolinetz, "Canada: Executive Dominance and Presidentialization," in *The Presidentialization of Politics: A Comparative Study of Modern Democracies*, ed. Thomas Poguntke and Paul Webb (Oxford: Oxford University Press, 2005).

13. Herman Bakvis, "Regional Politics and Policy in the Mulroney Cabinet, 1984–88: Towards a Theory of the Regional Minister System in Canada," *Canadian Public Policy* 15, no. 2 (1989): pp. 121–34.

14. Things are different in the consensus government model of Northwest Territories and Nunavut. The absence of political parties means that cabinet is chosen by a secret ballot process. See Graham White, *Cabinets and First Ministers* (Vancouver: UBC Press, 2005).

15. Matthew Kerby, "Worth the Wait: Determinants of Ministerial Appointment in Canada, 1935–2008," *Canadian Journal of Political Science* 42, no. 3 (2009): p. 594.

16. Linda Trimble and Manon Tremblay, "Representation of Canadian Women at the Cabinet Table," *Atlantis* 30, no. 1 (2005): p. 32.

17. Sharon Sutherland, "Responsible Government and Ministerial Responsibility: Every Reform Is Its Own Problem," *Canadian Journal of Political Science* 24, no. 1 (1991): pp. 91–120.

18. Paul Martin, "Verbatim: The Democratic Deficit," *Policy Options* (Dec./Jan. 2002): pp. 10–12.

19. Michael Chong, "Reform Act, 2014, passes Senate, 38–14," News release (23 June 2014). http://michaelchong.ca/2015/06/23/reform-act-2014-passes-senate-38-14/.

20. Savoie, *Governing from the Centre*.

21. Privy Council Office, "The Role and Structure of the Privy Council Office 2011" (2011), www.pco-bcp.gc.ca.

22. Donald C. MacDonald, "Ontario's Agencies, Boards, and Commissions Come of Age," *Canadian Public Administration* 36, no. 3 (2013): p. 350.

23. Government of Manitoba, "Agencies, Boards, and Commissions" (2013), www.manitoba.ca/government/abc/index.html.

24. Government of Nova Scotia, "Agencies, Boards, and Commissions" (2013), www.novascotia.ca/exec_council/abc/.

25. Government of Ontario, "Government" (2014), www.ontario.ca/government/government.

26. John C. Courtney, "In Defence of Royal Commissions," *Canadian Public Administration* 12, no. 2 (1969): pp. 198–212.

27. MacDonald, "Ontario's Agencies, Boards, and Commissions," p. 351.

CHAPTER 6

1. Michael Lusztig, "Federalism and Institutional Design: The Perils and Politics of a Triple-E Senate in Canada," *Publius: The Journal of Federalism* 25, no. 1 (1995): 35–50.

2. Jane Taber, "Brad Wall's Senate Wish: 'Reform It, Abolish It, Paint It Pink,'" *The Globe and Mail* (24 June 2011).

3. Alan Siaroff, "Seat Imbalance in Provincial Elections since 1900: A Quantitative Explanation," *Canadian Political Science Review* 3, no. 1 (2009): 77–92.

4. Peter Regenstreif, *The Appeal of Majority Government* (Toronto: Longmans, 1965); Peter H. Russell, *Two Cheers for Minority Government: The Evolution of Canadian Parliamentary Democracy* (Toronto: Emond Montgomery, 2008).

5. Eugene Forsey, "The Problem of 'Minority' Government in Canada," *Canadian Journal of Economics and Political Science* 30 (1964): 1–11; Howard Cody, "Minority Government in Canada: The Stephen Harper Experience," *American Review of Canadian Studies* 38 (2008): 27–42.

6. Garth Turner, *Sheeple: Caucus Confidential in Stephen Harper's Ottawa* (Toronto: Key Porter, 2009).

7. Alison Loat and Michael MacMillan, *Tragedy in the Commons: Former Members of Parliament Speak Out About Canada's Failing Democracy* (Toronto: Random House, 2014).

8. Hansard, "Canada, House of Commons Debates," 41st Parliament, 2nd Session (19 Nov. 2013), www.parl.gc.ca/HousePublications/Publication.aspx?Language=E&Mode=1&Parl=41&Ses=2&DocId=6307745.

9. Hansard, "Canada, House of Commons Debates," 41st Parliament, 1st Session (9 Feb. 2012), www.parl.gc.ca/HousePublications/Publication.aspx?DocId=5373230&Mode=1&Language=E.

10. Ailsa Henderson, *Nunavut: Rethinking Political Culture* (Vancouver: UBC Press, 2007).

CHAPTER 7

1. CBC Digital Archives, "1970: Pierre Trudeau Says 'Just Watch Me' during October Crisis," www.cbc.ca/archives/categories/politics/civil-unrest/the-october-crisis-civil-liberties-suspended/just-watch-me.html.

2. Beverley McLachlin, "Aspects of Equality: Rendering Justice" (conference presentation, Hull, QC, 17–19 Nov. 1995).

3. Office of the Commissioner for Federal Judicial Affairs Canada, "Number of Federally Appointed Judges as of July 1, 2014," www.fja.gc.ca/appointments-nominations/judges-juges-eng.html.

4. Royal Canadian Mounted Police, "Mission, Vision and Values" (2014), www.rcmp-grc.gc.ca/about-ausujet/mission-eng.htm.

5. Peter O'Neil, "Canadians' Faith in Police Has Plunged, Poll Finds," *Postmedia News* (25 April 2013), www.Canada.com/news/Canadians+faith+police+plunged+poll+finds/6518673/story.html.

6. Correctional Service of Canada, "Our Mission" (2012), www.csc
   -scc.gc.ca/about-us/index-eng.shtml.
7. Office of the Correctional Investigator, "Aboriginal Issues" (2014),
   www.oci-bec.gc.ca/cnt/priorities-priorites/aboriginals-autochtones
   -eng.aspx.
8. International Centre for Prison Studies, *World Prison Brief* (2012),
   www.prisonstudies.org/info/worldbrief.

CHAPTER 8

1. Fraser Institute, "Who We Are" (2014), www.fraserinstitute.org/
   about-us/who-we-are/overview.aspx.
2. Max Weber, *Economy and Society*, ed. Guenther Roth and Claus
   Wittich (Berkeley and Los Angeles: University of California Press,
   1978).
3. Christopher A. Simon, *Public Policy: Preferences and Outcomes*
   (New York: Pearson, 2007): p. 1.
4. William Kelso, *American Democratic Theory: Pluralism and Its
   Critics* (Westport, CT: Greenwood, 1978).
5. Stuart N. Soroka, *Agenda-Setting Dynamics in Canada* (Vancouver:
   UBC Press, 2002).
6. Eugene Bardach, *A Practical Guide for Policy Analysis: The Eightfold
   Path to More Effective Problem Solving*, 4th edn (Los Angeles: Sage,
   2011).
7. Aidan R. Vining and Anthony E. Boardman, "The Choice of Formal
   Policy Analysis Methods in Canada," in *Policy Analysis in Canada:
   The State of the Art*, ed. Laurent Dobuzinskis, Michael Howlett, and
   David Laycock (Toronto: University of Toronto Press, 2007).
8. Richard H. Thaler and Cass R. Sunstein, *Nudge: Improving Decisions
   about Health, Wealth, and Happiness* (New Haven, CT: Yale
   University Press, 2008).
9. Bardach, *A Practical Guide for Policy Analysis*.
10. Department of Advanced Education and Skills, Newfoundland and
    Labrador, "Program Overview," www.aes.gov.nl.ca/income-support/
    overview.html.
11. The earlier example of constitutional responsibilities did not iden-
    tify whether, as per section 94A, there is a federal department of
    old age pensions and benefits. There is not. Rather, the Department
    of Employment and Social Development Canada is responsible for
    administering the Old Age Security program.
12. CBC News, "Up the Skirt or in the Till: Top Ten Scandals in
    Canadian Political History" (10 Feb. 2005), www.cbc.ca/news2/
    background/cdngovernment/scandals.html.
13. Steven Chase, Erin Anderssen, and Bill Curry, "Stimulus Program
    Favours Tory Ridings," *The Globe and Mail* (21 Oct. 2009).
14. Public Service Commission of Canada, "Public Service Impartiality:
    Taking Stock" (Ottawa: 2008): p. 7. Available at www.psc-cfp.gc.ca/
    plcy-pltq/rprt/impart/impart-eng.pdf.
15. Jeffrey Simpson, *Spoils of Power: The Politics of Patronage* (Toronto:
    HarperCollins, 1988): p. 6.

CHAPTER 9

1. Otto Kirchheimer, "The Transformation of the Western European
   Party Systems," in *Political Parties and Political Development*, ed.
Joseph LaPalombara and Myron Weiner (Princeton, NJ: Princeton
   University Press, 1966).
2. Jack McLeod, "Explanations of Our Party System," in *Politics:
   Canada*, 4th edn, ed. Paul Fox (Toronto: McGraw-Hill Ryerson, 1977).
3. Jared J. Wesley, ed., *Big Worlds: Politics and Elections in the
   Canadian Provinces and Territories* (Toronto: University of Toronto
   Press, 2015).
4. Christopher Adams, *Politics in Manitoba: Parties, Leaders, and
   Voters* (Winnipeg: University of Manitoba Press, 2008).
5. Harold Clarke, Jane Jenson, Lawrence LeDuc, and Jon H.
   Pammett, *Absent Mandate: Canadian Electoral Politics in an Era of
   Restructuring*, 3rd edn (Agincourt, ON: Gage, 1996): p. 15.
6. John Courtney, "Reinventing the Brokerage Wheel: The Tory
   Success in 1984," in *Canada at the Polls 1984*, ed. Howard R.
   Penniman (Washington: American Enterprise Institute for Public
   Policy Research, 1988): p. 198.
7. Janine Brodie and Jane Jenson, "Piercing the Smokescreen:
   Stability and Change in Brokerage Politics," in *Canadian Parties
   in Transition*, 2nd edn, ed. A. Brian Tanguay and Alain-G. Gagnon
   (Scarborough, ON: Nelson, 1996).
8. Maurice Duverger, *Political Parties: Their Organization and Activity
   in the Modern State* (London: Methuen; New York: Wiley, 1954).
9. *Figueroa v. Canada (Attorney General)*, 2003, http://scc-csc.lexum.
   com/scc-csc/scc-csc/en/item/2069/index.do.
10. R. Kenneth Carty, "Three Canadian Party Systems: An Interpre-
    tation of the Development of National Politics," in *Party Democ-
    racy in Canada*, ed. G.C. Perlin (Scarborough, ON: Prentice-Hall,
    1988): pp. 15–30; R. Kenneth Carty, William Cross, and Lisa
    Young, *Rebuilding Canadian Party Politics* (Vancouver: UBC
    Press, 2000).
11. Rand Dyck, "Links between Federal and Provincial Parties and
    Party Systems," in *Representation, Integration and Political Parties
    in Canada*, ed. Herman Bakvis (vol. 14 of the Research Studies for
    the Royal Commission on Electoral Reform and Party Financing):
    pp. 129–77.
12. Joseph Wearing, *The L-Shaped Party: The Liberal Party of Canada
    1958–1980* (Toronto: McGraw-Hill Ryerson, 1981); Reginald
    Whitaker, *The Government Party: Organizing and Financing the
    Liberal Party of Canada 1930–58* (Toronto: University of Toronto
    Press, 1977).
13. Gad Horowitz, "Conservatism, Liberalism and Socialism in
    Canada: An Interpretation," *Canadian Journal of Political Science*
    32 (1966): p. 158.
14. Laura Payton, "NDP Votes to Take 'Socialism' out of Party
    Constitution," CBC News (14 April 2013), www.cbc.ca/news/politics/
    ndp-votes-to-take-socialism-out-of-party-constitution-1.1385171.
15. Rhéal Séguin and Daniel Leblanc, "Party's Over for the Bloc
    Québécois, Harper Says," *The Globe and Mail* (16 March 2013).
16. Anthony M. Sayers, *Candidates and Constituency Campaigns in
    Canadian Elections* (Vancouver: UBC Press, 1999).
17. Royce Koop, *Grassroots Liberals: Organizing for Local and National
    Politics* (Vancouver: UBC Press, 2011).
18. New Democratic Party of Canada, "Constitution of the New
    Democratic Party of Canada" (2013), http://xfer.ndp.ca/2013/
    constitution/2013_CONSTITUTION_E.pdf.

19. Liberal Party of Canada, "The Liberal Party of Canada: Constitution" (2011), http://convention.liberal.ca/files/2011/12/LPC-2009-Constitution-EN-revised-June-18-2011.pdf.

20. A notable case of leadership change saw Kevin Rudd lead the Australian Labour Party to victory in 2007, but within three years his public approval ratings had plummeted. In 2010, his colleague Julia Gillard announced that she would seek the leadership, prompting Rudd to immediately resign. Gillard led Labour to another election victory in 2012, and in 2013 Rudd attempted to coordinate a caucus vote against her. He was successful on the second attempt and once again became leader and prime minister. However, this time Rudd held the job for less than three months, as Labour was defeated in the 2013 election and was replaced by Liberal leader Tony Abbott.

21. Rick Mercer, *Rick Mercer Report: The Paperback Book* (Toronto: Anchor Canada, 2008): p. 189.

22. Joanna Everitt, Elisabeth Gidengil, Patrick Fournier, and Neil Nevitte, "Patterns of Party Identification in Canada," in *Election*, ed. Heather MacIvor (Toronto: Emond Montgomery, 2009).

23. Joseph Wearing, "Finding Our Parties' Roots," in *Canadian Parties in Transition*, 2nd edn, ed. Brian Tanguay and Alain-G. Gagnon (Toronto: Nelson Canada, 2009): pp. 14–31.

CHAPTER 10

1. José Antonio Cheibub, Jennifer Gandhi, and James Raymond Vreeland, "Democracy and Dictatorship Revisited," *Public Choice* 143 (April 2010): pp. 67–101.

2. Elections Canada, *A History of the Vote in Canada*, 2nd edn (Ottawa: Office of the Chief Electoral Officer of Canada, 2007).

3. Josh Wingrove and Chris Hannay, "Everything You Need to Know about the Fair Elections Act," *The Globe and Mail* (8 July 2014).

4. Jill Mahoney, "Joe Volpe Turfs Campaign Worker Caught Trashing Green Pamphlets," *The Globe and Mail* (25 April 2011).

5. Postmedia News, "Conservatives Drop Appeal of 'In and Out' Ruling," *National Post* (6 March 2012).

6. For instance, see Lawrence LeDuc, "The Leaders' Debates: (. . . and the winner is . . .)," in *The Canadian General Election of 1997*, ed. Alan Frizzell and Jon H. Pammett (Toronto: Dundurn, 1997): p. 207.

7. André Blais, Elisabeth Gidengil, Richard Nadeau, and Neil Nevitte, "Campaign Dynamics in the 2000 Canadian Election: How the Leader Debates Salvaged the Conservative Party," *Political Science and Politics* 36 (2003): pp. 45–50.

8. Statistics Canada, "Reasons for Not Voting in the May 2, 2011, Federal Election," *The Daily* (5 July 2011), www.statcan.gc.ca/daily-quotidien/110705/dq110705a-eng.htm.

9. Jon H. Pammett and Lawrence LeDuc, "Explaining the Turnout Decline in Canadian Federal Elections: A New Survey of Non-Voters," Elections Canada (2003), www.elections.ca/res/rec/part/tud/TurnoutDecline.pdf.

10. Timothy J. Feddersen, "Rational Choice Theory and the Paradox of Not Voting," *The Journal of Economic Perspectives* 18 (2004): pp. 99–112.

11. Donley T. Studlar, "Canadian Exceptionalism: Explaining Differences over Time in Provincial and Federal Voter Turnout," *Canadian Journal of Political Science* 34 (2001): pp. 299–319.

12. Elisabeth Gidengil, André Blais, Joanna Everitt, Patrick Fournier, and Neil Nevitte, "Back to the Future? Making Sense of the 2004 Canadian Election outside Quebec," *Canadian Journal of Political Science* 39 (2006): pp. 1–25.

13. Jack Layton, "A Letter to Canadians from the Honourable Jack Layton" (20 Aug. 2011), www.ndp.ca/letter-to-canadians-from-jack-layton.

14. Tom Brook, *Getting Elected in Canada* (Stanford, ON: Mercury Press, 1991).

15. Tom Flanagan, "Campaign Strategy: Triage and the Concentration of Resources," in *Election*, ed. Heather MacIvor (Toronto: Emond Montgomery, 2010).

16. R. Kenneth Carty and Munroe Eagles, "Do Local Campaigns Matter? Campaign Spending, the Local Canvass and Party Support in Canada," *Electoral Studies* 18 (1999): pp. 69–87.

CHAPTER 11

1. Hugh Heclo and Lester M. Salamon, *The Illusion of Presidential Government* (Boulder, CO: Westview, 1981).

2. CBC News, "Senator Mike Duffy, In His Own Words," (22 Oct. 2013), www.cbc.ca/news/politics/senator-mike-duffy-in-his-own-words-1.2159561.

3. CTV News, "Harper Signals Snap Election May Be Called" (26 Aug. 2008), www.ctvnews.ca/harper-signals-snap-election-may-be-called-1.319161.

4. Brian Topp, *How We Almost Gave the Tories the Boot: The Inside Story Behind the Coalition* (Toronto: Lorimer & Company, 2010): p. 57.

5. CBC News, "Liberals, NDP, Bloc Sign Deal on Proposed Coalition" (1 Dec. 2008), www.cbc.ca/news/Canada/liberals-ndp-bloc-sign-deal-on-proposed-coalition-1.700119.

6. John Geddes and Aaron Wherry, "Inside a Crisis That Shook the Nation," *Macleans* (11 Dec. 2009).

7. The Strategic Counsel, "Harper's Conservatives versus a Liberal–NDP Coalition: What Is the State of Canadian Public Opinion? A Report to *The Globe and Mail*" (4 Dec. 2008).

8. Josh Visser, "Liberals Apologize for Late Delivery of Dion Video," CTV News (3 Dec. 2008), www.ctvnews.ca/liberals-apologize-for-late-delivery-of-dion-video-1.347802.

9. Michael Laver and Norman Schofield, *Multiparty Government: The Politics of Coalition in Europe* (Oxford: Oxford University Press, 1990).

10. Allan Levine, *Scrum Wars: The Prime Ministers and the Media* (Toronto: Dundurn Press, 1993).

11. James N. Druckman, "The Power of Television Images: The First Kennedy–Nixon Debate Revisited," *Journal of Politics* 65, no. 2 (2003): pp. 559–71.

12. Canadian Radio-television and Telecommunications Commission, "Broadcasting Notice of Invitation CRTC 2013-563" (24 Oct. 2013), www.crtc.gc.ca/eng/archive/2013/2013-563.htm.

13. CBC News, "Public Doesn't Care about Spat with Press Gallery: Harper" (25 May 2006), www.cbc.ca/news/Canada/public-doesn-t-care-about-spat-with-press-gallery-harper-1.604422.

14. Paul Attallah and Angela Burton, "Television, the Internet, and the Canadian Federal Election of 2000," in *The Canadian General*

Election of 2000, ed. Jon H. Pammett and Christopher Dornan (Toronto: Dundurn, 2001): pp. 215–41.

15. Tamara A. Small, "Still Waiting for an Internet Prime Minister," in *Election*, ed. Heather MacIvor (Toronto: Emond Montgomery, 2010): pp. 173–98.

16. An excellent source for the role of information communication technologies in politics is Andrew Chadwick, *Internet Politics: States, Citizens, and New Communication Technologies* (Oxford: Oxford University Press, 2006).

17. Service Canada, "Service Canada: People Serving People" (2014), www.serviceCanada.gc.ca/eng/home.shtml.

18. Chadwick, *Internet Politics.*

19. "Canada Ranked 51st in Access to Information List," Toronto *Star* (22 June 2012).

20. Marshall McLuhan, *Understanding Media: The Extensions of Man* (New York: New American Library, 1964).

21. Joseph N. Cappella and Kathleen Hall Jamieson, *Spiral of Cynicism: The Press and the Public Good* (Oxford: Oxford University Press, 1997).

22. Robert Entman, "Framing Bias: Media in the Distribution of Power," *Journal of Communication* 57 (2007): pp. 163–73.

23. J.L. Granatstein and Norman Hillmer, *Prime Ministers: Ranking Canada's Leaders* (Toronto: HarperCollins, 1999).

24. J.P. Lewis, "If We Could All Be Peter Lougheed: Provincial Premiers and Their Legacies, 1967–2007," *British Journal of Canadian Studies* 25, no. 1 (2012): pp. 77–114.

25. The Teddy Awards are named after the former chair of the Canada Labour Relations Board (whose first name is Ted). In 1999, the auditor general revealed that the chair had skipped many days of work, had submitted expense claims for a second job, and had expensed the government for lavish meals, including a $733 lunch for two in Paris.

26. Public Works and Government Services Canada, "How It Works" (2014), www.tpsgc-pwgsc.gc.ca/pub-adv/roles-eng.html.

27. Jonathan Rose, *Making Pictures in Our Heads: Government Advertising in Canada* (New York: Praeger, 2000).

28. L. Fraser, *Propaganda* (Oxford: Oxford University Press, 1957).

29. Alex Marland, "If Seals Were Ugly, Nobody Would Give a Damn: Propaganda, Nationalism, and Political Marketing in the Canadian Seal Hunt," *Journal of Political Marketing* 13, no. 1/2 (2014): pp. 66–84.

30. Richard Nimijean, "Rebranding the Oil Sands," *Inroads* (Fall/Winter 2011): pp. 76–85.

31. "Stephen Harper's '24 Seven' Show Has North Korean Vibes," *Huffington Post Canada* (9 Jan. 2014).

32. Frank E. Dardis, Fuyuan Shen, and Heidi H. Edwards, "Effects of Negative Political Advertising on Individuals' Cynicism and Self-efficacy: The Impact of Ad Type, Ad Message Exposures," *Mass Communication and Society*, 11 (2008): pp. 24–42; William J. Schenck-Hamlin, David, E. Procter, and Deborah J. Rumsey, "The Influence of Negative Advertising Frames on Political Cynicism and Politician Accountability," *Human Communication Research*, 26, no. 1 (2000): pp. 53–75.

33. John G. Geer, *In Defense of Negativity: Attack Ads in Presidential Campaigns* (Chicago: University of Chicago Press, 2006).

34. Susan Delacourt, *Shopping for Votes: How Politicians Choose Us and We Choose Them* (Toronto: Douglas & McIntyre, 2013).

35. Jennifer Lees-Marshment, "The Product, Sales and Market-Oriented Party: How Labour Learnt to Market the Product, Not Just the Presentation," *European Journal of Marketing* 35, no. 9/10 (2001): pp. 1074–84.

36. For example, Margaret Scammell, "Brand Blair: Marketing Politics in the Consumer Age," in *Voters or Consumers: Imagining the Contemporary Electorate*, ed. Darren G. Lilleker and Richard Scullion (Newcastle, UK: Cambridge Scholars, 2008).

37. For instance, Simon Hudson and J.R. Ritchie, "Branding a Memorable Destination Experience: The Case of 'Brand Canada,'" *International Journal of Tourism Research* 11 (2009): pp. 217–28.

38. Alex Marland and Tom Flanagan, "Brand New Party: Political Branding and the Conservative Party of Canada," *Canadian Journal of Political Science* 46, no. 4 (2013): pp. 951–72.

39. Jared J. Wesley and Mike Moyes, "Selling Social Democracy: Branding the Political Left in Canada," in *Political Communication in Canada: Meet the Press and Tweet the Rest*, ed. Alex Marland, Thierry Giasson, and Tamara A. Small (Vancouver: UBC Press, 2014).

40. Tom Flanagan, *Harper's Team: Behind the Scenes in the Conservative Rise to Power*, 2nd edn (Montreal and Kingston: McGill–Queen's University Press, 2009); Tom Flanagan, *Winning Power: Canadian Campaigning in the 21st Century* (Montreal and Kingston: McGill–Queen's University Press, 2014).

41. David Soberman, "The Complexity of Media Planning Today," *Brand Management* 12, no. 6 (2005): p. 421.

CHAPTER 12

1. A. Paul Pross, "Pressure Groups: Adaptive Instruments of Political Communication," in *Pressure Group Behaviour in Canadian Politics*, ed. A. Paul Pross (Toronto: McGraw-Hill Ryerson, 1975): p. 1.

2. Rand Dyck, *Canadian Politics: Critical Approaches*, 5th edn (Toronto: Nelson, 2008): p. 392.

3. Pross, "Pressure Groups."

4. Robert M. Alexander, *The Classics of Interest Group Behaviour* (Belmont, CA: Thompson Wadsworth, 2006).

5. Brian A. Tanguay and Barry J. Kay, "Political Activity of Local Interest Groups," in *Interest Groups and Elections in Canada*, vol. 2 of the Research Studies of the Royal Commission on Electoral Reform and Party Financing, ed. F. Leslie Seidle (Toronto: Dundurn, 1991).

6. Lisa Young and Joanna Marie Everitt, *Advocacy Groups* (Vancouver: UBC Press, 2004): p. 6. See also Fraser Valentine, "Public Interest Groups: Some Important Facts" (2013), www.ilCanada.ca/article/public-interest-groups-251.asp.

7. Canadian Pharmacists Association, "What We Do" (2014), www.pharmacists.ca/index.cfm/about-cpha/what-we-do.

8. Assembly of First Nations, "Description of the AFN," www.afn.ca/index.php/en/about-afn/description-of-the-afn.

9. Council of Canadians with Disabilities, "Council of Canadians with Disabilities (CCD) Proposals Re: Expansion and Renewal of the Social Development Partnership Fund" (June 2008), www.ccdonline.ca/en/socialpolicy/access-inclusion/partnership-fund.

10. Conference Board of Canada, "About Us" (2014), www.conferenceboard.ca/about-cboc/default.aspx.

11. Government Relations Institute of Canada, "Code of Professional Conduct" (2014), http://gric-irgc.ca/about/code-of-professional-conduct-2.

12. Idle No More, "The Vision" (2014), www.idlenomore.ca/vision.

13. Jacquetta Newman and A. Brian Tanguay, "Crashing the Party: The Politics of Interest Groups and Social Movements," in *Citizen Politics: Research and Theory in Canadian Political Behaviour*, ed. Joanna Everitt and Brenda O'Neill (Don Mills, ON: Oxford University Press, 2002).

14. CTV News, "Masked Intruders Demand UQAM Students Follow Boycott" (3 April 2015), www.ctvnews.ca/Canada/masked-intruders-demand-uqam-students-follow-boycott-1.2311364.

15. Aaron Wherry, "Neda Topaloski Explains Why She Went Topless to Protest Bill C-51: Femen and the Theory of Toplessness as Protest," *Maclean's* (24 March 2015).

16. Colin Horgan, "'We Did Not Mean to Offend,' Creator Says of Anti-Wildrose Video," *iPolitics* (19 April 2012), www.ipolitics.ca/2012/04/19/we-did-not-mean-to-offend-creator-says-of-anti-wildrose-video.

17. Janet Hiebert, "Interest Groups and Canadian Federal Elections," in *Interest Groups and Elections in Canada*, vol. 2 of the Research Studies of the Royal Commission on Electoral Reform and Party Financing, ed. F. Leslie Seidle (Toronto: Dundurn, 1991), p. 4.

18. Elections Canada, "Third Party Election Advertising Reports for the 41st General Election" (2014), www.elections.ca/content.aspx?section=fin&document=index&dir=thi/advert/tp41&lang=e.

CHAPTER 13

1. The term is also commonly used to refer to the limited influence of backbenchers compared with the growing clout of the prime minister's office. However, here we refer to it in the context of population diversity and the representation of that diversity.

2. Warren E. Kalbach, "Ethnic Diversity: Canada's Changing Cultural Mosaic," in *Perspectives on Ethnicity in Canada: A Reader*, ed. Madeline A. Kalbach and Warren E. Kalbach (Toronto: Harcourt, 2000): p. 70 (emphasis added).

3. Kalbach, "Ethnic Diversity."

4. Karen Bird, "Obstacles to Ethnic Minority Representation in Local Government in Canada," in Caroline Andrew, ed., *Our Diverse Cities* (Ottawa: Metropolis and the Federation of Canadian Municipalities, 2004): pp. 182–6.

5. Jorgan Dahlie and Tissa Fernando, "Pluralism and Power: Some Perspective," in Dahlie and Fernando, eds, *Ethnicity, Power, and Politics in Canada* (Toronto: Methuen, 1981).

6. Nelson Wiseman, "The Pattern of Prairie Politics," in *Party Politics in Canada*, 8th edn, ed. Hugh Thorburn and Alan Whitehorn (Toronto: Prentice Hall, 2001); R. Kalin and J.W. Berry, "Ethnic and Multicultural Attitudes," in *Ethnicity and Culture in Canada: The Research Landscape*, ed. J.W. Berry and J. Laponce (Toronto: University of Toronto Press, 1994): pp. 308–9.

7. Joanna Everitt, "Gender and Sexual Diversity in Provincial Election Campaigns," in *Battlegrounds: Elections, Electors, and Electioneering in the Canadian Provinces*, ed. Jared Wesley (Vancouver: UBC Press, forthcoming).

8. Rick Mercer, "Rant: Teen Suicide," *CBCtv YouTube Channel* (18 Dec. 2013), www.youtube.com/watch?v=J1OvtBa2FK8.

9. Melanee Thomas, "Gender and election 2015: Continuity with no real change." *Canadian Election Analysis 2015: Communication, Strategy and Democracy* (Vancouver: UBC Press, 2015): pp. 46–7.

10. Meagan Fitzpatrick, "Supreme Court Should Have 4 Women, Says Retiring Justice," CBC News (15 Aug. 2012), www.cbc.ca/news/politics/supreme-court-should-have-4-women-says-retiring-justice-1.1163037.

11. "Federal Affirmative Action Policy Faces Review," CBC News (22 July 2010), www.cbc.ca/news/Canada/federal-affirmative-action-policy-faces-review-1.940237.

12. Joe Friesen, "Tories Take Aim at Employment Equity," *The Globe and Mail* (22 July 2011).

13. Daniel LeBlanc, "Marois Blasts Multiculturalism in Favour of 'Values' Charter," *The Globe and Mail* (6 Sept. 2013).

14. Aaron Derfel, "Quebec Doctors Already Being Recruited," *Montreal Gazette* (13 Sept. 2013).

15. CTV News, "Jacques Parizeau Opposes Charter of Values" (3 Oct. 2013).

16. All band members must be status Indians, but not all status Indians are band members. Prior to Bill C-31, band membership was automatically assigned with status. Since 1985, individual bands have the ability to define their own membership rules (or to remain under the old system of automatic designation).

17. Patrick Fournier and Peter John Loewen, "Aboriginal Electoral Participation in Canada," Paper commissioned by Elections Canada (2011), www.elections.ca/res/rec/part/abel/AEP_en.pdf.

18. Kiera L. Ladner and Michael McCrossan, "The Electoral Participation of Aboriginal People," Elections Canada Working Paper Series on Electoral Participation and Outreach Practices (2007), http://elections.ca/res/rec/part/paper/aboriginal/aboriginal_e.pdf.

19. James Youngblood Henderson, "Empowering Treaty Federalism," *Saskatchewan Law Review* 58 (1995): pp. 241–329; Kiera Ladner, "Treaty Federalism: An Indigenous Vision of Canadian Federalisms," in *New Trends in Canadian Federalism*, 2nd edn, ed. François Rocher and Miriam Smith (Peterborough, ON: Broadview, 2003): pp. 167–96; James Tully, *Strange Multiplicity: Constitutionalism in an Age of Diversity. Cambridge* (Cambridge: Cambridge University Press, 2003).

20. Tom Flanagan, *First Nations: Second Thoughts* (Montreal and Kingston: McGill–Queen's University Press, 2000): p. 195.

21. *Parents Involved in Community Schools v. Seattle School District No. 1*, 551 U.S. 701 (2007).

22. Ivona Hideg and D. Lance Ferris, "Support for Employment Equity Policies: A Self-enhancement Approach," *Organizational Behavior and Human Decision Processes* 123, no. 1 (2014): pp. 49–64.

CHAPTER 14

1. The cartoon was titled "Notre drapeau national"; see Charles Hou and Cynthia Hou, *Great Canadian Political Cartoons, 1820 to 1914* (Vancouver: Moody's Lookout Press, 1997).

2. Here is the full text of Ariana Cuvin's description of her winning design for Canada's 150th anniversary logo: "The maple leaf is the nation's most iconic symbol, and I used subtle design choices to represent Canada and its Confederation. The base of the leaf

is made up of four diamonds (diamonds are celebratory gems), with nine more expanding outwards from them, meant to represent the four provinces that formed Canada after Confederation in 1867, eventually growing to the 13 provinces and territories. The repeated shape is meant to create a sense of unity and the 13 shapes forming the leaf represents our togetherness as a country. In the coloured iterations, the centre four diamonds are similar in colour. From left to right, similar colours are used in a row to show the provinces and territories that joined Canada in the same year. The multi-coloured iteration gives a feeling of diversity while the red one shows pride and unity." (https://uwaterloo.ca/arts/news/gbda-students-design-chosen-Canadas-150-anniversary-logo)

3. Hugh Mellon, "Understanding Today by Starting with Old Tomorrow," paper presented at the Conference on Sir. John A. Macdonald, Queen's University (January 2013), www.queensu.ca/iigr/index/MellonPaperSirJohnFINAL.pdf.

4. Roy MacLaren, *Commissions High: Canada in London, 1870–1971* (Montreal and Kingston: McGill–Queen's University Press, 2006): p. 193.

5. F.R. Scott, "W.L.M.K.," in Donna Bennett and Russell Brown, eds, *An Anthology of Canadian Literature in English* (Don Mills, ON: Oxford University Press): pp. 412–13.

6. North Atlantic Treaty Organization, "The North Atlantic Treaty" (4 April 1949), www.nato.int/cps/en/natolive/official_texts_17120.htm.

7. Ekos, "Decisive Opposition to Canada's Afghanistan Mission" (16 July 2009), http://ekos.com/admin/articles/cbc-2009-07-16.pdf.

8. David Collenette, "David Collenette on 9/11," *Maclean's* (7 Sept. 2011), www2.macleans.ca/2011/09/07/up-in-the-air/.

9. Canada, "Key Findings of the Commission," Commission of Inquiry into the Investigation of the Bombing of Air India Flight 182 (2010), http://epe.lac-bac.gc.ca/100/206/301/pco-bcp/commissions/air_india/2010-07-23/www.majorcomm.ca/en/reports/finalreport/key-findings.pdf.

10. "Stephen Harper's Apology to Air Canada Victims' Families," *National Post* (23 June 2010).

11. Pierre Trudeau, "Appendix V: Prime Minister of Canada's Televised Statement on the War Measures Act, October 16, 1970," in Dwight Hamilton and Kostas Risma, *Terror Threat: International and Homegrown Terrorists and Their Threat to Canada* (Toronto: Dundurn, 1970): pp. 241–7.

12. Michael Friscolanti, "The Merciless and Meticulous Toronto 18 Ringleader Goes to Prison for Life," *Maclean's* (18 Jan. 2010).

13. "Some Politicians under Foreign Sway: CSIS," CBC News (22 June 2010), www.cbc.ca/news/politics/some-politicians-under-foreign-sway-csis-1.909345.

14. Craig Offman, "The Making of Michael Chan," *The Globe and Mail* (17 June 2015).

15. Colin Freeze, "How CSEC Became an Electronic Spying Giant," *The Globe and Mail* (30 Nov. 2013).

16. Colin Freeze, "'Five Eyes' Intelligence-Sharing Program Threatens Canadians Abroad, Watchdog Warns," *The Globe and Mail* (31 Oct. 2013).

17. Freeze, "How CSEC Became an Electronic Spying Giant."

18. "CSEC's Collection of Metadata Shows Ability to 'Track Everyone'," CBC News (5 Feb. 2014), www.cbc.ca/news/technology/csec-s-collection-of-metadata-shows-ability-to-track-everyone-1.2522916.

19. Dana Mattioli, "On Orbitz, Mac Users Steered to Pricier Hotels," *The Wall Street Journal* (23 Aug. 2012).

20. United Nations, "UN at a Glance" (14 Feb. 2014), www.un.org/en/aboutun/index.shtml.

21. Rick Mercer, *Rick Mercer Report: The Book* (Toronto, ON: Anchor Canada, 2008): p. 224.

22. Perry Beatty, "Canada's Next Free-Trade Agreement? How About a Deal Between the Provinces?" *The Globe and Mail* (2 Jan. 2014).

23. The Commonwealth, "Aso Rock Declaration on Development and Democracy" (2003), http://thecommonwealth.org/sites/default/files/history-items/documents/AsoRockDeclaration2003.pdf.

24. Canada, "Aid Effectiveness Agenda," Foreign Affairs, Trade and Development Canada (14 Feb. 2014), www.acdi-cida.gc.ca/acdi-cida/ACDI-CIDA.nsf/eng/FRA-825105226-KFT.

25. Mike De Souza, "Cities Say Stephen Harper Government Getting 'Cold Feet' on Fighting Poverty," *Postmedia News* (9 Feb. 2014).

26. José Miguel Insulza, "Twenty Years Later: Canada's Role in the OAS and the Hemisphere," Canadian Foundation for the Americas (2010), www.focal.ca/en/publications/focalpoint/321-october-2010-jose-miguel-insulza-en.

ADDITIONAL CREDITS

INDEX